THE

WILLARD J. GRAHAM SERIES

IN ACCOUNTING

BOOKS IN
THE WILLARD J. GRAHAM SERIES
IN ACCOUNTING

Cost Accounting:
Analysis and Control

COST ACCOUNTING

Analysis and Control

GORDON SHILLINGLAW, Ph.D.

PROFESSOR OF ACCOUNTING
GRADUATE SCHOOL OF BUSINESS
COLUMBIA UNIVERSITY

1967 · Revised Edition

RICHARD D. IRWIN, INC.

Homewood, Illinois

Revised Edition

First Printing, April, 1967
Second Printing, July, 1968

Printed in the United States of America

Library of Congress Catalog Card No. 67–15844

TO MY WIFE

PREFACE

THE FIRST EDITION of this book was written to provide a textbook which would give primary emphasis to the managerial uses of cost accounting information. All the textbooks then available emphasized either accounting procedures or the relationship of factory costs to the firm's published financial statements. Managerial needs were not totally ignored, but they took a back seat to the needs of the technician and to the requirements of public financial reporting.

In contrast, I have tried to approach cost accounting from the viewpoint of the managerial consumer of accounting information. The criterion that I have applied to accounting concepts and procedures is how well they are likely to meet the needs of management. The question of what costs are to be reported as the cost of balance sheet assets and what costs are to be taken to the income statement as deductions from revenues is important and has not been neglected, but it has not been the dominant concern. My primary interest is in what managers want or need to know and how best to provide this information.

I have addressed this book to all those who have an interest in internal accounting data—business executives, accounting majors, and other business students. I do not subscribe to the view that the accounting major has need for any different approach to this subject than is appropriate for other students in the broad field of management, assuming that the same amount of time is available for each. The future accountant has at least as great a need as the future line executive for a thorough understanding of the ways in which accounting data will be used because it is he who will be called upon to structure the accounting system to meet the demand for relevant information. The line executive, for his part, needs to be aware of the problems faced by the accountant in meeting managment's requests for information. Both groups should know the meaning and limitations of different kinds of accounting information. Although it may be desirable for the accounting specialist to proceed at a slower rate and to work more of the problems than the general management student, the overall approach and basic objectives should be the same for both.

The main purpose of the revision has been to improve the book's teachability. It has been completely rewritten and reorganized with this objective in mind; many new problems have been added; and many of the old problems have been reworded and revised. I have attempted to define terms more carefully and use them more consistently in text and problems. Several chapters have been split in two for greater teachability.

I have tried to write each chapter so that the average student will be able to understand the concepts and also apply them to practical problems. The student should realize, however, that he cannot read this book, or any accounting book for that matter, as he would a detective story or novel. For best results, he should copy key figures from the numerical illustrations on notepaper and make sure that he can trace the relationships among these figures as they are unfolded in the text.

In substantive terms, new material has been added on the motivational relationships between standards and performance, on distribution cost analysis, on profit variance analysis, and on resource allocation with more than one scarce resource. Problems of uncertainty have been given more explicit recognition, albeit at a very simple level.

The book is divided into six parts of unequal length. Part I, consisting of the first three chapters, is designed primarily to identify and describe the management processes of planning and control and the demands placed by these processes on the accounting process. Part II, six chapters in all, deals with factory cost finding—the measurement of the factory unit cost of manufactured products. Although the main purpose of this section is to describe various cost finding methods, the relevance to management of the resultant unit cost figures is given a good deal of emphasis.

Part III is the longest section of the book, and outlines ways in which accounting data can be generated and used in cost control, both in the factory and in other company operations. Part IV consists of one chapter only, devoted to the conversion of accounting data prepared for managerial uses to a form suitable for public financial reporting.

Part V, consisting of Chapters 19–23 and Appendix A, is concerned with cost analysis and the relevance of accounting data to decisions on such questions as capital expenditures, sales emphasis, customer selection, and product pricing. The final three chapters, Part VI, are concerned with internal profit reporting and evaluation, with particular emphasis on the measurement of the profits of organizational divisions of decentralized companies and the establishment of standards for evaluating the profit performance of such divisions.

One suggestion that I have resisted is to include specific instruction in linear programming and other similar techniques in the quantitative kit bag. Knowledge of these techniques is indispensable to the modern cost accountant, but in my opinion this material cannot be presented adequately in the amount of space that I could make available by condensing the coverage of other topics. In this case, and perhaps in this case alone, I am perfectly willing to leave something to be taught in courses other than cost accounting.

This book can serve as a textbook for either a one-semester or a two-semester course in cost accounting and controllership. Two semesters will give the instructor time to cover all of the chapters and perhaps to bring in additional cases and supplementary readings from outside sources. In line with the emphasis on concepts and uses of cost accounting rather than on accounting techniques and procedures, there are no lengthy practice sets. Instead, it is suggested that the two-semester course include a required term paper in which students, individually or in groups, report on some aspect of the cost accounting procedures in cooperating local companies.

If the book is used for a one-semester course, several chapters will have to be omitted if the coverage of each is to be adequate. Choice of the chapters to be omitted will of course depend on the preferences and interests of the individual instructor and on the coverage of complementary courses in controllership, budgeting, finance, business economics, and so forth.

Some of the practice problems were derived from published sources, some from personal observation in cooperating companies, and some from work done by my colleagues. I have made no attempt to provide the same number of problems for each chapter, but have attached larger numbers of exercises and problems to those chapters for which repetitive drill seemed especially appropriate or for which a summary of several chapters' work was in order.

Few of the problems can be regarded as direct preparation for the CPA examination. Even those problems which came originally from past CPA examinations have sometimes been modified to implement specific points raised in the text. Problems modified in this way are identified as "Adapted from a Uniform CPA Examination" and may differ materially from the actual problems from which they were derived. Passing the cost accounting portions of the CPA examination is a specialized objective that is best met by repetitive drill on the kinds of questions found in previous examinations, but only *after* a thorough briefing in the basic underlying principles.

An innovation in this edition is the set of representative problem solutions in Appendix B, provided for those students who have the time to work problems other than those assigned by their instructors. These selected problems are intended mainly to provide exercise in the rudiments of problem solving and for this reason have almost entirely numerical solutions. The more difficult problems are not well represented in Appendix B because they generally contain qualitative elements that can be worked out properly only through class discussion.

So many people have helped me along the way that I, cannot hope to name more than a small percentage. I owe a major debt to Myron J. Gordon for his advice and encouragement in the preparation of the first edition and for permitting me to use a number of problems originally prepared for our joint work, *Accounting: A Management Approach*. Thomas M. Hill, Zenon S. Zannetos, and Carl Devine were also very helpful to me in the writing of the first edition.

In revising the book I have benefited greatly from a host of comments made by users of the first edition and by my colleagues at Columbia University. My biggest debt is to Carl L. Nelson, who read early drafts of every chapter and whose criticisms were so unanswerable that whole chapters often had to be rewritten. In addition, I am especially grateful to Russell A. Taussig for his perceptive review of most of the manuscript and to Louis H. Jordan for his suggestions on the sequencing of the material in Parts II and III. Homer A. Black, John C. Burton, Tsvi Ophir, and Stephen A. Zeff also made comments on the first edition which I found particularly useful in writing the second. John Burton, Carl Nelson, David Solomons, and Russell Taussig were also most generous in allowing me to use or modify problems they had written. Charles H. Smith took on the herculean task of checking the solutions to most of the problems, and for this I am highly grateful.

My final acknowledgment is to the late Willard J. Graham, until his death last fall the editor of the Irwin accounting series. I am extremely fortunate to have had his advice and support through two editions, and I hope that some of his wisdom has rubbed off on its pages. He will be sorely missed, but fondly remembered.

New York, New York
March, 1967

GORDON SHILLINGLAW

TABLE OF CONTENTS

PART I. COST ACCOUNTING AND ITS SETTING

THE MANAGEMENT CONTROL PROCESS: Control through Planning. Control through Direction and Supervision. Control by Feedback Response. Control by Appraisal. Interrelationships among the Processes. Other Classification Systems. ACCOUNTING'S ROLE IN MANAGEMENT CONTROL. OTHER FUNCTIONS OF ACCOUNTING: External Reporting. Internal Control. Routine Services. THE PLACE OF COST ACCOUNTING.

FINANCIAL PLANNING THROUGH BUDGETS: The Budget Defined. Components of an Overall Budget System. Business versus Governmental and Personal Budgets. The Budget Span. Budgeting as an Iterative Process. The Role of Accounting in Budgeting. A BUDGETARY PLANNING AND CONTROL SYSTEM: Background Situation. Preparing the Operating Budget. The Cash Budget. The Advantages of Budgeting. CONTROL REPORTING: Responsibility Centers and Cost Centers. The Chart of Accounts: Organizational Classification. The Chart of Accounts: Descriptive Detail. The Financial Reporting System. Financial Reporting to Top Management. Divisional Reporting: Sales Management. Departmental Reporting: District Manager. Periodic Reporting: The Control Limit Concept.

Example of a Decision. THE STRUCTURE OF DECISIONS: Problem Diagnosis. Goals or Objectives. Alternative Actions. Environmental Conditions. Outcomes and Payoffs. Decision Rule. INCREMENTAL ANALYSIS: Profit versus Income. Incremental versus Absolute Profit. Incremental Revenues. Incremental versus Sunk Cost. Separate Costs for Separate Purposes. Avoidable Costs. Opportunity Cost. COST/VOLUME RELATIONSHIPS: Fixed Costs. Variable Costs. Types of Fixed Costs. Semivariable Costs. Economists' View of Cost Patterns. Accountants' View of Cost Patterns. Fixed Costs and Sunk Costs. Other Determinants of Cost Behavior.

PART II. MEASUREMENT OF PRODUCT COST

THE ESSENCE OF JOB ORDER COSTING: Components of Manufacturing Cost. The Job Cost Sheet. Burden Rates. Predetermined Burden Rates. MANAGERIAL USES OF UNIT COST DATA. COST FLOWS FOR INCOME DETERMINATION: Cost Flows in Trading Companies. Cost Flows in Manufacturing. Recording Materials Costs. Control Accounts and Subsidiary Ledgers. Recording Labor Costs. Recording Factory Overhead. Overhead Absorption. Product Completion. Recording the Cost of Goods Sold. Under- or Overabsorbed Overhead. Disposition of Overhead Variances.

PART III. CONTROL OF OPERATING COSTS

APPENDIXES

INDEX

Part I

Cost Accounting and
Its Setting

Chapter 1

THE ROLE OF
COST ACCOUNTING

THE ORIGINS of accounting can be traced back into prehistory. Accounting records of a sort have been found in Minoan palaces, Egyptian tombs, and Assyrian temples dating from more than two millenia before the age of Rome, and at all times organized society has found the need to maintain some kind of accounting records. Accounting concepts, systems, and procedures in use today are the outgrowth of a development that began to take formal shape in the accounts of merchants in the Italian city states during the Renaissance, and no end to this development process is yet in sight.

The oldest forms of accounting developed as a result of the need of commercial firms to keep track of their relationships with outsiders, to maintain records of how and where they had invested their money, and to permit an accurate determination of the amounts accruing to the various owners of the business. Cost accounting, on the other hand, is a much more recent development. It was born in response to the needs of the managers of manufacturing companies for detailed information about the cost of manufacturing individual products, and the task of providing this kind of information is still a fundamental concern of most cost accounting systems.

Demands for accounting information have multiplied, decade by decade, and both the methods and scope of cost accounting have grown to meet these demands. In the process, it has expanded into related areas that were never envisioned in the cost accounting systems of 50 years ago. These trends have also been reinforced by increasing needs for certain kinds of classified cost data for government agencies, shareholders, and other groups outside the management circle. The purpose of this chapter is to sketch in broad terms the management processes to which cost accounting data are addressed and the ways in which cost accounting relates to these and other purposes.

THE MANAGEMENT CONTROL PROCESS

The managerial processes which concern cost accounting most directly are those which center on planning for the future and controlling current operations. These may be characterized broadly as processes of *management control,* utilizing four separate though interrelated techniques:

1. Control through planning.
2. Control through direction and supervision.
3. Control by feedback response.
4. Control by appraisal.

Control through Planning

Control always begins at the planning stage. No other technique controls the firm's destiny as planning does, and the difference between effective and ineffective planning can be so great as to overshadow the effect of all other control techniques combined.

Planning is the process of deciding on a course of action, of finding and choosing among the alternatives available. It takes three forms: (1) *policy formulation*—establishment of the major ground rules that determine the basic direction and shape of the enterprise, the limits within which management is free to exercise its discretion; (2) *decision making*—the choice among alternative solutions to specific operating or financial problems within the prescribed policy limits; and (3) *budgeting*—the preparation of comprehensive operating and financial plans for specific intervals of time.

All of these are decision processes and all are subject to replanning as conditions change, better information becomes available, or the goals of the enterprise are revised. The decisions may be on a grand scale and deal with basic company strategies, or small in scope and concern only minor questions of operating tactics, but they are all alike in resting on comparisons of the expected costs and benefits of the various perceived alternatives.

Control through Direction and Supervision

The second control mechanism consists of the interrelated processes of direction, coordination, and supervision. These are the means by which plans are executed and results achieved. They consist of seeing to it that customer orders are obtained, that production and delivery schedules are met, that prescribed procedures are followed, and that expenditures are kept consistent with the established plans.

This mechanism, which might be called *direct control* or *concurrent control,* relies upon the leadership and human relations abilities of management to achieve its ends. It requires a capacity to anticipate potential trouble spots and to take action before trouble arises. It also presumes an ability to see when things are going wrong, without waiting for the more formal indications provided by specifically designed feedback linkages, and in this it shades imperceptibly into the third control process.

Control by Feedback Response

The third link in the chain of control techniques is *responsive control,* the actions taken on the basis of the observation and analysis of performance. The two elements in this process are the signal or *feedback* that action is necessary and the *response* to that signal. The feedback usually takes the form of observed differences or deviations between actual and planned performance. Routine weekly or monthly reports, for example, are *attention directing* in that they emphasize deviations from plans and signal the presence of conditions or problems that should be investigated.

Responses to feedback data are of two types: corrective and adaptive. The response should be a *corrective* action if direct control has been inadequate, and an *adaptive* action if the deviation was due to an inhospitable environment. Adaptive action is a kind of replanning, and this takes us back where we started.

It should be emphasized that performance reports or other information feedback mechanisms are not the control device. Control is accomplished by direct action, and all the reports in the world won't bring a deteriorating situation back under control unless they trigger some sort of action. Feedback, in other words, has an intermediate purpose—to improve the quality of the actions taken by management and to increase management's confidence that its actions are the right ones.

Control by Appraisal

The feedback mechanism serves another purpose—that of performance appraisal. The gap between actual and satisfactory performance helps management distribute rewards and penalties among its subordinates. Periodic performance reports thus serve a *scorecard* function for higher management in addition to the attention-directing function for management at the direct control level.

Appraisal performs three kinds of control tasks. First, the monetary and nonmonetary rewards accompanying consistent good performance and the penalties for poor performance inevitably affect the *motivation* of the affected personnel. If the reward structure is well conceived, this motivation should work positively to stimulate progress toward company goals.

Second, a soundly based appraisal system will lead to the promotion of the more effective managers to positions of greater scope and responsibility. This once again should contribute to company strength and profitability.

Third, the mere presence of an appraisal system can have a salutary effect on performance. People often behave differently—sometimes better, sometimes worse—if they know that their performance is being monitored.[1] Acceptance of the appraisal system is likely to improve performance, and management's task is to secure this acceptance.

The big problem here is that performance has many dimensions, many of them extremely difficult if not impossible to quantify. The things that can be easily measured may not be the most important aspects of performance, and emphasis on these aspects may direct performance in the wrong channels. When this happens, the blame is usually placed on the measurement system, but in truth the fault lies with management for misusing the measures that are available. Nevertheless, those who operate the feedback reporting system have an obligation to point out the shortcomings of their measures as well as to try to find ways of extending the scope of quantification.

Interrelationships among the Processes

The interrelationships among these processes are illustrated in Exhibit 1–1. Decisions and plans are made on the basis of information from various sources. These decisions are translated into action by the operating executives. Information on the results of these actions is recorded and compared with the planned results, and these comparisons then provide a basis either for corrective action (responsive control) or for adaptive action (replanning). They also serve in the appraisal of personnel.

Other Classification Systems

The few pages devoted here to the management control process can do no more than introduce the subject. A better understanding of the

---

[1] Some interesting evidence bearing on this point is provided by Neil C. Churchill, William W. Cooper, and Trevor Sainsbury, "Laboratory and Field Studies of the Behavioral Effects of Audits" in Charles P. Bonini, Robert K. Jaedicke, and Harvey M. Wagner, *Management Controls: New Directions in Basic Research* (New York: McGraw-Hill Book Co., Inc., 1964), pp. 253–67.

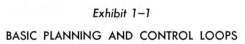

Exhibit 1–1

BASIC PLANNING AND CONTROL LOOPS

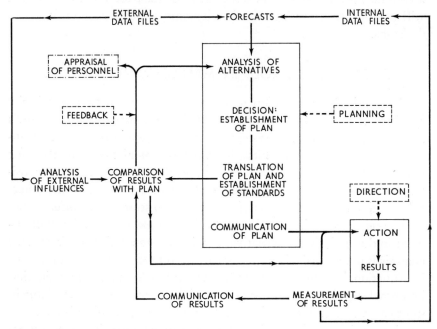

process requires both experience and exposure to the rather extensive literature that has developed over the years.

Various writers have chosen different ways of describing the structure of management controls. One of the most recent works, for example, uses a three-way breakdown—strategic planning, management control, and operational control—distinguishing largely on the basis of the scope of the decisions taken and their susceptibility to routinization.[2] Strategic planning concerns decisions with the largest scope and greatest potential impact (expansion into new markets), while at the other extreme operational control deals with actions that are narrow in focus and have short time horizons (eliminating excess inventories).

The choice of a classification scheme depends on its purpose, and our decision to describe management control in terms of a four-way classification of control mechanisms does not imply that other classification schemes are wrong—they just do not provide as good a background for the chapters that follow. For example, the principles underlying strategic planning decisions are the same as those that must be applied in

---

[2] Robert N. Anthony, *Planning and Control Systems: A Framework for Analysis* (Boston: Harvard Graduate School of Business Administration, Division of Research, 1965).

periodic budgeting, even though the impact of decisions of the former type may be potentially much greater than those of the latter. The accountant must provide the same kinds of data for both, and thus it will pay him to try to identify the elements common to both kinds of decisions.

ACCOUNTING'S ROLE IN MANAGEMENT CONTROL

Accounting's contribution to management control processes is the province of *managerial accounting.* An integral part of the company's management information system, managerial accounting serves management in several ways. First, it serves as a vital *source of data* for management planning. The accounts and document files are a repository of a vast quantity of details about the past progress of the enterprise, without which forecasts of the future can scarcely be made.

Second, it provides a cadre of *trained personnel* to assist management in the analysis of alternatives and in the preparation of plans. This analysis is not exclusively or necessarily even predominantly an accounting function, but attempting to plan without at least some participation by knowledgeable accounting personnel is a hazardous undertaking in most cases. In fact, the chief accounting officer or *controller* is an active and influential member of the top-management group in many companies, but he becomes so because of his personal qualities and the relevance of his experience. The title of controller does not necessarily carry with it direct control responsibilities except within the accounting organization.

Third, managerial accounting provides a *means of communicating* management plans upward, downward, and outward through the organization. At early stages in planning, this means identifying the feasibility and consistency of the various segments of the plan. At later stages it keeps all parties informed of the plans that have been agreed upon and their roles in these plans.

Fourth, it supplies *feedback reports,* for both attention-getting and scorecard-keeping purposes. This is often the most visible contribution of managerial accounting within the firm and perhaps for this reason gets the most attention.

Finally, managerial accounting has a role to play in the *interpretation of results.* Response to feedback data typically requires identification of the likely cause or causes of departures from plan and location of the responsibility for follow-up action. Within certain limits, this too can be an accounting function.

In short, managerial accounting is an important part of the company's management information system. Some would even maintain that the entire task of data gathering and information reporting is part of the accounting function. Others would not go so far, but few would deny that the management information system needs to be internally consistent, both for economy and for the quality of the information supplied. It makes no sense, for example, for a factory production department to collect its own figures on scrap recoveries while the accounting department is already doing the same thing. Furthermore, it can be a source of confusion if marketing management reports its performance in terms of orders booked while the accounting department bases its reports on products shipped. In other words, an effective management information system cannot be designed piecemeal. It must consider management's needs at all levels, and it should also provide a unified means of data accumulation and feedback.

OTHER FUNCTIONS OF ACCOUNTING

The accounting organization performs many functions other than those of managerial accounting. These may be classified for convenience into three groups:

1. *External reporting functions:* preparation of financial and statistical reports to shareholders, taxing authorities, and other interested parties.
2. *Internal control functions:* administration of systems to safeguard assets, maintain the accuracy of accounts, and review adherence to prescribed policies and procedures.
3. *Routine service functions:* maintenance of data and document files, preparation of invoices and payrolls, etc.

External Reporting

The external reporting functions are the province of *financial accounting,* designed to satisfy the information requirements of those whose focus of interest is the *company as a whole.* Its scope is largely limited to the development of historical reports summarizing the company's financial history and current financial position.

This contrasts sharply with managerial accounting, which tends to focus on segments of the company, such as product lines or divisions or branch territories. This is not to imply that management has no interest in financial accounting. On the contrary, management often uses data drawn from company income statements, funds statements, and balance sheets in making decisions on such matters as dividend distributions and new financing; but the dominant purpose of such statements is external rather than managerial, and the basic ground rules for external financial reporting are established by outsiders.

The breakdown of accounting information into internal and external categories is not always rigid. Sometimes the same figures are needed for both; sometimes internal figures that management does not use for decision making nevertheless need to be reported to outside groups to help justify the decisions that management has made.

For example, management would find cost data indispensable in preparing a bid for a special contract to supply a government agency with, say, 100,000 door latches. If the bid were accepted, the company might then need to use these same data in obtaining a bank loan to finance the project, and would probably use its records of actual costs incurred to secure payments from the government as work progressed.

Many other examples of the external usefulness of internal accounting data could be cited, but one or two more should be sufficient. Price justification in regulated industries or in response to allegations of antitrust law violations is one common need; labor contract negotiations may be another. Arguments for real estate tax abatement in some localities can be based largely on internal profit information.

Despite all these apparent inconsistencies, it remains useful to regard financial and managerial accounting as two separate components of the accounting program. This will help keep accounting methods and accounting purposes in clear relation to each other.

Internal Control

Internal control has been defined as "the plan of organization and all of the coordinate methods and measures adopted within a business to safeguard its assets, check the accuracy and reliability of its accounting data, promote operational efficiency, and encourage adherence to prescribed managerial policies."[3]

The asset-protection aspects of internal control constitute the system of *property control.* To help safeguard the company's cash balances, for example, only a limited number of persons should be granted the authority to approve the expenditure of company funds. In large or medium-sized companies and even in many small ones, these procedures generally also provide for the separation of the actual handling of cash and signing of checks from the authorization and approval process.

---

[3] Committee on Auditing Procedure, American Institute of (Certified Public) Accountants, *Internal Control* (New York: A.I.C.P.A., 1949), p. 6.

The accountant's responsibility for property control is pervasive, and references will be made throughout this book to procedures designed to perform this function. The main emphasis, however, is on the information functions of cost accounting, and the treatment of property control systems will be subordinated to this purpose.

Routine Services

Little need be said about the routine services provided by the accounting staff. It must maintain document files for evidentiary purposes and sometimes for later internal analysis as well. It must prepare a variety of command documents, such as employee payrolls and customer invoices.

All of these are important functions, and care must be exercised to insure that the system design is effective and economical. Typically the data input to the information system is produced in the document-preparation operation, which means that both objectives must be recognized in system design.

THE PLACE OF COST ACCOUNTING

With all this as background, we may at last be in a position to try to indicate what cost accounting is. Perhaps the most logical way to begin is with a definition of cost. *Cost represents the resources that have been or must be sacrificed to attain a particular objective.* For example, the objective may be to acquire a plot of land, and cost is measured by the amount of cash that will have to be paid to acquire the land. Other objectives may require different methods of *measuring* cost, as we shall see in Chapter 3, but the definition is universal.

Cost accounting, then, deals with the measurement of resource sacrifices. By itself, however, this definition is more pedantic than useful. A better approach is to ask what a company's cost accounting department is likely to do. It is typically concerned primarily with four activities, often though not exclusively in connection with factory operations:

1. *Cost finding:* measurement or estimation of the costs of individual products, departments, or other segments of the firm's operations.
2. *Cost analysis:* estimation of the relationships between costs and various determinants of costs.
3. *Cost recording:* classification and distribution of costs among the various ledger accounts.
4. *Cost reporting*: communication of cost data to various interested parties.

These four activities are the nucleus of cost accounting, no matter how much more broadly we may find it convenient to define the field. At least part of each of them is an element of financial accounting, while another part belongs to managerial accounting. Some features serve both branches.

Cost accounting's main contribution to financial accounting is in providing the data used to distinguish between those factory costs that are to be charged against current revenues as expenses and those that are to be assigned to the company-produced goods and services in end-of-period inventories. This is primarily a matter of cost finding, and we shall begin to examine this aspect of cost accounting in Chapter 4.

Cost accounting's role in managerial accounting is much more diffused and hence more difficult to pin down. For managerial purposes, cost data are often of limited usefulness by themselves, but need to be weighed in conjunction with revenue and investment data as well. Furthermore, the principles governing the processing and analysis of cost data for management cannot really be separated from those governing the recording, reporting, and analysis of other kinds of data. For these reasons the cost finding, cost analysis, cost recording, and cost reporting activities of managerial accounting cannot be developed or discussed in isolation but must be fully integrated into the planning and control framework into which they must fit.

Reflecting this view, cost accounting is defined here more broadly as *the body of concepts, methods, and procedures used to measure, analyze, or estimate the costs, profitability, and performance of individual products, departments, and other segments of a company's operations, for either internal or external use or both, and to report on these questions to the interested parties.*

Thus defined, cost accounting encompasses all of managerial accounting and the factory cost finding aspects of financial accounting as well. To objections that this is too broad a definition, the only reply is that it is intended primarily to delineate an area that must be studied as an interrelated whole. Narrower definitions would not succeed in narrowing the scope of the inquiry. Thus in a sense it doesn't matter how the subject is defined, as long as narrower definitions are accompanied by an appropriately wider selection of contributory material.

SUMMARY

Accounting is first and foremost a service function, centering on the provision of information. Financial accounting consists of providing companywide information, primarily to outsiders, while managerial accounting is devoted to supplying information to management on segments of the firm's operations, for use in the various processes of management control.

This chapter has distinguished four control techniques: planning, direction and supervision, feedback response, and appraisal. All of these require accounting data to some extent, and a major portion of the task of supplying such data is in the domain of cost accounting. Narrowly defined, cost accounting consists of the activities of cost finding, cost analysis, cost recording, and cost reporting, primarily in factory operations. These activities must be so closely integrated with the rest of managerial accounting, however, that the study of cost accounting requires a full understanding of the entire managerial accounting structure. In the next chapter we shall introduce a simple illustration to show how this is supposed to work.

Cost accounting also serves financial accounting by deriving product unit cost data for use in pricing end-of-period inventory balances and determining the cost of goods sold. One task of the following chapters will be to examine the methods used for this purpose in terms of their applicability to managerial problems.

DISCUSSION QUESTIONS

1. What is *cost?*
2. What service does the cost accountant perform for the company's shareholders?
3. To what extent is planning an accounting function?
4. What purposes are served by the accounting data files? What kinds of data would you expect to find in the cost accounting portion of the data files?
5. Distinguish between the attention-getting and scorecard purposes of accounting reports.
6. What is the relationship between planning and policy determination?
7. Describe the process of control by feedback response. What part does the cost accountant play in this process?
8. "Control information is provided by means of comparisons." What kinds of comparisons would you find most useful for this purpose?
9. What is *internal control?* How does it differ from the four types of management control processes outlined in this chapter?
10. A factory manager recently told the factory accountant to cost all factory materials at replacement cost. The accountant replied that he could not comply because this would violate generally accepted accounting principles. Is this a valid argument?

Chapter 2

ESSENTIALS OF FINANCIAL PLANNING AND CONTROL

A VITAL PART of the management control network in most companies of any size is provided by the system of periodic financial budgets and operating reports. The purpose of this chapter is to describe in broad outline what these budgets and reports are and how they can serve management. To permit us to focus on the process itself, discussion of the criteria by which management chooses from among alternative plans will be deferred to Chapter 3, together with other basic planning concepts.

FINANCIAL PLANNING THROUGH BUDGETS

Budgets are the expression, largely in financial terms, of management's plans for operating and financing the enterprise during specific periods of time. They are instruments of management control in three ways: (1) as the means of organizing and directing a large segment of the management planning process; (2) as continuing reminders of current plans and programs for the guidance of day-to-day management; and (3) as the bench marks against which to measure actual performance.

The Budget Defined

The definition of a budget may be summarized as *a predetermined, detailed plan of action developed and distributed as a guide to current operations and as a partial basis for the subsequent evaluation of performance.* For example, the operating budget of a service company might be summarized as in the following table:

	Actual Last Year	Budget This Year
Sales................................	$412,000	$450,000
Expenses:		
Executive salaries.................	$ 51,000	$ 55,000
Servicemen's salaries..............	214,000	225,000
Office salaries.....................	28,000	30,000
Rent............................	20,000	20,000
Supplies.........................	4,000	5,000
Other expenses...................	6,000	6,000
Total expenses.................	$323,000	$341,000
Net Income.......................	$ 89,000	$109,000

Components of an Overall Budget System

A complete budget system is made up of a number of individual budgets. These budgets may generally be classified into four categories: (1) physical budgets, (2) cost budgets, (3) profit budgets, and (4) finance budgets. Exhibit 2–1 shows some of the major components of each of these groups.

Exhibit 2–1

BUDGET COMPONENTS

Physical Budgets	Cost Budgets	Profit Budgets	Finance Budgets
Unit sales		Dollar sales	Cash
Unit production	Manufacturing costs		Capital outlays
Unit purchases	Selling costs	Cost of goods sold	Financing
Unit inventories	Administrative costs	Expenses	Balance sheet
Manpower	Financing costs		
Facilities	Research costs		

Most of these components will be further subdivided to show details that are necessary for planning or control. For example, the unit sales and dollar sales budgets will probably be broken down by sales divisions and by product lines. They may also be classified by sales territory, customer category, or any other desired grouping. Each plant will have its own manufacturing cost budget, classified according to organization lines within the factory and also according to the nature of the cost. Finance budgets are more likely to be restricted to the company as a whole, but a certain amount of subdivision is frequently encountered in these as well. A company which has incorporated subsidiaries may even have separate financing budgets for each subsidiary.

The process of segmenting the budget does not take place after the overall company budgets are established. Rather, the company budgets represent a consolidation and coordination of the detailed budget components. Most budgets start from forecasts of sales volume, detailed to fit the company's product line, organization, and operating characteristics. On the basis of forecasted sales, budgets are prepared for production and the related functions of purchasing, manpower, and facilities. On this basis, cost budgets are prepared and combined with the sales budgets into profit budgets. Cash, capital outlay, and other finance budgets are prepared in conjunction with the cost and profit budgets, and the end result is a complete financial plan for the operations of the company during the budget period.

Business versus Governmental and Personal Budgets

A distinction is often drawn between business budgets, on the one hand, and governmental and personal budgets, on the other. The latter, it is said, are limiting and restrictive, whereas the former are not. Rautenstrauch and Villers, for example, make the statement that "public budgets only *reflect* a policy, while industrial budgets *create* a policy."[1] Personal budgets are even more restrictive in that the ability of the individual to increase his total expenditures during a given period is even more limited than that of most business enterprises.

Perhaps a more fundamental difference is that the choice among alternative business plans often depends on the input/output relationships reflected in the budget, whereas criteria for acceptance of government or personal expenditure programs cannot be expressed precisely in budgetary terms.

The distinction should not be overdrawn, however. All budgets are to some extent an expression of policies and agreed-upon means to desired and acceptable goals. In this sense, all budgets are an expression of standards as to the best means of achieving certain objectives under expected conditions; but if conditions change or new opportunities arise, the budget can always be changed. Governmental budgets tend to be less flexible in execution than business budgets because the mechanism for securing authority to increase budget allowances is much slower and more cumbersome—most business executives can exceed budgeted expenditures within limits without consulting higher management—but

---

[1] Walter Rautenstrauch and Raymond Villers, *Budgetary Control* (New York: Funk & Wagnalls Co., 1950), p. 5.

in both cases the criterion for the change is that the added benefits exceed the added costs.

The Budget Span

Budgeting terminology generally distinguishes between *budgets* which are prepared to cover a period of a year or less in advance and *plans* which peer farther into the future. For a company that has both, the current budget is typically the current year's segment of the long-term plan and is wholly integrated with it.

Both long-range plans and short-range budgets are plans in the sense that we are using the term, and the process by which they are developed is essentially the same. They differ mainly in the degree of confidence with which they are advanced, in the detail in which they are presented, and consequently in the force of their impact on day-to-day operating decisions.

Annual budgets are typically prepared as a consolidation of a series of 12 monthly budgets, or if prepared as a set of annual figures, they are usually divided later on into monthly segments. Monthly figures are necessary to provide interim bench marks against which to compare actual results, particularly if seasonal influences are strong.

Budgeting as an Iterative Process

Few budgets can or should be prepared simply by adding together the various budget proposals made by each of the operating executives. As one executive was recently quoted as saying: "Every division wants to at least triple its research and double its sales force. If we let them get away with it, we'd have the damnedest profit and loss statements you ever saw."[2]

Even after discounting the financial man's bias in such matters, it must be acknowledged that few if any budgets are the same as the proposals originally submitted. The problem is threefold. First, budget proposals must be reviewed at higher levels for consistency with company objectives, current policies, and the plans of other parts of the organization. In a multi-tiered organization, this review process is likely to be repeated several times as the proposals move upward toward final approval.

The second problem is that the feasibility of each plan has to be tested. Does the company have the capacity to carry out the proposed plans? Different companies will face different kinds of capacity re-

---

[2] Donald P. Selleck, Controller of Minnesota Mining and Manufacturing Company, quoted in *The Wall Street Journal,* December 20, 1965, p. 1.

straints, but the most common are money, production facilities, and people. Without adequate funds to finance plans, production capacity to meet delivery requirements, or people to staff departments, proposed programs simply cannot be carried out. When this sort of situation arises, capacity has to be rationed in ways that will create the least conflict with the company's objectives.

The third reason for higher level scrutiny of budget proposals is really an offshoot of the first. Estimates and forecasts are subject to a variety of errors and biases, and therefore often need to be examined with a jaundiced eye.

The Role of Accounting in Budgeting

The budget is no more the creature of the controller than of the treasurer or the personnel manager, but the controller may have a good deal more to do with it than any other staff executive. The role of accounting in business planning of all sorts is to provide certain types of data and to assist in the analysis and interpretation of data. In budgeting, moreover, accountants on the budget director's staff join with production specialists, marketing specialists, and others to review budget proposals for technical accuracy and consistency. The budget director also has the responsibility of preparing and disseminating the documents embodying the agreed-upon, coordinated plan to the operating executives who have prepared and approved it. The budget director usually reports to the controller, although in some companies he serves as an independent staff advisor to top management.

A BUDGETARY PLANNING AND CONTROL SYSTEM

An illustration may be helpful in demonstrating the budgetary planning and control process. The Apex Lighting Company is in the business of designing and installing lighting systems for factories and commercial buildings, streets, and highways. As an adjunct of this work, it also does remedial and repair work on existing systems, mostly in rewiring older offices and apartment buildings. The company's organization chart is shown in Exhibit 2–2.

Background Situation

Early in 1967, the Apex board of directors decided that drastic action was necessary to arrest a decline in the company's fortunes. As Exhibit 2–3 shows, the company had reported annual operating losses for each of the three previous years, and these losses had been growing. Only a

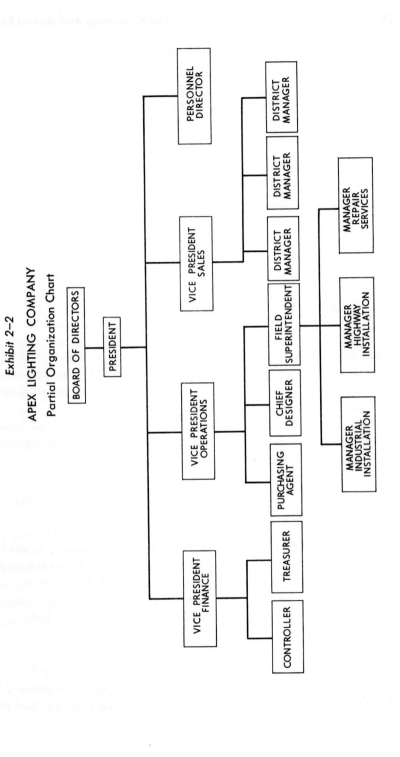

Exhibit 2–2

APEX LIGHTING COMPANY

Partial Organization Chart

BOARD OF DIRECTORS

PRESIDENT

VICE PRESIDENT FINANCE

VICE PRESIDENT OPERATIONS

VICE PRESIDENT SALES

PERSONNEL DIRECTOR

CONTROLLER

TREASURER

PURCHASING AGENT

CHIEF DESIGNER

FIELD SUPERINTENDENT

DISTRICT MANAGER

DISTRICT MANAGER

DISTRICT MANAGER

MANAGER INDUSTRIAL INSTALLATION

MANAGER HIGHWAY INSTALLATION

MANAGER REPAIR SERVICES

Exhibit 2–3

APEX LIGHTING COMPANY

Comparative Statement of Income
For the Years 1964 through 1966

	1964	1965	1966
Sales................................	$4,000,000	$4,100,000	$3,800,000
Less:			
Wages and salaries..............	$1,800,000	$1,875,000	$1,800,000
Materials and supplies..........	1,200,000	1,220,000	1,210,000
Travel expense.................	200,000	195,000	210,000
Depreciation...................	180,000	185,000	190,000
Other operating expenses.......	820,000	845,000	855,000
Interest expense...............	5,000	5,000	5,000
Total expenses..............	$4,205,000	$4,325,000	$4,270,000
Net Income (Loss)...............	$ (205,000)	$ (225,000)	$ (470,000)

small amount of interest-bearing debt was outstanding, but the poor earnings history limited the company's access to new capital funds and the company could not stand more than another year or two of losses on the recent scale without endangering its solvency.

This decision for drastic action was reached on the basis of accounting information—in this case the companywide financial statements. The accounting information was not sufficiently detailed, however, to show the directors what was wrong or what ought to be done, and the existing accounting system did not provide for more detailed reporting. At this point an outside consulting firm was called in to study the situation.

The consultants reported that the company's operating expense ratios were much higher than those of its competitors but that the existing accounting records were too fragmentary to reveal the source or extent of any inefficiencies. They also noted that whereas Apex Lighting had concentrated its efforts on new commercial and industrial lighting systems, its major competitors had been diversifying rapidly into other lines and had been able to report increasing profits.

Acting on the consultants' advice, the president brought in the management services division of the company's public accounting firm to begin work immediately on the design of an adequate internal financial planning and reporting system.

Preparing the Operating Budget

The consultants felt that the most urgent need was for a cash and profit plan for the company as a whole. To accomplish this, each of the company's operating executives was asked to prepare estimates for those budget elements falling within his jurisdiction.

The starting point was the sales vice president's forecast of sales, classified into three "product lines": industrial installations, highway installations, and repair services. The company's executives regarded these as three separate markets, and sales revenues had been classified on this basis for the past several years.

The sales vice president's first step was to circulate to his district managers an economic forecast of general business conditions that had been provided by the company's commercial bank. The record of monthly sales in each district for the three previous years, classified by product line, was also sent to the various district managers by the sales vice president. He told them to assume that the size of the sales force would remain unchanged for the remainder of the year but that increased promotional expenditures of other kinds could be proposed if strong evidence of their profitability could be presented.

With this information as background, each district manager prepared his own sales forecast and a tentative selling expense budget for the remaining months of the year. The entire sales management group then attended a meeting at which these forecasts were revised and consolidated into tentative sales and selling expense budgets for the year.

The sales budget was then turned over to the operating and design vice presidents, who were asked to prepare cost and manpower estimates for the volumes of work planned, using the limited amount of historical accounting data available and drawing on the results of their work with the consultants up to then. As they prepared these estimates, they also checked to make sure that adequate capacity existed in the installation departments and in the design division to service the volume of sales budgeted.

A tentative expense budget was also submitted by the personnel manager, and the controller drew up a similar proposal for his own department. Because of the small size of the company and the constant communication among the executives concerned during the planning process, no revisions were necessary at this point and the controller had only to add the various proposals together to derive the final *operating budget* or *profit plan* shown in Exhibit 2–4. This profit budget was also broken down on a monthly basis to facilitate purchasing and cash scheduling as well as to provide a basis for subsequent control reporting.

This profit plan reflected the basic expense breakdown incorporated in the new chart of accounts. Note that only three of these expense categories—productive labor, productive materials, and other field expenses—were assigned to individual product lines. None of the others

Exhibit 2–4

APEX LIGHTING COMPANY

Summary Profit Budget for the Year 1967

	Industrial Installations	Highway Installations	Repair Services	Total
Service revenues..................	$2,200,000	$500,000	$1,500,000	$4,200,000
Less: Productive labor..............	$ 620,000	$150,000	$ 390,000	$1,160,000
Productive material...........	920,000	70,000	370,000	1,360,000
Other field expenses...........	190,000	80,000	140,000	410,000
Gross margin.....................	$ 470,000	$200,000	$ 600,000	$1,270,000
Less: Depreciation................				$ 300,000
Sales salaries................				250,000
Other selling expenses.........				409,000
Administrative salaries........				200,000
Other operating expenses......				485,000
Interest expense..............				5,000
Total general expense.......				$1,649,000
Net Income (Loss)................				$ (379,000)

was readily traceable to any one product line. For example, all salesmen handled all lines, and salesmen were paid a straight salary and no commission on the volume sold. Tracing salary expenses to individual product lines was thus impossible. The accountants felt that a product line classification of some of the other expenses might be desirable later on, but for the time being they were satisfied to start with the three readily traceable items.

The Cash Budget

While the profit plan was being prepared, the president asked each division manager to submit proposals for expenditures on equipment, long-range market development, and other purposes not immediately concerned with current operations. The controller consolidated all of these proposals with his own estimates of the cash flows deriving from the profit plan and prepared the following tentative cash budget for the year:

Collections from customers...............		$4,100,000
Less: Payments on current operating expenses......		3,900,000
Net cash flow from operations..............		$ 200,000
Nonoperating expenditures:		
Market research and development............$100,000		
Equipment replacement....................... 250,000		
Additional equipment....................... 150,000		
Dividends (equal to 1966 total)............... 40,000		
Total nonoperating expenditures............		540,000
Net Cash Outflow...........................		$ 340,000

Although the controller knew that the company's cash resources were inadequate to finance all of the proposed expenditures, his task at this stage was solely to assemble the estimates and prepare them for review by top management. It is not feasible in this space to discuss the criteria by which management decided which proposals to accept and which to reject. The final decision was to omit the dividend, reject most of the equipment proposals, but maintain as much of the market research and development expenditures as the company's resources would permit. No cutback of operations was required. On May 15 the final operating and cash budgets were approved by the board of directors and distributed to the responsible executives.

The Advantages of Budgeting

The values of budgeting lie as much in the process as in the resulting documents. Perhaps the greatest advantage of the budgeting process is that it forces periodic *self-examination* as to functions, methods, objectives, and costs. Although a budget can be prepared simply on the basis of what was done last year, adjusted for any changes in conditions or scope of the activity that may be anticipated for the coming year, the soundly conceived budgeting plan should stimulate the supervisor or other executive to take a more critical view of his own operations than he is likely to do in directing day-to-day operations.

The budgeting process also forces executives to *quantify* their plans and to examine the feasibility of these plans in terms of both profitability and consistency with the plans of other segments of the company. The budget gives management a chance to *anticipate* and in many cases to consider revision of basic policies before the need for this revision might otherwise become apparent through the urgency of a deteriorating situation.

The hurry in which the Apex Lighting Company produced its first plan did not permit realization of many of these benefits. Furthermore, many of the estimates were much less reliable than would be normally expected. Even so, some progress had been made in both of these directions, and the final budget itself brought home to the entire management group just how far they had to go before the company would be out of its present difficulties. They were impressed by the greater percentage profit margins to be obtained on highway and repair work and by the need to increase sales volume to cover the company's heavy selling and administrative expenses.

Perhaps most important, more executives had been drawn farther into the management process than ever before. The firm's consultants and accountants had been insistent from the outset that company personnel *participate* in all stages of budget preparation. This caused a certain amount of stress and strain, but when the budget was finally submitted, it was in every sense the company's own budget, not one imposed by a group of outsiders. Every executive was to some extent committed to his portion of the budget. Furthermore, he was more familiar with the details of the budget than he would have been without participation.

CONTROL REPORTING

The heart of the new accounting system of the Apex Lighting Company was in the monthly expense and profit reports issued to management. Expenses were classified departmentally; profits were reported by product line.

Responsibility Centers and Cost Centers

Expense reporting for internal cost control is tied closely to the concept of responsibility—that is, costs should be reported to the executives who have authority to incur them and the obligation to keep them under control. In fact, responsibility can be defined as an *obligation to perform* specified tasks.

This concept is reflected in the company's organization structure in that each block in the organization chart represents a *responsibility center*—an organization unit headed by a single person, *answerable* to higher authority and obligated to perform certain tasks. The responsibility centers of the lowest level are known by different names in different companies, *department* being perhaps the most common.

Individual departments may be further subdivided into *cost centers,* the basic organization unit for cost accumulation. The purpose of any such subdivision is to increase the homogeneity of the basic accounting data. In other words, if a responsibility center encompasses both machine-paced and manual operations, it may be desirable to record separately the costs associated with each type. For discussion purposes, it is usually permissible to assume that each department consists of a single cost center, but it should be remembered that this is not always true in practice.

This fragmentation of responsibility is necessary whenever the business is too large and too complex for one man to have direct contact with all operations. The scope of the operations with which a supervisor can have adequate working familiarity, or the *span of control,* varies directly with the technical complexity of the operations and with the number of different kinds of activities to be carried out by the group. Thus the operations of 20 or 30 identical automatic machines may require only one supervisor, whereas a 30-man maintenance force may call for a half-dozen crew bosses.

The departments are ordinarily grouped in divisions on the basis of some unifying principle. The divisional structure in the Apex Lighting Company is based on the grouping of related functions (sales, operations, etc.) in a single division. Divisions organized on this basis are called *functional* divisions. In other companies the division structure may center on the company's various product lines, geographical regions, or classes of customers.

The Chart of Accounts: Organizational Classification

The responsibility unit structure sets the pattern that the budget and accounting structure must follow. Each element of cost or revenue, both in the budget and in the accumulation of results, must be traced to the organization segment in which responsibility lies. Thus at a minimum there should be one account or group of accounts for each responsibility unit. To facilitate data processing, each unit is normally assigned an identifying number or alphabetic code conforming to some systematic plan. Exhibit 2–5 lists the code designations of the responsibility centers of the Apex Lighting Company. In this case, the first digit indicates the division, the second the section of the division, and the third the department. A fourth digit is used for subsections of the various operating departments, but these are not reproduced in this condensed illustration.

Exhibit 2–5

APEX LIGHTING COMPANY
Partial List of Responsibility Centers

Number	Name	Number	Name
1100	Operations Executive	3100	Sales Executive
1200	Purchasing	3200	District A
1300	Design	3300	District B
1400	Field Operations	3400	District C
1410	Industrial Installation	4100	Finance Executive
1420	Highway Installation	4200	Controller
1430	Repair Services	4300	Treasurer
2000	Personnel		

This coding is not necessarily the most efficient for data processing, but it illustrates clearly the relationships of the responsibility centers to each other. It also helps point out that responsibility is cumulative; that is, although an executive can delegate certain tasks to his subordinates, he cannot thereby relieve himself of the responsibility for performing those tasks. He is always answerable to higher authority for the performance of the duties assigned to him. In this sense, the operations vice president's responsibility center actually encompasses all the responsibility centers subordinate to it.

The Chart of Accounts: Descriptive Detail

A single summary account for each responsibility center is seldom adequate to provide data either for planning purposes or for control reporting. Such a summary account is not homogeneous—it encompasses items subject to many different behavior patterns and different control actions. For example, if the costs of company-paid health insurance benefits depend solely on the age of the employee and the number of his dependents, they should not be charged to the same account as payroll taxes that vary with the employee's gross pay.

To provide data of greater homogeneity, each department's costs are typically classified by "natural elements" such as salaries, supplies, power costs, and so on. This classification can be more accurately termed a *descriptive* classification because there is nothing inherently "natural" about any particular breakdown. The scheme will depend on the nature of the activity and on human judgment as to the degree of detail that is necessary. For example, one company may recognize only one category of factory supplies, whereas another may subdivide this element into six or eight categories.

In addition to the natural element classification, the chart of accounts may also classify the costs of a responsibility unit in other ways—by operation performed, by product class, or perhaps by customer group in the case of marketing department costs. Revenue data may be similarly subclassified on several bases to provide adequate detail in the basic accounting records to facilitate analysis of sales by product line, customer group, territory, channel of distribution, and so on. This cross-classification of data permits management to obtain information pertinent to several dimensions of its operations—information which will be useful not only in the explanation of deviations from planned performance but also in the analysis of alternative courses of action. If these classifications are made at the time the transactions occur, it will be much easier to analyze the data later on.

The costs of achieving this ideal would very likely be prohibitive, however, even in the highly unlikely event that full knowledge of the underlying behavioral patterns and determinants of cost was available. The more accounts there are, the higher will be the recording costs and the greater will be the chance of clerical error in classification (it is much harder to make an error if only one account exists than if there are one hundred). Thus, compromise on this issue has considerable justification.

The elemental breakdown of operating costs in the Apex Lighting

Exhibit 2–6

APEX LIGHTING COMPANY

Chart of Accounts: Field Departments

Department / Element	1400 Field Super- intendent	1410 Industrial Installation	1420 Highway Installation	1430 Repair Services
01 Productive labor	1400.01	1410.01	1420.01	1430.01
11 Supervision	1400.11	1410.11	1420.11	1430.11
12 Labor—travel time	1400.12	1410.12	1420.12	1430.12
13 Labor—idle time	1400.13	1410.13	1420.13	1430.13
14 Clerical labor	1400.14	1410.14	1420.14	1430.14
15 Other labor	1400.15	1410.15	1420.15	1430.15
21 Overtime premium	1400.21	1410.21	1420.21	1430.21
22 Vacation and holiday pay	1400.22	1410.22	1420.22	1430.22
23 Payroll taxes	1400.23	1410.23	1420.23	1430.23
24 Pensions	1400.24	1410.24	1420.24	1430.24
31 Travel allowances	1400.31	1410.31	1420.31	1430.31
41 Productive materials	1400.41	1410.41	1420.41	1430.41
51 Tools	1400.51	1410.51	1420.51	1430.51
52 Supplies	1400.52	1410.52	1420.52	1430.52
53 Equipment rental	1400.53	1410.53	1420.53	1430.53
54 Depreciation	1400.54	1410.54	1420.54	1430.54
61 Insurance	1400.61	1410.61	1420.61	1430.61
71 Other expense	1400.71	1410.71	1420.71	1430.71

Company's new chart of accounts varied to some extent from division to division. The basic structure of costs for the three field departments of the operations division is shown in Exhibit 2–6, p. 27. Again, a numerical coding system was used. When a cost was incurred, it was identified by department and classified as to the nature of the goods or services consumed. For example, if John Jones worked a full eight hours in the repair service department at an hourly rate of $3, the account 1430.01 (Repair Service—Productive Labor) would be debited with $24.

The Financial Reporting System

The focus of the new internal accounting system was on a set of internal performance reports. Some of these were to provide current cost control information, while others had broader implications for managerial decision making.

The more comprehensive control reports were to be issued monthly, for the most part, although certain reports would go weekly or even daily to crew foremen in the field. These reports were to inform each manager of the major deviations between actual costs and the standard or budgeted amounts *within his own area of responsibility,* so that he could investigate the causes and take whatever corrective action seemed necessary. This is known as *responsibility accounting.*

In the absence of any such deviations, it would be presumed that operations were under control and management could devote its efforts to cost reduction programs or other worthwhile activities of an innovative nature. This focusing of attention on the areas most in need of it is the principle of *management by exception.*

Financial Reporting to Top Management

The reports issued to a company's top management are usually highly condensed. The company's management information system routinely accumulates a wide variety of statistical and financial data. Only the most important of these data should be summarized and reported to top management.

Most financial reports to top management summarize the company's profit performance for the most recent period. Because the main focus of management's attention in the Apex Lighting Company seemed likely to be on trends and profitability of the company's three product lines, the periodic top-management profit performance reports were organized on a product line basis.

Beginning with June, a summary income statement was prepared in the form illustrated in Exhibit 2–7. During the first six months the

Exhibit 2–7

APEX LIGHTING COMPANY

Condensed Comparative Income Statement
For the Month of June, 1967

	This Month			Year to Date		
	Planned	Actual	Deviation	Planned	Actual	Deviation
Service revenues...........	$400,000	$440,000	$40,000	$2,250,000	$2,320,000	$70,000
Field service expenses......	275,000	296,000	(21,000)	1,638,000	1,670,000	(32,000)
Gross margin.............	$125,000	$144,000	$19,000	$ 612,000	$ 650,000	$38,000
Less: Depreciation.........	$ 25,000	$ 25,000	...	$ 150,000	$ 150,000	...
Sales salaries.........	21,000	22,000	$(1,000)	130,000	132,000	$(2,000)
Other selling expenses.	31,000	33,000	(2,000)	215,000	219,000	(4,000)
Administrative salaries...............	18,000	17,000	1,000	110,000	108,000	2,000
Other operating expense.............	39,000	35,000	4,000	252,000	243,000	9,000
Interest expense......	1,000	1,000	...	3,000	3,000	...
Total general expense...........	$135,000	$133,000	$ 2,000	$ 860,000	$ 855,000	$ 5,000
Net Income (Loss)........	$(10,000)	$ 11,000	$21,000	$ (251,000)	$ (208,000)	$43,000

company not only met its immediate profit goals but surpassed them by $43,000. As the exhibit shows, almost half of this came in June, when the company actually reported a small profit instead of the $10,000 loss that had been budgeted. Although this reflected to some extent the immediate effects of the newly instituted cost control and cost reduction programs, most of the improvement came from an increase in total service revenues.

Informative though this report was, it was not very useful to management. First, it failed to throw any light on operations in the individual product lines. Second, expense variances were not divisionalized, so that management had no idea who was ahead of the plan and who wasn't.

To remedy these defects, the report was recast in the form shown in Exhibit 2–8. From this it can be seen that the increased volume came entirely from highway installations and repair services, the two high-margin lines. Industrial installations continued to account for the lion's share of total service revenues, but they failed to meet the sales targets incorporated in the budget. Profitability ratios in this line improved,

Exhibit 2-8

APEX LIGHTING COMPANY

Condensed Comparative Income Statement
For the Month of June, 1967

	This Month			Year to Date		
	Planned	Actual	Deviation	Planned	Actual	Deviation
Service revenues:						
Industrial installations	$220,000	$206,000	$(14,000)	$1,350,000	$1,282,000	$(68,000)
Highway installations	70,000	105,000	35,000	200,000	280,000	80,000
Repair services	110,000	129,000	19,000	700,000	758,000	58,000
Total Service Revenues	$400,000	$440,000	$ 40,000	$2,250,000	$2,320,000	$ 70,000
Product line margin:						
Industrial installations	$ 53,000	$ 51,000	$ (2,000)	$ 270,000	$ 260,000	$(10,000)
Highway installations	28,000	41,000	13,000	76,000	109,000	33,000
Repair services	44,000	52,000	8,000	266,000	281,000	15,000
Total product line margin	$125,000	$144,000	$ 19,000	$ 612,000	$ 650,000	$ 38,000
Less departmental expenses:						
Sales	$ 58,000	$ 59,000	$ (1,000)	$ 380,000	$ 382,000	$ (2,000)
Operations	39,000	35,000	4,000	250,000	244,000	6,000
Finance	21,000	22,000	(1,000)	130,000	128,000	2,000
Personnel	4,000	4,000	...	24,000	24,000	...
Executive office	12,000	12,000	...	76,000	77,000	(1,000)
Total departmental expenses	$134,000	$132,000	$ 2,000	$ 860,000	$ 855,000	$ 5,000
Operating income (loss)	$ (9,000)	$ 12,000	$ 21,000	$(248,000)	$ (205,000)	$ 43,000
Less other expenses:						
Interest expense	1,000	1,000	...	3,000	3,000	...
Income taxes	...	...	...	...	...	...
Net Income (Loss)	$(10,000)	$ 11,000	$ 21,000	$ (251,000)	$ (208,000)	$ 43,000

however, and the failure to meet sales targets had a much smaller effect on profit than would have been the case earlier because the cost of doing the industrial work declined substantially.

Reports of this type cannot solve management's problems but they do serve a vital purpose in calling attention to favorable and unfavorable developments that might otherwise go overlooked. In a company as small as Apex Lighting, no further detail might be provided to top management. In larger companies, on the other hand, the deviations from budget would often be subjected to further analysis intended to identify some of the major causes of the profit deviation. How much of the deviation was due to a change in service prices? Did the richer product mix result from a shift in sales emphasis induced by sales management's recognition of the greater profit margins to be had in the highway and repair service lines? Or was it merely a case of increased business activity in general, with the Apex Lighting Company merely sharing in the improved fortunes of its customers? To what extent did current revenues result from sales activity in the past? Knowing the reasons for deviations, management is in a far better position either to change its plans or to take actions within the company that will bring its goals within reach.

Divisional Reporting: Sales Management

The reports to top management are usually only the tip of the iceberg. Even a company as small as Apex Lighting will ordinarily have an extensive set of detailed reports on various phases of operations, each one limited to a particular area of the business and tied to a particular set of responsibilities.

Exhibit 2–9 illustrates one report that went to the sales vice president of the Apex Lighting Company. Two things in this report are worth noting. First, the upper half of the report deals with orders received rather than with service revenues. Apex recognizes revenues as work is performed, but in industrial and highway installation work this is usually considerably after the sales division has done its job. The divisional report in this case concentrated, therefore, on orders received.

Second, the expenses reported to the sales manager are limited to *controllable* items. Attention is thus focused on those items that the division head or his subordinates can do something about. Omission of an item from this report does not necessarily mean that it is not controllable by anyone, however. It merely means that the head of *this* responsibility center can exercise no significant amount of control over it.

Exhibit 2–9

APEX LIGHTING COMPANY

Sales Division Performance Report
For the Month of June, 1967

	This Month			Year to Date		
	Planned	Actual	Deviation	Planned	Actual	Deviation
Orders received, by district:						
District A...............	$100,000	$110,000	$ 10,000	$ 580,000	$ 600,000	$ 20,000
District B...............	100,000	106,000	6,000	610,000	649,000	39,000
District C...............	170,000	202,000	32,000	1,210,000	1,229,000	19,000
Total Net Orders Received.....	$370,000	$418,000	$ 48,000	$2,400,000	$2,478,000	$ 78,000
Orders received, by product lines						
Industrial installations........	$200,000	$184,000	$(16,000)	$1,350,000	$1,268,000	$(82,000)
Highway installations..........	50,000	95,000	45,000	300,000	400,000	100,000
Repair services...............	120,000	139,000	19,000	750,000	810,000	60,000
Total Net Orders Received.....	$370,000	$418,000	$ 48,000	$2,400,000	$2,478,000	$ 78,000
Controllable expenses:						
District A...............	$ 6,698	$ 7,310	$ (612)	$ 39,145	$ 38,438	$ 707
District B...............	7,214	7,007	207	44,550	44,398	152
District C...............	12,345	12,965	(620)	83,633	87,978	(4,345)
Division headquarters.......	18,417	17,970	447	124,492	116,831	7,661
Total Controllable Expenses....	$ 44,674	$ 45,252	(578)	$ 291,820	$ 287,645	$ 4,175

Departmental Reporting: District Manager

Direct responsibility for the sales force in the Apex Lighting Company is lodged in the three district managers. A report like that in Exhibit 2–10 is issued to each district manager at the end of each month.

Notice how much more detail is contained in this report than in the top-management profit summary or even in the division management report. This is because it is only at this level that the detail is relevant to management action. Many companies pass information copies of these detailed reports upstream so that higher management can pursue points of specific interest to the source, but the main purpose of the detailed reports is to assist lower level management in carrying out its responsibilities.

Periodic Reporting: The Control Limit Concept

Little purpose would be served by continuing this illustration through the various levels of the operations, finance, and personnel divisions. The specifics would differ but the basic concepts would be the same. One point needs emphasis, however. The input/output relationships that reflect themselves ultimately in a company's income and cost reports are not rigidly defined. A single-valued plan is merely one of a number of possible outcomes contained within a band that may be wide or narrow. The width of the band depends on the forecasting skill of the planners and on the uncertainty associated with the process. For example, the band of uncertainty is ordinarily much narrower in a prediction of the number of operations an automatic machine can perform in an eight-hour day than in a forecast of sales.

Nevertheless, for any given process there is a range within which the values of an item will fluctuate *purely as a result of random forces*. If the cause of the deviation from plan is purely random, then the deviation is not subject to management control. It is important, therefore, to divide deviations between those that are likely to be the result of random forces and those that are not. The basis for this distinction is provided by a set of *control limits*—values of a given variable such that observed values outside the limits will be investigated.

For certain processes the control limits can be stated in terms of statistical probabilities—e.g., in a particular operation purely random forces would be likely to cause a factory rejection rate as large as 10 percent only once in a thousand times. Thus if a 10 percent rejection rate is recorded, management should probably look for a specific cause or causes.

Exhibit 2-10

APEX LIGHTING COMPANY

District Manager's Performance Report
For the Month of June, 1967

District A	This Month			Year to Date		
	Planned	Actual	Deviation	Planned	Actual	Deviation
Orders booked.	$105,000	$113,000	$ 8,000	$620,000	$640,000	$ 20,000
Orders canceled.	5,000	3,000	2,000	40,000	40,000	. . . .
Net orders received. . .	$100,000	$110,000	$ 10,000	$580,000	$600,000	$ 20,000
Orders received, by product line:						
Industrial installations.	$ 60,000	$ 52,000	$ (8,000)	$360,000	$335,000	$(25,000)
Highway installations.	10,000	. . .	(10,000)	70,000	65,000	(5,000)
Repair services.	30,000	58,000	28,000	150,000	200,000	50,000
Controllable expenses:						
Sales salaries.	$ 3,000	$ 3,000	$ . . .	$ 18,000	$ 17,600	$ 400
Office salaries.	700	750	(50)	4,500	4,600	(100)
Payroll taxes (8%).	296	300	(4)	1,800	1,776	24
Pensions (6%).	222	225	(3)	1,350	1,332	18
Travel and entertainment.	1,800	2,450	(650)	10,000	11,200	(1,200)
Local advertising.	200	180	20	1,200	550	650
Supplies.	330	270	60	1,590	1,180	410
Other.	150	135	15	705	200	505
Total Controllable Expenses.	$ 6,698	$ 7,310	$ (612)	$ 39,145	$ 38,438	$ 707

For most items, unfortunately, the control limits have to be set intuitively. Thus the manager of sales district A might well feel that all of his expense items were within reasonable control limits during June except travel and entertainment, which was more than 35 percent in excess of budget. The investigation would then be concentrated on that item.

SUMMARY

One major task of cost accounting is to provide data for use in periodic financial planning and control reporting. Financial plans or budgets are prepared on an organizational basis and must be adapted to the current external environment as well as to the company's capacity to carry them out. This requires data designed for decision making.

The periodic financial reports serve both scorecard and attention-directing purposes and typically provide performance summaries both by line of activity and by responsibility. The responsibility reports are hierarchical, and the amount of detail provided diminishes progressively in the reports intended for higher and higher levels of management, while the scope of the operations covered expands commensurately.

The bulk of this chapter was devoted to a simple illustration of the structure and benefits to be derived from a budgetary planning and control system. For a heightened dramatic effect, it was assumed in this example that the company had been operating previously with virtually no internal information at all. It is unlikely that a real company of this size would ever be quite this far behind the times, but it has happened in some young and rapidly expanding companies.

The pace at which the new system was introduced was unrealistically rapid, as was the rate of executive acceptance of the new system. Furthermore, the rapid progress made by the company in translating its newly found information into improved profitability undoubtedly over-stressed the value of the kinds of information the accountant can provide. Finally, in the interest of providing a comprehensive view of the accounting structure as a whole, the illustration had to be considerably condensed, thus glossing over a number of difficult problems that must be examined later.

The purpose of the example, however, was to provide a picture of the whole before the study of the parts was begun. For this purpose, some exaggeration and condensation is permissible, and it is now up to the remaining chapters to fill in the details and supply the necessary qualifications.

DISCUSSION QUESTIONS

1. What is a business budget and what purposes is it intended to serve? How do business budgets differ from government budgets and personal budgets?
2. What is the role of the accounting staff in the budgeting process?
3. Describe the basic dimensions of a company's chart of accounts.
4. Distinguish between responsibility centers and cost centers. How do they relate to blocks in the company's organization charts?
5. What kinds of accounting reports would most likely be prepared routinely for top management? How would these reports be used?
6. What is meant by the statement, "Budgeting is an iterative process"?
7. Can variances that result from random influences be corrected by control responses? How can random variances be distinguished from nonrandom variances?
8. The economic analysis department of the Amalgamated Meat Packing Company prepares annual forecasts of livestock offerings, aggregate consumer income, and population by geographical regions, and distributes these to product and plant managers prior to budget preparation. What is the objective of this procedure?
9. "We don't use accounting reports for cost control. By the time a variance shows up in an accounting report, it is too late to control costs." Comment on this point of view.
10. The Sanders Electronics Company issues monthly cost reports to the head of each department. No detailed breakdown of costs is provided; each department head is merely notified of his total costs for the month, his budget, and the difference between the two. In support of this practice, the company's president stated: "We don't want our people to be pencil pushers. If costs are out of line, we expect them to know enough about their operations to find out what is wrong and to do something about it." Discuss this statement.
11. "We like to give our salesmen a sense of participation by asking them to prepare sales estimates for the coming year, but our budget is based on forecasts prepared by market research. If we keyed production to the salesmen's forecasts, we would have inventory bulging out of all of our warehouses." Discuss the implications of this statement. What safeguards are required to make participative budgeting work effectively?
12. Can a single supervisor be held accountable for the operations of two or more cost centers? Can responsibility for the operation of a single cost center be split equally among two or more supervisors? Explain.

EXERCISES AND PROBLEMS

1. Using any coding system that seems appropriate, sketch out the rough outlines of a chart of accounts for a company which has the following characteristics:

Balance Sheet:
   Three major asset categories, with 100 possible subcategories in each.
   Two major liability categories, with 50 possible subcategories in each.
   Ten ownership equity accounts.
Factory Costs:
   One factory.
   Twelve departments in the factory.
   Twenty cost elements in each department (e.g., salaries).
Administration Costs:
   One department.
   Ten cost elements.
Marketing:
   Three products.
   Two branch territories and home office.
   Ten cost elements.

2. The Montagu Company was originally established to distribute a new type of waterproof, heat-resistant glue to shoe manufacturers. The glue was produced under contract by a large chemical company, and product sales were made by a field sales force of four salesmen who contacted shoe manufacturers directly. These salesmen were all chemical engineers and had the responsibility of training their customers' personnel in the proper methods of applying the glue. The revenues and expenses of the company have been recorded in a fairly simple set of accounts:

Sales	Office Supplies
Sales Returns and Allowances	Rent
Cost of Goods Sold	Printing and Postage
Sales Salaries	Telephone and Telegraph
Sales Commissions	Retirement Expense
Travel Expenses	Insurance Expense
Office Salaries	Miscellaneous Expenses

The president of the company has just decided to expand operations in two ways: first by taking on the distribution of a line of shoe "findings" (miscellaneous small items used in shoe manufacture), and second by marketing the company's glue to furniture manufacturers. Two salesmen are to be added to the shoe trades sales force. The furniture trade sales force will consist initially of three new salesmen to be hired for that purpose. The president, who heretofore has also acted as sales manager and controller, has decided to promote his senior salesman to the position of sales manager. The present office manager will become controller and office manager, with a new assistant to be hired.
   a) What changes, if any, will the company need to make in its accounting system to meet the income measurement objective? To meet other management objectives?
   b) What problems do you foresee in the measurement of income for individual product lines?

3. During 19x3 and early 19x4, the managment of the Irvington Corporation became increasingly concerned about the declining profitability of one of its products. Data relating to this product for the first quarter of 19x4 and the three full years preceding are as follows:

	19x1	19x2	19x3	1st Qtr. 19x4
Units sold............................	100,000	110,000	80,000	20,000
Net revenue from sales....................	$495,000	$540,000	$474,000	$115,000
Manufacturing cost of goods sold:				
Materials............................	$ 59,400	$ 67,350	$ 54,500	$ 13,800
Labor...............................	136,300	155,000	123,900	31,000
Other manufacturing costs...............	121,500	149,800	146,300	39,700
Freight and delivery costs..................	25,200	30,600	31,000	8,200
Sales salaries and commissions..............	34,750	37,000	33,700	8,550
Other selling and office expenses...........	26,400	31,400	37,600	9,650
Total direct product expenses...........	$403,550	$471,150	$427,000	$110,900
Product profit............................	$ 91,450	$ 68,850	$ 47,000	$ 4,100
Share of the market:				
Units sold............................	15%	12%	8%	7.5%
Dollar sales...........................	18	16	15	14.5

Analyze these data and prepare a report that will help management decide where the major problems might lie or what course of action to take.

4. The Mongol Company's factory contains 17 production departments. Products typically require processing in five or more of these departments. All products are subjected to final inspection before they are either placed in inventory or shipped to customers. Units rejected by the inspectors are sold immediately as seconds.

The company's industrial engineers have studied past experience with production rejects and have established the following standards: for products A, B, D, G, and H, rejects of 10 percent of the number of units placed in process; for all other products, rejects of 5 percent are regarded as normal.

During May, the production record was as follows:

Product	No. of Good Units	No. of Rejected Units
A............................	470	50
B............................	820	60
C............................	1,460	110
D............................	320	40
F............................	540	40
G............................	990	60
H............................	80	20
K............................	3,400	300
M............................	650	70

a) Prepare a report that will provide management with information on the effectiveness of quality control in the plant.

b) What additional data would you regard as essential to good management information on this aspect of performance?

c) If the company were to manufacture 1,000 different products each month, would you find it necessary to make changes in the report structure? Explain.

5. The Canyon Corporation operates two stores that sell and install automobile seat covers and a few automotive supplies such as upholstery cleaner and auto washing compounds. The company's president has heard that budgetary planning is a good thing and has decided that a profit plan should be prepared for the coming year. The managers of the two stores have submitted the following tentative budgets:

	Downtown Store	Suburban Store
Sales revenue:		
Seat covers..................................	$100,000	$180,000
Auto supplies...............................	18,000	40,000
Total.....................................	$118,000	$220,000
Store expenses:		
Supervisory & clerical salaries....................	$ 11,800	$ 11,900
Installers' wages...............................	10,200	20,000
Store clerks' wages............................	4,600	4,700
Rent...	9,600	8,800
Utilities.....................................	1,500	2,100
Other..	700	1,300
Total.....................................	$ 38,400	$ 44,800

During the coming year, the purchase cost of the seat covers is expected to average 55 percent of selling prices, while the selling prices of auto supplies will be approximately double their purchase cost.

The president himself prepared a tentative head office budget for the coming year:

Executive salaries...	$25,000
Clerical salaries..	12,000
Advertising..	10,000
Rent..	6,000
Office supplies...	1,000
Utilities...	1,200
Legal and consultants' fees................................	1,700
Other..	500
Total..	$57,400

a) Assemble these data into a tentative profit plan for the coming year.

b) What problems do you think the president and the store managers encountered in preparing their tentative sales and expense plans? What is their principal source of information? What information would the president use in reviewing the acceptability of the store managers' figures?

c) When the president saw the figures assembled in (a) above, he said, "This won't do. I want another $10,000 in profit." The manager of the downtown store suggested that the company stock a line of auto floor mats. Many of his customers had asked for these, and he thought that having them in stock would increase his sales by $5,000 a year, with no increase in store expenses. The suburban store manager thought he could also increase his sales $5,000 a year if he stocked floor mats. The purchase price would be about 60 percent of selling price. The suburban store manager also said that he could increase his seat cover sales by $30,000 if he added another installer at $5,000 a year and if the president would increase his advertising budget by $6,000 a year. This advertising would have no effect on sales at the downtown store, which lacks space to increase its volume of seat cover business. Prepare a revised profit plan, reflecting these figures, and see whether it meets the president's profit objective.

d) Your answer to (c) was based on a number of assumptions as to what would happen to expenses if volume were to increase. State these assumptions, and indicate how reliable you think they may be.

6. The cost accounting department of the Bayou Refinery of the Bipex Petroleum Company prepared the following comparative summary of operating costs, exclusive of the costs of crude oil and other product ingredients, for the month of December:

	This December		Increase (Decrease) Over Last December	
	Amount	Per Barrel	Amount	% Change
Barrels per calendar day............	51,791	......	3,268	6.7
Controllable:				
Salaries and wages:				
Operating....................	$ 224,268	$0.1397	$ 16,419	7.9
Maintenance.................	43,973	0.0273	2,915	7.1
Accounting..................	10,358	0.0065	804	8.4
Administration..............	21,713	0.0135	434	2.0
Total payrolls..............	$ 300,312	$0.1870	$ 20,572	7.4
Operating material.............	26,947	0.0168	7,229	36.7
Maintenance material...........	39,421	0.0246	5,937	17.7
Catalyst......................	54,839	0.0342	28,138	105.4
Other processing supplies........	52,402	0.0326	3,674	7.5
Employee benefits..............	22,552	0.0140	3,723	19.8
Fuel consumed.................	195,269	0.1216	15,613	8.7
Contract costs.................	37,195	0.0232	8,573	30.0
Coker rental...................	67,073	0.0418	(1,797)	(2.6)
All other controllable...........	44,583	0.0278	2,997	7.2
Total controllable..........	$ 840,593	$0.5236	$ 94,659	12.7

	This December		Increase (Decrease) Over Last December	
	Amount	Per Barrel	Amount	% Change
Noncontrollable:				
Depreciation..................	$ 208,789	$0.1300	$ 13,554	6.9
Taxes......................	37,398	0.0233	14	...
Laboratory...................	15,436	0.0096	2,293	17.4
Process advisory...............	7,390	0.0046	1,053	16.6
Maintenance engineering........	3,487	0.0022	204	6.2
Head office administration........	10,415	0.0065	496	5.0
Other......................	3,774	0.0023	1,563	70.7
Total noncontrollable........	$ 286,689	$0.1785	$ 19,177	7.2
Total Operating Cost......	$1,127,282	$0.7021	$113,836	11.2
Increase (decrease) over cost per barrel last year...............		$0.0284		

Analysis of Major Increases:

Payrolls:

Increased salaries and wage rates............................	$12,422
Increased work force.......................................	5,152
Increased overtime..	1,055
Increased vacation and holiday pay.........................	1,078
Increased sickness and accident pay.........................	865
Total Increase in Payrolls.............................	$20,572

Operating supplies:

Low-value items formerly charged to warehouse, now charged to refinery when purchased..............................	$ 5,769
Other increases..	1,460
Total Increase in Operating Supplies......................	$ 7,229

Catalyst:

Reformer unit No. 1—catalyst change.......................	$ 6,213
Reformer unit No. 2—initial batch for start-up...............	17,888
Desulfurizer—initial batch for start-up.....................	3,418
Increased requirements.....................................	619
Total Increase in Catalyst.............................	$28,138

Fuel consumed:

Increased price of fuel gas.................................	$ 5,865
Increased quantity consumed..............................	9,748
Total Increase in Fuel Consumed........................	$15,613

a) Of what significance are the figures relating to increases or decreases over the comparable month in the previous year?

b) Do you feel that the analysis of major increases provides sufficient information for cost control purposes? What additional information, if any, would you like to have to assist you in evaluating the cost control performance in the refinery?

7. The Erskine Sales Corporation serves as a manufacturers' representative for
several manufacturers of automotive replacement parts. It has sales branches
in each of three major eastern cities. Sales and expense data for the current
fiscal year are expected to show the following totals:

	Boston	New York	Philadelphia	Head Office	Totals
Sales....................	$4,000,000	$10,000,000	$6,000,000	....	$20,000,000
Cost of goods sold.........	2,700,000	6,750,000	4,050,000	....	13,500,000
Gross profit..............	$1,300,000	$ 3,250,000	$1,950,000	....	$ 6,500,000
Expenses:					
Salaries and commissions	$ 900,000	$ 1,600,000	$1,200,000	$ 300,000	$ 4,000,000
Rent..................	20,000	60,000	40,000	50,000	170,000
Travel expense.........	100,000	120,000	110,000	40,000	370,000
Advertising............	10,000	20,000	20,000	30,000	80,000
Other expenses.........	5,000	15,000	10,000	20,000	50,000
Total expenses........	$1,035,000	$ 1,815,000	$1,380,000	$ 440,000	$ 4,670,000
Net income before taxes....	$ 265,000	$ 1,435,000	$ 570,000	$(440,000)	$ 1,830,000
Income taxes..............	xxx	xxx	xxx	xxx	950,000
Net Income..............	xxx	xxx	xxx	xxx	$ 880,000

In planning for the coming year, the company's budget director obtained
the following information:

(1) Expected automobile "population" in the region, classified by make and age
of car, was obtained from the company's suppliers and was distributed to
the branch managers.
(2) The company's suppliers announced their intention to raise list prices
(charged by Erskine Sales to its customers) by 5 percent. Prices paid by
Erskine Sales will be increased by 4 percent.
(3) Salaries and commissions per employee will be 3 percent higher next year.
(4) Sales forecasts received from the branches anticipated the following increases
in *physical* sales volume: Boston, 6 percent; New York, 10 percent; and
Philadelphia, 8 percent. The product mix, or relative proportions of total
sales represented by each of the company's products, is expected to be the
same next year as this year.
(5) To handle the increased sales volume, the following increases in personnel
are anticipated: Boston, 2 percent; New York, 4 percent; Philadelphia, 3
percent; and head office, 2 percent. (These increases will occur in the indicated proportions at all salary levels.)
(6) Rent will be the same at all locations except New York, where a $30,000
increase is expected on lease renewals.
(7) Travel expenses will be $10,000 greater in each of the branches and $5,000
greater in the head office.
(8) The New York office has asked for an increase in its advertising appropriation to $40,000. All other advertising appropriations are to remain at this
year's level.
(9) Other expenses are expected to increase next year by 5 percent at all locations.
(10) Income taxes are budgeted at 30 percent for the first $25,000 of income and
50 percent for all income in excess of that figure.

a) Prepare a tentative operating budget for each branch office, for the head office, and for the company as a whole for the coming year.

b) Each of the three branches has indicated that it could expand sales by an *additional* 10 percent next year (that is, 10 percent of this year's physical sales volume) if it were to be permitted to hire additional salesmen and clerical employees. The added salaries and commissions, in excess of those already budgeted for next year, would be $120,000 at any branch for which such additional hiring is approved. Travel, advertising, and other expenses would be increased by $30,000 for any such branch. Head office expenses would be increased by $10,000 for each branch for which expansion approval is granted. Prepare calculations to indicate which branch or branches, if any, should be permitted to make the requested additions to their sales forces.

8. During 1966, Peonel, Inc., has been operating two shifts a day plus overtime in its single factory but has been unable to meet the growing demand for its two products. To continue its tradition of fast delivery, the company has had to reduce its finished goods inventory levels below the established minimum. The company's executives are considering moving to three-shift operations, and they have asked the budget director to assemble a preliminary financial and operating plan for 1967 on that basis.

Using an economic forecast prepared by a consultant to the company, together with reports of customer activity gathered by salesmen in the field, the company's two product managers have submitted the following tentative budgets for 1967:

	Product A	Product B
1967 sales (in units).............................	400,000	300,000
Increase over 1966...........................	100,000	90,000
Price per unit.............................	$1.00	$3.00
1967 production costs:		
Material cost per unit........................	$0.25	$0.55
Labor cost per unit..........................	$0.15	$0.45
Machine-hours required per unit..............	0.10	0.30
1967 product promotion expense...............	$50,000	$60,000
Increase over 1966..........................	$12,500	$18,000
(Varies with the number of units sold)		
Increase in finished goods inventories required with no increase in sales...................	5,000 units	4,500 units
Increase in assets because of increased sales:		
Accounts receivable.........................	$20,000	$54,000
Materials inventories........................	$ 2,500	$ 4,950
Finished goods inventories...................	5,000 units	3,500 units
Work in process inventories.................	Negligible	Negligible
Increase in accounts payable accompanying increased sales...........................	$ 2,500	$ 4,950

The factory manager's estimates of maximum production capacity and general factory costs (all factory costs except materials, labor, and depreciation) are:

	Production Capacity (Machine-Hours)	General Factory Costs at Capacity Operating Rates
Two-shift operations..........	91,450	$ 90,000
Three-shift operations.........	122,900	118,000

These estimates include allowances for labor overtime and also provide for a normal amount of time lost due to machine breakdowns and other kinds of work interruptions.

Other estimates and budget proposals that have been submitted to the budget director are:

General sales and administrative expenses (except depreciation)..$105,000
Depreciation:
    Factory and factory equipment............................. 50,000
    Office and sales facilities.................................. 25,000
Interest on long-term debt (maturing in 1975)................. 50,000
Dividends on common stock................................. 30,000
Research and development expenses......................... 100,000
Equipment replacement expenditures......................... 90,000
Plant expansion expenditures (these additional facilities will not
    be completed in 1967)................................... 300,000
Interest on short-term bank loans is to be computed at a rate of 5%
    on the balance of the bank loans outstanding at the *end* of
    1966 and is to be paid in 1967.
Income taxes are computed at a rate of 50% of taxable income and
    are due in the first quarter of the year following.
Minimum cash balance..................................... 140,000

The budget director estimates 1967 opening balances for working capital as follows:

Cash.. $160,000
Accounts receivable...............................   186,000
Inventories.......................................   33,350
    Total....................................... $379,350
Less:
    Bank loan.....................................$30,000
    Accounts payable.............................. 19,050
    Income taxes payable.......................... 54,000   103,050
    Working Capital........................... $276,300

Prepare a profit plan for 1967 that will be both technically and financially feasible, taking into consideration the following:

(1) Factory capacity should be assigned to the products in such a way as to maximize company profits, subject to the following restrictions: (*a*) the sales of each product are to be at least as large as they were the preceding year; (*b*) inventories of finished goods must be built up to the established minimum if sales are to remain constant and must increase proportionately with sales.

(2) The company will have no access to long-term sources of funds. Cash must be paid for all assets and services purchased except that trade credit (i.e., accounts payable) is available to finance raw material inventories. Bank credit is available up to 50 percent of the sum of the face amount of accounts receivable and the

cost of the inventories. Finished goods are carried on the balance sheet at material and labor cost, manufacturing overhead being considered an expense. Bank credit is available in units of $10,000.

(3) In case of a shortage of funds, management has decided that cutbacks in disbursements will be made in the following order:

   (a) Decrease plant expansion expenditures, but to an amount not less than $100,000.
   (b) Decrease planned sales; adjust inventory and accounts receivable as appropriate to match these decreases. Inventories of finished goods must be built up to the established minimum if sales are to remain constant and must increase proportionately with sales.

The complete plan will encompass the following:

a) Planned production of products A and B (in units).
b) Planned sales of products A and B.
c) Planned cash receipts and disbursements statement.
d) Planned income statement (finished goods are stated at material and labor cost only).

9. Cycle World is a large retailer of bicycles, scooters, and motorcycles. Its showroom and parts department occupy the main floor of a modern building; a repair department is located in the basement.

Cycle World has never sold motor scooters, although it has serviced them in its repair department. The local representative of the Ivrea Scooter Company has been trying to induce Cycle World to act as its exclusive dealer in the area, so far without success. Ivrea's terms have become progressively more favorable in the hope of inducing Cycle World to accept, but it has now made what it says is its final offer. If Cycle World turns this down, Ivrea will set up its own sales branch.

Taking on the Ivrea line would require Cycle World to invest $20,000 in an inventory of scooters and repair parts. Adequate space is available to carry these added inventories. Ivrea would finance one half of this requirement, with no interest charge, but Cycle World would have to finance the remainder from other sources. Cycle World would also have to hire an additional mechanic who would be trained at Ivrea's expense before being transferred to the Cycle World payroll.

Judging from his experience in introducing a new line of light motorcycles a year ago, and using some figures provided by his bank, Cycle World's president has drawn up the following set of forecasts for the Ivrea line:

	First Year	Second Year
Revenues:		
Product sales..................................	$50,000	$75,000
Repairs.......................................	3,000	5,000
Product warranty payments by Ivrea..............	1,500	2,000
Less: Bad debt losses...........................	(1,000)	(1,500)
Net revenues.................................	$54,500	$80,500

	First Year	Second Year
Expenses:		
Cost of goods sold..........................	$33,000	$49,500
Mechanic's wages............................	6,500	6,800
Repair supplies.............................	1,000	2,100
Advertising.................................	4,000	4,000
Other.......................................	500	750
Total expenses..............................	$45,000	$63,150
Incremental Profit..........................	$ 9,500	$17,350
Investment in Receivables...................	$30,000	$20,000*

(* The $20,000 is the *increase* in receivables investment *during* the second year. The total increase during the two-year period would be $50,000.)

All of these figures represent increments to the figures arising from Cycle World's present business. The figures given for the second year seem likely to be representative of what later years would bring.

The owners of Cycle World have put their entire savings into the business and cannot sell shares to outsiders. The company is already substantially in debt, and the company's bankers would be willing to increase their loans to Cycle World by no more than $20,000, at an interest rate of 6 percent a year. If the company does not take on the Ivrea line, the bank will not increase the size of its loan.

Cycle World's present business is expected to generate a $15,000 excess of operating cash receipts over operating cash outlays in each of the next two years. The figures on operating cash outlays include interest on the present bank debt as well as the president's $14,000 salary. Reported net profit, before adjusting for the Ivrea addition, any additional borrowing, or any of the facts revealed below, would be approximately $14,000 a year.

Cash dividends to shareholders have been $12,000 a year, and the board of directors would encounter great opposition from several of the major shareholders (all close relatives of the president) if the dividend were to be reduced.

The head mechanic has put in a request for $2,000 to buy several pieces of shop equipment to replace equipment which no longer functions reliably. The annual depreciation charge would be about $100 greater if the replacements were made.

Finally, the Sussex Bicycle Company has notified Cycle World that it will no longer pay the full $5,000 cost of local advertising. Experience has shown that without this advertising, Cycle World's profits would be about $6,000 less than they are now. Sussex has offered to pay half of the cost of advertising, which it points out would still leave Cycle World with a $3,500 profit from sales of Sussex bicycles.

a) Prepare tentative profit estimates and cash forecasts from the above data for each of the next two years, assuming that the Ivrea line is taken on and that all the requested expenditures are made. By what amounts are the company's cash resources inadequate to finance all the requested expenditures? (Ignore income taxes.)

b) You do not have enough data to enable you to advise the president on a course of action. Identify some of the alternatives that he might consider and indicate what kinds of information you would like to have to help the president reach the decisions on which his final profit plan would be based.

Chapter 3

DECISIONS
AND COSTS

ROUTINELY ACCUMULATED accounting data are essential ingredients for a wide variety of managerial decisions. The purpose of this chapter is to examine briefly the major elements of the decision-making process and then, against this background, to examine the kinds of cost data that are relevant to managerial decisions.

Example of a Decision

The Peerless Spring Company is a small manufacturer of spring-closing devices and other household and industrial hardware products. It has a strong distribution organization, but intensified competition in recent years has cut into its sales volume, leaving the company with substantial idle productive capacity and a small annual operating loss.

Hearing that Peerless Spring was anxious to diversify, a bearded inventor recently walked into the office of Mr. B. T. Ersman, the company's president, with a newly patented idea for an improved window safety catch. The inventor was willing to grant Peerless Spring an exclusive license to manufacture and market this device in return for a royalty of 10 cents for each unit sold.

Mr. Ersman referred this proposal to his sales and production managers for their estimates of sales and costs. Both were enthusiastic. The sales manager recognized immediately that the safety catch could be sold to the company's present customers with only a slight expansion of the sales force. Furthermore, the market could be realized almost immediately, without a long period of costly promotional outlays. After discussions with his salesmen, he decided that a price of $1.50 per unit would be competitive. At this price, a sales forecast of 300,000 units a year seemed reasonable, assuming the following annual increases in total company selling and administrative costs:

Sales salaries and commissions	$33,000
Travel and entertainment	24,000
Secretarial and clerical salaries	4,000
Office supplies	500
Promotional aids and samples	3,500
Advertising	5,000
Total	$70,000

The production manager looked very favorably upon this new product as a means of taking up some of the idle capacity in one of his two factories. Working closely with the factory controller, he estimated that factory costs would be increased by the following amounts per year:

Production materials	$150,000
Payrolls (including payroll taxes)	120,000
Power	9,000
Equipment maintenance	15,000
Factory supplies	6,000
Total	$300,000

These estimates were summarized as follows for presentation to Mr. Ersman:

Sales		$450,000
Expenses:		
Factory	$300,000	
Selling and administrative	70,000	
Royalties	30,000	400,000
Added Yearly Profit before Taxes		$ 50,000

Mr Ersman was pleased at the prospect of the $50,000 added profit contribution, but before making a decision he asked the sales manager how reliable the sales forecast was likely to be. The sales manager replied that the 300,000-unit figure seemed reasonable in the light of the overall size of the market and the prices and quality of competing products, but of course he could not guarantee this volume of new business. Even so, he felt that the worst he could do would be 200,000 units a year, and if market conditions were exceptionally good he might even be able to go as high as 400,000 units. He saw no more reason to expect one of these outcomes than the other.

Mr. Ersman had always been able to rely on the sales manager's estimates of the range within which sales were likely to fall, and he accepted them this time, even though the product was a new one to the Peerless Spring Company. The production and accounting people then came up with alternative cost figures at the higher and lower sales volumes, as follows:

	200,000 Units		400,000 Units	
Sales........................		$300,000		$600,000
Expenses:				
Factory........................	$240,000		$360,000	
Selling and administrative............	60,000		80,000	
Royalties........................	20,000	320,000	40,000	480,000
Added Profit (Loss).................		$(20,000)		$120,000

On the basis of these figures, the risk of loss seemed bearable and the potential gains attractive. Accordingly, a contract was signed with the inventor, additional sales personnel were hired, and the new device was placed in production.

THE STRUCTURE OF DECISIONS

Whether or not this venture was successful is not particularly relevant here, nor is the reliability of the particular methods used to estimate sales and expenses and to set prices. Furthermore, the decision-making process is seldom as quick or as simple as this brief description may imply. The illustration was designed with only one purpose: to show all the elements of decision making in miniature and in their proper relation to each other.

Problem Diagnosis

The decision in this example was made in response to an *opportunity* which had arisen. Decisions also are required when *problems* arise. A problem has been defined as a gap between an existing or forecasted condition or result and a desired condition or result. Thus if an automobile fails to start in the morning, it might seem that the problem is to get it started. Alternatively, the problem might be stated as the discrepancy between the need to get to the office at nine o'clock and the present inability to use the car to accomplish this. The solution may be to get someone to start the car or it may even be to abandon the car and get to the office by some other means. This process of problem formulation is known as *diagnosis.*[1]

The existence of a problem is sometimes revealed by a review of attention-directing accounting reports or by the preparation of budgets. Sometimes an external event, such as the introduction of a new product by a competitor, causes management to recognize a need for a decision.

[1] William S. Newman and Charles E. Summer, Jr., *The Process of Management* (Englewood Cliffs, N.J.: Prentice-Hall, Inc., 1961), chap. xii.

Sometimes the event is internal: a machine becomes unreliable and a decision has to be made whether to repair it, replace it, use another machine more intensively, or curtail production.

Once recognized, there is no fundamental difference between problems and opportunities. Both are in a certain sense problems that must be solved by a decision-making process. This process consists basically of five elements:

1. Goals or objectives.
2. Alternative actions.
3. Environmental conditions.
4. Outcomes and payoffs.
5. Decision rule.

Goals or Objectives

The definition of a problem as a gap between a desired result and a present or anticipated result indicates the importance of objectives. Without a goal there can be no gap and thus no need for a decision as to how to close the gap.

It is usually accepted that one of the objectives of a business enterprise is profit. Mr. Ersman, for example, recognized profit as one of the key factors affecting his decision. Profit, in turn, was merely a means toward the goal of company survival, which in turn was a means toward other more fundamental goals. Survival and other more basic goals are too vague to provide much guidance to the decision maker, however, and this required the expression of more immediate or operational goals to provide such guidance. Increased profit is an example of an operational goal.

Alternative Actions

Once the problem or opportunity has been identified, the next step is to list the alternative actions that might be taken. Alternatives are not always obvious but must be sought out. Successful business management is often a matter of finding and exploiting opportunities that others have overlooked.

It is a well-established fact, however, that people do not search until they have found all the alternatives available. In fact, it is doubtful that anyone can ever be sure that he has identified all alternative courses of action open to him. Furthermore, the search cannot be allowed to take so much time that action is unduly delayed.

There is some evidence that people search until they find at least one alternative that promises a satisfactory solution of the problem. The term *satisficing* has been coined to describe this behavior.[2] It might have been possible, for example, for the Peerless Spring Company's engineers to design a better product or to obtain a better product from some other source. Mr. Ersman, however, was content to exclude these other possibilities because he had found one that was acceptable. In this case only two alternatives were recognized: accept the proposal on the terms offered, or reject it in its entirety.

Environmental Conditions

Environmental conditions, sometimes called *events* or *states of nature,* are usually more difficult to describe precisely than alternatives. Environmental conditions represent the uncontrollable variables bearing on the decision. Although Mr. Ersman was aware that the number of possible states of nature was very large, he found it necessary to recognize only three.

The number of recognized combinations of alternatives and states of nature was thus six, three for each alternative, represented by the boxes in the following diagram:

Alternative \ Event	Good Market 1	Anticipated Market 2	Poor Market 3
Accept proposal A	A–1	A–2	A–3
Reject proposal R	R–1	R–2	R–3

The existence of more than one possible state of nature is one of the main dimensions of *uncertainty.* Uncertainty may or may not be recognized explicitly in decision making, but it is always present to some degree.

Outcomes and Payoffs

The table above is not very useful as it stands. What it lacks is some measure of the results to be expected under each possible combination of actions and states of nature.

Results can be stated in two ways: first as the *outcomes* expected for each action/state of nature combination, and secondly as the *payoffs* stemming from these outcomes. The outcomes here were measured in added sales dollars; the payoffs were measured in dollars of added profit. These payoffs can be expressed in a *payoff table,* as follows:

      [2] James G. March and Herbert A. Simon, *Organizations* (New York: John Wiley & Sons, Inc., 1958), pp. 140–41.

Event \ Alternative	Good Market	Anticipated Market	Poor Market
Accept proposal	+$120,000	+$50,000	−$20,000
Reject proposal	0	0	0

Decision Rule

Once the payoff table has been constructed, the decision maker must apply a *decision rule*—a set of instructions for choosing a course of action that will meet the company's objectives. Mr. Ersman's decision rule was not very clearly stated. He wanted to pick the alternative that seemed most likely to yield the larger profit, so long as that alternative would not expose him to "too great" a risk of loss if the state of nature proved unfavorable. This risk/profit relationship was not expressed mathematically, however.

It should be clear that *profit maximization* is a meaningless decision rule under conditions of uncertainty. If the market was poor, then rejection of the proposal would have been the profit maximizing alternative; the reverse would be true for a good or average market. To apply this kind of decision rule, therefore, some means must be found to reduce the payoffs under each alternative to a single figure.

One possibility is to weight the possible payoffs according to the relative *probabilities* that the various states of nature will occur. The resultant *weighted* payoff is called the *expected value* of the alternative.

Suppose, for example, that Mr. Ersman decided that the $20,000 loss had a 20 percent chance of happening, the $50,000 payoff a 50 percent chance, and the $120,000 payoff a 30 percent chance. In technical language, the three states of nature had probabilities of 0.2, 0.5, and 0.3, the total being 1.0. The expected value of the outcomes for each alternative is found by multiplying each possible payoff by its probability and adding the products, as follows:

Probability	0.3	0.5	0.2	
Event \ Alternative	Good Market	Anticipated Market	Poor Market	Expected Value
Accept proposal	0.3 × 120,000 = +36,000	0.5 × 50,000 = +25,000	0.2 × −20,000 = −4,000	+57,000
Reject proposal	0.3 × 0 = 0	0.5 × 0 = 0	0.2 × 0 = 0	0

In this case the expected value was slightly in excess of the $50,000 forecast payoff because the probabilities were not symmetrically distributed.

The decision rule implicit in the expected value calculation is *maximization of the expected value* of the payoffs. This is not necessarily the decision rule that Mr. Ersman would have used if he had calculated the probabilities explicitly. For example, if a $20,000 loss on this project would have put the company in bankruptcy and Mr. Ersman out of a job, he might have been much more cautious, weighting the possible loss by a factor much larger than its relative probability.

This is not the place to discuss different decision rules or the profit maximization assumption. In what follows, the emphasis will be on the derivation of data relevant to decisions rather than on the decision rules applied to them. It is always assumed, however, that *for any given state of nature,* the decision maker is interested in knowing which alternative seems to promise the greatest profit. How he then weighs the outcomes associated with the various states of nature is left largely to more specialized works on decision making.

INCREMENTAL ANALYSIS

The comparisons in the previous example were based on the *incremental principle:* that data for decisions should represent the *differences* between alternative courses of action. In other words, the concept that is relevant in quantitative analysis for decision making is the concept of *incremental profit:* the difference in profit for the company as a whole that is expected to result from choosing one alternative instead of another.

Profit versus Income

Notice that this definition uses the term *profit* rather than *income.* Incremental profit is an economic concept and is not necessarily identical to incremental income, which is an accounting concept. Incremental profit is defined as the effect of the choice between alternatives on the company's *net cash flow*—the margin between receipts and outlays of cash or equivalent liquid assets. Because measurement of accounting net income often requires the recognition of expense and revenue in periods other than the period of receipt or expenditure of funds, it may differ significantly from cash flow in any given time period. It is cash flow, however, not income flow, that represents the resources made available to management by the outcome of a particular course of action. It is thus more relevant to decision making.

Many internal accounting systems use the term profit to refer to the accounting income reported or budgeted for individual segments of the company's business, and we shall not make a point of avoiding this usage of the term. When discussing *incremental* profit, however, or incremental revenue or incremental costs, we shall always be referring to differences in cash flows rather than differences in reported income.

Incremental versus Absolute Profit

The profit summaries in periodic accounting statements are useful in decision making, but they generally must be adjusted to make them fully relevant. The income budgeted or reported for a particular product line or other business segment is not necessarily the portion of the company's profit that can be attributed to that segment. In other words, absolute profit may not be a good measure of incremental profit.

For example, let us assume that a company's management is examining the profitability of its sales branches. The income statement for the Baltimore branch for the previous year showed an income contribution of $50,000, as follows:

Sales	$1,000,000
Cost of sales	600,000
Gross margin	$ 400,000
Branch expenses	350,000
Branch Income Contribution before Taxes	$ 50,000

Assuming that the future is like the past, and that sales, cost of sales, and branch expenses all represented current cash flows, it would seem that closing this branch would reduce company profit by $50,000 a year before taxes. Upon investigation, however, it is discovered that other sales branches in neighboring territories could service the Baltimore territory by adding only $270,000 a year to their branch expenses, and without any loss in Baltimore sales volume. This is $80,000 less than the annual cash operating expenses of the Baltimore branch. In *incremental* terms, therefore, the Baltimore branch is actually *losing* $80,000 a year instead of earning a $50,000 profit.

The absolute profit figures for a given segment of a company's business operations are relevant to decision making only if—

1. The choice is between continuing the operation as it is or discontinuing it entirely, with no other alternatives possible.
2. The costs and revenues recorded for this operation are those that would have been avoided or lost if the operation had not taken place.

3. The recorded costs and revenues are a reasonable approximation of the future costs and revenues that would be avoided or lost by discontinuing the operation.

These conditions are seldom met, and the problem, therefore, is to decide how much the historical figures must be adjusted to make them useful for decision making.

Incremental Revenues

Alternatives often differ in the amount of sales revenues that they will yield. Revenue effects of a choice between alternatives may be of three types:

1. Direct effects.
2. Complementary effects.
3. Substitution effects.

A direct effect would be a change in the revenues of the business operation itself. In the above example, the direct effect of abandoning the Baltimore territory completely would be to lose revenues of $1 million. Because other branch offices could serve the Baltimore territory with no loss in sales, however, the net direct effect can be said to be zero.

Complementary and substitution effects are changes in the revenues of other company operations. A complementary change moves in the same direction as the direct change (an increase in toothbrush sales resulting from a campaign to sell more toothpaste, for example); a substitution effect is a change in one operation that partially offsets the change in another. The increase in sales of neighboring branches could be construed as a substitution effect.

Whether an effect is direct, complementary, or substitution is of course unimportant. What is important is that all such changes be reflected in the estimates of incremental profit.

Incremental versus Sunk Cost

The increments most completely within the domain of cost accounting are cost increments. *Incremental cost* or *differential cost* is the difference in total cost that will result from selecting one alternative instead of another.

For example, the engineering department of a company has made a suggestion that substantial savings can be realized by purchasing a higher quality of castings to be used in one of the company's products. The higher cost of materials would be more than offset by the savings in machining time, electricity, and other costs. Estimated costs per month under the two alternatives are:

	Current Castings	Better Castings
Materials......................	$140,000	$170,000
Labor........................	80,000	55,000
Supervision...................	15,000	15,000
Taxes........................	14,000	14,000
Depreciation and insurance......	32,000	32,000
Other factory costs............	63,000	53,000
Total....................	$344,000	$339,000

The incremental cost is thus $344,000 minus $339,000, or $5,000 per month. In this case incremental cost is negative, indicating a saving rather than an addition to total cost.

The term "incremental cost" is often used in another sense, to refer to the *elements* of cost that will change as the result of the decision rather than to the net difference between two sets of cost totals. For example, in the illustration, the only costs affected by the decision are those recorded in the accounts for materials, labor, and other factory costs. These are the incremental costs as far as this analysis is concerned, and we may shorten the analysis by filtering out as irrelevant all of the other costs that will not be affected by the decision. Thus the above table reduces to the following comparison:

	Current Castings	Better Castings	Increment
Direct materials............	$140,000	$170,000	+$30,000
Machining labor............	80,000	55,000	− 25,000
Other factory costs..........	63,000	53,000	− 10,000
Total..................	$283,000	$278,000	−$ 5,000

The net increment remains the same, $5,000, but attention is focused sharply on the items that are important.

The complement of incremental cost is *sunk cost,* defined as any cost that will not be different if one alternative is chosen instead of another. The definition, therefore, depends on the specific problem being analyzed; what is incremental with respect to one decision may be sunk with respect to another. In the preceding illustration, three of the cost elements were treated as sunk costs for that particular analysis:

	Current Castings	Better Castings
Supervision........................	$15,000	$15,000
Taxes............................	14,000	14,000
Depreciation and insurance........	32,000	32,000
Total......................	$61,000	$61,000

The shift to a different grade of castings would leave all of these cost elements unchanged. Therefore, these sunk costs are irrelevant to that decision and can safely be left out of the analysis.

Separate Costs for Separate Purposes

It should be clear from these definitions that the magnitude of incremental cost (and of incremental profit) depends on the decision to be made and the alternatives being compared. For example, the plant manager's salary is a sunk cost if the problem is to decide whether to install additional materials handling equipment, but it is presumably an incremental cost if abandonment of the plant is in question, and it may be partly incremental if the question is whether to double the plant's capacity.

Avoidable Costs

A term frequently used to refer to incremental cost is *avoidable cost*. This term is used when the choice is between continuing and discontinuing one of the company's operations or activities or between keeping and disposing of certain of its facilities. Studies of plant abandonment, discontinuation of a product line, or withdrawal from a geographical market area all call for the application of the concept of avoidable cost. The complement of avoidable cost, *unavoidable cost,* refers to the sunk costs in this kind of analysis.

Opportunity Cost

Another term that crops up in discussions of incremental analysis is the concept of opportunity cost. In its broadest sense, opportunity cost is the net cash inflow that is lost by the diversion of an input factor from one use to another. It is the value of an opportunity foregone. The opportunity cost of the time that a salesman spends in an air-conditioned theater on a hot summer's day is the incremental profit that would have been obtained on the sales that he lost by not calling on customers. From the salesman's point of view, the opportunity cost is the amount of commission that he loses by not making sales.

The concept of opportunity cost is implicit in any comparison of alternatives. The merits of any particular course of action are *relative* merits, the difference between this action and some other. Opportunity cost is thus more an expression of a method of approach than a definition of cost.

The explicit introduction of opportunity cost figures into profitability calculations is often helpful, however, when one or more of the inputs required by one or more of the alternatives is already in the possession of the company and thus does not require a current outlay of cash. These inputs may nevertheless have a cost, and this cost is measured by what has to be given up in order to make them available for the current proposal—their value in their best alternative use. This is their opportunity cost.

For example, a variety chain paid $100,000 for a plot of land in 1955 for the construction of a shopping center. Uncertainty as to the highway relocation plans of state public works officials led to a postponement of the shopping center project, and the land has lain idle ever since. The route of the new highway has now been established, and the company is again considering the possibility of using the tract as a shopping center site. Only two alternatives are under consideration: either to build the shopping center or to sell the land. The value of the shopping center is derived from the stream of future net cash receipts that can be obtained from rentals to other tenants and from the sale of merchandise in a new company store in the center. The value of the second alternative is the net amount that could be realized from the sale of the land. The net advantage of the shopping center is the difference between these two values.

Suppose that the land can be sold now for a price that will yield the company $800,000 after deducting all commissions, fees, and taxes, and that the value of the future cash flows from the shopping center is $1,200,000. (The derivation of this latter amount is the subject of a later chapter.) The comparison is:

Alternative	*Value of Expected Net Cash Receipts*
Build shopping center................	$1,200,000
Sell land............................	800,000
Incremental Profit................	$ 400,000

An alternative way of reaching the same result is to charge the opportunity cost of the land as an explicit cost of the shopping center proposal:

Value of center.......................$1,200,000
Less: Cost of land....................   800,000
        Incremental Profit...............$ 400,000

The company could obtain $800,000 in liquid resources by selling the land, and thus this is the amount it *invests* by *not* selling the land. The price paid in the past is irrelevant.

This alternative approach is useful because the owned resources to be incorporated into a particular project are often a small part of the total project, and there may be several such resources. This makes it inconvenient to set up a full set of alternatives, one for each possible combination of resource uses. The better procedure is to compute opportunity cost for each resource and insert these into the calculation.

COST/VOLUME RELATIONSHIPS

One of the most important determinants of incremental cost in many situations is the relationship between cost and the *volume of operations*. Volume always is expressed as a *rate* per period of time; for most purposes it is meaningless to refer to a volume of, say, 10,000 units without indicating whether these are to be produced in a week or in a year.

Different measures of volume may be relevant for different segments or aspects of the firm's operations. For example, volume may be measured by the number of units of products produced per time period, by the dollar volume of sales, or by the total labor hours recorded for a particular department during a month. What is important for the moment, however, is the behavior of the costs rather than the selection of the volume index.

Fixed Costs

Many costs are incurred to provide the *capacity* to produce or sell its products. These are in addition to the costs incurred directly for the act of production or sales. Capacity has three dimensions: *physical capacity,* provided by buildings, machinery, furniture, etc.; *organizational capacity,* provided by management, supervisory, and staff personnel; and *financial capacity,* provided by working capital and other financial resources.

In all three senses, capacity can be changed only slowly. It takes time to conceive of the need for new facilities, arrange for financing, complete facilities construction or acquisition, provide the necessary staff and personnel, and put all of these resources to work. Capacity reductions also take time. This means that during any short period of time, the firm must operate with a relatively constant stock of productive resources, including organizational and financial resources.

The costs of providing capacity are known as *fixed costs* or *capacity costs*—those costs that do not change as a *necessary* result of small changes in volume. Fixed costs are budgeted at a specified amount per week or month or year and thus are sometimes called *time costs* or *period costs.*

Variable Costs

Variable costs are those that change as a necessary response to small changes in volume. These are the costs incurred by utilizing the available capacity to produce or sell goods or services. They may or may not average the same amount per unit as volume increases or decreases, but they are by definition variable in total, depending on the rate of activity.

Types of Fixed Costs

It is often assumed that fixed costs are established by some immutable law of nature and therefore cannot be influenced by management action. All that the word "fixed" means, however, is that the total amount of the cost will not be affected by *small* changes in *volume;* if volume changes are large or if other influences are felt, the total amount can change. To cite one minor example, heating and air-conditioning costs are generally fixed with respect to volume changes, and yet they obviously vary from season to season and can be influenced by a wide variety of other factors as well.

In planning and decision making, it is useful to recognize three categories of fixed costs:

1. *Caretaker costs:* Costs not subject to change unless sufficient time is provided to permit adjustment of physical capacity (e.g., depreciation).
2. *Enabling costs:* Costs necessary to provide operating capacity within certain volume ranges but subject to change if volume is expected to be outside the given volume range (e.g., supervision).
3. *Discretionary costs:* Costs which have no cause-and-effect relationship to current volume but are fixed by management decisions, usually when operating plans are approved (e.g., consultants' fees).

Caretaker Costs. Almost all costs in the first category will continue even if all company operations are temporarily closed down and the volume of activity is zero. Some of these are amortizations of costs incurred in prior periods (depreciation); others represent current cash outlays (property taxes and executive salaries). Changes in these costs occur only gradually, and in general they need to be considered only if management wishes to examine the probable long-range effects of shifting to a new level of operating capacity.

Enabling Costs. Costs in the second category reflect discontinuities and indivisibilities in the cost structure. If a steam plant is to provide any steam at all, it is necessary to hire an operating crew and burn a certain amount of fuel merely to maintain pressure. If the demand for steam is increased beyond a certain point, another boiler must be fired up. This introduces "steps" into the fixed cost function—steps that are in addition to the variable costs associated with the generation of varying amounts of steam within stated volume ranges. For example, a department's cost budget might show the following totals:

	Units of Output per Month			
	10,000	12,000	14,000	16,000
Variable costs ($1 per unit)........	$10,000	$12,000	$14,000	$16,000
Fixed costs......................	5,000	5,000	6,000	6,000
Total Costs...................	$15,000	$17,000	$20,000	$22,000

In this case, a step of $1,000 per month in the fixed costs is required whenever volume is to be increased from 12,000 to 14,000 units a month. If the steps are sufficiently close together they may be averaged out and treated as part of the variable costs.

Discretionary Costs. A substantial number of cost elements fall into the third category, discretionary fixed costs. In a sense, all fixed costs are the result of management decisions made at some time. Unlike enabling fixed costs, however, discretionary costs bear no technological relationship to current volume levels. They are established by management as part of its overall operating plan for the period. Many of them are incurred to obtain future sales—e.g., some kinds of advertising, research, and product development. Others are incurred to maintain a current position or to facilitate current managerial activity—e.g., legal services, market research, etc. Some do in fact vary with the volume of activity because management appropriates funds to these activities on the basis of anticipated sales volume, but this does not constitute cost variability for decision-making purposes.

Semivariable Costs

Some costs do not fall precisely into either the fixed or the variable category but contain elements of both. These are generally referred to as *semivariable costs*. A typical example is the cost of electric power: some power consumption is independent of operating volume, while another component is likely to vary directly with volume.

Economists' View of Cost Patterns

Economists have developed theoretical descriptions of the cost structure of the firm in a period of time long enough to permit a change in the quantity of goods produced but too short to permit a change in the operating capacity of the firm. In the graphic presentation of one such model, shown in Exhibit 3–1, total fixed costs are shown as a horizontal

Exhibit 3–1

ECONOMISTS' VIEW OF THE COST/VOLUME PATTERN

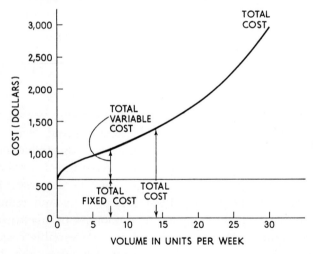

line, unresponsive to changes in volume. Total costs are drawn so as to rise sharply at first, then rise more gradually, and finally to rise more sharply again.

The shape of this curve is explained in terms of economies and diseconomies of the volume of operations. At low volumes, operations are performed in small lots. Simple equipment must be used because the cost of setting up higher speed machinery cannot be justified when only a few pieces are to be turned out. The cost curve tends to flatten out, however, when volume reaches the point at which economies of mass production can be achieved by a greater specialization of the work force and the use of higher speed equipment. Finally, some point is reached at which diminishing productivity is felt. Bottlenecks develop, production scheduling becomes more complex and is more likely to suffer interruptions, and the control process is subject to increasing strains.

Expressed in terms of cost per unit, the total cost curve of Exhibit 3–1 becomes the U-shaped unit cost curve of Exhibit 3–2, familiar to

Exhibit 3–2

EFFECT OF VOLUME ON AVERAGE COST PER UNIT

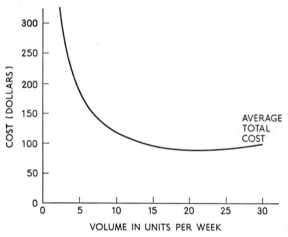

all students of elementary economics. Average cost per unit is high when volume is low because total fixed costs are spread over a relatively few units of product and because economies of mass production are not available to reduce variable costs per unit. As volume increases within the limits of constant capacity, average unit cost decreases, reflecting both a decrease in the average fixed cost per unit and reductions in average variable cost per unit due to economies of mass production. Later, diseconomies begin to set in and average variable cost per unit starts to rise. At some point, this increase just offsets the decline in average fixed costs, and the average total cost curve turns upward, as shown in Exhibit 3–2.

Changes in average variable cost per unit are the result of changes in *marginal cost*. Marginal cost is defined as the added cost that results from the production of one additional unit of output per unit of time.[3]

---

[3] A strict definition would equate marginal cost with the *rate of increase* of cost relative to the increase in volume. If the cost curves are continuous, as in the diagrams in this chapter, marginal cost can be obtained by measuring the mathematical derivative or slope of the total cost line at any point. Alternatively, total cost can be obtained by adding or integrating marginal costs for all volumes up to a given volume, including the costs that will be incurred if the facilities are not operated at all.

Exhibit 3–3 illustrates the relationships among marginal cost, average variable cost, and average total cost. The marginal cost curve is also conceived of as U-shaped. It is more sensitive to changes in volume than the average variable cost curve because averages reflect changes more slowly than individual observations. Even after marginal cost begins to rise, reflecting the onset of diminishing marginal productivity, average variable cost continues to fall because the increment or addition to cost is still lower than the average. This means that the marginal cost and the average variable cost curves must cross at the low point of the average variable cost curve.

The same relationship holds true between marginal cost and average

Exhibit 3–3

MARGINAL COST, AVERAGE VARIABLE COST, AND AVERAGE TOTAL COST

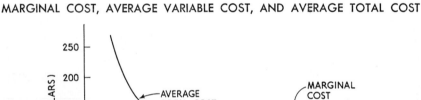
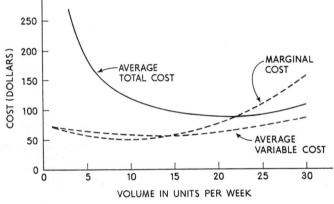

total cost. As long as the additions to cost resulting from additions to volume are less than average total cost, the average total cost curve will continue to fall, but when marginal cost goes above the average, the average must rise.

Accountants' View of Cost Patterns

The accounting view of the cost structure of the firm is in some ways simpler than the economists' view and in some ways much more complex. Most writers in economics are concerned with developing aggregate relationships in support of models of economic behavior. In such models a certain amount of simplification is necessary to reduce the number of variables to a workable level. Furthermore, to apply most techniques of mathematical analysis, it is necessary to assume continuous relationships and smooth curves. The curves shown in the preceding three diagrams are part of one of the simplest of economic models and assume that the firm is monolithic, with a single product and a single, homogeneous cost structure.

The accountant's interest is perhaps more pragmatic. His task is to describe the cost structure of the firm in all its complexity, recognizing the many products, many departments, and many elements to which costs are related. Nevertheless, in order to express the notion of variability, he often uses the very simple diagram shown in the left-hand portion of Exhibit 3–4 to represent cost variability. Total fixed costs are

Exhibit 3–4

ACCOUNTING VIEW OF THE COST/VOLUME PATTERN

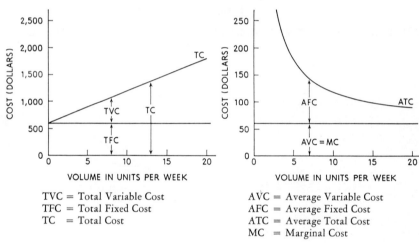

TVC = Total Variable Cost   AVC = Average Variable Cost
TFC = Total Fixed Cost   AFC = Average Fixed Cost
TC   = Total Cost   ATC = Average Total Cost
                                           MC = Marginal Cost

drawn on a cost/volume chart as a straight horizontal line; total variable costs are also drawn as a straight line, sloping upward to the right, as in the left-hand portion of Exhibit 3–4.

Taken at face value, this presentation has two simple meanings. First, *average variable cost per unit* is assumed to be constant for all volumes of activity up to full capacity, as shown in the right-hand portion of Exhibit 3–4. This means that marginal cost is also constant and equal to average cost. In fact, those two terms are often used interchangeably by accountants. Second, *average total cost* is assumed to decline continuously over the entire volume range up to full capacity, as in the right-hand portion of Exhibit 3–4, and will always be higher than average variable or marginal cost. Economies or diseconomies associated with increasing volume are assumed not to exist.

This does not mean that the accountant is unaware of diseconomies of increased utilization of capacity or of the limitations of the straight line assumption. He does ordinarily share the belief of many economists that within fairly wide volume ranges a straight line may be a reasonable approximation to the true cost/volume relationship. The straight line, constant average variable cost assumption produces what has been called a *general-purpose* variable cost, however, and if the specific purpose and circumstances dictate, the accountant must be prepared to make other assumptions.

For example, the assumed cost curve implicit in the budget for a manufacturing department may take the shape of the curve shown in Exhibit 3–5. This budget covers only a portion of the total possible

Exhibit 3–5

DEPARTMENTAL COST BUDGET

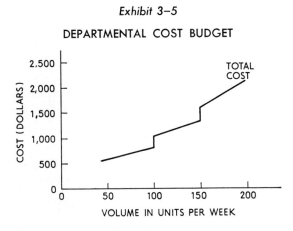

range of activity, encompassing the extremes of volume likely to be encountered. It rises in steps, but within each subrange it rises in relatively continuous fashion. The "slope" or rate of increase in cost may change from one segment of the volume range to another, and in Exhibit 3–5 the slope gets steeper at volumes in excess of 150 units per week, reflecting increasing use of overtime and nonpreferred machinery.

Whether the stepped increments in total cost should be treated as fixed or as variable costs is a matter of some dispute. Beyer, for example, treats these as variable costs,[4] whereas many other accountants view them as fixed. The distinction in many cases will have little practical significance, but when it does, a reasonable compromise is to include the stepped increments with the variable costs if the steps occur at fairly frequent intervals and as fixed costs if the steps are fairly broad.

---

[4] Robert Beyer, *Profitability Accounting for Planning and Control* (New York: Ronald Press, 1964), chap. vii.

Fixed Costs and Sunk Costs

The relevance of cost behavior patterns to incremental analysis is probably obvious. Whenever two alternatives differ in the rate of utilization of the existing facilities and organization, knowledge of cost variability is essential to the estimation of incremental cost. Confusion often arises, however, because it is often assumed that fixed costs are always sunk costs and that variable costs are always incremental. This is not always true. Fixed costs are those that don't change with relatively small changes of volume within the limits of existing capacity. Sunk costs are those that are unaffected by a choice between alternatives. Sunk cost is the much broader term of the two and may apply either to the fixed or to the variable costs.

For example, property taxes are fixed costs of plant operations in most instances. They will not be increased if the company is able to obtain additional volume to utilize plant capacity more fully. For a plant utilization decision, therefore, property taxes are not only fixed but also sunk costs. In studying the desirability of expanding the plant's operating capacity, however, these fixed costs are no longer entirely sunk because a larger plant will presumably carry a greater assessed valuation and therefore greater property taxes.

Similarly, when the problem is to compare the costs of operating at two different levels of output within the normal operating range, the only incremental costs may be the variable costs. To use the terms interchangeably, however, without specification of the problem under review, is inexcusable. A variable cost can also be a sunk cost under some circumstances. For example, if the company is considering whether to rent or own its manufacturing plant, total variable manufacturing costs are unlikely to be affected by the choice. Therefore, they may be treated as sunk costs for the purpose of reaching this specific decision. The criterion, here as always, is relevance to the decision at hand; and one of the problems in identifying sunk costs is to decide what costs are relevant in any particular case.

Other Determinants of Cost Behavior

Cost variability, of course, is not restricted to volume relationships. Much has been done in recent years to analyze the relationships between cost and lot size or between cost and the length of prior experience in performing a certain task, the so-called *learning curve*.[5] Provision for

---

[5] Learning curves are described and discussed briefly in Chapter 12.

some of these can be built into the accounting structure (for example, setup costs can be recorded separately from running time costs); others can be handled more conveniently by analysis outside the formal accounts (the learning cost pattern may be allowed for by predicting deviations from the cost standards that are based on mature operating conditions). Any further consideration of cost variability, however, must be deferred until it can be discussed in the context of the specific problems to which it relates.

SUMMARY

Decisions are made on the basis of anticipated payoffs of alternative courses of action. Payoffs depend, however, not only on the action selected but also on external environmental conditions. This means that it may be desirable to prepare more than one payoff estimate for each alternative, and the best course of action may not be at all obvious.

The role of accounting in this process is to provide data that can be used in forecasting the payoffs. These data must reflect the incremental principle that only differences between alternatives are relevant.

From this basic principle have come the concepts of incremental profit and incremental and sunk cost, together with a number of secondary concepts such as avoidable cost, opportunity cost, fixed cost, variable cost, and marginal cost. Of fundamental importance in the estimation of incremental cost is the probable behavior of costs in response to different variables, particularly the variability of costs with the volume of operations. Careful distinctions have to be made between fixed and variable costs, not only for decision making but for budgetary planning and other purposes as well.

It has been the purpose of this chapter to provide a broad introduction to the question of the relevance of financial data to decision making. Subsequent chapters will investigate how these matters relate to the design of accounting systems and the ways in which accounting data can be interpreted for incremental analysis.

DISCUSSION QUESTIONS

1. Distinguish among "marginal cost," "variable cost," and "incremental cost."
2. Many costs that are not constant for all possible ranges of operating volume are nevertheless referred to as fixed costs. Distinguish among the various types of fixed costs.
3. Which of the following costs would you expect to be generally classified as wholly fixed, wholly variable, or partly fixed and partly variable?

a) Depreciation.
b) Direct labor.
c) Superintendence.
d) Operating supplies.
e) Vacation pay.

f) Social security taxes.
g) Advertising.
h) Sales commissions.
i) Electric power.
j) Equipment maintenance.

4. When is a variable cost also a sunk cost? When is a fixed cost an incremental cost?

5. Is a sunk cost always one for which an expenditure has already been made or for which an obligation for expenditure has already been assumed? Explain.

6. "Marginal cost is only a short-run concept. If you allow enough time to encompass the retirement, replacement, or expansion of productive capacity, then all costs become marginal. Therefore, in any long-range cost analysis, you must use average total cost." Comment.

7. "As long as marginal cost is less than average cost, expansion of output will always reduce average cost, even if marginal cost is rising." Demonstrate the truth of this statement, using a numerical example.

8. The plant accountant for a machinery manufacturer recently stated that costs in his factory were 70 percent variable and 30 percent fixed. Assuming that his statement is accurate, what caution would you have to exercise in using these percentages next year in estimating the variable costs of specific products?

9. What is the relationship between the concepts of opportunity cost and incremental cost? Are they ever the same?

10. What is a decision rule?

11. Distinguish between outcomes and payoffs.

12. It has been stated that profit maximization cannot be used as a guide to decisions under conditions of uncertainty. Discuss this position.

13. An economist recently accused an accountant of using a naïve, oversimplified model of cost/volume relationships by assuming linear patterns in variable costs. The accountant countered by saying that the economist was just as bad, if not worse, because most economic models ignore variations in fixed costs. Each man now turns to you for support. What answer might you give that would tend to reconcile the differences between these two points of view?

EXERCISES AND PROBLEMS

1. "Dear Sir:

In your book you say that fixed costs are not necessarily unaffected by changes in the volume of activity. I have had three economics instructors, all of whom have their doctoral degrees, tell me that this definition is incorrect. They argue that if a cost is fixed it does not change. Would you please explain to me this difference of opinion?

Sincerely,"

How would you answer this letter?

2. From the following cost estimates, compute (*a*) average total cost, (*b*) average fixed cost, (*c*) average variable cost, and (*d*) marginal cost for each volume of activity. (Note: For this problem assume that fixed cost is the same at all volumes.)

Volume (Units per Hour)	Total Cost per Hour
0	$100
1	200
2	250
3	290
4	330
5	370
6	410
7	450
8	500
9	570
10	670

*3. From the following cost estimates, compute (*a*) average total cost, (*b*) average fixed cost, (*c*) average variable cost, and (*d*) marginal cost for each volume of activity. (Note: For this problem assume that fixed cost is the same at all volumes.)

Volume (Units per Hour)	Total Cost per Hour
0	$10
1	11
2	12
3	13
4	14
5	15
6	16
7	17
8	18
9	20
10	23

4. A motorist has computed that he can save money by leaving his car at home and flying from Boston to New York. Air fare and taxis, round trip, amount to $41. The motorist has found that it costs an average of 8 cents a mile to own and operate his car. The round trip requires him to drive 420 miles. Highway tolls and New York garage fees for a typical three-day trip amount to $9. Do you agree with the motorist's conclusions? Assume that he places no value on any time he might save by flying.

5. A methods analyst was assigned to study a particular operation to determine whether it could be performed at a lower cost. The cost of this operation, derived from the company's accounts, was $37,000 a month. The methods analyst completed his investigation and reported to his immediate superior: "This operation needs a complete revision of procedures. It is

---

* Solutions to problems marked with an asterisk (*) can be found in Appendix B.

costing us $20,000 to use the methods now in force, and that is worth 3 cents per share of common stock in after-tax earnings."

a) What did the methods analyst expect the operation to cost per month if procedures were revised according to his recommendations?

b) What cost concept did he use in his statement? What would you say is the monthly cost of this operation?

6. Your automobile battery is very old, and you are afraid that it will go dead during the coming winter if you don't replace it now. If you buy a new battery now, you can buy it at a price of $20. If you wait and the battery dies, you will have to pay $25 for a replacement.

    Cold weather is approaching, and you believe that the probability of the battery dying during the winter is 70 percent.

a) Construct a payoff table.

b) Describe the decision rule that you would apply in this situation and indicate what decision you would make.

*7. An outlay of $10,000 is proposed. Incremental cash receipts resulting from this outlay could be anywhere from zero to $25,000. The probabilities are:

Receipts	Probability
$ 0	0.1
5,000	0.2
10,000	0.4
15,000	0.2
20,000	0.05
25,000	0.05

a) Construct a payoff table.

b) Compute expected value for each alternative action.

*8. The Rise Company makes bumper jacks, and last year it sold 50,000 at a price of $3 and produced them at an average cost of $2.25. The sales manager states that at a price of $2.50 he could sell 75,000 units. The factory manager estimates that 75,000 could be produced at an average cost of $2 each. What is the incremental revenue, the incremental cost, and the incremental profit on reducing the price to $2.50 each?

9. The Potts Company is the exclusive dealer in Buffalo, New York, for frabbles, which it buys from the Amalgamated Frabble Company at the following prices:

In Lots of—	Unit Price Is—
Less than 100	$5.00
100 to 499	4.75
500 or more	4.50

    The Potts Company's practice has been to order frabbles monthly in the quantities necessary to meet the following month's requirements. The average monthly requirement has been 80 units, and the average price paid under this plan has been $4.90.

a) Potts is considering giving up its rights to serve the nearby city of Batavia. It now sells approximately 10 frabbles a month in Batavia. What unit cost figure should Potts use in evaluating the desirability of this move, assuming that Amalgamated is not expected to change its price schedule?

b) A customer has asked Potts to deliver 50 frabbles a month at a price of $6 each. What unit cost figure should Potts use in evaluating the desirability of this contract, again assuming that Amalgamated is not expected to change its price schedule?

10. Franklin Enterprises can ship product A to a customer for $40. Shipping charges for product B are $30. If both products are packed together, the total shipping cost is $50. Only one unit of product B may be packed with each unit of product A.

a) The customer now buys product A but not product B. What cost would you use in evaluating the desirability of getting the customer to buy product B?

b) Franklin Enterprises ships equal quantities of both products to its warehouse near the customer at the $50 combined shipping cost. The customer buys only product B, product A being sold to other nearby customers. The customer has found a use for product A and asks for a price quotation. What shipping cost would you use in calculating the profitability of any given price?

11. The Kabal Machine Works manufactures a number of repair parts that are used in maintenance of the company's production equipment. These parts are made in the company's maintenance shop. Cost data on the last three lots of a particular part were as follows:

Date	No. of Pieces	Costs				
		Setup	Labor and Material	Variable Overhead	Fixed Overhead	Total
1/6......	100	$4.50	$ 42.50	$14.00	$21.00	$ 82.00
4/8......	300	5.00	122.00	41.00	61.50	229.50
9/14.....	200	4.75	85.00	28.00	42.00	159.75

This part can be purchased from an outside supplier at a price, delivered, of 60 cents apiece.

a) Compute the "cost" per piece, using at least three alternative measures of cost.

b) The plant manager has asked you for a figure representing the cost of this part for use in deciding whether to buy it from the outside vendor. Select one of the figures you developed in (a) and state reasons for your selection.

12. A study of the costs of the Paltec Company's Pittsford factory produced the following estimates of costs at various volume levels:

Output per Hour	Total Costs per Hour
13	136
12	124
11	113
10	102
9	82
8	73
7	65
6	58
5	52
4	46
3	40

The analyst who prepared these estimates stated that the cost figures for all output rates in excess of nine units per hour included a provision for $10 per hour in additional fixed costs that need not be incurred at output rates of nine units per hour or less. (Note: Assume that the cost function is linear in the volume range of zero to six units per hour.)

a) Compute average total cost, average variable cost, and marginal cost for each output rate and plot the resultant figures on a single sheet of graph paper.

b) Discuss the problem you encountered in computing marginal cost for an output rate of 10 units an hour, and defend your solution of this problem.

*13. The Powwow Flour Milling Company is currently operating its mill six days a week, 24 hours a day, on three shifts. It could easily obtain a sufficient volume of sales at current prices to take the entire output of a seventh day of operations each week. The mill's practical capacity is 6,000 hundredweight of flour per day. Flour sells for $5.70 per hundredweight, and the price of wheat is $2.17 per bushel. Approximately 2.35 bushels of wheat are required per hundredweight of flour. Fixed costs now average $2,100 per day, or $0.35 per hundredweight. The average variable cost of mill operation, almost entirely wages, is $0.17 per hundredweight. Sunday operation would require the payment of double wages for Sunday work, which would bring the variable cost of Sunday operation to $0.33 per hundredweight. Total fixed costs per week would increase by $210 if the mill were to operate on Sunday.

a) Compute the average total cost per hundredweight for six-day operation. What is the net profit margin before taxes, per hundredweight?

b) Compute the average fixed cost per hundredweight for seven-day operation. Would it be profitable for the mill to operate on Sundays?

14. A manufacturing plant operates on a single-shift, five-day week. It can produce up to 8,000 units of output per week without the use of overtime or extra-shift operation. Fixed costs for single-shift operation amount to $30,000 per week. Average variable cost is a constant $10 per unit at all output rates up to 8,000 units per week. The plant's output can be increased to 12,000 units a week by going on overtime or adding Saturday operations or both. This entails no increase in fixed costs, but the variable cost is $12 per unit for any output in excess of 8,000 units per week up to the 12,000-unit capacity.

The plant also operates a second shift if sales volume warrants, and if second-shift operation is more efficient than overtime or Saturday operation. The maximum capacity of the second shift is 7,000 units per week. The variable cost on the second shift is $10.50 per unit, and operation of a second shift entails additional fixed costs of $4,500 per week.

a) At what operating volume does it become economical to operate a second shift? (Assume that the product cannot be inventoried in any substantial quantities.)

b) Prepare a schedule of marginal cost for output rates ranging from 5,000 units per week to 17,000 units per week, in 1,000 unit intervals, assuming that any overtime or Saturday operations are performed by the first shift.

15. A "direct mail" company would charge you $2,000 to print and mail to a list of 10,000 selected executives a brochure describing your new "exec-o-mat" desk calendar. You buy these from a manufacturer for $15 and sell them for $30. An incremental cost of $1 is incurred to pack and ship each exec-o-mat. Your annual profit from other sources is $3,000, and your bank balance is now $2,500.

Your previous experience with mailings of this kind has indicated that any sales made in response to the mailing will be made in the three months immediately following the mailing. Your experience also leads you to expect a 3 percent response to the mailing (in this case, 300 units sold). The probabilities that you assign to the various possible outcomes are:

Percent Response		Probability
Range	Average	
0.51–1.5..........	1.0	0.10
1.51–2.5..........	2.0	0.25
2.51–3.5..........	3.0	0.50
3.51–4.5..........	4.0	0.10
4.51 or more......	5.0	0.05

If you decide to undertake the mailing, you will increase your inventory and hire an additional stock boy, so as to be prepared for any orders that come in. The stock boy's wages and added inventory carrying costs on the *additional* inventory would amount to $500 a month. Costs of carrying the *current* levels of inventory and operating the stock room now total $3,000 a month.

The carrying cost figures included in the estimates quoted in the preceding paragraph apply only if sales made in response to the mailing total at least 300 units. In addition to these, extra incremental carrying costs of $0.50 would be incurred for each unit sold less than 300. (For example, if 200 units were sold, the extra carrying costs resulting from the failure to meet the 300-unit minimum would total $0.50 × (300 − 200) = $50. This figure covers the entire three-month period—it is not a cost per month.)

a) Prepare a profitability estimate on the basis of the forecasted 3 percent response.

b) Prepare a payoff table, with five states of nature.

c) Compute the expected value under each alternative management action.

d) Is this a situation in which the decision maker would be likely to use a decision rule that departs materially from maximum expected value? Comment.

16. The Penn Yan factory of the Marlman Products Company operates a five-day week. For cost accumulation and reporting purposes, the year is divided into 13 "months" of four weeks each. You are given the following information about this factory:

(1) Property taxes, insurance, depreciation, salaries, and miscellaneous costs amount to $12,600 a month when the plant is shut down.

(2) Salaries and the costs of telephone, electricity, steam, and heat are $6,300 a month greater when the plant is operating than when it is shut down, no matter what rate of output is achieved.

(3) Whenever production rates equal or exceed 120 units a day, management authorizes expenditures of $2,500 per month for employee recreation, window washing, and community services. If the production rate equals or exceeds 160 units per day, management authorizes additional expenditures of $3,780 a month for adult education and related activities.

(4) Labor and materials costs amount to $10 per unit.

(5) The costs of other items not previously mentioned above are:

Units Produced (per Day)	Other Costs (per Month)
80	$ 5,600
90	6,300
100	7,000
110	7,700
120	8,400
130	9,100
140	9,800
150	10,800
160	12,160
170	13,940
180	16,200
190	19,000
200	22,400

a) From the preceding information, compute for each operating volume from 80 units per day to 200 units per day the following figures: (1) total cost per month, (2) total fixed cost per month, (3) total variable cost per month, (4) average total cost per unit, (5) average fixed cost per unit, (6) average variable cost per unit, and (7) marginal cost per unit.

b) Plot the figures obtained in (*a*) on graph paper, using separate graphs for total costs and for unit costs.

c) The plant is now operating at a rate of 150 units per day. What is the incremental cost of increasing the output rate to 160 units per day?

d) The company can sell as many units as it can produce at a price of $24.10 per unit, after deducting selling and administrative costs. What is the most profitable rate of daily output? What if the net price is $14.10?

Part II

Measurement of Product Cost

Chapter 4

MEASUREMENT OF FACTORY UNIT COST: JOB ORDER COSTING

COST ACCOUNTING was born and grew to manhood on a diet of cost measurement, specifically measurement of factory cost per unit of manufactured products. Such figures are known as measures of *product unit cost* or simply *unit cost*. They are used in decision making and also in determining inventory costs and the cost of goods sold for enterprise financial reporting.

Various approaches to product costing are available. This chapter describes the basic outlines of the costing method known as *job order costing* and also indicates how unit costs are reflected in company financial statements.

THE ESSENCE OF JOB ORDER COSTING

The first step in measuring a product's cost is to decide on the *costing unit*—that is, whether to try to accumulate costs separately for each unit of each product, for each separately identifiable group of units of each product, or for all the units of product produced in a given department during a period of time.

This choice depends to a great extent on the way in which production is organized. In shipbuilding, for example, each ship typically represents a very large proportion of the producton volume at any one time. It is thus both easy and informative to trace many costs to one particular ship or another. The costing unit for unit cost determination in this case is the *job* or *production order,* and each job consists of one unit of product. In other cases, each job order covers the manufacture or assembly of a number of identical units of a given product. Even in shipbuilding, it is customary to cost parts of the job separately, and many subjobs

79

may consist of several identical units. In both of these situations, the method of unit cost determination is known as *job order costing.*

Job order production is typical whenever the production volume in any one product is too small to justify devoting production facilities exclusively to it for any significant length of time. Examples of this kind of situation abound in industries in which a sizable proportion of the output is to individual customer specifications (e.g., automotive repair shops, job printing plants, and management consulting firms and other service businesses). It is also common whenever the work in any time period is concentrated on a relatively small number of product units (e.g., shipbuilding and building construction).

Components of Manufacturing Cost

Three classes of manufacturing costs are ordinarily distinguished in job order costing:

1. Direct labor.
2. Direct materials.
3. Factory overhead.

Labor and materials costs that are *traced* specifically to the job are known as *prime costs* or, more specifically, as *direct labor* and *direct materials.* Direct labor cost is any labor cost that is directly traced to a particular job order. Similarly, direct materials costs are those costs of raw and processed materials, component parts, and subassemblies that are traced directly to specific jobs.

These definitions are based on the traceability of the *costs* and not necessarily on the physical relationship between the specific input and the product. Direct materials costs, for example, may include the costs of some materials that are not specifically incorporated in the finished product. All that is necessary is that the costs of these materials can be traced to the costing unit, in this case the individual job order.

All manufacturing costs that are not traced to the product costing unit are classified as *factory overhead,* also called *factory burden, manufacturing expense,* or *indirect cost.* They are distinguished from prime costs in that they are incurred either jointly for the benefit of more than one job order or in units that are individually too small to be traced readily to specific costing units.

Depreciation on the factory building, for example, is a cost that is incurred to permit production of all the products turned out by the factory. No portion of this cost can be traced unequivocally to any particular unit of product. The costs of thread, tacks, and glue, on the other hand, conceivably could be traced to individual job lots, but the clerical cost of tracing them is so high that in job order costing it is more *convenient* to group them with manufacturing overhead.

The Job Cost Sheet

Accounting for job lot production begins with the issue of a production order. This contains instructions to the production departments, indicating such information as the specifications of the items to be produced, the number of units required, a list of materials to be used,

Exhibit 4–1

JOB ORDER COST SHEET

DESCRIPTION: Cannister No. 278   JOB ORDER NO. 1234

DATE ORDERED 5/1/—   DATE DUE 5/15/—   DATE COMPLETED 5/12/—

QUANTITY ORDERED 2,000   QUANTITY COMPLETED 2,000

MATERIALS COST

Date	Item	Quantity	Price	Amount
5/3	Shell No. 14	2,000	$0.32	$640.00
5/4	Shell No. 14	50	0.32	16.00
5/5	Handle No. 142	2,000	0.12	240.00
5/10	Paint	2	2.75	5.50
	Total			$901.50

Cost summary:

Materials........$ 901.50
Labor...........   71.40
Overhead applied.   177.10
   Total.........$1,150.00
Average cost......$ 0.575 each

LABOR COST

Date	Operation	Hours	Rate	Amount
5/4	22	6.5	$2.20	$ 14.30
5/6	31	10.0	2.10	21.00
5/10	42	14.5	1.80	26.10
5/12	44	4.0	2.50	10.00
	Total			$ 71.40

the operations to be performed, the equipment to be used, and the required delivery date. At the time a job order is issued, the accounting department is notified, an identifying number is assigned to the job and a *job cost sheet* is prepared. This sheet is the focus of product costing in job order production.

A sample job cost sheet is shown in Exhibit 4–1. This shows the job number, the number of items to be produced, and delivery information, as well as columns in which the costs incurred in connection with this job can be recorded. As the work progresses, costs are entered on the cost sheets, as in the exhibit. When the job is completed, the finished products are assigned the average cost per unit of all units in the lot.

Burden Rates

Only direct labor and direct materials costs are entered directly on the job cost sheets. Because factory overhead is not traced to specific job orders, the only way of including it in product cost is to assign it to jobs on the basis of some average rate. An average of this kind is known as a *burden rate* or *overhead costing rate*.

One possibility would be to divide the actual overhead costs for the month by some measure of total production volume for that month. For example, if the month's factory overhead totaled $209,000 and the month's direct labor cost amounted to $95,000, a burden rate equal to the ratio between these two figures, $2.20 per dollar of direct labor, could be used. If this were done, a job on which direct labor cost totaled $100 would be assigned $220 in factory overhead costs. This amount would be shown on the job cost sheet as *overhead absorbed* or *overhead applied*.

This use of direct labor dollars to represent production volume deserves comment. Because the factory in job order production manufactures so many products of different size and complexity, it is almost never possible to measure production volume by the total number of units of product manufactured. Instead, volume is measured by some index of productive *input*, such as direct labor hours or machine-hours or, as in the example, direct labor cost.

Predetermined Burden Rates

In most job order costing systems, the burden rate is *predetermined*—that is, the rate is not the average overhead cost of each individual period but is rather the average of a "normal" or typical period:

$$\text{Burden rate} = \frac{\text{Estimated costs in a normal month}}{\text{Total volume in a normal month}}.$$

For example, assume that at normal production volume the factory would record $100,000 in direct labor costs each month and $210,000 in factory overhead. The burden rate would be:

$$\frac{\$210,000}{\$100,000} = \$2.10 \text{ per direct labor dollar.}$$

At this rate, each time a dollar of direct labor was recorded on a job order cost sheet, the job would also be charged for factory overhead at 210 percent of the direct labor cost.

The predetermined rate is used to simplify and speed clerical operations—that is, overhead can be applied to jobs as the work is performed, without awaiting the calculation of actual cost and actual volume at the end of the month. More importantly, the predetermined rate keeps temporary fluctuations in average overhead cost out of the product cost calculations, on the grounds that these fluctuations have nothing to do with specific products but only with production as a whole.

MANAGERIAL USES OF UNIT COST DATA

The applicability to decision making of unit costs derived by job costing techniques is the subject of considerable controversy. The argument is focused on the elements of fixed costs introduced into unit cost by way of the burden rate, but the issue is really under what circumstances, if any, average product unit cost is a good approximation to incremental product cost. For short-run, utilization-of-capacity decisions it clearly is not; for decisions with a longer time horizon it may be somewhat closer to the desired measure.

These issues will be taken up in a later chapter, but one use of unit cost data in decision making is unquestioned: the job cost sheets provide an invaluable source of data on direct product costs. Cost estimates for new jobs are typically based on the records of costs incurred on similar jobs in the past. For this reason, the costs charged to the job cost sheet are often coded to indicate type of materials, operation performed, and so forth.

Identification of trends in unit cost for standardized products may also be useful in decision making. The periodic cost reporting system seldom includes statistics of this kind, but there is no reason why they cannot be picked out if management finds them useful.

Unit cost data are less useful for control purposes because they represent the *combined* performance of a number of departments. Control reporting is departmental, following responsibility lines, and it is difficult to adapt job cost data to this basis. At best, unit costs can be identified as higher or lower than the advance estimates and investigation can reveal the cost centers responsible for most of the deviation. It is generally impractical, however, to derive departmental totals of these deviations when there are many cost centers and many jobs. Development of cost data for use in cost control will be discussed later, beginning in Chapter 10.

COST FLOWS FOR INCOME DETERMINATION

Unit cost measures derived from job order costing also play an important role in the determination of net income and inventory costs for companywide financial statements. The costing problem in income determination is to estimate the amount of cost that should be deducted from the revenues of the period. Such costs fall into two categories: expenses and losses. An expense is a cost that is judged to have expired during the specified time period in the creation of revenues. A loss is a cost that has expired during the period, but with no offsetting benefit or connection with the creation of revenue. In practice, the term "expense" is sometimes applied to manufacturing overhead costs that are not charged directly to the income statement, but in the interest of clarity the definition above should be observed strictly.

From this, the relationship between the income statement and the asset side of the balance sheet should be apparent. If a cost has not expired in the creation of revenues or as a loss, it remains as an asset on the balance sheet. This means that the problem of income determination is inseparable from the problem of inventory costing as long as inventory costing is kept within the confines of the double-entry bookkeeping system.

Cost Flows in Trading Companies

The wholesaling or retailing firm normally performs some combination of the functions of buying, storing, transporting, and selling a number of different products. Revenues are recognized at the time of sale, but the recognition of expense depends on the nature of the individual factor inputs.

Exhibit 4–2 is a simple schematic representation of the flow of costs

Exhibit 4–2

COST FLOWS FOR INCOME DETERMINATION IN TRADING COMPANIES

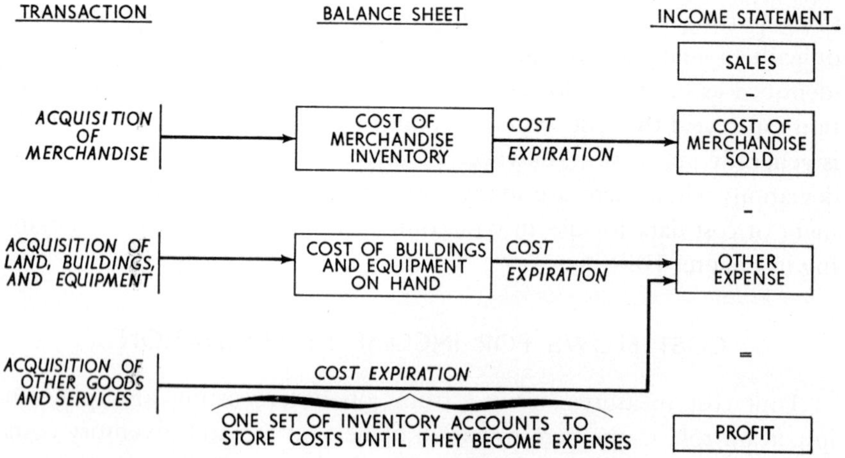

in a trading company for financial reporting purposes. This diagram shows only one intermediate stage between the incurring of a cost and its transfer to expense. Cost is inventoried either in long-life property or in physical inventories and is transferred to expense as the property depreciates or as the inventories themselves are sold.

Some other costs, such as the cost of insurance premiums paid in advance, are also inventoried on the balance sheet before being transferred to the income statement as they expire, but they have been ignored in the interests of keeping Exhibit 4–2 as simple as possible. Because this is not a manufacturing company, most other costs for wages, salaries, supplies, electric power, and so forth are not inventoried but are charged directly to the income statement as expense of the period in which acquisition takes place.

For example, assume that at the start of its operations the company purchases merchandise at a total cost of $800,000 and store fixtures at a cost of $100,000. Rent of $22,500 is paid in advance for 18 months' use of a store building. During the year the cost of the merchandise that is sold is $600,000, leaving a year-end inventory of goods that cost $200,000. Depreciation on the store fixtures is $10,000, and 12 months' prepaid rent amounting to $15,000 is transferred to expense. Other costs are charged directly to expense and consist of $250,000 for wages and salaries and $50,000 for taxes, purchased services, and operating supplies. The net income for the period, before provision for income taxes, is:

Sales...........................		$1,000,000
Expenses:		
Cost of goods sold.............	$600,000	
Salaries and wages............	250,000	
Depreciation.................	10,000	
Rent........................	15,000	
Other.......................	50,000	925,000
Net Income....................		$ 75,000

No portion of the cost of wages and salaries or miscellaneous costs is left on the balance sheet because it is assumed that they were incurred to enable the firm to obtain the sales of this period, with no measurable carry-over to future periods.

Cost Flows in Manufacturing

Whereas the wholesaler's business is primarily one of buying, storing, and selling, the manufacturer performs an additional economic service by converting the form of the materials that he buys into a product that is recognizably different. The costs that he incurs for this conversion process are the manufacturing costs that entered into the unit cost calculations earlier in this chapter.

The manufacturer's inventories are a mixture of items that are still in the state in which they were received, others that are undergoing conversion, and others that are in the state in which they will be sold. For income determination purposes, it is necessary to charge as expenses those manufacturing costs which can reasonably be associated with the revenue from the products that were actually sold, leaving on the balance sheet in inventory accounts the conversion costs associated with items still in semiprocessed and finished states.

The block diagram in Exhibit 4–3 illustrates this point. It will be

Exhibit 4–3

COST FLOWS FOR INCOME DETERMINATION IN MANUFACTURING

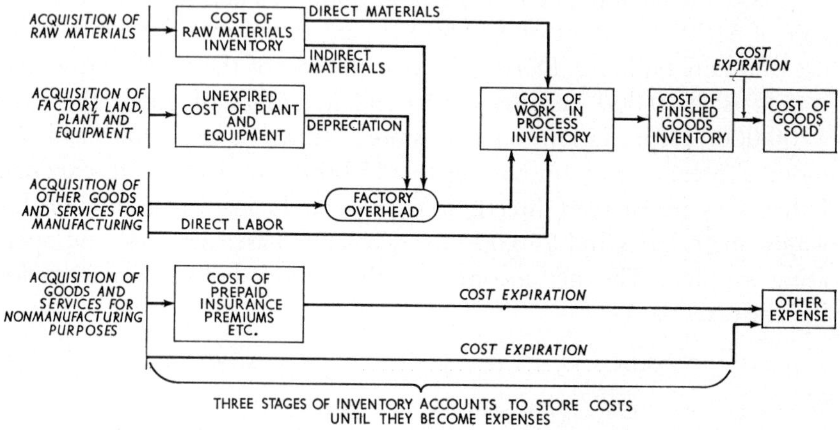

THREE STAGES OF INVENTORY ACCOUNTS TO STORE COSTS
UNTIL THEY BECOME EXPENSES

noted in comparing Exhibit 4–3 with Exhibit 4–2 that the flow of nonmanufacturing costs is the same in both charts. Some of them, such as prepaid insurance premiums or the cost of buildings and equipment not used in manufacturing, go through one "inventory" or balance sheet stage before transfer to expense. Others, such as salesmen's salaries and commissions, pass directly to the income statement as expense. These nonmanufacturing costs are generally referred to on the income statement as *selling and administrative expenses.*

It is only with respect to manufacturing costs that the requirements of income determination necessitate more than one intermediate stage between the incurring of a cost and its transfer to expense. At the first stage, costs may be lodged in materials purchased, plant and equipment acquired, or other goods or services bought prior to their use. At the second stage, materials may be in process in varying stages of completion—these states having been reached by the application of labor and other manufacturing inputs to the basic materials. At the third stage, the manufacturing function has been completed but the goods have not yet been sold.

Up to this point nothing has happened to justify identification of manufacturing costs with the revenues of the period. Only when the final stage is reached—the sale of the goods to outside customers—do manufacturing costs appear on the income statement as expense.[1]

Recording Costs: Materials

To illustrate, assume that a factory manufactures a wide variety of metal products. To simplify further, assume that there were no inventories of any kind in the factory at the beginning of May.

During May the company purchased materials at a cost of $200,000 and placed them in the factory storeroom. In summary form, the accounting entry to record these purchases was:

(1)

Materials Inventory..200,000		
Accounts Payable..		200,000

As in all illustrations in this book, these entries reflect the accounts used by this company and are not intended to exclude other possibilities. Other companies may use other account titles or follow somewhat different bookkeeping procedures. For example, the Materials Inventory account may be called Stores, or the cost of materials purchased may be debited initially to a Purchases account. During this month materials costing $113,000 were withdrawn from the storeroom and *issued* to factory departments. Of this sum, $105,000 represented the cost of materials issued specifically for individual jobs, to be charged as direct material on those jobs. The remaining $8,000 was the cost of supplies for general use in the factory, not traceable to any specific job or jobs. Supplies or materials used in this way are usually called *indirect materials,* and their costs are a subdivision of factory overhead costs.

The costs of direct materials were entered on the job cost sheets for the various production lots, and the total direct materials cost was charged to an inventory account entitled Work in Process. Indirect materials, on the other hand, were not charged directly to an inventory

---

[1] This presumes that revenues are recognized at the time of sale. If revenues are recognized on a production basis, slight alterations in the diagram will be necessary.

account but instead were first recorded in overhead accounts. These entries can be summarized as follows:

(2)

```
Work in Process..............................................105,000
Factory Overhead.........................................  8,000
    Materials Inventory........................................        113,000
```

Control Accounts and Subsidiary Ledgers

The Materials Inventory, Work in Process, and Factory Overhead accounts in this illustration appear in the company's *general ledger* or main file of accounts and are known as *summary* or *control* accounts. This means that the balances in these accounts correspond in total to the amounts shown in more detailed *subsidiary ledgers* or cost files.

For example, the detail underlying the Materials Inventory account balance is provided in the individual stock cards in the subsidiary ledger known as the stores ledger. Similarly, the balance in the Work in Process account should agree with the total of all the costs shown on the job cost sheets for jobs still in process, and the Factory Overhead control account balance should correspond to the total of the amounts shown in the detailed overhead accounts for the individual factory cost centers.

The main purposes of these summary or control accounts and their accompanying subsidiary files are (1) to reduce the bulk of the general ledger, and (2) to facilitate access to portions of the account file without temporarily immobilizing other portions of the file. The detailed accounts have been left out of this illustration for simplification only.

Recording Labor Costs

The factory payrolls for May totaled $157,000. This amount included $95,000 for the portion of production workers' time that could be traced to individual jobs (the direct labor), $22,000 for indirect labor, and $40,000 for the salaries of supervisory and clerical employees in the factory. The entry to record the May payrolls was:

(3)

```
Work in Process...............................................95,000
Factory Overhead............................................62,000
    Payrolls Payable...........................................        157,000
```

The direct labor costs were also entered on the individual job cost sheets.

Recording Factory Overhead

In addition to materials and payroll costs, the factory incurred other costs during the month of May. These costs, which totaled $139,000, could not be traced to specific jobs, so they too were classified as factory overhead:

(4)

Factory Overhead. 139,000
    Accounts Payable, etc.   139,000

Overhead Absorption

A predetermined burden rate of $2.10 per direct labor dollar, based on the calculation made earlier in this chapter, was used to assign factory overhead to job orders. Because direct labor costs amounted to $95,000 during the month, a total of $199,500 ($2.10 × $95,000) was assigned to jobs in process. This amount was also charged to the Work in Process control account by the following entry:

(5)

Work in Process. 199,500
    Factory Overhead.   199,500

In other words, costs initially and temporarily recorded in Factory Overhead were transferred by entry (5) from that account to Work in Process. This procedure is known as *overhead absorption* or *overhead application.*

Product Completion

In the typical case, many job orders would be in production each month. To keep the illustration simple, however, let us assume that our factory had only four jobs in process during May. The job cost sheets for these four jobs showed the following totals after the above transactions had been recorded:

Job No.	Direct Materials	Direct Labor	Overhead Applied	Total
1.	$ 28,000	$20,000	$ 42,000	$ 90,000
2.	57,000	30,000	63,000	150,000
3.	15,000	35,000	73,500	123,500
4.	5,000	10,000	21,000	36,000
Total. . . .	$105,000	$95,000	$199,500	$399,500

The first two of these jobs were completed during May, and the finished products were turned over to the sales division. The job order cost sheets for these two jobs were removed from the in-process file, and an entry was made to transfer the costs accumulated on these two jobs to the Finished Goods Inventory account (another control account):

(6)
Finished Goods Inventory...240,000
    Work in Process...   240,000

At the same time, entries were made in a subsidiary finished goods ledger to record the number of units finished and the cost per unit. For example, job No. 1 was the manufacture of 15,000 water pumps. A filing card was prepared for water pumps, and an entry was made to record the completion of 15,000 water pumps at a unit cost of $6. A second card was prepared for job No. 2, consisting of 5,000 oil burners at a unit cost of $30 each. (Once again, remember that the typical production lot is ordinarily much smaller than these, at least as a percentage of total factory output.)

Recording the Cost of Goods Sold

During May, the company shipped 6,000 water pumps and 3,000 oil burners to various customers. The cost of these goods was obtained from the finished goods ledger cards, as follows:

Item	Unit Cost	Number Sold	Cost of Goods Sold
Water pumps.......	$ 6.00	6,000	$ 36,000
Oil burners.........	30.00	3,000	90,000
Total.........			$126,000

These amounts were subtracted from the finished goods ledger cards, and an entry was made to record the transfer:

(7)
Cost of Goods Sold...126,000
    Finished Goods Inventory...................................   126,000

This entry completed the so-called "job order costing cycle." Materials were purchased, issued from inventory, processed into finished goods, and sold. After all these events were recorded, the factory cost accounts appeared as shown in Exhibit 4–4.

In other words, cost accounting not only arrived at a measure of unit cost but also distributed the costs of the various productive inputs among the various outputs in the manner shown in Exhibit 4–5. Notice that the two bars in this diagram are of the same height, corresponding to a total cost of $496,000. Inputs and outputs *must* be equal because the cost accounting system defines output in terms of inputs, and inputs and outputs are thus merely two ways of describing the same total.

Exhibit 4–4

MANUFACTURING COST ACCOUNTS

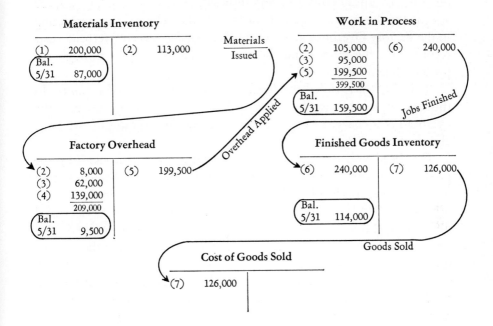

Exhibit 4–5

ACCOUNTING RELATIONSHIPS BETWEEN FACTORY INPUTS AND OUTPUTS

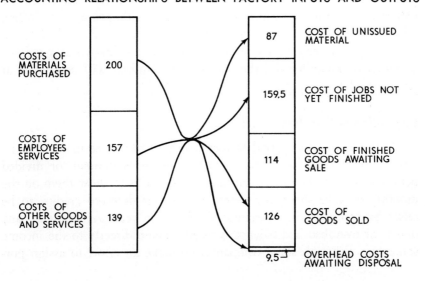

Under- or Overabsorbed Overhead

The only difficulty with this approach is that one of the so-called outputs, "overhead costs awaiting disposal," was fictitious. The $9,500 assigned to this fictitious output was merely the debit balance remaining in the Factory Overhead account, the difference between overhead costs recorded for the month and the amount charged to jobs through the predetermined burden rate.

This $9,500 is called the *burden variance* or *overhead variance*. In this case it would also be referred to as *underabsorbed* because the overhead cost charged to the factory exceeded the amount of overhead absorbed by production.

Overhead variances are likely to arise for three reasons: (1) the production *volume* achieved is different from the level defined as normal (in the example, direct labor cost was only $95,000 instead of the normal $100,000 per month); (2) the *prices* of indirect services used differ from those on which the burden rate was based; and (3) the *amounts* of indirect services used are larger or smaller than the production volume warrants.

The second and third of these are probably self-evident, but the first needs at least a partial explanation. The burden rate is based on estimated or budgeted costs at some specified volume. Some of these costs are fixed—that is, they will be the same for almost any likely production volume. Depreciation on the factory building, for example, will be the same whether the factory direct labor cost is $80,000 or $100,000 per month, but the total amount *charged to job orders* (absorbed) by means of the predetermined rate will vary with production. When production levels are low, fixed overhead will be underabsorbed (as in the example above), and vice versa. This effect is known as a *volume variance*. Its meaning and the calculations required will be studied at length in a later chapter.

Disposition of Overhead Variances

At the end of the period factory overhead variances may either be left on the balance sheet, taken to the income statement, or divided between the two. The most common procedure is to show them on the monthly balance sheet as deferred charges or deferred credits, to be offset by compensating variances later in the year. At year-end, any under- or overabsorbed balance is usually taken directly to the income statement, although some companies do make an effort to assign portions of it to uncompleted and unsold inventories. The validity of these procedures will be studied later.

SUMMARY

Job order costing is one of the two principal methods of factory product costing. It consists of identifying for each production lot the labor and materials costs directly traceable to that lot, adding to these a portion of the nontraceable overheads, and dividing the total of all these costs by the number of product units in the lot.

Unit costs determined in this way are used to measure the cost of goods sold and the cost of inventories for company financial reporting. Application of the predetermined burden rate in this connection creates differences or variances between actual overhead costs and the amounts charged to products, and the reasons for these variances must be studied.

Job costs are also often used in product pricing and other kinds of managerial decisions, but their relevance for these purposes must remain for the moment an open question. The main thing to remember at this stage is that unit cost calculations, like other elements of the cost accounting structure, are not ends in themselves. They must be justified by their usefulness to others, primarily to management, and their relevance to the problems to which they are applied should never be assumed without first examining the nature of the problem and the structure of the costs.

DISCUSSION QUESTIONS

1. What is the difference between *cost* and *expense?*
2. Why are burden rates necessary in job order costing?
3. What are the reasons for using predetermined burden rates?
4. Underabsorbed overhead in the Garfill Company amounted to $16,000 during March. What might have caused this?
5. What is the product costing unit in job order costing?
6. For what purposes is factory unit cost calculated? Do you think that one measure of unit cost can serve all of these purposes satisfactorily?
7. Under what circumstances would you expect factory overhead to be neither overabsorbed nor underabsorbed during a given time period?
8. What is the relationship between the file of job order cost sheets and the factory ledger or general ledger?
9. If the company has a factory ledger, what is the relationship between it and the company's general ledger?

10. Which of the following items would you expect to record directly on individual job order cost sheets? Explain why or why not in each case.

a) Direct labor.
b) Indirect labor.
c) Materials handling labor.
d) Machine maintenance labor.
e) Factory supplies.
f) Machinery depreciation.
g) Direct materials.
h) Electric power.

11. The Mander Company was organized in January to manufacture and sell small hand tools. During the first three months of operation, the company manufactured products with a total factory cost of $100,000. Selling and administrative costs for the period amounted to $15,000. Orders for April delivery, totaling $50,000, were obtained during the first quarter of the year, but no products were shipped to customers prior to April 1.

What income would be reported for the period through March 31? Comment briefly on the operations of the period and on the relevance of the reported income to the evaluation of these operations.

EXERCISES AND PROBLEMS

1. The Corbett Woodworking Company manufactures chairs and other pieces of wooden furniture. Production is on a job order basis. The factory burden rate is $2 per direct labor dollar. The following data relate to job No. 876 for 200 wooden footstools:

(1) Lumber issued from storeroom: $49.70.
(2) Direct labor: 35 hours at $2 an hour.
(3) Footstools completed: 196 (4 footstools were rejected in final inspection, broken up, and burned).
(4) Footstools sold on credit to Ye Olde Roadside Store: 10.

a) Compute unit cost to the nearest tenth of a cent.
b) Prepare journal entries to record these transactions.

2. Job order X150 was placed in production in December, 19x1. During December, materials costing $800 were issued for use on this job, and 60 direct labor hours were expended at an average wage rate of $2.20 an hour. The burden rate in 19x1 was $4 a direct labor *dollar*.

The company's new fiscal year began on January 1, 19x2. Job order X150 was finished in January with the additional expenditure of 90 direct labor hours at an average wage rate of $2.30 an hour, and additional direct materials amounting to $250 were issued for use in this job. The burden rate in 19x2 was set at $9 a direct labor *hour*.

The job consisted of 500 units of product.
a) Compute unit cost to the nearest tenth of a cent.
b) Prepare journal entries to record these transactions.

*3. The Basic Foundry prepares metal castings for specific orders, using a job order costing system. During the month of January, job No. 103 calling for 10,000 machine parts was started and completed. Information about this order is summarized as follows:

_____

* Solutions to problems marked with an asterisk (*) can be found in Appendix B.

(1) Materials issued: 21,000 pounds at $0.66 a pound.
(2) Labor hours expended: 2,000 at $2.15 an hour.
(3) Factory overhead charged to jobs: $4 a direct labor hour.
(4) Unused material returned to storeroom: 800 pounds.
(5) Castings completed: 9,800.

a) Compute unit cost of production to the nearest cent.
b) Prepare journal entries to record these transactions.

4. The following data have been collected in connection with job No. 7863, manufactured by the Belmont Machine Works:

(1) Materials issued:

August 4.........................$3,800
August 9......................... 1,700
August 20....................... 800

(2) Direct labor:

	Hours	Cost
Week of August 2..........200		$520
Week of August 9..........300		800
Week of August 16.........250		550
Week of August 23.........100		220

(3) Manufacturing overhead applied at a rate of $1.50 per direct labor hour.
(4) Order completed (100 units), August 25.

Prepare a job order cost sheet for this job, enter the appropriate information, and compute the cost per unit.

*5. Chailly, Inc., uses a job order costing system in its factory with a predetermined burden rate based on direct labor *hours*. You are given the following information:

(1) Job No. 423 was started on March 3, finished on March 28.
(2)

	Job No. 423	All Jobs (Month of March)	Budgeted for Entire Year
Direct labor hours............	60	10,000	100,000
Direct labor cost..............	$200	$ 40,000	$ 350,000
Direct materials cost.........	$800	$150,000	$1,300,000

(3) Factory overhead:

Budgeted, entire year.....................$900,000
Actual, month of March.................. 100,000

a) Compute the cost of job No. 423.
b) Compute the amount of factory overhead over- or underabsorbed during the month of March.

6. One of the jobs in the factory of the Gentry Company during June was job No. 422, calling for the manufacture of 100 Flister Blidgets, Polished, Large. The factory accountant had to record the following events, among others, during June:

June 1 Issued 200 pounds of material X for job No. 422, at $0.75 a pound.
    4 Issued 50 pounds of material Z for job No. 422, at $3.20 a pound.

5   Expended labor during week on job No. 422—76 hours in department A at $3 an hour.
8   Issued lubricants and cleaning compounds to department A, $100.
11 Returned 10 pounds of material Z to storeroom—quality not up to specification for job No. 422.
11 Issued 15 pounds of material Z for job No. 422, at $3.30 a pound.
12 Expended labor during week on job No. 422—33 hours in department A at $3, and 10 hours in department B at $2.50 an hour.
15 Discovered defects in five Flister Blidgets, which were then sent back to department A for reworking.
16 Issued 20 pounds of material P to department B for job No. 422, at $2 a pound.
17 Damaged 5 pounds of material P originally issued for job No. 422, and transferred them to scrap bin. These have only scrap value at 20 cents a pound.
18 Finished job No. 422.
19 Expended labor during week on job No. 422—3 hours in department A (reworking defective units) at $3 an hour, and 30 hours in department B at $2.50 an hour.
1–19 Burden rates for production departments: department A, $2 a direct labor hour; department B, $4 a direct labor hour.
30 Collected the month's scrap from both departments, 100 pounds with scrap value of 10 cents a pound (total materials processed by both departments during the month, 10,000 pounds).

a) Prepare a job order cost sheet, enter all the pertinent costs, and compute unit costs, by element, for job No. 422. (Note: Some of the items may not be reflected directly in the job order cost sheet.)

b) How useful for cost control purposes is the unit cost obtained in (a)? Explain.

7. A factory uses a job order costing system. The burden rate is $5 per direct labor hour. The direct labor wage rate is $2.50 an hour. A careless bookkeeper has lost the file of job order cost sheets covering the work done last week, but fortunately the underlying documents are still available. No jobs were in process at the beginning of the week, which was the first week of operations following the annual summer vacation plant shutdown.

a) Using the information below, prepare a summary table that will show the total cost assigned to each job to date, as well as unit cost for each job completed last week:

(1) Direct labor and direct materials used:

Job Order	Direct Materials	Direct Labor Hours
498............	$1,500	116
506............	960	16
507............	415	18
508............	345	42
509............	652	24
511............	308	10
512............	835	30
Total........	$5,015	256

(2) Actual overhead costs for the week, $1,480.
(3) Jobs completed: No. 498, 500 units; No. 506, 2,000 units; No. 509, 100 units.

b) What should the balance in the Work in Process account be at the end of the week?

c) What was the over- or underabsorbed overhead for the week?

d) Discuss possible reasons why management might be interested in the unit cost figures derived in (a).

8. The Sandrex Company uses a job order cost accounting system. Direct labor costs are charged daily to Work in Process and credited to Accrued Wages Payable on the basis of time tickets. Direct materials costs are charged to Work in Process and credited to Materials Inventory. Factory overhead costs are charged initially to a Factory Overhead account. Overhead costs are charged to the Work in Process account by means of a predetermined burden rate of $2 per direct labor hour. The costs of goods finished are transferred from Work in Process to a Finished Goods account at the time each job is completed. A perpetual inventory system is used for both materials and finished goods.

Prepare journal entries to record the facts described below. Each of these events should be regarded as independent of the others, and it should be assumed in each case that any pertinent prior recordings have been made correctly unless it is stated otherwise. If no entry is required, explain why.

a) Goods manufactured at a cost of $8,000 are sold for $14,000. Manufacture of these products was completed in the preceding accounting period. The job cost records show that the total manufacturing cost of $8,000 includes $2,000 of materials, $3,000 of direct labor, and $3,000 of overhead.

b) Factory overhead is charged to a job on which 480 direct labor hours have been recorded during this period.

c) It is discovered prior to the end of the period that an error has resulted in treating 500 hours of direct labor at $2.50 per hour as indirect labor (i.e., the charge was made to Factory Overhead). The job on which this labor was used has been finished but not yet sold.

d) Materials costing $5,000 and supplies costing $500 are issued from the factory storeroom. Of the materials, $1,000 is for use in constructing new display cases in the salesroom. The display cases are completed and placed in use this period. The remaining materials are issued to the factory for specific job orders. Of the supplies, $100 is for the immediate use of the sales office. The remainder are for factory use.

e) Prior to the end of the period, it is discovered that $1,000 of direct materials have been charged to the wrong job. At the time this error is discovered, both jobs have been completed but not yet sold.

f) Prior to the end of the period, it is discovered that an error was made in adding up the direct labor hours on a certain job which has now been completed and sold. The dollar amount of direct labor was added correctly, but the hours were overstated by 100.

9. The records of the Simmons Company showed the following information for 19x0:

Inventories, January 1:
Materials..$ 50,000
Work in process....................................... 12,000
Finished goods.. 63,000
Inventories, December 31:
Materials... 43,000
Work in process....................................... 16,000
Finished goods.. 61,000
Operating cost accounts (from December 31, trial balance):
Purchases of materials (for direct and indirect use).......... 169,000
Purchases returns and allowances   3,000
Direct labor.. 80,000
Indirect labor..   7,000
Indirect material (from materials inventories).............   3,000
Power and light.......................................   3,000
Heat..   4,000
Depreciation—buildings................................   5,000
Depreciation—equipment................................   8,000
Miscellaneous factory costs...........................   1,000
Overhead absorbed..................................... (33,000)

a) Set up the necessary operating cost and inventory accounts, enter the January 1 balances given above, and make entries to record the year's transactions, including the cost of goods sold.

b) What was the amount of under- or overabsorbed overhead for 19x0?

10. The opening April balances of the Apex Company inventory and overhead accounts were:

Raw material..$35,000
Work in process....................................... 8,000
Finished goods.. 26,000
Overhead (over-) or underabsorbed..................... (3,000)

During the month the following costs were incurred:

Raw materials purchased...............................$23,000
Direct labor.. 14,000
Indirect labor.. 8,000
Power... 1,500
Depreciation.. 1,500
Supplies.. 2,000
Other manufacturing costs............................. 5,000
Selling and office expense............................ 9,000

Raw material costing $31,000 was put into process during the month. At the close of the month the production orders still in process, all of which had been started during the month, had been charged with the following costs:

Direct material.......................................$4,000
Direct labor.. 1,500

Overhead is charged on the basis of 140 percent of direct labor cost. Finished goods inventory as of April 30 amounted to $18,000.

a) Present journal entries to cover the transactions indicated by the above information.

b) List the balances in the inventory accounts and the amount of the over- or underabsorbed overhead as of April 30.

*11. The Ace Appliance Company had the following inventories on October 1:

Raw material and stores....................................$12,650
Work in process... 8,320
Finished goods... 11,100

The following transactions took place during the month:

(1) Purchased material at a cost of $4,500.
(2) Issued material:
   Direct material, $6,320.
   Indirect material, $930.
(3) Payroll:
   Direct labor, $3,300.
   Indirect labor, $1,880.
   Selling and administrative salaries, $2,600.
(4) Miscellaneous manufacturing overhead, $2,700.
(5) Applied manufacturing overhead at 150 percent of direct labor cost.
(6) Goods completed during month cost $12,650.
(7) Miscellaneous selling and administrative expenses, $1,835.
(8) Ending inventory, finished goods, $9,250.
(9) Sales revenue from goods sold, $19,350.

a) Account for the above transactions, using T-accounts, and establish the closing balances in the inventory accounts.

b) Prepare an income statement for the month, with a supporting schedule of the cost of goods manufactured and sold. (Overhead over- or underabsorbed is to be included in the cost of goods sold.)

12. The cost accounts of the Moonray Appliance Company include a single Work in Process account, in which the costs of direct materials and direct labor are accumulated directly, and the following accounts for manufacturing overhead: Indirect Labor, Factory Supplies, Maintenance, Rent, Depreciation, and Miscellaneous. Overhead costs are charged directly to these latter accounts.

Overhead costs are charged to Work in Process at the rate of 25 cents for every dollar of direct materials cost; the accompanying credit entry is to a Factory Overhead Summary account. At the end of the month the balances in the six detailed overhead accounts are closed into the Factory Overhead Summary account.

The November 1 balances in the various inventory accounts were as follows:

Materials and supplies.....................................$39,000
Work in process... 18,900
Finished goods... 11,400

The Factory Overhead Summary account had a debit balance of $14,300 on November 1.

The following transactions occurred in connection with the manufacturing activities of the plant for the month of November:

(1) Purchased materials on account, $113,000.
(2) Materials issued:
     For job orders, $76,000.
     Factory supplies, $1,200.
(3) Factory payrolls accrued:
     For job orders, $44,000.
     Supervisory and other indirect labor, $8,000.
(4) Machinery repairs performed by outside contractor, on account, $900.
(5) Paid rent for the factory building for November and December, $3,000.
(6) Machinery depreciation for November, $3,500.
(7) Accrued miscellaneous factory overhead, $1,000.
(8) Jobs completed and transferred to finished goods stock room, $97,000.
(9) Finished goods inventory, November 30, $17,100.

a) Prepare journal entries to record these transactions in the appropriate accounts.

b) Prepare T-accounts for Materials and Supplies, Work in Process, Finished Goods, Cost of Goods Sold, and Factory Overhead Summary, and enter the opening balances, all items affecting these accounts during the month, and the closing balances.

13. The Nesbitt Company uses a LIFO basis for costing its finished goods inventories; materials and parts are costed on a FIFO basis, and work in process is inventoried on the basis of the cost of specific job lots. Annual increments to finished goods inventories are assumed, for LIFO purposes, to be from the first job lots completed during the year.

One of the company's products is the Model G Hand Stapler, and on January 1, 1963, the LIFO inventory cost of this product was:

	No. of Dozen	Cost per Dozen	Inventory Cost
Base quantity................	1,000	$25.20	$25,200
1957 layer..................	100	28.80	2,880
1961 layer..................	150	31.20	4,680
Total..................	1,250		$32,760

A burden rate of $2 per direct labor hour was used throughout the factory in 1963. No Model G staplers were in process on January 1, 1963.

The following transactions relating to production and sale of Model G Hand Staplers took place during 1963:

(1) Shipped 250 dozen to customers during January.
(2) Manufactured 1,000 dozen on job No. 2246 during February: direct materials, $9,800; direct labor, 6,000 hours at $2.20 an hour.
(3) Shipped 1,500 dozen to customers during March, April, May, and June.
(4) Manufactured 1,200 dozen on job No. 2873 during July: direct materials, $12,100; direct labor, 7,100 hours at $2.30 per hour.
(5) Shipped 900 dozen to customers during August, September, October, and November.
(6) Started job No. 3045 on November 21, but delays in receiving materials prevented completion of this job in 1963. This job order consisted of 1,000 dozen, with accumulated costs to December 31 of: direct materials, $10,200; direct labor, 5,900 hours at $2.30 per hour.

a) Compute total cost of Model G Hand Staplers sold for 1963 and the cost of staplers in process and in finished goods inventory on December 31, 1963.

b) The company wishes to keep perpetual inventory records on its finished goods. What problems would be encountered and how would you solve them?

14. The Subway Car Company manufactures railway and subway cars to customer orders. Revenues are recognized at the time finished products are shipped to customers. A predetermined burden rate of $3 per direct labor hour is used in the company's factory.

On March 1, $120,000 in materials and supplies were on hand. The company maintains no inventory of finished goods, but it had three jobs in process in its factory on March 1:

Job No.	No. of Cars	Costs Accumulated in Prior Months
6456..............................	1	$ 43,000
6457..............................	4	134,000
6459...,..........................	3	27,000

The following transactions affecting manufacturing costs occurred during the month of March:

(1) A new job order, No. 6460, was placed in production.
(2) Materials, supplies and parts in the amount of $97,000 were purchased on account.
(3) Materials, supplies, and parts were issued to production departments, as follows:

Job 6456...	$ 2,000
Job 6457...	20,000
Job 6459...	35,000
Job 6460...	5,000
General factory use..................................	18,000

(4) Labor time tickets showed the following totals:

Job 6456..................................	1,200 hours,	$ 5,000
Job 6457..................................	8,000 hours,	$20,000
Job 6459..................................	10,000 hours,	$26,000
Job 6460..................................	800 hours,	$ 3,000
Indirect labor............................	3,000 hours,	$ 5,400

(5) Factory depreciation for the month, $10,000.
(6) Other factory operating costs amounted to $35,000 (credit Accounts Payable).
(7) Job 6456 was finished and shipped to the customer on March 18.
(8) Two cars in job 6457 were finished and shipped to the customer on March 28. The remaining two cars in the job were one half completed on March 31.

a) Record the above information in appropriately titled T-accounts. Direct labor and direct materials costs are charged directly to a single Work in

Process account. All manufacturing overhead costs are charged, when incurred, to a Manufacturing Overhead account. Factory overhead absorbed is credited to this Manufacturing Overhead account.

b) Prepare a schedule showing March 31 balances in the Work in Process and Manufacturing Overhead accounts.

15. The Corgut Company uses a job order cost system in its manufacturing plants. During the first week of March, three jobs were in production in the machine shop of the Akron plant. Cost estimates for these three jobs were as follows:

	Job No. 1273	Job No. 1276	Job No. 1280
Materials.....................	$ 450	$ 500	$ 700
Labor........................	1,400	900	1,000
Total Prime Cost...........	$1,850	$1,400	$1,700

a) From the following data (1) prepare job order cost sheets for the three jobs, (2) prepare entries in journal form to record information in the general ledger, and (3) enter the indicated amounts in the job order cost sheets. (Manufacturing overhead costs are not charged to job orders in this company.)

	Job No. 1273	Job No. 1276	Job No. 1280	Indirect	Total
Work in process, March 2:					
Materials.....................	$200	$420	$ 0	$ 0	$ 620
Labor........................	650	400	0	0	1,050
Materials issued for week.........	300	100	800	200	1,400
Labor for week..................	900	600	500	550	2,550
Materials purchases for week......					1,800

During the week job Nos. 1273 and 1276 were completed and transferred to the finished goods stock room. It is estimated that all the materials required for job No. 1280 have been issued and that 40 percent of the labor required to complete this job has been performed.

b) Prepare a report on the operations of the machine shop during the week of March 2, emphasizing the differences between actual and estimated costs.

c) What problems would be encountered in obtaining useful cost control information if there were 50 jobs in process instead of the three assumed in this problem?

16. The Lagrange Company manufactures several types of pumps, partly to order and partly for stock. In both cases, work is done on the basis of production orders and costs are recorded by job. The company's balance sheet as of August 31, 1964, and its transactions for the month of September, 1964, are as follows:

THE LAGRANGE COMPANY

BALANCE SHEET

As of August 31, 1964

ASSETS

Current Assets:

Cash...	$ 23,280	
Accounts receivable................................	31,070	
Materials and supplies.............................	15,120	
Work in process...................................	8,300	
Finished goods....................................	6,730	$ 84,500

Long-Life Assets:

Machinery and equipment...........................	$248,600	
Less: Allowance for depreciation...................	83,200	165,400
		$249,900

LIABILITIES

Current Liabilities:

Accounts payable..................................	$ 27,650	
Accrued wages and salaries.........................	1,830	$ 29,480

NET WORTH

Common stock....................................	$150,000	
Retained earnings.................................	70,420	220,420
		$249,900

Transactions during September:

(1) Purchased: Materials and supplies....................... $28,310

                     Machine....................................... 21,000 $49,310

(2) Issued materials and supplies:

    Direct materials—job No. 17........................... $ 2,530

                     No. 18............................ 7,120

                     No. 19............................ 6,690

    Indirect materials.................................... 4,060   20,400

(3) Accrued wages and salaries:

    Direct labor—job No. 16, 1,200 hrs...................... $ 2,440

                   No. 17, 3,600 hrs....................... 7,370

                   No. 18, 5,600 hrs....................... 10,580

                   No. 19, 800 hrs........................ 2,000

    Indirect labor and supervision........................... 5,420

    Office salaries (administration and sales).................. 4,590   32,400

(4) Other manufacturing costs (credit Accounts Payable):

    Power, light, and heat............................... $ 3,830

    Repairs... 1,160

    Sundry... 790   5,780

(5) Administrative and sales expenses incurred................ 2,770

(6) Depreciation on equipment: Plant....................... $ 2,040

                         Office....................... 120   2,160

(7) Jobs finished during month: Nos. 16–18

(8) Sales during month: Job No. 15 (balance)................. $ 8,350

                   No. 16 (all)..................... 16,800

                   No. 17 (all)..................... 18,800

                   No. 18 (20 out of 50 pumps)....... 13,400   56,350

(9) Received payments from customers on account............. 47,800

(10) Paid: Accounts payable............................... $43,690

       Wages....................................... 31,850   75,540

(11) Received loan from bank on September 30

    (90-day note)......................................   30,000

Additional information:

(1) Payroll deductions and taxes are omitted for purposes of simplification.
(2) All costs incurred other than payrolls are in the first instance credited to Accounts Payable.
(3) Manufacturing Overhead is charged to jobs at the rate of $1.50 per direct labor hour.
(4) The opening balance of Finished Goods represents part of job order No. 15; that of Work in Process, job No. 16. (Materials, $4,500; Direct Labor, $2,100; Overhead, $1,700.)

a) Enter the above transactions in T-accounts and job order cost sheets. (Use a single T-account for all factory overhead costs.)
b) Prepare financial statements for the month. Over- or underabsorbed overhead is to be entered as a special item on the income statement.

17. The Farquar Corporation uses a job order cost accounting system in its factory. All property records are maintained at the head office, which also performs all purchasing, billing, payroll, and cash receipt and disbursement operations. The factory ledger showed the following balances on February 1:

Materials and Supplies.....................................40,000
Jobs in Process...57,000
Finished Goods...73,000
Cost of Goods Sold.......................................   xxx
Manufacturing Overhead...................................   xxx
      Head Office Control..................................   170,000

Manufacturing overhead is charged to jobs in process at a predetermined rate of $1.50 per direct labor dollar. The offsetting credit is to the Manufacturing Overhead account. At the end of each month the Manufacturing Overhead account is closed into the Cost of Goods Sold account, which is then closed into the Head Office control account.

On February 1, the job cost file listed the following jobs:

	Materials	Labor	Overhead	Total
No. D1762.......	$ 600	$ 1,900	$ 2,850	$ 5,350
No. D1783.......	2,900	3,200	4,800	10,900
No. E0004.......	4,000	1,400	2,100	7,500
No. E0010.......	6,500	1,000	1,500	9,000
No. E0011.......	14,000	2,000	3,000	19,000
No. E0013.......	4,000	500	750	5,250
Total...........	$32,000	$10,000	$15,000	$57,000

During February, the following transactions were recorded in the factory ledger:

(1) Materials and supplies received in the factory storeroom, $62,000.
(2) Materials and supplies issued by the storeroom to factory departments:

Job No. E0004....................................	$ 500
Job No. E0010....................................	1,000
Job No. E0013....................................	2,500
Job No. E0015....................................	8,000
Job No. E0016....................................	11,000
Job No. E0017....................................	6,000
Job No. E0018....................................	9,000
Indirect materials...............................	7,500
Total.......................................	$45,500

(3) Labor performed in factory departments:

Job No. D1762....................................	$ 200
Job No. D1783....................................	700
Job No. E0004....................................	7,200
Job No. E0010....................................	8,700
Job No. E0011....................................	12,000
Job No. E0013....................................	7,800
Job No. E0015....................................	3,600
Job No. E0016....................................	9,000
Job No. E0017....................................	15,000
Job No. E0018....................................	3,000
Indirect labor...................................	31,500
Total.......................................	$98,700

(4) Other overhead costs charged to the factory:

Supervision.......................................	$22,500
Maintenance......................................	8,800
Heat, light, and power...........................	4,600
Payroll taxes and pensions........................	10,300
Depreciation.....................................	9,500
Miscellaneous....................................	1,200
Total.......................................	$56,900

(5) Jobs completed and transferred to finished goods: Nos. D1762, D1783, E0004, E0010, E0013, E0017.

(6) Cost of finished goods sold, $138,000.

a) Enter February 1 balances in T-accounts representing the five factory ledger accounts and in the individual job order cost sheets.

b) Prepare journal entries to record February transactions and post them to the factory ledger accounts and job order cost sheets. Use only the five ledger accounts listed earlier.

c) Prepare a schedule showing the February 28 balances in each factory ledger account and job order cost sheet.

18. The Swanson Company produces its own line of products and also manufactures on order from other companies. On the afternoon of January 31, 1967, a fire broke out in the company's rented offices and destroyed the journal, the general ledger, the work in process ledger, and the finished goods ledger. You have been asked: (1) to reproduce the work in process and finished goods ledgers as of January 31, 1967, and (2) to prepare the January, 1967, financial statements.

Account balances as of January 1, 1967, were as follows:

THE SWANSON COMPANY

TRIAL BALANCE

As of December 31, 1966

Cash	$ 7,000	
Accounts receivable control	9,000	
Stores control	4,800	
Work in process control	3,600	
Finished goods control	4,200	
Prepaid insurance	800	
Plant and equipment	12,600	
Allowance for depreciation		$ 3,500
Accounts payable		2,800
Accrued payroll		300
Capital stock		30,000
Retained earnings		5,400
Sales		......
Sales returns and allowances	......	
Cost of goods sold	......	
Selling and administrative expense control	......	
Direct labor cost	......	
Direct material cost	......	
Indirect labor cost	......	
Factory supervision	......	
Factory supplies	......	
Factory depreciation	......	
Factory utilities	......	
Miscellaneous factory indirect cost	......	
	$42,000	$42,000

Schedule of work in process, December 31, 1966:

Job No.	Material	Labor	Overhead	Total
72	700	400	480	1,580
74	800	200	240	1,240
75	560	100	120	780

Schedule of finished goods, December 31, 1966:

Item No.	Quantity	Unit Cost	Total Cost
A 21	400	$3.00	$1,200
A 31	800	2.50	2,000
A 41	250	4.00	1,000

The following information is available relative to January, 1967, transactions:

(1) The last page of the purchase journal giving totals for the month:

	Total	Stores	Plant and Equipment	Selling and Admin. Expense	Factory Utilities
	·	·	·	·	·
	·	·	·	·	·
	·	·	·	·	·
Total	$8,760	$2,700	$1,500	$4,200	$360

(2) Analysis of materials issued:

Job	74	75	76	77	Factory Supplies
Amount	$400	$300	$600	$650	$200

(3) Analysis of the labor records for the month:

Job	72	74	75	76	77	Indirect Labor
Amount	$120	$320	$440	$400	$120	$300

(4) Spoiled work report (one only during January):

Date: Jan. 20, 1967	Estimated scrap value $20
Job order: 75	Disposal of scrap Deposited at
Material spoiled $50	stock room for later use
Labor hours spoiled 20 hrs.	as raw material.
Wage rate $2/hour	

The company usually charges Miscellaneous Factory Indirect Cost for the loss on spoiled work, which is the difference between the cost incurred and the scrap value.

(5) Factory production report for the month:

Job	Nature	Date of Completion
72.........	Special order for Co. X	Jan. 9
74.........	Special order for Co. Y	Jan. 12
75.........	500 units of A 41	Jan. 25
76.........	Construction order— equipment for own use	Jan. 21

(6) Sales journal showing all shipments for the period:

Detail	Quantity	Proceeds
Special order (job 72)............	100	$5,000
Special order (job 74)............	250	3,000
A 21.........................	150	630
A 31.........................	300	1,050
A 41.........................	350	2,100

The company's sales terms are net 30 days, and finished goods are transferred to expense on a first-in, first-out basis.

(7) Duplicate of a credit memorandum issued by the sales manager (one only during the month):

To: Co. Y
From: The Swanson Company
We are sorry to know that fifty pieces of the goods shipped to you on January 12 do not fit your specifications. The returned pieces have been received today. This is to inform you that both the sales price of these pieces and the return freight have been credited to your account. This total amounts to $620.

Further investigation substantiates the above statement and reveals:
a) Since the returned goods were in salable condition, they were charged to finished goods at cost.
b) Return freight is considered a selling expense.

(8) Payroll paid in January:

Factory direct and indirect workers.............$1,800
Factory supervision............................ 700
Selling and administrative salaries.............. 500

Only factory workers are paid by the week. The payroll clerk says that some accrued payroll exists on February 1, but that she has yet reconstructed the figures after that "exciting" afternoon.

(9) Monthly depreciation on plant and equipment is charged at the rate of 8 percent per *year*.

(10) Insurance expiration for January amounts to $50. The contract covers the plant and equipment only.

(11) Overhead is absorbed at the rate of $1.20 per dollar of direct labor cost.

(12) The first checkbook for January was burned, but the second one discloses that the January 31 balance is $3,000. Confirmation with the bank establishes the total deposits during the month at $7,500. Since some recipients of the company's checks may not cash them immediately, the actual disbursement figure cannot be secured from the bank's records.

Prepare an income statement for January, 1967, a balance sheet as of January 31, 1967, and work in process and finished goods ledgers.

Chapter 5

MEASUREMENT OF FACTORY UNIT COST: PROCESS COSTING

THE SECOND major type of production system is *continuous processing,* used whenever production facilities are devoted exclusively to the production of a single product or highly similar products for long periods of time. Petroleum refining, basic steel production, glass manufacture, and large portions of the chemical process industries utilize continuous processing techniques.

The cost finding method used in process production is known as *process costing.* The purpose of this chapter is to outline the most important features of process costing systems.

The Basis for Process Costing

If the nature of operations is suitable for process costing, each production cost center corresponds to one stage in the production cycle and has a relatively homogeneous output—that is, each unit of output is similar enough to every other unit to permit output to be measured by a simple unit count. (In this discussion the terms *process center* and *department* will be used interchangeably to refer to a cost center engaged directly in product processing.) Costs and output statistics are accumulated for each process center during a specified period of time such as a month. The average cost computed from these figures is then assigned to each unit of the process center's output for the period. This is repeated for all process centers, and the total unit cost of finished products is the sum of these unit costs.

The product costing unit, in other words, is the total output of a department or process center during a given time period. Because departmental output is assumed to be homogeneous, no attempt is made to assign costs to specific job lots or batches.

Process costing is also applied to *joint production,* in which the output of a processing stage consists of two or more separate products. In this case, the lack of a single common unit of output creates some difficulties in the calculation of average unit cost, requiring some means of weighting the outputs of the various joint products. The remainder of this chapter, however, deals only with independent production, leaving joint production to Chapter 9.

DERIVATION OF PRODUCT COST

Process costing techniques can be applied either in cost *estimation* before production takes place or in cost *measurement* after the fact. The procedure is identical.

The simplest application of process costs is in specialized sequential processing. For example, assume that a factory manufactures a single product. Production operations are performed by three production departments or process centers, each of which performs a single operation and then transfers its output to the next center, as shown in Exhibit 5–1.

Exhibit 5–1

WORK FLOWS IN PROCESS PRODUCTION

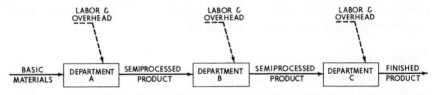

These three departments will be used to illustrate process costing under three sets of conditions: (1) no work in process at either the beginning or the end of the month; (2) work in process at the end of the month but not at the beginning; and (3) both beginning and ending work in process.

No Work in Process: The Basic Calculation

Department A had no work in process either at the beginning or at the end of May. During May, raw materials costing $28,500 were put into process in department A, thus starting the production cycle. During the month, department A processed all the material and transferred 95,000 pounds of partially completed products to department B for further processing. Departmental labor costs for the month were $9,-500, and departmental overhead totaled $19,000.

The unit cost of production in department A was thus $57,000 divided by 95,000 pounds, or $0.60 a pound:

	Total	Per Unit
Materials.....................	$28,500	$0.30
Labor.......................	9,500	0.10
Other.......................	19,000	0.20
Total...................	$57,000	$0.60

The three-way cost breakdown in this table does not correspond precisely to the direct materials–direct labor–overhead classification developed in Chapter 4. Overhead, for example, was defined in that chapter as factory cost not directly traced to the product costing unit. Because the product costing unit in process costing is the process center's output for a period of time, *any* cost traced to the process center can be referred to as a direct cost. The line is thus no longer between direct and indirect materials but between different classes of direct materials, and the term overhead loses most of its meaning. It is often used, however, to refer to processing costs other than process center labor and materials.

For control reporting and for the accumulation of planning data as well, the process center's costs are ordinarily classified into many more than three categories. The three categories recognized here, however, will be sufficient to demonstrate the method.

Effect of Ending Inventory

Department B also started the month of May with no inventory in process. Its costs for the month were $21,000 for labor and $15,000 for other processing costs. During the month it completed its operations on the 85,000 pounds of product received from department A and transferred this quantity to department C. This left 10,000 pounds of partially processed product in department B at the end of May, as shown in Exhibit 5–2. About half of department B's work had been done on these products.

The ending inventory introduces a new complication into the illustration. In process costing, unit cost is always determined by dividing a production center's costs by its output. In department A, output was easily measurable as the number of units completed. Not so in department B. It is no longer possible to obtain average unit cost by dividing total department cost by the number of units completed because this would ignore the units still in process. Nor is it possible to divide by the number of units received from department A, among other reasons because the department did not finish this much production. It would have had to incur still more costs to get a full 95,000 pounds of product.

Department B thus has two separate "output" figures, one used as a divisor for materials costs and the other as a divisor for labor and other costs (referred to hereafter as processing costs). As far as materials costs[1] are concerned, the correct divisor is 95,000 pounds and the unit cost is still 60 cents. This is because the number of units finished by department B plus the number still in process at the end of the month equaled the number received from departent A. Loss of units in production through spoilage or other causes or addition of other mate-

Exhibit 5–2

DEPARTMENT B PRODUCT YIELDS

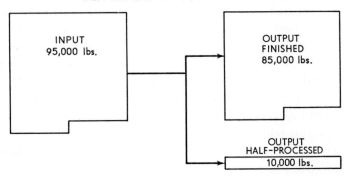

rials from sources other than department A would require the calculation of a new unit cost of materials.

The correct cost divisor for processing costs is 90,000 pounds, consisting of 85,000 pounds on which all work was completed and 10,000 half-completed units (assumed to be equivalent to 5,000 pounds of completed work). This 90,000-pound figure is also known as *equivalent production*.

The calculation of the two cost divisors can be readily summarized:

	Materials Cost	Processing Costs
Units completed (pounds).....................	85,000	85,000
Equivalent units in ending inventory............	10,000	5,000
Unit Cost Divisor (Pounds)....................	95,000	90,000

[1] Materials, labor, and overhead costs of department A were combined when the goods left the department and are treated as materials costs in subsequent departments.

On this basis, the average processing cost in department B is 40 cents a pound ($36,000 divided by 90,000 pounds). The 85,000 pounds transferred to department C therefore had an accumulated cost of $1 per pound—60 cents from department A and 40 cents from department B. The 10,000 pounds remaining in department B's inventory had an average cost of 80 cents per pound—60 cents from department A and 20 cents from department B (because they were only half processed in this department they were assigned only half the cost of completed units). These calculations are summarized in the following table:

	Total	Per Unit
Costs:		
Materials..........................	$57,000	$0.60
Labor.............................	21,000	0.23
Other.............................	15,000	0.17
Total Cost.......................	$93,000	$1.00
Cost distribution:		
To department C..................	$85,000	$1.00
To ending work in process.........	8,000	0.80
Total Distributed................	$93,000	xxx

Effect of Beginning Inventories

Department C is the finishing department. It completed 89,000 pounds of product during the month and had 6,000 pounds of half-completed product in process at the end of the month. Unlike the other two departments, however, department C began the month with an inventory of 10,000 pounds of product, half-processed in this department.

The work of the department for the month consisted of completing work on the 10,000 pounds in the opening inventory, completely processing an additional 79,000 pounds of product, and half processing another 6,000 pounds. Completing the processing of the initial 10,000 pounds was equivalent to processing 5,000 pounds from start to finish. Initial processing on the 6,000 pounds left in inventory at the end of April added another 3,000 pounds to equivalent production. Combining these with the 79,000 pounds started and completed during the month yields an equivalent production of 87,000 pounds.

Another and perhaps more convenient way of calculating equivalent production and the materials cost divisor as well is to start with (1) the units completed during the period, then add (2) any partially completed units in process at the end of the period, and subtract (3) the units in process at the beginning of the period. Using this formula, the cost divisors were:

	Materials Cost	Processing Costs
Units completed (pounds)........................	89,000	89,000
Equivalent units in ending inventory............	6,000	3,000
	95,000	92,000
Less: Equivalent of work done in prior period on beginning inventory.........................	10,000	5,000
Cost Divisor (Pounds)......................	85,000	87,000

The rationale for this calculation is diagramed in Exhibit 5–3. Of the 89,000 pounds completed during the month (upper two blocks in the diagram), the equivalent of 5,000 pounds was actually produced during the previous month, and thus must be subtracted (unshaded area at the left of the topmost block). This indicates that the work actually done during May on the units completed during the month was the equivalent of complete processing of 84,000 pounds of finished product (shaded areas in two upper blocks). To this must be added the 3,000-pound equivalent of the inventory still in process at the end of the month, represented by the shaded area in the lower block of Exhibit 5–3. The total of these figures is equivalent production.

To achieve this output, department C incurred $8,700 in labor costs and $13,050 in other processing costs. The processing costs therefore

Exhibit 5–3

CALCULATION OF EQUIVALENT PRODUCTION

PRODUCTS IN PROCESS, MAY 1	5000 5000
PRODUCTS STARTED AND COMPLETED DURING MAY	79,000
PRODUCTS IN PROCESS, MAY 31	3000 3000

WORK DONE IN APRIL   WORK DONE IN MAY (87,000 EQUIVALENT UNITS)   WORK TO BE DONE IN JUNE averaged 25 cents a pound ($21,750 divided by 87,000), making a total product cost of $1.25 a pound. This was the unit cost to be reported to management to represent the cost and efficiency of operations for the month.

Unlike the unit costs of the two previous departments, however, this figure could not be used for both income statement and balance sheet preparation because it did not reflect in any way the costs assigned to the semiprocessed inventory on hand at the beginning of May. Various possible costing rules are available for this latter purpose, the most common being the moving average and first-in, first-out (FIFO) methods. A brief discussion of these two methods is thus necessary.

First-In, First-Out Method

Under FIFO inventory costing, beginning-of-month inventory cost balances are transferred to the next department as part of the cost of the first units completed during the month. For example, assume that the cost recorded for the 10,000-pound initial inventory in department C was $11,600, made up as follows:

	Per Unit	Total Cost
Materials.	$1.05	$10,500
Processing.	0.11	1,100
Total.	$1.16	$11,600

Completion of these units in May added another $1,250 to this total (the 10,000 pounds were half processed at May's average cost of 25 cents a pound). Thus under FIFO the first 10,000 units completed would lead to a transfer of $11,600 plus $1,250 or $12,850 to the finished goods inventory account.

The other 79,000 units completed would then be costed at the average cost for the month, or $1.25. The total cost of output transferred to finished goods therefore would be:

	First 10,000	Next 79,000	Total
Materials.	$10,500	$79,000	$ 89,500
Processing.	2,350	19,750	22,100
Total.	$12,850	$98,750	$111,600

For convenience, no distinction would be made in finished goods inventories between the first 10,000 and the next 79,000 pounds of product. They would all be entered at an average cost of approximately $1.254 a pound ($111,600 divided by 89,000). This simplification would also be made if the work were transferred to another department rather than to finished inventories.

The inventory remaining in department C on May 31 would then be FIFO-costed at average cost for the month:

Materials: 6,000 lbs. at $1.............................$6,000
Processing: 6,000 lbs., half processed, at $0.125............   750
      Total..$6,750

The cost distribution of department C could then be summarized as in Exhibit 5–4.

Exhibit 5–4

DISTRIBUTION OF PROCESS COSTS: FIFO METHOD

Costs of Department C

	Total Amount	Per Equiva- lent Pound
Costs in department:		
Materials:		
In process, 5/1...............................	$ 10,500	$1.05
Received.....................................	85,000	1.00
Total.....................................	$ 95,500	xxx
Processing costs:		
In process, 5/1..............................	$ 1,100	$0.22
Labor.......................................	8,700	0.10
Other.......................................	13,050	0.15
Total.....................................	$ 22,850	xxx
Total Departmental Cost...........................	$118,350	xxx
Cost distribution:		
To finished products:		
Materials....................................	$ 89,500	$1.006
Processing...................................	22,100	0.248
Total finished products......................	$111,600	$1.254
In process, 5/31:		
Materials....................................	$ 6,000	$1.000
Processing...................................	750	0.125
Total in process, 5/31.......................	$ 6,750	$1.125
Total Cost Distributed...........................	$118,350	xxx

Moving Average Method

The calculation procedure can be simplified slightly by use of a single average (referred to below as a *moving average*) to apply to all products in a department during the month. For example, the total cost of materials in process in department C during May was $95,500 (opening balance plus $85,000 for materials received from department B during the month). Under the moving average method, this would be distributed evenly over the 95,000 pounds completed and still in process at the end of the month, at an average rate of $1.005 a pound:

Transferred, 89,000 pounds at $1.005..............................$89,445
In process, 5/31, 6,000 pounds at $1.005.......................... 6,030
  Total...$95,475

Due to the rounding error, this total is $25 less than the actual materials cost charged to the department. This could be eliminated by carrying the unit cost calculation to more decimal places or by adding or subtracting the rounding error in the amount transferred out or the amount remaining in process at month-end.

Similarly, the $22,850 in processing costs in department C's accounts at the end of May would be divided between the 89,000 pounds transferred and the 6,000 pounds remaining in process. The unit cost divisor in this case would be 92,000 pounds because the ending inventory was only half processed (89,000 pounds of fully completed products plus the equivalent of 3,000 pounds in the ending inventory). Average cost would be $0.248, to the nearest tenth of a cent.

The processing cost to be transferred would thus be $22,072 (89,000 pounds × $0.248), leaving $778 as the cost of the ending inventory in process. These calculations are summarized in Exhibit 5–5.

The unit cost divisor under the moving average approach differs from equivalent production by the number of equivalent units in the opening inventory:

	Materials	*Processing*
Units completed during period........................	89,000	89,000
Plus: In process, end of period.......................	6,000	3,000
Cost divisor, moving average......................	95,000	92,000
Less: In process, start of period......................	10,000	5,000
Equivalent Production.........................	85,000	87,000

The peculiarity of the average cost calculation is that the sum of the number of units finished and still in process at the *end* of the period is divided into the sum of the costs incurred during the period and the costs in process at the *beginning* of the period. The reason for this is

Exhibit 5–5

DISTRIBUTION OF PROCESS COSTS: MOVING AVERAGE METHOD

Costs of Department C

	Total Amount	Per Pound
Costs in department:		
Materials:		
In process, 5/1.....................	$ 10,500	$1.05
Received..........................	85,000	1.00
Total..........................	$ 95,500	$1.005
Processing costs:		
In process, 5/1.....................	$ 1,100	$0.22
Labor............................	8,700	0.10
Other............................	13,050	0.15
Total..........................	$ 22,850	$0.248
Total Department Cost..................	$118,350	$1.253
Cost distribution:		
To finished products:		
Materials.........................	$ 89,445	$1.005
Processing........................	22,072	0.248
Total finished products.............	$111,517	$1.253
In process, 5/31:		
Materials.........................	$ 6,055	$1.005
Processing........................	778	0.124
Total in process 5/31...............	$ 6,833	$1.129
Total Cost Distributed..................	$118,350	xxx

that the latter sum reflects all the cost inputs, while the former sum represents all of the units available to absorb these costs. Equivalent production, on the other hand, is used as a divisor for the current month's costs only, and this requires the subtraction of the opening inventory.

The differences between the moving average and FIFO methods should not be overstressed. The resultant unit costs will not depart materially from each other unless the production cycle is particularly long and monthly cost per unit of equivalent production changes rapidly. For this reason, the choice between the two ordinarily can be made on the basis of convenience. In principle, however, equivalent production is the only legitimate divisor in calculating current unit cost because it is the only one that measures the amount of work done, the amount for which the current period's costs were incurred.

Production Cost Summary

The previous calculations have been collected in the production cost summary illustrated in Exhibit 5–6. Notice in this case how the amount transferred out of each department becomes the materials cost of the next department. In other situations it may be desirable to recognize separate categories of materials, distinguishing between the costs of those materials transferred from the preceding department and the costs of materials coming from other sources. Similarly, processing costs

Exhibit 5–6

PRODUCTION COST SUMMARY

	Department A		Department B		Department C	
	Total Cost	Unit Cost	Total Cost	Unit Cost	Total Cost	Unit Cost
Costs in department:						
Materials:						
In process, 5/1	....	....	....	....	$ 10,500	$1.05
Received	$28,500	$0.30	$57,000	$0.60	85,000	1.00
Total	$28,500	$0.30	$57,000	$0.60	$ 95,500	$1.005
Processing costs:						
In process, 5/1	....	....	....	....	$ 1,100	$0.22
Labor	$ 9,500	$0.10	$21,000	$0.23	8,700	0.10
Other	19,000	0.20	15,000	0.17	13,050	0.15
Total	$28,500	$0.30	$36,000	$0.40	$ 22,850	$0.248
Total Departmental Cost	$57,000	$0.60	$93,000	$1.00	$118,350	$1.253
Cost distribution:						
Transferred out:						
Materials	$28,500	$0.30	$51,000	$0.60	$ 89,445	$1.005
Processing	28,500	0.30	34,000	0.40	22,072	0.248
Total	$57,000	$0.60	$85,000	$1.00	$111,517	$1.253
In process, 5/31:						
Materials	....	.....	$ 6,000	$0.60	$ 6,055	$1.005
Processing	....	.....	2,000	0.20	778	0.124
Total	....	.....	$ 8,000	$0.80	$ 6,833	$1.129
Total Cost Distributed	$57,000	xxx	$93,000	xxx	$118,350	xxx

might be broken for management's information into more than two categories.

The Need for Separate Cost Divisors

This illustration has assumed that two cost divisors would suffice for each department. This was based on two assumptions:

1. All the materials required for a unit of departmental output were placed in process at the same time, in this case at the beginning of processing in each department.
2. All departmental processing costs made their contribution to production in proportion to departmental labor, so that a single measure of degree of completion could be applied to all.

These assumptions are not always valid. Certain materials, such as containers, may be added at the end of processing or at some time other than at the beginning. Furthermore, some processes have two or more processing determinants. In processes in which products must age, for example, a distinction must be made between those costs that relate to the amount of physical work done on the products and those that relate to the amount of time they have spent aging in the department. A separate degree of completion figure can then be applied to each of these categories.

Because departments often add their own materials to products received from prior departments, it is common to distinguish between costs of materials received and costs of materials added. To simplify the illustration, however, it was assumed that departments B and C added no materials during processing, and thus this added cost element did not appear.

Lest all these calculations seem unduly formidable, it should be noted that in many processes inventories are sufficiently stable to justify using the number of units *completed* during the month as an approximate measure of departmental ouput. This simplifies matters considerably in that it makes it unnecessary to calculate separate cost divisors for different cost elements. Care should be taken, however, to insure that the assumption is not applied when the number of equivalent units in inventory changes materially from one month to the next.

Departures from Output Homogeneity

Although process costing is strictly applicable only when departmental output is homogeneous with respect to departmental operations, it is nevertheless often applied when this condition is not met. For example, process costing would probably be used in a process center which is engaged in filling pint, quart, and gallon containers with three different types of liquids. The output in this case is not homogeneous, but it is close enough to it to justify the simplifying assumption that it is. Output can be measured either in gallons or in numbers of containers filled, depending on whether costs are more likely to be related to gallonage or to the container count.

Whether the homogeneity assumption can be applied is of course a matter of judgment, and the tolerable limit of heterogeneity cannot be specified precisely. The main criterion is whether management loses significant information by not computing separate unit costs for separate products, information which cannot be obtained more cheaply in other ways. For the container-filling operation, for example, an inexpensive engineering study could probably provide adequate estimates of the differences in cost per gallon resulting from different container sizes or different liquid inputs. In other cases, subdivision of the process center into smaller, more homogeneous cost centers will be the answer. Job order costing should be adopted only as a last resort, because of its higher clerical cost and more complicated paper work.

CONTROL USES OF PROCESS COSTING

Unit cost figures obtained by process costing techniques have the same application in inventory costing and decision making as those coming from job order costing. Because *product* cost in process costing is also *departmental* cost, however, unit product cost is often used to provide departmental information in ways that are not possible under job order costing.

An example of a process center control report is shown in Exhibit 5–7. In this exhibit, departmental costs are classified into several descriptive categories and a unit cost is computed for each. Extra columns are provided to show last month, year to date, and prior year figures. Space is usually added for explanations of important changes in the figures.

Such reports are an attention-getting device that may lead immediately to corrective action or eventually to decisions on changes in methods, equipment used, and so forth. Furthermore, because these unit costs are descriptive both of the product and of the process, they can serve a wider variety of purposes than job order cost averages.

This kind of control report has a number of shortcomings, however. For one thing, the cost comparisons shown are entirely with what has happened in the past, not with what is expected or what should have happened. This violates the basic requirements of control reporting laid down in Chapter 2, unless it can be presumed that the prior period figures represent a satisfactory level of cost performance for the current period.

Exhibit 5–7

DEPARTMENTAL COST REPORT: PROCESS PRODUCTION

Cost Center: 5116—Coke Batteries						Month: October
Cost Item	Current Month, 44,000 Tons		Last Month, 40,000 Tons	Year Ago, 43,000 Tons	Year to Date	
					This Year	Last Year
	Cost	Per Unit	Per Unit	Per Unit	Per Unit	Per Unit
Direct materials.......	$981,200	$22.30	$22.38	$21.98	$22.54	$21.65
Recoveries...........	(230,121)	(5.23)	(5.22)	(5.26)	5.58	5.41
Net direct materials....	$751,079	$17.07	$17.16	$16.72	$16.96	$16.24
Indirect materials.....	1,463	0.03	0.03	0.03	0.03	0.03
Fuels.................	79,538	1.81	1.77	1.75	1.76	1.68
Labor................	13,251	0.30	0.31	0.26	0.31	0.27
Utilities..............	2,604	0.06	0.06	0.07	0.06	0.06
Services..............	41,623	0.95	1.05	0.88	1.03	0.85
Maintenance.........	5,190	0.12	0.13	0.16	0.11	0.12
Administrative........	8,095	0.18	0.22	0.17	0.19	0.17
Total...........	$902,843	$20.52	$20.73	$20.04	$20.45	$19.42

Second, because many process center costs contain fixed elements, unit cost will fluctuate inversely with fluctuations in volume. These fluctuations in unit cost are not relevant to the process center manager because volume fluctuations are not ordinarily within his control.

Third, unit cost can change due to changes in the unit prices of productive inputs charged to the process center. These price changes can arise in three ways:

1. Changes in the current prices of externally purchased goods and services, including wage rates.
2. Changes in the cost performance of prior process centers—an increase in unit materials cost, for example, may merely reflect an increase in the unit cost in a prior center rather than a poor materials yield in the process center being studied.
3. Changes due to the methods used to cost materials inventories—charges for materials costed on a FIFO basis, for example, can change from period to period even though purchase prices are currently stable.

Some means must be found for isolating the influences of these changes either from the accounts themselves or from the reports issued for control purposes. Various possibilities for accomplishing one or the other of these will be considered in later chapters.

RECORDING PROCESS COSTS

Cost recording in process costing is usually simpler than in job order costing. Costs need to be recorded by cost center only—product costing is effected by end-of-month adjustments of a fairly simple nature, and job order cost sheets are neither necessary nor in most cases possible to prepare.

Accounts Required for Inventory Costing

For inventory costing purposes, it is necessary only to record separately each category of costs subject to a different cost divisor. Because the same divisor was used for both labor and other processing costs in each cost center in the earlier illustration, only one account would be necessary in each cost center to record both categories of costs. Assuming that department A is not always free of in-process inventories, six summary accounts would be necessary:

Materials   Costs—Department A
Materials   Costs—Department B
Materials   Costs—Department C
Processing Costs—Department A
Processing Costs—Department B
Processing Costs—Department C

Recording Materials Costs

Departmental materials costs are ordinarily classified into several categories for control reporting and data accumulation, and separate subaccounts are established for each class. For product costing purposes, only the summary entry is usually necessary, and the summary entry to record the issuance of materials to department A in the previous example would be:

(1)

Materials Costs—Department A.................................28,500
   Materials Inventory..   28,500

Recording Processing Costs

Labor costs, too, are ordinarily classified both as to cost center and also as to the type of labor (e.g., operators, helpers, maintenance men, etc.). Once again, however, only a simple summary entry is required for product costing purposes:

(2)

```
Processing Costs—Department A...............................  9,500
Processing Costs—Department B............................. 21,000
Processing Costs—Department C...............................  8,700
    Wages Payable.............................................         39,200
```

Other processing costs would also be subdivided for management information, but for product costing purposes the following entry would be enough:

(3)

```
Processing Costs—Department A............................. 19,000
Processing Costs—Department B............................. 15,000
Processing Costs—Department C............................. 13,050
    Accounts Payable, etc.....................................         47,050
```

End-of-Month Adjustments

The end-of-month adjustment for product costing could then be done in steps, following the flow of products. First, to record the transfer of products from department A to department B:

(4)

```
Materials Costs—Department B............................... 57,000
    Materials Costs—Department A.............................         28,500
    Processing Costs—Department A...........................         28,500
```

Because there was no inventory in process in department A at the end of the month, this entry would reduce the balances in the department A accounts to zero.

Second, to record the transfer of products from department B to department C:

(5)

```
Materials Cost—Department C................................ 85,000
    Materials Cost—Department B.............................         51,000
    Processing Costs—Department B..........................         34,000
```

This would leave balances in the departmental cost accounts, representing the $8,000 computed cost of the work in process in department B at the end of May.

Finally, to record the transfer of products from department C to the finished goods storeroom (using FIFO figures):

```
Finished Goods Inventory....................................111,600
    Materials Costs—Department C............................         89,500
    Processing Costs—Department C..........................         22,100
```

This series of entries is summarized in Exhibit 5–8.

Exhibit 5–8

COST FLOWS IN PROCESS COSTING

Materials Costs—Department A			
(1)	28,500	(4)	28,500

Processing Costs—Department A			
(2)	9,500	(4)	28,500
(3)	19,000		
	28,500		

Materials Costs—Department B			
(4)	57,000	(5)	51,000
		Bal. 5/31	6,000
Bal. 6/1	6,000		

Processing Costs—Department B			
(2)	21,000	(5)	34,000
(3)	15,000		
	36,000	Bal. 5/31	2,000
Bal. 6/1	2,000		

Materials Costs—Department C			
Bal. 5/1	10,500	(6)	89,500
(5)	85,000		
	95,500		
		Bal. 5/31	6,000
Bal. 6/1	6,000		

Processing Costs—Department C			
Bal. 5/1	1,100	(6)	22,100
(2)	8,700		
(3)	13,050		
	22,850		
		Bal. 5/31	750
Bal. 6/1	750		

Finished Goods Inventory		
(6)	111,600	

SUMMARY

Whenever the output of a production center is sufficiently homogeneous to be measured in physical product units, unit cost can be determined by the process costing method. In process costing, unit cost is determined by dividing each cost center's costs by its output for a specified period of time.

These unit cost calculations are usually made separately for each cost element for control reporting and also to provide data for planning and decision making. For the latter purpose, forecasts of unit costs rather than the historical averages are relevant, but the same process costing procedure can be used in either case.

This is not to imply that the average unit cost of all cost elements is relevant to managerial decisions. As was pointed out in Chapter 3, fixed costs may be wholly or partially sunk with respect to some decisions. Furthermore, the variable costs may not change in direct proportion to changes in volume, and average cost therefore may not be a very good measure of incremental cost. Later chapters will give additional space to questions of this sort.

DISCUSSION QUESTIONS

1. What differences are likely to exist between job order costing and process costing with regard to the definition of direct labor?

2. How do job order costing and process costing differ with respect to the time at which unit product costs are computed?

3. What is the product costing unit in process costing?

4. If the only purpose of cost accounting were to be the derivation of factory unit costs for public financial reporting, how many cost accounts would have to be provided to record the monthly operating costs of any one process center?

5. Assuming that unit costs are to provide some kind of information for management, under what conditions can process costing be used?

6. Under what conditions would you tend to regard week-to-week fluctuations in average unit cost as meaningful indicators of the effectiveness of cost control within a production department, using process costing?

7. Indicate whether you would expect to find job order or process costing systems used in plants manufacturing the following kinds of products:

   a) Cotton yarn.   e) Textbooks.
   b) Frozen orange juice.   f) Briar pipes.
   c) Men's suits.   g) Cigarettes.
   d) Diesel locomotives.   h) Automobile tires.

8. What kinds of information relating to end-of-period inventories must be obtained to permit calculation of processing costs per unit?

9. What is meant by "equivalent production"? Under what circumstances is cost per unit of equivalent production used to cost production transferred out of a department? When is it used to cost inventories remaining in process in a department at the end of the period? Under what circumstances would you be willing to use departmental completion figures in place of equivalent production figures?

10. Why is it desirable to compute equivalent production even if transfers out of a department are costed by the moving average method?

11. What problems arise in determining unit costs in departments that add further processing materials to semiprocessed products received from previous departments? What changes in account structure would be required to deal with these problems?

12. Should the costs of units lost in process be spread over the remaining good units or be charged to the income statement as production losses?

13. The Lyndall Company uses a process cost accounting system, and a physical inventory of the work in process at the end of the month must be taken in each department. The practice of the company is to allow each department manager to take his own inventory. The methods used for this are crude in comparison with the methods used in taking the year-end physical inventory. The department head, for example, usually estimates rather than counts his inventory in process.

Do you feel that a department's monthly in-process inventory should be taken by someone outside the department and that more accurate methods should be used? Give your reasons.

14. A factory uses a process cost accounting system and reports unit cost to each department head each month. A separate unit cost is computed in department A for each of eight elements of departmental cost, including two classes of materials, four classes of labor, and two other cost accounts. Indicate how these unit cost figures might be used in cost control and what might be done to make them more useful for this purpose.

EXERCISES AND PROBLEMS

1. Department A finished work on 50,000 units during April and transferred them to department B. On April 1, department A's inventory consisted of 15,000 units, complete as to materials but only one-third processed. During April it received 58,000 unprocessed units from the storeroom, and on April 30, it had 20,000 units still in process, complete as to materials but only one-half processed.

Compute equivalent production figures for the month for materials and for processing costs.

2. Department Y received from department X semiprocessed products for which it was charged $30,000. This represented $20,000 in the cost of materials to department X and $10,000 in department X processing costs. Department Y received from the storeroom other materials which it mixed with the semiprocessed products received from department X as the first step in department Y operations. The cost of these added materials was $15,000, and processing costs charged to department Y totaled $40,000. Equivalent production in department Y was 10,000 units for materials and 8,000 units for processing costs.

Compute separate unit costs for department Y's materials and for its processing costs.

3. A department in a firm using a process cost system has the following costs charged to it during the month of October:

Materials	$76,000
Labor	3,000
Other processing costs	14,000
Total	$93,000

During the period 30,000 units were completed. In process at the end of the period were 8,000 units, which contained all the material but which were on the average only 50 percent processed. There was no opening inventory. Determine the cost of the ending inventory.

*4. In a particular process, all materials are placed in production at the beginning of the process. The following data relate to the month of May:

     Inventory in process, May 1............ 1,000 pounds, 40% complete
     Placed in process.....................10,000 pounds
     Completed........................... 9,000 pounds
     Inventory in process, May 31........... 800 pounds, 60% complete

a) Compute unit cost divisors for the month for materials and for processing costs, in a form suitable for the application of FIFO inventory costing.

b) Make similar computations in a form suitable for the application of moving average inventory costing.

5. Department T produces product 12X from semiprocessed material A24 which it receives from department Q. The material is received in liquid form; the final product is a precipitate obtained after several preliminary operations in department T.

On January 1, 4,000 gallons of A24 were in process in department T. As of that date, department T had done approximately three fourths of the amount of processing necessary to convert this material into finished product. An additional 20,000 gallons of A24 were received from department Q during January and 3,000 gallons, one-third–processed in department T, remained in inventory on January 31. 155,000 pounds of product 12X were completed during the month. The normal yield is 7.5 pounds of product 12X per gallon of material A24.

a) Compute the number of equivalent units for the month, giving separate figures for materials and for processing costs.

b) What were the moving average cost divisors (in pounds)?

6. The Tober Company's factory has two departments, A and B. Materials enter department A where they are processed; the processed materials are then transferred to department B for finishing.

There were no inventories on hand in either department at the start of operations on September 1. Costs and output data for the month were:

	Dept. A	Dept. B
Outputs (units):		
Finished and transferred out...............	9,000	7,000
Finished but still on hand, 9/30...........	1,000	.....
Unfinished, 9/30........................	.....	2,000
Costs:		
Materials..............................	$12,000	None
Labor.................................	5,000	$6,000
Processing supplies.....................	1,000	2,000
Other processing costs..................	4,000	8,000

* Solutions to problems marked with an asterisk (*) can be found in Appendix B.

"Processing supplies" are introduced at all the stages of the production process, whereas "materials" are introduced at the beginning of processing. It can be assumed that unfinished units still in process in a department at the end of the month have gone through one half of the processing to be performed in that department.

a) Compute unit cost in each department and in total for both departments for the month.

b) Prepare journal entries to record the transfer of product out of each department.

c) What is the inventoried cost of units on hand in each department at the end of September?

*7. The Cantrell Company uses a process cost accounting system to determine unit manufacturing costs. Its manufacturing operations are performed in a single production department in which materials A and B are combined to produce product X. Costs are determined weekly, and materials inventory is costed by the FIFO method. The company's chart of accounts provides two in-process inventory accounts: (1) Materials in Process and (2) Labor and Overhead in Process. The following information pertains to the week of March 7–11:

> Inventories, March 7:
>   Material A, 10,000 pounds at $2.40.
>   Material B, 30,000 pounds at $0.30.
>   Work in process, none.
> Material A received in inventory, 5,000 pounds at $2.50.
> Materials issued to production:
>   Material A, 4,000 pounds.
>   Material B, 11,000 pounds.
> Other costs for week:
>   Supervision.............................$ 200
>   Operating labor........................... 1,600
>   Helpers and cleanup.......................   300
>   Heat, light, and power....................   100
>   Depreciation..............................   400
>   Other.....................................   155
>   Total................................$2,755
>
> Inventories, March 11:
>   Material A, 11,000 pounds.
>   Material B, 19,000 pounds.
>   Work in process, product X, 1,500 pounds.
> Product X completed during week, 13,500 pounds.

The March 11 inventory of product X in process is complete as to materials and two-thirds complete as to processing costs.

a) Compute average cost per pound of product X for the week.

b) Record these transactions in appropriate T-accounts.

8. The Folger Company manufactures a product known as Andron in a single unified sequence of processing operations. Production costs for the month of January were as follows:

Materials:

A............10,000 lbs............	$ 20,800
B............ 1,000 gal............	5,200
C............20,000 lbs............	27,300
D............ 1,100 doz............	3,300
Labor............	15,000
Other processing costs............	33,000
Total Cost............	$104,600

Materials A, B, and C are mixed together at the start of processing. Material D is added at the very end of processing, whereupon the finished product is transferred immediately to the shipping department.

During January, 48,000 units of Andron were finished, packed, and sent to the shipping department. On January 31, 4,000 units were still unfinished, but approximately one half the necessary labor had been performed on these. Other processing costs vary with labor cost. There was no work in process on January 1.

a) What was the cost *per unit* of Andron for the month of January?

b) What was the *total* cost assigned to units finished during the month?

c) What was the *total* cost assigned to the units still in process at the end of the month?

*9. The Stanley Chemical Company uses a process costing system of unit cost determination. The company's factory consists of two departments: raw materials are first mixed in the mixing department and then transferred to the refining department for completion. Product still in process in a department at the end of a month is assumed to be 100 percent complete as to materials and 50 percent complete as to processing costs in that department. The costs of units lost in production are to be spread evenly over equivalent good production in that department. You are given the following data for the month of January:

	Mixing	Refining
Quantities:		
In process, January 1............	0	0
Transferred in............	100,000	92,000
Transferred out............	92,000	80,000
In process, January 31............	7,000	10,000
Lost in process............	1,000	2,000
Costs charged to department:		
Materials............	$ 49,500	$ 0
Labor............	57,300	42,500
Other processing costs............	38,200	38,250
Total............	$145,000	$80,750

Prepare a production cost summary and distribution sheet for each department, using a format similar to Exhibit 5–6.

10. Department X receives semiprocessed material from department W, processes it, and transfers its output to department Y for further processing. The materials received from department W are first subjected to heat, which reduces the moisture content. Weight losses during subsequent processing steps in this department are insignificant.

October, 19x3, operations in department X are summarized by the following data:

Work in process, October 1, 19x3................... None
Material received from department W.............. 60,000 lbs. @ $1
Processing costs for the month:
   Processing materials............................$13,500
   Processing labor............................... 40,500
   Supervision...................................... 6,750
   Other processing costs.......................... 15,750
Goods transferred to department Y................. 40,000 lbs.
Partially processed goods still in process, October 31,
   19x3....................................... 10,000 lbs.

The goods still in process in department X on October 31 were approximately one-half processed in this department. (Note: All anticipated shrinkage due to weight loss has already occurred.)

a) Compute the unit cost to be assigned to goods transferred to department Y during the month.

b) *Processing costs* per unit for selected prior months were as follows:

	Department X Processing
Month and Year	Costs per Unit
September, 19x3.........................$1.78
August, 19x3............................ 1.74
July, 19x3.............................. 1.75
June, 19x3.............................. 1.68
October, 19x2........................... 1.65
October, 19x1........................... 1.55

What conclusions, if any, can you reach from these data as to the effectiveness of cost control in department X during October, 19x3? What additional information, if any, would you like to have in using these unit cost figures for this purpose? Give your reasons.

11. The Patroon Company operates a plant in which a single product is manufactured passing through three processing departments. Basic materials are combined in the first department by means of a chemical reaction. The semiprocessed product is then transferred to the second department for further processing and from there to the third department for finishing.

During the first month of operations the following costs were accumulated in the departmental accounts:

	Dept. 1	Dept. 2	Dept. 3
Basic materials......................	$ 40,000	$ 0	$ 0
Processing materials and supplies........	0	6,600	2,960
Processing labor......................	60,000	19,800	15,170
Supervision..........................	3,000	1,100	1,110
Maintenance labor....................	2,400	550	592
Other departmental costs..............	15,000	8,250	6,253
Total............................	$120,400	$36,300	$26,085

The process yield reports for the three departments for the month showed the following:

	Dept. 1	Dept. 2	Dept. 3
Units completed and transferred to next department.....	23,000	19,000	17,000
Units in process, end of month...............	2,000	4,000	2,000

For product cost determination purposes, the company divides departmental costs into two categories: (*a*) materials costs, and (*b*) processing costs. In departments 2 and 3, the cost of product transferred from the previous department is treated as a materials cost; processing materials and supplies, however, are regarded as processing costs. The inventories of units in process at the end of the first month of operations were complete as to materials in all departments. They were estimated to be one-half processed in department 1 and three-quarters processed in departments 2 and 3.

During the month, 12,000 units of finished product were shipped to the company's customers. No finished goods were on hand at the beginning of the month, and 5,000 units remained in finished product inventory at the end of the month.

a) Compute equivalent production for each of the two cost categories in each department.

b) Compute the costs of units in process in each department at the end of the month, both in total and per unit, distinguishing between materials costs and processing costs in inventory.

c) Prepare a cost of production report, showing materials and processing costs per unit (to the nearest tenth of a cent) and total costs transferred out of each department.

d) Prepare journal entries to record the month's costs in departmental accounts and an end-of-month adjusting entry or entries to reflect interdepartmental transfers and the cost of goods sold during the month.

12. The operating centers of the Fergus Company's factory are grouped into three departments for product costing purposes. The output of department I is transferred to department II, where it is used in the manufacture of product A, and to department III, where it is used in the manufacture of

product B. There were no in-process inventories in any department at the beginning of August. The following production statistics were accumulated for the month of August:

	Dept. I	Dept. II	Dept. III
Materials used (pounds):			
Material W.............................	10,000	0	0
Material X.............................	20,000	0	0
Material Y.............................	0	5,000	0
Material Z.............................	0	0	8,000
Processed material (from department I).....	0	15,000	10,000
Goods finished and transferred out of department (pounds):			
Processed material......................	25,000	0	0
Product A.............................	0	16,000	0
Product B.............................	0	0	13,000
In process, August 31 (pounds):			
Processed material......................	5,000	0	0
Product A.............................	0	4,000	0
Product B.............................	0	0	5,000

The inventories in process at the end of August were complete as to materials and one-half processed in the departments in which they were located at that time.

The following costs were charged directly to the departmental accounts during August:

	Dept. I	Dept. II	Dept. III
Materials.............................	$ 24,000	$ 4,200	$10,800
Labor................................	55,000	25,200	18,600
Other processing costs.................	22,000	16,200	12,400
Total...........................	$101,000	$45,600	$41,800

Additional information for August:

(1) Materials inventories, August 1, $45,000.
(2) Finished goods inventories, August 1:
    Product A, 8,000 pounds at $5.10, $40,800.
    Product B, 10,000 pounds at $4.70, $47,000.
(3) Materials purchased, $48,000.
(4) Sales:
    Product A, 12,000 pounds.
    Product B, 14,000 pounds.
(5) Finished goods inventory is costed on a first-in, first-out basis.

(Note: All costs assigned to the units transferred out of department I are charged to the materials accounts of departments II and III.

a) Compute unit cost divisors for each department for the month.

b) Prepare a schedule showing materials and processing costs per unit and the cost distribution between transfers and work in process, in each department.

c) Prepare journal entries to record the month's costs in departmental accounts and an end-of-month adjusting entry or entries to reflect interdepartmental transfers and the cost of goods sold during the month.

13. Materials are received in department A, processed, and then transferred to department B, where final processing takes place. The following data relate to the operations of department A for December:

	Quantity	Cost
Inventory in process, December 1:		
Materials.....................................	95 {	$ 228
Processing costs............................		72
Materials added from stock room...............	520	1,242
Processing costs..............................	...	528
Units completed and transferred to department B	310	?
Inventory in process, December 31:		
Materials.....................................	190 {	?
Processing costs.............................		?

All materials are placed in process at the start of processing—thus all work in process is complete as to materials. A total shrinkage of 10 percent is regarded as normal in department A, however, and it is assumed that half of the expected shrinkage has already taken place in the inventory in process at any time.

Inventory in process is assumed to be half processed in the department, and the costs of lost units are to be spread over all equivalent good units produced.

a) What is equivalent production for the month with respect to (a) materials and (b) processing costs?

b) Compute the unit costs that you would report to management to reflect the efficiency of the department's operations for the month.

c) Using the moving average method, compute the costs to be transferred to department B and the costs of work still in process in department A at the end of December.

*14. The David Company uses a process cost accounting system for determining product costs. It has three departments, and at the end of each day the work in process in each department has been completely processed by that department and is ready for transfer to the next department. The amount of cost to be transferred from one department to the next is determined on a FIFO basis.

You are given the following information for the month of November:

	Mixing		Refining		Finishing	
	Units	Cost	Units	Cost	Units	Cost
Completed work in process, 11/1	10,000	$ 20,000	8,000	$24,000	12,000	$42,000
Units received..................	90,000	153,000	88,000	?	86,000	?
Operating costs...............	.....	31,500	.....	87,620	.....	45,040
Units transferred out............	88,000	?	86,000	?	89,000	?
Completed work in process, 11/30	12,000	?	10,000	?	9,000	?

Supply the information missing from the above table.

15. Dashing Dachshund Dippers are made in two sequential processes, bristle toning and assembly. The bristle toning department manufactures bristle sets while the assembly department assembles the final product. The data are:

Bristle toning department:

Opening inventory: 400 units, 100 percent complete as to materials ($1,900) and 50 percent complete as to processing costs ($1,860).
Units started during month: 3,150.
Bristle sets completed and transferred to assembly: 3,000.
Units spoiled: 50; this is considered normal; scrap recovery of $75 is credited against current period material cost.
Closing inventory: 100 percent complete as to materials, 40 percent complete as to processing costs.
Costs for the current period:
Materials, $9,375 (before credit for scrap recovery).
Labor, $6,000.
Other processing costs (variable), $4,500.
Other processing costs (fixed), $3,000.
Unit costs are determined by the moving average method.

Assembly department:

Opening inventory: 200 units, 100 percent complete as to materials ($5,300) and 25 percent complete as to processing costs ($975).
Materials required in this process (per finished unit):
Two bristle sets from bristle toning.
One bristle holder, at $3 (required at start of process).
Units started: 1,500.
Units transferred to finished goods: 1,500.
Units spoiled: none.
Closing inventory: 100 percent complete as to materials, 75 percent complete as to processing costs.
Costs for the current period:
Materials, to be computed from data given above.
Labor, $8,000.
Other processing costs (variable), $6,400.
Other processing costs (fixed), $4,800.
Ending inventories and transfers to finished goods are costed on a FIFO basis.

a) Prepare a production cost summary and distribution sheet for each department, using a format similar to Exhibit 5–6.
b) What unit costs should be reported to management as the cost of opera-

tions for the month? Should any distinction be made betwen fixed and variable costs in such calculations?

(Adapted from a problem by John C. Burton)

16. The following costs were charged to process 2 of the H Company during July:

Costs transferred from process 1..............................$184,000	
Materials added in process 2................................ 34,000	
Processing costs... 104,000	

Production figures for the month for process 2 were:

Work in process, July 1....................... 2,000 pounds, 60% completed	
Finished during July..........................20,000 pounds	
Work in process, July 31...................... 5,000 pounds, 40% completed	

Process 2 materials are not added to the semifinished product received from process 1 until the very end of processing in process 2. The work in process in process 2 on July 1 had a cost of $22,500.

a) Compute the number of equivalent units for the month, giving separate figures for materials and for processing costs.

b) Compute the July 31 cost of work in process and the cost of units transferred out of the process during July, using the first-in, first-out method.

17. The Butts Company has a two-process factory in which all materials are placed in process in department A at the start of processing and semi-finished products are transferred to department B for completion. No additional materials are introduced in department B. The following data relate to the month of June:

Department A:
Beginning inventory (50 units, one-fourth completed): materials, $50; processing costs, $50.
Raw materials received during month (100 units), $100.
Processing costs incurred during month, $390.
Ending inventory: 60 units, one-third completed.

Department B:
Beginning inventory (40 units, one-half completed): materials, $213; processing costs, $150.
Processing costs incurred during month, $540.
Ending inventory: 45 units, two-thirds completed.

No product units were lost in either department during the month.

a) Compute unit costs in each department for the month of June on a moving average basis.

b) Using these unit costs, determine the cost of the work still in process on June 30 and the cost of goods transferred out of each department during the month.

18. The Andrews Metals Company operates two refining units of equal size, with identical equipment, paying identical wage rates. The following data relate to the operations of these two units during the month of September:

	Selby Mill	Franklin Mill
Quantities:		
Pounds in process, September 1 (½ completed)........................	10,000	8,000
Pounds received........................	78,000	52,000
Pounds refined, completed..............	60,000	37,000
Pounds in process, September 30 (½ completed).......................	8,000	10,000
Costs:		
Materials in process, September 1........	$ 8,000	$ 6,400
Processing costs in process, September 1....	7,000	5,600
Materials............................	74,100	49,400
Supervision..........................	6,000	5,700
Operating labor.......................	59,100	35,900
Depreciation.........................	30,000	30,000
Scrap credit..........................	(2,000)	(1,300)

A certain amount of shrinkage is expected in the refining process inasmuch as the refined metal weighs less than the ore concentrate from which it is refined. This weight loss takes place continuously during processing and is assumed to be proportionate to the percentage of completion. For the purpose of costing materials in process, it is assumed that the refined metal constitutes 75 percent of the ore concentrate, by weight.

Prepare an analysis that will assist management in comparing the relative efficiency of the two plant managers in controlling operating costs. Indicate what additional information you would like to have, if any.

19. The Apex Brewery uses a process cost accounting system. It has four production departments: brewing, storage, racking, and bottling. Beer is brewed in the brewing department and transferred to the storage department for aging in large tanks, from which it is later drawn off and piped to the racking and bottling departments. The racking department places the product in stainless steel kegs or barrels, whereas the output of the bottling department consists of cases of bottles and cans. The following statistics relate to the month of August (all figures are in number of barrels):

	Brewing	Storage	Racking	Bottling
Opening liquid inventories........	15,000	70,000	4,000	12,000
Transferred in....................	46,000	45,400	12,300	35,300
Transferred out...................	45,400	47,600	11,100	37,900
Shrinkage*.......................	600	2,800	200	400
Ending liquid inventories.........	15,000	65,000	5,000	9,000

* Includes on-premises consumption, rejected batches, loss through damaged containers, leakage, and evaporation.

Operating costs for the month of August were accumulated in departmental accounts. These accounts showed the following balances for the month:

	Brewing	Storage	Racking	Bottling
Materials......................	$ 68,554	....	.....	.....
Salaries and wages.............	54,290	$ 2,390	$20,146	$108,563
Supplies......................	1,003	412	4,822	23,244
Keg rent......................	....	......	37,782	....
Containers....................	......	......	......	257,410
Depreciation..................	9,328	6,086	4,073	27,822
Service department charges.......	14,086	7,194	28,205	43,123
Sundry.......................	8,615	1,063	3,096	18,515
Total....................	$155,876	$17,145	$98,124	$478,677

The August 1 inventory accounts showed the following balances:

	Brewing	Storage	Racking	Bottling
Materials in process.............	$22,650	$243,554	$16,080	$48,240
Processing costs in process.......	14,775	18,900	......	......
Total....................	$37,425	$262,500	$16,080	$48,240

Inventories in the brewing and storage departments are assumed to be 100 percent complete as to materials and 50 percent complete as to processing costs. Inventories in racking and bottling are assumed to be 100 percent complete as to materials; no labor and overhead are inventoried in these departments. Unit costs are determined monthly by the moving average method. No costs are assigned to units lost in production.

a) For each department compute equivalent production and moving average cost divisors for the month.

b) Prepare a departmental cost summary similar to that described in this chapter. Show total costs and unit costs.

20. The King Process Company manufactures one product, processing it through two processes—No. 1 and No. 2.

For each pound of process No. 1 output, two units of raw material X are put in *at the start* of processing. For each gallon of process No. 2 output, three cans of raw material Y are put in *at the end* of processing. Two pounds of process No. 1 output are placed at the start of process No. 2 for each gallon of finished goods started. Spoilage generally occurs in process No. 2 when processing is approximately 50 percent complete, and the costs of the spoiled units are assigned to the good units produced during the period. The recovery value of spoiled units is deducted from prior department costs.

The company uses FIFO for inventory costing for process No. 1 and finished goods, and moving average cost for inventory costing for process No. 2. Separate accounts are maintained for each process for (1) raw materials, (2) processing costs, and (3) prior department costs (costs of semiprocessed products received by process No. 2 from process No. 1).

Data for March:

(1) Units transferred:
  From process No. 1 to process No. 2.....................2,200 pounds
  From process No. 2 to finished goods...................... 900 gallons
  From finished goods to cost of goods sold................. 600 gallons
(2) Raw material unit costs: X. $1.51 per unit; Y, $2 per can.
(3) Processing costs: process No. 1, $3,344; process No. 2, $4,010.
(4) Spoilage recovery, $100.
(5) Inventory data:

	Process No. 1		Process No. 2		Finished Goods	
	Initial	Final	Initial	Final	Initial	Final
Units of product........	200 lbs.	300 lbs.	200 gal.	300 gal.	700 gal.	1,000 gal.
Fraction complete, processing costs....	½	⅓	½	⅔		
Cost:					$13,300	
Materials...........	$560		0			
Processing costs.....	$108		$ 390			
Prior department costs..........	0		$2,200			

a) Prepare journal entries to record the transfer of costs from process No. 1 to process No. 2, from process No. 2 to finished goods, and from finished goods to cost of goods sold. Present the necessary schedules of unit production and unit cost to support your entries.

b) Compute the cost of the March 31 inventory in each process and in finished goods.

(Adapted from a Uniform CPA Examination)

21. The Incredible Gadget Company manufactures a single product. Its operations are a continuing process carried on in two departments—the machining department and the assembly and finishing department. Materials are added to the product in each department without increasing the number of units produced.

In the month of May, the records showed that 75,000 units were put in production in the machining department. Of these units, 60,000 were completed and transferred to assembly and finishing, and 15,000 were left in process with all materials applied but with only one third of the required processing costs.

In the assembly and finishing department, 50,000 units were completed and transferred to the finished stock room during the month. Nine thousand units were in process on May 31, 1,000 units having been destroyed in production with no scrap value. All required materials and two thirds of the processing costs had been applied to the 9,000 units still in process but only one half of the prescribed material and labor had been applied to the 1,000 units lost in process.

There was no work in process in either department at the first of the month.

The materials and labor cost of units lost in production is to be treated

as additional "other processing costs" in the assembly and finishing department.

Cost records showed the following charges during the month:

	Materials	Labor	Other Processing Costs
Machining....................	$120,000	$ 87,100	$39,000
Assembly and finishing..........	41,650	101,700	56,810*

* Does not include the cost of spoiled units.

a) Prepare a statement showing the unit cost for the month.
b) Prepare a schedule showing the amount of cost credited to each department during the month and the details of the work in process balances
   at the end of the month.
c) Do you agree or disagree with a procedure that includes a portion of
   the cost of lost units in the cost of ending inventories in process? Support your position.

(Adapted from a Uniform CPA Examination)

22. The Reese Extract Company produces flavoring extracts and spices for food
products. The company's major product, vanilla extract, is produced in two
process stages, percolating and mixing. The percolating process consists of
chopping vanilla beans, percolating them in an alcohol solution, and drying
the process residue to recover reusable alcohol.

In the chopping operation, a sufficient number of beans is chopped for
one batch of extract and the chopped beans are placed in a percolator. Ten
percolators are used, so that there is always some product in process in the
percolating process. After percolating, the extract is piped from the percolator to storage tanks in the mixing department, while the residue is carried to
a dryer. The alcohol in the residue is recovered in the drying process and
returned to storage. The dried residue is then discarded as waste.

A batch consists of 1,100 pounds of beans, 405 gallons of alcohol, and
sufficient water to make a 1,000-gallon solution. The yield from each batch in
percolation is 800 gallons of extract, 45 percent alcohol. The remainder of
the solution either goes to the dryer, where 35 gallons of alcohol are
recovered from each batch, or is lost in the percolating process.

The 45 percent strength vanilla extract is placed in storage tanks to
await further processing. From these storage tanks the extract is piped into a
mixing tank where it is mixed with a sugar and water solution in sufficient
quantities to reduce the alcohol content of the extract to 36 percent. No
alcohol is lost in this operation. The contents of the mixing tank are then
piped into another set of storage tanks, and from there, they are piped to
another location for packaging.

Separate inventory accounts are maintained for product in the percolating department and in the two sets of storage tanks. In addition, each of the
two departments maintains a materials account and a "conversion cost"
account in which to accumulate departmental charges. These accounts are
closed out by appropriate entries at the end of each year.

The first-in, first-out method is followed for inventories in the percolating process, but the moving average method is used for all other inventories, including those in storage tanks. In computing unit cost in the percolating process, it is assumed that alcohol recovery from any unfinished work in process will be at the normal level of 35 gallons from each batch.

Periodic inventory counts showed the following data for the beginning and end of last year:

	January 1		December 31
	Quantity	Cost	Quantity
In percolators:			
Extract, one-half finished.........	4 batches {	$6,228	8 batches
Alcohol recoverable..............		280	
In storage tanks, 45% strength.......	3,200 gal.	5,784	4,000 gal.
In mixing process..................	None		None
In storage tanks, 36% strength.......	2,000 gal.	3,477	2,500 gal.

During the year, 130 batches were started in the percolators. Product yields and alcohol recovery were normal. A total of 100,000 gallons of 45 percent strength extract was piped into the mixing process, and 250,000 pounds of sugar were used in the sugar-and-water solution required to bring the extract to a 36 percent basis. Average cost of vanilla beans was 50 cents a pound, alcohol cost $2 per gallon, and sugar cost 5 cents a pound. Conversion costs for the period were:

Chopping, percolating, and drying............................$36,096
Mixing.. 16,250

a) Prepare a schedule tracing the flow of product through the two departments and the two sets of storage tanks, in terms of physical units, and calculate the physical unit divisors to be used in computing average unit cost in each department.

b) Prepare a two-column manufacturing statement in the form illustrated in this chapter, one column for total cost and the other for unit cost, for each department and each storage tank, showing work in process balances and the amount of cost transferred out of each department and each storage tank.

(Adapted from a Uniform CPA Examination)

Chapter 6

CLASSIFYING

OPERATING COSTS

EVERY STUDENT of accounting is familiar with transactions analysis by which every event that is to be reflected in the ledger accounts is scanned to determine which accounts are affected and in what amounts. This presupposes a previously established classification scheme which is provided by the chart of accounts.

Previous chapters identified four possible dimensions of the cost sections of the account structure—the cost center or responsibility unit, the cost element, the product, and the asset/expense distinction—but passed over two thorny groups of problems:

1. How many separate cost elements should be recognized for each cost center?
2. How should direct labor and direct materials costs be measured?

The main purpose of this chapter is to examine these questions. In addition, a brief section at the end of the chapter describes some of the documents and procedures that are frequently used to provide cost data in the form desired by the accountant. Although much of the discussion will focus on factory costs, particularly in connection with the problem of measuring direct product costs, most of it is equally applicable to the operating costs of other kinds of cost centers.

BASIC CONSIDERATIONS

The preparation of financial statements for external reporting requires a very limited breakdown of costs by cost element. Certain categories of selling and administrative expense, for example, would have to be accumulated separately to satisfy the data specifications in income tax regulations, wages and hours legislation, or trade association statistical gathering plans, but none of these requires a great deal of detail. Factory costs would need to be even less detailed if inventory costing were the sole object—from this point of view telephone service charges are no different from the costs of lubricating supplies, and two different accounts would not be required.

The fineness of the descriptive or natural element breakdown, therefore, depends on management's need for planning and control information. A cost center may have one labor account or twenty, depending on management's perception of its needs for detail and the cost of obtaining it.

This flexibility in cost classification even extends to the definitions of direct and indirect labor and materials in job order costing systems. Any cost traceable to a specific job order *can* be defined as direct labor or direct materials, but there is no law to say it *must* be so classified.

Criteria for Cost Classification

Chapter 2 emphasized the *homogeneity* criterion in cost classification. Homogeneity has two dimensions. First, an account should embrace only those costs having a common set of determinants. This requirement has its origins in both the planning and the control applications of accounting data. The manager can control cost only by acting on the determinants of cost, and if an account includes items with different determinants, the manager can never be clear where his efforts should be directed. This separation is equally important for planning in that cost estimation ordinarily proceeds from estimates of cost determinants to estimates of cost via some estimated relationship. The more heterogeneous the account, the more difficult it will be to estimate cost relationships. For this reason, for example, office clerical salaries would ordinarily be separated from salesmen's commissions or sales branch managers' salaries.

Second, the costs assigned to a particular account should have the same pattern of response to the various determinants of cost behavior. This behavioral homogeneity requirement comes from the need for data for planning. If both lubricating oil and electric power consumption are determined by the number of machine-hours run but respond in different ways to changes in machine-hour levels, this differential response can be obscured by lumping both elements together in a single cost account.

In practice, most accounting systems try to record fixed and variable cost components in separate accounts insofar as possible. In fact, the advantages of this kind of breakdown are so great that many costs that could be treated as direct labor or direct materials are often transferred to overhead because they are not proportionally variable. Thus direct labor and direct materials are often proportionally variable, *by defini-*

tion. (In process costing, some of the departmental labor and materials accounts are given a similar meaning.)

Cost variability is not the only behavioral characteristic of costs that is important. It makes sense, for example, to classify office rent and equipment rent in two separate accounts, even if they are both fixed, because separate decisions are required to change them. Operating volume is probably the most important behavioral determinant, however, which accounts for the attention given it in system design. Thus a number of account classifications are introduced solely because the costs they are meant to accumulate vary to a different degree or in a different pattern from those in some other account category.

Behavioral homogeneity may in some cases require a finer account breakdown than control homogeneity. For example, payroll taxes and pension costs are controllable in the short run only as a by-product of control of cost center wages and salaries. If merging them would deprive management of information useful for decision making, however, they should be recorded separately.

Application of the homogeneity principle is subject to diminishing returns, of course, and should not be carried to the extreme. More accounts mean higher clerical and storage costs, slower access time, and added opportunities for error, and at some point any further trade-off of cost for homogeneity becomes unprofitable. Unfortunately, no one has yet devised a means of locating this point by quantitative means, and so perhaps this ought to be labeled the principle of common sense.

Recording Costs by Causes

Another application of the homogeneity criterion is in the assignment to separate accounts of costs denoting departures from preestablished norms. Although most such accounts are used in conjunction with standard costing systems such as those outlined in the next chapters, accounts drawn on roughly similar bases can be used even in the absence of standard costing. For example, it might be useful to charge the costs of spoiled materials to special accounts rather than to the specific job orders for which they were originally issued.

Devices of this sort are the first step in the direction of classifying costs by causes. Thus the quantity of labor regarded as normally required to produce a production order is charged to the product which is the cause of incurring the cost. Costs in excess of this quantity are regarded as resulting from other causes and are assigned to other accounts, each one relating to a specific cause for departures from the norm.

This kind of causal analysis is essential to the control process. In many cases, the manager already knows the causes but needs the accounting reports to let him know how serious their effects have been. In other instances, the causes are so far removed from the scene of operations that no accounting system can identify them—for example, crew performance is off because one of the crewmen has been staying up late too many nights with a sick friend.

It is often possible, however, to build some of the causal analysis into the account structure. For example, the fact that some labor time is spent in nonproductive uses is a symptom, not a cause. One way to provide additional control information is to set up several accounts for nonproductive or idle time, one for each major cause of idleness. Thus the idle time could be recorded at the time it occurred as caused by machine breakdowns, waiting for materials, and so forth. If these data can be determined accurately, they may be a very useful supplement to the supervisor's knowledge of his own operations.

CLASSIFYING LABOR COSTS

Corporate payrolls cover payments for a wide variety of services performed by employees. Although this section is phrased in terms of manufacturing payrolls, the arguments are equally applicable to sales, service, and administrative payrolls.

Employee Payment Plans

Broadly speaking, employee payrolls may be grouped into two classes—salary payrolls and wage payrolls. Salary payrolls include the earnings of those employees who are paid a flat sum each payroll period, regardless of the number of working hours during the period. Some salaried employees may also receive commissions, extra pay for overtime, or bonuses in addition to the base salary, but their base pay is not dependent upon the number of hours worked.

Wage payrolls, on the other hand, cover those employees who are paid by the hour, by the day, or by the piece—the total compensation varying according to attendance or production. Payment systems in which the employee's earnings depend at least in part on his output are called "incentive pay plans."[1]

---

[1] Other types of incentive plans are based not on individual output but on group output or company profit. The latter are more properly referred to as profit sharing plans. For an exposition of a group incentive plan, see Frederick G. Lesieur (ed.), *The Scanlon Plan* (New York: John Wiley & Sons, Inc., 1958). For brief, simple descriptions of a number of other incentive plans, see Robert I. Dickey (ed.), *Accountants' Cost Handbook* (2d ed.; New York: Ronald Press, 1961), Sec. 6, pp. 27–32, and Sec. 15, pp. 26–28.

The simplest example of an incentive-type payroll is the straight piecework system. The earnings of an employee on piecework are computed for each payroll period by multiplying the agreed rate per piece times the number of good pieces produced. This is usually accompanied by a minimum daywork rate of so much per hour, so that if an employee's production falls below the daywork minimum, he will be paid at the day rate rather than the piecework rate for that period. For example, if John Jones is paid on the basis of 10 cents a piece with a $1.25 an hour guarantee and he works 38 hours during the week, his minimum wage for the week is $47.50 (38 × $1.25), even though his week's output might be only 450 pieces, which would entitle him to only $45 on a piecework basis.

Overtime Premiums

Each payment plan has a simple basic pattern from which actual wage or salary rates depart only for specified reasons. Thus a salaried worker receives a fixed amount each week, the hourly worker gets a certain amount for each hour worked, and the piecework operator gets so much per piece as long as basic conditions are met.

Departures from the base sometimes occur, however, if the salaried employee works overtime, or if the hourly worker is on the night shift, or if the piece rate man's output falls short of an agreed minimum. These departures usually lead to a portion of the wage bill being charged to separate accounts.

Probably the most universal example of this kind of departure from base wage or salary rates is *overtime premium,* the amount added to the base rate for hours worked in excess of some specified number each day or each week. Overtime premiums are ordinarily charged to separate accounts, even if they apply to labor hours that can be identified as direct labor hours. For example, if the basic or "straight-time" wage rate is $2 an hour and the overtime rate is $3, each overtime hour will lead to a $2 charge to some labor account (direct or indirect) and a $1 charge to Overtime Premiums, an overhead account.

Overtime premiums are not charged directly to the specific jobs performed in overtime hours for two reasons. First, the jobs performed in overtime hours are not necessarily the ones responsible for the overtime. In some cases a direct charge to a job can be justified, as in the case of a rush order for a specific customer, but in general the overtime results from a *total* demand on the production facilities in excess of single-shift capacity. *All* production shares equally in the responsibility for the overtime.

The second argument for treating overtime premiums as overhead is that cost control efforts as well as many decisions focus on the cost center rather than on the product. For these purposes it is desirable to accumulate wage premium payments departmentally rather than by individual product units. For example, the need for second-shift operation may be evidenced by mounting overtime premium costs. Even though production requirements are now being met satisfactorily through the use of overtime, it may be more economical to substitute for the costly overtime operations a partial second shift or expanded first-shift work force.

Average versus Marginal Overtime Premium

Classification of overtime premiums as overhead serves a control reporting objective and also has the negative advantage of excluding spurious elements from the direct labor charge, but it still leaves one question unanswered: how much overtime premium should be included in product cost?

Like other overhead items, overtime premiums enter product costs through the burden rate. Ordinarily the burden rate includes provision for *average* wage premiums at normal volume. Decisions as to the profitability of individual segments of the business, however, call for information on *incremental* cost. If overtime premiums are substantial, it can be argued that *every* job should be costed at the *full overtime rate,* on the grounds that elimination of *any* job would lead to savings at this rate.

The relevance of this argument will depend on the facts in any particular situation. If an increase or decrease in output will lead straight time and overtime to change by identical percentages, then the average is appropriate. If an output change will affect only the overtime hours, then the full overtime rate should be used. In other cases, some intermediate assumption will best fit the facts. The point of this discussion is not to recommend a doctrinaire solution but to emphasize the need for flexibility. Each company should have its own system, and that system should change from time to time as the situation changes.

Shift Differentials

Shift differentials—wage premiums paid for work on second and third shifts—are very similar to overtime premiums. For decisions relating to the utilization of capacity, a strong argument can be made for charging all products with the *maximum* shift differential that will have to be paid. The *average* shift differential is relevant to this purpose only if the production technology requires round-the-clock operation, so that the marginal wage rate is a composite wage rate from all three shifts.

Most companies classify shift differentials as overhead and include a provision for an average differential in the burden rate. Segregation of shift differentials permits the measurement of the aggregate amount of these costs and thus presumably facilitates control comparisons, even though the average differential may not be a good measure of opportunity cost and thus may be less relevant to decision making.

Make-Good Pay

Piece rate wage plans are ordinarily subject to a guaranteed daily or weekly minimum. If aggregate piece rate wages are less than this minimum, the difference represents an overhead cost known as *make-good pay* or *day rate* differential. Such costs sometimes can be identified by product, but for the reasons cited earlier the usual treatment is to classify them as overhead. The burden rate ordinarily includes a provision for the normal amount of make-good pay to be expected.

Productivity Sharing Incentive Plans

Some incentive plans provide for a sliding wage scale under which an employee's wage increases as his hourly output increases, but less than in proportion to the increase in hourly output. This permits the company to benefit from lower wage costs per unit while still giving the employee the benefit of increased take-home pay for increased output.

In process costing systems, incentive wage supplements can be classified easily in cost center accounts, either as part of the basic labor cost or separately, and average wage cost can be computed each period. A similar possibility is available in job order production if the incentive pay is computed job by job—actual wage cost can be computed for each individual job.

Most job order incentive plans other than piece rate plans, however, measure output by some kind of point system, with each product assigned a given point value. For example, a plan might call for a basic wage rate of $2 an hour, plus one half a cent a point for production in excess of 200 points an hour during each week. The difficulty in job costing under a plan of this sort is that the total incentive pay and thus the average rate per hour or per point cannot be determined until the end of the pay period. The accountant, therefore, must either wait until the end of the period or cost individual jobs at an estimated wage rate. The estimated wage rate would presumably reflect estimated average productivity. For example, if hourly production averages 500 points, the wage rate would be:

$$\$2 + \$0.005 \times (500 - 200) = \$3.50 \text{ an hour.}$$

The average cost per point would be $0.007, instead of the one cent implicit in the base wage rate of $2. No control purpose would be served by segregating the incentive pay in an overhead account—in fact, it would be better to include it as part of the direct labor wage rate so that the actual wage rate could be compared with the estimated rate. Such comparisons are discussed at length in the chapters on standard costing.

It should be noted that this averaging procedure does not introduce any real conflict between average cost and incremental cost. Incremental cost is not one-half cent a point because a management-directed increase in output presumably means adding more man-hours, not ordering the work force to produce more each hour. If the incentive plan is doing its job, this latter avenue is presumably unavailable, and so additional output can be obtained only by adding man-hours, probably at a cost greater than the average cost of $0.007 if less-experienced workers have to be hired. If management has knowledge of the incremental cost structure, it can use incremental rates, but in most cases the average rate will be an adequate approximation to the incremental rate.

Accounting for Fringe Benefits[2]

Indirect forms of employee compensation, popularly referred to as *fringe benefits,* are accounting for an increasingly large fraction of total employment costs. Some of these costs are imposed by law—social security taxes, for example. Others have been and are being introduced either through the results of collective bargaining or on the initiative of employers. Examples include paid vacations, paid holidays, company-sponsored recreation and education programs, company contributions to pension plans, medical insurance, and supplemental unemployment benefit plans.

Most companies record the manufacturing portion of the costs of these items in factory overhead accounts, charged directly or allocated to departments and then assigned to product cost by inclusion in factory burden rates. To illustrate, one company pays five supplemental wage costs: (1) federal old-age insurance taxes at a rate of 5 percent of gross

---

[2] For a more extensive review of this topic, see the National Association of Accountants, *Accounting for Labor-Related Costs, Research Series No. 32* (New York: National Association of Accountants, 1957).

wages; (2) unemployment compensation taxes at an average rate of 3 percent of gross wages; (3) pension accruals at 5 percent of gross wages; (4) vacation and holiday pay at 6 percent of gross wages; and (5) college tuition payments for sons of employees, averaging 50 cents a week for each employee.[3]

John Richards, a machine operator in the company's factory with a base pay rate of $3 an hour, worked 40 hours during the week of March 15. Direct labor accounted for 32 hours and indirect labor for the remaining 8 hours. Under one alternative, the entry to distribute his gross pay for the week would be as follows:

```
Work in Process (32 hours at $3)...............................96.00
Indirect Labor—Department X (8 hours)..........................24.00
     Accrued Wages Payable.......................................      120.00
```

The various fringe benefits would then be accrued in a separate entry:

```
Payroll Taxes—Department X (8%)..................................9.60
Pensions—Department X (5%)........................................6.00
Vacation and Holiday Pay—Department X (6%)........................7.20
College Tuition Program..........................................0.50
     F.I.C.A. Tax Accrued........................................      6.00
     Unemployment Tax Accrued....................................      3.60
     Pension Liability...........................................      6.00
     Vacation and Holiday Pay Accrued............................      7.20
     Provision for Tuition Grants................................      0.50
```

Two objections could be raised to this treatment. First, the department head can control these fringe benefits only through his control of labor utilization in his department, and thus it serves no purpose to report them separately. Second, the base wage rate understates the cost of each labor application. Inclusion of a provision for fringe benefits in the burden rate is only a partial answer to this second objection, and the use of a labor *charging rate* which includes provision for fringe benefits might be a better solution.

In the example above, the costs of the first four fringe benefits vary with the employee's gross pay and total 19 percent of the base wage rate. The college tuition program costs vary only slightly with the number of employees and not at all with the number of labor hours worked in any year. Because their behavioral pattern is unique, they should probably be excluded from the charging rate. On this basis, the charging rate would be:

---

[3] Payroll tax rates are changed from time to time. The 1967 rate for federal insurance (F.I.C.A.) taxes was 4.4 percent on the first $6,600 of each employee's gross pay each year. To simplify the illustrations, arbitrary round-number rates have been assumed.

Base rate	$3.00
F.I.C.A. tax	0.15
Unemployment	0.09
Pension	0.15
Vacation and holiday pay	0.18
Charging Rate per Hour	3.57

Using this charging rate, the weekly wage distribution would take the following form:

Work in Process (32 hours at $3.57)	114.24	
Indirect Labor—Department X (8 hours at $3.57)	28.56	
Accrued Wages Payable (40 hours at $3)		120.00
F.I.C.A. Tax Accrued		6.00
Unemployment Tax Accrued		3.60
Pension Liability		6.00
Vacation and Holiday Pay Accrued		7.20

The college tuition grant provisions would have to be accrued by a separate entry and classified as overhead.

Implications of Stabilized Wage Plans

Many observers believe that an increasing number of companies will be turning to devices that will transfer production labor from the hourly wage payroll to the salary payroll. The increasing emphasis placed by unions on employment security, spearheaded by such actions as the bargaining for supplemental unemployment benefits in the automobile and other industries, lends support to this view.

This poses some interesting problems in the interpretation of direct labor cost data. Direct labor cost is now assumed to be directly proportional to the volume of production. If production doubles, then direct labor cost will double; if production is cut in half, direct labor cost can also be halved. Employees can be laid off temporarily and recalled when sales prospects require. Under a guaranteed employment plan, however, payroll costs cannot be adjusted this rapidly.

This raises the question of whether all labor costs should be classed as indirect and assigned solely on a departmental basis. There is a strong case against this treatment. Control criteria require a comparison of actual performance with some bench mark of satisfactory performance. To a large extent this means comparing the actual hours of labor with the labor hours that are reasonably necessary to produce the actual output. A failure to distinguish between hours of productive labor and hours of nonproductive labor would eliminate the basis on which these control comparisons can be made. A comparison of total labor costs with total output cannot reveal the sources of changes in labor efficiency because this overall comparison obscures a wide variety of conflicting causes, some of which may offset others. For example, total labor cost per unit may remain relatively constant even though productive labor time per unit may be declining as a result of the introduction of improved methods or equipment. The offsetting increase in idle time obscures the actual improvement in productivity and therefore hides the possibilities for cost reduction through rescheduling of the labor force.

The difficulties in seeing this point may stem from a confusion between a guaranteed wage per man and a stabilized total payroll. Labor cost adjustments under stabilized wage plans must increasingly take the form of adjusting the size of the permanent work force rather than the number of hours worked by individual employees. Some of this adjustment can be made painlessly by not hiring workers to replace workers who leave as part of the normal turnover for retirement or new jobs in other companies. Transfer of employees to other duties within the company is also possible in many cases. When these outlets are inadequate to meet the requirements for adjustment of the labor force, layoffs of workers become necessary. The separate accumulation of idle time costs in overhead accounts provides the necessary information foundation for appraising the effects of continued employment of excess labor as opposed to the costs that the company would incur as a result of discharging employees.

Classification of Setup Costs

Another example of the alternatives available in cost classification is in the recording of setup costs. In a job order or batch production system, the amount of setup time may be a significant portion of the total cost of the job. The question is whether setup costs should be included with direct labor or classified as indirect labor and charged to a departmental overhead account.

The arguments for charging the cost of setup labor to individual job orders are relatively straightforward. Such costs can be traced, in most instances, to specific job orders. Including them in the direct labor charge will produce a more precise record of historical product cost than can be obtained by including them with manufacturing overhead. Treating setup cost as overhead means that the charge to any one job will be based on average relationships which are unlikely to hold true for any one specific job.

There are, however, counterarguments. If lot size varies, the average setup time per unit is likely to vary inversely with the size of the batch. Under these conditions, classifying setup cost as direct labor destroys the proportionality between direct labor cost and units produced, an assumption that is particularly valuable in cost analysis for planning and decision making. Secondly, if setup labor is charged directly to jobs, variations in unit cost resulting from differences in lot size tend to be buried with variations due to all other causes. This reduces the usefulness of unit cost information for cost control purposes. Finally, one school of thought would also contend that unit cost for income determination purposes should not be influenced by lot-size variations. Unit cost should include a reasonable provision for setup cost, based on a normal lot size for each product, and deviations from the norm should be excluded from unit cost.

Compromises are possible, of course. Setup time may be charged to direct labor but with a distinctive coding that permits segregation of the setup charges and their accumulation in cost center accounts either on a routine basis or by special reruns of the cost cards. Systems which charge setup cost to individual jobs as direct labor may provide separate lines on the job cost sheet for setup costs of various operations. This permits later analysis by jobs and by departments. In any case, setup time should not be treated as unclassified direct labor unless the quantities involved are small for each job or difficult to distinguish from operating direct labor.

Labor Time Classification

Most costing systems provide for dividing each cost center's labor costs into several categories. In process costing, distinctions are typically among different job categories—operators, helpers, materials handlers, and so forth. Wages for individual employees are seldom divided among two or more accounts.

This kind of classification has its counterpart in job order costing, but in addition portions of the wages of direct production workers are often identified in the accounts with various nonproductive or indirectly productive activities. Nonproductive time of direct production operators is often referred to as *down time,* and typical classifications include rest time, waiting for repairs, and so forth.

The purpose of this kind of classification is to make a causal identification of costs, and it is justified whenever a particular event is likely to happen with a great enough frequency and a large enough effect to require routine feedback. For example, if machine breakdowns are likely to lead to a total of 10 hours of idle time a year in a 10-man cost center, this would hardly justify routine segregation of the cost of idle time from this scource. Management has enough figures to scan without adding another unless it is an important one.

Rework Labor

Although many examples of items classified as nonproductive time could be discussed, only one is of enough general interest to be covered here, and that is the cost of *rework labor.*

Not all units of product are completed in satisfactory condition. Some are spoiled and must be discarded or scrapped; some are spoiled but can be placed in salable condition by reperforming certain operations; and still others are spoiled but can be sold as seconds or irregulars. The cost of the labor expended to correct defects in workmanship in job order production can be charged to the work in process accounts as direct labor because it can be traced to specific jobs. In process costing, it can be merged with other labor costs in the regular cost center accounts. If it can be identified separately, however, it should ordinarily be separated from other labor cost and assigned to a cost center *overhead* account as rework labor. The objectives of this treatment are to produce *departmental* totals of rework labor costs for control purposes and to include such costs in the unit cost calculations only to the extent that burden rates include a provision for normal rework labor.

Some systems do not provide for the transfer of rework labor and similar costs to overhead. In such cases it is still desirable to code the cost records in such a way as to permit the derivation of departmental totals upon request. Some companies go even farther and code this kind of cost by product line and also by the machine and operator doing the original defective work, if these can be identified.

CLASSIFYING MATERIALS COSTS

The term "materials" in manufacturing applies to raw commodities, fabricated parts, and subassemblies. Although materials are generally acquired from outside vendors, parts and subassemblies that are manufactured in the company's plants and placed in inventory storage are also generally classified as materials.

Pricing Materials Quantities

Most cost accounting information is stored and reported in monetary terms. For this purpose, the quantities of materials received, issued, and on hand must be assigned dollar prices.

The relevant price for decision making is the opportunity cost of the materials. This will be expected replacement cost if materials stocks are to be replenished, or resale market value if replenishment is not contemplated and sale is the most profitable alternative to the proposed use of the materials. Historical cost is not relevant in any case, unless of course it happens to coincide with opportunity cost.

Opportunity cost unfortunately is an extremely difficult concept to apply in routine cost bookkeeping, and most systems do not attempt even a partial application of the concept. Instead, materials are priced either at outlay cost or, in standard costing systems, at predetermined or standard prices. Discussion of standard prices will be deferred to the section beginning with Chapter 10. For the moment, two issues arising when outlay costs are used need to be discussed:

1. Should "cost" be defined as purchase price or as net delivered cost?
2. In what sequence should costs be transferred from materials inventory accounts?

Inclusiveness of Cost.   Vendor prices are sometimes net delivered prices, sometimes factory prices, before adding freight and subtracting discounts. The issue is essentially the same as for labor fringe benefits—what does the input actually cost? Once again it seems clear that any cost that is dependent upon the acquisition of the materials is as much a part of the price of the materials as the amount payable to the vendor. Net delivered cost is thus the preferred basis for inventory unit costing.

The only questions are questions of materiality and convenience: are freight charges and discounts *large enough* to affect unit cost materially, and is it *convenient* to match them with purchases on an item-by-item basis? If they are immaterial, then freight costs and discounts can be recorded separately and closed out directly to the income statement, without passing through the inventory accounts. If they are material in amount, it may still be inconvenient to try to obtain net delivered cost, invoice by invoice and item by item, and in this case some predetermined average amount may be added or subtracted from gross invoice prices to get an approximation to net delivered cost.

For example, suppose that six different items ae included in a single shipment and covered by a single invoice. Dividing the actual freight bill among these items is time-consuming and expensive. Charging freight to purchase cost on the basis of a predetermined average is undoubtedly less accurate, but it may be close enough to guide management in materials usage decisions under most circumstances.

Sequence of Cost Releases.   The second problem is to choose a method of costing the materials issued from inventory. Most historical costing systems (that is, those that do not use standard prices) follow either the FIFO or moving average method.[4] Either of these will lead to departures of recorded materials cost from current replacement cost at the time of issuance. If inventory turnover is rapid, these departures will ordinarily be small. Otherwise, some thought should be given to departing from historical cost altogether for internal cost transfers, using an approximation to current replacement cost. Adoption of such a plan would require a relatively simple end-of-year adjustment to restore an outlay cost basis for external financial reporting. The adjustment would be similar to that discussed in Chapter 18 for standard costing systems.

Defective and Lost Units

Few problems are encountered in assigning the costs of issued materials to operating accounts. Indirect materials are seldom subdivided into many categories, and the main question is what to do with costs that were originally charged as direct materials but turn out to have been unproductive or wasted.

For example, upon completion of a job lot of 100 units of product, it is found that five units are defective and must be sold as seconds. The total cost of the job was $3,900, or $39 a unit. One way of looking at this is to say that some of the costs expended on the defective units were nonproductive and should be removed from the product cost accounts. Suppose that it is decided to assign a value of $15 a unit to the seconds, indicating a loss of $24 a unit. The accounting entry would be:

Finished Goods Inventory—Firsts (at $39)	3,705	
Finished Goods Inventory—Seconds (at $15)	75	
Loss on Rejects (at $24)	120	
Work in Process		3,900

The loss on rejects might be further classified by causes if a basis for such a classification exists and if the amounts are large enough.

A second alternative is to credit the job with the recoverable value of the rejected units, leaving the good units to bear the net cost of the job. For example, if $20 is the total net resale value of the seconds, unit cost for the 95 good units would be:

Total cost	$3,900
Less: Value of seconds	100
Net Cost	$3,800
Unit cost ($3,800 ÷ 95)	$ 40

The entry to record this would be:

---

[4] For a discussion of these and other methods, see Myron J. Gordon and Gordon Shillinglaw, *Accounting: A Management Approach* (3rd ed.; Homewood, Ill.: Richard D. Irwin, Inc., 1964), chapt. X.

Finished Goods—Seconds...100
    Work in Process.. 100

This second alternative is usually applied in process costing to units lost in production. For example, if enough materials are placed in process to produce 10,000 units of product but the process yields only 9,000 units, the cost of all materials inputs is ordinarily spread over the 9,000 good units. The low yield shows up in a high unit cost rather than in a specific charge to overhead.

The main defect of this second approach is that it fails to provide management with data on past product losses in usable form for both control and planning purposes. This is less serious in process costing than in job order costing because unit cost variations are computed departmentally and the effect of lost units on unit cost can be calculated fairly readily:

	Units	Total Cost	Unit Cost
Materials used.................	10,000	$18,000	$1.80
Equivalent production..........	9,000	18,000	2.00
Effect of Lost Units.........	1,000	......	$0.20

The loss of units does not add to total cost but it does increase unit cost, in this case by 20 cents.

This kind of analysis can be performed in job order costing only on a job-by-job basis. Departmental summaries would be very difficult to obtain for routine reporting to department heads. Furthermore, losses are often a function of the machine or operation rather than of the particular job or product. In the normal course of events, losses will occur on some jobs but not on others. To assign rejection losses to those jobs on which they happened to occur would result is less accurate rather than more accurate costing. The better procedure for planning purposes, therefore, is to accumulate such losses departmentally and include in product cost through the burden rate a provision for *normal* losses only.

Scrap

Scrap poses a somewhat different problem. Most scrap is traceable to departments but not to individual job orders, except at prohibitive cost. The *cost* of scrapped materials is seldom segregated by departments or cost centers, however. Instead, the net *market* value of scrap recovered is typically *credited* to a cost center overhead account:

Scrap Inventory. xxx
    Scrap Recovery—Department X.   xxx

The result is to overstate the cost of direct materials and understate average overhead costs. As long as materials costs and scrap recoveries are identified by cost center, however, an adequate basis for control reporting is available.

COST RECORDING PROCEDURES

The implementation of a cost accounting plan requires a well-conceived set of documents and procedures. To some extent this is simply a matter of adding a cost account code to the payment voucher or analogous document. Some procedures are designed expecially for use in cost accounting, however, and these need a very brief description.

Purposes of Documents and Procedures

Most materials flow into and through the factory on a river of documents processed by means of a specified set of procedures. One purpose of these documents is to help safeguard the inventories by making it possible to identify at all times the persons accountable for them and to insure against their unauthorized use. This is a property control objective.

A second purpose of most documents is to transmit action instructions. For example, one document might instruct a storekeeper to give a specific quantity of a certain material to a production department foreman, while another document might tell the foreman what to do with this material.

Finally, the documents provide the basis for data accumulation and information reporting. They indicate how much is needed, how much is ordered, received, and used, and often what has been produced from the materials. The information content of the documents constitutes the input to cost accounting.

Acquisition of Materials

Materials accounting begins with the issue of a *purchase requisition* or its equivalent—a request to the purchasing department to acquire certain items from outside vendors. Once a vendor is selected, a *purchase order* is prepared, detailing the amounts and specifications of the materials desired, usually together with a requested delivery date. For inventory control purposes, the quantities ordered are usually entered in the perpetual inventory records.

When the goods are shipped, the vendor sends an *invoice* to the purchasing department, together with other shipping documents. The invoice lists the actual quantities shipped, the prices charged, and the total amount of the payment due. When the goods are received, they are inspected and counted and a *receiving report* is prepared. This may be a separate form, or it may be merely the receiving department's copy of the original purchase order on which the goods received have been checked off. This provides the basis for recording the company's liability and for charging the materials inventory accounts.

The materials inventory accounts are ordinarily supported by a subsidiary *stores ledger* or *materials ledger* consisting of a set of detailed records, one for each kind of material kept in inventory. One such record is the simple stores ledger card illustrated in Exhibit 6–1.

Exhibit 6–1

STORES LEDGER CARD

PART NO. 1623 D
DESCRIPTION: Bearing Pin, Brass   UNIT: Dozen

Date	In			Out			Balance		
	Quantity	Price	Amount	Quantity	Price	Amount	Quantity	Price	Amount
May 1							106	$2.14	$226.84
4				70	$2.14	$149.80	36	2.14	77.04
10	200	$2.20	$440.00				236	2.19	517.04

Issuing Materials

Physical control of materials inventories is normally maintained by keeping the materials in specified stock rooms until they are required for use in production. In most cases it is desirable to issue materials only if a *materials requisition* form has been filled out and signed by an authorized person or if some other reliable device for attribution of materials consumption is available. The requisition shows the items issued, the quantities of each, and the job order number of cost center account number. It provides the basis for recording materials issues in the ledger accounts and in the stores ledger and job order cost sheet.

The requisition process is impractical and unnecessary whenever a production process utilizes large quantities of bulk materials, such as crude oil in petroleum refining or iron ore in pig iron production.

Instead, materials flows are determined by some form of metering or by periodic inventory counts.

Returned Materials

If a cost center finds that it has requisitioned either direct or indirect materials in excess of the amount actually required, it is normally obligated to return any such excess materials to the storeroom, accompanied by a *returned materials card.* This card identifies the nature of the materials, the quantity returned, and the job order or cost center account to which they were originally charged.

In job order costing, the costs of any direct materials returned are customarily credited to the individual job cost sheets. Thus the net materials cost shown on the job sheet represents the cost of the materials actually used on that job.

Payroll Accrual

Payroll accounting has two sides: the first dealing with the *liability-payment* aspects of the transactions and the second having to do with the identification of the cost with various segments of activity, usually referred to as the *distribution* of labor cost.

The liability-payment aspects of payroll accounting are not part of cost accounting, and only the briefest summary of procedures is necessary here. Wage and salary liabilities are accrued on the basis of information from two sources: personnel records and attendance or production records. For each employee, a *master personnel record* is maintained, showing his employment history with the company, job classification, title, current rate of pay, and authorized deductions for hospitalization insurance, pension plans, savings plans, union dues, and so forth. The master record may be filed on punched cards or on magnetic tape or other forms of electronic storage.

The attendance record is usually provided by an in-and-out *clock card* from which it is possible to compute the total elapsed time the employee has been in the plant and ready for work during the payroll period. Elapsed time is classified between regular time and overtime, and the clock card identifies the shift worked if the company operates more than one shift.

For salaried employees, the payroll liability is ordinarily taken directly from the master personnel record. Attendance cards may be checked for excessive absences or for paid overtime if the salary plan adjusts for these. For hourly employees, wage liability for the payroll period is computed by multiplying the rate shown on the personnel record by the number of hours worked, as shown on the clock card. If a shift differential is paid for workers on second and third shifts, the basic rate is adjusted to provide for this differential. Overtime hours are paid for at the overtime rate applicable to the particular employee and shift.

To illustrate, assume that the payroll register shows total wages of $12,276 for the week, including $658 for overtime premium. Various amounts will be withheld from gross pay for transmittal to the federal and state governments (for income taxes and social security taxes withheld), to insurance companies or trustees (for hospitalization insurance, savings or pension plans), or to others in whose favor employees have authorized deductions from their pay. Only the residual is payable directly to the employee. For cost accounting purposes this breakdown is irrelevant, and the payroll can be summarized simply as follows:

```
Factory Overhead..................................................    658
Labor Cost Summary............................................ 11,618
    Accrued Wages Payable.....................................         12,276
```

Notice that this entry already includes a partial labor cost distribution. Because overtime premium is calculated from the attendance records, it can be split off as a by-product of payroll preparation. Factory Overhead is a control account, of course, and cannot supply the detail required for control reporting. Entries would also be made in the overtime premium accounts for the various cost centers in one or more subsidiary ledgers. To save space, only the summary entry is given here.

The Labor Cost Summary account used in this entry is an example of a *suspense account* or *clearing account* created for the purpose of accumulating historical labor costs temporarily until they can be distributed to appropriate manufacturing cost accounts.

Distributing Wage Costs

Methods of labor cost distribution are determined largely by the nature of the production operation. In most process production systems, for example, most employees are assigned full time to a single cost center, and all the information necessary for cost distribution can be obtained from attendance cards and master personnel records.

In job shops as well as in some process production operations, however, it is often desired to divide the wage or salary costs of individual employees among two or more descriptive accounts.

The usual basis for this classification is the *time ticket*. The time ticket provides information as to (*a*) the job order number or descriptive labor account number, (*b*) the cost center, (*c*) the name and number of the employee, (*d*) the number of hours worked on the job or task, and (e) the basic wage rate. In many cases this last figure is inserted later from the master personnel record.

In process costing, time tickets are required only if individual employees divide their time between cost centers, or if the company wishes to classify the wages of individual employees between productive time and nonproductive time, or if the cost center for some reason encompasses more than one subprocess.

Because these time tickets are prepared as work is performed, the company has the option of distributing wage costs directly from the time tickets without waiting for reconciliation with the attendance records. For example, Exhibit 6–2 shows a daily cost distribution sheet with a separate line for each time ticket. This sheet, or the card file underlying it, provides the basis for entries in the control accounts on the individual job cost sheets and in the subsidiary cost ledger.

If all elapsed time is accounted for, the total cost distribution will equal the total payroll at straight-time rates. Thus the total payroll distribution for the week might show the following debits and credits:

```
Work in Process............................................8,849
Factory Overhead...........................................2,769
     Labor Cost Summary........................................        11,618
```

Once again, the debit to Factory Overhead would be supported by charges to the individual cost center indirect labor accounts in the subsidiary ledger, and direct labor charges would be entered in the individual job cost sheets. The summary entry shown above serves no cost accounting purpose beyond that of providing a data control total.

Concurrent Labor Cost Distribution

The foregoing illustration has assumed that the cost distributions and payroll accumulations are performed separately and reconciled later. Many systems, however, provide for a simultaneous processing of the attendance records and time tickets. The summary entry to record the payroll and distribute it at the same time is of course a consolidation of the two earlier entries, eliminating the Labor Cost Summary account entirely:

```
Work in Process............................................8,849
Factory Overhead (Indirect Labor).........................2,769
Factory Overhead (Overtime Premium)........................ 658
     Accrued Wages Payable......................................        12,276
```

Simultaneous preparation of payrolls and distribution of labor costs is facilitated by modern data processing equipment, but many systems still provide for separation of the two. One reason in less highly mecha-

Exhibit 6-2

LABOR COST DISTRIBUTION SHEET

DATE: May 11, 19—
WEEK NO. 19

PAYROLL GROUP M14

Employee No.		Name	Hours	Base Rate	Dept. Charge	Account No.	Job No.	Operation No.	Amount
Dept.	Serial								
1	316	J. C. Abrams	3.0	1.75	1	0301	1762	1	5.25
1	316	J. C. Abrams	1.0	1.75	1	0301	1762	2	1.75
1	316	J. C. Abrams	5.0	1.75	1	0301	1762	3	8.75
1	423	A. B. Allen	8.0	2.00	1	1412			16.00
1	437	T. P. Andrews	6.0	1.80	1	0301	1879	6	10.80
1	437	T. P. Andrews	2.0	1.80	1	1417			3.60

nized systems is that it may be more efficient to have different clerical personnel process the payrolls and distribute the costs. Another reason is that many companies insist upon daily labor distributions for next-day reporting to department heads and supervisors. Still a third reason is not to delay the processing of the job cost sheets for completed jobs. Finally, the labor rates used in cost distribution are often predetermined and are not expected to equal the actual payroll for the period. The choice, in other words, rests as always on the questions of economy, convenience, and timeliness.

SUMMARY

The foundation of any cost accounting system is a good framework and set of procedures for cost classification. The framework is provided by the chart of accounts, specifying how the distinctions among various categories of cost are to be made.

The bulk of this chapter has been devoted to a discussion of how the homogeneity principle of account construction might be applied in particular situations. Given management's wide latitude in designing the account structure, the choice should be guided by the usefulness of the classification to management processes, measured against the cost of obtaining added detail.

The question of classification is often closely allied with the question of the price at which productive inputs will be charged against specific operations. Overtime premiums, for example, could be charged as part of the direct labor rate or as part of overhead or even excluded from product or cost center costs entirely. In deciding such questions the primary criterion must be that of relevance to current decision making and control, and the solution is to be found in using incremental costing rates for decision making while obtaining departmental cost totals for any items that are controllable separately from the total labor or materials quantities involved.

Cost classification of this sort can make a great contribution to the control process, but this contribution is bound to be limited unless appropriate cost standards are developed. These are the subject of Chapters 10 through 13.

DISCUSSION QUESTIONS

1. Can you conceive of any circumstances in which some of the labor hours that could be traced to a particular job order might be classified as departmental overhead instead? Explain.

2. Will it make any difference whether such items as vacation pay and company pension costs are included in the direct labor charging rate or are classified as departmental overhead? Which method will produce the more accurate product unit costs?

3. Should direct labor costs be classified by department in a job order costing system?

4. Should overtime premiums be charged to the specific jobs produced during overtime hours? For decision making, would it ever be appropriate to charge *every* job with the *full overtime rate,* even though only 10 percent of the jobs are done on overtime?

5. In reconciling clock cards with timecard totals for a particular payroll period, it is discovered that the clock cards show a total of 100 hours more than the total of the timecards. What should be done about this discrepancy?

6. Why are employers' payroll taxes normally assigned to manufacturing overhead as separate items rather than as part of the charge to specific jobs or overhead accounts to which the payroll itself is distributed?

7. Describe a procedure that would result in charging labor-related costs such as payroll taxes, vacation pay, pension accruals, and employer hospitalization insurance contributions as part of the regular labor charge.

8. What are the reasons for costing materials inventories at net cost, after adding freight and handling costs and subtracting discounts and allowances?

9. What characteristics of the last-in, first-out method of inventory valuation make it difficult to apply this method to routine daily inventory accounting.

10. Coal is the principal fuel used in electric power generation. Coal is typically delivered by ship, barge, or rail and stored at the power plant in open storage areas. It is fed into furnaces by a system of continuous hoists and automatic conveyors. Discuss the problems of securing an adequate record of receipts, consumption, and inventories of coal.

11. What classification scheme might be substituted in process costing for the direct labor/indirect labor distinctions appropriate to job order costing? Why is there a need for any subclassification of departmental labor in process costing?

12. The Riddle Company uses a job order costing system to account for the manufacture and assembly of electronic components. Completed units that are rejected in inspection are delivered to a rework man for correction of the defects. If the volume of rejects is large, one or more assemblers are transferred temporarily to assist the rework man. Should rework labor be classified as direct or indirect labor?

13. The placing of a purchase order with a supplier of material or parts does not customarily give rise to an entry in the Materials Inventory Control account. The amount of goods already on order, however, is an important factor in the decision to place a new order. Furthermore, the placing of the order creates a legal obligation of the purchasing company either to accept delivery or to pay damages to the supplier. In view of these facts, what justification is there for the customary accounting treatment? How might goods on order be reflected in a company's inventory and financial records?

EXERCISES AND PROBLEMS

1. The workweek of employees in the foundry department of the ABC Company ranges between 42 and 50 hours, with all hours in excess of 40 per week being paid at a rate of one and one-half times the basic hourly wage rate of $3.60 per hour. On the average, each worker works 45 hours a week.

   a) What is the foundry labor cost per hour that should be included in product unit cost for public financial reporting? How much of this should be shown as direct labor? Explain your answer.

   b) Management is trying to decide whether certain products are profitable enough to continue manufacturing. From this point of view, what is the foundry labor cost of a product that requires 10 hours of foundry labor? Explain.

2. The Burns Machinery Company manufactures a wide variety of machined parts and a small number of specialized assemblies. In manufacturing a certain part, it has the option of using machine A, which requires three hours for initial setup and adjustment, or machine B, which requires only one hour of initial setup. Once the setup is completed, machine A can turn out approximately 50 parts an hour, whereas machine B's output is at an average rate of 30 parts an hour.

   a) How large a production lot would be necessary to justify the use of machine A, assuming that wage rates are the same for setup and operating labor on both machines?

   b) Should the cost of setup labor be classified as direct labor or as indirect labor? Support your answer.

*3. The Plane Company uses a job order costing system. Metal scrap is collected weekly from each department and stored in a bin near the loading dock. A scrap dealer empties the scrap bin once a month and makes payment on the basis of the current market price of scrap.

   During March, 200 pounds of scrap were collected from department X and 1,000 pounds of scrap were collected from all departments combined. The price paid by the scrap dealer was 10 cents a pound. During March, department X worked on three jobs, weighing 10,000, 5,000 and 1,000 pounds, respectively. The costs of materials used on these jobs totaled $30,000, $5,000 and $2,500, respectively.

   Indicate how you would account for scrap in this situation.

4. In a job order for 500 piece parts, 80 parts are damaged beyond repair in the production operation and must be junked.

   a) Should the costs of these parts be removed from the job order cost sheet? Indicate the criteria by which you judged this question and the reasons why application of these criteria led to the course of action you have chosen.

---

* Solutions to problems marked with an asterisk (*) can be found in Appendix B.

b) If the costs are removed from the job order cost sheet, what form should the journal entry take? State your reasons.

*5. The Branby Company uses "net delivered cost" as the basis of entries in the stores ledger and in the Raw Materials control account. Net delivered cost is defined as gross invoice price minus discounts plus an allowance for the costs of purchasing, freight-in, and receiving room. Discounts are deducted directly in the processing of invoices; the remaining items are added to net purchase price by means of a "purchase burden rate," based on estimated annual purchasing, freight-in, and receiving costs per dollar of estimated purchases.

Annual planning budgets approved last December showed the following estimates for the current year:

Purchases..	$2,400,000
Purchasing department cost............................	42,000
Freight-in...	80,000
Receiving department cost.............................	22,000

During January of this year, the costs actually incurred were:

Purchases..	$225,000
Purchasing department cost............................	3,600
Freight-in...	4,500
Receiving department cost.............................	1,900

a) Compute the purchases burden rate for the current year.
b) Prepare a summary journal entry to record January materials purchases.
c) Compute the amounts of purchasing, freight, and receiving costs under- or overabsorbed by purchases during the month. What explanations might you offer for these?

6. The Canton Plastics Company manufactures injection molded plastics on a job order basis. Many jobs require the purchase of plastic powders of a special color or chemistry, and if the quantity purchased exceeds that required to fill the order, its cost is charged to the job and the excess powder is scrapped. In addition there are scrap losses in production.

After a simple grinding and mixing operation, the scrap is reusable on certain products which do not have rigid color and chemistry specifications. The sales of these products are large enough so that Canton buys scrap on the open market fairly frequently and rarely sells its scrap.

Material cost is a very high fraction of total cost to manufacture, and scrap averages about 10 percent of material consumed. The Canton Company can sell its scrap at about $0.15 per pound and buy scrap at about $0.20 per pound. The price of new plastic powders ranges from $0.30 to $0.50 per pound, depending on the color and chemistry of the material.

How should the Canton Plastics Company cost scrap in its accounts and in developing cost data for management's information?

*7. The Gray Company capitalizes all freight charges relating to materials purchased and deducts all discounts in computing the amounts to be entered in the stores ledger. A perpetual inventory is maintained. On April 1, the company had 200 units of material No. 1476A in inventory at a cost of 50 cents each. The following transactions in material No. 1476A occurred during April:

April 2　Received 500 units from Alpha Company at a price of 55 cents each, delivered; terms, net 30 days.
 4　Issued 50 units for use in job No. N1346.
 8　Issued 200 units for use in job No. N1402.
 12　Received 500 units from Beta Company at a price of 48 cents each, F.O.B. Cleveland; freight charges, $20; terms, 2 percent, 10 days, net 30 days.
 16　Issued 400 units for use in job No. N1481.
 18　Issued 50 units for use in job No. N1346.
 25　Issued 250 units for use in job No. N1417.
 28　Received 1,000 units from Beta Company at a price of 47 cents each, F.O.B. Cleveland; freight charges, $40; terms, 2 percent, 10 days, net 30 days.

 a) Prepare a stores ledger card for material No. 1476A and make the necessary entries, using a moving average method of inventory valuation.
 b) Repeat this procedure using a FIFO inventory valuation method.

8. The Collins Company costs its raw materials inventories by the moving average method. Freight-in is distributed to materials purchased in proportion to purchase prices. The stores ledger cards show the following balances at the beginning of March:

Material A, 700 pounds at $0.252............................$176.40
Material B, 400 pounds at $0.165............................　66.00
Material C, 26,000 feet at $0.03............................　780.00
Material D, 5,000 feet at $0.125............................　625.00

The following events occurred during March:

March 2　Issued:　　200 lbs. material A
 5,000 ft. material C

 5　Received: 20,000 ft. material C at $0.031 per foot
 10,000 ft. material D at $0.124 per foot
 (Freight for above two items, $186.)

 9　Issued:　　300 lbs. material A
 150 lbs. material B
 8,000 ft. material C
 5,000 ft. material D

 16　Received:　1,000 lbs. material A at $0.24
 500 lbs. material B at $0.16
 (Freight for above two items, $64.)

 22　Issued:　　700 lbs. material A
 400 lbs. material B
 20,000 ft. material C
 3,000 ft. material D

 a) Prepare stores ledger cards for these four materials and make the necessary entries.
 b) Prepare summary journal entries to record the above transactions.

*9. The Durgin Corporation operates a large machine shop. All employees are paid either monthly or twice a month. Holiday and vacation pay is expected to average 7.5 percent of straight-time pay for all factory employees.

On an annual basis, the employer's share of F.I.C.A. and unemployment insurance taxes (also referred to as "payroll taxes") is expected to average 6 percent of straight-time pay for hourly employees and 5 percent of straight-time pay for salaried employees, not including holiday and vacation pay.

The employer's share of hospital insurance premiums averages 2 percent of straight-time pay, again not including holiday and vacation pay. Overtime premiums average 12.5 percent of the straight-time pay of hourly employees and 10 percent of the straight-time pay of salaried employees.

The factory payrolls for the month of March showed the following totals:

	Hourly Employees	Salaried Employees	Total
Direct labor at straight-time rates.............	$20,000	$	$20,000
Indirect labor at straight-time rates..........	4,000	5,000	9,000
Overtime premiums........................	3,000	500	3,500
Withholding taxes deducted.................			4,800
F.I.C.A. tax deducted.....................			1,465
Hospitalization insurance premiums deducted..			600

In addition, the Durgin Corporation was obligated to pay F.I.C.A. taxes on March payrolls equal to those deducted from the employees' gross pay and unemployment insurance premiums of 3 percent of the month's gross pay. It was also required to pay hospital insurance premiums equal to the amounts deducted from employee payrolls for the month.

a) How much should be charged directly to the job order cost sheets and to indirect labor accounts to reflect factory labor operations for the month of March?

b) Prepare summary journal entries to record and distribute the payrolls and labor-related costs for the month of March in a manner consistent with your answer to (a).

c) P. T. Jones took two weeks' paid vacation during June, for which the gross pay amounted to $200. The withholding tax applicable to Mr. Jones's vacation pay amounted to $13.80, the F.I.C.A. tax was $8.40, and his hospitalization insurance deduction was $3.10. No unemployment tax had to be paid on this vacation pay. Prepare whatever journal entry or entries would be necessary to record Mr. Jones's vacation pay and any related costs.

10. The Pride Corporation manufactures a line of high-quality curtains for sale to jobbers and department stores. Production is on a job order basis, and no jobs were in process at the beginning of the week in which the following events took place:

(1) Ordered 3,000 yards of cloth at $0.30 a yard. (The company already had 2,000 yards of cloth in inventory at $0.30 a yard.)

(2) Received this order in satisfactory condition.

(3) Issued 3,100 yards of cloth to production (800 yards for job No. 163, 1,800 yards for job No. 164, and 500 yards for job No. 165).

(4) Distributed labor costs as follows: job No. 163, 150 hours; job No. 164, 350 hours; job No. 165, 70 hours; rework labor on job No. 163, 10 hours; and time spent waiting for materials, 20 hours—all by workers whose straight-time wage rate was $2.20 an hour. Supervision, 44 hours; and maintenance, 66 hours—all by workers whose straight-time wage rate was $3 an hour. Janitorial services, 35 hours; and stock clerks, 40 hours—at a straight-time wage rate of $1.60 an hour.

(5) Prepared labor payroll, as follows (overtime paid at time and a half):

Straight-Time Wage Rate	Regular Hours	Overtime Hours	Total Hours
$3.00 an hour.......	100	10	110
2.20 an hour.......	550	50	600
1.60 an hour.......	70	5	75

(6) Absorbed overhead at a rate of $2.50 per direct labor hour.

(7) Completed job No. 163, consisting of 190 pairs of first-quality curtains and 10 pairs of "seconds." Seconds are carried in inventory at $2 a pair.

(8) Completed job No. 164, consisting of 400 pairs of first-quality curtains.

(9) Collected scrap cuttings from production floor and sold them to a waste dealer for $20 cash.

Prepare journal entries to record each of the above events, using as many overhead accounts as you feel are necessary, and indicate what documents might arise in connection with each event. If no journal entry would be required, merely list the necessary document or documents. Justify your method of dealing with the problem raised by the completion of second-quality curtains in item (7) above.

11. The firm of Rundell Associates does a number of kinds of drafting, lettering, and commercial artwork for outside clients. A system of requisitions and time sheets is used to accumulate the costs of materials and personal services consumed on individual job orders.

   Although a few jobs are accepted on a flat fee basis, most jobs are priced to customers on a cost-plus-time basis. On these jobs, the customer's bill includes four elements:

   Costs of materials used;
   Personal service fees (at predetermined hourly rates, including markup over hourly cost);
   Overtime premiums paid for work on specific jobs;
   Miscellaneous out-of-pocket costs incurred on specific jobs.

   Materials costs on some jobs are substantial, and occasionally a customer will complain that he is being charged for too many spoiled materials. In general, however, materials costs amount to less than 10 percent of the gross amount of the customer invoice.

   Customers complain frequently about the size of the personal service fee, but this appears to be part of a bargaining strategy to impress on Rundell Associates the need to watch costs carefully on subsequent orders. Complaints about the overtime premiums are considerably stronger and often lead to downward revision of the invoices. During recent months these downward revisions have been large enough to cut the firm's net profit in half, and the managing partners are worried.

Indicate any changes that you would make in the company's cost accounting and billing procedures, giving reasons for your changes. If you wish to leave any or all of the present system unchanged, indicate briefly why you think no improvement is called for.

12. The Upget Company employs five men in its stamping department. All work is done on a job order basis. During the week of August 15, each man worked a full 40-hour week, with output as follows:

Name	Guaranteed Hourly Minimum	Units Produced
Brackett, S. J.	$1.50	1,840
Emery, P. L.	1.60	1,900
Evans, E. C.	1.50	1,960
Forest, T. A.	1.70	2,050
Simmons, F.	1.50	1,650

a) Compute the gross earnings of each worker and prepare a summary journal entry to record the week's wages, assuming that wages are paid on a piecework basis at $0.033 per unit produced, subject to the guaranteed hourly minimum.

b) Compute the gross earnings of each worker, assuming that a group incentive plan is in operation and that the standard output of the department is 7,200 units per week. Each member of the group receives the guaranteed hourly minimum if production is equal to or less than the standard output. The hourly rate for each worker is increased 1 percent for each 200 units per week in excess of standard production.

c) Would you charge the incentive bonus in (*b*) as part of the direct labor cost or as factory overhead? Why?

13. John Taft is paid a straight-time wage rate of $2 an hour. Excluding vacation periods and holidays, the factory normally operates 250 days a year. Seven of these days are Saturdays. The factory operates an eight-hour day, with occasional overtime. A worker in Mr. Taft's job classification will ordinarily work 50 hours of overtime in addition to the Saturday work. Overtime and Saturday work are paid at 150 percent of the straight-time wage rate.

In addition to direct wages for time spent on the job, the company is responsible for the following labor-related costs:

(1) A two-week paid vacation; this is provided to any employee who is employed throughout the year; vacation pay for other employees is in proportion to the period worked. Vacation pay is computed on the basis of a 40-hour week at straight-time pay. All employees take their vacations at the same time, during August, when the factory is closed for two weeks.

(2) Eight paid holidays a year, at straight-time wage rates; these holidays are provided to employees on the payroll at the time of each holiday. The factory does not operate on holidays.

(3) A maximum of five days' sick leave during a year; the average employee takes three days' sick leave during a year. Employees who are not employed for a full year are eligible for sick leave in proportion to their number of weeks on the payroll.

(4) The portion of payroll taxes (F.I.C.A., etc.) to be paid by the employer is 8 percent of the first $6,600 of each employee's gross pay.

(5) Private pension contributions equal to 3 percent of gross pay, including overtime and Saturday work premium, holiday pay, vacation pay, and sick pay.

(6) An employee recreation program, which averages $10 per employee per year; most of this goes to pay for equipment and to pay the salaries of coaches and athletic instructors.

(7) A cafeteria subsidy; the prices of meals in the factory cafeteria are adequate to cover the cost of the food served and to pay the wages of cafeteria personnel. The company supplies space and equipment and pays the salaries of a dietitian and a bookkeeper, at a combined cost which averages $15 per employee per year.

a) Compute the number of hours Mr. Taft would be expected to work during a normal year.

b) Compute a "labor charging rate" for Mr. Taft, based on the working hours calculated in (*a*) and including any of the labor-related costs you feel should be included.

c) Give your reasons for including or excluding each item.

14. Department X performs a variety of machining operations, using eight machines of various capabilities and work speeds. The machines are generally interchangeable, but variations from machine to machine in setup and operating time are substantial.

The foreman of department X is responsible for assigning specific jobs to specific machines, for the control of departmental costs, for maintaining product quality, and for meeting delivery schedules. Scheduled completion dates for each department are ordinarily set by the production scheduling department after consultation with the department foreman. To maintain quality standards, department X's output is subjected to either sampling or 100 percent inspection and defective units are returned immediately for rectification ("rework").

Department X employs six men regularly and operates a single shift. Four of the six are paid on piece rates, subject to an hourly minimum rate; the other two are paid a straight hourly wage. All workers are paid a premium for overtime work (in excess of 40 hours a week) of 50 percent of the minimum or base hourly rate. The amount of this premium is not affected in any way by the amount of piecework earnings.

Piece rate earnings for a trained worker are expected to average 125 percent of the minimum hourly rate, and piece rate workers are also paid 125 percent of the minimum hourly rate when they are required to work on orders for which no piece rates have been established ("nonrated work"), when they are idle for 15 consecutive minutes or longer because work is temporarily unavailable, or when they are assigned to maintenance, cleanup, or other auxiliary tasks. No compensation is paid for rework labor time.

Five categories of departmental labor time are recognized in the accounts:

	Normal Weekly Hours
Piece-rated production....................	150
Nonrated production....................	16
Work flow and cleanup..................	64
Setup.................................	20
Waiting..............................	10
Total............................	260

All setup labor is performed by one of the hourly paid workers, T. F. Jones, and no overtime premium is budgeted for this operation. Mr. Jones devotes the rest of his time to routine maintenance, materials handling, and so forth (described by the company as "work flow and cleanup labor"), along with the other hourly paid worker, R. J. Selden. No overtime hours are budgeted for either of these workers.

Piece rates are established on the basis of the machines with the shortest operating cycle that can be adapted to the particular product. When a piece rate worker is forced to use slower machines, he is given a premium in addition to the regular piece rate, based on the amount necessary to equalize earnings per hour under normal conditions. This "substitute equipment premium" is expected to average 2 percent of the regular piece rate earnings during a normal month.

The daily hourly minimum for piece rate production is computed only on the hours spent on piecework, including rework labor hours—in other words, total hours minus hours spent on setup, waiting time, and all other kinds of nonrated work except rework time. The total, called *net piecework hours,* is multiplied by the man's hourly base rate to find the guaranteed minimum piecework earnings. If this is more than the man's actual piece-work earnings, including premiums for use of nonpreferred equipment, he is paid the guaranteed minimum. The make-good differential is expected to average 2 percent of regular piecework earnings plus substitute equipment premiums.

Employer payroll taxes average 8 percent of gross pay, vacation and holiday pay approximate 4 percent, and company pension contributions amount to 5 percent. Health insurance premiums paid by the company total 10 cents an hour up to 40 hours per man per week. Workmen's compensation insurance premiums amount to 1 percent of gross payrolls other than the overtime premium portion of the payrolls. Overtime premiums are expected to average 10 percent of the minimum hourly pay rates.

The following data relate to the operation of department X for the week ending January 28:

Worker	Hourly Base Rate	Total Actual Hours	Nonrated Production Hours	Work Flow and Clean-Up Hours	Setup Hours	Waiting Time Hours	Regular Piecework Earnings	Substitute Equipment Premium
Adams, P...	$2.00	44	5	..	..	..	$ 78	$20
Jones, T. F..	4.00	40	..	8	30	2	...	..
Marron, J. N.	2.00	46	..	2	..	1	125	..
Peters, W. G.	2.00	42	14	..	..	6	48	5
Selden, R. J.	2.00	32	..	32	..	..	...	..
Terrill, B. E.	2.00	40	5	..	..	..	66	..
Total...		244	24	42	30	9	$317	$25

a) Compute the total gross payroll for the week of January 28, exclusive of employer payroll taxes and other fringe benefit costs.

b) Prepare a summary classification of labor costs to be shown in the weekly report to the department foreman. Indicate how much you would show as direct labor and how much in each of the indirect labor categories you select. Also indicate how, if at all, you would reflect payroll taxes and other payroll related costs in the departmental cost report. Be prepared to justify your choices.

15. Bob Cullen, industrial relations director of the Campion Company, asks the accounting department for a statement of labor costs for use in wage negotiations. "The statements you buzzards give me put labor costs in many different places. I'd like to see them all in one spot, so we can see just how much labor is costing us."

Your supervisor suggests the following pattern for a statement to fill Mr. Cullen's request.

```
Basic labor cost:
    Direct labor.............................      $————
    Indirect labor..........................      ————
        Total labor cost....................                $————
Labor-related costs:
    Related to payroll dollars:
        Employee welfare and security........$————
        Premium payments for time worked.... ————
        Payments for time not worked........ ————
        Company policy payments............. ————
            Total...........................      $————
    Related to number of employees:
        Company policy payments.............$————
        Employment administration.......... ————
            Total...........................      $————
                Total labor-related costs...........        $————
Total Labor and Labor-Related Costs.......                  $————
```

Mr. Cullen has been receiving the income statement and the cost of goods manufactured statement.

THE CAMPION COMPANY
STATEMENT OF COST OF GOODS MANUFACTURED
For the Year Ending December 31, 1966

Cost of manufacturing:		
Direct materials...		$3,100,000
Direct labor...		2,205,000
Overhead absorbed (100% of direct labor cost)..............		2,205,000
		$7,510,000
Less increase in inventory:		
Work in process, January 1..............................	$600,000	
Work in process, January 31.............................	810,000	210,000
Cost of Goods Manufactured.............................		$7,300,000

THE CAMPION COMPANY

INCOME STATEMENT

For the Year Ending December 31, 1966

Sales......................................		$12,000,000
Cost of goods sold:		
Cost of goods manufactured...................	$7,300,000	
Less increase in inventory:		
Finished goods, January 31................$1,000,000		
Finished goods, January 1................. 900,000	100,000	
	$7,200,000	
Plus underabsorbed overhead..................	26,900	7,226,900
Gross margin................................		$ 4,773,100
Selling and administrative expenses..............		3,580,000
Net Income.................................		$ 1,193,100

THE CAMPION COMPANY

STATEMENT OF OVERHEAD INCURRED AND APPLIED

For the Year Ending December 31, 1966

Overhead incurred:	
Indirect materials...$	400,000
Indirect labor...	315,000
F.I.C.A. taxes (only on factory payroll)..............................	64,600
Unemployment compensation taxes....................................	21,000
Workmen's compensation insurance premiums.........................	72,000
Group life insurance premiums (paid by company)......................	10,500
Overtime premiums..	60,000
Vacation pay..	176,000
Cost of living adjustment..	124,800
Superintendence (not included in factory payroll)......................	500,000
Heat, light, and power...	100,000
Depreciation of building, machinery, and equipment.....................	150,000
Christmas bonus...	17,500
Overtime meal reimbursement...	52,500
Funded pension and annuity payments.................................	168,000
Total overhead incurred...$2,231,900	
Overhead absorbed..	2,205,000
Overhead Underabsorbed (Closed to Cost of Goods Sold)...................$	26,900

The schedule of selling and administrative expenses for 1966 included, among others, the following:

Company contributions to employee savings plan (for factory employees).....$	57,616
Suggestion system payments (all made to factory employees)................	5,000
Factory dispensary and plant doctor costs................................	19,000
Safety campaigns and posters..	2,000
Employee magazine...	25,000
Tuition or other allowances to employees attending trade schools, universities,	
or taking special courses outside the plant (all factory employees)..........	1,500
Social, athletic, and other recreational costs (all factory employees).........	10,000
Employment office, personnel and industrial relations department costs........	200,000

Prepare the statement requested by Mr. Cullen, using the form suggested by your supervisor.

16. A factory consists of several departments, three of which are used in the manufacture of product X. Department A is operating a single shift of 40 hours a week with a crew of 15 men any one of whom can do any of the work normally done in this department. Each of these 15 men is now working about six hours of overtime each week. Overtime in department A is shared equally by these men—that is, if only 30 hours of overtime work is available each week, each man will ordinarily work two overtime hours a week. Second-shift operations are not feasible in this department because additional workers with the requisite skills are not available locally. The basic wage rate in department A is $2.50 an hour.

Department B is on two-shift operation, with 40 hours a week in each shift and no overtime. Workers in the first shift are paid $3 an hour; second-shift men earn $3.30 an hour. The first shift has three men for every two men on the second shift, and this ratio is maintained continuously—that is, if department B's scheduled rate of output is increased or decreased, men are added to or subtracted from each shift in proportion to current employment. Adequate numbers of workers are available to expand employment in this department by as much as 20 percent at the current wage rates.

Department C is operating a single shift, 40 hours a week. It has two groups of employees: 10 first-grade men at $4 an hour; and five second-grade men at $3.50 an hour. Each first-grade man is now working five hours of overtime each week; second-grade men do not work overtime. First-grade men cannot do the work of second-grade men, and second-grade men cannot do the work of first-grade men. Additional first-grade men cannot be hired, but the existing force of first-grade men will work as much as 10 hours of overtime each week if necessary to meet production schedules. Additional second-grade men can be hired locally on a short-term basis at $3.50 an hour as the need arises.

Overtime hours in each department are paid at a wage rate equal to 150 percent of the regular-time wage rate. (All wage rates given above are regular time rates.) If work is not available, the company's practice is to put its employees on a short workweek.

The company is now producing product X at the rate of 100 units a week. A unit of product X requires two labor hours in department A, four labor hours in department B, and three first-grade and one second-grade labor hours in department C.

a) Compute the labor cost per unit that should be used in computing the profitability of product X. Explain the reasoning you followed in deriving this figure.

b) A new customer for product X has just asked the company if it can supply him with 10 units of this product each week. What labor cost per unit should be used in deciding whether to undertake to meet this customer's requirements?

Chapter 7

MEASURING FACTORY UNIT COST: THE VARIABLE COSTING CONCEPT

THE UNIT COST CALCULATIONS in Chapters 4 and 5 were based on the *full costing* or *absorption costing* concept. In recent years, more and more companies have been turning to an alternative costing concept known variously as *direct costing, marginal costing,* and *variable costing.* The purpose of this chapter is to examine this concept to see what it is, what advantages it might have over the older and more popular absorption concept, and what problems it gives rise to.

THE NATURE OF VARIABLE COSTING

Variable costing is a device to permit the segregation of the variable component of manufacturing costs in product records and subsequently in internal profit performance reports. *Under variable costing, unit cost is defined as the average variable cost of manufacturing the product.* Fixed manufacturing costs are ordinarily excluded from product cost completely, although in some dual systems both variable cost and full cost are computed.

Impetus for Variable Costing

Many types of managerial decisions require comparisons of the profitability of different methods of utilizing existing capacity. For this purpose, the analyst needs estimates of short-run variable costs. Under absorption costing, the only way to get the data upon which to base such estimates is to go back to the data from which unit costs were prepared and try to extract the fixed elements. Variable costing is the outgrowth of the search for a more efficient way of providing these estimates.

Application to Process Costing

One way of applying the variable costing concept to process production is to divide each production center's cost elements into two groups—fixed and variable—and compute unit cost only for the variable elements. This is probably the most common method of application.

To illustrate, Exhibit 7–1 shows the calculation of unit cost in the

Exhibit 7–1

DEPARTMENTAL COST REPORT: VARIABLE COSTING BASIS

DEPT. Mixing and Grinding

PRODUCTION   201,000 Bbls.   MONTH OF November

	This Month		Prior Period Unit Cost	
	Total Cost	Unit Cost	Last Month	Last Year
Variable costs:				
Direct labor..................	$ 6,541	$0.0327	$0.0329	$0.0304
Indirect labor*..............	303	0.0015	0.0024	0.0018
Payroll charges..............	1,298	0.0065	0.0066	0.0056
Fuel and water..............	2,527	0.0126	0.0119	0.0115
Light and power............	9,806	0.0490	0.0486	0.0487
Grinding supplies............	953	0.0048	0.0049	0.0046
Dust collector...............	427	0.0021	0.0011	0.0015
Total variable..............	$21,855	$0.109	$0.108	$0.104
Fixed costs:				
Supervision...................	$ 712			
Maintenance labor............	2,299			
Maintenance materials........	1,956			
Total fixed.................	$ 4,967			

* All labor is traceable to the department and thus is direct labor, as that term has been defined here. This company uses the term to identify those classes of work performed directly in production, while indirect labor is identified as the costs of miscellaneous departmental chores such as cleaning and messenger work.

mixing and grinding department of a cement mill. Eight cost elements are classified as variable, and an average unit cost is computed for each element each month. All of these costs are completely traceable to the department in this particular case. No service department costs are allocated to the mixing and grinding department, and the fixed costs traceable to the department are not averaged over the units produced.

The unit costs in Exhibit 7–1 are used as a measure of departmental cost performance for the month, and for this purpose production is measured in terms of *departmental* output, the number of barrels of mix completed and transferred to the next department. For product costing, however, costs in this particular factory are averaged over the number of barrels of finished products (cement) produced by the *factory* during the month. This computation is illustrated in Exhibit 7–2. The costs of

Exhibit 7–2

PRODUCT COST SUMMARY: VARIABLE COSTING BASIS

PRODUCT Portland Cement				
PRODUCTION 198,000 Bbls.			MONTH OF November	
	This Month		Prior Period Unit Cost	
	Total Cost	Unit Cost	Last Month	Last Year
Purchased materials:				
Gypsum......................	$ 17,085	$0.086	$0.086	$0.085
Additives....................	3,276	0.017	0.017	0.016
Total materials...............	$ 20,361	$0.103	$0.103	$0.101
Departmental costs:				
Limestone/marble...............	6,951	0.035	0.034	0.030
Cement rock...................	15,266	0.077	0.079	0.076
Shale.........................	2,486	0.013	0.014	0.015
Mixing and grinding...........	**21,855**	**0.109**	**0.108**	**0.104**
Burning.......................	71,229	0.360	0.352	0.342
Finish grinding................	20,098	0.102	0.104	0.099
Total Product Cost.................	$158,246	$0.799	$0.794	$0.767

each department are shown as departmental totals only, and the figures given for the mixing and grinding department (boldface type) are the column totals from Exhibit 7–1.

Notice that in this case the costs of semiprocessed product are not transferred from department to department in parallel with the flow of goods. To facilitate costing, it is assumed that changes in departmental work in process are negligible, so that a single measure of output can be used to compute the unit cost in all departments. This cuts down on the bookkeeping costs and also reduces the chance of clerical error in recording interdepartmental transfers.

Handling Semivariable Costs

The main defect with the method just described is that it doesn't provide for semivariable costs. Maintenance costs, for example, may be subject to minimum requirements, no matter what the level of operating volume, plus increments in response to higher and higher rates of capacity utilization. It may be impossible, however, to determine how much of a given maintenance job is the fixed part and how much is the variable.

In these circumstances, the only approach is to use a predetermined burden rate, at least for those components of cost that cannot reasonably be assumed to be completely and proportionately variable. It might be a single rate for all semivariable elements or a series of rates, one for each semivariable element. Because the purpose of the predetermined rate is to determine average variable cost for product-oriented decisions, subdivision of the rate is not essential except insofar as it facilitates review and revision of the rates when conditions change.

Exhibit 7–3 illustrates how this change might affect unit costing in

Exhibit 7–3

VARIABLE UNIT COST REPORT USING PREDETERMINED RATES FOR SEMIVARIABLE COST ELEMENTS

DEPT. Mixing and Grinding PRODUCTION 201,000 Bbls.			MONTH OF November	
	This Month		Prior Period Unit Cost	
	Total Cost	Unit Cost	Last Month	Last Year
Variable costs:				
Direct labor.....................	$ 6,541	$0.0327	$0.0329	$0.0304
Indirect labor...................	303	0.0015	0.0024	0.0018
Payroll charges..................	1,298	0.0065	0.0066	0.0056
Fuel and water..................	2,527	0.0126	0.0119	0.0115
Grinding supplies................	953	0.0048	0.0049	0.0046
Dust collector...................	427	0.0021	0.0011	0.0015
Total variable..................	$12,049	$0.060	$0.059	$0.055
Semivariable costs:				
Light and power................	$ 9,806	$0.042*		
Maintenance labor...............	2,299	0.005*		
Maintenance materials...........	1,956	0.009*		
Total semivariable.............	$14,061	$0.056*		
Total product cost...............	xxx	$0.116		
Fixed costs:				
Supervision.....................	$ 712			

* Predetermined rates for variable component only.

the cement mill's mixing and grinding department. One item previously classified as variable has now been reclassified as semivariable on the grounds that it includes a fixed cost component, while two items not previously included in product cost have been moved from the fixed to the semivariable category. For each element, actual costs for the month are shown for the information of the department head, but the unit cost figures shown in this section of the exhibit are predetermined and represent the variable component only. *They do not reflect the current month's cost experience in any way.*

The unit cost figure of $0.116 a barrel is a hybrid: partly predetermined and partly based on cost performance for the month. The notion of predetermining a portion of unit cost is already familiar from the discussion of job order costing, and the possibility of going still farther and predetermining unit cost in its entirety will be discussed later in the chapters on standard costing.

Application to Job Order Costing

Job order costing differs from process costing in that it is not possible under job order costing to identify departmental cost totals with individual products. Job order output is so heterogeneous that even under variable costing a burden rate must be used to derive product cost. This burden rate could be based on the actual overhead costs charged to a department each month, but the virtually universal practice is to use a predetermined rate.

Labor and materials accounting is not affected by the choice between variable costing and full costing. Direct labor and direct materials costs are assumed to be fully variable with volume and therefore are assigned to product units in the manner described in Chapter 4. Only the treatment of overhead is different.

In a sense, this makes it easier to develop a meaningful variable costing system. Since burden rates must be set anyway, there need be no temptation to define every cost element as either wholly fixed or wholly variable. Variability can be recognized wherever it exists.

For example, suppose that departmental volume is measured in machine hours and departmental overhead costs are expected to vary as follows:

	Fixed per Month	Variable per Machine-Hour
Supervision............................	$1,400	....
Indirect labor...........................	.....	$0.10
Indirect materials.......................	.....	0.05
Maintenance............................	100	0.08
Power..................................	......	0.02
Total...........................	$1,500	$0.25

Maintenance costs are semivariable and are expected to average $100 a month plus eight cents for each machine-hour. The variable costing burden rate would include the eight cents but not the $100. A job order which required 10 machine-hours in this department would thus be charged $2.50 (10 hours × $0.25) for variable overhead. No charge would be made for any portion of the $1,500 in fixed cost.

Terminology: Variable Costing versus Direct Costing

Product costing systems of the kind just described are generally referred to as *direct costing* systems, but this term is misleading. As it is used in other contexts, the word "direct" implies a high degree of *traceability* of the cost to specific costing units. Thus direct labor is labor cost that is traceable to specific job orders or process flows; direct departmental charges are those that can be identified specifically with a given department. Much overhead that is variable in response to changes in production volume, however, is not specifically traceable to individual products or even to specific production departments. For this reason we prefer to use the term *variable costing* in describing cost absorption systems that recognize the distinction between fixed and variable costs.

FULL COSTING VERSUS VARIABLE COSTING

While there are those who maintain that cost estimates for short-run decisions should reflect the full costing concept, most of the opposition to variable costing is focused on the thesis that it fails to provide management with guidance for decisions that have a longer time horizon, particularly product pricing, marketing policy, and capacity expansion or contraction problems. The question is whether full cost provides a better measure of incremental cost for these purposes than average variable cost.

Long-Run Cost Behavior

The assumption implicit in the use of full cost figures for estimating incremental costs is that given a large enough change in volume and enough time to adjust to the new situation, total cost will vary in direct proportion to changes in operating volumes and average cost will remain constant.

Two factors stand in the way of this happy solution. The first of these is cost *indivisibility,* stemming from the availability of certain resources in large aggregates only. In one company's maintenance shop, for example, a reduction of 90 percent in the work load would not have permitted the disposal of a single piece of equipment—each piece had to be available to do its own specialized work whenever an emergency arose. The cost of keeping these machines in working order was thus an indivisible cost.

Indivisibilities lead to lower average costs for higher rates of utilization of the indivisible elements and incremental costs that are less than average costs—the more highly indivisible the fixed cost, the farther the increment will be from the average.

The second factor that leads incremental cost away from average cost is that changes in capacity change not only the total but the structure of the fixed costs. Average fixed costs will decline as capacity increases, at least up to a point, not only because the indivisible cost elements are spread over larger and larger volumes but also because larger volumes permit the company to change the technology being employed. Adding machines give way to bookkeeping machines and bookkeeping machines to computers.

Economists have speculated for many decades on the effect on average cost of changes in capacity. They have assumed that this average cost will decrease as capacity increases up to some point, after which it will tend to increase. Some empirical studies have tended to support this assumption; none has disproved it.[1] If the assumption is valid, then, the *long-run marginal cost*—the change in total cost resulting from a change in the scale of operations—is not constant.

Full cost, in other words, is useful for decision making only if it approximates long-run marginal cost, and most evidence seems to indicate that the long-run cost curve is not sufficiently linear to justify this assumption.

The Argument for Variable Costing

How, then, is average variable cost any better? It will almost certainly understate long-run marginal cost and may in some cases be farther from this figure than full cost. The argument for variable costing rests basically on two premises: first, that it is more pertinent to short-term, capacity-utilizing decisions; and second, that it serves as a clearer, less ambiguous base on which to build estimates of incremental costs when fixed costs are likely to change. In other words, it makes the simplifying assumption that average variable cost is an acceptable approximation to incremental variable cost, but it forces the analyst to make specific, explicit assumptions in each case about the impact of the decision on fixed costs.

Full cost has another weakness which may be even more fundamental than the one discussed above. Full unit cost figures cannot be derived except on the basis of a relatively arbitrarily selected measure of normal volume. Furthermore, in multiproduct factories, the methods used to

---

[1] Two summaries of empirical studies in this area are to be found in P. J. D. Wiles, *Price, Cost, and Output* (Oxford: Basil Blackwell & Mott, Ltd., 1956), chap. xii, Appendixes A and B; and J. Johnston, *Statistical Cost Analysis* (New York: McGraw-Hill Book Co., Inc., 1960), chap. v.

divide fixed costs among the various products ordinarily must be quite arbitrary. Thus even if the firm is operating in a volume range in which long-run marginal cost is approximately constant, full cost cannot be assumed to be equal to long-run marginal cost. We shall return in the next chapter to an examination of some of the measurement difficulties which impair the usefulness of full cost data.

Variable Costing and Internal Profit Statements

Variable costing has another advantage over full costing in that it facilitates the preparation of internal profit budgets and reports in a format that will focus management's attention on profit variability. Full discussion of these budgets and reports must be deferred to later chapters, but a few words may be useful here.

The difference between net revenues and total variable costs for any segment of the business—known by some term such as *variable profit, marginal income,* or *P/V income*—rises as sales increase and falls as sales decrease, assuming constant prices and manufacturing methods. The response of profit to volume changes, other things being equal, is thus indicated much more clearly than in a statement based on full costing, in which terms such as "reduction in underabsorbed overhead" are likely to appear.

Along similar lines, it can be argued that variable costing not only does not ignore fixed cost but in fact emphasizes it. Profit budgets show the aggregate amount of fixed cost that must be covered, which serves not only to dramatize the relative significance of fixed costs but also to point out the effects of decisions which establish fixed costs.

For example, suppose that product X has a high variable profit per unit, as shown in the following table:

	Amount	% of Sales
Sales.....................................	$100,000	100%
Variable expenses:		
Manufacturing........................	$ 40,000	
Selling.............................	5,000	
Total Variable Expenses.............	$ 45,000	45
Variable profit...........................	$ 55,000	55%
Traceable fixed costs.....................	10,000	10
Profit Contribution.......................	$ 45,000	45%

A decision to expand the amount of selling effort being devoted to this product is likely to entail increases in fixed costs. This effect on fixed costs can be shown directly, without confusion:

	Present Effort	Expanded Effort	Change
Sales......................	$100,000	$130,000	+$30,000
Variable expenses...........	45,000	58,500	+ 13,500
Variable profit..............	$ 55,000	$ 71,500	+$16,500
Traceable fixed costs.........	10,000	20,000	+ 10,000
Profit Contribution..........	$ 45,000	$ 51,500	+$ 6,500

In absorption costing, in contrast, this increment would be derived by first obtaining net product margin and then adjusting this for differences in under- or overabsorption of fixed costs. Absorption costing works with full cost averages, and the derivation of increments from such data can be extremely difficult.

Handling Step Functions

Cost functions are seldom as simple as the previous illustrations have implied, although often we don't know enough about them to specify more complex relationships with any confidence.

Suppose, however, that a department's overhead costs are expected to vary as shown in the upper portion of Exhibit 7–4. This is a form of *step function* in which some elements of cost vary discontinuously with volume, going up in irregular steps. Most authorities would agree that these steps should be reflected in the variable cost burden rate, and this is shown as a dashed line in the exhibit. The slope of this line represents the average rate of variability within the normal limits of volume variation—in other words, the variable overhead cost burden rate. In this case the burden rate is 40 cents a machine-hour.

The situation represented in the lower half of Exhibit 7–4 is not as clear-cut. For fairly large ranges of volume variation, the rate of cost variability is represented by the slope of line *A*. If the entire volume span from zero to capacity is included, however, the "leveled cost" line would be the one labeled *B* and the rate of cost variability would be twice as high, 20 cents a machine-hour instead of 10 cents.

Most advocates of variable costing would probably use line *A* in a case of this sort, on the grounds that average variable cost figures are

Exhibit 7–4

STEP FUNCTIONS IN OVERHEAD COSTS

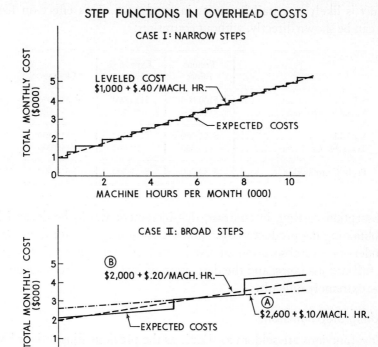

typically applied to decisions encompassing fairly small increments in operating volume, and that averaging the step functions would cloud the meaning of unit cost when the steps are this large.

PITFALLS IN VARIABLE COSTING

Despite its advantages, the application of the variable costing principle is not without pitfalls. Three of these deserve mention:

1. To reduce bookkeeping costs, variable unit cost may be measured in ways that understate short-term cost variability.
2. Variable unit costs may be used as measures of incremental costs at inappropriate times.
3. Variable unit cost figures may provide management with poor guidance for marketing policy decisions.

Understated Cost Variability

One danger in variable costing is that product cost will be defined in such a way as to understate true cost variability. The behavior of overhead cost is exceedingly complex, and there is a strong temptation to follow the line of least resistance and include in product cost only those costs that are obviously and fully variable. In some cases, variable overhead has been excluded completely from product cost. This simplifies the bookkeeping at the cost of producing misleading variable profit data.

To illustrate, assume that two products have the following margins over direct labor and materials costs:

	Product A	Product B
Selling price............................	$4.50	$3.00
Standard prime cost......................	2.00	1.20
Margin..................................	$2.50	$1.80

This comparison would lead to the conclusion that product A is more profitable than product B, at least on a unit basis. But suppose that product B requires very little processing and therefore has very low variable factory overhead per unit, whereas product A is a relatively complex product, requiring substantial manufacturing effort (indicated by a high ratio of labor to materials cost). The variable overhead cost on product B might be only $0.05 per unit, as opposed to $1 for product A. The correct variable profit comparison would thus show:

	Product A	Product B
Selling price............................	$4.50	$3.00
Variable costs:		
Labor and materials...................	$2.00	$1.20
Variable overhead.....................	1.00	0.05
Variable profit...........................	$1.50	$1.75

Thus it can be seen that the relative incremental profitability of the two products is just the reverse of that indicated by the margins over prime costs.

This is not really an argument against the variable costing principle. Rather, it points up a danger that stems from misapplication of the concept which must be recognized and guarded against.

Variable Cost as a Substitute for Incremental Cost

Perhaps a more serious danger is that variable cost will be assigned a broader meaning than it deserves. That is, it is possible that average variable cost will be *assumed* to be equal to incremental cost without further investigation. As we have pointed out earlier, some decisions call for estimates of increments in fixed costs, while others may even require some of the variable costs to be regarded as sunk.

This again is more an indictment of the user than of the system. An accountant who routinely churns out average variable cost figures no matter what problem is at hand is no better than his brother who does the same with full cost or prime cost figures.

Inapplicability of Short-Run Costs

Not all of the objections to variable costing are based on the misapplication of the direct costing principle or on the inadequacy of any historical statements to provide guides for current decision making. The most serious substantive objection is that it yields product cost figures that provide no basis for long-range pricing policy. This argument stems from the proposition that in the long run the price of every product must cover not only its variable costs but also a "fair share" of the fixed costs of the company and leave enough margin to provide an adequate profit on capital investment. According to this school of thought, assignment of fixed cost to products is necessary to reflect the long-run marginal cost associated with each product.

Unfortunately, the issue is not this simple. As we pointed out in the opening pages of this chapter, long-run marginal cost is unlikely to be equal either to current average full cost or to average variable cost. The relevance of cost data to product pricing and marketing policy decisions is too important a question to pass off with a few sentences here, and anything we say now will merely anticipate the discussion in Chapters 21–23. A possible compromise is worth mentioning here, however, and that is to supplement the variable cost figures with estimates of what might be called *attributable cost*.

Attributable cost includes not only the short-run variable costs but also those fixed costs that are significantly divisible, in other words those that rise in steps in the manner illustrated in the lower half of Exhibit 7–4.[2] For example, assume that a department with a normal operating volume of 10,000 machine-hours has the following budgeted costs at normal volume:

---

[2] A somewhat different definition is embodied in an earlier article on this subject. See Gordon Shillinglaw, "The Concept of Attributable Cost," *Journal of Accounting Research*, Spring, 1963, pp. 73–85.

	Total Cost per Month	Normal Cost per Hour
Variable costs..........................	$3,000	$0.30
Divisible fixed costs....................	2,000	0.20
Indivisible fixed costs..................	1,000	0.10

A full cost burden rate would be 60 cents a machine-hour, while a rate based on attributable cost would be 50 cents and a rate for the variable costs would be only 30 cents.

Attributable cost is not necessarily a good measure of long-run marginal cost, but it is likely to be closer to measuring the cost impact of certain classes of decisions than either full cost or average variable cost. For example, the quality control staff may be entirely salaried, and the program's cost may be regarded as entirely fixed, but a significant change in production volume will almost unquestionably lead to a change in total quality control costs as the size of the inspection force is increased or decreased.

Once again, attributable cost should not be regarded as an all-purpose measure of incremental cost. If the decision is important enough to warrant a full-scale investigation of cost effects, the assumption that divisible fixed costs will vary roughly in proportion to volume needs to be questioned. For other decisions, however, it can be used as an approximation that is accurate enough in the circumstances.

VARIABLE COSTING AND EXTERNAL REPORTING

The objective of variable costing is to provide product unit costs for use by management. It was not designed to provide data for public financial reporting and in fact has been specifically rejected for this purpose by the bulk of the accounting profession. The following statement of a committee of the American Accounting Association is representative: ". . . the cost of a manufactured product is the sum of the acquisition costs reasonably traceable to that product and should include both direct and indirect factors. *The omission of any element of manufacturing cost is not acceptable.*"[3] Variable costing for public financial reporting does have its supporters, however, and this section will be devoted to examining the implications of this possibility.

---

[3] Committee on Accounting Concepts and Standards, "Accounting and Reporting Standards for Corporate Financial Statements: 1957 Revision," *The Accounting Review,* Vol. XXXII (October, 1957), p. 539 (italics added). Two members of the committee dissented from this portion of the statement.

Application to Income Measurement

Product costs are defined as those assigned to products; period costs are those that are expensed as they are incurred. If the variable costing concept is reflected in corporate financial statements, only variable factory costs are charged to balance sheet accounts; all fixed costs are period costs, treated as expenses of the accounting period in which cost expiration is recognized, and are thus taken directly to the corporate income statement without passing through product inventory accounts.

Effects on Reported Income

Under certain conditions, variable costing and absorption costing will produce different figures for reported income. To illustrate, let us assume that a company manufactures only one product. Normal production volume is 50,000 units a year, at which volume fixed costs average 25 cents a unit. For the year 19x1, both sales and production volumes were expected to be at the normal levels, and budgeted gross margin was as follows:

	Total	Per Unit
Sales (50,000 units).....................	$60,000	$1.20
Cost of goods sold:		
Variable costs.......................	$37,500	$0.75
Fixed costs.........................	12,500	0.25
Total cost of goods sold............	$50,000	$1.00
Gross Margin......................	$10,000	$0.20

If sales, production, and costs are at the planned levels, gross margin will be the same whether absorption costing or variable costing is used. If production exceeds sales, however, absorption costing will inventory some of the fixed cost that variable costing would charge off as an expense. For example, if production for 19x1 was 55,000 units, a total of $13,750 would be charged to products (25 cents $\times$ 55,000 units). If actual fixed costs were as budgeted, fixed costs would be overabsorbed by $1,250 under absorption costing:

```
Absorbed fixed costs...........................................$13,750
Actual fixed costs.............................................  12,500
    Under or (Over) Absorbed .....  ...........................$(1,250)
```

Alternative methods of treating this overabsorbed balance in corporate financial reporting will not be discussed until Chapter 18. In this series of illustrations all such balances will be charged or credited to the income statement for the period in which they arise. Thus in this case, assuming a sales volume of 47,000 units in 19x1 (8,000 units less than the number produced), absorption costing would produce the following income statement:

	Total	Per Unit
Sales (47,000 units).....................	$56,400	$1.20
Cost of goods sold:		
Variable costs.......................	$35,250	$0.75
Fixed costs.........................	11,750	0.25
Total cost of goods sold.............	$47,000	$1.00
Under or (over) absorbed overhead.......	(1,250)	xxx
Gross Margin.........................	$10,650	xxx
Ending Inventory (8,000 Units)..........	$ 8,000	$1.00

The reported gross margin would thus be $650 greater than the amount budgeted, even though sales volume fell short of the budget by 3,000 units and actual costs departed from expected totals in no other way. The explanation, of course, is that production was more than adequate to absorb the fixed costs. (The same effect would be observed if a postdetermined burden rate were used. Assuming a zero opening inventory, the fixed costs assigned to the units sold would be 47/55 of $12,500, or $10,680. In this case, reported gross margin would be reduced to $10,470, but it would still exceed the amount budgeted.)

An income statement prepared in accordance with the variable costing principle would give an entirely different impression:

	Total	Per Unit
Sales (47,000 units).....................	$56,400	$1.20
Cost of goods sold.....................	35,250	0.75
Variable profit........................	$21,150	$0.45
Fixed manufacturing expense............	12,500	xxx
Gross Margin.........................	$ 8,650	xxx
Ending Inventory (8,000 Units)..........	$ 6,000	$0.75

Here it can be seen that the decline in sales reduced company profits by $1,350 (3,000 units times $0.45 per unit).

Continuing this example to show what happens when sales exceed production, assume that production in 19x2 was cut back to 48,000 units, while sales went up to 52,000 units. The absorption costing statement would show:

	Total	Per Unit
Sales (52,000 units)...................	$62,400	$1.20
Cost of goods sold:		
Variable costs.......................	$39,000	$0.75
Fixed costs.........................	13,000	0.25
Total cost of goods sold.............	$52,000	$1.00
Under or (over) absorbed overhead.......	500	xxx
Gross Margin.........................	$ 9,900	xxx
Ending Inventory (4,000 Units)..........	$ 4,000	$1.00

Sales have gone up by 5,000 units, but reported profits have gone down from last year by $750, the result of charging this year's operations with *all* of this year's fixed cost plus a portion of last year's.

Again the variable costing statement presents a more sensitive reflection of the response of profit to sales:

	Total	Per Unit
Sales (52,000 units)....................	$62,400	$1.20
Cost of goods sold.....................	39,000	0.75
Variable profit........................	$23,400	$0.45
Fixed manufacturing expense...........	12,500	xxx
Gross Margin.........................	$10,900	xxx
Ending Inventory (4,000 Units)..........	$ 3,000	$0.75

This shows a $2,250 increase in profit as a result of the increased sales.

Taken over a long enough period of time, these profit differences will tend to cancel out, but in any one year the effects may be substantial.

Pros and Cons of Variable Costing Financial Statements

Two principal arguments have been advanced in support of using variable costing in public financial reporting. First, it is argued that sales volume is a better basis on which to judge the firm's economic success than production volume, and that under absorption costing reported income can be influenced significantly by the level of production, independent of current sales volume.[4] This gives management an opportunity to influence reported income as it sees fit by varying the rate of production so as to smooth or accentuate year-to-year variations in reported income.

The potential impact of such variations was demonstrated in the illustration in the preceding paragraphs. This potential varies inversely with the rate of inventory turnover and with the length of the reporting period. In other words, monthly financial statements are more vulnerable to this effect than annual statements; statements of companies with slow-moving inventories are more vulnerable than those of high-turnover firms.

The second argument of the variable costers is doctrinaire rather than pragmatic. It is that inventories ought to reflect only those costs that are optional in timing, the so-called "relevant costs."[5] In other words, the goods in inventory could have been produced by expenditures either in the period just ended or in future periods. By producing them now, the company has enabled itself to avoid future expenditures. The amount of the costs thus avoided is the measure of "relevant cost." Those fixed costs that will not be avoided in the future because production has already taken place in the past, it is argued, should not be treated as product costs and therefore should be taken directly to the income statement as expenses of the period.

This is not precisely an argument for variable costing in financial statements because some fixed costs could be avoided if no production at all took place and thus should be included in "relevant cost." Variable cost is ordinarily closer than full cost to the cost avoidability criterion, however, and the argument has been used to support variable costing for public financial reporting.

The arguments against variable costing for corporate financial reporting are also doctrinaire rather than pragmatic. The full costers argue that all factory costs are necessary to production and that there-

---

[4] In some cases production volume is more significant than the volume of products shipped, but in such cases an effort should be made to recognize revenue on a production basis. See Myron J. Gordon and Gordon Shillinglaw, *Accounting: A Management Approach* (3rd ed.; Homewood, Ill.: Richard D. Irwin, Inc., 1964), chap. v.

[5] For a discussion of these issues, see David Green, "A Moral to the Direct Costing Controversy?" *Journal of Business,* July, 1960, pp. 218–26; Charles T. Horngren and George H. Sorter, " 'Direct' Costing for External Reporting," *The Accounting Review,* January, 1961, pp. 84–93; and George J. Staubus, "Direct, Relevant, or Absorption Costing?" *The Accounting Review,* January, 1963, pp. 64–74.

fore every fixed cost should be reflected in one burden rate or another for inclusion in product cost.

The difficulty with this argument is that it cannot be tested. Because some overhead costs are truly common costs, not traceable to any one product, any allocation contains an inescapably arbitrary element. This means that it is impossible to cite any figure as an unequivocal measure of unit cost, and the variable cost/full cost argument can never be resolved on doctrinaire grounds. The real question is what difference it makes to the user of the financial statements, and no evidence on this point is yet available. For the moment, however, it is clear that a substantial shift in viewpoint will be necessary to achieve recognition of variable costing as a satisfactory basis for financial reporting.

Reconciling Internal and External Statements

Whenever variable costing is used for internal costing but external financial statements reflect the full costing principle, some means must be found for bridging the gap between the two.[6] Three possibilities suggest themselves. First, the variable costing figures could be memorandum figures only, in the form of unit cost estimates for each product; routine product cost accumulations and internal financial statements would be on a full cost basis. Inasmuch as at least that portion of full cost representing allocated costs and burden rates is based on estimates, the only apparent purpose of recording them in the books is to facilitate external financial reporting on a full cost basis. This objective would not seem to justify the clerical effort required to make large numbers of allocations and overhead applications, unless these are required to meet the audit requirements of cost-plus contracts.

A second possibility is to maintain a dual system, with product cost records showing both variable cost and full cost figures. This, too, is clerically expensive and can only be justified if the full cost figures have commensurate managerial significance, or if they are needed for cost-plus contracts.

The third alternative is to maintain product cost records on a variable cost basis only, with a supplemental account to reflect some average aggregate amount of fixed overhead appropriate to the level of inventory on hand. The balance in this account would be updated periodically by applying some formula to the variable costs in inventory as of the statement date. This can be done economically, and the resultant inventory cost totals will ordinarily serve the purposes of external financial

---

[6] For some evidence on this point, see *Current Application of Direct Costing, Research Report No. 37* (New York: National Association of Accountants, 1961).

reporting as well as carefully worked out, fully allocated unit cost figures.

It is worth repeating, however, that the most important distinction between variable costing and absorption costing is not that they lead to different measures of periodic income but that they provide different measures of the relative profitability of individual products, territories, or other segments of the company's business. This point was admirably expressed in a report issued by the National Association of Accountants: "Direct costing has sometimes been described as a plan for eliminating fixed costs from inventories. This description stresses an incidental feature rather than the prime objective of the plan, which is provision of information about cost-volume-profit relationships."[7]

VARIABLE COSTING PROCEDURES

When variable costing is applied as in the cement mill example described at the beginning of this chapter, the cost bookkeeping is simple. Costs are simply accumulated in departmental accounts and then averaged at month-end over the month's production. Suppose, however, that the company were to recognize the existence of semivariable costs, as in the final part of that example. This would require a slightly more complex procedure, and one that deserves some illustration.

Basic Procedure

The basic variable costing procedure comprises four steps. First, costs are accumulated departmentally. In the cement mill example, the journal entries for the mixing and grinding department for November can be summarized as follows:

Variable Cost Summary—Mixing and Grinding......................12,049
Semivariable Cost Summary—Mixing and Grinding.................14,061
Fixed Cost Summary—Mixing and Grinding........................ 712
    Wages Payable, etc...   26,822

(These summary accounts would of course be supplemented or replaced by detailed elemental accounts, but these are omitted here for ease of presentation.)

Second, if service department costs are expected to vary in response to changes in the level of production activity, the production departments could be charged for the variable component of service depart-

[7] "Direct Costing, Research Series No. 23," *N.A.C.A. Bulletin,* Vol. XXXIV (April, 1953), p. 1080.

ment cost. Our cement mill example contains no service cost variability, and so further discussion of this point can be deferred to Chapter 8.

Third, the costs assigned to departmental output are credited to departmental accounts. In the example, all of the wholly variable costs would be credited to the department, plus $0.056 per barrel for the variable portion of the semivariable cost elements. The month's production in this case was 198,000 barrels, and thus the total absorption of semivariable costs was $11,088 (198,000 × $0.056). The entry can be represented by the following:

```
Finished Goods Inventory........................................23,137
     Variable Cost Summary—Mixing and Grinding..................    12,049
     Semivariable Cost Summary—Mixing and Grinding.............    11,088
```

The existence of end-of-month departmental work in process balances would of course require a proportionate division of the costs between goods still in the department and goods transferred to other departments or finished goods.

Fourth, the unabsorbed balances in the semivariable cost summary and fixed cost summary accounts must be transferred to income statement accounts:

```
General Factory Expense.........................................2,724
     Semivariable Cost Summary—Mixing and Grinding..............     2,012
     Fixed Cost Summary—Mixing and Grinding......................       712
```

Discussion of the nature of the unabsorbed balances in the semivariable cost accounts will be deferred to Chapter 15, but for the moment it can be assumed that these represent the fixed component of the semivariable costs for the month of November.

End-of-Period Inventory Adjustment

In the illustration, no information was given on those fixed costs that were not traceable to the mixing and grinding department. Conditions in this company are ideally suited to a simple end-of-year adjustment for external financial reporting. At the end of the year, all of the factory costs that have not been assigned to products during the year are added together and averaged over the year's production. This average is multiplied by the number of barrels in the year-end inventory (the company prices its inventories on a FIFO basis), and an adjusting entry is made to record the difference between this amount and the year-beginning balance in the Fixed Costs in Inventory account.

For example, on January 1 the balance in the Fixed Costs in Inventory account was $27,000. The appropriate year-end balance, derived by the averaging method just described, was $19,000. Thus $8,000 had to be transferred from the balance sheet to an income statement account, as follows:

General Factory Expense...8,000
   Fixed Costs in Inventory.......................................   8,000

Most situations are more difficult than this one, with changes in work in process balances and a multiplicity of products, but simple end-of-year adjustments ordinarily can be worked out for public financial reporting on a similar averaging basis without elaborate bookkeeping procedures.

SUMMARY

Variable costing is an alternative to the full costing basis described in previous chapters for developing factory unit cost for manufactured products and services. It defines product cost as the average variable cost of producing the goods or services.

The main argument for variable costing is that it provides information that is more readily useful for decision-making purposes. Although incremental cost with respect to a particular decision may not be equal to either variable cost or full cost, it is easier to move from variable cost to incremental cost than to take full cost figures and convert them into estimates of incremental cost. Furthermore, estimates of short-run variability can be derived from a variable costing data bank, while under absorption costing special studies are required to obtain these data.

It can be argued, of course, that variable cost data may be just as misleading as full cost data because of the existence of increments in fixed costs. Temptations to oversimplify analysis are always present. The fact remains, however, that differences in profit contribution are more significant for analysis than differences in absorption costing totals. When product costs are obtained by absorption costing techniques, there is a strong temptation to deal with averages rather than with the margins that are required in incremental analysis. Because variable costing forces the analyst to deal explicitly with fixed costs, these items are much less likely to be overlooked.

Variable costing is not now generally acceptable for public financial reporting. Arguments have been advanced both for and against such acceptance, but they are largely irrelevant to the question of the desirability of variable costing. Variable costing must stand or fall on its managerial advantages. It is still possible to use variable costing for routine recording of transactions while at the same time using absorption costing for public financial statements. The adjustment of inventory figures for changes in the inventoried portion of fixed costs is a relatively simple task, and the need to report income on an absorption costing basis should not preclude the use of variable costing if management finds it more useful for internal purposes.

DISCUSSION QUESTIONS

1. What is the purpose of variable costing?
2. How does variable costing differ from full costing?
3. Is the usefulness of variable costing impaired by nonlinearities in the cost structure?
4. The term "direct costing" is often used to describe unit costing systems of the type described in this chapter. The controller of one company, however, has described his company's costing system as a "direct costing system, but not a variable costing system." What did he mean by this statement?
5. Comment briefly on the following statement: "We believe in absorption costing because each unit of each product must bear its fair share of overhead."
6. Would you expect reported profit to fluctuate more widely under variable costing or under absorption costing? Explain.
7. "Direct costing produces income statements that are a more accurate reflection of the true profit fluctuations than the income statements produced by absorption costing." State briefly why you either agree or disagree with this statement.
8. Does variable costing bring the costs of idle factory capacity to the income statement more promptly than absorption costing?
9. One businessman has argued as follows: "Variable costing is great for process accounting; it is nonsense in the job order plant." Discuss.
10. "A burden rate that includes fixed as well as variable manufacturing overhead costs is not very helpful in short-run decision making but is very valuable for long-term decisions because it reflects long-run cost variability." Do you agree or disagree? Why?
11. "Variable costing has no value in costing process production because most costs can be classified as either direct material or direct labor. Indirect overhead is of relatively little significance." Explain why you either agree or disagree with this statement.
12. Some authorities have stated that the need for variable costing could be eliminated easily by providing a better chart of accounts for classifying and accumulating actual costs and by improving the format of periodic financial statements so that the effects of volume on costs and income would be more readily apparent. Discuss this argument.
13. It is a fact that fixed factory overhead costs are essential to production. Does it not follow logically, therefore, that a portion of such costs should be

included in product cost for any use to which product cost data are to be applied?

EXERCISES AND PROBLEMS

1. The company uses a job order costing system. Factory overhead costs for the coming year are expected to be as follows:

Fixed..	$ 50,000
Semivariable..	30,000
Variable...	20,000
Total..	$100,000

Production volume is expected to be 50,000 direct labor hours. The variable components of semivariable costs average 50 cents a direct labor hour.

a) Compute unit cost under the variable costing principle for a job lot of 1,000 units requiring $1,000 in direct materials and 500 direct labor hours at an average wage rate of $3 an hour.

b) If actual operating volume is at the level budgeted and actual overhead costs total $105,000, how much factory overhead would be charged to all jobs combined?

c) How much would be charged to all jobs combined if the company were using full costing?

2. The company uses a process costing system. Variable costs in process 1 totaled $20,000 last month; fixed costs amounted to $5,000. Process output totaled 64,000 pounds.

a) What was unit cost under variable costing?

b) Suppose that output would have been 80,000 pounds if a trainee had not forgotten to close a drain valve. This sort of accident or error occurs very seldom. How, if at all, does this change your answer to (a)?

3. The company used a factory overhead burden rate of $2.50 a machine-hour, both in 19x4 and in 19x5, based on the absorption costing principle. Under- or overabsorbed factory overhead cost is closed out to the income statement at the end of each year.

In 19x5 the company recorded a total of 200,000 machine-hours. Actual overhead amounted to $275,000. Overhead costs included in inventories totaled $50,000 on January 1, 19x5, and $75,000 on December 31, 19x5, using the method followed by the company.

Budgeted variable factory overhead costs averaged $1 a machine-hour both in 19x4 and 19x5. Reported income for 19x5 was $100,000.

What would reported income have been if the company had reported income on a variable costing basis? (Ignore income taxes.)

*4. The Adams Plastics Company recorded the following data for the years 19x5 and 19x6:

---

* Solutions to problems marked with an asterisk (*) can be found in Appendix B.

	19x5	19x6
Production—pounds	5,000,000	6,000,000
Sales—pounds	5,000,000	5,100,000
Direct labor	$ 50,000	$ 60,000
Direct materials	100,000	120,000
Fixed factory overhead	60,000	60,000
Variable factory overhead	40,000	48,000

Assuming that 5,000,000 pounds is the normal production volume and that all under- or overabsorbed overhead is closed at the end of the year to cost of goods sold, compute the amount of factory cost charged against revenue for each year, using (*a*) absorption costing and (*b*) variable costing.

*5. The company has four products, with direct costs and selling prices as follows:

Product	Selling Price	Direct Costs per Unit	
		Materials	Labor
A	$20	$7	$2
B	19	5	3
C	18	3	4
D	17	1	5

The burden rate is 200 percent of direct labor—50 percent for variable costs and 150 percent for fixed costs.

a) Compute a profit margin for each product, per unit and as a percentage of selling price, using full cost absorption.

b) Perform the same computations, using variable costing.

6. Factory overhead costs are expected to be as follows:

Monthly Output (in Units)	Factory Overhead Costs		
	Group A	Group B	Group C
5,000 or less	$1,000	$ 500	$2,000
5,500	1,100	600	2,000
6,000	1,200	600	2,000
6,500	1,300	700	2,000
7,000	1,400	700	2,000
7,500	1,500	800	2,000
8,000	1,600	800	2,000
8,500	1,700	900	2,700
9,000	1,800	900	2,700
9,500	1,900	1,000	2,700
10,000	2,000	1,000	2,700
10,500	2,100	1,100	2,700
11,000	2,200	1,100	2,700
11,500	2,300	1,200	2,700
12,000	2,400	1,200	3,400

Production need not be in multiples of 500 units but can be any volume from zero to 12,000 units a month.

a) Assuming that volume ordinarily fluctuates between 8,500 and 11,000 units a month, what figure would you use to represent the variable cost per unit? Explain your reasoning for each group of costs.

b) How, if at all, would your answer differ if you were asked to supply attributable cost per unit?

7. A company owns two factories: factory No. 1 and factory No. 2. Costs for an output of 14,000 units of product X in factory No. 1 are:

Materials..............................	$35,000
Labor.................................	14,000
Variable overhead.....................	12,600
Fixed overhead........................	8,400
Total..............................	$70,000

The raw materials cost in this table is the amount charged to factory No. 1 for product A, which is manufactured in factory No. 2. Each unit of product X requires two units of product A as a raw material.

Factory No. 2 sells part of its output to factory No. 1 and part to outside customers. Its normal monthly volume is 50,000 units of product A, and the costs of producing this volume are:

Materials..............................	$10,000
Labor.................................	5,000
Variable overhead.....................	2,500
Fixed overhead........................	45,000
Total..............................	$62,500

a) Compute the unit cost of product X on a variable costing basis, (1) assuming that only factory No. 1 uses variable costing, and (2) assuming that both factories use variable costing.

b) Account for the difference between the figure you derived in (a) and average full cost.

*8. The Axelrod Company prepares its income statements on a variable costing basis. The following data relate to last year's operations:

Sales..	$172,000
Variable manufacturing costs of goods finished...............	86,000
Fixed manufacturing overhead.............................	30,000
Inventories, January 1 (at variable cost)....................	20,000
Inventories, December 31 (at variable cost).................	25,000
Sales commissions and other variable selling expenses.........	35,000
Fixed selling and administrative expenses...................	29,000

a) Prepare an income statement for the year in variable costing form.

b) The Axelrod Company's auditors will not certify the company's financial statements unless a supplementary inventory account is established to reflect the difference between the full cost and variable cost of year-end inventories. This account, "Fixed Costs in Inventories," had a balance of $5,000 on January 1. Assuming that the company uses a FIFO inventory valuation and that fixed costs are to be inventoried at the ratio of

fixed manufacturing overhead to variable manufacturing costs of the
period, calculate the required balance in the Fixed Costs in Inventories
account as of December 31 and the effect of this procedure on reported
income for the year.

9. The Dowd Company operates one small factory in which it manufactures a
single homogeneous product for sale to customers in the chemical and
plastics industries. The company's costing system is based on the full
costing principle and therefore inventories are stated at full cost.

Although there have been some increases in materials prices and wage
rates during the past few years, the company has been able to offset these to
a large extent by a vigorous program of cost reduction. Accordingly, the
variable cost of the company's product has remained unchanged for the
past three years at $7 a unit. The selling price of the product has also
remained constant at $20 per unit, and factory fixed costs have been
assigned to production on the basis of a burden rate of $8 a unit. All
underabsorbed or overabsorbed manufacturing costs are taken to the income statement for the year.

The company had no inventories of finished goods on January 1,
19x1, and the following results were reported for the years 19x1 and
19x2:

	19x1	19x2
Sales—units..................................	25,000	37,500
Beginning inventory—units.....................	5,000	15,000
Ending inventory—units........................	15,000	7,500
Production—units..............................	35,000	30,000
Fixed factory overhead costs.....................	$280,000	$290,000
Fixed selling and administrative expenses...........	20,000	21,000
Variable selling and administrative expenses.........	10,000	15,000

a) Compute reported income for the two years by (1) full costing and
(2) variable costing.

b) What would the company's reported income have been in 19x2 if
production had been 37,500 units under (1) full costing, and (2)
variable costing. Assume that total fixed costs would have been as
stated above and that the same burden rates were used in both years.

*10. Sales and profits of the Feaster Manufacturing Company for the first two
quarters of the year were as follows:

	First Quarter	Second Quarter
Sales............................	$300,000	$450,000
Net profit......................	55,000	57,000

The directors are concerned that a 50 percent increase in sales has
resulted in only a small increase in profit. The chief cost accountant

explains that unabsorbed overhead was charged to second-quarter operations. His statement is based on the following data:

	First Quarter	Second Quarter
Sales—units.....................................	20,000	30,000
Production—units............................	30,000	24,000
Ending inventory—units.......................	10,000	4,000
Selling price per unit...........................	$ 15	$ 15
Variable manufacturing cost per unit..............	5	5
Fixed manufacturing overhead costs..............	180,000	180,000
Fixed overhead per unit (burden rate).............	6	6
Selling and administrative expenses...............	25,000	27,000

The company uses a first-in, first-out (FIFO) method for costing inventory. All underabsorbed or overabsorbed manufacturing costs are closed out to Cost of Goods Sold at the close of each period.

a) Prepare income statements for the two periods, using the method now employed by the Feaster Manufacturing Company. Indicate the book value of the ending inventory for each period.

b) Prepare similar statements, using the variable costing method.

c) What would second-quarter net profit have been under each method if production in that period had been 30,000 units?

11. The Leininger Corporation follows the variable costing principle in job order costing. The following transactions occurred in the factory during the month of July:

(1) Purchased materials on account, $22,500.
(2) Issued materials:
    Direct materials, $18,000.
    Factory supplies, $3,500.
(3) Accrued hourly payrolls for four weeks (to be paid by home office), $40,000.
(4) Accrued salary payrolls for the month, $10,000.
(5) Distributed labor costs:
    Direct labor, $36,000.
    Supervision and clerical, $10,000.
    Indirect labor, $7,000.
(6) Incurred other factory overhead, $70,000.
(7) Applied variable overhead to work in process: $0.75 per direct labor dollar.
(8) Transferred finished goods to inventory: There was no work in process at either the end or the beginning of the month.

a) Prepare journal entries to record these transactions.

b) Compute the unabsorbed overhead for the month. Why does this arise?

c) No distinction between fixed and variable overhead costs was made in items (1) through (5). How is it possible to operate a variable costing system without making such distinctions?

12. The company has three small factories, each specializing in a single product. Because the factories are so small, a single factory superintendent is responsible for all three factories. Annual costs are:

	Factory A	Factory B	Factory C
Direct materials...............	$ 15,000	$ 15,000	$ 15,000
Direct labor..................	45,000	60,000	75,000
Variable overhead.............	30,000	45,000	60,000
Fixed overhead...............	90,000	75,000	60,000
Total Costs..............	$180,000	$195,000	$210,000

In addition, the factory superintendent's office has fixed costs of $63,000 a year.

The volume of activity in the three factories can be measured in three ways: by direct labor hours, by machine-hours, and by units of output. Normal annual volumes are:

	Factory A	Factory B	Factory C
Direct labor hours..............	10,000	20,000	30,000
Machine-hours.................	20,000	20,000	20,000
Units of output.	30,000	20,000	10,000

a) Compute unit cost for each product on a variable costing basis.
b) Prepare a table showing the relative profitability of the three products which sell at the following prices: A—$7; B—$13; and C—$19. Ignore selling and administrative expenses and income taxes.
c) Devise some method of calculating full cost for each product and discuss the problems you encountered in developing these figures. Does it make much difference which method you select?

13. The company has three factories for which the following data are available:

	Factory 1	Factory 2	Factory 3
Normal monthly volume..........	50,000 Labor hours	30,000 Machine-hours	100,000 lbs.
Expected overhead costs at normal volume:			
Variable......................	$75,000	$30,000	$20,000
Fixed........................	25,000	90,000	80,000

All three factories use predetermined burden rates for product unit costing.

Factory 1 makes product X, with the following input requirements per unit:

Materials:
2½ pounds of material A, from factory 3.
2 units of material B, from factory 2.
1 unit of material C, from outside vendor, $5.
Direct labor in factory 1: 3 hours, at $2.50 an hour.

Direct labor and materials costs in factory 3 average 70 cents a pound. A unit of material B has a direct labor and direct materials cost in factory 2 of $2 a unit, and requires 1½ hours of machine time in factory 2.
a) Compute the unit cost of product X, following the full costing principle.

b) Compute the unit cost of product X, following the variable costing principle.

c) The manager of factory 1 is also in charge of a small sales force who have the responsibility of bringing in orders to keep the factory busy. Business has been very slack lately throughout the industry, and being anxious to secure additional business, the manager of factory 1 has authorized his salesmen to quote prices only slightly higher than the costs of his labor, materials, and variable overhead. His products are of recognizably competitive quality, but the low price quotations have not been low enough to get the orders. Can you offer any suggestions as to why this may be the case?

14. The Jonas Good Company uses the variable costing principle for internal cost accounting but reports inventories and income to the public on a full cost FIFO basis. It uses a predetermined burden rate for variable overhead costs.

For convenience, the inventory accounts are maintained on a cost element basis rather than a stage-of-completion basis. That is, the balance in the Materials in Inventory account represents the cost of raw materials, the cost of the direct materials content of work in process, and the cost of the direct materials content of finished goods inventory. Three such accounts are maintained for the variable costs: Materials in Inventory, Labor in Inventory, and Variable Overhead in Inventory.

A fourth inventory account—Fixed Overhead in Inventory—is maintained for fixed overhead costs, to permit full cost public reporting. No entries are made in this account during the year; thus the January 1 balance remains in the account until the year-end adjustments are made. At the end of the year, the fixed costs applicable to the year-end inventories are determined by using a predetermined burden rate, based on that year's budgeted ratio of fixed cost to direct labor cost at normal volume. A year-end adjustment is then made to bring the balance in the Fixed Overhead in Inventory account up to date.

For public reporting purposes, any under- or overabsorbed overhead remaining after inventory accounts have been adjusted to their correct year-end balances is carried directly to the income statement as an adjustment to the cost of goods sold.

The following data are available (all figures are in thousands of dollars):

	19x1	19x2
(1) January 1 inventory:		
Materials in inventory	$ 70	$130
Labor in inventory	60	180
Variable overhead in inventory	30	?
Fixed overhead in inventory	45	?
(2) Actual costs for the year:		
Materials purchased	180	100
Direct labor employed	210	60
Factory overhead costs	220	150
(3) Revenue from sales	400	600
(4) Operating expenses	50	55
(5) December 31 inventory:		
Materials in inventory	130	30
Labor in inventory	180	90

(6) Budgeted variable overhead during each of these two years amounted to 40 percent of direct labor cost. *At normal volume,* budgeted fixed overhead was equal to 150 percent of variable overhead in 19x1 and 160 percent of variable overhead in 19x2.

(7) Production volume was normal in 19x1, but production schedules in 19x2 were cut back drastically to permit the company to correct a serious overstocking of inventory.

a) Compute the variable and fixed overhead cost components of year-end inventories for both years.

b) Prepare income statements for each year according to (1) variable costing and (2) full costing.

c) Assuming that financial statements are to reflect the full costing concept, what adjusting entry must be made as of December 31, 19x1, to correct the balance in the Fixed Overhead in Inventory account? What entry should be made as of December 31, 19x2?

d) The company pays an executive bonus equal to a fixed percentage of the net income reported to the public and to the stockholders of the Jonas Good Company. Do you believe that the bonus would be more equitable if it were based on the income reported internally to management on a variable costing basis? Give your reasons.

Chapter 8

ALLOCATING FACTORY OVERHEAD
COSTS FOR PRODUCT COSTING

PRODUCT UNIT COSTING is seldom as simple as one might infer from the preceding chapters, mainly because they ignored almost completely the departmental dimension of overhead costs. Even in job order production, overhead costs are usually applied to products departmentally, through the use of departmental burden rates for the production departments through which individual job orders pass.

The difficulty is that some overhead costs are not readily traceable to production departments; if they are to be included in the burden rates, they must first be *allocated* or *redistributed* among the various production departments. The purpose of this chapter is to see why and how this might be done. Because process costing raises no unique problems in this regard, most of the following discussion will focus on job order costing systems.

The Case for Departmental Burden Rates

The burden rate used in the illustrations in Chapter 4 was a plantwide burden rate—that is, all factory costs of all departments were included in one single average. In practice, however, departmental burden rates are ordinarily preferred on the grounds that they yield more *accurate* estimates of product unit costs.

The accuracy issued is raised because individual manufacturing operations vary widely in the depth of mechanization and in the amount of overhead cost per unit of activity. Highly mechanized departments ordinarily have high overhead cost/direct cost ratios, and vice versa. Plantwide burden rates average out these differences.

For example, the illustrative job cost sheet in Chapter 4 (Exhibit 4–1) showed an overhead charge of $177.10, representing a plantwide burden rate of $5.06 per direct labor hour. This yielded a product unit cost of $0.575 each. This same job has been recosted in Exhibit 8–1, using departmental burden rates. Because most of the work on this job was done in cost center No. 4, with a relatively low burden rate, use of departmental burden rates reduces the overhead charge to $126 and reduces unit cost to $0.549, a reduction of $0.026, or about 5 percent.

The revised unit cost figure derived from Exhibit 8–1 is regarded as

Exhibit 8–1

JOB ORDER COST SHEET

DESCRIPTION: Cannister No. 278   JOB ORDER NO. 1234
DATE ORDERED 5/1/—   DATE COMPLETED 5/12/—
QUANTITY ORDERED 2,000   QUANTITY COMPLETED 2,000

MATERIALS COST					Cost Summary:
Date	Item	Quantity	Price	Amount	Materials.....$ 901.50
					Labor........ 71.40
5/3	Shell No. 14	2,000	$0.32	$640.00	Overhead..... 126.00
5/4	Shell No. 14	50	0.32	16.00	Total........$1,098.90
5/5	Handle No. 142	2,000	0.12	240.00	Unit cost.......$ 0.549 each
5/10	Paint	2	2.75	5.50	
	Total			$901.50	

LABOR COST						OVERHEAD	
Date	Cost Center	Opera-tion	Hours	Rate	Amount	Rate	Amount
5/4	2	22	6.5	$2.20	$14.30	$6.00	$39.00
5/6	3	31	10.0	2.10	21.00	5.00	50.00
5/10	4	42	14.5	1.80	26.10	2.00	29.00
5/11	4	44	4.0	2.50	10.00	2.00	8.00
	Total				$71.40		$126.00

more accurate than the unit cost obtained in Chapter 4 because it reflects the operating costs of the facilities actually used for this particular production order. Thus a product that passes through only a series of manual assembly departments will not be assigned any of the overhead costs of the highly mechanized machining departments.

THE ALLOCATION PROBLEM

Once it has been decided to use departmental burden rates (or departmental cost averages in process production), the question arises of how to handle costs that are not readily traceable to individual direct production departments. Two groups of these costs can be distinguished:

1. *Direct service department costs:* the direct costs of departments which provide services to production departments and often to other service departments.
2. *General factory overheads:* common costs, such as property taxes on the factory building which cannot be traced to any one department but are shared in some sense by two or more factory departments.

The issue is how to get service department costs and general factory overheads into product unit costs.

For example, suppose that service department S provides services to production departments M and P. The budgeted direct or traceable costs of these three depatments (excluding direct materials and direct labor for the two production departments) are:

Department	Direct Costs	Normal Volume
M................	$25,000	10,000 direct labor hours
P................	50,000	50,000 machine-hours
S................	20,000	......

If burden rates were limited solely to the overhead traceable to production departments, department M would have a burden rate of $2.50 per direct labor hour, department P would have a burden rate of $1.00 per machine-hour, and department S costs would never get into product costs at all.

The method usually adopted to include in product cost a provision for all or part of service department and general factory overheads is to build it into the production department burden rates. In other words, each production department's overhead cost budget ordinarily covers both direct and indirect departmental overheads. The latter represent the *allocation* or *redistribution* of budgeted service department and general factory overhead costs among the production departments.

Service Department Charging Rates

Interdepartmental cost allocation is accomplished through the use of *charging rates:* figures representing the average cost of individual service departments. The charging rate is to the service department what the burden rate is to the production department, with one modification—all service department costs are overhead, and therefore the charging rate reflects both the direct and indirect costs of providing services.

Transfer Prices. Probably the most obvious base for a service department charging rate is a measure of *usage*—the number of units of service performed by the service department. Typical usage or consumption indexes are:

Department	Usage Index
Electric power	Kilowatt-hours
Maintenance	Maintenance labor hours
Stock room	Requisitions

A charging rate expressed as an amount per unit of service performed is known as a *transfer price*.

Activity Charges. If a reliable index of usage is unavailable, and if service department costs are variable, the correct approach is to find a measure of the volume of activity in departments receiving or creating the need for the service. The measure selected should be one that seems to correlate well with variations in service department costs. For example, if some costs of the payroll department vary with the total number of labor hours in the factory, it would be appropriate to use a charging rate of so much per factory labor hour. A charging rate of this sort is known as an *activity charge.*

Capacity Charges. Unlike the variable costs, the fixed costs of a service department are incurred to provide service *capacity* rather than the services themselves. Examples include the costs of providing floor space, heat and light, and plant management. In such cases, the cost to be allocated to a given department should be based on its relative share of the total service load during peak load periods, if this can be ascertained or estimated.

Because in most cases the service facilities are provided jointly for the joint use of a number of departments, it is difficult to determine with any precision just what percentage of capacity each department is responsible for. The problem, in other words, is to obtain an index of total service capacity and then to obtain some measure of each department's *occupancy* of that capacity. Thus the charging rate in this case can be called an occupancy charge, capacity charge, or possibly a potential-activity charge, and it is based on a measure of the *facilities provided* rather than facilities used.

Ability-to-Pay Charges. The lack of a reasonable index of use or of any clearly defined pattern of cost variability leaves a gap in the cost allocation structure. This gap is filled, whenever possible, by measures of relative occupancy of the facilities provided. Occupancy indexes are often difficult to find, however, and in situations of this sort the capacity of the service department is often *assumed* to correlate with the *size* of the other departments or with their *ability to absorb* service department charges.

The ability-to-pay criterion is often justified on the grounds that each department and each product must bear its "fair share" of all costs and that if no other basis can be found for allocation, the ability-to-pay criterion is better than nothing. Unfortunately, this begs the question. If it is impossible to find a reliable index of usage, occupancy, or variability, then the overhead cost must be truly a common cost of the various departments and *any* allocation is bound to be arbitrary and potentially misleading. Under these circumstances the use of the ability-to-pay charging rate lends to the allocation an aura of precision and objectivity that is completely unjustified. Either no allocation should be made or some basis should be chosen that will be instantly recognizable as arbitrary and of no managerial significance.

Multistage Allocations

In most factories, service departments serve each other as well as the production departments. This creates interrelationships that can be extremely complex. To cite the simplest of these relationships, suppose that management wants to cost a product that uses two hours of machine time in production department P. Department P uses department X services, which in turn require the services of department Y. Thus we might allocate a portion of Y's cost to X and a portion of X's cost to P so that X and Y costs are included in appropriate proportions in the cost of product A.

This sequence of events is illustrated in Exhibit 8–2. Under this

Exhibit 8–2

ILLUSTRATIVE COST ALLOCATION SEQUENCE

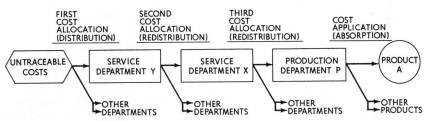

scheme, the unit cost of each department's output includes the direct costs of that department, plus a portion of the costs of departments providing services to it, plus a portion of the untraceable costs of the factory as a whole, and this is true whether the output is a physical product or a service.

Full Costs, Partial Costs, or No Costs?

Of all the issues in cost accounting, probably none is as controversial as the advisability and extent of interdepartmental allocations of budgeted costs. Some companies regard the whole process as an unnecessary nuisance; others go all the way to make sure that every budgeted cost finds a home in one production department burden rate or another.

The main issue here is the same one faced in the discussion of variable and full costing in the preceding chapter: which method will provide figures that are more useful to management in decision making? An advocate of full costing will support allocation of all service department and general overhead costs, both fixed and variable, while the variable coster will argue for allocating variable costs only. Still another possibility is to allocate some but not all of the fixed costs, applying the concept of attributable cost developed in Chapter 7.

The only valid reason for omitting allocations altogether from product unit costing procedures is on the grounds of immateriality—either overhead costs are entirely fixed or the variability is so small that it can be ignored, at a consequent saving in bookkeeping costs. It should be clear from the preceding chapter that adoption of the variable costing principle is not an argument for excluding *all* factory overhead costs from product cost. Variable overhead costs are just as much a part of variable cost as direct labor and materials.

For example, assume that a service department has the following budget for a normal monthly service output of 10,000 service units:

Fixed costs	$ 4,000
Variable costs	20,000
Total Costs	$24,000

In this case the variable cost charging rate to production departments would be $2 a service unit ($20,000 divided by 10,000 units). The burden rate of each production department would include a provision for the variable portion of the services consumed, costed at $2 a service unit.

In the remainder of this chapter, we shall follow the widespread practice of allocating full costs, primarily to examine the problems encountered in such measurements, and secondarily because they may be required for cost-plus contract pricing and public financial reporting. For the reasons outlined in the preceding chapter, as well as to effect some reductions in clerical costs, routine measures of product costs developed for use in managerial decision making should not go beyond attributable cost. Furthermore, any charging rates that include a provision for fixed costs should preferably be subdivided into fixed and variable components to make them more readily adaptable to decision making.

AN ALLOCATION PLAN

The methods of applying these concepts can best be presented through a simple illustration. The Standoff Company's factory is divided into three service and three production departments. Budgeted allocations are based on the budget and statistical data shown in Exhibit 8–3. These data will be used for all the illustrations in the remainder of this chapter.

First Step: Primary Distributions

The first step is to distribute the unassigned overhead among the six departments. Electric power, for example, is purchased from a public utility company. Meters in the three production departments and in the equipment maintenance department record the amount of electricity consumed for motive power in those departments. The remaining power is used for lighting the factory and factory office and for operating a few simple pieces of office equipment. Separate metering of office power consumption has been deemed uneconomical, and all such power passes through the buildings department meter, along with power for lighting.

Electric power, in other words, is partly traceable to specific departments, but the company finds it more *convenient* to record power costs initially in a single factorywide account and then distribute them among the five departments in which meters are installed.

The distribution of budgeted costs in this instance is based on budgeted power consumption. The Standoff Company purchases electricity at a flat rate of two cents a kilowatt-hour (kwh), and at this rate the budgeted power cost distribution is:

Department	Kwh Used	Amount Charged
Buildings.............................	10,000	$ 200
Factory administration..................	......	......
Equipment maintenance.................	2,000	40
Machining............................	50,000	1,000
Welding and plating...................	5,000	100
Assembly............................	13,000	260
Total............................	80,000	$1,600

The costs of building depreciation, taxes, and insurance are a different matter. These are common costs of the entire building, and no

Exhibit 8–3

STANDOFF COMPANY: DATA FOR BUDGETED ALLOCATIONS

	Total	Service Departments			Production Departments		
		Buildings	Factory Administration	Equipment Maintenance	Machining	Welding and Plating	Assembly
Budgeted operating statistics:							
Floor space (sq. ft.)	50,000	....	5,000	3,000	20,000	7,000	15,000
Direct labor hours	20,000	....	....	....	6,000	2,000	12,000
Total labor hours	32,900	900	....	....	10,000	4,000	16,000
Power consumed (kwh)	80,000	10,000	....	2,000	50,000	5,000	13,000
Maintenance hours used	2,000	....	....	2,000	1,500	300	200
Departmental overhead:							
Salaries	$10,200	$1,000	$6,100	$ 600	$ 900	$ 500	$1,100
Indirect labor	20,200	1,900	....	5,100	5,700	2,500	5,000
Operating supplies	2,600	600	700	400	400	300	200
Equipment depreciation	1,500	100	100	200	800	200	100
Miscellaneous	1,640	200	500	300	275	75	290
Total	$36,140	$3,800	$7,400	$6,600	$8,075	$3,575	$6,690
Unassigned overhead:							
Electric power	$ 1,600						
Building depreciation, taxes, and insurance	2,000						
Total Factory Overhead	$39,740						

metering is possible. In this case allocation is on the basis of an index of facilities provided, the relative amount of floor space occupied. The budgeted allocation is:

Department	Floor Space		Cost Allocated
	Amount	Percent	
Buildings......................	......	...	......
Factory administration............	5,000	10	$ 200
Equipment maintenance...........	3,000	6	120
Machining......................	20,000	40	800
Welding and plating..............	7,000	14	280
Assembly.......................	15,000	30	600
Total.......................	50,000	100	$2,000

These two allocations are often referred to as *primary* distributions because they do not require the transfer of costs from one department to another and can be made in any sequence as long as they are made before any secondary distributions are made.

Redistribution by Sequential Allocation

The Standoff Company completes its factory budget by making secondary distributions of the budgeted cost data. For this purpose, it uses what is known as a *sequential allocation* procedure. Under sequential allocation, the service departments are ranked in terms of the relative amounts of services or facilities they provide to the other service departments. Costs of the department providing the most universally used services or facilities are distributed first, and so on.

Selection of Sequence. In the Standoff Company scheme, buildings department costs are distributed first, to all five other departments. Factory administration costs, including the costs received in the buildings department allocation, come next, and are spread among the equipment maintenance and factory production departments only—no further charges are made to the buildings department accounts. Finally, equipment maintenance costs, both direct and allocated, are charged to the three production departments.

The sequence selected is inevitably somewhat arbitrary. Either factory administration or buildings costs could have been chosen for the first cut because each of these departments uses the services or facilities of the other. In this case, buildings was chosen because it was felt more useful to management to have some indication of the costs of space used for administrative purposes.

Buildings Department Allocation. Budgeted buildings costs total $4,000 a month, including $200 for electric power. Analysis has indicated that these costs are almost entirely fixed for the volume ranges within which the company expects to operate. Furthermore, no index of service consumption by the other departments is obtainable. For these reasons the controller has selected floor space occupied as an index of capacity or facilities provided, even though he recognizes that factory administration probably uses more than its proportionate share of the buildings department employees' time. The average budgeted cost per square foot of floor space is eight cents a month ($4,000 divided by 50,000 square feet), and the resulting budgeted allocation is:

Department	Floor Space %	Cost Allocated
Factory administration...............	10	$ 400
Equipment maintenance................	6	240
Machining...........................	40	1,600
Welding and plating..................	14	560
Assembly............................	30	1,200
Total........................	100	$4,000

Factory Administration Department Allocation. A facilities provided criterion is also used for allocating factory administration costs. Here the index of occupancy is even less clear than for buildings department costs, but budgeted total labor hours is regarded as likely to have a reasonably close correlation to the factors that require administrative capacity in the factory, and this is the index that has been selected.

Budgeted factory administration costs amount to $8,000 a month, including $7,400 in direct charges (from Exhibit 8–3), $200 in building occupancy charges, and $400 in buildings service charges. This amounts to 25 cents a labor hour, and at this rate the budgeted allocation is:

Department	Total Labor Hours Amount	Percent	Cost Allocated
Equipment maintenance.........	2,000	6.25	$ 500
Machining....................	10,000	31.25	2,500
Welding and plating	4,000	12.50	1,000
Assembly.....................	16,000	50.00	4,000
Total....................	32,000	100.00	$8,000

Equipment Maintenance Department Allocation.   Finally, equipment maintenance costs are allocated on the basis of an index of usage—maintenance labor hours. The charging rate is thus a transfer price and is broken down into fixed and variable components for the planning files. Let us assume that the costs budgeted for maintenance are divided into fixed and variable components as follows:

	Fixed	Variable	Total
Direct charges (Exhibit 8–3).......	$1,640	$4,960	$6,600
Electric power.....................	......	40	40
Space charge......................	120	......	120
Building service...................	240	......	240
Factory administration.............	500	......	500
Total......................	$2,500	$5,000	$7,500

This is for a budgeted volume of 2,000 maintenance labor hours, and at this volume the charging rates are $1.25 an hour for fixed costs and $2.50 an hour for variable costs, a total of $3.75 an hour.

Strictly speaking, the fixed costs of operating the maintenance department should be allocated on the basis of service consumption during peak service periods because this is the measure of required capacity, and fixed costs represent the costs of providing capacity. In this case, however, as in many others, budgeted consumption can be regarded as an adequate index of facilities required, and thus can be used for both the fixed and the variable portions of maintenance department cost.

Completed Allocation Sheet.   The completed factory cost budget is shown in Exhibit 8–4. The sequential or step-down procedure shows clearly in this exhibit, and at the end of the process all budgeted factory costs[1] have been reassigned to one or another of the three production departments. The production department totals are then used to establish departmental burden rates for the year, and these are shown at the bottom of Exhibit 8–4 as rates per direct labor hour in each case.

An Alternative: Cross-Allocations

Sequential allocation plans are anathema to many accountants who prefer either to allocate service costs directly to production center accounts, without intermediate allocations of one service center's costs to another service center's accounts, or to set up a set of simultaneous

---

[1] Although this should represent the normal monthly costs of operating the department rather than the costs budgeted for a particular year, the two figures have been assumed equal here to simplify the illustration.

Exhibit 8–4

STANDOFF COMPANY: BUDGETED OVERHEAD DISTRIBUTION SHEET USING SEQUENTIAL ALLOCATIONS

	Total	Service Departments			Production Departments		
		Buildings	Factory Administration	Equipment Maintenance	Machining	Welding and Plating	Assembly
Direct overhead:							
Salaries	$10,200	$1,000	$6,100	$ 600	$ 900	$ 500	$ 1,100
Indirect labor	20,200	1,900	.....	5,100	5,700	2,500	5,000
Operating supplies	2,600	600	700	400	400	300	200
Equipment depreciation	1,500	100	100	200	800	200	100
Miscellaneous	1,640	200	500	300	275	75	290
Total	$36,140	$3,800	$7,400	$6,600	$ 8,075	$3,575	$ 6,690
Primary distributions:							
Electric power	1,600	200	.....	40	1,000	100	260
Building depreciation, taxes, insurance	2,000	.....	200	120	800	280	600
Total Factory Overhead	$39,740	$4,000	$7,600	$6,760	$ 9,875	$3,955	$ 7,550
Secondary distributions:							
Buildings		(4,000)	400	240	1,600	560	1,200
Factory administration			$8,000 (8,000)	500	2,500	1,000	4,000
Equipment maintenance				$7,500 (7,500)	5,625	1,125	750
Allocated Totals					$19,600	$6,640	$13,500
Normal volume (direct labor hours)					6,000	2,000	12,000
Burden rate/direct labor hour					$ 3.267	$ 3.32	$ 1.125

equations to permit *cross-allocations*—e.g., charging building service costs to the factory office and factory office costs to the buildings department.

This approach derives from the mutual interdependence of the various service centers. They do provide services or facilities to each other and thus, it is argued, each should be charged with a portion of the costs of each of the others. The result will be more accurate cost center charging rates and product costing rates.

The cross-allocation approach is easy to apply to the Standoff Company example. The only service departments in the Standoff Company that provide service to each other are the buildings and factory administration departments. Buildings has a total labor hour budget of 900 hours out of the factory grand total of 32,900 hours. Its costs are $4,000, after the primary distributions but before any secondary distributions, so its full budget would be:

Buildings budget = $4,000 + 9/329 × Factory administration budget.

Factory administration, on the other hand, occupies 10 percent of the total floor space, and its full budget would be:

Factory administration budget = $7,600 + 0.1 × Buildings budget.

With two equations and two unknowns, it is a simple matter to determine the full budgets for these two departments:

Department	Monthly Budget	Charging Rate
Building	$4,219.50	$0.08439 per square foot
Factory administration	8,021.95	0.24386 per labor hour

These rates should be rounded off, but we shall use them in this form so that the argument will not be confused by the presence of rounding errors.

When these rates are used, the equipment maintenance department budget becomes:

$$\text{Equipment maintenance budget} = \$6,760 + 3,000 \times \$0.08439 + 2,000 \times \$0.24386 = \$7,500.89 .$$

The revised charging rate for equipment maintenance is thus $7,501 divided by 2,000, or $3.7505 per maintenance labor hour.

The final allocations under this method are shown in Exhibit 8–5. A quick glance back at Exhibit 8–4 will reveal that in this case the effect of the change in allocation method on the departmental burden rates is insignificant. This will not always be true, however, and with more

Exhibit 8-5

BUDGETED OVERHEAD DISTRIBUTION SHEET
USING CROSS-ALLOCATIONS

	Service Departments			Production Departments		
	Buildings	Factory Administration	Equipment Maintenance	Machining	Welding and Plating	Assembly
Direct overhead............	$3,800	$7,400	$6,600	$ 8,075	$3,575	$ 6,690
Primary distributions......	200	200	160	1,800	380	860
Total factory overhead.....	$4,000	$7,600	$6,760	$ 9,875	$3,955	$ 7,550
Secondary distributions:						
Buildings................	(4,220)	422	253	1,688	591	1,266
Factory administration....	220	(8,022)	488	2,438	975	3,901
Equipment maintenance....	.....	.....	(7,501)	5,626	1,125	750
Allocated Totals..........	.....	.....	.....	$19,627	$6,646	$13,467
Normal volume (direct labor hours).....				6,000	2,000	12,000
Burden rate/direct labor hour..........				$ 3.271	$3.323	$ 1.122

service departments and more interrelationships between service departments the effect could be material in amount.

Interest in this approach has revived in recent years with the availability of high-speed digital computers. When they had to use desk calculators, accountants shrank from the task of finding a mutually inclusive set of charging rates for a factory with ten or more service departments. It is fairly simple to program a computer to perform the necessary operations, however, and this is likely to stimulate a more widespread adoption of cross-allocation plans.

Merely because something can be done does not necessarily mean that it should be done, as enthusiasts in any field are prone to conclude. The case for cross-allocations would be stronger if it were clear that the added accuracy was more than an illusion. The unfortunate fact is that the errors inherent in full cost allocations are ordinarily much larger than the errors inherent in sequential allocation. In most situations, the accountant would do better to turn his efforts toward simplifying and rationalizing the existing structure of allocations rather than toward achieving greater mathematical precision.

Spurious Accuracy in Burden Rates

The underlying objective of departmentalizing the burden rate is to produce product costs that are more nearly representative of the total short-run and long-run costs necessary to manufacture each product. From this point of view it would seem that accuracy of product costing can be improved by multiplying the number of cost centers, each of them consisting of a single operation or series of related operations.

From the discussion in this chapter, however, it should be apparent that this added accuracy may be more apparent than real. The narrower the segment of plant operations, the greater is the proportion of allocated costs. Because many of these allocations must be made in a highly arbitrary fashion, the gain from a greater homogeneity of operations may be largely offset by the lessened significance of the cost center cost totals.

This is not to imply that burden rates are more accurate for larger cost centers. It simply means that further subdivision of a responsibility unit into smaller cost centers for product costing may not add to the accuracy of product costs and may also mislead some people into believing that it does.

SUMMARY

Most factory burden rates are departmental burden rates, with the work done in each production department being costed at the average overhead cost of that department rather than the average for the factory as a whole. Because products do not pass through service departments, however, the costs of these departments will not be included in product costs when departmental burden rates are used unless special provision is made for them.

The technique most commonly used to accomplish this is to include in budgeted production department overheads amounts derived by allocating budgeted service department costs and general factory overheads among the production departments. The variable portion of budgeted service department costs can be allocated to the departments expected to use the services on the basis of budgeted service department consumption or usage. If an index of consumption is not available, the charging rate can be based on the index of activity with which service cost variations correlate most closely. Fixed service department costs, on the other hand, should be allocated on the basis of *potential* usage—that is, usage during periods of peak service department operation, the percentage of the service department's capacity required by each of the other departments.

The purpose of these allocations is to get more accurate product costing rates for inventory costing and managerial decision making. This does not necessarily mean that fixed cost allocations are relevant to all decisions utilizing unit cost data. Indeed, our earlier discussion should have indicated that they are often not relevant in decision making. Further examination of this issue, however, must await a later chapter.

DISCUSSION QUESTIONS

1. Why should factory overhead costs be departmentalized? Why should departmental burden rates be developed?

2. In what sense does the use of departmental burden rates improve the accuracy of product unit costs? In what sense is the added accuracy spurious or illusory?

3. The costs of factory service departments are normally included in the amount of overhead to be assigned to products. Why is it necessary or desirable to accumulate these costs initially in service department accounts instead of assigning them directly to production department accounts?

4. It is generally believed that manufacturing overhead now represents a much larger proportion of total manufacturing costs than it did 10 or 15 years ago and that this is a trend that can be expected to continue. What explanation can you advance for this trend?

5. What are the shortcomings of allocations based on the criterion of "ability to pay"?

6. Discuss the problems that arise in conjunction with sequential distributions of service department costs. How would you choose the sequence in which such distributions are made?

7. What purposes, if any, are served by including allocated costs in departmental burden rates?

8. Select a measurement unit that you feel would be a reasonable basis for distributing the costs of each of the following service departments. Indicate which allocation criterion you believe is appropriate in each case.

a) Medical.   f) Maintenance.
b) Personnel.   g) Power.
c) Buildings services.   h) Cafeteria.
d) Labor timekeeping.   i) Cost accounting.
e) Storeroom.   j) Receiving.

9. What distinguishes a producing department from a service department?

10. How can the concept of cost attributability be reflected in interdepartmental cost allocations?

11. What is the main argument for cross-allocations? How would you decide how much weight to give to this argument?

12. A certain chemical company includes in product unit cost only the costs of direct materials, direct labor, and other costs directly traceable to the processing departments. General factory overhead and service department costs are taken to the income statement as expenses of the period. Compare this system with variable costing and also with absorption costing as to (a) differences in product unit cost, and (b) differences in reported net income of the period.

EXERCISES AND PROBLEMS

*1. The costs of department X are $2,000 a month plus $0.20 for each department X service unit consumed. Monthly service consumption and volume of production activity in the factory's four direct production departments are normally as follows:

Department	Service Units Consumed	Production Volume
1......................	1,000	10,000 direct labor hours
2......................	5,000	8,000 direct labor hours
3......................	8,000	20,000 machine-hours
4......................	6,000	15,000 direct labor hours
Total................	20,000	

---

* Solutions to problems marked with an asterisk (*) can be found in Appendix B.

Each batch of 1,000 units of product A requires 10 direct labor hours in department 1, 20 direct labor hours in department 2, 100 machine-hours in department 3, and 5 direct labor hours in department 4.

Using departmental burden rates, how much department X cost should be included in a measure of the "full cost" of a unit of product A?

2. Department S has the following monthly budget at its normal volume of 1,400 service hours:

Service labor	$4,000
Supervision	700
Supplies	300
Depreciation	1,750
Other costs	250
Total	$7,000

All of these except supervision and depreciation are proportionately variable with volume. Supervision costs represent the salary of the department head, while depreciation is on a set of equipment all of which must be kept available as long as department S stands ready to provide its services.

Departments 1 and 2 use 200 department S hours and 300 department S hours, respectively, in a typical month. Department 1's production volume is measured in direct labor hours, with a normal volume of 10,000 direct labor hours a month. Department 2's output is measured in pounds of product, with a normal volume of 30,000 pounds a month.

A unit of product X weighs 10 pounds and requires 5 direct labor hours in department 1. How much department S cost should be included in the cost of a unit of product X on a full cost basis, an attributable cost basis, and a variable cost basis?

3. The Langdon Company has two producing and two service departments. Estimated monthly cost and operating data for the year 19x1 are:

	Department			
Cost	Producing Able	Producing Baker	Mainte- nance	General Plant
Direct labor cost	$15,000	$20,000	$6,000	
Indirect labor	8,000	14,000	1,500	$13,900
Indirect materials	3,000	7,000	900	1,500
Miscellaneous costs	4,000	4,000	1,400	1,000
Maintenance hours	1,800	1,200		

General plant costs are entirely fixed; it is assumed that the other three departments benefit from general plant services in proportion to their total budgeted direct labor cost.

Develop full cost burden rates for the two producing departments, including a provision for absorption of budgeted service department costs. Use direct labor cost as your index of volume.

4. Analysis of the four departments in the Langdon Company (see the preceding problem) established the following additional information:

(1) The fixed indirect labor cost in each producing department is: Able, $2,000; and Baker, $4,000.
(2) Indirect materials are completely variable in both producing departments.
(3) Miscellaneous costs are completely fixed in both producing departments.
(4) Maintenance hours required by each producing department increase by one hour for every $10 increase in direct labor cost (output) in Able department and one hour for every $20 increase in direct labor cost in Baker department.
(5) In the maintenance department direct labor cost and indirect materials are considered variable while indirect labor and miscellaneous costs are fixed.

Prepare departmental burden rates on the variable costing principle.

5. The Five-Star Company has two production departments, A and B, but it uses a single plantwide burden rate of $3 a direct labor hour. Experience has shown that overhead costs in deparment A vary with the number of direct labor hours, while those in department B vary with the number of machine-hours in the following proportions:

	Department A	Department B
Fixed overhead costs..................	$12,500 per month	$23,000 per month
Variable overhead costs...............	$ 0.75 per direct labor hour	$ 0.10 per machine-hour
Normal volume......................	10,000 direct labor hours per month	20,000 machine-hours per month

Two products, X and Y, have the following production requirements:

	Department A	Department B
Product X:		
Direct labor hours...........	1	5
Machine-hours..............	—	20
Product Y:		
Direct labor hours...........	4	2
Machine-hours..............	—	3

a) Compute overhead cost per unit for each product, using the plant-wide burden rate and following the *full costing* principle.
b) Compute overhead cost per unit for each product, using departmental burden rates and following the *full costing* principle.
c) Compute overhead cost per unit for each product, using departmental burden rates and following the *variable costing* principle.
d) Which of these cost figures do you think management would find useful in decision making? Explain the reasons for your choice(s).

6. The Robertson Company has been using a blanket or overall overhead rate for the entire company. An alternative has been proposed: departmental overhead rates. You are given the following information:
(1) Three products (A, B, C) are produced in three departments (1, 2, 3).
(2) Labor hours required for each product are:

LABOR HOURS REQUIRED PER UNIT OF PRODUCT

Product	Department			Total
	1	2	3	
A....................	2	1	1	4
B....................	0	2	2	4
C....................	2	3	3	8

(3) Product produced in a normal year: A—40,000 units; B—40,000 units; and C—10,000 units.

(4) Overhead incurred in a normal year: department 1—$400,000; department 2—$300,000; and department 3—$100,000.

(5) Sales this year: A—20,000 units; B—40,000 units; and C—10,000 units.

(6) The company's inventories are listed on a full cost LIFO basis, and the year-end inventories of product A were 10,000 units greater than the year-beginning quantities.

Should the company use a companywide or departmental burden rate? Why? (In either case the burden rate would be based on direct labor hours.)

*7. The Hubbard Woods Company applies manufacturing overhead to all orders by use of departmental burden rates. The divisions of the factory for this purpose are (1) melting and pouring, (2) molding, (3) core making, and (4) cleaning and grinding. From the data shown below, prepare an overhead distribution sheet showing in detail the manufacturing overhead chargeable to each department under an absorption costing system.

NORMAL MANUFACTURING COSTS PER MONTH

Indirect labor:
Melting and pouring..................................$1,000
Molding.. 300
Core making....................................... 100
Cleaning and grinding.................................. 300
Supplies used:
Melting and pouring.................................. 50
Molding.. 50
Core making....................................... 200
Cleaning and grinding.................................. 100
Taxes (equipment, $12, building, $24)..................... 36
Compensation insurance..................................... 65
Power.. 50
Heat and light... 80
Depreciation—building...................................... 64
Depreciation—equipment.................................... 60
　　　Total.......................................$2,455

Department	Floor Space (Sq. Ft.)	Cost of Equipment	Direct Labor	Compensation Insurance*	Horsepower Rating
Melting and pouring..........	500	$2,000	....	$2.00	10
Molding...................	2,000	500	$1,200	1.00	..
Core making..............	500	1,500	500	1.00	10
Cleaning and grinding.......	1,000	2,000	1,300	1.50	30
Total.................	4,000	$6,000	$3,000	...	50

* Rate per $100 of payroll.

8. A company's factory has three producing departments, a maintenance department, and a steam electric power plant. Because the company produces a variety of products, some of them highly seasonal, and because some of the products do not require work in all departments, a considerable variation occurs from month to month in the proportion of power consumed by the various departments.

The following statistics are taken from the company's annual budget:

	Horse-power of Motors	Annual Power Consumption in Kilowatt-Hours	Annual Direct Labor Costs
Maintenance department.........	20	30,000	....
Producing department A..........	200	480,000	$250,000
Producing department B..........	300	540,000	200,000
Producing department C..........	80	150,000	500,000
Total.....................	600	1,200,000	$950,000

Departmental burden rates are used for product costing in the three producing departments.

The annual budget for the power plant shows the following:

Fixed costs..$50,400
Variable costs.. 21,600
Total..$72,000

a) What provision for electric power costs should be made in the budget of each of the four power-consuming departments if the company follows the variable costing principle in product costing? Explain.

b) How would your answer to (a) differ if the company were to use full absorption costing but still wanted variable cost information available? Show your calculations and state your reasons.

9. The Fragile Company absorbs manufacturing overhead by means of departmental burden rates. Inventories of materials and parts are valued at average full cost, including absorbed overhead. The burden rates in the company's three factory departments are:

Machining.............................$1.00 per direct labor dollar
Wiring............................... 1.50 per direct labor dollar
Assembly............................. 2.00 per direct labor dollar

The company now has an opportunity to submit a bid covering the requirements of a state agency for 1,000 units of a custom product. This product is an assembly of four parts, two of which are now carried in stock. The average costs per unit for the two inventoried items are:

Base No. 101..$ 0.66
Subassembly No. 463....................................... 10.55

The remaining two parts, a gauge and a cover, can be purchased from an outside supplier at a unit price of $2.50 and $1.80, respectively.

To manufacture this custom product, the Fragile Company will have to attach the gauge to the subassembly in the wiring department and assemble this with the base and cover in the assembly department. The estimated labor costs of these operations are $0.10 and $0.30 per unit, respectively.

a) Prepare a cost estimate for this custom product, following the full costing principle.

b) Analysis of the most recent job cost sheets for base No. 101 and subassembly No. 463 shows the following cost breakdown:

	Base No. 101	Subassembly No. 463
Cost per unit:		
Materials...........	$0.30	$ 1.80
Labor:		
Machining..........	0.12	0.50
Wiring.............	....	2.50
Assembly...........	0.04	0.50
Overhead...........	0.20	5.25
Total............	$0.66	$10.55

Assuming that variable overhead costs per direct labor dollar in the three departments are $0.50, $0.70 and $1.00, respectively:

(1) Compute the cost of the two manufactured parts on the basis of the variable costing principle.

(2) Prepare a cost estimate for the custom product based on the variable costing principle.

10. The management of the Kleinhans Company is now reviewing the profitability of several of the company's products. The company's president is particularly concerned about product Y, which has the lowest apparent profitability per unit of any of the company's products. The sales department believes that this product must remain in the company's line, but the sales manager is prepared to instruct his salesmen to concentrate their selling effort on other products and not to make any effort to sell product Y. The company's products are manufactured in three factory departments, each of which has a full cost burden rate of 240 percent of direct labor cost. The direct costs and selling prices of three of the company's products are as follows:

| Product | Selling Price | Direct Product Cost per Unit | | | |
| | | Direct Materials | Direct Labor | | |
			Dept. A	Dept. B	Dept. C
X..............	$34	$5.00	$4.00	$1.00	$1.00
Y..............	29	3.00	1.00	4.00	1.00
Z..............	32	4.00	1.00	1.00	4.00

The departmental burden rates per direct labor dollar are as follows:

	Dept. A	Dept. B	Dept. C
Variable overhead..............	$1.20	$0.40	$1.00
Fixed overhead.................	1.20	2.00	1.40
Total.....................	$2.40	$2.40	$2.40

a) Compute gross profit per unit and as a percentage of selling price for each of these three products, using full absorption costing procedures.

b) Compute variable profit contribution per unit and as a percentage of selling price for each of these three products, as they would appear under variable costing procedures.

c) Comment on the differences that you have found between the two costing methods. What recommendation would you make to the company's management? What additional information, if any, would you like?

*11. In calculating the machine-hour cost of the Winston engine lathe No. 14, the accountant of the Horton Machine Works considered the following data:

BUDGETED COST OF MAINTAINING BUILDINGS

Depreciation on buildings.................................	$18,000
Care of grounds...	1,200
Repairs and upkeep......................................	13,730
General factory lighting.................................	470
Cleaning...	380
Heating..	1,500
Insurance on buildings..................................	10,600
Taxes on buildings......................................	14,120
Total...	$60,000

Area available for manufacturing: 75,000 square feet. Area required by Winston engine lathe No. 14, including share of aisle space: 120 square feet. Original cost of engine lathe No. 14: $4,000. Depreciation: 10 percent, straight line.

Work reported on engine lathe No. 14 during the previous year totaled 2,080 hours. The normal running time for this lathe was computed at 2,500 hours per year. The cost of power for the factory was $0.015 per kwh. The lathe required 20 kw per hour of operation.

Part of the budgeted charges against the Winston engine lathe No. 14 at normal volume were as follows:

Proportion of taxes..	$ 10
Proportion of insurance.........................	12
Proportion of stores and supplies............................	38
Repairs..	35
Tools and jigs used..	169
Proportion of planning cost...................................	69
Proportion of functional foremen............................	131
Indirect labor used...	70
Total..	$534

From the data given, compute a full cost machine-hour rate for Winston engine lathe No. 14. Show all computations.

12. The Franklin Press Company has in its factory a drill press department in which are located six style A, three style B, and two style C machines. A few facts with reference to the nature of these machines and their operations are given in the table below:

	Machine Style A	Machine Style B	Machine Style C
Original purchase price—each machine..............	$2,000	$3,000	$4,500
Horsepower rating—each machine..................	5	10	20
Space occupied—each machine (sq. ft.).............	20	50	60
Labor rate per hour, machine operators..............	$2.00	$2.50	$3.20
Normal hours operated per month—each machine.....	170	160	150

The normal operating costs of the drill press department for one month are as follows:

Indirect labor and supervision.............................	$1,375
Depreciation, taxes, and insurance—buildings.................	910
Depreciation, taxes, and insurance—machinery................	600
Heat and light...	260
Power..	545
Miscellaneous...	300
Total..	$3,990

Indirect labor varies roughly with the number of direct labor hours in the department. Supervision is a fixed cost, but in burden rate calculations it is assumed to be related to the number of direct labor hours. Miscellaneous operating expenses are also related roughly to the number of direct labor hours.

One hour of direct labor is required for each machine-hour on each machine.

a) Calculate a department wide, full costing burden rate on a direct labor cost basis.

b) Calculate separate full costing burden rates for the various machine styles, on a machine-hour basis.

c) Assuming that job No. 2051 was run on one of the style C machines and required 15 hours' time, compare the amounts of overhead that would be charged to the job using the two rates developed above. Which figure is right?

13. The Premier Company's factory has four production departments and four service departments—office, buildings, maintenance, and shipping room. All cost accounting, scheduling, and storage functions are performed in the office department. The buildings department is responsible for heating, lighting, and maintaining the factory building and grounds. The maintenance department handles repairs of all equipment except office equipment, the latter being serviced on contract by an outside firm. Shipping handles all incoming shipments and assembles finished products for distribution to the company's customers and sales branches.

The annual budgets of the direct charges of the service departments, reduced to a monthly basis, are as follows:

	Office	Buildings	Main-tenance	Shipping Room
Supervision....................	$ 2,000	$ 500	$ 900	$ 400
Salaries......................	12,000	.....	.....	.....
Indirect labor.................	.....	3,500	6,200	1,500
Supplies......................	4,500	1,000	920	1,900
Depreciation—building.........	.....	2,500	.....	.....
Depreciation—equipment.......	100	100	210	.....
Heat and light................	.....	6,000	.....	.....
Other direct charges...........	17,920	3,400	1,700	540
Total Direct Charges.......	$36,520	$17,000	$9,930	$4,340

Budgeted or normal operating data for the year, also on an average monthly basis, are:

	Floor Space (Square Feet)	Total Employees	Maintenance Labor Hours	Machine-Hours
Department 101........	18,000	50	560	8,000
Department 102........	16,000	40	610	12,000
Department 103........	33,000	100	930	16,000
Department 104........	20,000	60	500	10,000
Office.................	10,000	34	...	.....
Buildings.............	1,000	11	...	.....
Maintenance..........	1,000	17	...	.....
Shipping room........	2,000	6	...	.....
Total.............	101,000	318	2,600	46,000

Prepare a cost distribution sheet, allocating service department costs sequentially in the following sequence and on the following bases:

> Buildings—floor space.
> Office—number of employees.
> Maintenance—maintenance labor hours.
> Shipping room—machine-hours.

14.† The Aywun Tool Company, which was started some years ago, at present employs some 80 men in its own factory on the production of electrically driven hand tools. Three different models are made. About 55 men work in the machine shop making the parts, and about 25 are employed in an assembly shop putting together the machined parts and components, such as small electric motors, which are bought outside. A foreman, who is responsible to the general manager, is in charge of each shop.

The company sells its tools direct to large industrial users, employing two salesmen to obtain orders, and advertising in the engineering journals. It also sells through wholesalers to hardware stores for the nonindustrial market.

In April 19x2, the general manager died and his successor, a Mr. Harold Bright, was recruited from a larger firm in the same industry. On taking over, he found that industrial sales were running at a level which represented only about 70 percent of the factory single-shift capacity. The company's audited accounts for the last complete financial year showed a small profit, representing a quite unsatisfactory return on the capital employed.

One of the first things that Bright called for, on taking over his new duties, was an up-to-date statement showing the costs and selling prices of the company's products, together with comparative figures for a period 12 months earlier. After considerable delay, the firm's accountant produced the following statement relating to three of the company's most popular models:

	Direct Materials	Direct Labor	Factory Overhead	General Overhead	Selling Expenses	Total Cost	Selling Price
Model A:							
March, 19x2	$ 4.00	$3.30	$2.50	$1.50	$0.75	$12.05	$15.00
March, 19x1	3.40	3.30	2.35	1.50	0.55	11.10	14.00
Model B:							
March, 19x2	7.60	8.40	4.55	3.00	1.65	25.20	28.00
March, 19x1	6.30	8.40	4.20	3.00	1.45	23.35	26.50
Model C:							
March, 19x2	13.50	9.60	7.05	4.50	2.45	37.10	42.00
March, 19x1	13.00	9.60	6.60	4.50	2.25	35.95	42.00

Being himself well versed in the complexities of cost accounting and knowing that the company only kept rather crude historical cost records,

---

† This problem was prepared by Professor David Solomons of the University of Pennsylvania.

Bright felt that before he could safely begin to draw any conclusions from the figures, he must know a good deal about the bases on which they had been prepared. He therefore drew up a list of questions for the accountant to answer.

What *questions* did Bright need to ask in order to satisfy himself as to the bases on which the cost schedule had been prepared? You are not required to draw any conclusions from the figures.

*15. The Tisket Tasket Casket Company, manufacturers of burial caskets and morticians' equipment, has three service departments and eight production departments. The company has decided to use predetermined rates as the basis for service department cost allocation. The budgeted direct departmental charges for the three service departments for the current year are as follows:

> Department A....................$12,000 per month
> Department B.................... 18,000 per month
> Department C.................... 20,000 per month

The estimated numbers of service units budgeted for this year are as follows:

Service Department	Budgeted Monthly Service Consumption by Departments				
	A	B	C	Production	Total
A.............	....	1,200	800	6,000	8,000
B.............	600	....	1,400	8,000	10,000
C.............	2,000	1,000	....	12,000	15,000

This table should be read as follows: service department A provides 1,200 units of service to service department B, 800 units of service to service department C, and 6,000 units of service to the various production departments.

a) Compute, for each of the three service departments, a charging rate per service unit that covers only the costs directly traceable to that department (direct departmental charges). In other words, the charging rate will not include any provision for the costs of other service departments, nor will service departments be charged for their use of other service departments' services.

b) Compute charging rates by sequential allocation, taking the service departments in alphabetical order.

c) Compute charging rates which give full recognition to the interdependence of the three service dpartments, using cross-allocations. Three equations must be solved simultaneously, one for each service department. The equation for department A is:

$$\text{Charging rate}_A = \frac{\$12,000 + 600 \times \text{Charging rate}_B + 2,000 \times \text{Charging rate}_C}{8,000 \text{ total service units consumed}},$$

16. From the following information, prepare an overhead cost distribution sheet and predetermined labor hour burden rates for each of the Sender Company's four producing departments (machine No. 1, machine No. 2, assembly, and painting) on a full costing basis.

ESTIMATED OVERHEAD COSTS

Indirect labor and supervision:
Machine No. 1...$33,000
Machine No. 2... 22,000
Assembly... 11,000
Painting... 7,000
Material storage..................................... 44,000
Maintenance... 32,700
Indirect materials and supplies:
Machine No. 1.. 2,200
Machine No. 2.. 1,100
Assembly... 3,300
Painting... 3,400
Maintenance... 2,800
Other:
Rent of factory...................................... 96,000
Depreciation of machinery and equipment.............. 44,000
Insurance and taxes on machinery and equipment....... 2,400
Compensation insurance at $2 per $100 of labor payroll...... 19,494
Power.. 66,000
Factory office salaries.............................. 52,800
General superintendence.............................. 55,000
Miscellaneous office costs........................... 21,620
Heat and light....................................... 72,000
Miscellaneous storage charges (insurance, etc.)...... 3,686

PROJECTED OPERATING DATA

Department	Area (Sq. Ft.)	Cost of Machinery and Equipment	Raw Materials Used	Horse-power Rating	Direct Labor Hours	Direct Labor Payroll	Number of Employees
Machine No. 1.....	65,000	$220,000	$520,000	2,000	120,000	$440,000	200
Machine No. 2......	55,000	110,000	180,000	1,000	44,000	220,000	120
Assembly..........	44,000	55,000		100	60,000	110,000	60
Painting..........	32,000	22,000	90,000	200	27,500	55,000	30
Storage...........	22,000	11,000					28
Maintenance.......	11,000	16,500					20
Office............	11,000	5,500					22
Total.........	240,000	$440,000	$790,000	3,300	251,500	$825,000	480

(Note: Allocate office and general superintendence costs on the basis of direct labor hours, maintenance on the basis of machinery and equipment cost, and storage costs on the basis of materials [direct and indirect] used.)

17. A manufacturing firm has four departments, two of which are producing departments (A and B) and two of which are service departments (C and D). Volume in each producing department is measured in direct labor hours (DLH). Costs are:

Department	Direct Fixed Costs	Variable Direct Costs		Units of C's Services Required	Units of D's Services Required
		Per Direct Labor Hour	Per Unit of Service		
A............	$50,000	$2.00	...	0.010 per direct labor hour	....
B...........	30,000	1.50	...	0.035 per direct labor hour	0.0475 per direct labor hour
C...........	19,350	...	$2.00	....	0.050 per unit of C's services
D...........	9,780	...	3.00	0.010 per unit of D's services	....

This is to be read as follows: for department A, direct fixed costs are $50,000, direct variable costs are $2.00 per direct labor hour, and, in addition, 0.01 of a unit of service provided by department C is needed for each direct labor hour in department A.

Expected production volume is:

A.................29,000 direct labor hours.
B.................20,000 direct labor hours.

a) Compute a full cost burden rate for each producing department, to the nearest tenth of a cent. (Note: This requires cross-allocations.)

b) Compute burden rates for use in a variable costing system.

18. M. Lebec has a small factory consisting of two production departments, a machinery maintenance department (serving the machines of the two production departments), a methods and scheduling department, and a small factory office. The building is rented at a monthly rental that covers the cost of heat, light, building maintenance, etc. For a typical month, the costs of general factory overhead and of the service departments are as follows:

Plant manager's salary...................................$1,560
Rent... 2,400
Direct departmental costs—service departments:
  Factory office....................................... 1,260
  Methods and schedules department..................... 1,530
  Maintenance department............................... 1,800

All of these costs are regarded as wholly fixed and indivisible except those of the factory office and the maintenance department. The factory office costs include the salaries of the factory accountant and the bookkeeper ($1,140 a month) and forms, paper supplies, etc. ($120 in an average month—$30 fixed and $90 variable with factory direct labor hours).

Of the direct maintenance department costs, $800 represents the salaries of the maintenance supervisor, depreciation on shop equipment, and other costs of providing maintenance capacity. The remaining $1,000 represents the wages of the maintenance men and the costs of maintenance supplies required for a maintenance volume of 200 maintenance labor hours a month; this $1,000 is regarded as a variable cost in that in periods of low maintenance requirements the maintenance men are assigned to other productive work in the factory.

The overhead costs traceable to the two production departments are:

	Production Dept. A	Production Dept. B
Fixed..........	$ 7,600	$1,880
Variable........	4,260	1,920
Total......	$11,860	$3,800

Physical statistics for a typical month are:

	Factory Office	Methods and Schedules	Maintenance	Production Dept. A	Production Dept. B
Direct labor hours..	...	...	....	4,000	6,000
Employees........	2	2	3	18	27
Machine-hours.....	...	...	....	6,000	3,000
Maintenance hours.	...	...	....	120	80
Floor space (sq. ft.)	900	300	1,200	6,400	3,200

The amount of maintenance required in each production department is partly variable with machine-hours. Routine maintenance amounts to 30 hours a month in production department A and 50 hours in production department B. The rest is proportionately variable with production department volume.

a) Compute a full cost burden rate for each production department, first distributing the plant manager's salary and factory rent among the five departments, and then redistributing service department costs sequentially, in the left-to-right sequence shown in the table above. The allocation bases are:

> Plant manager's salary..........Employees
> Rent..........................Floor space
> Factory office..................Employees
> Methods and schedules.........Machine-hours
> Maintenance...................Maintenance hours.

A machine-hour burden rate should be used in production department A; the burden rate for department B should be based on direct labor hours.

b) M. Lebec is considering whether to accept an order for 100 units of product X at a reduced price for delivery six months from now. Adequate capacity will be available to handle this order, and fixed costs will be essentially the same whether the order is accepted or rejected.

Each unit of product X requires one hour of department A labor and one hour of department B labor, three machine-hours in department A and one-half machine-hour in department B. How much of the overhead costs listed should be allocated to *each unit* of product X for purposes of this decision? You need not necessarily use the burden rates developed in (*a*) above, but you should explain briefly your reasons either for using these rates without adjustment or for using different figures.

Chapter 9

COSTING JOINT PRODUCTS

PREVIOUS CHAPTERS have dealt with the problems encountered in the measurement or estimation of the costs of products produced independently of each other. Now it is time to recognize another class of products: those produced jointly with each other. The purpose of this chapter is to examine the methods used to derive unit costs for joint products and to study the relevance of these unit costs to management decisions.

The Nature of Joint Products

When the processing of a single input or set of inputs yields two or more products, these products are referred to as *joint products.* Gasoline and fuel oil are joint products. So are beefsteaks and cowhides, although both of these are the products of separate processing of the raw outputs of the joint process.

Three different types of joint processing situations should be distinguished:

1. *Fixed yields:* the joint products are derived in proportions which are fixed by formula, as in certain chemical reactions.
2. *Materials-determined yields:* the percentage yield of each of the joint products depends on the quality or composition of the joint materials inputs.
3. *Processing-determined yields:* the relative yields of the various joint products can be varied by alterations in the processing methods employed.

The individual outputs in any one of these processes may be marketed "as is" or subjected to further processing, depending on the nature of the immediate output and the profitability of separate processing.

The Nature of Joint Costs

The existence of joint products creates the phenomenon of *joint costs.* These may be defined as the costs of those input factors that are necessary for the manufacture and separation of all the joint products as

238

a group and not specifically for any one of them alone. In other words, not all the costs of joint products may be classified as joint costs. Livestock, purchasing, and slaughtering costs are true joint costs of all the products that will eventually be marketed by the meat-packer, but many of the later processing costs can be attributed specifically to one product or another.

For example, the cost of curing ham is not a joint cost of ham and lard but is specific to the ham. This provides us with a basis for a distinction between joint costs and *separable costs*—costs specifically traceable to a particular joint product. Some of these will be prime costs, others will be overhead, and the methods described in the preceding chapters can be applied.

Joint costs pose two questions for the accountant. First, how are they to be allocated to the joint products for inventory valuation? Second, how should they be treated for decision making? Although we shall discuss the decision-making aspects more fully later, this chapter will consider both of these questions briefly.

JOINT COSTS IN DECISION MAKING

Managerial decisions that must be made in connection with joint products are essentially of two types:

1. Decisions relating to the joint products as a group—e.g., discontinue total production or expand total production.
2. Decisions relating to the depth of additional processing to be applied to individual joint products—e.g., sell the product as it stands or process it further before sale.

Joint Products as a Group

For the group of joint products as a whole, the question is whether the total revenue to be derived from the sale of all joint products, less any processing and distribution costs necessary to place these products in marketable form, is adequate to cover the incremental costs of the joint inputs. For example, the decision to work a mine which produces ore containing gold, zinc, and lead must be based on consideration of the market prices of all three metals. Inasmuch as the price of gold is fixed by law, some marginal mines are worked only when zinc and lead prices are high. The amount of newly mined gold flowing into the U.S. Treasury fluctuates with the prices of other metals that are mined jointly with gold.

Another related problem is to determine the maximum price that the company can afford to pay for joint inputs of a given grade or specification. This will depend on the relative yield of each product to be derived from the joint input. For example, in buying raw materials that vary in quality, the price that can be paid will be higher on grades that yield a greater proportion of high-value products. The maximum purchase price is a function of the total value of all the joint products, less all the joint costs of processing or conversion.

Individual Joint Products

Once it has been determined that joint production is profitable, there is a further question of how far to process each of the joint products. For example, should cowhides be tanned or should they be sold on the market untanned? For this kind of decision, the question is whether the sale value of the product can be increased by more than the additional costs of separate processing—the separable costs. The cost of the steer no longer has any meaning for this decision. What is relevant is *opportunity cost,* in this case the amount that could be realized from the sale of the untanned hides. If hides can be sold untanned for 30 cents a pound, then 30 cents a pound is the opportunity cost of any hides that are retained for further processing. (Not selling the hides at 30 cents requires the same economic sacrifice as buying hides at 30 cents: this is the meaning of opportunity cost.) The relevant comparison is:

Market value of tanned hides............................		$0.40
Less: Market value of untanned hides..................$0.30		
Incremental separate processing cost................ 0.08		0.38
Incremental Processing Profit..........................		$0.02

The stage of production at which the joint products are separated for further independent processing or sale is commonly referred to as the *split-off point.* Exhibit 9–1 shows a process with two split-off points. Raw materials are first cooked, after which three separate products are split off: grease, a glue and water mixture, and a residue. Both the glue-water mixture and the residue are subjected to separate processing. Processing the mixture yields one product only: glue. Processing the residue, on the other hand, yields two products: grease and tankage stock. The latter is then cooked once again to yield fertilize tankage.

The costs of operating the primary cooker are joint costs to all the outputs. The costs of operating the evaporator, on the other hand, are specific costs of the glue and have no connection with the grease and tankage outputs. Conversely, the cost of operating the press is a joint cost of grease and tankage stock but cannot be regarded as a cost of the glue.

This illustration should demonstrate that identification of a split-off point is possible even if no outside markets exist for the individual products at this point. Location of a split-off point is a purely technological question. The absence of an intermediate market for one of the joint products merely means that opportunity cost for that product is zero. The desirability of further processing of this product, therefore, can be

Exhibit 9–1

SPLIT-OFF POINTS IN JOINT PRODUCTION

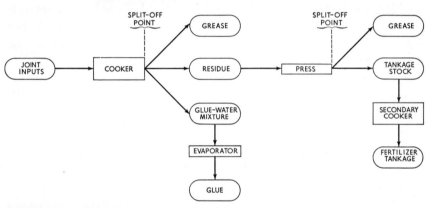

determined by comparing the costs of further processing with the net market proceeds from the product after processing. No allocation of the joint costs will assist in this decision.

Separable Costs and Joint Production Decisions

The separable costs of further processing and distribution of individual products may in some cases have a bearing on the decision as to whether to manufacture the joint products as a group. In making this decision, the incremental *profit* from further processing should be considered but processing *losses* should be ignored. For example, suppose that processing a certain material will yield 2,000 tons of product A and 500 tons of product B a week at a total joint cost of $60,000 a week. Product A can be sold for $40 a ton, but product B is unsalable without further processing. After further processing, product B can be sold for $15 a ton, but incremental separable processing costs total $6,000 a week. The decision to continue joint production should be based on the following comparison:

	A	B	Total
Sales	$80,000	$7,500	$87,500
Incremental separable processing cost		6,000	6,000
Product contribution	$80,000	$1,500	$81,500
Joint processing cost			60,000
Joint Profit			$21,500

But suppose that product B can be sold for only $10 a ton, or total revenues of only $5,000. In this case further processing of B cannot be justified, and the joint production decision must be based on the revenue for product A alone. Product B will be obtained along with A, but management is under no compulsion to process it further. In this case the comparison might take the following form:

Sales, product A		$80,000
Less: Joint processing costs	$60,000	
Removal costs, product B	500	60,500
Joint Profit		$19,500

Any costs of disposing of the unwanted by-product must be charged against product A revenues, but any losses that would occur if the by-product were processed further can be disregarded.

The dangers attendant upon inappropriate cost allocation procedures can be illustrated by modifying our example slightly. Now let us assume that product B can be sold "as is" for $5 a ton or for $20 a ton if further processing costs of $6,000 a week are incurred. This company has adopted an arbitrary formula for allocating the joint processing costs to the joint products on the basis of percentage of total tonnage, 80 percent or $48,000 to product A and 20 percent or $12,000 to product B. This produces the following product profit statement:

	Product A	Product B	Total
Sales	$80,000	$10,000	$90,000
Less: Joint processing cost	$48,000	$12,000	$60,000
Separable processing cost	.....	6,000	6,000
Operating Profit	$32,000	$(8,000)	$24,000

This statement makes product B look unprofitable. By disregarding the arbitrary cost allocation, however, it can be seen that further processing of product B will produce a contribution to company profit:

Sales, product B (processed)............................		$10,000
Less: Separable processing cost.....................$6,000		
Market value, product B (unprocessed)......... 2,500		8,500
Profit Contribution, Product B Processing.............		$ 1,500

Without further processing of product B, total revenues from the joint products would be only $82,500, less joint processing costs of $60,000, or a joint profit of $22,500. Further processing of product B adds $1,500 to the total profit, which now becomes the $24,000, shown in the preceding table. The method used to allocate the joint costs served to obscure this fact.

ASSIGNING JOINT COSTS TO PRODUCTS

Unit cost finding for independently produced products serves, to varying degrees, decision making, control, and inventory costing purposes. Because joint costs are incurred to yield the joint products *as a group,* however, it is not possible to divide them among the products in any managerially meaningful way. Thus unit costs serve only in inventory costing purpose.

The most commonly used bases for joint cost allocation fall generally into two broad categories:

1. Physical bases.
2. Market value bases.

Physical Allocation Bases

If the joint products can be measured in terms of some common physical unit of measure, the joint input cost may be allocated to each product on the basis of its proportion of the total joint physical output. For example, the cost of lumber milling might be apportioned to the various grades of lumber on the basis of each grade's relative proportion of the total number of board feet produced during the period, as in Exhibit 9–2.

The physical unit basis is also used in some cases even though the output of the various joint products is not ordinarily measured in terms of a common physical unit. For example, one of the joint products may be a liquid, measured in gallons, and another may be a solid, measured in pounds. For cost allocation, conversion factors may be used to express output of both products in pound or gallon equivalents. Such methods are usually referred to as "equivalent unit" methods, but they are fundamentally no different from other physical unit measures.

Allocation of joint costs on a physical unit basis is generally unsatisfactory and should be avoided. The most glaring weakness of the physical unit basis is that it assumes implicitly that the production of each of the joint products is equally desirable. In the case of timber costs, for example, the price paid for timber or for timbering rights will vary with the expected lumber yield. If a given stand of timber is expected to yield a high proportion of the higher valued grades of lumber, the timber rights will command a higher price than if the lower grades predominate. Although we have already said that cost allocations should not influence the acquisition decision, it is unrealistic to assign to low-grade lumber the same unit cost that is assigned to high-grade lumber. If all the lumber in a given stand of timber were of the lower

Exhibit 9–2

LUMBER COST ALLOCATED ON PHYSICAL UNIT BASIS

Product	(1) M Feet Produced	(2) Percentage of Total	(3) Total Cost Allocated (2) × $3,500	(4) Allocated Cost per M Feet (3) ÷ (1)
Clear.........	10	12.5%	$ 437.50	$43.75
Industrial.....	12	15.0	525.00	43.75
No. 1.........	30	37.5	1,312.50	43.75
No. 2.........	20	25.0	875.00	43.75
No. 3.........	8	10.0	350.00	43.75
Total.....	80	100.0%	$3,500.00	xxx

grades, cost would almost certainly be lower than indicated by the average cost per board foot for mixed grades obtained by the method illustrated in Exhibit 9–2.

To put this another way, average cost per physical unit is a poor measure of the opportunity cost of obtaining each of the joint products, and opportunity cost, if we could measure it, would provide a sound basis for valuing each joint product. For example, if we could purchase and process timber containing clear lumber only at a cost of $70 per thousand board feet, then $70 would be a valid basis for product costing, useful for decision making as well as for inventory valuation.

A second but related argument against physical unit allocations arises from the application of the financial accounting principle of conservatism in balance sheet valuation. Assignment to low-valued products of the same cost per unit assigned to high-valued products will in many cases yield inventory valuations in excess of market values. Thus some products will be overvalued and others will be undervalued on company balance sheets. Only an allocation method that considers market values can avoid this.

Value-Based Allocation

There are several ways of introducing market values into the allocation process, but the basic approach can be established by examining the two most common methods:

1. Relative market value method.
2. Uniform percentage net-back method.

Relative Market Value Method. One method is to multiply the physical output of each product by its market price at the split-off point, add the resulting market values for all products, and find the percentage of the total represented by each product. These percentages are then used to allocate the total input cost among the joint products.

For example, this method might be used to allocate lumber costs among the various grades of lumber produced, as shown in Exhibit 9–3.

Exhibit 9–3

JOINT COST ALLOCATED ON RELATIVE MARKET VALUE BASIS

Product	(1) M Feet Pro- duced	(2) Price per M Feet	(3) Market Value (1) × (2)	(4) % of Total Market Value	(5) Total Cost Allocated (4) × $3,500	(6) Allocated Cost per M Feet (5) ÷ (1)
Clear............	10	$100	$1,000	20.0%	$ 700	$70.00
Industrial........	12	80	960	19.2	672	56.00
No. 1............	30	60	1,800	36.0	1,260	42.00
No. 2............	20	50	1,000	20.0	700	35.00
No. 3............	8	30	240	4.8	168	21.00
Total........	80	xxx	$5,000	100.0%	$3,500	xxx

The total cost of producing 80,000 board feet of lumber is $3,500. The clear grade lumber represents 20 percent of the total value of the lumber produced, and by this method of allocation 20 percent of the joint cost of all grades of lumber, or $700, is assigned to clear lumber. Total cost is fully allocated, and each product shows the same percentage gross margin, in this case 30 percent of selling price. If this method is used, inventoried cost can never exceed market unless all products in total cost more than the aggregate market value.

Uniform Percentage Net-Back Method. Another variant of the market value approach is frequently used whenever one or more of the joint products is not readily marketable at the split-off point but can be marketed effectively after further processing. For example, a chemical process may yield two products, one of which can be packaged and sold without further processing, whereas the other is produced in a liquid solution that cannot be sold because of high transportation costs. A ready market for the second product exists, but only if it can be recovered from the water in which it is dissolved. In this case, market value at the split-off point cannot be obtained directly, but it can be approximated by subtracting the costs of the drying operation from the market value of the dried product. This derived market value can be referred to as the "net realization" or "net-back" to the joint process from the sale of the ultimate product. By performing this operation for each of the joint products which cannot be sold readily without further processing, approximate market values at the split-off point can be determined for all products, and allocation of joint cost proceeds in exactly the same manner as in the previous illustration.[1]

An example of this kind of calculation is shown in Exhibit 9–4. In

Exhibit 9–4

JOINT COST ALLOCATED ON UNIFORM PERCENTAGE NET-BACK BASIS

Product	(1) Price	(2) Separable Processing Cost	(3) Contribution to Joint Cost (1) − (2)	(4) Units Produced	(5) Total Contribution (3) × (4)	(6) % of Total	(7) Allocation of Joint Cost (6) × $300,000	(8) Allocated Joint Cost per Unit (7) ÷ (4)
A.........	$50	$10	$40	10,000	$400,000	66.67%	$200,000	$20.00
B.........	40	12	28	5,000	140,000	23.33	70,000	14.00
C.........	20	5	15	4,000	60,000	10.00	30,000	7.50
Total......	xxx	xxx	xxx	xxx	$600,000	100.00%	$300,000	xxx

this example, joint processing costs amount to $300,000 and there are three joint products, each of which requires additional processing before it can be sold. After further processing costing $10 per unit, product A can be sold for $50. Its contribution to joint cost, therefore, is $40 per unit, or $400,000 for the production yield of 10,000 units. This represents two thirds of the net-back from all three products combined, and thus product A is assigned two thirds of the joint processing cost, or $200,000. This averages $20 per unit, as shown in the last column of Exhibit 9–4.

This method is basically similar to the relative market value method. Either method can be defended as producing a "reasonable" allocation of joint costs for public financial reporting. Both can be attacked as

---

[1] Any marketing costs that can be traced to individual products should also be deducted in the same manner as separate processing costs. For simplicity these have been ignored in this illustration.

arbitrary. The only real difference between them is that the uniform percentage net-back method assigns no profit to subsequent operations, whereas such operations can show either a profit or a loss under the relative market value method. In both cases the percentage profit margins for all of the company's products are identical at the split-off point. (In Exhibit 9–4, for example, the profit margin for each product is shown as 50 percent of the net-back from further processing.)

The critical point to remember here is that joint cost allocations of the kinds just described are made solely for public financial reporting and have no relevance in managerial decision making. Physical unit allocation, for example, can easily assign more cost to a product than it can be sold for, but this does not necessarily mean that management should not sell the product at going market prices. The relative market value method, which equalizes the percentage profit on sales for each of the joint products at the split-off point, serves to increase the *apparent* profitability of further processing by the amount of the discount of average allocated cost below market value at the split-off point. The uniform percentage net-back method goes to the other extreme and in effect assigns zero profitability to separate processing of the joint products. This is just as bad. As we have already seen, decisions as to the desirability of joint production should be based on total costs and total revenues for all the joint products combined. Decisions as to the depth of separate processing should depend on the relationships between market value increments and the incremental cost of further processing and distribution. For neither of these purposes is cost allocation by any of the methods that we have outlined thus far of any relevance.

Variable Proportions and Incremental Cost

The general rule that the cost of an individual joint product cannot be measured is subject to one exception—the case of variable proportions. Many joint products are joint in the sense that they are produced simultaneously from one set of material inputs in a single series of manufacturing operations, but their relative proportions can be altered by changes in the way the materials are processed or by changes in the quality or composition of the raw materials. Thus the gasoline yield from a barrel of crude oil can be altered within limits by adjustments in the refining process or by purchase of different grades of crude oil. Under these circumstances, the incremental costs of increasing the yield of each of the refined products can be determined or at least estimated with a fair degree of accuracy. This permits the analysis of the economic effects of varying product proportions, although for reasons we shall see shortly it does not provide a handy mechanism for routine allocations of joint costs.

To illustrate, let us assume that a department produces two products, X and Y, from a single process. Product X sells for $5 a pound; product Y is priced at $2 a pound. Production of these two products is currently in the ratio of 40 percent product X and 60 percent product Y, but by varying production techniques the yield of X can be increased to a maximum of 60 percent if conditions warrant.

This may be treated as a problem in the desirability of further processing. First, let us assume that the increased yield of product X results from subjecting product Y to an additional processing operation (as in subjecting gas-oil distillates to catalytic cracking to increase the gasoline yield). If 60 pounds of product Y can be processed further to yield 20 additional pounds of product X, at an incremental processing cost of $0.75 per pound, we get the following comparison:

Revenues after processing:		
Product X, 20 pounds at $5...		$100
Product Y, 40 pounds at $2...		80
Total...		$180
Less:		
Processing cost, 60 pounds at $0.75................................	$ 45	
Market value of Y before processing...............................	120	165
Incremental Profit..		$ 15

Phrasing this in another way, the incremental cost of another 20 pounds of product X is the sum of $45 processing cost and $40 in lost revenues from the sale of 20 pounds of product Y, or $85. The incremental cost of product X is thus $4.25 per pound.

A similar set of calculations can be prepared if the increased yield results not from further processing of one of the original joint products but from modifications in the basic processing techniques themselves. The incremental cost of increasing the yield of any product is still the sum of incremental processing costs plus the sale value of the other joint products lost by the shift in product mix.

Two major difficulties are encountered in efforts to apply this approach in practice. First, incremental cost is not a constant but varies, depending on relative yields. If the crude run is yielding 35 percent gasoline, the cost of increasing the yield to 36 percent will probably be less than it would be for increasing the yield from 40 percent to 41 percent. This requires the development of a schedule or table of incremental costs, one for each assumed product mix. Second, the opportunity cost of products sacrificed to increase the yield of others is the net revenue lost by this sacrifice. This is not necessarily equal to the product price. For example, if existing market prices are rigid and increased output of product Y will merely result in increased inventories of product Y, then the opportunity cost component of the incremental cost of product X is zero. (It may even be negative to allow for inventory carrying costs.) Even if market prices are flexible, if the company's share of the market is so large that increases in sales volume can be achieved only by price reductions or greater promotional effort or both, the opportunity cost of product Y will almost certainly be less than its market price. It is much more difficult to estimate opportunity cost than to estimate selling price.

These difficulties can sometimes be overcome, and this sort of calculation is made routinely in oil refining and other industries. It is not generally available for public financial reporting, however, for two reasons. First, of course, the incremental cost calculation is not applicable to joint production in which relative product proportions are fixed. No amount of manufacturing can increase the amount of beefsteak recoverable from any given steer, and the cattle market is not sensitive enough to provide measures of incremental cost from changes in materials specifications.

Second, the total costs of all of the joint products determined by this method are highly unlikely to equal total joint cost. As long as outlay cost continues to be the basis for inventory costing for public financial reporting, therefore, this method cannot be used for this purpose.

THE COSTING OF BY-PRODUCTS

Cost accounting systems generally distinguish between two classes of joint products—(1) *coproducts* or *main products* and (2) *by-products*. The distinction is important in accounting for only one reason: coproducts are costed by some variant of one of the methods described earlier in this chapter, while by-products are costed on a different basis.

Defining By-products

Although the distinction between the two types of products is inevitably imprecise, a reasonable working definition is that a by-product is a joint product for which the market value is an immaterial proportion of the total market value of all the joint products. Some have added to this definition a further qualifying clause that by-products are *incidental* to production, whereas coproducts are the main *purpose* of production, but this is not very helpful. Although the revenues from any one by-product may be immaterial, by-product revenues in total often represent the difference between profitable and unprofitable operations. Furthermore, history is replete with examples in which the relative positions of main products and by-products have been reversed. For example, gasoline was originally a by-product in the manufacture of kerosene, but with the growth of the automobile and electric lighting, kerosene shrank to the status of a by-product. The age of the jet airliner has brought kerosene back into the picture, and future developments are likely to produce further changes. Thus any distinction between joint products and by-products must be regarded as strictly temporary, to be reconsidered as conditions change.

Illustration of By-product Costing

Although considerable variation can be found in practice, the costing method known as the *by-product method* consists of crediting a process with the market value of the by-products at the time of production and dividing the residual among the main products.

For example, suppose that a process yields three products, A, B, and C. C is to be treated as a by-product, A and B as main products. The total cost of processing a 1,000-pound batch of products is $934. Yield and market value data are as follows:

Product	Yield (Pounds)	Market Value per Pound	Total Market Value
A.............................	200	$1.90	$ 380
B.............................	500	1.50	750
C.............................	300	0.10	30
Total.................	1,000	xxx	$1,160

The first step in the by-product method is to subtract the market value of the by-product from the total joint cost:

Joint cost.......................................$934
Less: Value of by-product........................ 30
Cost Assigned to Main Products.................$904

The remainder of the joint cost is then apportioned between the main products by one of the methods described earlier. A relative market value distribution is as follows:

Product	Percent of Total Market Value	Total Cost Allocated	Allocated Cost per Pound
A........................	33.6%	$304	$1.52
B........................	66.4	600	1.20
Total..................	100.0%	$904	xxx

This method serves to assign to the by-product a cost equal to its anticipated value:

Product	Anticipated Value	Allocated Cost	Percent Margin
A........................	$ 380	$304	20.0%
B........................	750	600	20.0
C........................	30	30	0
Total..................	$1,160	$934	19.5%

The immateriality of the by-product is evident from this table. If product C were to be treated as a coproduct, it would be allocated a total of $24.15 (30/1,160 of $934) instead of $30, leaving only $5.85 to be redistributed between the other two products. This is only about two thirds of 1 percent of the costs already assigned to these products.

Determination of Market Value

If the market value of by-products is to be introduced into the accounts, it should represent the net amount that the company can expect to realize from the sale of the product. If market price is independent of the company's activities, then market price can be taken as a very close approximation to net realization or market value. If by-product markets are not well organized, however, so that firm market prices are not available, then estimates of net realization must be made. Furthermore, if marketing effort will be necessary to find customers for the by-product and negotiate sales, then an estimate of the costs of marketing the by-product should be deducted in arriving at market value.

Timing of By-product Recognition

By-product revenues may be recognized in the accounts either at the time of split-off or at the time the by-products are sold. In an earlier chapter we saw that scrap values may be credited to production either in the period during which the scrap is produced or at the time of sale. Deferral until point of sale has the advantage of avoiding the need to estimate sale value. It has the disadvantage of introducing into the accounts irregularities that have nothing to do with the production operations in the periods in which the by-products are sold. Although again the low total value of by-products may render this effect immaterial, whenever possible the value of by-products should be recognized in the periods in which they are produced.

Inventory Valuation of By-products

The selection of the time for recognition of the value of by-products carries with it an implicit assumption as to the method of valuing by-product inventories on the corporate balance sheet. Delay in recognition to the point of sale implies that by-products will be carried as memorandum quantities only. Recognition of value at the time of split-off implies valuation at market, in violation of the cost basis for inventory valuation in general. Because by-product values are immaterial, by definition, this departure from cost can be tolerated. When by-product values are material, then one or more of the by-products should be treated as a main product.

CONTROL OF JOINT PRODUCT INVENTORIES

Stocks of individual joint products are likely to get out of balance unless continuing efforts are exerted to keep them in line. Although it is sometimes possible to control relative yields in joint production, this control can ordinarily be exercised only within limits. Seasonal demands for gasoline and fuel oil, for example, create the need for large inventories of the off-season product, and this in turn creates pressures on product price structures. Other products in which relative demand is not primarily seasonal pose an even greater problem. There is no guarantee that inventory buildup in one product as a result of increased demand for other joint products will cure itself through a shift in relative demand.

The problem boils down to this. Increased sales of one joint product lead to increases in inventories of other joint products which cannot be sold at existing selling prices with the amount of selling effort now being expended on them. Lower prices or increased selling effort or both might bring inventories back down to desired levels, but sales management has not taken the initiative to achieve this. The possibility of price reductions may be ruled out temporarily on the grounds that the company wishes to maintain a stable price structure. The possibility of price increases in the product with the greater demand may also be ruled out for the same reason. Increased selling effort on the slower moving products or reductions in selling prices, if these are not ruled out by company policy, are inhibited by inadequate margins between selling prices and inventoried costs. Sales management is content to let these items remain in inventory rather than dilute average net profit on sales by taking the necessary steps to sell them. So inventories continue to build up until there is a shift in relative demand or until the situation becomes so bad that management takes some drastic action to restore the balance.

It should be noted that the inventory buildup may in fact be the most profitable thing to do. There are occasions on which it is more profitable to throw away some of the joint products or even pay to have them removed in order to continue to enjoy the profits on other joint products. Certainly steel production is not going to be cut back to permit clearance of slag inventories, nor will petroleum refining cease because there is no market for asphalt. The question of operating versus not operating is, as we have pointed out, a problem in total costs and total revenues and not a matter of the profitability of any one item alone.

But assuming that there are costs associated with the maintenance of inventories, the control of inventory levels is a matter of managerial concern. From an accounting viewpoint, there are two weapons that can be used to influence inventory levels. One weapon is to make a charge in the accounts of those executives who have responsibility for sales volume to cover the carrying costs of inventory. The amount charged is a direct function of the level of inventories carried. This has been used in some companies to provide an incentive for inventory control.

Another possibility is to recognize that *market price* may not be a valid measure of *market value* and to adjust the cost allocation formula so as to assign a smaller share of the joint cost to the slower moving items. Although the change in allocation by itself does not make it more or less desirable to sell the product, this action may serve to increase management's interest in disposing of excessive inventories of such items. The inventory carrying charge is likely to be a more effective device or rather one that permits a more rational approach to the question of product emphasis and pricing. The shift in allocation, however, does serve to illustrate the effect that allocation methods can have on the company's sales policy and the essential arbitrariness of the allocation of joint costs. What is really relevant is a comparison of the incremental revenue that can be obtained from increased product sales with the net increase in costs necessary to achieve this increase. For this purpose, savings in inventory carrying costs can be treated as partial offsets to the incremental cost of selling the product, but in no case is the amount of joint cost allocated to the product of any real economic relevance.

SUMMARY

When products are produced independently, a large number of costs can be attributed clearly to one product or another by the methods described in the preceding chapters. When two or more products are produced jointly from a single set of inputs, however, no such identification is possible. Unit costs can be computed by methods outlined in this chapter, but they have no relevance in decision making and should be ignored for that purpose. The sole purpose of joint cost allocation is for public financial reporting or to find "reasonable" solutions for such purposes as price determination under cost-plus pricing contracts or value estimation for insurance or tax purposes.

DISCUSSION QUESTIONS

1. What are joint products?
2. Distinguish between a by-product and a coproduct. What is the justification for treating these two types of joint products differently in cost accounting?
3. What difference, if any, does it make whether a given joint product is classified as a coproduct or as a by-product?
4. What is the split-off point? Of what significance is it in costing joint products? In decision making?
5. This chapter has been concerned with joint product costs. What other kinds of joint costs are encountered in manufacturing companies?
6. An executive recently remarked that the allocation of joint costs among joint products is essential "so that we can know just how profitable each of our products is." Comment on this statement.
7. It is common accounting practice to assign no joint costs to certain joint products. Under what circumstances is this a meaningful treatment?
8. Discuss each half of the following statement: "The task of the accountant in joint-cost situations is to allocate the joint costs among the joint products in the most realistic way so that they will be appropriate to management decision making. The best allocation method for this purpose is ordinarily some variant of the relative market value method."
9. What managerial justification exists for assigning to each joint product at the split-off point its market value less the estimated costs of selling or otherwise disposing of that product? If this treatment were to be applied to all the joint products, what would have to be done to insure conformity with the "cost basis" for public financial reporting?

10. "Allocation of joint costs to products is inescapably arbitrary. Therefore, I see no reason why we have to allocate at all." Prepare an answer to the second half of this statement.

11. A certain company classifies the output of a joint process into two product categories: "firsts" and "seconds." The joint production costs are assigned to the two types on the basis of relative market values. The company's cost accountant has suggested that all products should be assigned the same unit cost and that any margin of this cost over the net market value of seconds should be transferred to the income statement as an expense. The company's sales manager has countered with the suggestion that the loss on seconds, chargeable to the manufacturing division, should be based on the difference between the market price of firsts and the market price of seconds. Which of these three methods do you prefer? Why?

12. When the problem is to decide whether or not to process a joint product further, how much of the joint cost should be allocated to this product? Why?

13. The Emilia Company allocates joint costs on the basis of relative market values. The costs assigned to "firsts" and "seconds" of a particular product on this basis are: firsts, $1.50 per unit; seconds, $1.20 per unit. Seconds are then reworked and can be sold as first-quality products. The rework costs amount to $0.40 per unit. How would you handle rework costs in the company's cost and inventory accounts?

14. The Omar Meat Company is a "breaker." It inspects meat carcasses in packing houses to find top prime grade carcasses which it cuts and either sells immediately or cures. All cuts except ribs and loins are sold to the chains and retail meat markets at cost or below. The ribs and loins are cured from two to four weeks at 33 degrees and kept free of mold, and are then sold as "Omar's vintage beef." The cured boneless prime loin strip sold in November for $2.33 per pound in 100-pound minimum lots to restaurants and clubs. The price for smaller lots was $4 per pound, dry-iced and prepaid. The Omar Meat Company's profits run $75,000 on a gross of $2,500,000.

   a) What kind of cost calculation would result in the statement "sold to the chains and retail meat markets at cost or below?"

   b) Explain the usefulness of the calculation described in (*a*) for (1) guiding management in pricing the other cuts to chains and retail meat markets, and (2) costing any inventory of such other cuts on hand as of a balance sheet date.

EXERCISES AND PROBLEMS

1. During the past year the Atom Chemical Company converted certain raw materials into 500,000 pounds of material "A" and 1,000,000 gallons of liquid "B." The total joint cost of production was $388,000. After separation, material "A" was further processed and converted into material "C" at an additional cost of 3 cents a pound. The sales price of material "C" was 40 cents a pound and that of liquid "B" 30 cents a gallon. On December 31, the inventory showed 20,000 pounds of material "A," 50,000 gallons of liquid "B," and 35,000 pounds of material "C."

At what costs should the above quantities of "A," "B," and "C" be carried in end-of-year inventory?

2. The Juno Refining Company processes an ore into three metals. During the past month, the company processed 150,000 tons of ore and incurred the following costs:

Ore...	$600,000
Direct labor..................................	80,000
Other variable processing costs..................	50,000
Fixed processing costs..........................	70,000
Total Costs...............................	$800,000

The output and price per ton at which it was sold were:

Product	A	B	C
Output in tons.................	20,000	10,000	3,000
Price per ton..................	$20.00	$30.00	$50.00

Compute the cost per unit of each metal, stating any assumptions you had to make.

3. The Paycock Chemical Company has a plant which jointly produces two chemicals, X–16 and Y–32. The total cost incurred to point of separation is $864,000 a month at normal volume. Monthly production is two million gallons of X–16 and 300,000 pounds of Y–32. X–16 is processed further to make one of the company's branded products, Z–48. Based on the price of Z–48 less the further processing costs, the net-back on X–16 is $0.45 a gallon. The price of Y–32 is $0.20 a pound.

Compute the cost of X–16 on the assumptions:

a) Y–32 is a joint product.
b) Y–32 is a by-product.

*4. The total cost of processing 100,000 barrels of crude petroleum—including raw material, labor, and overhead—is $440,000. Expected yields and market values of products are as shown below. Compute unit product costs for inventory costing purposes.

Product	Barrel Yield	Estimated Market Values	
		Per Barrel	Total
Aviation gasoline............................	8,000	$ 6.25	$ 50,000
Motor gasoline..............................	42,000	5.00	210,000
Kerosene....................................	10,000	4.40	44,000
Distillate fuels..............................	20,000	4.00	80,000
Lubricants..................................	5,000	10.00	50,000
Residual fuels...............................	10,000	2.60	26,000
Gases and loss...............................	5,000	...	.....
Total.......................................	100,000	xxx	$460,000

---

* Solutions to problems marked with an asterisk (*) can be found in Appendix B.

5. A company processes soybeans to make soybean meal and soybean oil. After initial processing, soybean oil is separated from a cake-like residue. The cake is then ground and moisturized to form soybean meal. During a certain week the company processed 10,000 bushels of soybeans to yield 90,000 pounds of soybean oil and 450,000 pounds of cake. The cake was then processed further to yield 500,000 pounds of meal, the increase in weight resulting from added moisture.

The cost of the beans was $2.20 per bushel, the costs of joint processing amounted to $2,702, and the costs of processing the cake into meal amounted to $400. The market price of meal was $55 a ton, and the market price of oil $0.15 a pound.

a) Using the uniform percentage net-back method of cost allocation, compute unit costs for the week.

b) Compute unit costs, allocating joint costs on a physical unit basis. Would you find this method acceptable for inventory costing in this case? Explain.

*6. The General Chemical Company manufactures a broad range of chemicals. In one of its processing units two materials are combined to make three joint products. The relative market value method is used to allocate the joint costs among the products, and the relevant cost, price, and quantity information is given below.

Input	Quantity	Cost per Unit
Material A.	100 lbs.	$0.12
Material B.	50 gals.	0.15
Direct labor.	3 hrs.	2.00
Manufacturing overhead.	3 hrs.	3.50

Output	Quantity	Price per Unit
Product I.	30 lbs.	$0.60
Product II.	60 lbs.	0.40
Product III.	20 gals.	0.30

What is the unit cost of each product, using the company's method?

7. A process yields two products, Nix and Pox. Ten pounds of raw materials cost $42 and yield 7 pounds of Nix and 3 pounds of Pox. Costs of processing the materials average $22 for each 10 pounds of materials. Nix sells at a price of $9 a pound. Pox sells for $4 a pound, but only after the company spends $1 a pound to process it into salable form.

a) Using the "uniform percentage net-back" basis, compute a unit cost for each of the two products.

b) A new proposal has just been made to use 10,000 pounds of Nix to manufacture 10,000 pounds of a new product each month. The new product would yield $15 a pound in revenues; incremental costs to produce and sell the new product would average $6.25 a pound, excluding the cost of Nix. Should the proposal be accepted?

*8. The Standard Philatelic Service purchased a stamp collection from the heirs of a well-known collector. A price of $132,000 was paid for the entire collection. The company's appraiser divided the collection into the following categories:

Category	Expected Sales Value
Sheets, unused..	$ 10,000
Plate number blocks, unused............................	40,000
Singles, rare..	84,000
Singles, unused, common................................	20,000
Singles, used—for catalogue sale.......................	5,000
Singles, used—for bulk sale............................	1,000
Total..	$160,000

Compute the inventory cost of each category.

9. The following data summarize the factory operations of the Umbrage Hosiery Company for the month of June:

Production:

Firsts...	6,840 pairs
Seconds..	900 pairs
Rejects..	100 pairs

Costs:

Joint processing costs................................	$7,077.34
Packing and trademarking—firsts......................	68.40
Packing—seconds.....................................	6.00

Sales:

Firsts: 6,840 pairs at $1.26 a pair.
Seconds: 900 pairs at $0.51 a pair.

Scrap Recovery:

From rejects...	$12.00
From other scrap.....................................	43.00

a) Compute the cost of hosiery, using the uniform percentage net-back method and treating firsts and seconds as coproducts.

b) Compute the cost of hosiery on the assumption that seconds are by-products.

c) The factory accountant has decided to exclude losses on seconds and rejects from product cost. Compute such losses for the month of June:

   (1) Measuring the loss by the differences between average unit cost and the sales value of seconds and rejects at the split-off point.

   (2) Measuring the loss by the difference between the sales value of firsts and the sales value of seconds and rejects at the split-off point.

*10. The Andrews Creamery Company receives bulk milk from farmers. The largest portion of this milk is pumped into holding tanks for subsequent pasteurization, homogenization, and bottling. The remainder is fed into cream separators, in which the cream is separated from skim milk. Some of the cream is then pasteurized and bottled for sale. The remainder is churned into butter. Skim milk is sold to a local cheese factory. During January the Andrews Creamery received 20,384 hundredweight of bulk milk, with a butterfat content of 820 hundredweight, for which it paid farmers $75,625. The output of the creamery for the month was as follows:

	Total Cwt.	Butterfat Content Cwt.
Whole milk...............	13,580	522
Cream for sale.............	569	228
Cream for butter...........	167	67
Skim milk................	5,968	...
Losses....................	100	3
Total.................	20,384	820

The estimated market value of the creamery's output for the month was $1.01 per hundredweight plus $78 per hundredweight of butterfat content. Processing costs for the month amounted to $4,484.

a) Compute the cost per hundredweight for each class of the creamery's products on a relative market value basis and prepare a summary showing the total costs allocated to each product class. No cost is to be assigned to lost product.

b) How would you cost product losses in a management report for the month?

11. Products A, B, and C are joint products. Products A and B are treated as main products; product C is treated as a by-product, its market value of $20 a pound being subtracted from joint costs at the time of split-off. The remaining joint costs are allocated between the main products on the basis of relative market values less completion costs.

During July, joint product costs amounted to $85,000 and costs of separate processing of product B totaled $10,000. The month's production was as follows:

```
Product A............................30,000 lbs.
Product B............................10,000 lbs.
Product C...........................   200 lbs.
```

Product A sells at a net price of $2 a pound; product B is sold at a price of $4 a pound.

a) How much of the joint cost is assigned to each unit of product C?

b) How much of the joint cost is assigned to each unit of product A?

c) In view of its high price per pound, do you agree with the company's decision to treat product C as a by-product? Explain briefly.

d) A proposal has been made to cost inventories of product A at $2 a pound and unprocessed product B at zero, on the grounds that these figures represent their "opportunity costs." Comment briefly on this proposal.

12. Martino, S.p.A., buys material X to make product A. Material X is available only in 10-kilogram bars at a price of 20,000 lire (the Italian monetary unit) per bar. Three units of product A, weighing 2 kilograms each, are made from each bar. The remainder of the bar is sold as scrap at a price of 500 lire per kilogram.

The average cost of processing each bar is approximately 60,000 lire, and the scrap is recovered only at the very end of the processing operation.

Product A is sold at a price of 30,000 lire per unit, after deducting selling costs.

The company is trying to evaluate a proposal to purchase equipment to process this scrap so that it can be sold at a higher price than 500 lire per kilogram.

a) How much of the joint materials and processing costs would you assign to each kilogram of scrap in computing the profitability of this proposal? Explain your answer.

b) A customer has asked Martino to supply it with 1,000 units of product B, at a price of 48,000 lire per unit. A unit of product B is obtained by melting a unit of product A, adding another ingredient, and letting the mixture cool in molding forms. The cost of the other ingredient and the additional labor and processing costs required to produce 1,000 units of product B amount to 20,000 lire. Martino cannot increase its purchases of material X, and it will have to reduce its sales of product A by 1,000 units if it accepts the customer's proposal. What unit cost of product A should be used in evaluating the desirability of this proposal? Should the proposal be accepted? Explain.

*13. A department processes materials to yield two joint products, A and B. The following data relate to the month of May:

(1) Materials issued to the department, $7,920.
(2) Departmental processing costs, $9,240.
(3) Finished production:
    10,000 gallons of A (market value, $8,000).
    5,000 gallons of B (market value, $12,000).
(4) Work in process, May 1: none.
(5) Work in process, May 31: 2,000 gallons, complete as to materials and half processed in the department (each gallon is assumed to yield one-half gallon of A and one-fourth gallon of B—the other one-fourth gallon of materials is lost through evaporation).

Compute unit cost per unit of each product by the relative market value method. (Note: You will need to compute equivalent production in dollars of market value.)

14. The Madison Company produces two products jointly, Tincon and Awlcon. These products emerge from the joint process in coarse form and require further finishing before they are salable. In processing the Awlcon, a waste material is generated. This waste material has no market value, but the Madison Company has developed a process for converting the waste into a salable product which it calls Griscon.

Production of these three products for the month of June was:

	Quantity	Market Value
Tincon.................	400,000 lbs.	$191,000
Awlcon...............	100,000 lbs.	92,000
Griscon...............	10,000 lbs.	3,000
Total..............		$286,000

Manufacturing costs for the month were:

	Before Separation	After Separation		
		Tincon	Awlcon	Griscon
Materials..............	$ 64,000	$26,000	$ 9,000	$ 200
Labor.................	30,000	45,000	18,000	1,100
Overhead.............	16,000	15,000	6,000	700
Total.............	$110,000	$86,000	$33,000	$2,000

a) Treating unrefined Tincon and unrefined Awlcon as coproducts of the first process and the waste material to be converted into Griscon as a by-product of Awlcon finishing, compute unit cost for each of the three products for the month, using the uniform percentage net-back method of allocating joint costs to coproducts. No selling costs are traceable specifically to any of these products. (Note: you should recognize two different joint processes here, and you should cost the second of these before costing the first.)

b) If you were a manager in the Madison Company, how if at all would you use the unit costs developed in (a)? Explain.

15. Materials are received in department A, where they are processed into two joint products which are then transferred: finished product X to finished goods inventory, and semiprocessed product Y to department B, where it is processed further and from which finished product Y is transferred to finished goods inventory.

Product X is sold at a price of $1 a pound; product Y at a price of $5 a gallon. Average processing cost in department B is $1.50 for each pound of product Y. Selling expenses are negligible.

The following data pertain to department A's operations during December:

	Quantity	Cost
Inventory in process, December 1..................	10,000 gals.	$17,000
Materials added.....................................	50,000 gals.	53,970
Processing costs.....................................	....	16,710
Units completed:		
Product X.......................................	20,000 lbs.	?
Semiprocessed product Y.......................	20,000 gals.	?
Inventory in process, December 31.................	4,000 gals.	?

The opening and closing inventories were complete as to materials and half processed in department A. Inventory costing is on a FIFO basis, and for unit costing purposes it is assumed that each gallon of materials will yield two fifths of a pound of product X and one half of a gallon of product Y. Under normal conditions, no product Y is lost in department B.

a) Compute unit costs for department A's output, treating the two products as joint products and using the uniform percentage net-back method. For what purpose(s) could these unit costs be used? (Note: Equivalent production must be measured in dollars of net-back to the joint process.)

b) Fill in the blanks in the table above.

c) Additional units of product Y can be obtained from department A by increasing processing costs by $1.75 for each additional gallon of product Y that is desired. Each such additional gallon obtained reduces the output of product X by one pound. Departmental capacity is inadequate to process any more raw materials than were processed during December. Use this information to compute unit costs for products X and Y. State any assumptions underlying your calculations.

16. The Lendrim Company has been manufacturing product X by a certain process for more than 30 years. In 1954 the company discovered a new method of producing X which involved producing Y jointly with X. Y is a new product that is a substitute for Z. Since the joint production of X and Y seemed profitable if Y could enter the markets for Z, production was initiated under the new method, and a new sales organization was set up to sell Y.

Last year about 40 percent of the company's output of X was obtained by the new method and Y had won a small but secure and promising share of the market formerly limited to Z. This market has been expanding at a relatively rapid rate, whereas the market for X has shown a much smaller rate of growth.

When the new method was first put into production in 1955, the accounting department decided to cost the output of X at the cost under the old method and to charge the remainder of the joint cost to Y. For example, X is manufactured by the old method at a unit cost of 25 cents a pound, and the yield of X from the new process is 40,000 pounds a week. The cost assigned to the pounds of X yielded by the new process is thus $10,000 per week, and the cost that the company assigns to Y is the total cost of processing X and Y by the new method, less this $10,000.

For the last few years Y has been earning a higher return on sales than X. The product sales manager responsible for sales of X is convinced that his product is actually more profitable to the company than Y, no matter what the accounting records may show. He has argued that it is unfair to assign all the cost savings of joint production to Y and none to X, particularly in view of the fact that X is well established and is much more important to overall company profitability than Y. He wants the method of allocation changed.

The manager of the department producing X under the old method is also unhappy because his production of X has been cut back by 20 percent during the last few years, while production under the new method has been expanding sharply. He feels that if costs are the same under the two methods, one should not be favored over the other.

A typical week's production consists of 60,000 pounds of X, produced by the old method, and 40,000 pounds of X and 20,000 pounds of Y, produced by the new method. Materials, labor, and variable factory overhead costs are proportional to the total quantity of materials processed. The costs of a typical week's production are as follows:

	Old Method		New Method	
	Total Cost	Cost per Pound	Total Cost	Cost per Pound
Materials..........................	$ 8,400	$0.14	$10,800	$0.18
Labor.............................	1,800	0.03	2,400	0.04
Variable factory overhead............	2,400	0.04	3,000	0.05
Fixed factory overhead..............	2,400	0.04	1,800	0.03
Total Cost....................	$15,000	$0.25	$18,000	$0.30
Cost of X........................	15,000	0.25	10,000	0.25
Cost of Y........................	.....	...	$ 8,000	$0.40

What recommendation would you make to the company?

17. The Wilde Corporation operates a factory with two production departments. Materials first pass through department I, where a substantial loss in weight takes place at the start of processing. The semiprocessed materials pass on to department II, where they are processed further to form two separate products, Elong and Ulong, together with a waste material known as "tailings." The following data refer to the month of April:

	Department I	Department II
Quantities:		
Materials received........................	100,000 lbs.	80,000 lbs. (from Dept. I)
Work in process, April 1 (materials 100% complete, one-half processed in department).....	20,000 lbs.	None
Work completed..........................	80,000 lbs.	20,000 lbs. Elong / 50,000 lbs. Ulong / 8,000 lbs. tailings
Work in process, April 30 (materials 100% complete, one-third processed in department).....	15,000 lbs.	None
Costs:		
Costs in process, April 1:		
Materials..............................	$ 8,100	None
Processing costs........................	6,000	None
Materials received........................	28,000	?
Processing costs incurred....................	46,700	$31,050

Sales and selling costs during April were as follows:

	Elong	Ulong	Tailings
Selling price...........................	$3.00 per lb.	$2.00 per lb.	$0.10 per lb.
Units sold.............................	18,000 lbs.	70,000 lbs.	8,000 lbs.
Traceable costs of packing, selling and delivery*...............................	$2,700	$14,000	0

* Assumed to be wholly variable with respect to the number of pounds sold. In addition, there were fixed selling and administrative costs, not traceable to any product, in the amount of $40,000 for the month.

The company uses the moving average method of inventory costing. Joint cost is to be allocated on the basis of a uniform percentage net-back at the split-off point. Tailings are to be treated as a by-product.

a) Compute the total cost and cost per unit of department I inventory in process on April 30.

b) Compute the unit costs that would be used in recording the transfer to finished goods inventory of Elong, Ulong, and tailings, respectively.

c) Prepare unit cost figures for department I that can be used by management as rough indicators of departmental efficiency during the month of April.

d) Inventories of Elong have been increasing during recent months, and it is now believed that it will not be possible to sell more than 18,000 pounds a month in the foreseeable future. Sales of Ulong are expected to average 50,000 pounds a month. Two pounds of Elong are produced for every five pounds of Ulong, and these proportions cannot be altered.

The production manager has recently figured out a way of treating Elong to make it acceptable to a few customers who use a competing product. Approximately 2,000 pounds of treated Elong can be sold each month to these customers, at a price of $2.50 a pound. The costs of treatment would be $0.50 a pound, and the costs of selling the product would be $0.20 a pound. Should the 2,000 pounds of Elong be treated in this way? Support your conclusion with figures from this problem and a concise statement of your reasoning.

18. The Zandrum Company processes a group of raw materials in a single processing operation. The output of this operation consists of three products destined for further processing in the company's factory and one by product that is sold "as is" to fertilizer manufacturers. None of the three products that are processed further is salable in the form in which it emerges from joint production.

The company's policy is to treat by-product values as reductions of joint cost and to allocate net joint cost to the three main products by a variant of the relative market value method. From the final selling price of each of the three products after further processing, the company deducts the estimated cost of further processing. It also deducts 25 percent of selling price, representing the company's average gross margin on sales. The resulting "net prices to main process" are used to allocate the net joint costs of the main process to individual products.

During July the costs of raw materials and joint processing in the main process amounted to $21.410. Production and related data were as follows:

Product	Quantity Produced (Units)	Final Selling Price per Unit	Estimated Cost per Unit to Complete
A......................	1,000	$ 6.20	$0.91
B......................	2,000	3.80	0.87
C......................	2,500	10.08	1.84
D (by-product).........	10,000	0.05	...

a) Compute the amount of the net joint cost to be allocated to each of the three products A, B, and C.

b) Recompute the allocations made in (*a*) on the basis of costs of raw materials and processing amounting to $23,410 during July, all other data remaining the same. What conclusions could you draw from your calculations?

19. Chemco, Inc., has perfected a process for producing from the three raw materials A, B, and C, two chemical compounds, Yip and Zip. The raw materials are required in the following proportions, by weight:

A................................. 3 parts
B................................. 5
C................................. 2
                                 ──────
                                 10 parts

The following diagram illustrates the manufacturing process:

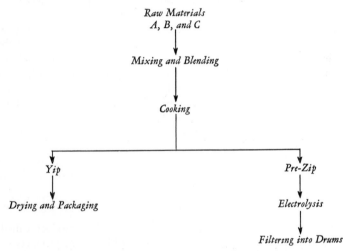

One hundred thousand (100,000) pounds of raw material will be processed each month. The unit costs of the three raw materials are as follows:

A...................................$ 2 per lb.
B................................... 50 per ton
C................................... 4 per gal.

One gallon of raw material C weighs 8 pounds.

It is estimated that the monthly costs of processing and packaging will be:

Mixing, blending, and cooking..................$16,350
Yip: drying and packaging...................... 4,960
Zip: electrolysis and filtering................... 6,880

The cooking process reduces the weight of the combined raw materials by 40 percent. From the 100,000 pounds of original raw materials, 20,000 pounds of pre-Zip and 40,000 pounds of wet Yip will be obtained. Wet Yip will be subject to a further weight reduction of 10 percent in the drying operation. Pre-Zip cannot be sold without further processing. Of the pre-Zip electrolyzed, 25 percent by weight becomes a nonmarketable precipitate; the remainder, a liquid, is filtered into 50-gallon drums without further attention. One gallon of Zip weighs 7.5 pounds.

The cost of drums, which are returnable and for which customers are to be charged separately, is not to be included in either the cost or the price of Zip.

Both products will be sold through distributors. The prices charged to the distributors are to be 64 percent of the list prices of the two products.

a) The company wishes to establish prices that will allow the company to earn 20 percent of the net price received by the company. It estimates that 25 percent of net selling price will be necessary to allow for selling and administrative expenses (including provision for income tax). Prepare schedules showing the list and net selling prices per unit of each product that will meet the company's profit objectives if the indicated volumes can be sold at these prices. The prices for Yip are to be prices per pound; the prices for Zip are to be prices per gallon.

b) Assuming that the prices (net selling prices charged to distributors) that will permit the company to dispose of its entire monthly production are $2 per pound for Yip and $40 per gallon for Zip, will it be profitable for the company to undertake the manufacture of Yip and Zip? Assume selling and administrative expenses of 25 percent of sales. Show your calculations.

c) Using the allocation method developed in (a) above and the selling prices and selling and administrative expenses assumed in (b), prepare a pro forma income statement for each of the two products and for both together. What changes, if any, should be made in the allocation procedure?

(Adapted from a Uniform CPA Examination)

20. The Holmes Corporation manufactures one principal product, called "Sagron." Material is started in process 1, from which three products emerge: Sagron, which is processed further in process 2; "Wanelon," which is processed further through process 3; and "Bylon," which is sold without further processing. The following data for February are available:

    (1) Material put into process 1, $12,000.
    (2) Conversion costs:
        Process 1...$8,000
        Process 2... 4,000
        Process 3... 300
    (3) There were no beginning or ending in-process inventories.
    (4) Production and sales data:

	Quantity Produced	Quantity Sold	Sales Value of Units Sold	February 28 Market Price
Sagron...........	5,000	4,000	$24,000	$6.00
Wanelon.........	3,000	2,000	2,000	0.90
Bylon............	1,000	900	450	0.55

    (5) Selling and administrative expenses average 50 cents per unit for Sagron, 40 cents per unit for Wanelon, and 4 cents per unit for Bylon.

The company regards production of Wanelon and Bylon as incidental to the manufacture of Sagron. In computing the costs to be assigned to Wanelon, a standard net profit of 10 percent of sales is assumed. Costing of Bylon is based on the assumption that there will be no profit or loss on sales of this product.

a) Compute the cost of the Bylon inventory and the costs transferred from process 1 to Bylon units during the month.

b) Compute the cost of the Wanelon inventory and the cost transferred from process 1 to Wanelon units during the month.

c) Copy and complete the following entries:

    (1) Process 1
           Process 2
           Process 3
                Materials Inventory and Sundry

    (2) Process 2
           Process 3
           Bylon Inventory
                Process 1

    (3) Finished Goods—Sagron
                Process 2

    (4) Finished Goods—Wanelon
                Process 3

    (5) Cash
           Sales—Sagron
           Cost of Goods Sold—Sagron
                Finished Goods—Sagron

    (6) Cash
           Sales—Wanelon
           Cost of Goods Sold—Wanelon
                Finished Goods—Wanelon

    (7) Selling and Administrative Expenses
                Cash and Sundry

    (8) Cash
           Bylon Inventory
           Selling and Administrative Expenses

d) Copy and complete the following income statement for the month:

	Sagron	Wanelon	Bylon	Total
Sales				
Cost of goods sold				
Gross profit				
Selling and administrative expenses				
Net Profit				

(Adapted from a Uniform CPA Examination)

21. The Abel Chemical Company has four processing departments, I, II, III, and IV, and three final products, D, E, and F. The following diagram shows product flows between departments:

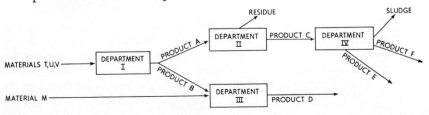

The semiprocessed products A and C can be sold or bought in outside markets at firmly established prices of 50 cents and 80 cents per pound, respectively. Semiprocessed product B has no outside market value; the Abel Chemical Company developed product D as a means of utilizing the output of product B that formerly had been given free to anyone willing to haul it away.

Department II's production residue is sold on contract at a price of 5 cents a pound. Sludge from department IV is pumped into settling beds where the moisture content is allowed to evaporate. Moisture content is approximately 30 percent by weight. The dried sludge is then sold at a price of 7 cents a pound.

During the month of March the following transactions were recorded by the Abel Company:

(1) Materials issued:
    Materials T, U, V..$ 6,000
    Material M.. 3,000
(2) Processing costs:
    Department I...$ 2,160
    Department II... 3,555
    Department III.. 1,800
    Department IV... 4,282
(3) Production:
    Product A...20,000 lbs.
    Product B...10,000 lbs.
    Product C...18,000 lbs.
    Product D...14,000 lbs.
    Product E...12,000 lbs.
    Product F... 500 gals.
    Department II residue................................... 1,500 lbs.
    Department IV sludge (wet).............................. 2,000 lbs.
(4) Sales:
    Product D...11,000 lbs.
    Product E...10,000 lbs.
    Product F... 300 gals.
    Residue... 1,500 lbs.
    Sludge (dry).. 1,000 lbs.

There were no inventories of finished goods on hand as of March 1. In-process inventories were assumed to remain constant during the month.

The Abel Chemical Company does not allocate costs to products. Instead, it transfers products internally at estimated market values. Each department is credited monthly for the net market value of its output, priced at the following prices:

    Product D......................................$0.40 a lb.
    Product E...................................... 1.20 a lb.
    Product F...................................... 8.00 a gal.

These credits are made to departmental "production value" accounts. The accompanying debits are made to the operating cost accounts of departments receiving semiprocessed products or to inventory accounts for finished products, residue, and sludge.

The difference between the amounts charged to a department and the amounts credited to it represent the department's "profit" for the period. To the extent that the period's production remains unsold at the end of the period, this "profit" must be excluded from company financial statements for external reporting. This is accomplished by the following series of month-end adjustments:

(1) Departmental cost and production value accounts are offset against each other and the difference credited to the following three accounts:

Internal Profit—Product D
Internal Profit—Product E
Internal Profit—Product F

Department III's "profit" is transferred to the Internal Profit—Product D account; the "profits" of the other three departments are divided between the other two product profit accounts in proportion to the relative market values of the month's output of the two products.

(2) The finished goods inventory accounts are credited for the quantity of goods sold at market prices; the accompanying debits are to the Cost of Goods Sold account.

(3) The internal profit accounts are debited for the average processing profit applicable to the quantities sold; the accompanying credits are to the Cost of Goods Sold account, to reduce that account to a cost basis. The remaining balances in the internal profit accounts are treated on the month-end balance sheets as deductions from the finished goods inventory balances, which are stated at market prices.

a) Prepare entries to record the costs and cost transfers for the month of March and the end-of-month adjustments.

b) Comment on the probable objectives, the strengths, and the weaknesses of this system.

CASE 9–1: THE WILLIAMSON CHOCOLATE CO., LTD.*

The Williamson Chocolate Co., Ltd., which has its headquarters and principal factory in Leicester, England, has been engaged in the production of chocolate and cocoa products since the beginning of this century. Subsidiary companies have been established in Canada, Australia and South Africa, and each of the subsidiaries manufactures the more important of the company's products and markets them in its home market.

The Australian company is located in Melbourne, where all of its manufacturing activities take place, and warehouses for local distribution are also maintained in Sydney, Adelaide and Perth. The main output at the factory is chocolate in bars. Cocoa beans, the principal raw material for the manufacture of chocolate, are imported from abroad. As a rule, the beans are cleaned, roasted, ground and then passed through a press. In the press, cocoa butter is separated from cocoa powder, which comes out of the press in the form of cocoa cake. The cocoa butter leaves the press in liquid form because of the heat that is generated during the press operation. The cocoa butter is then stored in large tanks, ready for use in the current production of chocolate.

The Melbourne factory was a net user of cocoa butter, i.e., its chocolate

---

* This case was written by Professor David Solomons, Copyright 1964 by l' Institut pour l' Etude des Méthodes de Direction de l' Entreprise (IMEDE), Lausanne, Switzerland. Reproduced by permission.

production called for more cocoa butter than could be obtained from the pressing of cocoa beans for powder manufacture. This extra cocoa butter could have been imported but it was subject to a heavy import duty, and the local management believed that it was cheaper to import beans and extract the cocoa butter from them. As a result of implementing this policy the factory found itself with a steadily mounting stock of cocoa powder.

The following figures show how the stock of cocoa powder increased during the period 1960–62:

	Pounds	Pounds
1960:		
Stock at January 1, 1960..........................		30,500
Output of press................................		416,975
		447,475
Less: Usage in 1960............................		324,500
Stock at December 31, 1960.....................		122,975
1961:		
Output of press................................		638,750
		761,725
Less: Usage in 1961............................	506,420	
Sales in 1961............................	35,500	541,920
Stock at December 31, 1961.....................		219,805
1962:		
Output of press................................		792,125
		1,011,930
Less: Usage in 1962............................	641,600	
Sales in 1962............................	43,385	684,985
Stock of cocoa powder, December 31, 1962........		326,945

These large stocks of cocoa powder held at the factory caused a serious storage problem, and the local management made continuous efforts to find profitable outlets for the excess cocoa powder. However, the sale of this powder on the Australian market raised a question as to its proper valuation. In accordance with accounting instructions issued by the head office in London some time before the last war, the cost of the cocoa beans purchased together with the labor and overhead costs of the pressing process had to be allocated between the cocoa butter and the cocoa cakes on the basis of the fat content remaining in these two products after the pressing operations. This gave a cost for cocoa powder of about 23 Australian pence a lb. or about 50% above its current market price at the end of 1962†. The company was therefore unable

---

† The Australian £ stands at a discount in relation to the English £. All values mentioned in this case are expressed in Australian currency.

to dispose of its excess stock of cocoa cakes without incurring a considerable loss. For balance sheet purposes, however, the company made a provision in its accounts in order to bring the book value of its stock of cocoa down to the market value.

During 1963, cocoa prices fell further and the subsidiary was unable to sell any large quantities of its excess stocks, because its costs were too high. There was practically no internal market for cocoa cakes. It did succeed, however, in exchanging 13,000 lbs. of cake against 2,000 lbs. of cocoa butter with another manufacturer.

In the middle of 1963, Mr. Cannon, the marketing manager, brought forward a scheme to market a new cocoa preparation for making a hot chocolate drink. The marketing prospects seemed good so long as the selling price could be kept low enough. This new product offered a promising means of disposing of the excess stocks of cocoa powder but only if they were costed out at substantially less than the cost allocated to them in the books.

The production manager, Mr. Parker, supported this proposal with enthusiasm. He had drawn the attention of the subsidiary's managing director, Mr. Woodstock, repeatedly to the storage problem created by the cocoa stocks, and he welcomed the possibility which now opened up of dealing with this problem once for all. Besides, he said, he had never been able to see the logic of basing the cost of cocoa powder on its fat content. It was its flavor which was important, and fat content had little to do with flavor.

Both Cannon and Parker were surprised to find that Mr. Woodstock was not unreservedly enthusiastic about Cannon's proposal. He pointed out that if cocoa powder were charged to the new product at present cost levels, the product would never show a profit; and without a drop in the price of cocoa beans greater than anyone could at present foresee, the only way to reduce the cost of cocoa powder would be to change the basis of cost allocation between cocoa powder and cocoa butter. This could not be done without permission from London and he was by no means certain that such permission would be given unless some basis of cost allocation which was clearly better than the present one could be proposed. It was all very well to attack the present basis of allocation, as Mr. Parker had done. But unless he or somebody else could suggest a better one, why should London agree to a change?

Mr. Woodstock went on to point out that there was another aspect of the matter which made him reluctant to approach London. If the allocation of costs to cocoa powder were reduced, with a consequent increase in the cost of cocoa butter, the calculation which had been supplied to London in 1959 to support the expenditure of £A40,000 on a new cocoa press would be completely undermined. Only on the basis of the present cost of producing cocoa butter as compared with the cost of importing it could investment in the press be justified. If more cost were to be allocated to cocoa butter, it might be shown that it ought to be imported after all, and the investment in the press would be shown to have been misguided.

Part III

Control of Operating Costs

Chapter 10

BASIC STANDARD COSTING
FOR MATERIALS AND LABOR

PRODUCT UNIT COSTS derived by either process or job order costing often fail to satisfy management's needs for cost data for product pricing and other decisions, at least partly because they represent the past and partly because they may reflect inefficiencies that cannot be recuperated in competitive markets. Furthermore, without comparable bench marks, neither unit costs nor departmental cost totals are adequate for cost control reporting.

Both of these gaps can be filled in part by the development of standard costs for factory direct materials and direct labor.[1] The purpose of this chapter is to explain what standard costs are, why they may be more relevant to decision making than historical costs, and how they might be used to provide useful cost control information for management.

STANDARD PRODUCT COSTS

Standard product cost typically comprises factory costs only and is the sum of three elements:

1. *Standard materials cost:* the quantities of direct materials that are deemed necessary, on the average, to manufacture one unit of product, multiplied by preselected or standard materials prices.
2. *Standard labor cost:* the quantities of direct labor that are deemed necessary, on the average, to manufacture one unit of product, multiplied by preselected or standard wage rates.
3. *Standard overhead cost:* the amount of factory overhead to be absorbed by the production of a unit of product.

These figures are typically stored in a *standard cost file* which serves as a data bank from which data can be withdrawn when needed either

---

[1] Standard product costs can also be developed for factory and nonfactory overhead costs, but for various reasons overhead standards need to be discussed separately.

for decision making or for use in control reporting. The standard cost file usually consists of one file card or other storage unit for each type of material, each part, each operation, and each product manufactured.

The Bill of Materials and Operations Flow Sheet

The standard cost files consist of three parts: (1) standard materials and parts prices; (2) standard labor (and overhead) costs for individual production operations; and (3) standard product costs. Items in the third category—standard product costs—are derived from the first two by means of the standard *bill of materials* and the standard *operations routing sheet* or *flow sheet*.

Materials quantity standards start from product specifications as to size, shape, appearance, desired performance characteristics, and permissible tolerance limits. These are reflected in the bill of materials, which describes and indicates the quantity required of each of the various

Exhibit 10–1

BILL OF MATERIALS

STANDARD MATERIALS REQUIREMENTS

ITEM   Base Plate No. 423   DRAWING NO.   9463
STANDARD QUANTITY   1,000   DATE   11/14/—

MATERIALS			REMARKS
No.	Description	Required for Standard Lot	
176	Steel plate	4,200 lbs.	

PARTS

Part No.	Description	Specs. per Unit	Required for Lot	Part No.	Description	Specs. per Unit	Required for Lot
201	Anchor	1	1,010				
217	Brace	2	2,080				

materials and parts that will go into the creation of the finished product. A sample bill of materials form is shown in Exhibit 10–1.

Labor quantity standards also start from product specifications, which determine the factory operations necessary to manufacture the product. These operations are summarized on a flow sheet such as the one shown in Exhibit 10–2. This flow sheet specifies the operations to

Exhibit 10–2

OPERATIONS ROUTING SHEET

STANDARD OPERATIONS LIST					
ITEM Base Plate No. 423				DRAWING NO. 9463	
STANDARD QUANTITY 1,000				DATE 11/14/—	
Dept.	Operations		Job Class	Hours Allowed	Remarks
	No.	Description			
P	1731	Setup	1	2.0	
M	2146	Cut	2	5.5	
M	2172	Drill	2	21.0	
M	2175	Bevel	3	6.0	
M	2304	Polish	3	14.5	
A	2903	Press	5	2.5	
A	2905	Slip	5	2.5	

be performed and the labor quantities required for each. The standard labor time allowance, including specification of the employee classification appropriate for the operation, is obtained from the standard cost file, or if the operation is a new one, it is developed from a study of the operation to be performed.[2]

Standard Cost Sheet

Standard product costs are computed by entering the data from the standard bill of materials and the standard routing sheet, together with

---

[2] Typical bills of materials and operations flow sheets contain more detail than is appropriate here. For more realistic illustrations, see Robert I. Dickey (ed.), *Accountants' Cost Handbook* (2d ed.; New York: Ronald Press, 1960), sec. 15, pp. 8–19.

standard materials prices and wage rates obtained from the standard cost files, on a standard product cost sheet such as that shown in Exhibit 10–3. This shows the operations, materials, and costs deemed reasona-

Exhibit 10–3

STANDARD COST SHEET

STANDARD COST SHEET									
DESCRIPTION Base Plate No. 423						STANDARD COST $797.00			
QUANTITY 1,000						STANDARD COST PER UNIT $0.797			

Operation or Item	Dept.	Materials			Labor			Cumulated Cost	
		Quan- tity	Price	Cost	Hours	Rate	Cost	Mate- rials	Labor
Setup	P				2.0	$3.50	$ 7.00		$ 7.00
Steel Plate	M	4,200	$0.06	$252.00				$252.00	
Cut	M				5.5	3.00	16.50		23.50
Drill	M				21.0	3.00	63.00		86.50
Bevel	M				6.0	3.00	18.00		104.50
Polish	M				14.5	3.00	43.50		148.00
Anchor	A	1,010	0.14	141.40				393.40	
Press	A				2.5	2.00	5.00		153.00
Brace	A	2,080	0.07	145.60				539.00	
Slip	A				2.5	2.00	5.00		158.00

bly necessary for a lot of 1,000 piece parts described as base plates. The first column specifies the types of materials required and the operations to be performed, while the second identifies the departments responsible. The remaining columns list the quantities and costs of these various standard inputs. The "cumulated cost" columns at the right of this form are used primarily for costing inventories of partly processed orders at the end of the month. They can also be used to cost the transfer of partially completed work from one department to the next if more than one department works on the job.

STANDARD COSTS AND STANDARD COSTING

The standard cost file is a mine of data for cost estimation. These data also serve cost control purposes by informing operating personnel of the appropriate cost allowances for individual products and individual operations. For control reporting, however, the standards are not enough by themselves. They must be compared with the actual costs incurred in manufacturing. These comparisons are ordinarily accomplished through *standard costing systems.*

The Concept of Standard Costing

Like the under- or overabsorbed overhead balances mentioned in Chapter 4, differences between actual and standard production costs are known as *variances.* Materials and labor variances may be classified into two main categories: quantity variances and price variances. *Quantity variances* are the differences between actual and standard input quantities for the output actually achieved; *price variances* are the differences between actual and standard input prices.

The basic objective of a standard costing system is to assist the department head by identifying and describing the variances over which he has some degree of control. Price variances are seldom controllable at the departmental level; thus the variances reported to the department head or foreman ordinarily consist of quantity variances only.

Under most circumstances, quantity variances that are within prescribed control limits can be presumed to be the product of random forces and no action is called for. When larger quantity variances occur, a search for causes is ordinarily deemed necessary. If the causes are beyond the department head's control, then adaptive action or replanning may be appropriate; otherwise, corrective action is called for.

Departmental quantity variances are also used by the department head's superior as a means of judging his effectiveness in cost control. Some systems require explanations of major variances each period; others call for explanations from the department head only if the variances persist. Higher executives will also review price variances and determine whether corrective action or replanning is needed.

The Concept Illustrated

Standard costing systems generate quantity variances by charging a cost center for the actual quantities of inputs consumed and crediting it for the standard input equivalents of the cost center's actual output. The difference represents the quantity variance, expressed in physical input units. When these are multiplied by standard input prices, the result is the dollar quantity variance that appears in the accounting records.

For example, department A manufactures product Y, utilizing only material X and labor. The standard production relationships are expressed in the equation:

1.2 tons of X + 0.3 hours of labor → 1.0 tons of product Y.

During February, department A consumes 1,400 tons of X and 350 hours of labor to produce 1,100 tons of product Y. In physical units, therefore, the department's account shows:

Department A

Input:	Output:
1,400 tons X	1,100 tons Y
350 hours labor	

But 1,100 tons of product Y can also be expressed in terms of their *standard input content* of 1,320 tons of X (1,100 times 1,2) and 330 hours of labor (1,100 times 0.3). Substituting these equivalents and splitting the account into two, we have:

Department A—Materials

Input:	Output:
1,400 tons X	1,320 tons X
Bal. 80 tons	

Department A—Labor

Input:	Output:
350 hours labor	330 hours labor
Bal. 20 hours	

The balances in these accounts now represent the *quantity variances* in physical terms, 80 tons of X and 20 hours of labor, both on the debit side. This means that actual costs have exceeded standard; credit balances would mean that the cost center's activities have been carried out at less than standard cost. A debit variance is referred to as *unfavorable;* a credit variance is *favorable.*

These quantity variances can be expressed in monetary terms by multiplying the physical quantities by standard prices. Standard prices are used instead of actual prices so that the monetary measure of the quantity variance will represent quantity deviations only. This can be accomplished only if all physical quantities are measured in terms of the same input prices. For example, if the standard price of X is $7 per ton and the standard wage rate is $2 per hour, the quantity variances become $560 for materials (80 times $7) and $40 for labor (20 times $2). The accounts now show:

Department A—Materials

9,800	9,240
Bal. 560	

Department A—Labor

700	660
Bal. 40	

In most companies, of course, the departmental inputs and outputs are far more heterogeneous than in this simple example, but the basic relationships are similar. Each cost center is charged for its physical inputs and credited for its physical outputs. The differences between the physical input equivalents of the department's output and the actual physical inputs represent the quantity variances.

When there are many different kinds of inputs and many different kinds of products, the statement of variances in physical terms becomes unwieldy and only the dollar variances are reported. It should always be remembered, however, that these dollar totals are merely convenient ways of summarizing the underlying physical deviations from standard performance.

A STANDARD COSTING PLAN

The simplest basis for standard costing is provided by what might be called the *basic plan*.[3] Under this plan, each cost center or department has its own work in process accounts which are charged with the actual quantities of labor and materials inputs, priced at *standard* prices, and credited with the standard cost of the cost center's output. Quantity variances for labor and materials are determined *in total* for each cost center *at the end* of each reporting period, usually a month or a week.

Information Requirements

The information required to apply the basic plan to a factory cost accounting system consists of—

1. A record of the physical quantities of labor and materials charged to a cost center during the accounting period, together with the standard prices of these inputs.
2. A record of the physical quantities of the goods completed by the cost center during the accounting period, together with the standard input costs of these goods.
3. Data on physical quantities of work in process in the cost center at the beginning and end of the accounting period, priced at standard prices.

The Galahad Company, which is engaged in simple job order production operations, uses a basic plan system. The company's factory contains two production departments, machining and assembly, and each department has separate work in process accounts for labor and for materials. Inventory quantities on hand at the beginning of September, priced at standard cost, were:

---

[3] In the first edition of this book, this plan was referred to as the *modified partial plan*, adapted from the terminology in Robert I. Dickey (ed.), *Accountants' Cost Handbook* (2d ed.; New York: Ronald Press, 1960), sec. 16.

Materials and parts..$30,000
Materials in process—machining.................................. 5,000
Labor in process—machining...................................... 8,000
Materials in process—assembly................................... 7,000
Labor in process—assembly....................................... 3,000

Computing Materials Price Variances

The first feature of the Galahad Company's standard costing system is that it isolates materials price variances at the time the materials are received.

For example, suppose that the Galahad Company receives a shipment of 1,000 widgets and 500 flibbets. The standard price files indicate that the standard price per unit (including an estimated amount for discounts and surcharges) is $0.75 for widgets and $1.15 for flibbets. At these prices the items purchased have a standard cost of $1,325:

1,000 widgets at $0.75...$ 750
500 flibbets at $1.15.. 575
    Total..$1,325

Suppose further that the actual cost of this shipment is only $1,286, computed as follows:

1,000 widgets at $0.73...$ 730
500 flibbets at $1.14.. 570
    Total f.o.b. cost..$1,300
Freight..   12
Less 2% cash discount (2% of total f.o.b. cost)................ (26)
Net Purchase Cost..$1,286

The price variance in this case is $1,325 minus $1,286, or $39, and *favorable* (actual price less than standard).

Recording Materials Purchases

In the Galahad Company's system, the price variance is reflected in the ledger accounts at the time of purchase. When goods are purchased, the inventory accounts are charged for the *actual quantities received,* multiplied by the *standard prices* of the individual items. The difference between the total of these amounts and the net cost of the goods (including all discounts, freight, and other surcharges) is the materials price variance. The Galahad Company enters this in the Purchase Price Variance account.

During September, Galahad purchased materials from outside vendors at a total net purchase cost of $12,600. The standard prices of these materials totaled $12,000, and therefore an *unfavorable* price variance of $600 was recorded:

```
Materials and Parts..............................................12,000
Purchase Price Variance........................................   600
      Accounts Payable..........................................        12,600
```

Separating the price variances at the time of purchase makes it possible to report them promptly to management. An unfavorable price variance does not necessarily mean that the purchasing department is not doing its work well, but it may signal the need for new pricing, product, or procurement decisions. For these purposes price variances are often classified by product line, class of vendor, or other classification scheme.

Recording Materials Issues and Returns

Galahad's main reason for isolating the price variance at the time of purchase is to get it out of the materials cost accounts. Once the materials have been checked in, all subsequent transactions are recorded at standard price.

For example, direct materials requisitioned by the machining department during the month of September amounted to $11,300; those requisitioned by the assembly department totaled $4,000, all at standard prices. These materials issues were recorded by entries with the following effect:

```
Materials in Process—Machining....................................11,300
Materials in Process—Assembly.................................... 4,000
      Materials and Parts........................................        15,300
```

In addition, the machining department returned to the storeroom various materials that it had requisitioned but found it didn't need. These returns amounted to $400 at standard prices:

```
Materials and Parts................................................400
      Materials in Process—Machining.................................        400
```

Aside from updating the records of *physical* stocks in the storeroom each time goods are received, issued, or returned, Galahad makes no materials entries other than the summary entries illustrated above. A job cost sheet is prepared for each job at the time the job order is issued, but this job cost sheet is completely filled in at that time with the *standard* quantities and prices of labor and materials for the specific quantity of parts or products to be manufactured to fill the order. Actual quantities of labor and materials used on the job are never recorded on the job cost sheet.

Computing Labor Rate Variances

Variances from standard wage rates are also removed by the Galahad Company before labor costs are charged to the departmental accounts. The labor rate variance is the difference between the actual wage rate and the standard wage rate for the actual number of hours worked.

Factory employees of the Galahad Company fall into several pay grades, but for clerical convenience Galahad has chosen to use only three rates in distributing labor costs in the two production departments: $3 an hour for all direct production workers in machining, $2 an hour for direct production workers in assembly, and $1.50 an hour for indirect employees in both departments. Maintenance, supervisory, and service department employees are paid from separate payrolls and do not enter this illustration.

Direct production workers in the Galahad Company often work on indirect tasks, and the labor time tickets for September showed the following distribution:

	Direct Labor		Indirect Labor		Total Hrs. × Std. Rate
	Actual Hours	Act. Hrs. × Std. Rate	Actual Hours	Act. Hrs. × Std. Rate	
Production employees—machining.....	6,200	$18,600	700	$2,100	$20,700
Indirect employees—machining........	....	.....	2,000	3,000	3,000
Total labor cost—machining......	xxx	$18,600	xxx	$5,100	$23,700
Production employees—assembly......	4,900	$ 9,800	250	$ 500	$10,300
Indirect employees—assembly........	....	.....	400	600	600
Total labor cost—assembly........	xxx	$ 9,800	xxx	$1,100	$10,900
Total Labor Cost at Standard Rates......................	xxx	$28,400	xxx	$6,200	$34,600

The *actual* payroll for the month totaled $34,900, and thus the rate variance was $300, and unfavorable:

```
Actual hours × actual rates.......................................$34,900
Actual hours × standard rates.....................................  34,600
    Labor Rate Variance.........................................$    300
```

Recording Labor Costs

Direct and indirect production workers in the Galahad Company are paid weekly. The first weekly pay period in September began on the first day of the month, and the four weekly payrolls prepared during the month totaled $33,000. Of this, overtime premiums accounted for $900 in machining and $400 in assembly.

All labor costs except overtime premium are charged initially by

Galahad to a temporary suspense account called Payroll Cost Summary, and the entries to record the month's payrolls had the following effects:

```
Payroll Cost Summary.........................................  31,700
Overtime Premium—Machining...............................     900
Overtime Premium—Assembly.................................     400
    Accrued Wages Payable.....................................          33,000
```

If the payroll period and the reporting period do not coincide, as they do not in this case, an accrual has to be made to include all wages earned during the period. This accrual can be made either from the clock cards or the time tickets, costed at actual wage rates. (Standard wage rates may be used if they are more readily available; the resulting error is unlikely to affect the size of the variances materially.)

In the Galahad Company, wages payable for the last two days of September amounted to $3,200, recorded as follows:

```
Payroll Cost Summary...........................................3,200
    Accrued Wages Payable.......................................         3,200
```

This brought the actual wage cost at straight-time wage rates up to the $34,900 figure quoted earlier.

Distributing Labor Costs

Labor charges to the Galahad production departments reflect the actual number of labor hours, multiplied by standard wage rates. The labor cost distribution summarized earlier can be represented by the following entry:

```
Labor in Process—Machining......................................18,600
Labor in Process—Assembly.......................................  9,800
Indirect Labor—Machining........................................  5,100
Indirect Labor—Assembly.........................................  1,100
    Payroll Cost Summary........................................          34,600
```

The Payroll Cost Summary account now shows a debit balance of $300, representing the labor rate variance for September:

Payroll Cost Summary

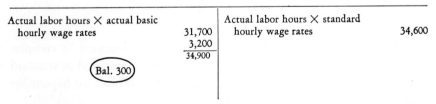

Actual labor hours × actual basic hourly wage rates		Actual labor hours × standard hourly wage rates	
	31,700		34,600
	3,200		
	34,900		
Bal. 300			

The balance in this account is the labor rate variance that we calculated earlier. If desired, the cost summary account can be closed out by transferring the balance to a variance account:

Labor Rate Variance..300
    Payroll Cost Summary...   300

It should be noted that this rate variance reflects differences between standard wage rates and actual straight-time pay rates. It does not include elements such as overtime premiums or shift differentials. These are segregated in payroll preparation and charged directly to overhead cost accounts. Thus the labor rate variance is actually only a portion of the complete variation of actual rates from standard rates, the residual after the effects of some of the more significant causes of rate deviations have been isolated.

Calculating Departmental Output

A department's output for any given period consists of the number of product units completed during the period, adjusted for any change in the amount of work in process between the beginning and end of the month. This is essentially the same calculation used to determine equivalent production in Chapter 5, except that now output is measured by the *standard cost* of the work done rather than in physical units.

For example, the machining department's output for September was as follows:

	Standard Materials Cost	Standard Labor Cost
Products completed and transferred out of department.............................	$ 9,000	$19,000
Add: Work in process, end of month..........	6,200	6,600
Less: Work in process, start of month.........	(5,000)	(8,000)
Output at Standard Cost.................	$10,200	$17,600

This represents the actual quantity of work done during the month, measured by its standard cost (standard input quantities $\times$ standard input prices).

Calculating Quantity Variances

The departmental quantity variances can be determined by comparing output, measured as above, with actual inputs, measured at standard prices. In the machining department, the input quantities for September were:

    Materials issued, at standard prices..............................$11,300
    Less: Materials returned to storeroom............................   400
        Net materials cost, at standard prices........................$10,900

    Actual Labor Hours, at standard wage rates......................$18,600

Because both inputs and outputs are measured at the same set of standard input prices, the differences between them represent the quantity variances (also referred to as yield, usage, or performance variances):

	Materials	Labor
Output, at standard prices and standard quantities.........	$10,200	$17,600
Input, at standard prices and actual quantities............	10,900	18,600
Quantity Variances..............................	$ (700)	$(1,000)

In this case, because the inputs exceeded the outputs, both variances were *unfavorable*.

Recording Product Completions—Machining

In the Galahad Company's basic plan standard costing system, the quantity variances are derived from the ledger accounts. To accomplish this, each department is credited each month with the standard cost of the work completed during the month. This is determined by multiplying the number of completed units of each product by the standard unit cost.

Units completed by a department may be transferred to another department, to the finished goods storeroom, to the materials and parts storeroom, or directly to customers. During September the standard cost of work completed by the machining department was as follows:

	Materials	Labor	Total*
To finished goods...........................	$2,000	$ 5,000	$ 7,000
To parts storeroom.........................	2,200	2,800	5,000
To assembly department.....................	4,800	11,200	16,000
Total......................	$9,000	$19,000	$28,000

*In practice, standard product cost will ordinarily include a provision for factory overhead, but this chapter deals only with materials and labor costs.

The entry to record these transfers would be:

```
Finished Goods......................................................  7,000
Materials and Parts.................................................  5,000
Materials in Process—Assembly......................................16,000
    Materials in Process—Machining............................           9,000
    Labor in Process—Machining................................          19,000
```

Notice that standard labor costs of the machining operations become part of the materials costs in the assembly department. As far as the assembly department manager is concerned, he receives processed materials, not unprocessed materials and labor. His labor cost account should show only the labor used in his department.

Computing Quantity Variances—Machining

After the standard cost of completed production was recorded, the machining department's work in process accounts showed the following:

Materials in Process—Machining				Labor in Process—Machining			
Bal. 9/1	5,000	Returns	400	Bal. 9/1	8,000	Completions	19,000
Issues	11,300	Completions	9,000	Charges	18,600		
	16,300		9,400		26,600		
(Bal. 6,900)				(Bal. 7,600)			

The work *completed* is not the same as the work *done,* of course, unless no change in work in process has taken place. The balances in the work in process accounts represent a mixture of the standard cost of physical inventories still in process at the end of the month and materials quantity variances for the month. At the end of September, a check of the standard cost sheets for uncompleted jobs revealed that the work still in process in machining had a standard materials cost of $6,200 and a standard labor cost of $6,600 (2,200 standard direct labor hours). The differences between these figures and the respective account balances of $6,900 and $7,600 were the materials and labor quantity variances for the month. The variances computed in this way are identical to the figures obtained in our earlier calculations. They can be transferred to special variance accounts by the following entries:

Materials Quantity Variance—Machining	700	
Materials in Process—Machining		700
Labor Quantity Variance—Machining	1,000	
Labor in Process—Machining		1,000

Recording Product Completions—Assembly

A comparable set of entries was made in the assembly department accounts. All of the finished output of the assembly department during September was placed in the finished goods stock room. The standard cost of these transfers was $20,500 for materials and $9,500 for assembly labor. The entry is:

Finished Goods	30,000	
Materials in Process—Assembly		20,500
Labor in Process—Assembly		9,500

The standard materials costs, as explained earlier, included the standard machining labor costs of any parts that went through the company's machining department prior to their use in assembly.

Computing Quantity Variances—Assembly

The balances in the assembly work in process accounts as of the end of September were as follows:

Materials in Process—Assembly

Bal. 9/1	7,000	Completions	20,500
Issues	4,000		
From machin- ing	16,000		
	27,000		
Bal. 6,500			

Labor in Process—Assembly

Bal. 9/1	3,000	Completions	9,500
Charges	9,800		
	12,800		
Bal. 3,300			

Once again, the department has been charged with actual input quantities priced at standard prices and credited with actual output, priced at the equivalent standard input cost (standard hours times standard wage rates). The balances in the departmental accounts, therefore, consist of a combination of the quantity variances and the standard labor content of ending in-process inventories. The quantity variances are determined by deducting the standard costs still in process. An inventory count indicates that the standard cost of materials in process in assembly at the end of September was $6,700; standard labor cost was $3,400. The variance calculation is:

	Materials	Labor
Product completions..................................	$20,500	$9,500
Add: Ending work in process.........................	6,700	3,400
Less: Beginning work in process.....................	(7,000)	(3,000)
Output, at standard cost.............................	$20,200	$9,900
Input, at standard prices............................	20,000	9,800
Quantity Variances..................................	$ 200	$ 100

Alternatively:

	Materials	Labor
Ending work in process, at standard....................	$6,700	$3,400
Account balances, from ledger.........................	6,500	3,300
Quantity Variances..................................	$ 200	$ 100

In this case both variances are favorable in that the output did not require as much input as the standards called for. The entry to adjust the work in process accounts to a standard cost basis is:

```
Materials in Process—Assembly.......................................200
Labor in Process—Assembly...........................................100
    Materials Quantity Variance—Assembly...........................        200
    Labor  Quantity  Variance—Assembly.............................        100
```

Basic Plan: Summary

The essence of the basic plan standard costing system is shown schematically in Exhibit 10–4. When materials are purchased, they are charged to the inventory accounts at standard prices. The differences between standard and actual prices are charged or credited at the time of purchase to a price variance account. (The exhibit shows only a debit or unfavorable variance.)

Next, the actual quantities of direct materials issued to the production departments are charged to the departmental materials in process accounts at standard prices. (To conserve space, only the transactions related to the machining department are shown.) Third, the standard materials cost of work completed by each production department is credited to the departmental materials in process account for that department.

The final requirement is to determine the standard materials content of the jobs still in process at the end of the period. The difference between this and the balance in the materials in process account is the departmental materials quantity variance for the period, and this is reported to the department head. (Both variances in the exhibit are unfavorable; favorable variances appear as credit balances in the variance accounts.)

Application of the basic plan is easiest whenever some simple assumption as to the level of in-process inventories is justified. For example, if inventories can be assumed to be negligible, the in-process account balances can be regarded as representing quantity variances only. Or, if inventory quantities are virtually unchanged from month to month—as they are in many process production systems—the changes in the account balances during the month can be interpreted as quantity variances. Even if in-process inventories are large and changing, however, the need to determine inventory quantities at the end of each reporting period is not ordinarily a formidable task nor a cause of any significant reporting delay.

The reporting interval, of course, need not be one month. It can be a week or even a day if the delay associatd with a longer interval impairs

Exhibit 10–4

BASIC PLAN STANDARD COSTING

Materials and Parts

		Actual quantity issued × standard prices:	
Beginning Balance: Actual quantity × standard prices	30,000	To machining	11,300
Actual quantity purchased × standard prices	12,000	To assembly	4,000
Returned to storeroom	400		
Ending Balance: Actual quantity × standard prices	27,100		

Issues

Materials in Process—Machining

Beginning Balance: Actual quantity at standard cost (standard quantity × standard price)	5,000	Actual quantity of goods finished at standard cost (standard materials quantity × standard price)	9,000 — Completions
Actual quantity received × standard prices	11,300	Returned to storeroom	400
Ending Balance: Actual quantity at standard cost	6,200	Excess of actual quantity used over standard usage × standard prices	700

Materials Quantity Variance—Machining

Excess of actual quantity used over standard usage × standard prices	700

Purchase Price Variance

Excess of actual over standard prices of materials purchased	600

the value of the information to an excessive degree. If in-process inventories do not change materially from day to day, the cost of obtaining daily quantity variance reports by the basic plan will be relatively small. If departmental in-process inventories fluctuate, however, daily reporting will probably require the adoption of the more costly standard costing plan described in the next chapter. Under these conditions, the benefits to be derived from more frequent reporting need to be weighed very carefully against the costs.

THE ADVANTAGES OF STANDARD COSTING

This illustration may have paved the way for a discussion of some of the advantages of standard costing: better control information and more timely reporting. Some systems provide additional benefits through increased clerical economy, and these possibilities also should be discussed.

Better Control Information

By far the most important is the advantage of better control information. Paradoxically, this argument is strongest in situations in which standard costing is most difficult to apply, specifically when the product line is broad, product mix is constantly changing, and production is on job orders. In the absence of standard costing, the only control comparisons that can be obtained in a job order system are for individual jobs or perhaps individual operations. The total labor and materials cost accumulated for a specific job can be identified as greater or less than standard. Large differences can then be traced to specific operations or operators by analysis of the job time tickets.

Apart from the clerical effort required to accumulate these data and tabulate the comparisons, the major objection to this procedure arises from the fact that the apparent precision of these detailed comparisons is an illusion. Deviations from standard on individual iterations of a particular task are expected and unavoidable. The significant question is whether these deviations are positive or negative in the aggregate and large enough to suggest that the operation is out of control.

In other words, variations due to random causes are not controllable, and random influences have much more opportunity to cancel each other out in larger aggregates. Reporting deviations in detail on a routine basis presents a mass of indigestible data and obscures the really essential features of the overall picture. Detailed comparisons can still be made when there is good reason to anticipate deviations on a specific operation or specific job, but this does not mean that routine comparisons must follow the same pattern. Standard costing provides a meaningful way to aggregate the deviations from standard costs to show how effectively costs have been controlled during a given time period.

Another and closely related point in favor of standard costing is that only by reflecting standard costs in the cost center accounts is it feasible to departmentalize the variances from standard performance. In job order production, individual jobs flow from department to department and responsibility for control of the cost of any particular job is diffused. The unit of control is the responsibility unit, although the unit of valuation is the job. It is relatively meaningless under these conditions to compute the total deviation between actual costs and standard costs unless these deviations can be traced further to the control centers in which they arise. To accomplish this, both actual costs and standard costs must be assigned to control centers, and the most economical way to make these assignments is by incorporating the standard costs into the procedural routines for accumulating accounting information.

Applicability to Process Production

The argument for standard costing is weaker for process production than for job order production. Departmental unit cost data can be compared to some extent with budgeted unit cost or unit costs of previous periods to give a measure of cost effectiveness. Comparisons of this sort are far from perfect, however. In addition to variations due to changes in physical yields, unit cost may fluctuate for any of three other reasons:

1. Input prices may vary.
2. Departmental volume may vary.
3. Product mix may vary if output is not completely homogeneous.

The use of unit cost figures in control reporting therefore requires careful analysis to separate the effects of these various influences. Furthermore, historical comparisons imply that prior period averages constitute a valid cost standard, and the error in this assumption may be the most important reason for applying standard costing to process production. Historical cost standards provide a bench mark for judging improvement, nothing more.

Faster Reporting

The second major reason for standard costing is that it may permit faster reporting of operating data. This is important because the value of any information declines as it relates to a period farther and farther in the past. Operations do not come to a halt while reports are being prepared. The longer it takes to develop these reports, the longer will be the time for any unfavorable trends to develop before corrective action can be taken.

The age of information depends on two elements: the *interval,* or length of the reporting period, and the *delay,* or elapsed time between the end of the interval and the issuance of the report. Age can be reduced by shortening the interval, generally at the price of sharply increased data processing costs, or by reducing the delay. There are many ways of reducing delay, some of them requiring greater data processing costs; standard costing, however, makes a contribution in this direction by predetermining certain portions of the data and by dealing with deviations in the aggregate.

For example, if actual costs do not have to be recorded on job order cost sheets, the time required to process actual costs can be reduced substantially. Furthermore, if the job cost sheets can be completely filled out with quantities and prices before the jobs enter production, the reporting process will not be held up while the job cost sheets are brought up to date and tabulated.

Lower Clerical Costs

A third major advantage provided by some standard costing plans is their ability to effect reductions in clerical costs. One source of economy has already been mentioned. By pricing materials inventories at standard, Galahad is able to reduce the costs of materials accounting by eliminating actual costs from the stores ledger. In fact, the inventory ledgers can be maintained in physical quantities only; it is a simple matter to determine aggregate standard cost whenever this is required. This avoids the need for time-consuming and partly arbitrary allocations of discounts and surcharges among the various items covered by an invoice. It also eliminates recomputation of average unit cost after each purchase (moving average method) or the separate tracing of the costs of successive lots of inventory (FIFO method), thus reducing the clerical time required for cost recording and file maintenance.

The same benefit accrues from pricing other quantities at standard. Issues and returns of materials, interdepartmental transfers, and shipments and returns of finished goods can all be recorded faster, at lower cost, and with less chance of clerical error. Cost estimates also can be prepared faster and at far less cost if a standard cost file is in being.

Another source of economy stems from the elimination of the historical job cost sheet. This eliminates a detailed posting operation, an operation that can be very costly.

Not all standard costing systems, of course, are cheaper to operate than the systems they replace. Even a basic plan system can increase total clerical costs if the costs of developing standards and keeping them up to date are extremely high. By and large, however, the basic plan is cheaper than any other kind of standard costing plan, and it may lead to a significant clerical cost reduction. An example of a more elaborate standard costing plan, with higher costs and greater information output, is discussed in Chapter 11.

Standard Costs for Planning

The advantages of standard costs for decision making can be obtained without the incorporation of these standard costs in the ledger accounts. In product pricing, contract bidding, and other types of analytical applications, management needs costs that can be regarded as typical of the products or operations that will be affected by managerial decisions, and standard costs may satisfy this requirement.

Historical product costs may be far from typical for several reasons. First, they may be out of date because operating conditions have changed or are expected to change. This requires some means of modifying historical data to reflect future expectations. Second, the quantity of input factors consumed during a particular time period or on a particular job may be atypical due to special and temporary circumstances. Costs that reflect past inefficiencies are particularly inappropriate for pricing decisions because they give a poor guide to the amounts that can be recovered in competitive markets. Conversely, costs that are exceptionally low due to temporary circumstances may point toward prices that are lower than the market will bear.

Third, the method used to price these input quantities may produce unit or total costs that are either out of date or fluctuate erratically. For example, whenever materials issued for a job or process are priced at historical acquisition costs, the cost of the job or process will be influenced to some extent by variations in materials purchase prices. It will also be affected by the inventory pricing method adopted. In a job order cost system, for instance, it is not uncommon to find the materials cost per unit on a series of successive lots of the same product varying over a wide range. These variations may reflect fluctuating materials yields, fluctuating materials prices, or merely time lags resulting from the use of FIFO or moving average inventory pricing.

The fourth reason is that unit cost fluctuates as a result of such factors as differing lot sizes, different production methods or equipment used, or purely random influences on production. For example, assume that setup time for a part is four hours whether the production run is for 100 units or 500 units. Also assume that setup time is treated as a direct labor cost. If running time is approximately 10 hours per 100 units and production wage rates average $2.50 an hour, both on setup and running, the unit costs of two separate lots will be substantially different, as shown in the following table:

| | Labor Hours | | | Labor | Labor Cost |
Lot Size	Setup	Run	Total	Cost	per Unit
100.......	4	10	14	$ 35	$0.35
500.......	4	50	54	135	0.27

Variations in unit cost arising from these various causes make planning difficult because without standards there is no way of determining how much the unit *should* cost. A well-designed standard cost file can provide this information and can therefore give the analyst a sounder base for cost estimating. This is not to say that cost standards are always relevant to decisions. Standards get out of date or do not fit the lot sizes or other conditions expected to prevail in the future. Nevertheless, figures representing standard cost relationships can be adjusted for changes in prices or other conditions much more readily than historical cost figures because cost elements are determined in detail and can be transformed in any way that a particular decision calls for.

SUMMARY

Product unit costs derived by process or job order costing techniques ordinarily come too late for many planning purposes and by themselves provide no basis for judging departmental cost control effectiveness. The development of standard product unit costs for labor and materials helps fill both these gaps in factories with repetitive manufacturing operations. The standard cost files provide data relevant to some pricing and other management decisions, while recording the standard cost of production in departmental accounts provides a basis for useful control comparisons on a departmental basis.

Factory costing systems to accomplish these objectives are known as standard costing systems. Differences between standard and actual costs, known as variances, are isolated in the ledger accounts. The portions of the total variance representing differences between actual and standard input quantities for actual outputs—that is, the quantity variances—are accumulated by responsibility units and, in the system described in this chapter, reported to responsible executives as departmental totals for a given period of time.

The justification for reporting the variances in lump sums rather than by jobs or causes is that some variation from standard is unavoidable. Standards are by their very nature averages, and the fact that averaging is necessary implies the possibility of deviation. What is important is that these deviations be kept within limits, and lump-sum reporting can indicate at a glance whether this has been accomplished. Investigation of the causes of the deviations is typically justified only if the control limits have been exceeded.

DISCUSSION QUESTIONS

1. What is the primary purpose of the bill of materials? The operations routing sheet?
2. What is the structure and content of the standard cost file?
3. Primarily for whose information are factory cost variances prepared?
4. What purposes are served by pricing materials inventories at standard prices rather than at actual prices?
5. What purposes are served by a standard cost file in a company in which operations consist of manufacturing custom products on customer orders and to customers' specifications?
6. In view of the fact that materials prices and labor rates are largely outside the control of factory operating personnel, why is it necessary to have standard prices and wage rates?
7. One company claims that it has achieved the advantages of standard costs by developing physical input standards. "Whenever we want to know dollar standards, we can multiply physical standards by currently applicable prices. For control purposes we compare actual physical inputs with standard inputs. The spreads between the two are more meaningful to our operating people than any dollar comparisons could be." Comment on this statement.
8. Assuming that standard costs can be prepared for each job entering a job shop, what additional control information can be obtained by incorporating these standard costs into the formal accounting records instead of merely listing them on the job order cost sheets and accounting for actual costs by job order costing procedures?
9. Much of the bookkeeping economy achieved with a standard cost system is accomplished by giving up information obtained with an actual cost system. State three types of information lost under a basic plan standard cost system, indicate how giving up this information reduces bookkeeping costs, and discuss the problems connected with giving up the information.
10. From what source or sources are standard cost credits to departmental direct labor and direct materials accounts obtained?
11. Under what circumstances would you want to supplement a standard cost system by recording actual costs on individual job orders?
12. How is the materials quantity variance determined under basic plan standard costing?

13. Some companies make comparisons of costs incurred in one period with those incurred in prior periods and interpret the deviations as evidence of favorable or unfavorable results of cost control. To what extent is this practice valid and what are its shortcomings?

14. One observer has claimed that the specific wage rates and materials prices selected as standard are relatively unimportant in the use of standard costs in operating cost control. From this viewpoint, standard price is only a constant multiplier to be applied to physical input and output quantities so that variances can be stated in dollars. Comment on the merits and shortcomings of this argument.

EXERCISES AND PROBLEMS

1. The Coolrite Company, a manufacturer of air-conditioning equipment, purchases mechanical control mechanisms (control knobs, cable, and connectors) of unique design from the Trolflex Company. These control mechanisms are specially tailored to the requirements of the Coolrite Company's air conditioners, different mechanisms being used in different products. Engineers from both companies work closely in preparing the specifications for new air-conditioner models. Should materials price variances on these mechanisms be charged to the Coolrite Company's purchasing department?

2. A flour miller purchases wheat and rye grains of various grades for processing into flour. The company "hedges" its grain and flour inventories by selling contracts for future grain delivery to speculators in grain "futures" markets. Inventories are completely hedged if the company's contracts for future delivery equal the grain content of the company's physical inventories. The company's policy is to cover 100 percent of its inventories at all times by hedging, but the purchasing department is allowed to leave some inventories unhedged if, in its judgment, market conditions seem to warrant such action. Should the purchasing department be charged or credited with materials price variances? With gains or losses on futures contracts? Would your answer differ if the company's policy required a continuous 100 percent hedge?

3. The Clearsite Company manufactures plate glass in a continuous series of processes. Cooled glass flows in a continuous stream into the polishing department, where it passes between two sets of polishing wheels and emerges ready for final cutting and packing. An interruption of the electric current activating these polishing wheels creates a difficult problem because the flow of cooled glass from the previous operation cannot be halted. When an unscheduled power interruption occurs, as it does once or twice a year, three men from the polishing department crew must be assigned immediately to score, break, and destroy the unpolished glass before it enters the polishers and jams the entire product flow. How would you account for the cost of cooled glass thus destroyed, and for the polishing department labor costs incurred during the period of interrupted production?

4. Application of the basic plan of standard costing to certain continuous production operations, such as blast furnace production of pig iron, is facilitated by the reasonable assumption that physical quantities of inventory in process remain constant as long as the operation continues. What problems arise in measuring quantity variances in a cost center during a month in which the operation is shut down so that no inventory remains in process at the end of the month? What problems arise during the following month when operations are resumed? Can you suggest an accounting device that would alleviate these problems?

5. One problem that is imposed on the accounting system by the adoption of standard costs is the isolation of the causes of cost variances.

   a) Assuming that there are no work in process inventories, prepare a set of accounts that will permit the accounting staff to take directly from the account balances, without further analysis, a materials price variance, a materials quantity variance, a labor rate variance, and a labor quantity variance. Indicate for each account what is to be debited and credited to that account. Also state what the balance in each account represents.

   b) What changes in procedure or interpretation would the existence of work in process inventories force you to make in your solution to (a)?

*6. The standard labor cost of a particular product is two labor hours per unit at a standard wage rate of $1.80 an hour. A particular lot of 1,000 units of this product required 1,900 labor hours at $1.85 an hour. Compute the variances.

7. The Hillman Company manufactures a single product known as Quik-Tite. Production of Quik-Tite requires the use of material A. Transactions in material A for the month of June are summarized in the following table:

	Standard	Actual
Units of Quik-Tite produced...............		61,000 units
Pounds of material A required to produce one unit of Quik-Tite.......................	1.6 lbs.	1.5 lbs.
Cost of material A purchases during June....	$2.00 per lb.	$2.05 per lb.
Inventory of material A on June 1, priced at $2 a pound..........................	4,000 lbs.	4,000 lbs.

Compute materials quantity variances for the month.

*8. Products A and B have standard direct labor requirements of two hours and three hours per unit, respectively. The standard wage rate is $3 per hour. During April, 1,500 units of product A and 4,000 units of product B were manufactured. Direct labor for the period totaled 14,500 hours and cost $44,000. Compute the labor variances.

*9. Standard direct labor cost of the product is $3 a unit. Operating data for the month of July are:

---

* Solutions to problems marked with an asterisk (*) can be found in Appendix B.

Units in process, July 1 (one-half processed)............................ 500
Units finished during July..3,000
Units in process, July 31 (one-fourth processed)........................ 800

Compute the standard direct labor cost of the month's output.

10. Standard direct labor cost is $1 a unit for product A and $2 a unit for product B. The standard labor cost of work in process was $2,000 on September 1 and $5,000 on September 30. The standard wage rate is $3 an hour, and there were 7,500 direct labor hours during September. The direct labor payroll for September totaled $23,000, and 4,000 units of product A and 7,000 units of product B were completed during the month.

   a) Compute the standard direct labor cost of the month's output.
   b) Compute the direct labor quantity variance.
   c) Compute the direct labor rate variance.

11. The standard bill of materials for 100 units of product A is:

	Standard Quantity	Standard Unit Price	Standard Cost of Materials
Material X.................	105 lbs.	$0.70	$ 73.50
Material Y.................	560 ft.	0.40	224.00
Part Z.....................	102 units	1.20	122.40
Standard Materials Cost..			$419.90

The purchases and consumption of materials were as follows:

Item	Purchases	Price	Units Consumed
X........	40,000 lbs.	$0.65 per lb.	33,000 lbs.
Y........	150,000 ft.	0.45 per ft.	161,000 ft.
Z........	32,000 units	1.30 per unit	31,200 units

The output was 30,000 units of product.

Determine and identify the various materials variances for the month.

*12. The factory uses a standard costing system. The following facts were recorded for one department for November:

   (1) Materials purchased and placed in storeroom:
       At actual prices, $106.
       At standard prices, $100.
   (2) Materials received from storeroom (at standard prices), $105.
   (3) Labor used:
       At actual wage rates, $70.
       At standard wage rates, $68.
   (4) Products finished (at standard cost):
       Standard materials cost, $85.
       Standard labor cost, $63.
   (5) Work in process, November 1—none.
   (6) Work in process, November 30 (at standard):
       Standard materials cost, $15.
       Standard labor cost, $8.

a) Compute the variances.

b) Enter the month's transactions in T-accounts, including any entries necessary to prepare the accounts to accumulate December transactions.

13. Department M performs two operations in the manufacture of product P. Standard costs for these operations are:

	Materials	Labor
Standard cost of semifinished product transferred from department K...................	$4.50	
Operation 44.............................	5 lbs. at $0.20	1.5 hours at $2.50
Operation 49.............................	...	2.0 hours at $3.00

The following information relates to the month of July:

(1) On July 1, 500 units of product P were in process in department M. Operation 44 had been performed on these units, but operation 49 had not been started.

(2) Department M received 2,000 units of semifinished product from department K.

(3) Department M transferred 2,200 completed units of product P to department N.

(4) The July 31 work in process inventory consisted of 300 units on which no department M work had been performed.

(5) Department M received 9,500 pounds of material for use in operation 44.

(6) Department M's direct labor hours totaled: operation 44 labor, 3,000 hours; operation 49 labor, 4,000 hours.

a) Compute quantity variances for the month for labor and materials.

b) Prepare journal entries to record the above transactions.

14. The company uses a basic plan standard costing system in its factory. Prepare journal entries to reflect the following information:

(1) Material with a standard cost of $63,000 is purchased at a cost of $58,500.

(2) The mixing department requisitions material with a standard cost of $14,300 for use on production order No. 8265.

(3) The finishing department delivers 4,000 units of item No. 3728 to finished goods. Reference to the standard cost card for item No. 3728 reveals that its standard cost is: material, $2.40; labor $0.65.

(4) At the end of March, the winding department's Materials in Process account shows a balance of $8,500, and a physical count of the materials in process, costed at standard cost, is $9,300.

(5) For the painting department, the hours worked in each job category and the standard hourly rates are:

Job Category	Hours	Rates
I.............	400	$1.60
II.............	1,800	1.90
III............	1,400	2.60
IV............	600	3.40

(6) At the end of the month, the Payroll Cost Summary account has a credit balance of $5,600. The last payroll of the month was three working days before the end of the month, and during these days the men on the hourly payroll put in 1,620 hours. Their average wage rate is $2.60 an hour.

*15. The Durabilt Company, manufacturer of men's work clothes, employs a standard cost system similar to that discussed in this chapter. You are given the following information concerning the month of September:

(1) Inventory September 1:
Raw material.....................................$58,500
Material in process.............................. 6,700
Labor in process................................. 2,400
Finished goods................................... 32,100
(2) Purchases during September:
Actual cost...................................... 42,380
Standard cost.................................... 44,620
(3) Deliveries to finished goods:
Standard material cost........................... 40,350
Standard labor cost.............................. 22,300
(4) Direct labor employed at standard rates....... 23,600
(5) Material put in process....................... 46,650
(6) Inventory October 1:
Raw material.....................................   ?
Material in process.............................. 12,300
Labor in process................................. 4,700
Finished goods...................................   ?
(7) Shipments at standard labor and materials cost........ 63,500
(8) Direct labor payroll for month...................... 24,400

a) Account for the above transactions, using T-accounts and journal entries.

b) Prepare a list of variances, and briefly state the meaning of each.

16. Using a basic plan of standard costing and carrying materials inventories at standard net delivered prices, record the following information in appropriate T-accounts and list any variances you are able to identify, indicating for each whether it is favorable or unfavorable.

(1) Actual cost of materials purchased:
Gross invoice price..............................$50,000
Discounts received on purchases..................   800
Freight and delivery charges on materials purchased. 2,300
(2) Standard cost of materials purchased.......... 51,000
(3) Materials issued (at standard prices)......... 47,000
(4) Direct labor:
At actual wage rates............................. 30,000
At standard wage rates........................... 28,000
(5) Cost of goods finished (at standard):
Materials.. 40,000
Labor.. 26,000
(6) Cost of goods in process, end of month (at standard):
Materials.. 5,200
Labor.. 5,100
(7) There was no work in process at the beginning of the month.

17. The following data relate to the month of July:

	Actual Cost	Standard Cost
(1) Materials purchased.	$ 80,000	$ 77,000
(2) Materials used.	140,000	139,500
(3) Materials in process, July 1.	20,000	21,000
(4) Materials in process, July 31.	25,000	22,800
(5) Materials cost of product completed in July.	135,000	135,700

(6) The Materials Inventory account is carried at standard cost.

a) Calculate the variances. (Note: You will not need all the data supplied.)

b) What managerial action would be expected in response to the reporting of these variances to management?

18. Tufwun Products Company manufactures a limited line of machined products in its Albany factory. A basic plan of standard costing is in use at the factory, with materials inventories being carried at standard prices. The following information pertains to the operations of the Milling Department for the month of September:

(1) Direct labor in the department is divided into three basic pay grades, as follows:

Grade	Standard Wage Rate per Hour
101.	$2.00
102.	2.50
105.	3.00

(2) Wages actually paid to employees will differ from these standard rates due to seniority provisions, etc. Actual hours worked and actual gross pay during the month were as follows:

Grade	Hours	Gross Wages
101.	1,250	$ 2,520
102.	1,500	3,900
105.	1,520	4,200
Total.	4,270	$10,620

(3) Production and product cost standards for the month:

Product	Standard Materials Cost per Unit	Standard Milling Department Labor per Unit 101 Hours	102 Hours	105 Hours	Standard Labor Cost	Units Completed
A.	$2.00	0.5	1.0	..	$3.50	400
B.	4.00	1.0	0.5	1.5	7.75	800
C.	5.00	0.5	1.0	0.5	5.00	600

(4) Direct materials charged to the department, $7,600.

(5) There was no unfinished work in process in the department either at the beginning or at the end of the month.

a) Record the above information in appropriate T-accounts.

b) Prepare a list of the variances for the month, identifying each one clearly, in as much detail as you deem appropriate.

c) To whom would you report each of the variances you identified in (*b*)? What action; if any, would be taken in response to your reports?

19. The HRV Manufacturing Company uses a standard cost system in accounting for the cost of its single product. Standard product cost has been set on the following basis:

> Standard direct labor per unit, 8.5 hours at $1.90 per hour...............$16.15
> Standard direct material per unit:
> Material T, 10 pounds at $0.42 per pound........................... 4.20
> Material V, six units at $0.80 per unit.............................. 4.80
> Total...$25.15

The following operating data were recorded for the month of April:

> In process, April 1, none.
> Completed during April, 9,000 units.
> In process, April 30, 500 units, one-half complete as to labor, 100 percent complete as to material T, and 30 percent complete as to material V.
> Direct labor charged to the factory at standard wage rates during April, $153,-000.
> Materials purchased during April:
> 100,000 pounds of T at $0.45 a pound.
> 80,000 units of V at $0.78 a unit.
> Materials issued to operating departments during April:
> Material T, 96,000 pounds.
> Material V, 60,000 units.

a) Enter these transactions in appropriate T-accounts.

b) List all variances of actual costs from standard costs, with a description of each kind of variance that you can identify.

20. Eiseman, Inc., manufactures a line of children's sleds. Its standard cost system separates price variances at time of purchase. Factory overheads are regarded as wholly fixed and are charged to expense as incurred, without passing through the product inventory accounts. Factory overhead is budgeted at $69,000 a month.

Standard costs and production and inventory data for the four models manufactured in the sled department during September were:

	Model 3	Model 5	Model 22	Model 30
Standard cost per unit:				
Materials.......................	$0.80	$1.20	$1.50	$2.00
Labor...........................	1.00	2.00	3.00	5.00
Total........................	$1.80	$3.20	$4.50	$7.00
Units completed...................	5,000	10,000	4,000	2,000
Units in process, Sept. 1.............	None	1,000	None	200
Units in process, Sept. 30...........	None	1,000	None	None

Units in process on any given date are assumed to be 100 percent complete as to materials and 50 percent complete as to labor.

The following transactions relate to the sled department during the month of September:

(1) Purchased materials on account (standard cost, $35,000), $35,400.
(2) Issued materials:
    Direct materials, at inventory cost, $24,500.
    Indirect materials, at inventory cost, $3,000.
(3) Accrued payrolls for the month (including indirect labor), $64,200.
(4) Direct labor hours (standard wage rate, $2 an hour), 23,800 hours.
(5) Indirect labor, $20,000.
(6) Other factory overhead, paid in cash, $50,000.

a) Record the above information in appropriate T-accounts. Be sure to enter any opening balances.

b) Prepare a list of variances for the month, with titles that are sufficiently descriptive to identify the nature of each variance.

21. The Shawmut Company makes two products in its Irvington factory. Standard labor and materials costs for these two products are as follows:

	Product A	Product B
Department X:		
Materials from stock room:		
4 lbs. material P @ $1.....................	$ 4.00	$ 4.00
2 lbs. material Q @ $5....................	10.00	....
3 lbs. material T @ $2....................	....	6.00
Labor, 0.5 hour @ $3......................	1.50	1.50
Subtotal............................	$15.50	$11.50
Department Y:		
Materials from stock room:		
1.1 containers @ $0.10....................	0.11	0.11
Labor:		
1.0 hour, grade PF–1 labor @ $3.50........	3.50	....
0.2 hour, grade PF–2 labor @ $2.50........	0.50	0.50
Total Standard Cost...................	$19.61	$12.11

Both products are processed initially in department X and finished in department Y. Overhead costs are not included in standard product costs. The following transactions took place during February:

(1) Materials purchased:
    Material P, 40,000 pounds, $39,200.
    Material T, 20,000 pounds, $42,000.
    50,000 containers, $4,700.
(2) Materials issued:
    Material P, 21,500 pounds.
    Material Q, 3,800 pounds.
    Material T, 9,200 pounds.
    Containers, 4,700 units.
(3) Labor:
    Department X, 2,700 hours, $8,370.
    Department Y: 2,020 PF–1 hours, $7,070.
              950 PF–2 hours, $2,470.

(4) Units finished:

	Product A	Product B
By department X.................	2,000	3,000
By department Y.................	2,100	2,500

Standard costs of work in process were as follows:

	February 1	February 29
Department X.......................	None	None
Department Y:		
Materials in process................	$7,750	$9,300
Labor in process...................	800	800

a) Compute any labor and materials variances that you can identify and indicate which of these should be shown on the February performance reports issued to the manager of department Y.

b) Each department has separate materials in process and labor in process accounts. There is a factory ledger. Materials purchases are paid for by the head office, but labor payrolls are accrued and paid at the factory. A basic plan of standard costing is in use. Prepare journal entries to record the transactions listed in items (1) through (4) above.

22. The Prentice Company manufactures two products in its Denver plant. The plant uses a standard cost system for direct labor and direct materials costs. Factory overhead costs are not taken into product costs and are not introduced into this problem in any way.

The factory contains two production departments, X and Y. Production on both products is initiated in department X and completed in department Y. Materials inventories are carried at standard cost. Each department has two work in process accounts—materials in process and labor in process. The standard cost of materials received by a department from the storeroom is charged to the materials in process account of that department. The standard labor and materials costs of the operations performed in department X are charged to the materials in process account of department Y at the time the semifinished goods are transferred.

The standard costs for the two products are shown below. Note that operations and costs are listed in the order in which the work moves through the plant.

Operation	Department	Labor Cost	Materials from Storeroom	Cumulative Cost
14....................	X	$2.00	$5.00	$ 7.00
12....................	X	1.50	0.10	8.60
20....................	X	1.00	0.50	10.10
18....................	Y	3.00	...	13.10
32....................	Y	1.00	0.90	15.00

Product B: Standard cost per unit.

Operation	Department	Labor Cost	Materials from Storeroom	Cumulative Cost
11..................	X	$0.10	$0.30	$0.40
16..................	X	0.25	...	0.65
27..................	X	0.20	0.05	0.90
32..................	Y	0.05	0.05	1.00

The following data pertain to the factory's operations during the month of July:

	Actual Prices	Standard Prices
(1) Materials received from suppliers and placed in storeroom................................	$31,402	$30,100
(2) Materials issued from storeroom:		
To Department X...........................	xxx	20,530
To Department Y...........................	xxx	4,260
(3) Actual direct labor:		
Department X..............................	21,470	21,400
Department Y..............................	15,351	14,620
(4) Goods finished and transferred:		

Product	From Dept. X to Dept. Y	From Dept. Y to Finished Goods
A..............................	3,100 units	3,000 units
B..............................	14,000 units	15,000 units

(5) Work in process, July 1:
Department X: 200 units of product A, complete through operation 12.
Department Y: 1,000 units of product B, complete through operation 27.
(6) Work in process, July 31:
Department X: none.
Department Y: 100 units of Product A, complete through operation 18.

a) Prepare journal entries to record the month's transactions, including interdepartmental transfers.

b) Prepare a list of variances, indicating for each whether it is favorable or unfavorable and the level of management at which control responsibility is likely to lie.

23. The Covered Wire Company manufacturers copper insulated electrical wire of various specifications on a job order basis. Physical inventory records are relatively complete. There is a stores record card for each category of raw material, and this card is kept up to date, in physical quantities only, by daily entries to record receipts and requisitions for the day. Similarly, finished goods inventory cards are kept up to date by daily postings of orders completed and goods shipped, again in physical quantities only.

The company has no cost accounting system. In preparing bids for new business, the company utilizes a file of product cost estimates for each of about 200 products. The remainder of the company's products differ from these 200 only in such minor respects as the color of the insulating material. The file consists of estimated materials requirements and direct labor hours, which can be extended at current prices and wage rates at any time a cost estimate is desired.

During the year all materials purchased are charged to a purchases account and direct labor costs are charged to a direct labor account. Overhead costs are accumulated in a series of descriptive accounts. Quarterly income statements are prepared for management and for the company's bank creditors.

No inventory count is made quarterly, and quarterly cost of goods sold is the sum of direct labor and overhead for the quarter plus an allowance for materials based on the ratio of the materials component of the cost of goods sold to total sales during the previous year.

The quarterly income statements for the first three quarters of 19x0 indicated profits of $120,000, $145,000, and $75,000, respectively. When the physical count of inventories was made at the end of 19x0, however, the audited income statement for the year revealed a loss of $56,000. Although part of this was due to a poor fourth quarter, management came to the conclusion that something would have to be done to improve the accounting system so that the quarterly statements would be a more accurate reflection of the operations of the company. The controller suggested that a job order costing system be established, with perpetual dollar inventory records for materials and finished goods and job cost sheets for work in process. Management rejected this idea because of the clerical cost it would entail. The controller then suggested that some form of standard costing be introduced if this could be done with little addition to clerical cost.

Outline your suggestions for such a system.

Chapter 11

VARIATIONS IN
STANDARD COSTING

MOST standard costing systems in use today are more complex than the basic plan system described in the preceding chapter. This greater complexity is designed to permit the reporting of variances more frequently and in greater detail. This chapter deals with methods of accomplishing these twin objectives and also includes some discussion of the applicability of standard costing to joint production.

SINGLE PLAN STANDARD COSTING

Greater detail and more frequent reporting of variances typically require identification of variances as they occur, operation by operation, rather than as end-of-period residuals. Standard costing systems designed to accomplish this objective fall into the general category of *single plan* systems.

Nature of the Single Plan

The principal feature of the single plan is that each charge for direct materials and direct labor is broken down into standard cost and variance components. In other words, it must be possible to compute not only the standard cost of production completed in a department during the period but also both the actual and the standard input quantities *at the time the work is performed.*

For example, if an operation calling for 5.0 standard labor hours is performed in 5.5 hours, two accounts will be charged, one for the standard hours and the other for the half-hour quantity variance. This requires a greater amount of data preparation time than basic plan standard costing because the input documents must show both standard and actual quantities.

Because variances are identified as they arise, they never enter the work in process accounts, which are *always* valued at standard input quantities and prices for the uncompleted work still in process. In other words, debits as well as credits to single plan work in process accounts are for standard quantities of labor and materials, multiplied by standard prices and wage rates, as shown in Exhibit 11–1.

Exhibit 11–1

SINGLE PLAN COST FLOWS

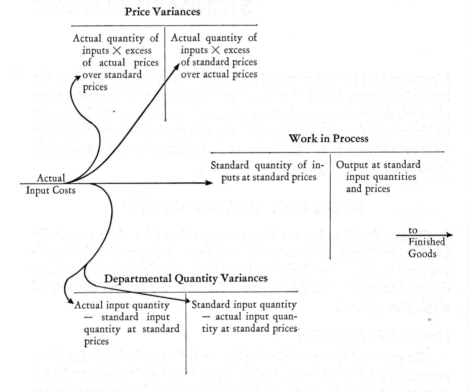

Single Plan Illustration

Standard costing at the Faultless Company follows the single plan. Priced at standard cost, September 1 inventory balances were:

> Materials and parts....................$30,000
> Work in process........................ 23,000

To simplify the illustration, the Faultless Company is assumed to be identical in all respects to the Galahad Company described in Chapter 10. It has two production departments, and the same costs and the same output figures for September. Only the standard costing plan is different.

Accounting for Materials Costs

Identification of the materials quantity variance when it arises requires some means of identifying the actual materials consumption for each operation. The Faultless Company accomplishes this by classifying materials requisitions into two categories: standard and supplemental. Standard requisitions generate entries to the work in process accounts; supplemental requisitions refer to off-standard quantities and lead to entries in variance accounts.

At the time a production order is prepared, a set of requisition cards is prepared for the standard quantities of materials shown on the standard cost sheet. The Faultless Company uses punched cards for this purpose, and a separate card is punched for each class of materials listed on the standard cost sheet. When a cost center commences work on a job, the cost center foreman presents to the stock room the cards for the materials that he will require and obtains the standard quantity of materials specified.

As the job progresses, it may become necessary to requisition additional materials quantities to cover excessive spoilage. In this case the standard prepunched requisition card cannot be used. Instead, a supplemental requisition card, usually of a different color and with a distinctive code designation, is issued. This gives rise to an entry debiting a materials quantity variance account and crediting stores inventory.

During September, the machining department requisitioned $11,-300 of materials and parts, $10,200 on standard requisitions and $1,-100 on supplemental requisitions. The assembly department requisitioned from the storeroom standard quantities amounting to $4,200 and supplemental quantities priced at $400. The entries to record these transactions are:

```
Work in Process.............................................14,400
    Materials and Parts.........................................        14,400

Materials Quantity Variance—Machining......................... 1,100
Materials Quantity Variance—Assembly..........................   400
    Materials and Parts.........................................         1,500
```

Notice that the Faultless Company uses only one work in process account instead of the four required by the Galahad Company system. Because the work in process accounts are not used to accumulate departmental variances, they need not be departmentalized or subdivided by cost element. Some systems do not even record the issuance of materials that are issued on standard requisitions, but keep all unissued materials and the standard materials content of work in process and finished goods in a single inventory account to reduce clerical cost and eliminate one source of clerical error.[1]

Materials returns are handled by procedures analogous to those used for supplemental requisitions. If a job is completed without consuming all the materials issued, the excess materials are returned to the store-room where a returned materials card is filled out with the quantity of each material returned. This is then extended at standard prices to provide a basis for crediting the department's variance account.

During September the machining department returned materials with a standard cost of $400, while returns from the assembly department amounted to $600, at standard prices. The entries are:

```
Materials and Parts.............................................1,000
    Materials Quantity Variance—Machining........................        400
    Materials Quantity Variance—Assembly.........................        600
```

Once all the requisitions for a given day, week, or month have been posted, the balances in the variance accounts are a direct measure of quantity variances for the period:

Materials Quantity Variance—Machining				Materials Quantity Variance—Assembly			
Supplemental		Returns	400	Supplemental		Returns	600
requisitions	1,100			requisitions	400		
Bal. 700				Bal. 200			

In this case the aggregate variances are the same as for the Galahad Company—$700 unfavorable for machining and $200 favorable for assembly—but the file of supplemental and returned materials cards provides a basis for more detailed analysis of these variances by operation, job, machine, or operator than was possible for Galahad.

Accounting for Labor Costs

In order to transfer labor costs to the single plan work in process accounts, some means must be found for identifying the standard quantity of labor at the point of application. The most common device used for this purpose is the prepunched or preprinted time ticket. If the job is of a standard lot size, these tickets may be prepared long before the job is scheduled, but in any event it is possible to prepare standard labor

---

[1] See Robert L. Beyer, *Profitability Accounting for Planning and Control* (New York: Ronald Press, 1963), pp. 77–80, 128.

time tickets before the work begins. For the base plate job represented by Exhibits 10–1 through 10–3, for example, seven separate tickets probably would have been prepared, one for each of the operations called for on the standard cost sheet.

Identification of the labor quantity variance in a single plan system is ordinarily accomplished by entering actual labor time on the standard labor time ticket for each operation. This means that a labor variance could be reported for each operation performed; and with suitable coding, variance totals could be obtained for each type of operations, each operator, each job, each product, or each machine. The Faultless Company, however, uses the single plan primarily to get daily departmental labor variance reports on a routine basis, and it prepares variance summaries by operation or other classification only if a special need arises. The routine reports, in other words, differ from those in the Galahad Company only in that they are issued daily instead of monthly.

In summary, the accounts in the Faultless Company show the following labor cost flows:

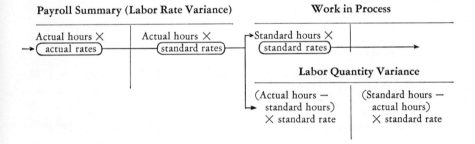

The payroll summary account serves the same purpose it was designed to fulfill under the basic plan—that of segregating the labor rate variance. Each cost center, of course, has its own quantity variance accounts.

During September the standard labor cost of work performed in the machining department totaled $17,600, at a standard wage rate of $3 an hour, and this is the amount that was debited to the Work in Process account. An additional $1,500 in direct labor costs, again at the standard wage rate, was charged directly to the machining department's labor quantity variance account, but this was partially offset by favorable variances on other jobs amounting to $500.

The standard labor cost of operations performed in assembly during September was $9,900. Excessive labor hours on some operations during the month amounted to $450, but these were more than offset by favorable variances on other operations amounting to $550. These figures can all be summarized in a single entry:

```
Work in Process...........................................27,500
Labor Quantity Variance—Machining...........................  1,500
Labor Quantity Variance—Assembly............................    450
    Labor Quantity Variance—Machining.......................              500
    Labor Quantity Variance—Assembly........................              550
    Payroll Summary (Labor Rate Variance)...................           28,400
```

Recording Completed Production

During September the machining department finished goods with standard materials costs of $9,000 and standard labor costs of $19,000, a total of $28,000. Of this, $7,000 represented finished goods, $5,000 was for fabricated parts, and the remaining $16,000 applied to goods transferred to the assembly department.

Because the Faultless Company uses only a single work in process account for all departments, no entry is required to record the interdepartmental transfers. Completion of finished goods and machined parts by the machining department is recorded by entries with the following effect.

```
Finished Goods............................................7,000
Materials and Parts.......................................5,000
    Work in Process.......................................           12,000
```

The finished output of the assembly department amounted to $30,000, recorded as follows:

```
Finished Goods...........................................30,000
    Work in Process.......................................           30,000
```

The balances in the inventory accounts are now entirely up to date, without need for further adjustment. The entire process is summarized in Exhibit 11–2.

Single Plan Reporting to Management

The structure and frequency of cost reports to management should be tailored continuously to the needs of current management. In many factories, for example, a tabulator run of the previous day's labor performance is placed on each foreman's desk at the start of each workday, with a separate line or lines for each operator. A truncated example of such a report is shown in Exhibit 11–3. Notice that the variances are stated in physical and percentage units only, with no dollar conversion. Most companies prefer to use physical units whenever possible, on the grounds that they are more readily understood by operating personnel.

Physical measures may not tell the whole story, of course. If a man

Exhibit 11-2

SINGLE PLAN COST ACCOUNTS ILLUSTRATED

Materials and Parts

Bal. 9/1	30,000	Std. req.	14,400
Purchases	12,000	Supp. req.	1,500
Returns	1,000		15,900
From Mach.	5,000		
	48,000		
Bal. 32,100			

Purchase Price Variance

Purchases	900	Purchases	300
Bal. 600			

Work in Process

Bal. 9/1	23,000	Fin. parts	5,000
Std. req.		Fin. goods	7,000
mach.	10,200	Fin. goods	30,000
Std. req. ass'y.	4,200		42,000
Std. DL mach.	17,600		
Std. DL ass'y.	9,900		
	64,900		
Bal. 22,900			

Materials Quantity Variance—Machining

Supp. req.	1,100	Returns	400
Bal. 700			

Materials Quantity Variance—Assembly

Supp. req.	400	Returns	600
		Bal. 200	

Payroll Summary (Labor Rate Variance)

Payroll	31,700	DL mach.	18,600
Accrual 9/30	3,200	DL ass'y.	9,800
	34,900	Ind. lab. mach.	5,100
Bal. 300		Ind. lab. ass'y.	1,100
			34,600

Labor Quantity Variance—Machining

Unfav. var.	1,500	Fav. var.	500
Bal. 1,000			

Labor Quantity Variance—Assembly

Unfav. var.	450	Fav. var.	550
		Bal. 100	

in a $3 pay bracket is used to perform work normally assigned to a $2 man, costs will be out of line even if the work is completed in standard time. Furthermore, the relative importance of different materials is not reflected in physical unit variances. Finally, if many kinds of materials are used, the data processing problem can become extremely difficult and the resulting variance lists can become so long and unwieldy as to be virtually useless to management.

For these reasons, comprehensive variance reporting ordinarily utilizes monetary figures, both at the first-line supervisor level and in the
more condensed higher management reports. Physical unit reporting is
usually limited to some portion of direct labor, direct materials, and
physical output, with the bulk of factory cost variances reported in
monetary terms.

A daily labor report such as the one shown in Exhibit 11–3 is not
always necessary or desirable. Although single plan standard costing is
particularly well suited to the task of generating daily labor variances,
this is not a sufficient reason to report these variances daily. There is

Exhibit 11–3

DAILY LABOR VARIANCE REPORT

DEPARTMENT Machining				DATE 3/6
SUPERVISOR P. B. Naum				

Operator	Standard Hours Earned	Actual Direct Hours (Including Personal Time)	Variance	
			Hours	Percent of Standard
Brown, P...................	8.2	8.0	0.2	2.4%
Conrad, T. T...............	8.6	8.0	0.6	7.0
Ennis, J...................	3.3	4.0	(0.7)	(27.2)
Gordon, L..................	8.4	9.5	(1.1)	(13.1)
King, M....................	7.9	8.0	(0.1)	(1.3)

such a thing as overcontrol, and too frequent reporting may actually
defeat its own purpose by not making sufficient allowance for normal
fluctuations in productive efficiency. It may be better to report less
frequently, applying the exception principle to weekly or even monthly
variances, and using the detailed variance data provided by single plan
procedures solely as raw material for special analyses whenever aggregate quantity variances appear to be getting out of line.

Comparison with Basic Plan

The use of single plan standard costing presupposes considerable
amounts of clerical preparation and standardization of operations. It is
likely to be most effective in terms of rapid processing of data if the
typical production operation is of standard products in standard lots or
batches, but it can be applied whenever individual inputs can be identified with standard input quantities at the time of performance. A
single plan in which both actual and standard labor times are recorded
has advantages when detailed analysis of variances by operation, machine, operator, or product is desired. Systems of this type require

considerably more clerical time than basic plan systems, but they reduce the calculation and search time necessary to detail the variances. A single plan system is also likely to permit prompter preparation of monthly statements.

Finally, the actual cost data recorded under the single plan provide a much broader data base for cost estimating. While it is true that one purpose of the standard cost files is to facilitate rapid cost estimation without the need for special cost studies, standards are not always up to date and they may even be wrong. Furthermore, some products or some operations may be subject to a wider variation in cost than others, and this may be an important factor in such questions as contract bidding. For all these reasons, the actual cost file may produce benefits.

Basic plan systems deliberately sacrifice this additional information in the interest of reducing clerical costs. Such plans are particularly well suited to operations in which in-process inventories either are negligible or do not change materially from period to period, but it is usually practicable to apply them to the variable inventory case. All that is required is an economical way of approximating the standard input costs of the work still in process at the end of the period.

Many modifications of these two plans are possible, of course. In some basic plan systems, for example, actual costs are accumulated on a sampling basis to widen the data base. Despite all such variations, however, the elements of similarity among the various systems are greater than the points of difference. The choice of method depends on the nature of the operations and the kinds of information that management is willing to pay for.

ANALYSIS OF QUANTITY VARIANCES

Standard costing systems often rely on the first-line supervisor to provide an explanation of the major sources of quantity variances. His close contact with the operation, it is reasoned, should permit him to know when variances arise and why; the accounting system merely gives a quantitative measure of the overall result. Even so, line management responsibility for variance analysis can be and usually is supplemented by more formal means of identifying the sources and causes of factor variances, and some of these methods are discussed in the following paragraphs.

Classification by Causes

One means of separating certain important kinds of variances from the quantity variance accounts is to classify them as overhead when they occur. This means, for example, that the size and importance of the labor quantity variance depends on company practice in classifying some portions of the variance as overhead. Many direct production workers, as we have indicated, devote part of each day to activities not directly connected with a specific job. The standard hourly cost of this portion of labor time can be assigned either to the variance account or to various overhead accounts, each one descriptive of a particular type of activity or cause of deviation from standard.

If most of the major causes of variances are reflected in charges to these classified overhead accounts, then the labor quantity variance is likely to be small and added information provided by a complete record of all actual labor hours, both direct and indirect, may be very small indeed.

A highly elaborate scheme for causal identification of variances is illustrated in Exhibit 11–4. This form provides for a virtually complete classification of labor quantity variances by cause. It presumes a single plan system and requires the foreman to assign a reason for each variance in excess of 10 percent. These classified variances are then tabulated and reported monthly to the foreman and to plant management.

Few systems go this far, but this illustration shows how far the routinization of variance analysis can go if management is willing to pay for it. Most companies are content to limit routine variance separation to a few main items, such as those discussed in the next few paragraphs, leaving more detailed investigation of residual variances to special analysis if and when required.

Effects of Materials Yields on Labor Variances

In materials-paced operations, such as much of process production, the amount of labor required varies as a function of the materials used rather than as a function of output. For this reason, an unfavorable materials quantity variance would normally be accompanied by an unfavorable labor quantity variance.

To illustrate, assume that one pound of materials is expected to yield five units of product. One hour of processing labor is required for each 10 pounds of materials processed, and the standard wage rate is $3 an hour. The standard labor cost of a unit of product is thus:

$$(0.1 \times \$3) \div 5 = \$0.06 \text{ per unit.}$$

Suppose now that 10,000 pounds of materials are processed, using 1,000 labor hours and yielding 45,000 units of product. The labor quantity variance will be:

Standard cost of output: 45,000 × $0.06.............................$2,700
Actual labor hours at standard wage rate............................ 3,000
    Labor Quantity Variance (Unfavorable)........................$ (300)

In this case, however, the entire labor quantity variance is a reflection of the materials quantity variance, because actual labor hours are exactly one tenth of the number of pounds of materials processed, which is the precise relationship assumed in the product cost standard. Thus the two quantity variances might reasonably be combined in a single quantity variance for management reporting.

In other words, whenever labor costs are governed by materials input flows rather than by output quantities, three components of the direct labor cost variance might be identified:

(1) Actual hours × actual wage rates
(2) Actual hours × standard wage rates
    LABOR RATE VARIANCE: (1) − (2)
(3) Required hours × standard wage rates
    LABOR PERFORMANCE VARIANCE: (2) − (3)
(4) Earned hours × standard wage rates
    EFFECT OF MATERIALS VARIANCE ON LABOR COST: (3) − (4)

(The term *required hours* has been coined to refer to the standard hours required by the given quantity of materials inputs; *earned hours* refers to the standard hours reflected in product standard cost.)

Whether the labor quantity variance is subdivided into these two components should depend on the materiality of the component referred to above as the *labor performance variance,* a term that has no standard meaning in practice but which we have adopted here to distinguish this component from the materials-related portion of the labor quantity variance. Only this performance component is affected by causal factors other than those leading to variances in materials yields, and thus the presumption is that in causal analysis the materials-related component should be extracted from the labor quantity variance.

Labor Substitution Variances

Labor variances sometimes arise not because workers are paid at a higher or lower rate than the standard rate for their particular pay grade, and not because the number of labor hours differs from standard, but because work which is supposed to be performed by a worker in one pay grade is actually performed by a worker in another grade. Variances of this latter kind are known as labor *substitution variances.*

To illustrate, suppose that workers in the machining department fall into two pay grades, each with its own standard rate. Suppose further that the cutting and drilling operation for the base plate job referred to in Exhibit 10–1 called for operators with a standard rate of $3.40 an hour, while the leveling and polishing operations utilized labor with a

Exhibit 11–4

DEPARTMENTAL DIRECT LABOR VARIANCE REPORT

Code	Reason for Variance	Control-ability	Month of			Year to Date		
			Actual Hours	Variance Hours	Cost	Actual Hours	Variance Hours	Cost
0	No reason. Variances less than 10 percent.	C						
1	Estimated running time too high. Reported to standards department.	N						
2	Estimated setup time too high. Reported to standards department.	N						
3	Men's effort and/or ability above average.	C						
5	New machine, standard has not been changed.	N						
6	Change in methods, standard has not been changed.	N						
7	New or improved tools, standard has not been changed.	N						
8	Used setup from previous jobs.	C						
9	Time set for man operating one machine. Ran two.	C						
10	Time clock registers to 0.1 hour only.	N						
11	Work done under special supervision.	C						
	TOTAL GAINS							
0	No reason. Variances less than 10 percent.	C						
51	Standard too low. Reported to standards department.	N						
52	First time job was made.	C						
53	Slow or obsolete machine used.	N						
54	Planning not correct. Was changed. Standards department notified.	N						
55	Could not follow operation as planned, delivery requirements.	N						
56	Operations in previous departments not performed as planned.	C						
57	Time set for man operating two machines. One available.	N						
58	Quantity too small.	N						
59	Extra setup result of machine break down.	N						
60	Extra work.	N						

61	Two men had to be assigned to job due to nature of job.	N
62	Learner, apprentice, or student.	N
63	Man inexperienced. Undergoing instructions.	N
64	Different operators used due to difficulty of job.	C
65	Assisting inexperienced operator on another machine.	N
66	Man's effort and/or ability below average.	C
67	Operation not performed correctly. Additional time required.	C
68	Parts spoiled. Had to make additional parts.	C
69	Tools not available at time job was started.	N
70	Trying out new tools.	N
71	Tools not correct when job was started. Had to be corrected.	N
72	Broke tool. Time lost redressing and sharpening.	C
73	Oversized material used.	N
74	Castings warped, but are within foundry tolerances.	N
75	Casting not to dimensions. Time lost waiting for instructions.	N
76	Material too hard. Frequent sharpening of tools required.	N
77	Improper supervision.	C
79	Illegible blue prints.	N
80	Blowholes and porous casting.	N
81	Sheet stock—secondary material or scrap ends used.	N
99	Full quantity or operations not complete.	N
	TOTAL LOSSES	
	GRAND TOTAL	

Efficiency % Controllable by Foreman   C

Efficiency % Noncontrollable   N

Efficiency % Overall

Reproduced by permission from "The Analysis of Manufacturing Cost Variances, Research Series No. 22," *N.A. (C.) A. Bulletin*, August 1952, pp. 1545–84.

standard rate of $2.60 an hour. The standard labor cost for 1,000 base plates is now:

Operation	Hours	Rate	Cost
Cutting.................................	5.5	$3.40	$ 18.70
Drilling.................................	21.0	3.40	71.40
Beveling................................	6.0	2.60	15.60
Polishing..............................	14.5	2.60	37.70
Total..............................	47.0	xxx	$143.40

Suppose now that the operators normally assigned to polishing are fully scheduled and that to meet delivery schedules on this order one of the drill press operators is assigned to perform the polishing operation. The operator's time will be charged to the department at the standard wage rate for his own pay grade ($3.40). The 80 cents an hour difference between this and the standard rate for the operation is due to a nonstandard labor assignment.

To summarize, if the worker's actual rate is $3.50 and he spends 16 hours on the polishing operation, the following variances can be distinguished:

(1) Actual hours × actual rate.................... 16 × $3.50 = $56.00
(2) Actual hours × standard rate for actual pay grade. 16 × $3.40 =   54.40
    LABOR RATE VARIANCE (1) − (2)............. $ 1.60
(3) Actual hours × standard rate for specified pay
    grade.................................... 16 × $2.60 =   41.60
    LABOR SUBSTITUTION VARIANCE (2) − (3)......   12.80
(4) Standard hours × standard rate for specified pay
    grade....................................14.5 × $2.60 =   37.70
    LABOR QUANTITY VARIANCE (3) − (4).........   3.90
    TOTAL VARIANCE (1) − (4)................ $18.30

The bulk of the total variance in this case is thus seen to be a substitution variance. If departmental charges are priced at the standard wage rates for each pay grade, the substitution variance will appear as part of the labor quantity variance unless it is removed. Isolation of the variance can be accomplished by classification in the accounts (e.g., charge the substitution differential to an overhead account as each substitution is made), if this is deemed desirable. The alternative of end-of-period analysis also requires documentation of each substitution as it is made.

Labor Mix Variance

Quite similar to the substitution variance is the labor mix variance that arises when a single standard wage rate is used to price labor of various pay grades. A single rate presumes a given mix of the various pay grades, and departures from this mix will give rise to a variance.

For example, suppose that the $3 standard wage rate in the machining department presumed an equal mix of workers in the two pay grades. The 6,900 direct and indirect labor hours worked by direct production workers during September included 3,300 hours of labor in the $3.40 grade and 3,600 hours in the $2.60 grade. Thus total hours at grade standard wage rates were:

$$
\begin{array}{rl}
3,300 \times \$3.40 = & \$11,220 \\
3,600 \times \$2.60 = & \underline{9,360} \\
\text{Total} & \$20,580
\end{array}
$$

The difference between this sum and the actual gross wages for period is the adjusted labor rate variance. The difference between the $20,580 and the amount charged to the department (6,900 hours $\times$ $3 = $20,700) is the labor mix variance. (This included both the direct and the indirect time of the direct production workers.)

Notice that in this example the amounts charged to the department were the same as in the earlier illustrations. The labor mix variance here is broken out of the labor *rate* variance rather than out of the quantity variance and thus does not affect the departmental charges. Whether the labor mix variance should be reported to the department head depends on whether he has significant control over the labor mix.

This analysis can be built quite easily into the bookkeeping routine or can be carried out by end-of-period calculations if desired. Many companies are satisfied, however, to leave both mix and substitution variances as part of the quantity or rate variances, particularly if the amounts of substitution and the amounts of mix variation are likely to be small, and defer any detailed analysis until a large variance is reported for a particular time period.

Product Rejection Variances

Some variances arise from defects in materials or workmanship that cause quality control inspectors to reject individual product units or even whole production lots. In a basic plan system, such variances remain part of the residual quantity variance unless provision is made for transferring costs to separate accounts during the period. Single plan systems require immediate separation of the variances from the work in process accounts, but may either leave them as part of the overall quantity variance or transfer them to separate overhead accounts.

If the production losses are recouped by issuing and processing new materials to bring the production lot up to the specified quantity, then the costs of these extra materials and operations can be charged directly to the departmental variance accounts as they are incurred. Similarly, the costs of rework labor and other costs of reprocessing defective goods to bring them up to specifications should also be charged to variance or overhead accounts. The temporary error in the work in process account balance thus disappears as soon as the deficiency is made good, and no adjustment of the work in process account is necessary.

If the lost units are not replaced, the work in process account must be relieved of the cumulated standard costs of all operations prior to the point of rejection. Here again, management has the option to enter the amounts in separate overhead accounts or to mix them with variances from other sources in the residual variance accounts. The choice probably hinges on the probable frequency of occurrence: the more frequently this sort of thing happens, the greater is the need to keep tabs on it.

Equipment Substitution Variances

Many other causes may contribute to the labor quantity variance, but we shall discuss only one more, the variance resulting from the use of nonpreferred equipment. Many factories, particularly job shops, contain a considerable variety of multipurpose equipment. Product cost standards are generally based on the use of a particular type of machine to do each operation, but scheduling difficulties may cause department foremen or the scheduling department to use substitute equipment in order to meet delivery schedules when the preferred equipment is fully utilized by other work. Use of standard operation timecards for the charge to work in process will leave an amount in the labor quantity variance account representing the effect of the use of nonstandard equipment.

This problem may be serious enough to justify considerable attention. If use of nonstandard equipment is frequent enough, separate cost standards may be prepared for each type of equipment used for performing each operation. When nonstandard equipment is used, the departmental accounts are credited with the standard cost of the operation on the machine actually used. Inventory accounts, however, are debited only for standard product cost, based on the use of standard equipment. The difference is debited on an overhead account, attributed to the scheduling function.

For example, assume that a drilling operation on a piece part is normally assigned to a new drill press in a standard time of 21 hours for a standard lot. It can also be performed on a slower machine in 23 hours. The standard wage rate on both machines is $3 an hour. The standard cost of the operation when performed on the slower machine is thus 23 hours at $3 an hour, or $69 instead of $63. A charge of $6 could therefore be made to an overhead account bearing a title such as Use of Nonstandard Equipment—Machining.

Even if this variance is not separated formally from other sources of labor quantity variances, labor timecards may be marked in some distinctive way so that the standard operation cost on nonstandard equipment can be computed. In a piece rate system this is normally required by the terms of the piece rate agreement. This kind of variance may also be identified routinely in an hourly wage plan, but it should be remembered that this results in an increase in clerical cost, an increase that may not be justified by the added information it provides.

A similar problem arises in automobile assembly plants. It is common practice to credit assembly with the standard cost of an "average" automobile. If the product mix in any period varies from that on which the average standard was computed, a variance will arise. To permit isolation of this variance, data on differences in the standard costs of different models must be available in the standard cost files.

Departmental Attribution of Variances

A delicate problem arises when variances occur in one department as the result of delays or defective workmanship in prior departments. For example, in the assembly operation it may be found that 30 of the base plates, with a standard cost of $0.393 each, were incorrectly cut and must be scrapped. On the surface, this seems like a simple problem which can be solved by charging $11.79 to the machining department and crediting the same amount to the appropriate inventory account.

The difficulty which is not obvious in this simple illustration is that it is frequently either impossible or too costly to determine which one of a number of previous departments was responsible for the defective work. Furthermore, the practice of charging departments with events that occur outside their jurisdiction may lead to argument and bitterness and undermine confidence in the validity of the variance accounts. For this reason, it is probably better to charge the cost of defects to a special variance or overhead account in the department in which the defect is found.

Even this can be dispensed with if materials defects are rare. That is, the company may choose to leave the costs of defective material in the materials quantity variance figures, accepting the slight information loss rather than incur the clerical costs necessary to achieve greater accuracy.

Direct Labor and Materials Classification

Departmental direct labor and direct materials totals are often so large that single departmental variances for each cannot meet the department heads' needs for control information. In process production, for example, all departmental labor is direct labor, by definition. Similarly, all departmental materials are direct materials because they are all traceable to the department. Furthermore, even if the term is restricted to those portions of departmental labor and materials that ought to vary in proportion to production volume, the definition implicit in this chapter, a single pair of variance accounts may not be enough.

Two major solutions to this problem are available. In process production, the usual answer is to establish separate accounts for each labor skill class and for each major type of materials used. Separate standards are set for each category, and actual costs are coded accordingly.

In job order production the subcategories are more likely to apply to groups of machines or work stations within the cost center. If the cost center is small and homogeneous, this kind of subdivision is generally unnecessary and a breakdown by grade and class is the only alternative.

Nonstandard Products

Some portion of each month's output in job order production is typically of new products or product modifications for which no standards have previously been set. This is not serious as long as these nonstandard products do not constitute a large proportion of total output.

Most nonstandard products in most companies are merely new combinations of operations and materials already listed in the standard cost file. These create no special problem. For more novel products, two solutions are possible. First, new standards might be developed for the new operations. If accuracy is attempted, the establishment of new standards is costly and could even delay production. Using rough approximations avoids these problems but may cloud the meaning of overall departmental variances.

The widely used alternative is to grant actual time allowances for unrated work. Actual costs can be accumulated on time tickets and totaled either for each job order or for each department in total. Job order totals can be compared with estimates, if desired, but the latter are not used as the basis for departmental credits. Departmental variances therefore pertain only to that portion of total production represented by input-rated operations.

STANDARD COSTING FOR JOINT PRODUCTS

All of the illustrations of standard costing thus far have been of products that are produced independently. Standard costs can also be developed for joint products, even though it is not possible to identify specific portions of the joint inputs with specific products. These standard costs serve no decision-making purposes but they can be useful in evaluating processing yields.

Deriving Standard Costs

The development of standard product costs for joint products requires three kinds of information:

1. Standard percentage physical yields for each of the joint products.
2. Standard prices and quantities for the joint inputs.
3. A standard cost apportionment formula (e.g., based on relative market values).

To illustrate, assume that a given process utilizes a single raw material for which a standard price of $4 per pound has been established. The standard labor cost of processing this material is $100 per hundred pounds of material input, for a total joint input cost of $500 per hundred pounds. The process yields products in three grades, and under present operating techniques the normal expected production consists of 60 percent firsts, 30 percent seconds, and 10 percent culls.

In this case the formula chosen to derive standard unit costs is a relative market value formula. The application of this formula to the standard input and standard output data is illustrated in Exhibit 11–5. (Once again, overhead costs are to be ignored in the interest of simplicity.) It will be recalled that the relative market value method apportions cost among the joint products in proportion to their respective percentages of the total market value of all joint products combined. Thus "firsts" account for 72 percent of total market value and thus are assigned 72 percent to total joint cost, or $360. This works out to $6 a pound, and this is adopted as the standard cost of "firsts." The standard unit costs of all three products are shown in column (6) of Exhibit 11–5. These can be further subdivided into standard materials and standard labor costs whenever a detailed variance analysis is desired.

Exhibit 11-5

ESTABLISHING STANDARD UNIT COSTS FOR JOINT PRODUCTS

Grade	(1) Standard Pounds Output per 100 Pounds Materials	(2) Estimated Market Price per Pound Output	(3) Market Value per 100 Pounds (1) × (2)	(4) Percent of Total Market Value	(5) Total Cost Allocated (4) × $500	(6) Standard Cost per Pound (5) ÷ (1)
Firsts.............	60	$13.20	$ 792	72%	$360	$6
Seconds...........	30	8.80	264	24	120	4
Culls.............	10	4.40	44	4	20	2
Total...........	100	xxx	$1,100	100%	$500	xxx

Analyzing the Quantity Variances

The departmental labor and materials quantity variances are computed by methods now familiar to us. First, actual input quantities are charged to the department at standard prices. Second, the department is credited with actual output quantities of each product at standard cost. The difference is the quantity variance.

For example, during November actual inputs at standard prices were as follows:

	Input Quantity	Input Cost at Standard Prices
Materials............................	10,000 lbs.	$40,000
Labor..............................	3,200 hrs.	11,200
Total............................	xxx	$51,200

Actual yields for the month were:

	Quantity (Pounds)	Standard Cost per Pound	Standard Cost Earned
Firsts......................	6,200	$6	$37,200
Seconds....................	2,800	4	11,200
Culls......................	500	2	1,000
Total...................	9,500	xxx	$49,400

The total quantity variance was thus $51,200 minus $49,400, or $1,-800 and unfavorable.

This figure can be further subdivided into *mix variance* and *yield variance* components by computing the cost that would have been "earned" by the department if the same total output had been in standard proportions—that is, the standard cost of the same output quantity at the standard mix. In this case the output totaled 9,500 pounds. If this had been distributed among the three products in the normal proportions of 60–30–10, the yield would have been as follows:

	Standard Mix Quantity (Pounds)	Standard Cost per Pound	Total Standard Cost at Standard Mix
Firsts......................	5,700	$6	$34,200
Seconds....................	2,850	4	11,400
Culls......................	950	2	1,900
Total..................	9,500	xxx	$47,500

In other words, if the process had yielded the same output (9,500 pounds) but in standard proportions, the standard cost earned would have been $47,500. The standard cost earned by the actual yield was $49,400. Thus the mix variance amounted to $1,900 and was favorable, reflecting the higher percentage yield of firsts than in the standard mix.

Offsetting this favorable mix variance was an unfavorable yield variance of $3,700, computed as follows:

	(1) Standard Input Cost per 100 Pounds Output	(2) Standard Input Cost per 9,500 Pounds Output	(3) Actual Inputs at Standard Prices	(4) Yield Variance (3) − (2)
Materials..........	$400	$38,000	$40,000	$2,000
Labor.............	100	9,500	11,200	1,700
Total.........	$500	$47,500	$51,200	$3,700

The standard input cost for 9,500 pounds of output is, of course, the same as the standard cost of 9,500 pounds of a standard output mix referred to in the preceding table, and the variance analysis can be summarized briefly:

(1) Standard cost, actual mix.................................$49,400
(2) Standard cost, standard mix.............................. 47,500
    MIX VARIANCE (1) − (2)..................................... $1,900
(3) Actual inputs, standard prices............................. 51,200
    YIELD VARIANCE (2) − (3)...............................   (3,700)
        TOTAL QUANTITY VARIANCE (1) − (3)..................... $(1,800)

The mix variance can be further subdivided by product, if desired:

	Standard Cost of Actual Yield, Actual Mix	Standard Cost of Actual Yield, Standard Mix	Product Mix Variance
Firsts...............	$37,200	$34,200	$3,000
Seconds.............	11,200	11,400	(200)
Culls...............	1,000	1,900	(900)
Total..........	$49,400	$47,500	$1,900

The same kind of information could be shown in a tabulation of percentage yields, but the conversion into dollar equivalents has the advantage of showing the relative desirability of physical yield variances in the various grades. Furthermore, it permits tying the physical comparisons in with the accounting records so that the entire variance can be analyzed.

Yield variance analysis using standard cost is particularly applicable when there is a definite heirarchy of the joint products in terms of relative desirability. If the joint output consists of several grades of product in which it is always desirable to produce as large a proportion as possible of the higher grades, under a given processing technique, then we can interpret variations from standard yields as favorable or unfavorable. If the relative market prices of the various coproducts are subject to frequent and pronounced shifts, no such simple interpretation is possible, but the variance figures will continue to emphasize the differences between actual and standard yields.

Variations in Input Quality

Up to now we have ignored two problems that arise frequently in costing joint production. First, the material input may be subject to variations in quality, and this will introduce yield variances that are not controllable in processing. Second, it is often possible to influence relative yields by varying the processing method. Some brief mention must be made of both of these problems.

Adjustments for variations in the quality of materials input can be made if the input can be analyzed chemically or by inspection and if relationships between input quality and product yields can be established. The overall mix variance can then be broken down into two parts: one representing variations in input quality, and the other representing variations from the expected mix for the actual input quality.

For example, suppose that in the previous illustration the materials used during the month should have yielded firsts, seconds, and culls in the ratio of 70–25–5. One hundred pounds of output in these proportions would earn standard costs of $530, or $30 more than for materials of standard quality:

	Product Yield (Pounds)	Standard Cost per Pound	Standard Cost Earned
Firsts........................	70	$6	$420
Seconds......................	25	4	100
Culls........................	5	2	10
Total.....................	100	xxx	$530

In other words, a favorable mix variance would be expected to arise from the higher quality of the materials used.

The mix variance for 9,500 pounds of output can be subdivided as follows:

(1) Standard cost, standard mix, standard quality (95 × $500)......$47,500
(2) Standard cost, standard mix, actual quality (95 × $530)......... 50,350
    INPUT QUALITY VARIANCE (1) − (2)........................ $2,850
(3) Costs earned... 49,400
    OPERATING MIX VARIANCE (2) − (3)........................   (950)
    TOTAL MIX VARIANCE (1) − (3)........................... $1,900

This shows that the total mix variance should have been even more favorable than it was, given the quality of the materials used. Thus operating performance was actually unfavorable this month.

Intentional Yield Variations

The possibility of altering the production process consciously to achieve desired changes in relative product yields raises a different kind of problem. Some variations of this kind require substantial changes in production facilities or techniques or both, but even within the constraints imposed by existing facilities, management may be able to alter the product mix within limits. Petroleum refineries, for example, typically produce more fuel oil per barrel of crude in the fall and winter and more gasoline during the spring and summer. Variations of this kind are not costless, however, and it may be necessary to make adjustments, either to the cost data or in analysis of cost variances.

Whenever yield variations are achieved by increasing or decreasing the flow of product through higher stage processing operations, the resulting cost variations are built into the existing standard costing system. In other words, there is a separate standard processing cost of each operation, and each has its own joint inputs and joint outputs. Petroleum refining is largely in this category. If the variation is achieved by adjusting the structure of specific operations, however, variances in processing costs and in product mix can no longer be considered independently as we have assumed in all the illustrations we have used thus far. A favorable yield variance may be the result of an unfavorable processing cost variance, and vice versa.

To illustrate, processing material K to yield products A, B, and C in the ratio of 60–30–10 has a variable processing cost of $1.04 a pound. The standard cost of material K is $2 a pound. By making adjustments in processing techniques, management can alter the output proportions to 70–25–5, but this requires variable processing costs of $1.20 a pound, an increase of 16 cents a pound.

Let us assume that standard product cost has been established at $4 a pound for product A, $2 a pound for product B, and $0.40 a pound for product C. If production yields are in the standard proportions, standard materials and variable processing costs will just be absorbed, as in the following table:

Product	Yield (Lbs.)	Standard Cost per Pound	Costs Earned by Production
A......................	60	$4.00	$240
B......................	30	2.00	60
C......................	10	0.40	4
Total................	100	xxx	$304 = $3.04 per lb.

If output is adjusted to a 70–25–5 ratio, however, the following situation arises:

Product	Yield (Lbs.)	Standard Cost per Pound	Costs Earned by Production
A......................	70	$4.00	$280
B......................	25	2.00	50
C......................	5	0.40	2
Total................	100	xxx	$332 = $3.32 per lb.

In other words, the shift in mix results in crediting the department for 28 cents a pound more than the standard mix would provide. The net effect is to permit the department to overabsorb cost by 12 cents a pound merely by increasing the relative output of product A:

Added "earnings" from shift in mix..................................$0.28
Added processing costs to achieve shift in mix.......................0.16
Net Overabsorption per Pound.................................$0.12

This shift in product mix is desirable only when the demand for product A is strong enough to support additional sales of the product without depressing the price significantly. If this is not the case, then the departmental variance should be adjusted to eliminate the effect of intentional yield variation.

SUMMARY

Standard cost plans differ largely in terms of when and how variances are isolated in the accounts. The most elaborate standard costing systems, those falling in the general category of single plan systems, attempt to determine all variances at the time the transactions are recorded. This is accomplished by coding the production input documents for actual as well as standard input quantities for each direct production operation.

The variances under this kind of plan ordinarily can be reported more frequently than those in the basic plan systems outlined in the previous chapter. They can also be reported in more detail and classified on several bases, if desired, but these detailed breakdowns and analyses often can be dispensed with until large unexplained variances occur.

Most standard costing systems, whether single plan, basic plan or something else, provide for identifying certain kinds of variances at the source and recording them in special variance accounts classified as part of factory overhead. Examples include overtime premiums and shift differentials, separated from the labor rate variance, and setup time, rework labor, and equipment substitution variances, separated from the labor quantity variance. Classifications such as these not only reduce the size of the residual unexplained variance but also eliminate from direct materials and direct labor most of the influences that cause them to vary disproportionately with volume.

Standard costs can also be used in joint production to provide indexes of the shifts in relative product yields. The calculations in the final section of this chapter are suggestive of what can be done in this connection, but whether this sort of thing should be done depends, as always, on management's ability to use this kind of information productively.

DISCUSSION QUESTIONS

1. How do single plan standard costing systems differ from basic plan systems? Which plan is likely to be more expensive to administer? Which can provide the greater amount of information?

2. How is the labor quantity variance determined under single plan standard costing?

3. Do individual work in process accounts for each of the various factory production departments serve any useful purpose when a single plan system of standard costing is in use? Explain.

4. What are the advantages and disadvantages of the procedure of accumulating variances separately for each type of operation performed within a cost center? Discuss the problems encountered in making these accumulations.

5. It has been suggested that single plan standard costing is more generally feasible for materials costs than for labor costs. Do you agree or disagree? Why?

6. Under what conditions can materials quantity variances affect the labor quantity variance?

7. How can the analysis of the causes of variances be built into the procedures for routine cost recording under single plan standard costing? Can similar techniques be used in conjunction with basic plan systems?

8. How does a labor substitution variance differ from a labor mix variance? Which is more likely to be subject to management control efforts?

9. What information is necessary to compute equipment substitution variances?

10. What purpose or purposes are served by standard costs for joint products? Describe how you would proceed to establish such standard costs.

EXERCISES AND PROBLEMS

1. The Nelson Company employs three grades of production labor in its factory. Standard wage rates are $1.80 per hour for grade 1 labor, $2.20 per hour for grade 2 labor, and $2.50 per hour for grade 3 labor.

   When a given operation can be performed equally well by employees in more than one grade, the standard cost for that operation is based on the standard wage rate of the least costly labor grade. It is frequently necessary, however, to schedule higher paid men to perform operations that normally call for lower paid operatives.

   a) What is the nature of the variance, if any, that results from this kind of substitution?

   b) To what department or departments would this variance be assigned? How would you make this decision?

2. A process yields three products: A, B, and C. A batch of 100 pounds of materials has a standard yield of 100 pounds of products: 50 pounds of A, 30 pounds of B, and 20 pounds of C. All three products are classified as

joint products. Materials and labor costs are $400 for a 100-pound batch, and the products sell for $2.20, $11, and $22 a pound, respectively.

Compute standard unit costs for products A, B, and C.

*3. The standard unit costs and standard yield ratios of three joint products are as follows:

Product	Standard Yield Ratio	Standard Cost per Pound
A..................	30%	$2
B..................	45	3
C..................	25	5

The total weight of product output is expected, under normal conditions, to equal the weight of the materials processed. Processing costs vary as a function of the weight of the materials processed.

During August, 5,000 pounds of materials were processed. At standard prices and wage rates, materials and labor cost $17,300. Output for the month totaled 1,600 pounds of A, 2,400 pounds of B, and 950 pounds of C. Fifty pounds of materials were lost in processing.

a) What is the standard cost of processing 100 pounds of materials?

b) Calculate the total quantity variance for August and break it down into mix and yield components.

4. Department M completed work on 5,000 pounds of A and 10,000 gallons of B during September. Work in process consisted of 6,000 gallons of material on September 1 and 4,000 gallons of material on September 30. A gallon of material is normally expected to yield one pound of A and one-half gallon of B. Half of the processing labor had been applied to the beginning and ending inventories of work in process. Standard materials costs are $5 a pound for A and $3 a gallon for B. Standard labor costs are $1.25 for A and $0.75 for B.

Compute the costs earned by production during the month.

*5. A department's employees are grouped into three pay grades, with standard wage rates as follows:

Pay Grade	Standard Hourly Wage Rate
1...............	$2.50
2...............	3.00
3...............	4.00

A single department-wide standard wage rate of $3.50 an hour is used for product costing. Data for October are:

(1) Actual department wages, $30,000.
(2) Standard labor cost of the month's output, $32,000.
(3) Actual labor hours: grade 1—2,000; grade 2—4,000; grade 3—3,000.

Analyze the departmental labor variances for the month.

---

* Solutions to problems marked with an asterisk (*) can be found in Appendix B.

6. Actual wages total $15,000. The standard wage rate used for product costing is $4 an hour. Actual labor time totals 4,000 hours: 2,500 hours of grade A labor, with a standard wage rate of $5 an hour; and 1,500 hours of grade B labor, with a standard wage rate of $3.50 an hour. The month's output has a standard labor cost of $15,800.

   a) What are the standard proportions of grade A and grade B labor implicit in the $4 standard wage rate used for product costing?
   b) How much labor cost would be charged to the Work in Process account to reflect the month's operations if the company were on a single plan standard costing system? A basic plan system?
   c) Compute and analyze the variances.

7. The Dade Corporation operates a single plant, manufacturing molded plastic products. It uses a standard cost system in which all price variances are removed at the time of purchase or payroll preparation. Production in the molding department is performed by crews of men in three separate wage rate classifications. A "standard crew hour" consists of 10 man-hours, distributed among the three pay grades as follows:

Pay Grade	Hours	Standard Rate	Standard Cost
FA–1....	2	$3.50	$ 7.00
FA–2....	3	2.80	8.40
FA–3....	5	2.40	12.00
Total..	10	xxx	$27.40

Standard output is 1,000 pounds of finished product per standard crew hour, and on this basis standard labor cost per 1,000 pounds of product is $27.40.

During February charges to the molding department included 650 hours of FA–1 labor, 1,000 hours of FA–2 labor, and 1,600 hours of FA–3 labor. Output of the molding department totaled 330,000 pounds of finished product. There were no in-process inventories either at the beginning or at the end of the month. The department operated 160 hours during February, using two production crews throughout the period. All of this was classified as productive time except for five hours of idle time recorded by one crew while machinery was being repaired. The departmental payroll for the month totaled $9,000.

   a) Compute any variances that you can identify.
   b) Trace the labor costs of the molding department through T-accounts. Indicate for each T-account what the ending balance represents. If possible, design your accounts so that only one variance remains in each. Assume a basic plan system.

*8. The Irwin Seating Company manufactures a line of metal and wooden chairs for sale to large institutional buyers. Its standard cost system is similar to the single plan system described in this chapter. During September the following events occurred relating to the wood chair department:

Materials purchased and placed in inventory:
Standard prices...$123,000
Actual prices.. 131,000
Direct materials (at standard prices):
Standard requisitions....................................... 140,000
Supplemental requisitions..................................... 12,000
Returned to storeroom.. 8,000
Direct labor (at standard wage rates):
Standard hours.. 80,000
Actual hours... 85,600
Direct labor payrolls:
Accrued wages payable, September 1............................. 8,200
September payrolls, covering period of August 30–September 24, inclusive (paid entirely in cash)................................. 79,500
Accrued wages payable, September 30........................... 16,300
Chairs finished (at standard cost):
Direct materials.. 122,400
Direct labor... 76,500

a) Prepare a list of cost variances for the month, in as much detail as the data permit.

b) Account for the above transactions using journal entries and T-accounts, with a separate account for each cost variance that you identified in part (*a*).

9. The Rushby Chemical Company manufactures a certain product by mixing three kinds of materials in large batches. The blendmaster is charged with the responsibility of maintaining the quality of the product, and this often requires him to alter the proportions of the various ingredients. Standard costs are used to provide materials control information.

The standard materials inputs per batch are:

	Quantity (Pounds)	Price (per Pound)	Standard Cost of Materials
Bulk material...........	420	0.06	$25.20
Coloring material.......	70	0.12	8.40
Setting material........	10	0.25	2.50
Total Batch........	500	xxx	$36.10

The finished product is packed in 50-pound boxes; the standard materials cost of each box is therefore $3.61.

During January, the following materials were put in process:

Bulk material..................181,000 lbs.
Coloring material.............. 33,000
Setting material............... 6,000
Total....................220,000 lbs.

Inventories in process totaled 5,000 pounds at the beginning of the month and 8,000 pounds at the end of the month. It is assumed that these inventories consist of materials in their standard proportions. Finished output during January amounted to 4,100 boxes.

a) Compute the total materials quantity variance for the month and break it down into mix and yield components.

b) Who, if anyone, in the management of the company would be interested in seeing this breakdown of the quantity variance?

10. A department has two kinds of machines which are interchangeable but not equally efficient. Standard labor hours per unit of product on each type of machine are:

Product	Model X Machines	Model Y Machines
A..............	1.0	1.2
B..............	2.0	2.6
C..............	3.0	2.8
D..............	4.0	5.0

Standard product cost is based, in each case, on the more efficient machine model for that product—that is, C's standard cost is based on model Y machine time, while standard cost for the other three products presumes the use of model X machines.

The data for March are:

(1) Actual labor hours, including items (4) and (5) below, 2,200.
(2) Standard wage rate, $3.50 an hour.
(3) Actual wages, $8,000.
(4) Labor hours, waiting for machine repair, 40 hours.
(5) Labor hours, correcting defects in products rejected in inspection: product B, 50 hours; product C, 30 hours.
(6) Production (units of product):

Product	Produced on Model X Machines	Produced on Model Y Machines
A..............	500	...
B..............	200	100
C..............	...	150
D..............	140	50

a) Compute and analyze the labor variance for the month in as much detail as the data permit. Explain the meaning of each variance component that you identify.

b) Assuming that a maximum of 1,460 hours on model X machines and 1,200 hours on model Y machines were available for production during the month, after subtracting waiting and rework time and allowing an adequate margin for variations in efficiency, did the department achieve the most efficient scheduling of its equipment? How is any scheduling inefficiency reflected in the labor variance? Explain and quantify if possible.

c) If this company has a single plan standard costing system, how much labor cost would be charged to the Work in Process account during the month?

*11. The Ace Chemical Company uses material B in the manufacture of the joint products Y and Z. The manufacturing operation is continuous, and a process cost system is used. The raw material equivalent of the work in process at any time can be estimated accurately, and it is reasonable to assume that the labor is one half applied on any work in process. Overhead costs are ignored in this problem.

The company uses the market values of products Y and Z at the start of year to derive standard product costs which remain in effect throughout the year.

a) From the following information establish the standard unit cost of Y and Z.

(1) Standard prices:

Material B................................$0.12 per lb.
Direct labor for four-man crew............$9.00 per crew hr.

(2) Market value and standard production of Y and Z per 100 pounds of B:

Product	Output	Price per Unit	Value
Y.........	50 lbs.	$0.40	$20.00
Z.........	20 gals.	0.20	4.00

(3) The standard production rate is 600 pounds of material B per crew hour.

b) The firm's inventory on May 1 and operating data for the month of May are given below. From this information, establish the standard costs of the opening and closing inventories and cost variances for May. Indicate any assumptions you had to make.

(1) Inventory on May 1:

Item	Quantity
B.........................	70,000 lbs.
B in process...............	5,000 lbs.
Y.........................	17,000 lbs.
Z.........................	16,000 gals.

(2) Operating data:
Purchased: 400,000 pounds of B at $0.13, $52,000.
Put in production: 380,000 pounds of B.
Produced: 205,000 pounds of Y, 62,000 gallons of Z.
Direct labor cost, $5,800.
Mill operation during month, 600 crew hours.
Ending inventory of B in process, 10,000 pounds.
Sold: 210,000 pounds of Y and 64,000 gallons of Z.

12. The output of the Noble Metals Company's foundry consists of metal castings and scrap metal, or "remelt." The input consists of a metal "charge" plus coke, limestone, and labor. A standard charge consists of 2,019 pounds of metal. When this is combined with standard quantities of

the other inputs, it is expected to yield outputs in the following standard proportions:

Input		Output	
Metal............2,019 lbs.		Good castings.......1,372.92 lbs.	
Coke.............. 200 lbs.		Remelt............ 585.51 lbs.	
Limestone........ 50 lbs.		Loss.............. 60.57 lbs.	
Labor............0.53 crew hrs.			

Good castings, in other words, are expected to average 68 percent of the metal charge, by weight; remelt is expected to average 29 percent; and the remaining 3 percent is expected to be lost.

The Noble Metals Company charges its foundry department for materials consumed at standard prices and for labor at standard hourly rates for each job classification. Price and wage rate variances are extracted separately and do not appear in the foundry department accounts. The standard materials prices for the current year are:

> Metal..............$2.80 per cwt.
> Coke............... 1.52 per cwt.
> Limestone.......... 0.10 per cwt.

The standard wage rate is $42 a crew hour.

The foundry is credited for the standard labor and materials cost of good castings and also for the remelt recovered. Scrap recovered can be reprocessed to regain its desired chemical content, and this recovered and reprocessed scrap can then be used in the foundry at a later date. Unprocessed scrap is therefore credited to the foundry's materials account at the standard price for metal less estimated reprocessing cost. The net scrap credit on this basis is $2.74 for each hundredweight of scrap recovered.

Labor hours are expected to vary with the number of metal "charges," and during the week of October 6, a total of 158.5 charges were processed.

During the week of October 6, the following data were recorded:

> Metals charged..320,000 lbs.
> Coke... 60,000 lbs.
> Limestone... 13,000 lbs.
> Remelt recovered.....................................102,000 lbs.
> Good castings produced...............................208,000 lbs.
> Labor crew hours (including downtime)................. 100 hrs.
> Labor crew hours (excluding downtime)................. 95 hrs.
> Labor cost charged to foundry (including downtime)...... $4,240

a) Compute the standard labor and materials cost per hundredweight of good castings produced, to the nearest tenth of a cent.

b) Prepare an analysis of labor and materials variances for the week, using as detailed a breakdown as possible.

13. The Glocken Steel Company has a standard cost system for direct labor and materials, the essentials of which as applied to the rolling mill are outlined below:

(1) The rolling mill is charged with:
    a) Steel ingots consumed at standard unit cost.
    b) Actual direct labor hours at standard rates for individual workers.

(2) The rolling mill is credited with or "earns":
   a) Good product at standard unit cost.
   b) Scrap at $18 a ton.
(3) The standard labor and material cost per ton of good product for each type (size, thickness, chemistry) of steel rolled is arrived at as follows:
   a) The standard cost per ton of ingots is multiplied by the standard yield rate to obtain the gross material cost per ton of product. The standard scrap production per ton of good product at $18 per ton is deducted from the gross material cost to obtain the net material cost.
   b) The standard rolling time per ton of good product for each type of steel rolled is multiplied by $37, the standard direct labor cost per hour of mill operation, to obtain the standard direct labor cost per ton of product. Standard rolling time includes no provision for idle time or downtime.
(4) The mill's "profit" or "loss" on labor and material in any month is the difference between its earnings and its costs, as defined above.
(5) Labor cost per ton varies widely from product to product, and total labor cost for any period will depend on the composition of the product mix during that period. Actual labor cost, therefore, correlates more closely with the standard labor cost earned than with either tons of ingots or tons of rolled products.

The operating data for the eighth month (the mill uses a 13-month year of four weeks each) are given below:

(1) Ingots consumed: 13,000 tons; standard cost, $325,000.
(2) Actual direct labor hours at standard rates: $14,720.
(3) Good product at standard cost:

	Quantity	Cost
a) Material	10,500 tons	$285,360
b) Labor	410 mill hrs.	15,170
Total		$300,530

(4) Scrap production: 2,500 tons.
(5) Including downtime caused by production interruptions, the mill operated 400 hours. The downtime was 14 hours. The actual direct labor time listed in (2) above included the costs of labor crews made idle by machine downtime.

a) Prepare the transactions (in T-accounts) which show the mill's operations.

b) Prepare whatever reports and analyses you feel would be helpful to management in reviewing the mill's operations.

14. The company's factory has two departments and operates a single plan standard costing system. Separate accounts are maintained for (1) raw materials and parts, (2) work in process, and (3) finished goods inventories. The following data relate to the month of January:

(1) Direct materials issued and returned (at standard prices):

	Department A	Department B
Standard requisitions	$30,000	$45,000
Supplemental requisitions	4,800	2,700
Returns	2,500	3,100

(2) Direct labor distribution (at standard wage rates):

	Department A	Department B
Actual time.....................	$21,000	$18,000
Standard time..................	21,700	20,600

(3) Work completed:

	Department A		Department B	
	Standard Materials Cost	Standard Labor Cost	Standard Materials Cost	Standard Labor Cost
Transferred to department A	.....	.....	$ 2,200	$ 1,000
Transferred to department B	$18,000	$12,000	.....	.....
Transferred to materials and parts inventory...........	4,200	3,000	9,300	5,000
Transferred to finished goods inventory..........	6,900	5,500	35,000	15,000

(4) Standard cost of goods sold: materials, $42,000; labor, $23,000.
(5) Direct labor payrolls, $42,000, including $750 overtime premiums in department A and $1,400 overtime premiums in department B.

a) Prepare a list of variances for the month in as much detail as the data permit.
b) Prepare journal entries to record the transactions.
c) Prepare the journal entries that would be appropriate if the company replaced its present inventory accounts with the following two accounts: Materials Costs in Inventories and Labor Costs in Inventories.
d) A run of the month's labor time tickets in department A showed that the following amounts, among others, were included in the labor quantity variance for the month (the department has a single standard wage rate of $3.50 an hour):

(1) Defective setup, 30 hours.
(2) Inferior materials, 50 hours.
(3) Standby machine used, 100 hours.
(4) Inexperienced operator, 80 hours.
(5) One operator on two machines, 250 hours (favorable).
(6) New machine, 120 hours (favorable).

Prepare a revised list of labor variances for department A.

15. The M & J Corporation is a textile company producing cotton cloth. It has for many years utilized standards to keep management informed as to the level of cost performance in the mill. Actual costs recorded for each department in the mill are compared with predetermined standards on reports distributed both to the department heads and to the mill superintendent. A different standard cost per yard is developed for each construction of cloth manufactured. This means that a standard based on the actual

volume of operations in any single week must consider the kinds of cloth manufactured ("product mix") as well as the total quantity of all products manufactured.

Product standards are accumulated on standard cost sheets—one for each type or construction of cloth. This sheet is subdivided by department and shows a detailed breakdown of materials, labor, and other departmental costs. The labor cost section shows the total standard cost of each type of labor required per yard of cloth, taken from the labor standards book, which lists the standard labor allowance for each processing operation in each department. The weaving room labor section of the standard cost sheet for style No. 2000 is shown in the following table:

	Labor Cost	
Classification	Cents per Loom Week	Cents per Yard
Twisting-in..................................	43.64	0.10
Changing, $14.50 per 4,300...................	.....	0.34
Weaving piecework...........................	.....	2.38
Loom fixers.................................	353.36	0.82
Smash piecers...............................	43.04	0.10
Battery hands...............................	112.30	0.26
Inspectors..................................	50.23	0.12
Filling carriers............................	29.51	0.07
Other labor.................................	101.28	0.23
Total Weaving Room Labor Cost per Yard....	xxx	4.42

The standard output for style No. 2000 is 431 yards per loom week. Except for the costs of changing and weaving piecework labor, the cost figures shown on this exhibit are based on standard labor costs per loom week, assuming an 80-hour workweek of two shifts of 40 hours each. For example, the standard loom fixers' cost per loom week for style No. 2000 is 353.36 cents, or $3.5336. This is shown in the first column of figures in the table above. Dividing this by the standard output of 431 yards per loom week yields a loom fixers' cost of 0.82 cents per yard, which is shown in the right-hand column of the table above. The standard setup labor cost for the type of loom used on style No. 2000 is $14.50, shown on the standard cost sheet as "changing" cost. Because 4,300 yards is the average run between changes, this gives the changing cost of 0.34 cents per yard shown in the right-hand column of the table. Weavers are paid on a piecework basis, the amount depending on the nature and complexity of the operation, with a guaranteed minimum daily wage. The standard weaving cost per yard is based on the piecework rates, taken directly from the labor standards book. This totals 2.38 cents per yard for style No. 2000.

During the week ending on February 3, the weaving room produced a total of 674,550 yards of cloth, in four different styles, with the following standard weaving room labor cost per yard:

Description	Style No. 2000	Style No. 2413	Style No. 2425	Style No. 2600
Twisting-in................	0.10¢	0.12¢	0.12¢	0.09¢
Changing....................	0.34	0.42	0.48	0.45
Weaving piecework..........	2.38	2.31	2.18	2.26
Loom fixers..................	0.82	0.90	1.04	1.05
Smash piecers...............	0.10	0.11	0.12	0.09
Battery hands...............	0.26	0.34	0.51	0.42
Inspectors..................	0.12	0.12	0.13	0.12
Filling carriers..............	0.07	0.05	0.07	0.06
Other labor.................	0.23	0.22	0.25	0.23
Total Cents per Yard.....	4.42¢	4.59¢	4.90¢	4.77¢
Production for week (yds.)....	142,050	206,500	155,600	170,400

Actual labor costs charged to the weaving room during the week were as follows:

Acct. No.	Title	Amount
123	Weavers (piece rate + make-up)	$15,822
135	Twisters In	971
150	Changing	1,785
206	Loom Fixers	6,968
260	Smash Piecers	883
261	Battery Hands	2,973
265	Inspectors	1,319
266	Filling Carriers	555
290	Other Labor	2,318
	Total	$33,594

a) From the information provided, prepare a summary report for the weaving room superintendent, showing cost deviations from standard for the week.

b) Comment briefly on the possible reasons for these deviations.

c) Would you wish to report information on the operations of this department in greater detail than is possible from the data supplied? If so, specify the kinds of added detail you would like to see.

Chapter 12

SETTING

COST STANDARDS

THE OPERATION of standard costing systems such as those described in the previous chapter presumes the availability of cost standards that will do what is required of them. The purpose of this chapter is to examine the basis on which standards can be developed, the constraints imposed by environmental conditions, and the kinds of problems that are likely to be encountered in applying the standard costing concept in practice.

SETTING PRICE STANDARDS

The two major elements in any standard cost are (1) the physical inputs required to produce a given physical output and (2) the unit prices of the input factors. For example, standard materials costs specify a given number of pounds or feet or gallons of materials at a specified price per pound or foot or gallon. Different criteria underlie the selection of these two elements, and separate discussion is therefore necessary.

Setting Labor Rate Standards

The derivation of standard labor costs requires the multiplication of standard labor time by the applicable standard wage rate. For planning purposes the rate standard presumably should be the average rate expected to prevail during the planning period. For administrative convenience, this is usually defined as the fiscal year, but for some decisions affecting longer (or shorter) periods, current year standards have to be adjusted.

Departures from expected average rates are sometimes made to keep unusual influences out of the rate standard. For example, if company wage rates are out of line with rates prevailing elsewhere in the indus-

345

try, management may wish to use industry rate standards rather than company standards. This requires budgeting the aggregate rate variance for overall profit planning and cash budgeting purposes.

Viewed in isolation, the level at which the standard wage rate is set is relatively unimportant for departmental cost control. The only requirement is consistency. For example, if a cost center earns 240 standard labor hours during January but uses only 230 labor hours, the important fact is the 10-hour favorable labor quantity variance. It makes little difference for control reporting whether this is priced at $2.50 or $2.80 an hour. The choice of standard rate affects the total dollar amount of the variance but neither its direction nor its percentage relationship.

The defect with this reasoning is that a department manager's cost control efforts must be balanced, with the most important item dealt with first, followed by others in order of descending importance. Furthermore, his performance in this area is ordinarily judged on an overall basis rather than item by item, and once again the weights assigned to individual items should indicate relative importance. Thus for control as well as for planning, standard prices should be those prevailing in the period during which the standards are applied.

Single versus Multiple Rates

The basic illustrations in the previous chapters assumed a single standard wage rate for each department. Multiplying this by actual and earned labor hours yielded a dollar measure of the labor quantity variance. The defect of the single rate is that it is appropriate to one labor mix only. As we pointed out in the previous chapter, if labor mix control is a departmental responsibility, the mix variance should be reported to the department head. This means that it should not appear as an element of the wage rate variance, as it will if a single department-wide rate is used.

Therefore, in order to reflect mix variances in departmental cost reports, as well as to produce more accurate costs for planning, many companies assign different standard wage rates to different types of labor. This increases the mechanical complexity of data processing and probably should be undertaken only if mix variation is likely to be great.

Use of separate rate standards for each pay grade, it should be noted, does not eliminate rate variances entirely. For one thing, not all workers in a given pay grade are paid the same amount. Seniority, for example, often confers a slight wage premium, and the standard wage rate can only average the expected rates within each pay grade.

Another possibility, also noted in the previous chapter, is that a worker in one pay grade will be assigned to work calling for an operator of a different grade. The worker must be paid at the rate for his own grade and seniority, but the amount absorbed by production is based on the standard rate for the job. This kind of substitution cannot and should not be considered in setting the standard rate but should be dealt with as part of manufacturing overhead.

Standard Rates for Wage Supplements

A somewhat different question is raised by so-called "fringe benefits" and other labor-related costs, such as payroll taxes, provision for pensions, holiday and vacation pay, group insurance benefits paid by the employer, and so on. The conclusion was reached in Chapter 6 that the labor charging rate could be expanded to include a provision for those elements that respond in the short run to the same actions that are taken to control labor costs. Proportional pension costs and payroll taxes meet this prescription and therefore could be included in the standard wage rate. Supplements to piece rate wages to bring them up to the daywork minimum, on the other hand, presumably are controllable separately and thus should be classified as overhead so that separate departmental totals can be observed.

Setting Materials Price Standards

Standard materials prices are generally built up from supplier price lists, catalogues, and the like, utilizing any information available as to probable future changes in these prices. The standard presumably should include some provision for freight-in and variable handling costs, less expected discounts from gross purchase prices. For example, the standard price of a metal stamping might be determined as follows:

```
Purchase price, in 500-piece quantities..........$3.45 each
Freight from supplier's plant...................  0.04
   Less: Purchase discounts.....................(0.07)
Standard Materials Price......................$3.42 each
```

It should be noted here that deviations of actual from standard materials prices do not necessarily indicate the relative efficiency or inefficiency of the purchasing department. To a limited extent, materials prices are controllable in that the purchasing department must exert its skill in selecting and bargaining with suppliers. Many price deviations, however, are beyond the company's control in that they merely represent differences between actual market conditions and those on which standards have been predicated.

Current, Expected, or Normal Prices

One question that often arises in the development of standard costs is the selection of the level at which to set standard materials prices and standard wage rates. The main alternatives are:

1. Prices expected to prevail during the coming period, usually one year.
2. Prices prevailing at the time of preparing the standard.
3. Prices expected to be "normal" during an extended period.

The choice among these alternatives depends in part on the kind of price fluctuation expected and also on the purpose for which the costs are to be used. If fluctuations tend to be frequent, with no discernible trend either upward or downward, the normal price concept is appropriate. Prices of raw metals, for example, typically fall into this category. On the other hand, if the direction of future price changes can be predicted with reasonable assurance, a strong argument can be made for using the average price predicted for the period in which the standard costs will be used.

The main argument in favor of using expected prices is that these are the relevant prices to use if the standard costs are to be used primarily in decision making. Pricing and other alternative choice decisions are based on forecasts of future costs and prices. To the extent that the estimates underlying these decisions are based on or utilize standard cost data, the standard costs should reflect expected future conditions rather than the conditions of the past.

It can be maintained, of course, that the level at which standard prices are established is immaterial for planning purposes because costs for planning can always be obtained by multiplying standard physical input quantities by up-to-date prices. If reference to the files is frequent, however, there are substantial advantages in pricing standard input quantities at expected price levels in computing standard product costs.

Standard prices used in cost control reporting also should represent expected prices. As with labor costs, although control of materials costs is often exercised primarily in terms of physical units, standard costs indicate the relative importance of the various materials items. In this way standard prices can influence the relative emphasis in departmental cost control efforts as well as managerial appraisal of these efforts. For this reason the weights assigned to individual materials quantities should have current relevance.

The only advantage of price standards established on the basis of the prices prevailing at the time standards are prepared is in identifying in the accounting records all changes that take place—that is, any price variance that occurs is the result of price changes alone, unobscured by forecasting errors. Price standards of this kind are not relevant to decisions, however, and thus have a very limited usefulness.

Impact of Split Purchasing

Policy or market considerations often require the purchasing agent to divide his purchases of an individual part or material between two or more suppliers, even though delivered prices may vary from supplier to supplier. The premium that must be paid over the delivered price quoted by the lowest cost vendor in some cases arises from the low-cost vendor's inability to supply the buyer's full requirements. In other cases, it represents the fee paid to insure that supplier competition will not atrophy or to insure continuity of supply in the event of interruption of shipments from one source.

No matter what the reason, this use of multiple sources raises an issue in standard pricing. Most companies probably resolve this issue by setting the standard at the average expected price, on the grounds that changes in the overall volume of purchases will not change the proportions coming from the various sources. Others prefer to set the standard at the lowest delivered cost so as to isolate in the accounts the cost penalty of using multiple sources. In this case, of course, the anticipated variances ordinarily should be included as a separate item of standard overhead cost or at least as a budgeted variance.

It can also be argued that standard cost should reflect the cost from the *most* costly source. The argument used is the one we applied to overtime premiums in Chapter 6—that standard cost represents the incremental materials cost and thus is more relevant to decision making than average cost. In most cases, however, expansion or contraction of purchase volume is unlikely to affect the highest cost or marginal source only. If so, marginal cost will be closer to average price than to the highest price paid, and the conventional treatment will be appropriate.

SETTING QUANTITY STANDARDS

Setting materials and labor quantity standards is more than a problem of applying scientific methods to determine the underlying physical laws of relationship between input and output. For one thing, the relationships are almost never rigid, and thus management has some power of choice. Second, both the level of the standard and the method of establishing it may influence the motivation and performance of affected personnel. Both of these points need to be considered.

The Concept of Normal Variation

Actual costs will be exactly equal to standard solely by chance, no matter how high or low the standard is set. Variation in input/output ratios is normal rather than the exception, and quantity variances therefore are virtually inevitable.

For example, under normal conditions, 100 typical 12-ton batches of material may be expected to yield the quantities shown in Exhibit 12–1.

Exhibit 12–1

EXPECTED DISPERSION IN MATERIALS YIELDS

Tons of Good Product per Batch	Percentage of Batches	Total Yield (Tons)
12...................	5	60
11...................	20	220
10...................	40	400
9....................	15	135
8....................	10	80
7....................	6	42
6....................	3	18
5....................	1	5
Total...............	100	960

In this case the average yield is 9.6 tons per batch and the modal yield is 10 tons. Setting the standard on the basis of either the mean or the mode—1.25 or 1.2 tons of materials for a ton of product—does not imply that this variation can be eliminated.

Selecting Standard Yield Levels

This statistical dispersion, resulting from random influences on the process, creates a major issue in standard costing. No matter how well standardized the operation or how simple the product, some variation in operating time (or materials consumption) is inevitable. Thus any standard set somewhere within the probable performance range will be exceeded some of the time and not met some of the time. The question is where in this range the standard should be set.

It has long been accepted doctrine that standards should represent "attainable good" performance. This has been interpreted to mean something in excess of average past performance, on the grounds that the latter includes the output of poorer workers and perhaps nonstandardized conditions as well. For this reason, observed quantity variances are more likely to be unfavorable than favorable.

In other words, the most commonly accepted definition of standard costs is that they represent a level of performance that is *reasonably attainable by an average experienced worker under expected conditions.*

The Motivation Question

This definition derives from one view of the relationship among standards, motivation, and performance. It holds that individuals will be motivated to achieve standards that they perceive to be within their reach, but that they will not exert much effort to exceed standards and that standards perceived to be out of reach will cease to exert a motivating influence. In other words, standards should be neither "too loose" nor "too tight," but "just right."

Until recent years, neither the cost accountant nor the industrial engineer gave much attention to the validity of this point of view. Although most accountants are still handicapped by a lack of familiarity with psychological concepts and research techniques and by the failure of research psychologists to communicate their findings to outsiders in understandable terms, recent years have witnessed a rapid growth among accountants in the awareness of the motivation problem and in the amount of attention given to it by accounting writers.

Despite the difficulty of proving psychological laws, several points seem to be emerging from this discussion. First, standards affect performance through their influence on the *aspiration level* of the affected individuals. The aspiration level is in a sense the individual's own tailor-made standard against which he measures success or failure. Other things being equal, the higher the aspiration level, the higher the performance.

Second, performance that is significantly different from the aspiration level will lead to an adjustment of the aspiration level in the direction of the level of performance achieved.[1]

Third, standards affect aspiration levels only to the extent that they represent organization goals that are accepted by the individual. This acceptance is best achieved by first getting the company goals accepted

---

[1] A notable attempt to test the relationships among standards, aspiration levels, and performance was carried out by Andrew Stedry, *Budget Control and Cost Behavior* (Englewood Cliffs, N.J.: Prentice-Hall, Inc., 1960).

by the group of factory personnel with which the individual identifies himself. This synchronization of group goals with company goals ordinarily requires strong company leadership, best provided by the supervisor directly in charge of the group, particularly if he is free to adapt his methods and the reward structure to the needs of his group. Failure to provide this kind of leadership can lead to rejection of the standard and even to negative effects on productivity.[2]

Attempts to use the aspiration level concept directly in setting standards are probably doomed to failure, not only because the aspiration level is virtually impossible to measure but also because it differs from individual to individual. Management can still try to raise aspiration levels and thereby improve performance, but it cannot base its standards on measurements of the aspiration levels of its employees.

Engineering Methods of Setting Labor Standards

In the absence of any valid measures of aspiration levels, most cost standards are based on records or estimates of actual achievement. Sometimes these are derived by some kind of engineering method, notably through observation of test runs (time study) or from a synthesis of preexisting time standards for individual work elements of specific operations (Methods-Time Measurement).

For example, a time study man may be sent down to observe and time the workers performing a given operation. The workers assigned to the test run are usually seasoned operators who know the equipment and who will work at a steady pace. The time study man must exercise his judgment both in the selection of the operators and in the exclusion of observations that reflect abnormal conditions. The remaining observations, presumably reflecting normal or random variations only, are the raw data from which a standard can be derived.

Nonproductive Time Allowances

So-called ideal or perfection standards can be obtained from the engineering data by some such device as averaging the best 10 percent of the observations or selecting the observation representing some high percentile such as the ninetieth.[3] The starting point for a reasonably

---

[2] This brief outline was derived from a first-rate article summarizing the results of a survey of the literature by George J. Benston, "The Role of the Firm's Accounting System for Motivation," *The Accounting Review,* April, 1963, pp. 347–54.

[3] Some companies use these ideal standards to get an absolute measure of departures from perfection. Ideal standards have no relevance for decision making, and their use for control purposes requires a great deal of sophistication.

attainable standard, on the other hand, is ordinarily the arithmetic average of the observations.

These observations typically do not include any provision for non-productive time except for small amounts inherent in the workers' operating methods. A certain amount of specifically nonproductive time—waiting for work, attending to personal needs, etc.—is ordinarily inevitable, and provision for this is usually incorporated in the standards. Similar allowances for the effects of worker fatigue are also introduced.

Such allowances may be based (*a*) on statistical studies of the past incidence of nonproductive time and the effect of fatigue, (*b*) on work sampling observations,[4] or (*c*) on supervisory judgment. Even if historical or test data are used, the engineer must decide which observations to include and how to interpret them. The element of judgment is never absent, even in the most sophisticated quantitative methods.

Standards and Statistical Control Limits

The amount of judgment required to establish standards even by engineering methods may indicate why the concept of the statistical control limit is not used more widely in cost control.

The notion of the statistical control limit is based on the assumption that the standard is set equal to the average performance recorded during a series of test observations that represent behavior under standard conditions. From the pattern of these observations, the statistician can state the probability that a deviation from the standard in excess of a specified amount is due to nonrandom forces and is thus subject to corrective or adaptive action. Some convention is then adopted as to how high a probability is necessary in order to require an investigation of the variance. Variances of a lesser magnitude are then assumed to result from random forces and are not investigated.[5]

Unfortunately, it is almost impossible to know whether the test observations, fatigue allowances, and so forth represent normal or abnormal experience. Since judgment is required in any case, most companies prefer to set control limits for departmental variances by judgment rather than by formula. The control limit technique is used widely, however, in quality control work and to some extent in such tasks as identifying pieces of equipment that may require adjustment or overhaul.

---

[4] Work sampling techniques are described briefly in Chapter 17 below.

[5] See, for example, Harold Bierman, Jr., *Topics in Cost Accounting and Decisions* (New York: McGraw-Hill Book Co., Inc., 1963), chap. i.

Historical versus Test Data

Engineered standards, based on observations of test runs or on predetermined time values, are generally regarded as the most accurate standards. They are also the most expensive to develop, and the tests themselves may become a source of worker misunderstanding.

For these reasons controlled test runs are seldom undertaken except to meet other objectives, such as work standardization and methods improvement. When studies are made for these purposes, accurate usage standards for control purposes can be obtained as a by-product at little additional cost. Otherwise, a cruder approach based on historical data should probably be adopted.

One possibility is to review the quantity data reported on job cost or departmental process costing records in the past. Preliminary standards derived from these can then be used to get the system going. The next step is to use these tentative standards to accumulate departmental variances during a trial period. So long as a department's variances are small and no other evidence of consistent inefficiency is shown, it may be presumed that the usage allowances are satisfactory.

Some chance always exists, of course, that the absence of significant variances covers up large compensating errors in the standards and that the department head is not perceptive enough to discover this. The probability that this kind of condition can long prevail is fortunately very small. It is also possible that a department head may keep methods improvements secret and thus avoid showing favorable variances so that his section may operate at a more leisurely pace. When this is true, however, the fault is in higher management's policies, attitudes, or communication skills. Almost any system can be "beaten" if those affected do not accept or misunderstand its objectives.

Large variances during the trial period may indicate either that the standards are inappropriate or that control was inadequate or that environmental conditions were temporarily abnormal or not well standardized. Accordingly, the causes of the variances need to be studied. The department heads themselves are the first source of information on this point, and analysis sometimes need go no further.

If this is not the case, or if confirmation of the foreman's opinion is required, additional data can be obtained by accumulating job costs for a *sample* of job orders for the *departments in question.* For the length of time needed to obtain accurate information on labor and material usage for each product, a job cost system is used in the department and care is taken to insure that costs are charged to the sample jobs as accurately as possible. The resultant information is more accurate and less expensive than data obtained by collecting job costs at actual prices for all products in all departments.

The Role of Participation

Standards intended for use in planning or for internal cost bookkeeping do not need the acceptance or concurrence of factory personnel. If standards are to be used for control, however, their impact on the attitudes and performance of operating people cannot be ignored.

Earlier in this chapter we cited the conclusion that acceptance of company goals can best be achieved by harnessing the tendency of people to identify with groups. One way to get greater group acceptance of company goals is to provide for group participation in goal setting. Participation is a means to the end of greater group cohesiveness which, in turn, may increase goal acceptance if leadership is effective.[6]

The techniques just described for deriving standard costs do not necessarily require participation, and in many companies what participation there is goes no deeper than the foreman level. Successful participation is difficult to achieve, requiring as it does a delicate combination of strong leadership with a true willingness to allow group opinion to affect the standard, and management may decide that it cannot meet these conditions at the operator level. Too often, however, failure to meet these conditions is regarded as a defect of participation itself. Participation alone cannot be expected to work miracles. A group's unwillingness to accept a standard that engineering or historical data indicate is reasonable is not evidence that participation has failed. Instead, it indicates a more basic failure in communication or in management-employee relations or in the incentive structure which participation may or may not help to correct.

Cost Reduction through Tight Standards

It has been implied earlier that a standard set higher than the individual is willing to accept as a meaningful goal may cease to become a motivating force and may even have negative effects. Tight standards are nevertheless often justified on the grounds that they will stimulate the search for cost reduction.

Unfortunately, this overlooks the fundamental distinction between cost *control* and cost *reduction*. Standards are essentially a tool of cost control. Cost reduction involves a reduction in standard cost; cost control means achieving costs that will meet preexisting standards. If the

---

[6] For a good, brief summary of the relationships between participation and performance, see Selwyn Becker and David Green, Jr., "Budgeting and Employee Behavior," *Journal of Business,* October, 1962, pp. 392–402.

two are confused, the setting of tight standards may fail to achieve either goal because no matter how effective cost reduction efforts may be, the revised cost standards will still be out of reach and thus cease to serve as a means of stimulating operating performance.

It should be pointed out that special circumstances may justify the establishment or retention of standards at levels that are not currently attainable. For example, one of the automobile manufacturers is said to have maintained its cost standards throughout World War II in the knowledge that they would not be met during the war period. The purpose of this was to provide a basis for the reestablishment of effective cost control after the war, with fewer labor problems than would arise if a completely new set of standards had to be established.

In another instance, in a newly opened plant, an aircraft equipment manufacturer established standards that it did not expect to meet for a period of several years. The reasons given in this case were that plant management was relatively unfamiliar with the operations to be carried out by the new plant and that it would take two or three years to develop a stable working force of an adequate quality. Standards set at the currently attainable level would have produced costs that the company could not sustain competitively on any long-term basis.

Impact of the Learning Curve

The technique just mentioned is very difficult to work into a participative standard. It is likely to work best in a situation in which performance is related to the duration of a learning process—in other words, whenever the so-called learning curve phenomenon is applicable. Aircraft manufacturers during the 1939–45 war discovered that unit cost declined as a function of the cumulative number of units produced, and that this decline could be predicted fairly accurately. These patterns were reflected in learning curves, showing the percentage decline in unit cost that could be expected from a given percentage increase in *cumulative* output. Thus an 80 percent learning curve was one in which doubling cumulative output would reduce cumulative unit cost by 20 percent. If the first 1,000 units cost a total of $10,000 to produce, or $10 a unit, the average cost of the first 2,000 units would be expected to be $8. (To achieve this, of course, the cost of the second 1,000 units would have to be only $6,000, or $6 each. Learning curve improvement ratios are usually stated as percentage reductions in cumulative unit cost.)

Most of the reported applications of the learning curve technique have been in the defense industries. They typically imply that cost standards are set by technicians and no mention of participation is made.

There is no reason why learning curve data cannot be introduced into the participation process, although it may be more difficult to induce workers to accept an improvement factor that seems as mechanically derived as this one.[7]

Incentive Wage Plans

For hourly wage plans the hourly wage rate is not affected by changes in hourly output; thus standard rates and standard quantities can be discussed separately. Putting an incentive wage on production destroys the independence of these two variables, and they must be discussed jointly.

For straight piecework plans, no problem is encountered. Standard cost is determined by the piece rate, and the amounts paid in certain circumstances to bring piecework wages up to the hourly minimum are charged to overhead. Compensation that is proportional to earned standard hours (another way of measuring output) similarly offers no problems. A problem exists only when pay is not proportional to output.

In such cases the standards used for control reporting and for planning is likely to be very different from the standard or base rate from which incentive pay is derived. For example, suppose that for each 40 hours devoted to incentive-rated work, an employee's weekly pay is $2 for each earned standard hour plus $1 for each earned standard hour in excess of 35. Rest time and personal time are included in elapsed time for this purpose; waiting time in excess of 15 minutes and time spent on nonrated work are paid at a straight hourly rate of $2 and are thus excluded from the elapsed time total. A worker who records 42 earned standard hours plus 3 hours of nonrated work in a 40-hour workweek would be paid as follows:

Incentive pay:
(1)	Gross elapsed time.....................	40	hours
(2)	Less: Nonrated time..................	3	hours
(3)	Net elapsed time (1) − (2)............	37	hours
(4)	Base output (3) × 35/40..............	32.375	hours
(5)	Earned standard hours................	42	hours
(6)	Base incentive pay (5) × $2..........	$84.00	
(7)	Bonus pay [(5) − (4)] × $1...........	9.63	
(8)	TOTAL INCENTIVE PAY..............	$93.63	

Hourly pay:
(9)	Nonrated time (2) × $2................	6.00
(10)	TOTAL GROSS PAY (8) − (9).........	$99.63

---

[7] For a more complete description of the learning curve concept, see Rolfe Wyer, "Learning Curve Techniques for Direct Labor Management," *N.A.A. Bulletin,* July, 1958, pp. 19–27.

If this represents standard hourly output, then the standard wage rate for incentive work is $93.63 ÷ 42 = $2.23 for each earned standard hour. Variances computed on this basis appear to be rate variances, but because they stem from variations in output performance they are really quantity variances and should be reported as such.

Setting Materials Quantity Standards

Materials quantity standards raise no conceptual issues other than those already discussed under the heading of labor quantity standards, and thus can be disposed of quite quickly. From a technical point of view, standard materials allowances may be derived by engineering methods or by analysis of historical accounting data. Participation has just as large a place in setting materials quantity standards as in setting labor quantity standards, and they are subject to the same provisos.

If perfection standards are used, then some provision must be made for budgeting standard variances, and thus the perfection standard differs only in a procedural sense from the reasonably attainable standards discussed here. As with labor standards, however, the management by exception principle would seem to imply that normal waste allowances should be incorporated in the standard so that variances will indicate relative success or failure in keeping costs within predetermined limits.

REVISION OF STANDARD COSTS

No matter how much care is devoted to the development of cost standards, they are bound to become more and more out of date with the passage of time. Prices and wage rates change, new equipment and new techniques are adopted, and product specifications are changed. Some mechanism is required to permit an orderly adaptation of standards to these changes in conditions.

This statement presumes that some kind of current, expected, or normal pricing concept is implicit in the cost standards. If fixed "basic" or "bogey" standards are used, the standards themselves will not be changed but budgeted variances will have to be updated, and this amounts to approximately the same thing.

Quantity standards for materials yield and labor performance are changed less frequently than price and wage rate standards. Changes in quantity standards are made only in the case of technological changes in the conditions of production. For example, the introduction of a new and faster type of machinery would result in a technological change in the operating characteristics of the plant, whereas the breakdown of equipment requiring the use of substitute equipment for extended periods of time would be regarded as a temporary change. Similarly, a general increase in materials prices would be permanent and therefore the cause of revisions of standards, whereas a strike in a supplier's plant which forces temporary diversion of purchases to other suppliers would not result in revision of standards.

Changes in standards may also be made because the existing standards are incorrect. Persistent, unexplained variances, coupled with continuing complaints by the foreman that particular standards are too tight, presumably should be studied, either by engineering methods, by temporary reinstatement of job costing procedures, or by analysis of work documents if these permit identification with products or operations. The usual outcome of these studies is to change either the work methods or the standards.

The real question to be answered in connection with revision of standards is not whether they will be revised, but when. Should standards be reviewed continuously or only once a year? And if standards are reviewed and revised within the year, should the standard cost files be updated? In view of the fact that planning and decision making require up-to-date standards, prompt and frequent revisions would seem desirable. File maintenance is an expensive operation, however. Furthermore, it may be necessary to deny access to the files while changes are being made. For these reasons, the typical solution is to accumulate revisions in a subsidiary file, without immediate reflection in the main file that is used in the accounting routine. For planning purposes these revisions can be incorporated into the cost estimates, even though they do not enter into the calculation of periodic variances from standard costs. Then, after some specified period, usually a year but sometimes more or less than a year, the revisions can be incorporated into the main file.

This is a compromise solution, and like all compromises, it may not be completely satisfactory for every application of standard cost data. It is likely to be more satisfactory than letting standards get progressively more out of date, however, and it is undoubtedly less costly than piecemeal file revision. Furthermore, it permits variances to be reported periodically on a consistent basis so that trends in these variances can be observed.

SUMMARY

Standard costing requires the development of standard input quantities and standard input prices for individual operations, materials, and products. Standard prices ordinarily should reflect all dimensions of price that depend solely on time worked or output achieved. On these grounds employer pension contributions could ordinarily be subsumed in the standard wage rate, while overtime premiums could not. Standard prices also should be established at the levels expected to prevail during the planning period, so as to permit the standard cost to be used for cost estimates and so that the relative importance of individual cost elements will be readily apparent.

The basic concept underlying quantity standards is that they should represent the performance expected of an average experienced worker, using the work methods and facilities available. These may be derived initially by engineering methods or by analysis of historical accounting records, but to be fully effective they must be accepted as attainable and relevant goals by the operating personnel themselves. This may require their participation at some stage in setting or revising standards.

Although this discussion has focused implicitly on the direct labor and direct materials costs of departments producing physical products for ultimate delivery to customers, it is equally applicable to departments producing physical products and measurable services for internal consumption. Company steam plants and repair shops, for example, perform repetitive services and are not inherently different from machining or assembly departments. Costs of these internal service departments are classified as factory overhead for product costing, but for control purposes many of them are the direct costs of service department products. The same principles are thus applicable.

DISCUSSION QUESTIONS

1. To what extent could management ever hope to eliminate labor and materials quantity variances entirely?
2. Supply a quantitative definition of a "tight" direct labor standard.
3. Should quantity standards be set deliberately "tight" for motivational purposes?
4. The establishment of standard labor times is often thought of as simply a matter of sending an engineer into the factory with a stop watch and recording his findings. Assuming that this has been done, what issues remain to be resolved before the time standard can be set? Discuss.
5. To what extent should allowances for waste, rest time, fatigue, and other departures from maximum physical performance be built into the materials and labor quantity standards?
6. How would you interpret variances from ideal or perfection standards?
7. Many processes utilize raw materials of uncertain and irregular quality. How

can standards be established under such circumstances, and how useful are they likely to be?

8. The establishment of standards for materials and labor costs presumes a direct proportionality between input and output quantities. What problems arise in setting standards when the number of units manufactured in separate lots of the same product varies widely from lot to lot? How can these problems be solved?

9. What are the advantages of basing a labor rate standard on the average base pay rate for a large group of employees instead of the base pay rate for the specific type of worker expected to perform each given operation? What are the disadvantages?

10. Comment on the statement that whereas materials standards can be established accurately through the analysis of product specifications, labor performance varies so widely from operator to operator and from day to day for any one operator in labor-paced operations that labor standards in these operations are of little usefulness.

11. Two processes making identical products have the same standard cost per unit of product. Over a period of several months the average quantity variances in the two processes tend to be identical. One of these processes is said to be under control, however, while the other is said to be out of control. On what grounds could such a statement be based?

12. It is sometimes suggested that if labor and materials quantity standards are set equal to the mean value of a set of representative observations, then quantity variances can be compared with statistically derived control limits, thereby eliminating human judgment as the basis on which significantly large variances are identified. Indicate your reasons for agreeing or disagreeing with this statement.

EXERCISES AND PROBLEMS

1. Many companies hesitate to introduce standard costs because of the expense of developing carefully detailed physical input standards for individual operations or products. Some companies have tried to bypass this drawback by setting tentative standards initially on the basis of recent past performance, revising these annually as more recent experience becomes available. How effective do you think this practice is likely to be in achieving the objectives of standard costs?

2. The Dandy Paint Company recently discontinued the use of labor and materials cost standards because variations from standard were large and inconsistent, unfavorable in one period and favorable in the next—the differences apparently not attributable to differences in management's effectiveness in cost control. What suggestions might you have made to management before it abandoned its standard cost system?

3. The Seegall Company is engaged in the heat-treating of various metal items supplied by local customers who lack heat-treating facilities of their own.

Many different items are processed simultaneously, but the treatment time per item varies widely, depending on the customer's specifications. For example, if two items are placed in the treating unit at the same time, one may be removed from the unit at the end of 15 minutes, whereas another may remain in the unit for an hour or more. How would you go about establishing a standard labor cost per unit?

4. You have been asked to prepare a standard container cost per unit for a certain product, given the following data:

> (1) Each unit of product requires one container.
> (2) Average performance last year: 1,050 containers used per 1,000 units of product.
> (3) Average performance of engineering department test run using average experienced workers: 1,030 containers used per 1,000 units of product.
> (4) Best performance found by engineering department: 1,015 containers used per 1,000 units of product.

> a) Select a standard performance level for use in computing standard cost and indicate the reasons for your choice.
> b) Standard cost could be set on any of the four bases referred to above. Indicate how you would interpret a debit balance in the quantity variance account in each of these four cases.

*5. Materials can be purchased for $1 a pound. Under normal conditions, 10 percent by weight of the materials placed in production will be recovered as scrap, with a scrap value of $0.10 a pound. The remaining 90 percent of the materials shrinks to half its weight in processing. The final product weighs 6.3 pounds. What is the standard net materials cost per pound of finished product?

*6. The Egbert Company buys a raw material in powdered form, dissolves it in water, concentrates the solution by boiling, adds sugar, and then packages the final product in one-pint jars. In the initial mix, one pound of raw material added to 0.95 gallons of water yields one gallon of mix. In the boiling operation, a 25 percent reduction in volume is achieved.

Addition of one-half pound of sugar per gallon of concentrate completes the blending operation, and the mixture is allowed to cool. The addition of sugar and the cooling operation do not affect the total liquid volume. A loss of 2 percent of volume is expected during the filling operation due to spilling, evaporation, overfilling of some jars, and residue left in the blending kettles. The raw material costs 80 cents a pound, and sugar has a standard price of 8 cents a pound.

Compute the standard materials cost per one-pint jar of finished product, to the nearest tenth of a cent.

7. The Duncut Company manufactures electronic components. Inspected products are moved on conveyors into the packing department. The packing department crew is covered by a group incentive plan whereby each employee's hourly earnings are equal to his hourly base rate plus 1 percent of the base rate for each 20 units packed per crew hour in excess of a base packing

---

* Solutions to problems marked with an asterisk (*) can be found in Appendix B.

rate of 1,000 units per crew hour. The crew consists of the following workers, with their respective hourly base rates:

>One counter-supervisor at $3.40
>One trucker at $2.25
>Three packers at $2.30

a) Compute the standard labor cost per unit, based on a standard packing rate of 1.24 times the base packing rate. (Round off to the nearest hundredth of a cent per unit.)

b) Assume that in one eight-hour day the crew packs 8,800 units. What are the actual and standard packing labor costs for the day?

8. The Midland Company utilizes a certain raw material in one of its products. The standard purchase price of this material is 40 cents per pound. The material is cleaned and then formed under pressure into the shape required for the end product. A shrinkage of 8 percent of its original weight has been established as normal during these operations. The formed material incorporated into the finished product weighs 2.3 pounds. What is the standard cost of this material per unit of product?

9. A steel rolling mill processes steel ingots with a standard price of $40 a ton. Scrap losses are expected to average 18 percent, by weight, of ingots received in the mill. This scrap is entirely recoverable and is valued at $30 a ton. What is the standard ingot cost per ton of rolled product?

10. The manufacture of a certain product requires the cutting of doughnut-shaped rings from a rectangular strip of material. The material is bought in strips of four-foot length, each weighing two pounds. The strip of material is fed into a machine which cuts the rings, leaving circular discs (like the holes in doughnuts) and a perforated strip of material or "skeleton" (what is left of the material after the rings and discs have been removed). Six rings and six discs are cut from each strip of material. Each ring weighs two ounces, and each disc weighs 1.2 ounces.

The standard price of the material is 64 cents a foot. The skeletons remaining after the rings and discs have been removed are sold as scrap at 20 cents a pound. Rings can be purchased from outside vendors at a price of 36 cents each; discs would cost 24 cents apiece if bought outside. Standard costs are necessary for cost control reporting.

a) Assuming that both the discs and the rings are useful in production and that no damage occurs in cutting, compute standard materials costs for rings and for discs. Explain the basis of your calculations and indicate why you chose this method in place of others that you might have considered.

b) Repeat the calculation described in (a) but assume that 10 percent of the discs and rings will be improperly cut and must be sold as scrap.

c) Repeat the calculation described in (b), assuming a 10 percent cutting loss and also assuming that the company has no use for the discs and that they, too, will be sold as scrap at 20 cents a pound.

d) Assuming that the company has been operating under the conditions specified in (c) and that it has now found a way to utilize half of the discs in the manufacture of a new product, what would you recommend be established as the standard materials cost of the discs? Explain.

11. The Peermore Products Company is considering the adoption of a system of standard costing to obtain more reliable information for the control of its operations. Employees in department 231 are classified in the following categories with their corresponding base pay rates:

> General foreman..............$180 a week
> Foremen.....................$160 a week
> Assistant foremen.............$140 a week
> Operators—grade 1............$3.20 an hour
> Operators—grade 2...........$2.90 an hour
> Helpers.....................$2.00 an hour
> Cleanup men.................$1.75 an hour

All department employees get time and a half for work in excess of 40 hours per week. A 10-cent per hour differential is awarded to workers operating a second shift if this is needed.

Operations are of continuous process type, but equipment may be shut down overnight and started up again the next day without additional start-up cost or damage to equipment or product. Men work in crews, the normal crew consisting of one assistant foreman, two grade 1 operators, four grade 2 operators, three helpers, and one cleanup man. The general foreman works the day shift only, but one foreman is on duty in the department for each shift worked. Although the available equipment permits a maximum of five crews in any one shift, the department frequently operates with only four crews and in some cases with only three crews. A second shift is never operated with less than three crews.

In preparing for the change over to standard costs, the methods department has accumulated output data, by crew, for the past four weeks. Each crew worked 40 hours in each week. These data are as follows:

	Pounds Produced in Week Ending—				
	4/7	4/14	4/21	4/28	Total
Day crew A....................	24,106	26,095	21,734	23,052	94,987
Day crew B....................	18,641	25,348	24,219	23,830	92,038
Day crew C....................	25,214	20,900	22,462	20,585	89,161
Day crew D....................	27,116	24,238	25,003	23,812	100,169
Day crew E....................	21,306	19,681	22,146	19,046	82,179
Night crew F..................	22,862	20,193	22,712	17,571	83,338
Night crew G..................	16,796	20,523	18,618	21,222	77,159
Night crew H..................	20,000	17,982	22,105	18,890	78,977
Night crew I..................	23,148	24,267	19,473	21,049	87,937

a) Develop a standard labor cost per pound.

b) Defend your method of deriving (1) standard output per crew hour and (2) standard labor cost per crew hour.

12. Many operations or processes are based on labor crews rather than individuals performing separate operations. The Daily Foods Company, which prepares frozen precooked dinners, has organized its kitchen on a crew basis,

each crew normally consisting of one head cook, two assistant cooks, and three helpers. Variations in crew size and composition are frequent, however, depending on the items being processed and the size of the batch. Furthermore, the company's wage structure provides for seniority pay differentials within each job classification. Thus, although the base pay for an assistant cook is $3 an hour, some assistant cooks are paid at a rate of $3.25 an hour. The average straight-time pay rates for the three job classifications are:

Head cooks...........................$3.80 an hour.
Assistant cooks...................... 3.15 an hour.
Helpers.............................. 1.80 an hour.

To prepare standard labor costs for the operation of breading chicken breasts, the company maintained a record of actual operating hours during a test period, averaging as follows:

Items processed in batch........	1,000	1,500	2,000	2,500
Man-hours and wage rates:				
Head cooks.................	2.3 at $3.50	2.6 at $3.60	3.0 at $3.70	3.7 at $3.90
Assistant cooks.............	2.3 at 3.20	5.7 at 3.10	6.0 at 3.25	7.4 at 3.15
Helpers....................	4.6 at 1.60	5.2 at 1.80	9.0 at 1.75	11.1 at 1.80

a) Prepare a standard cost per item for the breading operation, using the portions of the above data that seem most appropriate and assuming that most lots will consist of between 1,800 and 2,200 items.

b) Shortly after standards were adopted by this company, the kitchen breaded a batch of 1,500 chicken breasts. A crew of one head cook at $3.60, one assistant cook at $3.10, and three helpers at $1.80 worked three hours on this batch. Compute the deviation from standard and explain, insofar as possible, the causes of this deviation.

13. Historical job order cost records show the following labor costs per unit for product A:

Production Date	Labor Hours	Labor Cost
June, 19x2.................	1.8	$4.50
January, 19x3..............	1.5	4.15
April, 19x3...............	2.1	5.87
October, 19x3.............	1.9	5.20
February, 19x4............	1.6	4.80
June, 19x4.................	2.3	6.70
August, 19x4..............	1.8	5.20
February, 19x5............	1.7	5.00
May, 19x5.................	2.0	6.20
September, 19x5...........	1.9	5.75

No change in work methods took place during this time.

Employees are paid on an hourly basis, with seniority differentials based on length of service. Studies have indicated that output per man-hour does not correlate significantly with length of service, although of course not all workers are equally productive. The wage rate agreed on for 19x6 is $3 an hour, plus 10 cents for every five years of service. The employees' length of service will be distributed as follows during 19x6:

Length of Service	% of Employees
0–4	15
5–9	40
10–14	25
15–19	15
20–24	5

As part of the preparation for the company's adoption of standard costing, an industrial engineer timed three of the work crews selected by the department foreman as average experienced workers. Each of these crews processed five of the September, 19x5, batches of 100 units each, with the following results:

	Total Man-Hours per Batch		
	Crew 1	Crew 2	Crew 3
Batch 1	165	150	160
Batch 2	170	175	185
Batch 3	150	170	180
Batch 4	155	180	170
Batch 5	170	185	185
Total	810	860	880

a) What standard labor cost would you recommend in this case? Give reasons for your recommendation.

b) The standard that you developed in (*a*) was probably based on staff work of a quantitative nature. In a practical case, would you expect to have to consider any variables that are difficult to express in numerical terms? How would you deal with any such variables?

14. The Amdur Company recently completed development work on a new product and commenced production on a limited scale. The product has found favor with the company's customers, and the company intends to expand production to a rate of 1,000 units a week.

Labor costs for the first 2,000 units have totaled $20,000. Judging from past experience, the company's industrial engineers have estimated that a 90 percent learning curve will be applicable to this product until cumulative production reaches 128,000 units.

With a 90 percent learning curve, a doubling of *cumulative* production will reduce cumulative *average* labor cost by 10 percent. Thus if the first 100 units cost $100 (averaging $1 each), the first 200 units will cost $180 (averaging 90 cents each), and the first 400 units will cost $324 (averaging 81 cents each, which is 90 percent of the previous cumulative average of 90 cents each).

No further improvement in cost performance can be expected after the

128,000 unit total has been reached—that is, the 150,000th unit should have the same labor cost as the 128,000th unit.

a) Compute cumulative total labor cost and cumulative average labor cost for the first 128,000 units.

b) On a sheet of graph paper, prepare a diagram showing cumulative total cost for various cumulative volumes between 2,000 and 128,000 units.

c) From the diagram in (b), prepare a schedule showing the additional labor costs of producing each additional 4,000 units of product from zero to 128,000 cumulative units.

d) What labor cost standard would you establish for cost control reporting for the first year of full-scale production? Indicate why you favor this solution over other alternatives that you might consider.

15. The Sanders Company's molding department consists of a group of injection molding machines with interchangeable dies. Machine setup consists of removing a die from the machine and inserting another in its place. Because the cost of this operation is relatively high, a die tends to remain in place for a considerable period of time.

Each die has a number of openings or "cavities" in the shape of the product to be molded. The molding operation consists of closing the machine, whereupon melted polystyrene is forced under pressure into the die. There it is cooled into solid form by the circulation of cold water until it reaches a predetermined temperature, at which point the die opens and the molded products are ejected. The operator then closes the machine, and the process is repeated.

The labor cost of the molding operation is thus a function of (1) the number of cavities per die, (2) the length of the molding cycle (interval between closings), and (3) the number and compensation of operators tending each machine. The number of cavities per die is determined largely by the size and shape of the molded product, although the number of cavities actually in use may be reduced by blocking off one or more cavities that have developed defects that would lead to the rejection of finished products. Because of the high costs of die removal and setup, a die may be kept in operation with a fairly substantial number of its cavities blocked off.

The length of the molding cycle depends on how quickly the operator responds to the opening of the die. While the die is closed, he is engaged in inspecting the molded products and separating them from the plastic framework to which they are attached when ejected, and he may delay clearing and closing the machine as he is busy with these tasks when the machine opens.

The Sanders Company typically assigns one worker to a machine, with a relief man for each 10 machines. This relief man also keeps the machines supplied with raw material. The machine operators and relief men are paid at the rate of $1.70 per hour, with time and a half for overtime. Each man is entitled to a 15-minute rest period each morning and afternoon and a half-hour lunch period, as part of a normal eight-hour shift. His machine is operated by the relief man during the smoking period, but it remains idle during the lunch period. A study of recent experience revealed that each operator was idle for an average of 15 minutes a day while minor repairs or adjustments were being made to his machine. This idle time is not recorded separately on a routine basis. If a machine is to be out of operation for a half-hour or more, the operator is assigned to other tasks, such as correcting minor defects in rejected products.

 a) Compute a standard labor cost per machine-hour. Would you show this as a single figure or subdivide it?

 b) How would you proceed to establish a standard labor cost per unit of finished product? Indicate how you would deal with such factors as blocked cavities, rejected products, and operator delays in closing the machines.

 c) It is possible to prepare some dies with cavities of different sizes and shapes so that more than one product can be run simultaneously. How would you set standard labor costs for each of the products molded in this way?

16. The Sanders Company, whose operations were described in the previous problem, faces an additional difficulty in establishing standard labor costs. Its molding machines are not identical but fall generally into two categories: (1) newer machines, providing for automatic ejection of molded products; and (2) older machines, capable of taking only smaller dies and requiring manual "clearing" or removal of molded products after the machine opens. The output capacity of the older machines, therefore, is lower than that of the newer machines, measured in terms of pieces per machine-hour.

 How would you set standard labor cost per unit of product in the face of these differences?

17. Elise Toiletries, Inc., is introducing a new product, known as Lano-Lov Skin Lotion, to be sold in four-ounce bottles. Cost and engineering studies have produced the following estimates:

Item No.	Description	Cost	Quantity Used per 125-Gallon Batch
2147..............	4-ounce bottle	$5.50 per gross	102% of minimum
315..............	Label	$3.30 per 1,000	103% of minimum
	(Product will be reshipped in bottle cases—no cartons required.)		
4247..............	Compound 34A	$40 per 100 lbs.	70.0 lbs.
3126..............	Alcohol and glycerine	$40 per 100 lbs.	76.0 lbs.
4136B............	Perfume oil	Manufactured	3.5 lbs.

To allow for normal overfilling, waste, and breakage, standard materials cost (excluding containers and labels) is to be established on the basis of materials consumption at a rate of 104 percent of the quantities indicated in the table above. Waste allowances for the containers and labels are included in the percentage figures given in the right-hand column of the table.

Standard direct labor per gross is to be based on the following estimates:

Compounding....................0.12 hours at $1.90
Filling and packing..............1.00 hours at $1.60

Manufacturing overhead is to be included in standard cost at the following rates:

Compounding......................$3.00 per standard labor hour
Filling and packing.................$1.50 per standard labor hour
                                   plus $0.90 per gross

Perfume oil is mixed by the company according to its secret formula. The standard cost of a 90-pound batch of 4136B perfume oil is as follows:

Ingredients......................$2,169.95
Direct labor......................4.4 hours at $2.28 per hour
Manufacturing overhead..........$7.50 per batch plus
                                 $1.95 per standard labor hour

Prepare a standard cost sheet for one gross of bottles of this product. Calculations should be made to the nearest cent per gross. (One gallon contains 128 fluid ounces; a gross is 144 bottles.)

(Adapted from a Uniform C.P.A. Examination)

18. The Dundrum Chemical Company processes a raw material into a finished product which is then poured into gallon cans for shipment to wholesalers. The raw material is received in liquid form and goes to department A for initial processing. A 15 percent shrinkage in volume is regarded as normal in this department, although the actual shrinkage may be greater or less than this, depending on the quality of the material and the closeness of the control exercised by the operating crew. The semiprocessed product then passes into department B in which it is "cured" for five days and then placed in gallon cans. A shrinkage of 5 percent of the volume entering department B is regarded as normal for the curing operation. There is a certain amount of spilling due to overfilling in the packaging operation, but spilled liquid is collected and fed back into the filling pipes—the net amount lost through spilling is thus negligible.

Government regulations require that a gallon can must contain at least 0.97 gallons of liquid. The filled cans pass onto a weighing device before entering the can-closing machine, and any can not meeting the weight equivalent to the 0.97-gallon minimum is automatically tipped onto a moving screen over a drain. The liquid is then returned automatically to the filling pipes, and the container is dropped into a scrap bin. The company's can-filling equipment is sufficiently accurate to permit the company to set the automatic valves to place 0.98 gallons in each gallon can. The number of underfilled and therefore rejected cans is kept thereby at approximately one half of 1 percent of all cans filled. The average filled can contains 0.98 gallons of product.

The standard cost of raw material is $1.44 per gallon. Standard processing cost in department A is $0.50 per gallon of *semiprocessed* product. The gallon cans and lids are purchased from can manufacturers at a standard price of $0.05 per can and lid. It is normally expected that eight cans per thousand will prove defective, not including those scrapped as a result of underfilling. Scrap values of rejected cans are regarded as negligible.

a) Compute department A's standard materials cost per gallon of semi-processed product.

b) The standard materials and processing cost per gallon in department A is charged as materials cost to department B. Compute the standard materials cost, including standard container cost, per filled gallon can (to the nearest hundredth of a cent).

19. The Rytac Company has operated its factory for many years with a job order costing system. The company manufactures a broad line of machined metal products, both standard catalogue items and special items to customers' specifications. Approximately 30 percent of the annual production volume consists of standard items produced to stock, another 40 percent is made up of items that are essentially modifications of stock items, differing primarily in size or maximum tolerances or alloy composition, and 20 percent consists of standard catalogue items that are produced only to meet customer orders. The remaining 10 percent is accounted for by unusual items, experimental designs, and so forth.

Under the present system, the production planning department issues a job order specifying the number of units to be manufactured, catalogue number, if any, the production operations to be performed, and the kind of machines on which each operation is to be performed. A number is assigned to the job, and a set of punched cards is prepared, one for each type of materials to be used and one for each operation to be performed. These cards are placed in an envelope which then accompanies the job as it passes through the plant. Actual operating times and materials quantities requisitioned are recorded on these cards which are sent to the tabulating room for keypunching and sorting by job number.

At the end of each month a tabulator run summarizes costs for all jobs worked on during the month, and this provides a basis for summary entries to work in process and finished goods inventory accounts. A second tabulator run by catalogue number provides information that management uses to check trends in unit costs for standard items. For nonstandard items a monthly ratio of labor cost to product weight is computed and compared with similar ratios of prior months.

Manufacturing overhead is departmentalized but is not entered on the job order cost sheets. At year-end an average overhead cost per pound is computed for the fourth quarter, and this rate is used as the basis for year-end financial reporting of the overhead content of inventories.

Item inventory records for raw materials, parts, and finished goods are kept on a perpetual basis. Dollar credits to the inventory accounts are based on the moving average method, with average unit cost recomputed at the end of each month for any item in which additions to inventory have been made during the month.

A graduate student was employed last summer as a temporary assistant to the controller, assigned to the task of reviewing the company's cost system. Year-end inventory adjustments for the past few years had been unexpectedly large, resulting in substantial adjustments to fourth quarter income, much to the controller's embarrassment. Furthermore, although labor, materials, and overhead costs per pound had been increasing steadily, no one had been able to identify the causes with any confidence.

The graduate student's study revealed that the size of the year-end inventory adjustments was largely due to two factors: fluctuations in the percentage of capacity utilization and variations in the product mix. Some products were relatively light in weight but required substantial machining time, whereas other heavier products were machined only to wide tolerance limits or were primarily assemblies of purchased parts and thus utilized relatively little plant capacity.

The student also reported that the cost per pound figures were of little use for cost control and in fact were not used by factory personnel. Because he had to return to classes in September, he did little more than scratch the surface of the rising average cost problem, but he learned enough to be able to report that the isolation of the effects of price and wage rate changes would be a time-consuming task.

In his final report to the controller, the student suggested that a standard cost system be developed. He suggested that standards be set initially on the basis of the available historical data, without any significant use of the industrial engineering staff to develop engineered standards at this point.

a) Outline a standard costing system that will meet the controller's objectives, subject to the constraint that any increases in clerical costs should be minor, offset whenever possible by the elimination of clerical operations now being performed. Indicate what kinds of documents would be needed to meet the data requirements of your system. Comment on the kinds of information your proposed system would generate. Discuss any problems that you think would arise in putting your system into effect.

b) Do you think it is wise to establish standard costs without detailed engineering studies, as recommended by the student in this case? Give the arguments both for and against this practice and indicate which set of arguments you feel is stronger.

Chapter 13

FLEXIBLE BUDGETS AND THE CONTROL OF MANUFACTURING OVERHEAD COSTS

STANDARD COSTING PROCEDURES constitute a highly effective means of generating information for use in the control of direct labor and direct materials costs. When both standard and actual costs are incorporated into the accounting records, any deviations from standard can be identified and subjected to analysis, thus permitting the prompt initiation of corrective action wherever it is necessary and feasible. The purpose of this chapter is to examine the means by which similar kinds of control information can be generated for manufacturing overhead costs.

OVERHEAD COST STANDARDS

Cost control reports presume the existence of cost standards or comparison bench marks. Such standards must take into consideration the characteristics and behavior of the cost elements for which they are to be developed.

Characteristics of Overhead Costs

Control reports for manufacturing overhead costs could be simplified greatly if the control bench mark could be based on standard product costs. Standard product costs have an appealing simplicity. A given quantity of physical inputs is expected to yield a standard quantity of physical outputs. The only problems are to discover these relationships and to find a way of applying them to control reporting. Unfortunately, two characteristics of overhead costs reduce the relevance of standard product costs to control reporting:

1. Overhead costs are *common costs* with respect to individual lots or units of product.
2. Overhead costs include *fixed elements* that do not vary in strict proportion to changes in production volume.

Manufacturing overhead costs, also referred to as *indirect* manufacturing costs, factory *burden,* or manufacturing *expenses,* despite the ambiguity of these terms, are defined as those that either are not or cannot be traced to specific product costing units—in other words, *common costs.* This means that standards must be derived from *departmental* figures rather than from data relating to specific products or operations.

The second characteristic of manufacturing overhead costs that is relevant here is that they are not necessarily proportional to the volume of production activity. Standard product costs imply that average cost per unit of product will be the same at both high and low levels of production activity and that deviations from this average represent deviations from normal or standard performance. In contrast, manufacturing overhead includes many fixed costs,—costs that do not vary in proportion to changes in production volume. This is also true of many of the direct departmental costs in process costing which therefore need to be treated by techniques appropriate to overhead costs.

Standard overhead costs per unit, therefore, do not provide an adequate basis for control comparisons. Such standards are too restrictive at low volumes of production and too lenient at high volumes. Conversely, fixed budget appropriations make excessively generous cost allowances at low volumes of production and unduly tight allowances at high volumes. This means that meaningful standards of manufacturing overhead cost must be stated in terms of *totals* for a given time period, adjusted to levels appropriate to *current volume conditions.*

The Nature of Flexible Budgets

Taken together, these two characteristics of overhead costs require the development of *departmental flexible budgets* to serve as control bench marks. The flexible budget, also known as a *semivariable expense budget,* is actually a set of fixed budgets, one for each of a number of alternative production volumes.

Flexible budgets reflect the amount of cost that is *reasonably necessary* to achieve each of several specified volumes of activity. More specifically, flexible budget allowances express standards of what costs should be at each level of volume, on the assumption that production is stabilized at this volume.

For example, in Exhibit 13–1 the standard budget allowance for a

Exhibit 13–1

DEPARTMENTAL FLEXIBLE BUDGET

DEPT. NO. 10 DATE 12/1/66   NAME Drills   EFFECTIVE 1/1/67   APPROVED BY

Account No.	Title	Allowance Factor		Budget Allowances						
		Fixed Amount	Variable Rate	7,000 Hrs. Amount	8,000 Hrs. Amount	9,000 Hrs. Amount	10,000 Hrs. Amount	11,000 Hrs. Amount	12,000 Hrs. Amount	13,000 Hrs. Amount
01	Supervision	700	Step	$ 700	$ 700	$ 1,400	$ 1,400	$ 1,400	$ 2,100	$ 2,100
03	Service Labor		0.40	2,800	3,200	3,600	4,000	4,400	4,800	5,200
05	Idle Time		0.02	140	160	180	200	220	240	260
07	Shift Differential		0.08	560	640	720	800	880	960	1,040
09	Overtime Premium		Step	.....	200	200	400	400	600	800
11	Payroll Taxes		0.12	840	960	1,080	1,200	1,320	1,440	1,660
13	Vacation Accrual		0.20	1,400	1,600	1,800	2,000	2,200	2,400	2,600
	Total Payroll			$ 6,440	$ 7,460	$ 8,980	$10,000	$10,820	$12,540	$13,660
20	Supplies	20	0.01	$ 90	$ 100	$ 110	$ 120	$ 130	$ 140	$ 150
25	Perishable Tools		0.05	350	400	450	500	550	600	650
40	Maintenance	500	0.09	1,130	1,220	1,310	1,400	1,490	1,580	1,670
80	Depreciation	2,000		2,000	2,000	2,000	2,000	2,000	2,000	2,000
	Total Budget			$10,010	$11,180	$12,850	$14,020	$14,990	$16,860	$18,130

production rate of 10,000 direct labor hours per month is $14,020. As long as production activity is relatively constant from month to month, 10,000 direct labor hours should be accompanied by $14,020 in monthly overhead cost.

From this description, it should be apparent that flexible budgets represent *static* cost standards in that they do not attempt to standardize the dynamic effects of moving from one production level to another. This means that some deviations from the flexible budget standards are to be expected when volume changes rapidly. A 10 percent reduction in production schedules, for example, requires adjustments that may not be achievable overnight. Furthermore, it must be recognized that complete adherence to flexible budget allowances may not be desirable if the change in volume is expected to be of short duration. The effects on costs and on employee morale of violent fluctuations in the work force may far offset any short-period savings that might be achieved by forcing a rigid adherence to flexible budget standards.

Even under these circumstances, however, flexible budget comparisons are useful. They provide a basis for highlighting off-standard performance for further analysis and corrective action if necessary. They permit management to make an informed appraisal of the effects of decisions which may produce or eliminate deviations from budgeted performance. Furthermore, they provide a guide to be used in planning changes in the level of production.

REPORTING BUDGET DEVIATIONS

Department managers receive a wide variety of different reports during the course of a month. Some of these are prepared daily, some are prepared weekly, some monthly, and some at irregular intervals. Each is designed to serve a particular purpose, although only too often the original purpose has been lost in antiquity. The department head, however, typically receives only one summary report encompassing the results of all his operations, and it is on this report that we wish to concentrate at this point.

Departmental Cost Reports

The form of the periodic budget report varies widely from company to company. One example is shown in Exhibit 13–2. This statement makes no distinction between controllable and noncontrollable charges, but it does emphasize deviations between actual cost and the budgeted allowances. Year-to-date comparisons emphasize the cumulative effect of the monthly deviations.

These deviations of actual costs from the flexible budget allowances are most commonly referred to as *spending variances,* although other terms such as *budget variances* and *performance variances* are also used. The term "spending variance" is a misnomer because many cost center costs do not reflect current spending by the cost center manager, but it probably conveys the meaning more readily than any alternative.

Exhibit 13-2

DEPARTMENTAL OVERHEAD COST REPORT

DEPARTMENTAL OVERHEAD STATEMENT					
DEPARTMENT 10—Drills				PERIOD May, 1967	
				VOLUME 10,000 Hours	
Account		Current Month			Year to Date	
No.	Title	Actual	Budget	*Over, Under	Actual	*Over, Under
01	Supervision	$ 1,400	$ 1,400	. . .	$ 6,200	$ 600*
03	Service Labor	3,800	4,000	$200	19,200	800*
05	Idle Time	330	200	130*	740	180
07	Shift Differential	870	800	70*	3,580	100
09	Overtime Premium	650	400	250*	1,750	150*
11	Payroll Taxes	1,360	1,200	160*	5,720	200*
13	Vacation Accrual	2,040	2,000	40*	9,440	240*
	Total Payroll	$10,450	$10,000	$450*	$46,630	$1,710*
20	Supplies	30	120	90	540	20
25	Perishable Tools	260	500	240	2,410	110*
40	Maintenance	1,030	1,400	370	7,120	480*
80	Depreciation	2,150	2,000	150*	10,300	300*
99	Apportioned Charges	2,650	2,650	. . .	13,250	. . .
	Total	$16,570	$16,670	$100	$80,250	$2,580*

In most cases the budget allowances are adjusted to the actual level of volume achieved during the month rather than to the volume of activity that was anticipated at the beginning of the month. Under most circumstances, deviations between actual volume and anticipated volume will be relatively small, but even when they are large, the general philosophy is that the spending variances should reflect the ability of the department manager to adapt his operations to changes as they occur. As we have said earlier, the department manager may not be expected to adapt his cost structure instantly to any change in volume, but computing budget allowances on the basis of actual volume rather than anticipated volume focuses attention on the departure of actual performance from ideal performance for these volume conditions. This should provide the basis for a more intelligent approach to adjustments in the cost structure.

The Controllability Criterion

Departmental cost reports should be designed to emphasize the items that are subject to control by the department managers. One way of achieving this is to exclude from the departmental statements all items that are not controllable, either directly or indirectly, by the department heads. Exhibit 13–3 presents an illustration of a statement

Exhibit 13–3

DEPARTMENTAL REPORT ON CONTROLLABLE COSTS

DEPARTMENT COST SUMMARY				
DEPARTMENT Small Machining			PERIOD March 1967	

Direct Costs	Actual		(Over) or Under Standard	
	This Month	Year to Date	This Month	Year to Date
Direct materials	$16,250	$54,140	$1,020	$(740)
Direct labor	22,960	65,690	1,640	910
Direct labor hours	8,200	22,650	800	320

Controllable Overhead*	Actual		(Over) or Under Budget	
	This Month	Year to Date	This Month	Year to Date
Setup labor	$ 1,830	$ 5,210	$ 220	$(100)
Rework labor	450	1,300	(80)	(250)
Maintenance	620	1,850	350	70
Overtime	1,500	4,400	(110)	(300)
Supplies	860	2,520	(60)	(20)
Small tools	150	440	20	40
Other	100	300	(10)	10
Total	$ 5,510	$16,020	$ 330	$(550)

* The department manager's own salary is ordinarily recorded in such a way that it can be identified with the department when data for decisions are required, but it is ordinarily not classified as a controllable cost.

of this type. In this report, standard cost variances for labor and materials are shown along with the overhead cost variances. A summary figure for the month is prepared for incorporation in the report prepared for the next higher echelon of management, as in Exhibit 13–4, which is prepared in this case for the general superintendent. A similar summary report might be prepared for the manufacturing vice president, showing all service and staff departments as well as the totals for the production departments.

The exclusion of noncontrollable items from these reports reflects the general rule that performance reports should be restricted to items over which the manager has some degree of control. Despite this, noncontrollable elements are frequently shown on the monthly statements because management feels that for other reasons the departmental cost reports should include all costs traceable to a department plus a portion of centrally administered and service department costs. Whenever this is done, however, the distinction between controllable and

Exhibit 13–4

FACTORY PRODUCTION COST SUMMARY

CONTROLLABLE OVERHEAD SUMMARY—GENERAL SUPERINTENDENT				
				PERIOD March 1967
Department	Amount		(Over) or Under Budget	
	This Month	Year to Date	This Month	Year to Date
Superintendent's office	$ 3,560	$10,200	$ (160)	$ 300
Small machining	5,510	16,020	330	(550)
Large machining	12,480	32,170	(1,240)	(2,180)
Welding	3,340	8,060	260	130
Large assembly	6,910	19,520	310	80
Painting	2,530	7,910	(50)	(350)
Inspection and crating	1,440	4,360	(130)	100
Total	$35,770	$98,240	$(680)	$(2,470)

Explanatory remarks:
  Variance in large machining department mostly in excessive overtime on rush orders.

noncontrollable costs should be made quite clearly on the performance reports, as in Exhibit 13–5.

Variances in noncontrollable elements may be due to a poor system of cost allocation, or to decisions made by executives elsewhere in the company, or to events that are completely outside the control of company personnel. No matter what the cause, these variances are subject to the danger of misinterpretation. Large noncontrollable variances tend to obscure the effectiveness of the department manager in cost control. Furthermore, the presence of a large noncontrollable element in a department's cost report may lead the manager to believe that his cost control efforts are unimportant. For these reasons, one of two possible courses of action should be taken. First, we might eliminate noncontrollable elements from control reports altogether, as we did in Exhibits 13–3 and 13–4. As an alternative, we might design the reporting system so that noncontrollable costs charged to each department are

Exhibit 13–5

DEPARTMENTAL OVERHEAD COST SUMMARY REPORT

MONTHLY OVERHEAD SUMMARY

DEPARTMENT Finishing   PERIOD July 1967

Item	Current Month			Year to Date	
	Budget	Actual	(Over) Under	Actual	(Over) Under
Controllable overhead:					
Supervisory	$ 3,600	$ 3,600	...	$ 28,420	$ 360
General labor	4,320	3,980	$ 340	33,650	(1,430)
Employee benefits	2,670	2,590	80	22,370	(710)
Maintenance labor	1,450	870	580	12,430	200
Perishable tools	360	410	(50)	3,050	560
Operating supplies	1,070	1,230	(160)	8,140	(80)
Maintenance materials	1,200	1,040	160	9,220	380
Utilities	450	420	30	3,190	190
Total Controllable	$15,120	$14,140	$ 980	$120,470	$ (530)
Noncontrollable overhead:					
Equipment depreciation	$ 3,200	$ 3,300	$ (100)	$ 22,800	$ (400)
Occupancy charges	6,450	6,030	420	43,260	1,890
General proration	4,960	5,210	(250)	35,440	720
Total Charges	$29,730	$28,680	$1,050	$221,970	$ 1,680

equal to the budgeted amounts, thus eliminating variances in these items from the periodic performance reports. In Chapter 14 we shall suggest methods of predetermining cost allocations in such a way that the variances shown for the last three items in Exhibit 13–5 would disappear.

Approved Departures from Budget

We noted earlier that many fixed costs are programmed by management on the basis of forecasts of conditions likely to prevail during the operating period. If the forecasts are not borne out, then changes in some fixed costs may be necessary. In addition, higher management may authorize departures from flexible budget allowances for various reasons: substitute equipment has to be used temporarily, workers are to be kept temporarily on standby rather than laid off when volume drops, and so forth.

Such changes in allowances can be introduced in variance analysis or they can be incorporated into the budget reports themselves, as in Exhibit 13–6. Here both the original flexible budget allowances and the approved adjustments are shown, mainly to permit the foreman or

Exhibit 13–6

BUDGET ALLOWANCE ADJUSTMENTS

DEPARTMENT Drills   PERIOD   September, 1966

OPERATING VOLUME 11,000 Hours

	This Month					Year to Date		
Item	Budget Allow- ance	Ap- proved Vari- ance	Ad- justed Budget	Actual Cost	Oper- ating Vari- ance	Actual Cost	Ap- proved Vari- ance	Oper- ating Vari- ance
Supervision	$1,400	$(100)	$1,500	$1,500	. . .	$12,400	$(200)	$(600)
Service labor	4,400	400	4,000	3,800	$ 200	36,200	600	(800)
Idle time	220	. . .	220	350	(130)	1,680	. . .	180
Shift differential	880	. . .	880	950	(70)	7,100	. . .	100
Overtime premium	400	. . .	400	650	(250)	3,450	(100)	(150)

department head to see for himself where the adjusted budget figures have come from.

The Role of the Planning Budget

In Chapter 2, we illustrated how a budget that is prepared in advance as the end-product of a planning process could serve as a fixed point of reference for later performance comparisons. The coexistence of such *planning budgets* and flexible budgets for cost control reporting poses some analytical problems. Departmental cost performance may be completely in line with flexible budget allowances month after month, but total factory performance may be deviating farther and farther from the planning budget.

This apparent discrepancy arises because these two kinds of budgets are prepared to serve two different purposes. The persistence of deviations from the flexible budget over several reporting periods is some indication that costs are not being controlled adequately. The deviation between the planning budget and the flexible budget allowances, however, is primarily an indicator of deviations in production volume. For example, if the factory cost planning budget is $90,000 a month and the total of the departmental flexible budget allowances is $80,000, then we might say that the effect on cost of the deviation in volume is a reduction of $10,000 a month.

Deviations of actual performance from the financial plan are useful only at organizational levels high enough to permit an integral view of operations. Thus the $10,000 reduction in budgeted cost cannot be evaluated without some consideration of what this means to the overall profit plan, including revenue effects and other cost effects as well. The use of the flexible budget does not conflict with the development of planning budgets, but it is a mistake to report deviations from the planning budget to executives who have no responsibility for sales as well as for costs. Profit variance analysis is discussed in Chapter 24.

SELECTING THE ACTIVITY INDEX

Flexible budgets represent assumed relationships between cost and level of activity. The first step in flexible budgeting, therefore, is to select a measuring unit or index of the volume of activity for each cost element in each cost center.

Criteria for Selection

An ideal volume index is one that measures the factors that cause the costs. For example, if employees earn pension and vacation pay rights in proportion to their gross earnings, then labor dollars is a perfect index of volume because they are the *cause* of pension and vacation overhead costs. Similarly, if the company has to pay a lessor 5 cents every time a machine operation is performed, then the number of machine operations is a perfect index of volume with respect to machine rental costs. Cause and effect are both clear and measurable.

Unfortunately, causes are seldom this easy to identify. The most we can hope for is to find an index that *correlates* closely with changes in cost and therefore presumably correlates well with the underlying causal influences. For example, the labor costs of handling materials may be a function of the number, weight, and shape of the materials moved and the distances and routes they must travel through the factory. This function is probably too complex to measure. It may be, however, that the number of direct labor job tickets issued seems to correlate well with total materials handling costs, and if so it is a good index of volume.

Alternative Kinds of Indexes

Volume may be represented either by production output or production input. The possibilities are:

1. Planned output.
2. Actual output.
3. Planned input.
4. Actual output.

It may seem strange to include planned input and planned output among the possible measures of volume, but there is nothing illogical about it. Some overhead costs such as supervisory services are incurred on the basis of planned volume rather than actual volume, and under these circumstances it may be desirable to compute variances on both of these bases.

Indexes of Production Output

This does not resolve the main issue, the choice of the units in which to express cost center activity. Perhaps the most obvious measure is a count of units of output, such as pounds, gallons, or dozens of boxes. An index of this type is generally available for process industries, but elsewhere cost center output is too diverse in the sense that production of a gallon of one product will have a different effect on cost than production of a gallon of another.

One possibility is to express the volume of activity in terms of the number of operations performed by the responsibility unit. Again, this alternative is of limited applicability because the operations of most responsibility units are too diverse and cannot be reduced to a single common denominator.

Synthetic Output Indexes

Another possibility is to prepare a synthetic index of output. For example, product differences may be merely a matter of the size of the finished product. Quantities of the different sizes produced cannot be added together because larger units require more overhead costs than smaller units. In this case a synthetic output index may be computed by expressing each size in terms of the equivalent number of units of some standard size. Thus a manufacturer of links of chain may determine that one link of a given size is equivalent to 0.8 of a link of the standard size and a link of another size is equivalent to 1.2 links of the standard size chain.

The determination of these equivalence factors or conversion factors should be based on an examination of the relationship between size and overhead costs. If additional output of one link of chain will increase variable overhead costs by \$1 and added output of a link of chain of different size will increase variable overhead by \$1.20, then a 1.2 conversion ratio will be valid. Budget allowances developed on this basis will provide an automatic adjustment to changing product mix.

This presumes that some intermediate measure can be found that can be related both to cost and to product characteristics. Thus if costs tend to vary with the total physical weight of the cost center's output, this relationship can be measured and the results converted into equivalent units by dividing all weight figures by the weight of the arbitrarily selected standard size unit.

The main difficulty here is to derive equivalence multipliers that will be valid for all cost elements. If different equivalence factors are necessary for different cost elements, it is more confusing to talk of equivalent units than to use the intermediate index itself. In some cases this can be an output index, such as weight of good units finished, but production is ordinarily so diverse that the direct use of a measure of productive inputs is necessary.

Indexes of Production Input

The most common input indexes are direct labor hours, machine-hours, and direct labor cost, although in some cases pounds or other units of materials input are appropriate.

The problem here is to find an index that correlates closely with costs, no matter which product outputs are being produced. For example, if direct labor hours is the base, it is assumed that overhead cost will vary with direct labor hours no matter what kind of operation is being performed in the cost center or which product is being produced. Alternatively, it might be said that *the use of an input index assumes that neither variations in the operations mix nor variations in the output mix will influence the level of overhead cost.* If mix variations influence cost materially, then a different volume index should be sought.

It can be maintained, of course, that an input index is inherently inferior to an output index even if costs vary as a function of input rather than as a function of output. An input index permits relative efficiency or inefficiency in input usage to be reflected in the flexible budget allowances for the period, and the fear is that costs may be within the input-based allowances but still be too high from a competitive point of view. Unfavorable deviations from output-based standards eat into company profits even if costs are in line with input-based standards.

For example, referring back to the flexible budget in Exhibit 13–1, if direct labor in this department rises from 9,000 hours to 10,000 hours without a commensurate increase in output, the budget allowance for service labor will go up from $3,600 to $4,000. This will increase average budgeted cost per unit of product. In other words, use of an input index may provide a more accurate basis for *predicting* costs, but it does not show what costs are *justified* by the output achieved.

Unfortunately, to impose output-based standards when costs vary with input quantities is to attack the symptom rather than the disease. The fault, if any, lies in the control of the direct inputs rather than in the control of overhead costs, and remedial action should be directed there. Input indexes of volume should be used for deriving overhead cost budgets if they correspond more closely to the underlying relationships.

Standard Cost Indexes

The complete integration of input and output indexes comes with the adoption of standard product costing. Standard input figures provide an activity index that is impervious to changes in the relative efficiency of input usage; for example, total standard direct labor hours is completely unaffected by changes in the ratio of actual direct labor hours to standard. In this respect, such an index may be regarded as another form of synthetic output index, the conversion factor for each product being supplied by the standard input required.

To illustrate, suppose that departmental service labor is budgeted on the basis of direct labor hours. The department produces only two products, A and B, with departmental direct labor standards of two hours and four hours per unit, respectively. Production volumes, equivalent standard labor hours, and actual direct labor hours for three months are:

Month	Units Produced		Total Standard Direct Labor Hours			Total Actual Direct Labor Hours
	Product A	Product B	Product A	Product B	Total	
June.............	2,000	2,000	4,000	8,000	12,000	12,000
July.............	2,200	1,400	4,400	5,600	10,000	11,000
August..........	2,000	1,500	4,000	6,000	10,000	11,500

Use of total standard direct labor cost as the activity index assumes that two units of product A are equivalent to one unit of product B insofar as their effect on departmental service labor cost is concerned. Use of actual labor hours, on the other hand, assumes that the two products affect cost in proportion to actual labor inputs, which may vary from month to month.

The effect of these differences on the service labor budget allowances is significant. From Exhibit 13–1, we find that service labor is budgeted at 40 cents a direct labor hour. This yields the following budget allowances:

Month	Budget Based on—	
	Standard Direct Labor Hours	Actual Direct Labor Hours
June................	$4,800	$4,800
July................	4,000	4,400
August..............	4,000	4,600

If the causal factors underlying overhead costs are more closely correlated with output (standard direct labor cost) than with direct inputs (actual direct labor hours)—in other words, if overheads are relatively unaffected by changes in direct input yields—then only the allowances in the left-hand column should be used for any purpose. If costs are a function of input, however, cost allowances should be based on the figures in the right-hand column, even though this seems to violate the standard cost concept.

The point is that the difference between the total of the input-based allowances and the total based on the month's output (figures in the left-hand column) is a variance due to off-standard usage of *input* factors; only the variance between actual cost and input-based standards is in any way attributable to the manager's control over this element of overhead cost. This distinction will be explored further in Chapter 15.

Single Index versus Multiple Indexes

The discussion thus far has assumed that a separate index will be used for each cost element in each cost center. Only if all cost elements in a given cost center correlate more closely with one particular index than with any other will a single index be appropriate for all elements.

In practice, however, most cost centers use a single index only for all cost elements, the one index that best correlates with the *sum* of the cost center's costs. Following this pattern, single indexes were used for each of the cost centers referred to in the illustrations earlier in this chapter.

In part, this use of the single index is due to the need for a single departmental index for use as the burden rate base. In part, it can be explained by the data processing problems that multiple indexes introduce into less highly mechanized data processing systems. Neither of these reasons seems particularly persuasive today. The growing awareness that product costing and flexible budgeting are independent of each other, together with the ubiquity of versatile electronic computer systems, have largely destroyed whatever validity these arguments ever had. The main question today is whether the added accuracy provided by multiple indexes is sufficient to justify the inconvenience, additional cost, and additional complexity of presentation they entail.

On the one hand, there is no question that the use of two indexes rather than one would improve budget accuracy in most cost centers. Three might be even better. Many cost elements tend to fluctuate with *physical* input quantities, for example; whereas others, such as the cost of fringe payroll benefits to employees, vary as a function of *dollar* inputs. To the extent that the two indexes are closely correlated with each other, the difficulty is minimized, but it can seldom be eliminated altogether.

Multiple indexes are subject to some dangers, however. For one thing, they increase the apparent complexity of the system and therefore may impair its usefulness by decreasing its chance of acceptance by operating foremen. Secondly, addition of a second index is costly, both in establishing the budget allowances and in periodic computation of the budget allowances. Finally, the techniques available for estimating cost relationships are far from perfect, and the use of multiple indexes may give an impression that the estimates are more accurate than they actually are.

In short, it may be preferable to continue with single cost center indexes except for staff analytical work. Whenever changes in input mix are big enough to affect cost variances materially, they can be removed in variance analysis. At other times the errors can be ignored in the interests of simplicity.

ESTABLISHING FLEXIBLE BUDGET ALLOWANCES

Setting the flexible budget allowances is not really a separate task from selecting the activity index; analysis of cost/volume relationships is essential to both. Unless the nature of operations changes radically, however, volume indexes generally remain unchanged for long periods of time, whereas the budget allowance schedules are typically revised once a year and sometimes more often. This makes it meaningful to discuss flexible budget determination on the assumption that the volume index has already been chosen.

Approach to Analysis

Application of the participation principle to flexible budgeting means delegating authority for budget origination to operating management. Under this approach, each department head is requested to study the relationships between cost and the index or indexes of activity selected for his department. In most cases he is free to call for statistical or engineering assistance, generally through a budget department in the controller's office. The final budget is then the joint product of line and staff, with approval authority resting in a budget committee or other top-management group.

No matter what analytical method is used to determine reasonable cost allowances, it is ordinarily useful to start by plotting historical cost observations on a *scatter chart* like the one shown in Exhibit 13–7. Each point on this chart represents the amount charged cost center X for supplies in a specific month in the past. Whenever possible, adjustments

Exhibit 13–7

SAMPLE SCATTER CHART: COST CENTER X SUPPLIES COSTS

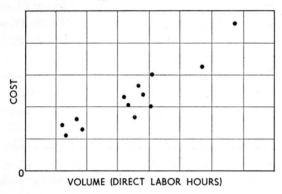

should be made for changes in outside influences such as changes in the unit prices charged for supplies, so that all the points plotted will be roughly comparable, but the main purpose here is to get an initial feel both for the apparent shape of the relationship and for the amount of accuracy likely to be achieved.

Preconceptions as to the shape of the cost pattern should always be questioned. Most of the illustrations of flexible budgets in this textbook portray very simple cost functions, mostly straight lines. Initially, the data available may not even be sufficient to document the slight refinements in the form of cost "steps" that we have introduced, and straight lines may be accepted as a first approximation. Once a system has been installed, however, and people have had experience in thinking about cost patterns, additional refinements are likely to appear if adequate encouragement is given.

The techniques for estimating cost variability patterns fall generally into three broad categories:

1. Inspection of accounts.
2. Statistical analysis of historical costs.
3. Engineering studies.

Inspection of Accounts

The inspection of accounts method might also be called the personal judgment method. The foreman or staff analyst goes down the chart of accounts, classifying each account as wholly fixed, wholly variable, or a mixture of both. These decisions are based on the foreman's personal knowledge and intuition, perhaps aided by rough scatter diagram plottings of historical data.

Having made this classification, the foreman or analyst estimates the monthly amount for each fixed cost element and the average unit cost for each proportionally variable element. The estimate of variable cost is often based on average historical cost per unit of activity, adjusted for any changes in prices, wage rates, or other conditions that may have occurred or are expected to occur.

Semivariable elements are usually submitted to analysis by one of the other methods, although the inspection of accounts method can be applied if some clear basis for planning exists. For example, social security taxes contain a fixed element for the fixed portion of total payrolls and a variable element for the variable payroll. The budget for social security taxes is complicated by the existence of a ceiling on taxable wages, but even so, social security taxes can be budgeted more accurately by formula than by any analysis of historical data.

It may also be possible to budget step functions largely by the inspection of accounts method rather than by the more elaborate statistical or engineering methods. For example, the number of foremen required in a responsibility unit is likely to vary only with fairly substantial changes in volume. Without going to the trouble of detailed cost analysis, the department head should be able to specify the volume level at which additional foremen will be required.

It is dangerous to carry the inspection of accounts method too far, of course, because underlying cost/volume relationships may exist without being apparent on the surface. The foremen may believe, for example, that the amount of electric power consumed should vary in direct proportion to the volume of activity, whereas careful analysis will indicate that there is a substantial fixed element of this cost. When properly applied, however, inspection of accounts is a highly useful work-saving device.

Statistical Analysis of Historical Costs

In the absence of any clear indication that a cost is either wholly variable or wholly fixed or that it varies with volume in some readily predictable way, statistical analysis of historical cost data may become necessary. The statistical techniques that have been applied to this task are relatively simple. Essentially, they are designed to estimate the straight-line relationship between cost and volume that seems to provide the most reasonable explanation of cost behavior in the past. Once determined, this relationship can be stated in the form:

$$\text{Total cost} = F + aV$$

in which F is the total fixed cost for the period, V is the index of volume for the period, and a is the rate of variable cost per unit of volume. Thus if monthly fixed costs are expected to total $10,000, the normal variable cost rate is $0.50 per machine-hour, and the department operates 12,-000 machine-hours per month, the cost budget should be $10,000 + $0.50 $\times$ 12,000, or $16,000.

As we observed in Chapter 3, an expression in this form need not be valid over the entire volume range from zero to full capacity—the only requirement is that it provide meaningful cost estimates within the range of normal operating volumes. Volumes above or below the limits of the normal range may be accompanied by changes in fixed costs and perhaps by changes in the variable cost rate as well. If any changes in fixed costs occur within the normal range, then the statistical techniques will have to be modified to reveal the steps in fixed costs.

Data Preparation

Before the relationship between cost and volume can be derived, some way must be found to eliminate from the historical data the effect on cost of changes in other nonrandom variables. Examples of these are changes in wage rates or materials prices, changes in methods, facilities, or working conditions, or changes in managerial policy governing the level of fixed costs. If the change is definite and measurable in both timing and amount, as in a change in wage rates, it may be possible to increase the comparability of historical observations merely by adjusting the data for the effect of the change. Or, if one or more historical periods were abnormal, as in the case of plant shutdowns due to strikes or materials shortages, the observations for these periods can be excluded from the analysis.

Graphic Projections

One of the simplest forms of statistical analysis is the graphic projection. This technique consists of plotting on a sheet of graph paper the cost/volume combination observed in each of a number of previous time periods and then drawing a line on this chart that seems to provide the best fit to the observed points. To illustrate, assume that the following amounts of indirect labor costs and standard direct labor hours were recorded in a department during the previous 12 months:

Month	Standard Direct Labor Hours	Indirect Labor
January......................	8,500	$2,600
February....................	8,000	2,500
March.......................	8,200	2,550
April.......................	7,000	2,500
May.........................	6,500	2,400
June........................	6,800	2,500
July........................	5,000	2,000
August......................	6,000	2,200
September...................	8,000	2,600
October.....................	9,000	2,700
November....................	9,500	2,900
December....................	8,400	2,700

The scatter diagram showing these observations appears in Exhibit 13–8. A freehand line of average relationship has been fitted to the plotted points. Reading from the line, the apparent variability is 18.75¢ per standard direct labor hour, fixed costs are $937.50 a month, and the flexible budget allowances are:

Standard Direct Labor Hours	Budgeted Indirect Labor
5,000.........................	$2,000
6,000.........................	2,187
7,000.........................	2,375
8,000.........................	2,562
9,000.........................	2,750
10,000........................	2,937

This is an extremely simplified application of the graphic method. Frequently it is necessary to correct for changes in conditions or to make preliminary plottings to remove the effects of variables other than volume. Even if these adjustments are not necessary, however, the position and slope of the line will be influenced by personal judgment

Exhibit 13–8

GRAPHIC METHOD FOR ANALYZING COST VARIABILITY

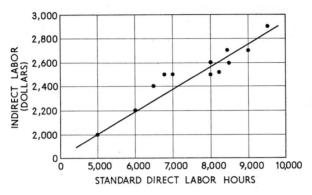

and visual perception. Others might have fitted a different line to the data plotted on Exhibit 13–8. For these reasons, the graphic technique should probably be limited to cases in which the plotted points cluster closely around a straight line. Even if the relationship is not to be estimated by this method, however, it is often useful to prepare the scatter diagram before using other methods. The visual evidence of the presence or absence of an obvious relationship, of apparent step functions, or of observations that appear to be abnormal can be very helpful in applying other statistical techniques.

Least Squares Regression

The most elaborate statistical method is the *method of least squares,* usually referred to as "regression analysis." This consists of finding a line such that the sum of the squares of the vertical deviations from the line will be at a minimum. A standard statistics textbook should be consulted before this method is applied, but a simple explanation of the approach is possible. The first step is to list the historical cost/volume observations in the first two columns of a work sheet and get a total for each column. The next step is to square each cost figure and sum these squares. Next multiply each cost figure by its associated volume and total the products. These figures can then be substituted in the two following equations:

$$\Sigma C = Na + b\Sigma V$$
$$\Sigma(CV) = a\Sigma V + b\Sigma(V^2)$$

where $V = $ volume,
$\quad\quad C = $ total cost at that volume,

N = number of observations,
a = total fixed cost per period at zero volume,
b = average variable cost per unit of volume.

These equations can be solved algebraically for a and b, and these values can then be inserted in the following equation:

$$C = a + bV .$$

The least squares regression line that fits the data given above is described by the formula:

Indirect labor cost = \$1,230 + \$0.17 × Standard direct labor hours.

This produces the following budget allowances:

Standard Direct Labor Hours	Budgeted Indirect Labor
5,000	\$2,080
6,000	2,250
7,000	2,420
8,000	2,590
9,000	2,760
10,000	2,930

Least squares estimates have the advantage of not relying on visual judgment for the location of the cost function. Furthermore, to the extent that deviations from the line of "best fit" result purely from random causes influencing cost, the least squares formula provides the best available estimate of the true relationship. Although it is generally the best method to use, its limitations should be recognized clearly. First, it too is influenced by extreme items, although to a much lesser degree than the high-low points method. Second, the accuracy or reliability of the line is dependent on the number of observations. Other things being equal, the greater the number of observations, the more faith we can place in the resulting formula, and in most instances the number of observations is too small to satisfy the rigid requirements of statistical tests of significance. Third, and this holds true for the other statistical methods as well, the historical data to which the line is fitted may be biased or distorted by the effects on cost of variables other than volume—effects that we cannot screen out by simple adjustments of the data.

To isolate the effects of more than one variable, the technique of *multiple correlation analysis* may prove useful. For example, in a plant which generates its own steam and uses this steam for both heating and motive power, two of the important variables might be temperature (or degree-days) and machine-hours. In order to discover the relationship between steam costs and volume as indicated by the number of machine-hours, it is necessary to adjust the data for temperature variations which impose varying demands on the steam plant for heat. The analysis might yield a formula of the form:

$$\text{Budgeted cost} = a + bX + cZ ,$$

in which X represents the number of degree-days ($65°$ Fahrenheit minus average outside temperature for each day) and Z represents the number of machine-hours. The coefficient c would be the amount of cost variation per machine-hour.

Limitations of Statistical Methods

The main limitation of statistical analysis is that it deals always with the past. If the past has been inefficient, the line of relationship will reflect these inefficiences. In other cases, goods or services are not consumed during the periods in which their costs are charged to operations. Statistical analysis, therefore, should be only the first step. Mere satisfaction of a mathematical formula does not guarantee that the flexible budget allowances will be reasonable. Budget allowances should be based on the best estimates of future relationships, and these may or may not coincide with the relationships indicated by mathematical equations derived from historical data.

Statistical methods are often used in the initial installation of flexible budgets to get a first approximation. The introduction of step functions or other departures from linearity often comes later. Whenever they are used in this way, care should be taken to emphasize the tentative nature of the indicated relationships. Statistical analysis is a valuable tool to assist responsibility unit heads in budget preparation, but it does not provide an automatic solution to the cost estimation problem.

Engineering Studies

The third approach to the development of flexible budget allowances is the industrial engineering approach. This consists of an effort to determine cost variability through engineering analysis of the physical relationships between various physical inputs and the volume of activity. Engineering studies frequently incorporate statistical analysis, but their typical application is in situations in which the available data are inadequate to support a valid statistical estimate of costs.

Engineering studies are perhaps the most expensive of the three methods that we have discussed. The superiority of the engineering approach is that it attempts to work with physical relationships rather than with observed historical patterns which may be distorted by the operation of a myriad of variables other than volume. Its main weakness, apart from the relatively high cost of estimation, is that the practical feasibility of the estimates cannot be pretested. Physical input /output relationships in overhead cost are likely to be considerably weaker than in prime costs, so that the accompanying cost estimates will be subject to a greater degree of error. Experience with actual cost behavior after the flexible allowances have been developed will lead to modifications of these allowances, but both the original estimates and the later modifications must be tempered by the application of human judgment. Because of the inherent nature of overhead costs, the use of judgment is no less important under the engineering approach than under either of the other approaches we have mentioned.

Because of the high cost of engineering studies, flexible budget allowances are ordinarily derived by this method only as a by-product. That is, the studies are usually for the primary purpose of work simplification, methods improvement, or cost reduction, not for cost estimation.

Grouping of Cost Elements

The normal procedure is to study each cost account separately and prepare a series of budget allowances for each. In some cases, however, it may be desirable to group two or more cost elements for analysis or reporting, or both. For example, there might be one group entitled "payroll charges" covering such items as:

Social security taxes
Unemployment compensation taxes
Holiday pay
Vacation pay
Sick leave
Health insurance
Pension accruals

One reason for a grouping of this kind is that the individual cost elements exhibit similar behavior in response to changes in volume and that they are not separately controllable. The principal weapon of control over the various payroll charges listed above, for instance, is control over the amount of labor used. Once this is determined, the size of the payroll charge in any given month is virtually automatic.

Another reason for account grouping is that fluctuations in some cost items may be erratic in short time periods with the irregularities tending to offset each other over a period of several months. If two or more cost elements of this type are grouped for analysis, the resulting relationship to volume may show up more clearly than if each item is studied individually. For example, although we may wish to classify indirect labor into such categories as waiting for materials, waiting for repairs, cleanup, and so forth, it may be useful to consolidate several of these categories for budgeting purposes into a single group. The relationship of the total of all items in the group to the index of volume may be relatively stable, despite the fact that the relative composition of the group shifts materially from month to month. Analysis of the individual items may fail to reveal a clear-cut pattern of cost variability—a pattern that becomes visible when the entire group is analyzed together.

There is, of course, a danger in finding by this method relationships that either do not exist or are of no use for control. The consolidation of cost elements should be limited to those which can be controlled by the same control actions and for which some *a priori* reason exists for assuming similar cost behavior. For example, direct and indirect materials ordinarily should not be added together, both because they must be controlled separately and because they do not exhibit the same variability response to volume changes.

SUMMARY

Product unit standard costs are not relevant for control of factory overhead costs because factory overheads are neither wholly variable nor traceable to individual products. Instead, control standards are reflected in departmental flexible budgets, consisting of a series of budget allowance schedules for various volume levels within the normal operating range.

For this purpose, activity indexes must be selected which most closely correlate with short-run cost variations. These are mostly input indexes, such as direct labor hours, although output and synthetic output indexes are often used when available if they correlate with overhead cost better than with input figures.

Methods used to estimate cost relationships depend on the nature of the operation and on the resources available for cost estimation. Of ultimate importance is the understanding and acceptance of the estimates by operating personnel, and this cannot be achieved by any doctrinaire adherence to a single formula.

Finally, it must be recognized that flexible budget techniques can never be expected to relieve management entirely of the difficult task of interpreting performance figures. It is impossible to design a reporting system such that the controllable variances reflect only the department head's performance and not the effects of causes and conditions outside his control. Causal analysis of variances is still necessary and may require the accumulation of supplementary statistics such as machine load factors, the length of production runs, and the mix of operations within each department. It also requires a considerable amount of informed judgment, and it is at this point that the real test of the cost accountant's experience and analytical skill begins.

DISCUSSION QUESTIONS

1. "Standard costs are most useful for the control of labor and material costs, but control of manufacturing overhead generally must be achieved by other means." Comment.

2. Why is it impossible to charge manufacturing overhead costs directly to products?

3. How does a semivariable overhead budget serve as an instrument for the control of manufacturing overhead costs if these costs are not simply a function of output but depend on other factors as well?

4. What factors other than output may be expected to cause variations in a manufacturing department's overhead from one month to the next?

5. Most methods used to establish flexible budget allowances presume that the relationship between cost and volume can be expressed as a straight line. Discuss the validity and meaning of allowances determined in this way.

6. What justification exists for the statement that standard cost provides an index of the volume of production output in situations in which product output is too diverse to permit direct aggregation of physical output data.

7. Assuming that both input and output indexes are available, under what circumstances would you base budget allowances on indexes of physical input rather than on indexes of physical output?

8. One writer has objected to the principle of the flexible budget on the grounds that the cost of securing short-period adherence to a flexible budget when volume declines may be greater than the cost saving achieved. He suggests that the fixed budget principle be followed and that when volume declines, corrective action be applied to the source of the trouble—volume—rather than to its symptom—underabsorbed manufacturing overhead. Comment briefly on this proposal.

9. It is common practice to select a single measure of volume for each department, with flexible budget allowances established for each cost element at different levels of volume, measured in this common denominator.

What assumptions underlie this practice? Under what circumstances would flexible budget standards prepared on this basis provide a poor basis for control information? What factors make it difficult to employ different volume indexes for different cost items?

10. "Departmental overhead cost reports should include only those items over which the department heads can exert some substantial measure of control." Comment.

11. How does the introduction of flexible budgets affect the desirable scope of the cost centers to which manufacturing overhead costs should be assigned?

12. What factors should govern the choice of weekly, biweekly, or monthly intervals for departmental cost reporting?

EXERCISES AND PROBLEMS

1. An electronic computer manufacturer says that his machine is versatile enough so that when properly programmed it can analyze past operations and prepare a multifunctioned (based upon a number of variables) detailed overhead budget that will not vary from actual overhead by more than 2 percent. In other words, the problem of budgeting will be solved because of more precise calculations.

    a) How useful would this budget be for planning purposes?
    b) How useful would it be for operating control purposes?

2. Using the method of graphic correlation, from the following data prepare a set of flexible budget allowances at 1,000 labor hour intervals between 26,000 and 30,000 labor hours. Do you think you could get a more accurate picture of the cost/volume relationship by a mathematical approach such as the least squares equations?

Labor Hours	Cost
30,000	$3,300
21,300	2,070
27,000	2,730
26,100	2,550
28,800	2,760
26,700	2,400
28,200	2,820
26,400	2,070
28,500	2,400
27,300	2,340
26,700	2,430
27,000	2,370

3. A department foreman has control over three items of overhead cost:

    Item A: This should amount to $300 per period plus 1 percent of the cost of materials used.
    Item B: This should amount to $200 per period plus 5 percent of the cost of labor used.

Item C: This should amount to $400 per period plus 20 cents per hour of labor used.

It is considered impracticable to use more than one index of the volume of activity. In a typical period, the following activity takes place:

Materials used......................................$60,000
Labor used (at an average wage of $3 per labor hour)....... 18,000

a) What measure of activity should be selected? Why?
b) What should the budget equation be?
c) Data for the first period under the plan are:

Materials used......................................$72,000
Labor used (at an average wage of $3.20 per labor hour)..... 16,000
Total controllable overhead.......................... 3,500

Prepare a report (3 lines) comparing actual cost with the budget.
d) Comment on any problems that might arise when the foreman and the factory superintendent receive your report.

*4. Monthly power cost and machine-hour data for the Shelby Company for the 12 months of 19x0 were as follows:

Month	Machine-Hours	Cost
January....................	3,500	$1,000
February..................	4,200	1,100
March.....................	4,900	1,300
April.....................	4,400	1,200
May.......................	4,300	1,200
June......................	3,800	1,100
July......................	3,300	1,090
August....................	4,100	1,280
September.................	4,700	1,400
October...................	3,800	1,210
November..................	3,000	1,080
December..................	4,000	1,230

Power costs during 19x0 were affected by a 10 percent increase in power rates (prices paid for power). This rate increase was effective on July 1, 19x0. No further increase is expected during 19x1.

a) Using any method you wish, derive from the preceding data budget allowances for power costs during 19x1 at operations levels of 3,500, 4,000, and 4,500 machine-hours a month.
b) Prepare similar budget allowances for 2,500 and 5,500 machine-hours. Comment on any problem or problems you encountered in preparing these allowances that you did not face in preparing the allowances called for in (a).

5. The monthly flexible budget allowances for the assembly department of the Boyce Furniture Company are shown in the following table:

---

* Solutions to problems marked with an asterisk (*) can be found in Appendix B.

	10,000 Direct Labor Hours	10,500 Direct Labor Hours	11,000 Direct Labor Hours	11,500 Direct Labor Hours	12,000 Direct Labor Hours
Supervision................	$ 1,800	$ 1,800	$ 1,800	$ 1,800	$ 1,800
Indirect labor.............	7,000	7,350	7,700	8,050	8,400
Supplies.................	4,000	4,200	4,400	4,600	4,800
Power, fuel, and water......	1,000	1,050	1,100	1,150	1,200
Depreciation..............	2,000	2,000	2,000	2,000	2,000
Space occupancy...........	3,000	3,000	3,000	3,000	3,000
General plant overhead.....	2,800	2,800	2,800	2,800	2,800
Total................	$21,600	$22,200	$22,800	$23,400	$24,000

Actual charges to the department for the month of March were as follows:

Supervision..............................	$ 1,900
Indirect labor............................	7,700
Supplies.................................	4,020
Power, fuel, and water....................	930
Depreciation.............................	1,950
Space occupancy..........................	3,000
General plant overhead....................	3,000
Total................................	$22,500

The actual volume of production during March totaled 10,500 direct labor hours.

a) Prepare a departmental overhead cost report for the month.

b) Comment on the possible causes of each of the variances shown on the report.

6. The following maintenance labor cost and statistical data were recorded for department 10 of the Finkle Paint Company during the first six months of last year:

Month	Maintenance Labor Cost	Actual Direct Labor Hours	Gallons Processed	Standard Direct Labor Cost
January...........	$1,500	12,000	26,000	$30,000
February.........	1,800	13,200	23,400	34,500
March...........	1,350	15,600	28,600	25,500
April............	1,200	15,600	33,800	22,500
May.............	1,800	18,000	24,700	31,500
June............	2,250	14,400	26,000	37,500

a) Using graphic methods, select the index of volume that appears to show the closest relationship to department 10's maintenance labor cost.

b) Prepare flexible budget allowances for this item within the volume range experienced. If you select a volume index other than the one chosen in (a), indicate why you have made the substitution. If you use the volume index chosen in (a), indicate why you think it is best of those available.

c) A statistician would object to the procedure used in (*a*) because six observations are generally insufficient evidence on which to base a formula of relationship. How would you answer the statistician's objections?

*7. The Riptide Company has a system of departmental flexible budgets for cost reporting. The fiscal year is divided into 13 "months" of four weeks each. The cost reports for one department for two successive months are summarized in the following table:

	Month 4			Month 5		
	Budget	Actual	Variance	Budget	Actual	Variance
Direct labor hours.....	xxx	4,000	xxx	xxx	3,000	xxx
Nonproductive time, direct labor........	$1,000	$ 800	$ 200	$ 750	$1,200	$(450)
Other indirect labor..	4,000	3,700	300	3,500	3,600	(100)
Operating supplies....	600	650	(50)	450	430	20
Depreciation.........	2,000	2,100	(100)	2,000	2,150	(150)
Building service charges...........	700	770	(70)	700	730	(30)
Total...........	$8,300	$8,020	$ 280	$7,400	$8,110	$(710)

a) Comment on the various items in these reports, indicating which items are likely to be of greatest significance in evaluating the cost control performance of the department supervisor.

b) Looking only at those items for which cost performance was poorer in month 5 than in month 4, what would be your reaction to the statement that the manager of this department had been lax in enforcing cost control during month 5? What remedial action would you suggest, if any?

8. Production volume in department X is measured by the number of standard direct labor hours earned by the department's output during any given period. Normal volume is 40,000 standard direct labor hours a month (each "month" consists of four consecutive weeks), and the flexible budget allowances for this volume of activity are:

Supervision—fixed...........................$ 2,000
Indirect labor—variable...................... 16,000
Supplies—variable........................... 12,000
Maintenance—variable portion.............. 2,000
Maintenance—fixed portion................. 2,000
Depreciation—fixed......................... 10,000
Floor space charges—fixed.................. 8,000

All variable cost elements are expected to vary in direct proportion to departmental output.

The department earned 45,000 standard direct labor hours during the "month" of March 2–March 29. The following costs were charged to the department during the month:

Supervision..................................$ 2,100
Indirect labor............................. 19,000
Supplies...................................... 13,200
Maintenance.............................. 3,900
Overtime premiums........................ 500
Depreciation.............................. 10,000
Floor space charges........................ 8,500

a) Compute the month's flexible budget allowances and cost variances for each of these seven items. (Use the letters U and F to denote unfavorable and favorable variances.)

b) For each of the seven cost items listed above, indicate whether any variances are likely to be wholly or partly controllable by the department foreman. How might variances arise in the noncontrollable items?

9. The assembly department of the ABC Company requires the following "indirect" personnel, no matter what level of operations is attained, at least within the volume range usually experienced:

One timekeeper at $3.50 an hour.
One tally clerk at $85 a week.
Two handlers at $2 an hour.

The department operates with a 40-hour week and a four-week month. The department's indirect labor account shows the following totals for the past 10 months, *including* the wages and salaries of the four employees listed above. The monthly standard cost credits to the department's labor in process account are also shown in this table:

"Month"	Indirect Labor	Standard Direct Labor Cost
1................	$3,570	$ 9,860
2................	3,510	9,680
3................	3,580	9,980
4................	3,670	10,250
5................	3,490	9,620
6................	3,520	9,870
7................	3,450	9,470
8................	3,420	9,420
9................	3,430	9,350
10................	3,360	9,000

a) Prepare flexible budget allowances for indirect labor for the assembly department, assuming that wage rates for both direct and indirect labor will be 5 percent higher next year than this year and that standard costs will be revised to reflect higher wage rates for direct labor. Use any method that you wish in preparing your estimates.

b) Prepare a similar set of allowances on the assumption that indirect labor cost is wholly variable with the exception of the wages of the four employees listed separately above.

c) The ABC Company makes no attempt to record the fixed and variable portions of indirect labor charges in separate accounts. What obstacles might be faced in attempting to make such a classification?

10. It is now February, 19x3. The Wyman Company has been working for the past several months on the installation of a system of flexible budgets in its Rutherford factory. A figure representing normal operating volume has been established for each department, and each department foreman has been asked to prepare a set of tentative cost allowances for operations at that level. Data on costs and volume in prior periods have been supplied to the foremen. Members of the corporate controller's staff have assigned to the factory temporarily to give the foremen any assistance they request.

The normal monthly operating volume for one department is 10,000 direct labor hours. Indirect labor costs for the past two years were:

	19x1		19x2	
Month	Direct Labor Hours	Indirect Labor Costs	Direct Labor Hours	Indirect Labor Costs
January...................	9,000	$12,820	12,000	$18,800
February..................	8,000	11,290	10,000	14,730
March....................	6,000	12,400	11,000	17,050
April.....................	7,000	13,100	10,000	15,220
May......................	8,000	11,540	11,000	16,350
June.....................	7,000	10,600	12,000	17,900
July......................	8,000	11,580	12,000	15,700
August...................	9,000	12,600	9,000	11,860
September................	7,000	9,820	10,000	13,050
October..................	6,000	8,800	8,000	10,120
November................	7,000	9,680	6,000	7,960
December................	9,000	12,430	7,000	9,180

a) Plot these observations on a sheet of graph paper and derive a tentative budget allowance for indirect labor cost at a normal operating volume of 10,000 direct labor hours a month.

b) Draw a line that seems to show most accurately the cost/volume relationship, and prepare tentative indirect labor cost allowances at operating volumes of 6,000, 7,000, 8,000, 9,000, 11,000 and 12,000 direct labor hours.

11. Further investigation reveals certain additional facts relating to the data given in problem 10:

(1) Rearrangement of the department's machines on July 1, 19x2, made it possible to reduce materials handling time. The factory's industrial engineer estimates that this reduction has led to an indirect labor cost saving of approximately 20 cents a direct labor hour every month since that time. The rearrangement has had no effect on the amount of overtime worked.

(2) Employees are paid a premium of 50 percent of their regular hourly wage rate for each hour of overtime work. Overtime premiums paid on direct and indirect labor have been included in the cost figures given in problem 11. Analysis of payroll documents shows that overtime premiums were as follows during the two years:

Month	19x1	19x2
January.....................	$520	$2,400
February.................	290	930
March....................	0	1,750
April.....................	0	920
May......................	340	1,250
June......................	100	1,800
July.......................	280	1,500
August....................	600	560
September.................	120	1,150
October...................	0	320
November.................	80	0
December.................	630	80

(3) Wage rates were 5 percent higher in 19x2 than in 19x1. Wage rates will remain at their 19x2 level throughout the current year.

(4) A fire destroyed a machine in March, 19x1. Direct production workers were not laid off but instead were assigned to other tasks classified as indirect labor until the replacement machine was ready for operation on April 10, 19x1.

Separate overtime premiums from other components of indirect labor costs, make any other adjustments that seem appropriate, plot the adjusted observations on graph paper, and prepare tentative flexible budget allowances for overtime premiums and for the other components of indirect labor cost.

12. The Broadbeam Foundry, Inc., manufactures precision castings from metal alloys. All production is to customer specification; no products are manufactured for stock. The company has been using a system of flexible budgets for some years to provide information for use in the control of foundry overhead costs. This system has the wholehearted support of the company's controller, chief engineer, and treasurer, but the plant superintendent has been increasingly antagonistic toward the system and now has proposed that the flexible budget be discontinued. He is supported in this position by the sales manager. In the opinion of the plant superintendent, existing standard cost data would provide an adequate device for the control of overhead cost.

Normal flexible budget allowances for each of several levels of operation for each production department have been developed, modified, and revised by careful analysis of historical data during the past 15 years. These allowances are revised annually on the basis of changes in production methods or facilities and changes in wage rates and purchase prices. Standard direct labor hours in each department are used as indexes of volume. Each month a departmental overhead cost budget is supplied to each department foreman, based on the production scheduled for his department during that month. In general, each foreman is expected to conform to these standards, although under special circumstances off-standard variances are approved in advance and shown on the monthly cost reports as "approved adjustments."

The plant superintendent has two basic objections to the present system. First, he says that a number of department foremen do not believe that the budget allowances prepared by the budget director are reasonable. As a result, they try to explain away the monthly budget variances and make little effort to conform to the budgets. Second, production costs are influenced heavily by the kind of orders being processed during any given month. Some metals require more machining than others; some orders have closer tolerance requirements and therefore lead to more rejects and rework labor than others. Variations of this sort are too complex to be built into the normal flexible budget allowances, which assume that the relationship of overhead costs to standard direct labor hours is unaffected by changes in product mix. The plant superintendent maintains that he and his foremen can estimate the effects of these variations and that they can make their own mental adjustments to standard cost to reflect these influences.

The sales manager's principal concern is that a flexible budgeting procedure might undermine his pricing policy, which is generally based on standard cost. He is disturbed by the fact that profits tend to fall when volume falls even though he continues to cover full standard cost in the prices that he quotes to his customers. He would rather see production department foremen concentrate their efforts on finding ways to keep within standard overhead cost per unit when volume reductions occur, and he feels that flexible budget allowances are too lenient under such circumstances.

a) Do you believe that the company should abandon its flexible budgeting system and adopt the plant superintendent's suggestions?

b) Suggest ways in which the company's present cost control program could be improved to meet the objections raised by the plant superintendent.

c) How would you reply to the sales manager's arguments?

13. The Broken Bend Manufacturing Company uses a standard costing system in its main factory. Direct labor and direct materials are charged to departmental work in process accounts which are credited for the standard cost of work completed. Factory overhead costs are also accumulated departmentally. Overhead budget allowances for department 23 are prepared on the following bases:

Account	Monthly Budget Allowance	
	Fixed	Variable per Standard Direct Labor Hour
Supervision.........................	$ 900	.....
Inspection.........................	200	$0.080
Helpers............................	300	0.250
Rework Labor......................	...	0.050
Labor Downtime...................	...	0.200
Other Indirect Labor..............	...	0.020
Overtime Premium.................	...	0.100
Supplies...........................	...	0.150
Power.............................	250	0.030
Vacation and Holiday Pay..........	102	0.150
Payroll Taxes......................	84	0.156
Pensions..........................	70	0.130
Total........................	$1,906	$1.316

During November, department 23 earned a total of 3,000 standard direct labor hours. The following transactions occurred during the month:

(1) Labor time tickets, extended at standard wage rates:

Direct labor............................	$5,810
Inspection.............................	220
Helpers................................	980
Rework labor..........................	270
Labor downtime........................	325
Other indirect labor...................	90

(2) Additional charges to department 23 from the factory payrolls for the month:

Supervision.............................	$920
Overtime premiums......................	430

(3) Supplies issued, $310.
(4) Power consumed, $380.
(5) Additional payroll charges:
   Vacation and holiday pay: 8 percent of supervisory payrolls, 6 percent of all other departmental wages and salaries except overtime premium.
   Payroll taxes: 6 percent of departmental wages and salaries.
   Pensions: 5 percent of departmental wages and salaries.

a) Prepare a cost report for the month showing budget allowances, actual charges, and variances (to the nearest dollar).

b) Comment on any variances that are of particular interest.

CASE 13–1—SOCIETÀ RIGAZIO*

Società Rigazio manufactures a wide variety of metal products for industrial users in Italy and other European countries. Its head office is located in Milan and its mills in northern Italy provide about 80 percent of the company's production volume. The remaining 20 percent is produced in two factories, one in Lyon, France, and the other in Linz, Austria, both serving local markets exclusively through their own sales organizations.

Until 1964, the methods used by the Milan headquarters to review subsidiary operations were highly informal. The managing director of each subsidiary visited Milan twice a year, in October and in April, to review his subsidiary's performance and discuss his plans for the future. At other times the managing director would call or visit Milan to report on current developments or to request funds for specified purposes. These latter requests were usually submitted as a group, however, as part of the October meeting in Milan. By and large, if sales showed an increase over those of the previous year and if local profit margins did not decline, the directors in Milan were satisfied and did nothing to interfere with the subsidiary manager's freedom to manage his business as he saw fit.

During 1963, Società Rigazio found itself for the first time in twelve years with falling sales volume, excess production capacity, rising costs, and a shortage of funds to finance new investments. In analyzing this situation, the Milan top management decided that one thing that was needed was a more detailed system

---

* Copyright 1965 by l'Institut pour l'Etude des Méthodes de Direction de l'Entreprise (IMEDE), Lausanne, Switzerland. Published by permission.

of cost control in its mills, including flexible budgets for the overhead costs of each factory.

The Lyon mill was selected as a "pilot plant" for the development of the new system. Because the Lyon mill produced a wide variety of products in many production departments, it was not possible to prepare a single flexible budget for the entire mill. In fact, Mr. Spreafico, the company's comptroller, found that the work done in most of the production departments was so varied that useful cost/volume relationships could not even be developed on a departmental basis. He began, therefore, by dividing many of the departments into cost centers so that a valid single measure of work performed could be found for each one. Thus a department with both automatic and hand-fed cutting machines might be divided into two cost centers, each with a group of highly similar machines doing approximately the same kind of work.

The establishment of the cost centers did not change the responsibility pattern in the factory. Each department had a foreman who reported to one of two production supervisors; the latter were responsible directly to Mr. Forclas, the plant manager. Each foreman continued to be responsible for the operations of all the cost centers in his department. In some cases a cost center embraced an entire department, but most departments contained between two and five cost centers.

Once he had completed this task, Mr. Spreafico turned to the development of flexible budgets. For each cost center he selected the measure or measures of volume that seemed most closely related to cost (e.g., machine hours) and decided what volume was normal for that cost center (e.g., 1,000 machine hours per month). The budget allowance at the normal level of operations was to be used later as an element of standard product costs, but the budget allowance against which the foremen's performance was to be judged each month was to be the allowance for the volume actually achieved during that particular month.

Under the new system, a detailed report of overhead cost variances would be prepared in Lyon for the foreman in charge of a particular cost center and for his immediate superior, the production supervisor; a summary report, giving the total overhead variance for each cost center would be sent to the plant manager and to Mr. Duclos, the managing director of Rigazio France, S.A., Lyon. The Milan top management would not receive copies of any of these reports, but would receive a monthly profit and loss summary, with comments explaining major deviations from the subsidiary's planned profit for the period.

The preparation of the budget formulas had progressed far enough by mid-1964 to persuade Mr. Spreafico to try them out on the September cost data. A top management meeting was then scheduled in Milan to discuss the new system on the basis of the September reports. Mr. Duclos and Mr. Forclas flew to Milan to attend this meeting, accompanied by the comptroller of Rigazio France and a production supervisor responsible for some thirty cost centers in the Lyon factory.

Mr. Enrico Montevani, Società Rigazio's managing director, opened the meeting by asking Mr. Spreafico to explain how the budget allowances were prepared. Mr. Spreafico began by saying that the new system was just in its trial stages and that many changes would undoubtedly be necessary before everyone was satisfied with it. "We started with the idea that the standard had to be adjusted each month to reflect the actual volume of production," he continued, "even though that might mean that we would tell the factory they were doing all right when in fact we had large amounts of underabsorbed burden. In that case the problem would be that we had failed to provide enough volume to keep the plant busy, and you can't blame the foremen for that. When you have fixed costs, you just can't use a single standard cost per hour or per ton or per unit, because that would be too high when we're operating near capacity and too low when we're underutilized. Our problem, then, was to find out how overhead cost varies with volume so that we could get more accurate budget allowances for overhead costs at different production volumes.

"To get answers to this question, we first made some preliminary estimates at headquarters, based on historical data in the accounting records both here and in Lyon. We used data on wage rates and purchase prices from the personnel and purchasing departments to adjust our data to current conditions. Whenever we could, we used a mathematical formula known as a "least squares" formula to get an accurate measure of cost variability in relation to changing volume, but sometimes we just had to use our judgment and decide whether to classify a cost as fixed or variable. I might add that in picking our formulas we tried various measures of volume and generally took the one that seemed to match up most closely with cost. In some cost centers we actually used two different measures of volume, such as direct labor hours and product tonnage, and based some of our budget allowances on one and some on the other. These estimates were then

Exhibit 1

OVERHEAD COST SUMMARY—COST CENTER 2122
September, 1964
(In Francs)

	Standard Allowance at Normal Volume (500 Hours, 25 Tons)	Budgeted at Actual Volume (430 Hours, 23 Tons)	Actual, Month of September	(Over) Under Budget
Supervision....................	180	180	145	35
Indirect labor..................	1,500	1,360	1,610	(250)
Waiting time...................	105	90	177	(87)
Hourly wage guarantee..........	70	60	30	30
Payroll taxes, etc...............	1,614	1,416	1,504	(88)
Materials and supplies..........	150	129	141	(12)
Tools..........................	750	645	638	7
Maintenance...................	1,600	1,536	1,876	(340)
Scrap loss.....................	2,110	1,941	2,456	(515)
Allocated costs................	5,260	5,260	5,305	(45)
Total.....................	13,339	12,617	13,882	(1,265)
Per ton....................	533.56	548.57	603.57	(55.00)

discussed with Mr. Forclas and his people at Lyon, and the revised budget formulas were punched into tabulating cards for use in monthly report preparation.

"Although you have a complete set of the cost center reports, perhaps we might focus on the one for cost center 2122, labeled Exhibit 1 (p. 407). You can see that we have used two measures of volume in this cost center, direct labor hours and product tonnage. During September we were operating at less than standard volume, which meant that we had to reduce the budget allowance to fr. 12,617, which averaged out at fr. 548.57 per ton. Our actual costs were almost exactly ten percent higher than this, giving us an overall unfavorable performance variance of fr. 1,265, or fr. 55 per ton.

"I know that Mr. Duclos and Mr. Forclas will want to comment on this, but I'll be glad to answer any questions that any of you may have. Incidentally, I have brought along some extra copies of the formulas I used in figuring the Septem-

Exhibit 2

FLEXIBLE BUDGET FORMULA—COST CENTER 2122

(Figures in Francs)

	Allowance Factors		Remarks
	Fixed Amount per Month	Variable Rate	
Supervision...............	180	....	% of foreman's time spent in cost center
Indirect labor.............	500	2.00/DLhr.	....
Waiting time.............	...	0.21/DLhr.	Wages of direct labor workers for time spent waiting for work
Hourly wage guarantee.....	...	0.14/DLhr.	Supplement to wages of workers paid by the piece to give them guaranteed minimum hourly wage
Payroll taxes, etc..........	204	2.82/DLhr.	Payroll taxes and allowances at 30% of total payroll, including direct labor payroll*
Materials and supplies......	...	0.30/DLhr.	....
Tools...................	...	1.50/DLhr.	....
Maintenance..............	800	32.00/ton	Actual maintenance hours used at predetermined rate per hour, plus maintenance materials used
Scrap loss...............	...	84.40/ton	Actual scrap multiplied by difference between materials cost and estimated scrap value per kilogram
Allocated costs...........	5,260	....	Actual cost per month, allocated on basis of floor space occupied

* Budgeted direct labor at standard volume, 500 hours at fr. 7.00 per hour; actual direct labor cost for September was 3,053 francs.

ber overhead allowances for cost center 2122, just in case you'd like to look them over."

a) Do you agree with Mr. Spreafico that 548.57 francs per ton (see Exhibit 1) is a more meaningful standard for cost control than the "normal" cost of 533.56 francs?

b) Comment on the variances in Exhibit 1. Which of these are likely to be controllable by the foreman? What do you think the production supervisor should have done on the basis of this report?

c) What changes, if any, would you make in the format of this report or in the basis on which the budget allowances are computed?

d) In developing the budget allowances, did Mr. Spreafico make any mistakes that you think he could have avoided? Does his system contain any features that you particularly like?

Chapter 14

FACTORY OVERHEAD
COST ALLOCATIONS IN
PERFORMANCE REPORTING

INTERDEPARTMENTAL cost allocations of the sort described in Chapter 8 are often carried beyond the development of departmental burden rates for product costing into the routine periodic departmental cost reporting structure. That is, all or part of the costs of service departments are charged each month to other service departments and to production departments.

This chapter has three purposes: (1) to examine various possible reasons for periodic cost allocations; (2) to describe a set of allocation methods that will best accomplish these objectives; and (3) to examine the variances that are likely to arise in departmental accounts under these and other methods.

Reasons for Allocation

The overhead content of product unit cost in standard costing systems and in most job order costing systems is based on predetermined burden rates. General overhead and service department costs are often included in these burden rates by allocation processes such as those described in Chapter 8.

In process costing systems and in some job order costing systems, on the other hand, unit overhead cost is determined *ex post* and often includes a provision for the *actual* service department and general overhead costs of the current period. This may be required by the terms of some of the firm's sale contracts, or to meet regulatory requirements, or merely to carry on a practice established for reasons long since forgotten.

Although product unit costs reflecting after-the-fact overhead allocations may be required by special conditions such as cost-plus contracts, they are unlikely to be superior to predetermined costs for product-oriented decisions and should not be undertaken for that purpose. Decisions require projections of future costs, and these generally must be normalized rather than be tied to the costs of any one prior period.

After-the-fact allocations can serve a managerial purpose under certain conditions, however, if they reflect in one department's accounts and periodic performance reports that department's consumption of another department's services. Although a specific cost may not be *directly* controllable by the department head, he may have a considerable amount of *indirect* control over it. For example, the manager of a machining department has no jurisdiction over the amount of *fuel* consumed in producing electric power in the company's power plant, but he may be able to exercise considerable control over the amount of *power* consumed in his department.

Allocations may also serve an attention-directing and decision-making purpose even if service consumption is not controllable but is measurable. The maintenance manager, for example, often has the sole responsibility for maintenance costs, which are nevertheless classified by department and even by individual pieces of equipment. These data can serve to identify trouble spots and also can be used by higher management in equipment replacement and similar decisions. They should be reported to the operating department heads, however, only if the latter are expected to share cost control responsibility.

Finally, after-the-fact allocations are sometimes defended on the grounds that they make each department head aware of costs incurred outside his jurisdiction but directly or indirectly on his behalf. This argument has validity only if this increased awareness leads to some kind of action by the department head, either to redouble his efforts on the costs he can control or to exert pressure on his counterparts in service departments to take action to reduce their costs. The effectiveness of allocations in this connection is highly questionable, but to whatever extent they can serve these objectives they can do it just as well by allocations made in annual budget preparation.

In short, except in special contract or regulatory situations calling for fully allocated, after-the-fact product unit costs, the only real objective of postdetermined interdepartmental cost allocations is to assist operating management by providing feedback data on controllable service consumption. The question is what allocation methods will best provide data of this kind.

ALTERNATIVE ALLOCATION METHODS

Data for control reporting should reflect differences between actual input quantities consumed and the input quantities budgeted under current conditions. The inputs here are the number of units of service department services consumed by a specific department. Any cost allocation, therefore, should reflect the department's *use* of service department services. The question is how the measures of usage should be costed.

Postdetermined Transfer Prices

Allocations based on indexes of service consumption require the use of *transfer prices,* defined in Chapter 8 as charging rates per unit of service consumed. The most common variant of the transfer price method, reflecting a bias against leaving any undistributed or overdistributed balances in service department accounts, is to compute the average actual service department cost per unit of service consumed. This average cost is an after-the-fact or *postdetermined transfer price,* and it changes every period.

For example, suppose that during October the maintenance department's costs totaled $24,000 on a work load of 4,000 service hours, an average of $6 an hour. Department M used 500 maintenance labor hours. Using the after-the-fact transfer price, the amount charged department M for maintenance labor for October would be 500 × $6 = $3,000.

The advantage of this method is that it does reflect service consumption, which is presumably the only variable subject to even partial control by the managers of service-consuming departments. It does this only imperfectly, however. For example, suppose that department M's flexible budget allows 100 maintenance department labor hours a month plus one maintenance labor hour for every 20 direct labor hours. The normal work load for the maintenance department is 5,000 maintenance labor hours a month, and at this level it has an operating cost budget of $25,000 a month, an average of $5 a maintenance labor hour. (This does not include repair parts, which are ordinarily charged separately.)

On this basis, department M's monthly maintenance labor allowance is computed from the formula:

$$\text{Budget} = \$500 + \frac{\$5 \times \text{Direct labor hours}}{20}.$$

If department M recorded 10,000 direct labor hours during October, its maintenance labor budget allowance would be:

$$\text{Budget} = \$500 + \frac{\$5 \times 10,000}{20} = \$3,000 \, .$$

This is just equal to the amount charged to the department, and thus the monthly cost report would show a zero maintenance labor variance. If the budget allowance were expressed in *hours,* however, a *favorable* variance of 100 maintenance hours would appear.

The problem is probably obvious. Unless physical flexible budget allowances are recomputed on a $6 basis, the departmental variance will reflect both a price effect (variation in cost per hour) and a quantity effect (variation in hours used). In other words, the amount charged against one department depends not only on the amount of service consumed but also on the total amount of service provided to all departments and on the efficiency with which the service department is managed. Thus a variance can appear in the periodic cost report even though service consumption by the department has been kept under control.

Predetermined Transfer Prices

The main defect in the actual cost transfer price method can be eliminated by fixing the transfer price in advance. For example, if maintenance hours are to be charged to other departments at a fixed rate of, say, $5 an hour, the charge for maintenance will depend solely on this rate and on the number of maintenance hours spent in each department. The figures are:

Charged to department M (500 hours × $5)........................	$2,500
Budgeted (as above)...	3,000
Spending Variance (100 hours × $5).............................	$ 500

In other words, the use of predetermined transfer prices keeps price effects from creeping into the overhead spending variances calculated for service-consuming departments. The alternatives to this are to segregate the price effect in variance analysis or to adjust the budget allowances each period to the new average cost figures. Both of these procedures are cumbersome and thus inferior to the predetermined transfer price.

A maintenance department illustration was used here for simplicity and because maintenance costs are usually allocated by transfer prices. It is not always clear, however, just how much responsibility production department managers have for the amount of maintenance work performed. Directly they may have none, with responsibility for both preventive maintenance and repairs lodged in the maintenance manager or managers. Even so, there is often much the operating manager can do to affect the amount of maintenance required, and this is therefore often regarded as an item to be controlled jointly by the maintenance and operating managers.

Other Allocation Bases

A second argument for periodic cost allocations is that they serve to make departmental managers aware of the effects of their actions on costs elsewhere within the company. If it is not possible to measure the department's service consumption, it may still be possible to find some other index that will correlate with the underlying cost relationships.

The merits of this cost awareness argument are open to dispute, as we observed earlier. Some authorities feel that allocations of this sort are self-defeating in that they merely serve to distract the manager's attention from the items he can control, but empirical evidence on this point is lacking. In any case, demands for these allocations are so widespread that the accountant must be prepared to devise schemes that will afford the least possible danger of misinterpretation.

The other two types of indexes available for this purpose are indexes of activity and indexes of facilities provided, previously described in Chapter 8. An *activity* index (factory labor hours, machine-hours, etc.) is appropriate if service center costs vary with the volume of activity in other departments. This suggests that the charging rate might either be restricted to the short-run variable cost elements or else be split into two components, one for the short-run variable costs and the other for costs that are fixed in the short run but variable over a longer interval. (Strictly speaking, the latter component ought to represent attributable fixed costs only—those that vary with changes in service center capacity—but it is common to allocate all budgeted costs, whether attributable or not.)

A *facilities provided* index, on the other hand, implies that the service center is operated to support other activities in a general sense and that its costs will go on in the short run even if none of its services are actually used. It is applicable to the fixed costs of providing service department capacity, and the amount charged to a department presumably should change when its needs for service capacity change.

Activity Charge Methods of Allocation

Most activity charges are based on postdetermined charging rates—that is, the charging rate is determined on the basis of cost and activity data for the current period. When this is done, it is almost inevitable that the production center's accounts will show a variance from flexible budget allowances which is totally meaningless for control purposes.

This variance arises from two sources. First, the existence of fixed service department costs means that the amount charged to production center X depends not only on the volume of activity in that center but also on the volume of activity *in all cost centers combined.* Thus production center X's charge for service may rise if other cost centers reduce their rate of activity, irrespective of what happens in production center X.

For example, if factory office costs are entirely fixed, a reduction in total labor hours in all cost centers from the normal 30,000 to 25,000 would increase the charging rate from 10 cents to 12 cents a labor hour ($3,000 divided by 25,000 equals $0.12). Thus the charge to X would increase from $600 to $720 (6,000 hours times $0.12), even if X logged its normal 6,000 labor hours during the month. The $120 would appear as an unfavorable variance on the monthly performance report issued to X's manager.

The second source of variance inherent in postdetermined activity charges is variation in the cost of operating the service center itself. If this increases, the charge to X will increase even if total labor hours in X and other cost centers remain constant. Once again, a variance could appear in X's accounts, bearing no relation to the manager's effectiveness in cost control. The manager still has no control over the amount of service provided, nor does he have any incentive to reduce his demands for service. The only way in which he can reduce his allocation is to reduce the index of his volume of activity (e.g., total labor hours), and his control over labor usage is better reflected in the variances in his labor cost accounts than in the service department charge.

Charges for Facilities Provided

When the costs of the service department are fixed, it makes little sense to vary the charge each month on the basis of current levels of factory activity. Instead, each cost center should be charged a fixed amount per month, determined in advance on the basis of the proportion of the service center's capacity provided for each of the beneficiary cost centers—in other words, a *capacity charge.*

For example, assume that factory office costs are fixed and that factory office capacity is closely related to the total labor hours budgeted for the factory. The factory office is staffed to meet the following normal service load:

Department	Labor Hours per Month at Budgeted Volume
M.	1,500
P.	7,000
X.	6,000
Y.	8,000
Z.	5,000
AA.	2,500
Total.	30,000

Under the fixed charge or lump-sum method, department M would be assigned 1,500/30,000 of the $3,000 budgeted monthly factory office cost, or $150. Department P would be assigned 7/30 of the total ($700), and so on. *These charges would not be changed, no matter what the total labor hours or service costs were in any month.*

This method reflects the application of the *facilities provided* criterion. Its advantage is that the amount charged to each department for noncontrollable fixed costs can be budgeted in advance and no variance in this charge will appear in the monthly cost statements. Thus the monthly report for department P would show budgeted costs of $700, "actual" costs of $700, and no variance.

Substitute Indexes of Service Consumption

The application of the usage criterion in transfer price allocation requires the availability of a satisfactory measure of the current use of services. Power may be metered, service hours may be counted, or services may be measured in some other units. It is not always possible or economical to set up adequate metering devices, however, and in these circumstances, substitute measures are often adopted.

One possibility is to substitute an activity index for a consumption index. To justify this substitution, there should be strong evidence that activity and consumption are highly correlated. For example, in an electroplating operation the amount of power consumption is likely to vary in close sympathy with the number of plating hours, in which case a power charge per hour would not be a serious oversimplification. However, in a machining department it is unlikely that power consumption will vary proportionately and automatically with the number of direct labor hours or with machine-hours.

Substitutions of this kind are fairly obvious, and their limitations may be readily apparent. Not so with another class of measures—those in which current allocations are based on past studies or estimates of consumption. For example, one company several years ago asked its factory executives to prepare detailed breakdowns of their working hours for a period of several months. From this the accounting department developed a scheme for allocating factory administrative costs among production departments on the basis of relative executive time spent in these departments during the test period. This ratio was then used for several years with the explanation that "this is the best measure of use that we have."

The trouble with an allocation method of this type is that it is likely to be misleading. It reflects not the criterion of use but the criterion of facilities provided, and as we have seen, allocations on these grounds have no meaning either for control or for decision making. They serve only to create an awareness of the existence of these costs and to get them into the departmental accounts from which they can be applied to products through departmental burden rates. To say that charges computed on this basis represent usage of services is to impute to them a meaning they do not have.

But suppose that the factory executives maintain a continuous record of time spent. Doesn't this provide an adequate basis for distribution of factory administrative costs to the departments? Doesn't the fact that the general superintendent spends one eighth of his time in the foundry helping to iron out production problems justify a charge of one eighth of his salary to this department? To answer this we must look once more at the purpose of the allocation. On control grounds there is little if anything that the foundry manager can do about the amount of time that the general superintendent spends in his department. True, if he is able to solve his own problems satisfactorily, the general superintendent may spend less time with him, but he still has no real control over this cost element.

Furthermore, for most types of decision making, the allocation of the superintendent's salary to departments has no significance. The superintendent's salary will be the same whether he spends most of his time in the office or on the factory floor. To the extent that costs are used in product pricing, it is unlikely that competition will permit price increases to cover the costs of excessive executive trouble shooting. At best, this kind of allocation emphasizes the fact that some departments are more troublesome than others, but this fact should be apparent without going through the expensive process of cost allocation.

AN ALLOCATION ILLUSTRATION

To illustrate the application of these methods in a systematic way, let us continue the Standoff Company illustration that we began in Chapter 8.

Exhibit 14-1

STANDOFF COMPANY: BUDGETED OVERHEAD DISTRIBUTION SHEET
USING SEQUENTIAL ALLOCATIONS

	Total	Service Departments			Production Departments		
		Buildings	Factory Administration	Equipment Maintenance	Machining	Welding and Plating	Assembly
Direct overhead:							
Salaries..........	$10,200	$1,000	$6,100	$600	$900	$500	$1,100
Indirect labor......	20,200	1,900	.....	5,100	5,700	2,500	5,000
Operating supplies.....	2,600	600	700	400	400	300	200
Equipment depreciation......	1,500	100	100	200	800	200	100
Miscellaneous......	1,640	200	500	300	275	75	290
Total..........	$36,140	$3,800	$7,400	$6,600	$8,075	$3,575	$6,690
Primary distributions:							
Electric power.......	1,600	200	.....	40	1,000	100	260
Building depreciation, taxes, insurance.....	2,000	.....	200	120	800	280	600
Total Factory Overhead.....	$39,740	$4,000	$7,600	$6,760	$9,875	$3,955	$7,550
Secondary distributions:							
Buildings........		(4,000)	400	240	1,600	560	1,200
Factory administration.......			$8,000 (8,000)	500	2,500	1,000	4,000
Equipment maintenance......				$7,500 (7,500)	5,625	1,125	750
Allocated Total........					$19,600	$6,640	$13,500

Basic Data

It will be recalled that the Standoff Company factory has three service departments and three production departments. The budgeted cost distribution sheet is reproduced here as Exhibit 14–1, showing budgeted cost allocations at normal volume.

In addition to these figures, a set of flexible budget schedules was prepared for each of the six departments. The buildings and factory administration department budgets were treated as completely fixed, while those of the other four departments contained both fixed and variable components.

No purpose would be served by reproducing here the full flexible budget schedules of each department. Consequently, only the allowances appropriate to the volume levels actually achieved during the month of October are presented in Exhibit 14–2.

Exhibit 14–2

STANDOFF COMPANY: FLEXIBLE BUDGET ALLOWANCES FOR THE MONTH OF OCTOBER

	Service Departments			Production Departments		
	Build-ings	Factory Admin-istration	Equip-ment Mainte-nance	Machin-ing	Welding and Plating	Assembly
Operating volume.......	....	....	1,960 main-tenance labor hours	6,400 direct labor hours	1,800 direct labor hours	10,000 direct labor hours
Salaries.................	$1,000	$6,100	$ 600	$ 900	$ 500	$ 1,100
Indirect labor...........	1,900	....	5,000	6,080	2,250	4,200
Operating supplies.......	600	700	392	427	270	167
Equipment depreciation..	100	100	196	853	180	83
Miscellaneous...........	200	500	294	293	68	242
Electric power..........	200	....	39	1,067	90	217
Building depreciation, etc...................	....	200	120	800	280	600
Buildings department charges..............	....	400	240	1,600	560	1,200
Factory administration charges..............	....	....	500	2,500	1,000	4,000
Equipment maintenance charges..............	....	....	....	5,700	1,045	650
Total..............	$4,000	$8,000	$7,381	$20,220	$6,243	$12,459

Exhibit 14-3

STANDOFF COMPANY: OVERHEAD DISTRIBUTION SHEET, OCTOBER USING PREDETERMINED CHARGING RATES

	Total	General Factory		Service Departments			Production Departments		
		Electric Power	Building Depreciation, Taxes, Insurance	Buildings	Factory Administration	Equipment Maintenance	Machining	Welding and Plating	Assembly
Costs incurred:									
Salaries.............	$10,400	....	....	$ 1,000	$ 6,200	$ 600	$ 900	$ 500	$ 1,200
Indirect labor.........	20,600	....	....	2,100	....	5,400	6,000	2,500	4,600
Operating supplies........	1,650	....	....	300	500	50	450	150	200
Equipment depreciation......	1,500	....	....	100	100	200	800	200	100
Miscellaneous............	900	....	....	300	130	730	80	100	150
Electric power............	1,686	$ 1,686							
Building depreciation, taxes, insurance....	2,070		$ 2,070						
Total Factory Cost.......	$39,396	$ 1,686	$ 2,070	$ 3,800	$ 6,930	$ 6,980	$ 8,230	$3,450	$ 6,250
Cost distributions:									
Electric power*............		(1,686)		220	....	38	1,120	88	220
Building depreciation, etc.†......			(2,000)	....	200	120	800	280	600
Building service†...........				(4,000)	400	240	1,600	560	1,200
Factory administration†.......					(8,000)	500	2,500	1,000	4,000
Equipment maintenance‡.......						(7,350)	6,750	375	225
Allocated Total............	$39,396	....	$ 70	$ 20	$ (470)	$ 528	$21,000	$5,753	$12,495
Absorbed overhead..........	38,026						20,800	5,976	11,250
Under- or (over-) distributed........	$ 1,370	....	$ 70	$ 20	$ (470)	$ 528			
Under- or (over-) absorbed........		....					$ 200	$ (223)	$ 1,245
Operating statistics:									
Direct labor hours........	18,200						6,400	1,800	10,000
Power consumed (kwh)........	84,300			11,000	....	1,900	56,000	4,400	11,000
Maintenance hours..........	1,960			....	....		1,800	100	60

* 2 cents per kwh.
† Fixed charge.
‡ $3.75 per maintenance hour.

Allocations for October

The cost distribution sheet for October is shown in Exhibit 14–3, reflecting the following allocation rules:

Power.....................................actual usage at 2¢ per kwh.
Building depreciation, etc...................as budgeted (fixed)
Buildings department charges...............as budgeted (fixed)
Factory administration charges..............as budgeted (fixed)
Equipment maintenance...................actual usage at $3.75 per
maintenance labor hour.

In other words, *all service department cost distributions are based on budgeted costs rather than on historical cost totals.* The two allocated cost items that the department managers can control to some extent— electric power and equipment maintenance—are charged at *predetermined transfer prices.* The other three items are charged as *predetermined lump sums* equal to the budget allowances for the period. The only deviations from flexible budget allowances, therefore, can be attributed to deviations between the actual consumption of services and the service quantities provided for in the flexible budget.

For example, the October cost performance report of the machining department is shown in Exhibit 14–4. The only large variance in

Exhibit 14–4

STANDOFF COMPANY: MACHINING DEPARTMENT COST REPORT
FOR THE MONTH OF OCTOBER

	Actual	Budget	(Over) Under Budget
Controllable and partially controllable:			
Indirect labor...................................	$ 6,000	$ 6,080	$ 80
Operating supplies............................	450	427	(23)
Electric power................................	1,120	1,067	(53)
Equipment maintenance........................	6,750	5,700	(1,050)
Miscellaneous................................	80	293	213
Total controllable........................	$14,400	$13,567	$ (833)
Noncontrollable:			
Salaries..	900	900	. . . .
Equipment depreciation.........................	800	853	53
Building depreciation, taxes, insurance............	800	800	. . . .
Buildings department charges....................	1,600	1,600	. . . .
Factory administration charges..................	2,500	2,500	. . . .
Total Costs................................	$21,000	$20,220	$ (780)

allocated costs is in equipment maintenance. Because a predetermined transfer price was used as the charging rate, this can be immediately interpreted as a variance due to the *quantities* of maintenance services consumed by the machining department during the month. Efficiencies or inefficiencies in running the maintenance department or variations in the total maintenance department load are not reflected in the charge made to the machining department. In this case, because all maintenance was charged at a single rate of $3.75 an hour, it is apparent that the department used 280 maintenance labor hours more than its flexible budget allowed for the production volume achieved in October ($1,050 divided by $3.75 equals 280).

Equipment maintenance costs are regarded by the Standoff Company as partially controllable by the production department managers and thus are reflected in the periodic cost reports. In many companies, full control responsibility is vested in the maintenance department managers. In the latter case, the company will probably wish to keep some record of the departmental distribution of the maintenance load, but no allocations need to be shown in the monthly cost reports of the production departments.

Service Department Variances

Under the Standoff Company's allocation system, the amounts charged for service department services or facilities in any given month will differ to some extent from the service department costs for the month. October, for example, saw the following service department variances (from Exhibit 14–3):

	Actual	Distributed to Other Departments	Under- (Over-) Distributed
Building depreciation, etc............	$2,070	$2,000	$ 70
Buildings department costs..........	4,020	4,000	20
Factory administration costs.........	7,530	8,000	(470)
Equipment maintenance costs........	7,878	7,350	528

Discussion of these variances must be postponed to the next chapter, but it is well to recognize here that they do not necessarily indicate favorable or unfavorable performance efficiency on the part of the department managers. Seasonal patterns in cost recognition, volume fluctuations, and external price changes, to mention only a few of the possible causes, may account in large part for under- or overdistribution of service department costs.

The equipment maintenance department, for example, had a $528 variance in October. This may mean that this department was experiencing some problems in controlling costs, but it may also mean that wage rates and supplies prices exceeded budgeted levels or that part of the maintenance force was idle due to a lack of work to be done. In other words, further analysis is necessary to identify the effects of individual factors influencing costs.

Actual Cost Alternative

The Standoff Company system is only one among many that might be used. One very common alternative is to base the monthly allocations on actual service department costs for the month rather than on budgeted costs. Exhibit 14–5 shows the cost allocations that would have been made if the company had used the sequential-allocation variant of this method for the month of October.

The charge for buildings services, for example, is computed on the basis of the average of the costs charged to the buildings department during the month, 0.804 cents a square foot or $40.20 for each 1 percent of total floor space. The result is to distribute service center costs completely, leaving no undistributed balances in service center accounts at the end of the month.

The defects of this substitute plan were given a good deal of attention earlier in this chapter, but several points are worth repeating in the context of this specific problem. First, the *total* amount absorbed by the month's production is unchanged because the predetermined burden rates are not affected by the amounts charged to production departments during any month. Second, the *relative* amounts charged to the various production departments for factory administration services changed because their relative man-hour totals were different from those budgeted. This served to shift some of the underabsorbed overhead from the assembly department to the machining department.

Finally, the maintenance charge for each production department was increased because the average cost of maintenance services was $4.03 an hour instead of the budgeted $3.75. This had the effect of increasing the amount charged to the machining department by more than $500, with proportional increases in the charges to the other two production departments.

The variation in the charging rate for maintenance is an example of the most serious weakness of the actual cost procedure. Variances shown in production centers' accounts for factory administration and building services can be ignored in performance reporting because these items are

Exhibit 14-5

STANDOFF COMPANY: ALTERNATIVE OVERHEAD DISTRIBUTION, OCTOBER

(Based on Actual Cost Averages for the Month)

	Total	General Factory		Service Departments			Production Departments		
		Electric Power	Building Depreciation, Tax, Insurance	Buildings	Factory Administration	Equipment Maintenance	Machining	Welding and Plating	Assembly
Allocation statistics:									
% of total labor hours*	100%					6.84%	34.53%	13.03%	45.60%
Power consumed (kwh)	84,300			11,000		1,900	56,000	4,400	11,000
Maintenance hours	1,960				....	....	1,800	100	60
Percent of floor space	100%				10%	6%	40%	14%	30%
Direct costs (Exhibit 14-3)	$ 39,396	$ 1,686	$ 2,070	$ 3,800	$ 6,930	$ 6,980	$ 8,230	$ 3,450	$ 6,250
Cost distributions:									
Electric power†		(1,686)		220		38	1,120	88	220
Building depreciation, etc.‡			(2,070)		207	124	828	290	621
Building service‡				$ 4,020 (4,020)	402	241	1,608	563	1,206
Factory administration§					$ 7,539 (7,539)	516	2,603	982	3,438
Equipment maintenance‖						$ 7,899 (7,899)	7,254	403	242
Total	$ 39,396						$21,643	$ 5,776	$11,977

* Excludes labor hours in buildings department.
† 2 cents per kwh.
‡ Percent of floor space × actual cost for month.
§ Percent of total labor hours × actual cost for month.
‖ $4.03 per maintenance hour (actual average maintenance department cost for month).

in no way subject to the control of the production center managers. Equipment maintenance is another matter, however. Operations in the Standoff Company factory are of such a nature that most maintenance other than routine preventive maintenance results from improper usage of the equipment. Thus a good deal of the control responsibility for maintenance is vested in the production center managers. The monthly maintenance variances, therefore, have significance in appraising this aspect of the production center managers' performance. Under the method followed here, however, approximately $549 of the amounts charged to the production centers represents price variances rather than quantity variances in the use of maintenance services, as shown in the following table:

Department	(1) Actual Maintenance Hours	(2) Actual Hours at Standard Rate (1) × $3.75	(3) Actual Hours at Actual Rate (1) × $4.03	(4) Price Variance (3) − (2)
Machining.....................	1,800	$6,750	$7,254	$504
Welding and plating.............	100	375	403	28
Assembly.....................	60	225	242	17
Total....................	1,960	$7,350	$7,899	$549

The amounts shown in column (2) are the amounts charged by the Standoff Company in Exhibit 14–3, while those in column (3) come from Exhibit 14–5. The difference is a price variance and has no place in the performance reports of the production center managers.

SUMMARY

Reassignment or allocation of overhead costs from one cost center or department to another is an important feature of most cost accounting systems. Many such allocations are carried out with little understanding of the purposes they are intended to serve.

Allocations *before-the-fact* serve an *inventory costing* purpose by placing service department costs into the production department budgets used for burden rate determination. Before-the-fact allocations can also serve a *planning* purpose by indicating long-run or short-run cost variability in response to changes in production volumes or capacities. Finally, allocations *after-the-fact* serve a *control* purpose if they reflect service consumption by other departments.

Because after-the-fact allocations serve only a control objective, the design of the allocation system should reflect the desired characteristics of control information. An allocation scheme that meets this specification consists of:

1. *Predetermined transfer prices* for services with measurable consumption units (consumption charges);
2. *Predetermined fixed charges* for the fixed component of the costs of service centers without readily traceable outputs (capacity charges); and
3. *Predetermined activity charges* for the variable component of the costs of service centers without readily traceable outputs (activity charges).

The predetermined rates and amounts should be developed as part of periodic financial planning; for planning purposes the fixed and variable components of departmental transfer prices should also be identified. After-the-fact allocations of the second and third classes can be omitted unless management feels that they serve to keep department heads aware of the costs of ancillary activities, thus possibly stimulating suggestions for methods improvement and cost reduction.

DISCUSSION QUESTIONS

1. Discuss the issues involved in including allocated costs such as rent and service department costs in a producing department's flexible budget and monthly overhead cost performance reports.
2. What are the shortcomings of monthly allocations based on the criterion of individual departments' current "ability to pay"?
3. To what extent can the manager of a factory production department control the costs of factory service departments?
4. What purpose, if any, is served by the monthly redistribution of service department costs?
5. For what kinds of service department costs would the appropriate monthly allocations consist of predetermined fixed amounts? On what basis would the amount be established?
6. What is a transfer price? How does it differ from an activity charge? When would you use it in place of an activity charge?
7. What are the advantages of predetermined transfer prices over postdetermined transfer prices for use in factory service department cost allocations?
8. A company uses predetermined departmental burden rates in product costing, based on full allocation of all factory service department costs. The monthly cost reports issued to the factory department heads, however, include charges only for those service departments for which usage indexes are available. Are the costs that are not allocated each month likely to be forgotten by management?
9. Does the concept of attributable cost have the same relevance to periodic

cost allocations as it has to allocations for burden rate determination? More relevance? Less relevance?

10. Comment on the kinds and locations of service department variances that are likely to arise when monthly allocations are based on predetermined rates. Do the same for variances arising under postdetermined rates (average actual cost).

11. What is the relevance of the facilities provided criterion to routine periodic service department cost allocations?

12. What method of cost allocation would you recommend if service department costs are entirely fixed and indivisible?

EXERCISES AND PROBLEMS

1. The Lilkas Corporation recently installed a medium-sized electronic computer to be used jointly by the accounting department and by the factory schedules and methods department. Each of these departments has its own programmer, but the computer rental and the salaries of machine operators are charged directly to the accounting department. The computer is now being used on a single-shift basis, but it is idle on the average of one hour a day. How would you allocate the cost of idle time between the two departments?

2. Most companies maintain property records that permit the identification of the original cost of equipment installed in each location or department. Charges for depreciation and property taxes and insurance on equipment are often accumulated in factorywide accounts, however, and are assigned to departments on the basis of the original cost of equipment installed. Do you feel that this procedure is likely to be generally satisfactory? State reasons for your conclusions.

3. Outline a basis for allocating the costs of a factory service department which has the following characteristics:

(1) It provides a wide variety of services to other factory departments.
(2) The clerical cost of keeping track of the amount of service time spent for the benefit of any one department would be prohibitively high.
(3) Approximately half of the costs of the service department at normal volume tend to vary in response to changes in the volume of factory activity.

Give reasons for your recommendations.

4. General manufacturing overhead and manufacturing service department costs may be allocated or recirculated to production departments in many ways. All costs may be allocated or just the variable costs. If all costs are allocated, separate treatment may be given the fixed and variable components. They may be allocated on the basis of a rate per unit of activity in the production departments or on the basis of a rate per unit of service performed. The rates may be determined in advance or after actual general and service department costs are accumulated.

Discuss the relative merits of the three following methods of allocation:

a) *After-the-fact* allocations of *full* service department costs on the basis of a single rate *per unit of activity* in the production departments.

b) *Predetermined* allocations of *full* service department costs on the basis of a single rate *per unit of activity* in the production department.

c) *Predetermined* allocations of *variable* service department costs on the basis of a single rate *per unit of service performed* by the service departments.

5. Given below are the details pertaining to the power service department. During the month of April, the costs of operating the power service department amounted to $9,300; of this amount $2,500 was considered to be a fixed cost.

SCHEDULE OF HORSEPOWER HOURS

	Producing Departments		Service Departments	
	A	B	X	Y
Needed at capacity production.....	10,000	20,000	12,000	8,000
Used during the month of April....	8,000	13,000	7,000	6,000

a) What dollar amounts of the power service department costs should be allocated to each producing and service department?

b) What reasons might you suggest for allocating the costs of one service department to other service departments as well as to producing departments?

(From a Uniform CPA Examination)

6. The costs of a service department, such as maintenance, are frequently distributed to the departments which utilize its services by multiplying a "charging rate" by the number of man-hours of service provided to each other department. The charging rate is computed so as to provide for a complete distribution of service department costs, using the following formula:

$$\frac{\text{Actual direct service dept. costs} + \text{Actual costs allocated to service dept.}}{\text{Total man-hours of service provided to all other departments}}$$

During the month of July, the milling department of the Grope Company called for very little maintenance service, but its monthly budget report showed that the maintenance department's charge for services performed for the milling department during July was in excess of the milling department's budget allowance for the month.

a) What conclusions would you draw from this "unfavorable variance"?

b) Can you suggest any improvements in the company's accounting treatment of maintenance department costs?

7. A company uses the following bases for allocating general overhead costs to organization segments:

Original Cost Center	Distributed to—	Basis
Head office administration.................	Division	Division sales dollars
Manufacturing division management........	Plants	Estimated time spent by manufacturing division management
Plant A building services department (depreciation, heat, maintenance, custodial, etc.)	All departments	Floor space
Plant A power department (wages, salaries, fuel, water, depreciation, occupancy charges, etc.)........................	Production depts.	Metered kilowatt-hours

a) Following the classification set forth in this chapter, state the allocation criterion used in each of the above.

b) State the probable purpose or purposes which each of these allocations is designed to achieve. In each case will the method achieve its desired objectives? Why or why not?

c) For each allocation which you believe is unlikely to achieve its objectives, suggest a better alternative.

8. Service department S provides services to other departments of the company's manufacturing division. The amount of service provided depends on the needs of the other manufacturing departments, as determined by their respective managers.

The normal operating volume for department S is 10,000 service hours a month. Budgeted cost for department S is $20,000 plus $2.50 per service hour. Actual department S cost for February was $42,000, at a volume of 8,000 service hours, including 1,100 service hours performed in production department M.

The normal operating volume for department M is 15,000 direct labor hours a month. At this volume, department M's budget allows for the consumption of 1,000 department S hours. During February, department M operated at a volume of 12,500 direct labor hours, and at this volume it had a budget allowance of 900 department S hours.

a) How much should department M be charged for department S services for the month of February? State your reasons.

b) Compute the variance in the charge for department S services that would appear on department M's cost performance report for the month, using the allocation method you developed in (a). Give a one-sentence explanation of the meaning of this variance.

c) Compute the variance in departmental costs that would appear on department S's cost control reports for the month.

d) Compute the *total* amount of department S costs to be charged during February to all other departments combined. What is the total amount over- or underdistributed for the month? If this differs from the amount computed in (*c*) above, try to explain how this difference arose.

*9. The Warren Manufacturing Company has four producing departments —milling, machining, assembly, and painting—and three service departments—factory office, plant operation, and storeroom. The company's records contain the following information for the month of July:

Department	Actual Direct Overhead Costs	Square Feet Floor Space	No. of Employees	Average % of Requisitions
Milling..............	$40,000	18,000	28	26%
Machining............	35,000	12,000	14	10
Painting.............	42,000	15,000	11	24
Assembly.............	30,000	9,000	9	40
Factory office.........	19,490	3,000	7	
Plant operation........	22,110	5,000	3	
Storeroom............	24,460	10,000	2	

The actual costs of the services departments for the month are to be redistributed, using a sequential allocation procedure. The departments are to be dealt with in the following sequence, using the indicated bases for cost allocation:

> Plant operation—square feet of floor space
> Factory office—number of employees
> Storeroom—average percentage of requisitions

a) Prepare an overhead cost distribution sheet for the month.
b) Prepare journal entries to record the actual costs for each department (credit "Head Office Control") and the redistribution of service department costs.

10. The following data have been taken from a department's overhead cost budget and from its account balances for the month of December:

	Budgeted		Actual Cost
	At Normal Volume	At Actual Volume	
Cleanup labor...............................	$ 400	$ 400	$ 550
Indirect labor..............................	3,000	3,600	3,400
Overtime premium..........................	300	500	750
Steam......................................	1,500	1,800	1,700
Heat, light, depreciation, and insurance........	2,000	2,000	2,400
Factory administration......................	800	800	800

The following additional information is available:

---

* Solutions to problems marked with an asterisk (*) can be found in Appendix B.

(1) All budgeted figures are at standard prices and standard wage rates.

(2) Indirect labor and cleanup labor are charged to the department at standard wage rates.

(3) Steam is purchased from a local utility at a price which varies with the price of soft coal; steam costs are charged to the departments on the basis of the average steam price for the month, multiplied by consumption determined on the basis of meter readings.

(4) Heat, light, depreciation, and insurance costs are charged to the departments on the basis of the percentage of the factory's floor space occupied at the beginning of the year.

Indicate what figures you would report to the department head, how you would arrange these figures on the department head's report, and what further data you would like to obtain to make the report more useful to the department head and his superiors. Give your reasons.

11. The management of Blake-Emmich desires to have departmental cost statements that will be all-inclusive so that the department head will be cognizant of his share of the total costs of operating the factory, but which will be used primarily for control purposes. The monthly budget of the machining department includes the following categories of costs:

(1) Fixed costs which are distributed among the factory's departments on a "fair and equitable" basis: the machining department's share of these costs is $12,000 a month.

(2) Fixed costs which are direct to the department, the amount of the cost being determined by the factory superintendent: $2,000 a month.

(3) Fixed costs which are direct to the department, the amount of the cost being determined by the department head: $600 a month.

(4) Variable direct costs for which the department head determines the amount of inputs used but not input prices: $4 a standard direct labor hour.

(5) Variable costs of service departments for which the machining department head determines the amount of service used: 5 units of service per standard direct labor hour, at an average variable service department cost of $0.20 a unit.

(6) Variable costs of service departments for which the service department head or the factory superintendent determines the amount of service used: 4 units of service per standard direct labor hour, at $0.30 a unit.

The machining department's output for July was the equivalent of 2,000 standard direct labor hours.

a) Compute a flexible budget allowance for July for each of the six cost categories listed above.

b) Comparisons between these flexible budget allowances and the "actual costs" charged to the department for July will be embodied in a monthly departmental cost report. Indicate for each category how "actual cost" should be measured and reported. Remember that the report is to be used for control purposes.

12. The Zeta Company operates a factory with six production departments, three service departments, and a plant office. Any cost which can be traced to one of these departments is charged to that department at the time it is incurred. All other costs are charged to the plant manager. The costs of the service departments are charged to the production departments on the following bases:

Department	Amount Distributed Monthly	Basis of Distribution
A.........	Total budgeted cost	Fixed amount to each production department, determined in advance
B..........	Total actual cost	Average service cost per service hour times service hours used by each production department
C..........	?	Fixed amount per service department hour, determined in advance, times actual service hours used by each production department

Costs charged to the plant manager are of two kinds: (1) those relating to building occupancy, such as building depreciation, insurance, and taxes; and (2) general administration costs, such as the plant manager's salary. Actual occupancy costs for the month are allocated to all departments on the basis of floor space, prior to the distribution of service department costs. General administration costs, together with plant office costs, are not distributed.

The factory uses a flexible budget and issues reports to each of the ten departments showing variances between actual costs and the flexible budget standard for the volume of activity in each department during the month. The flexible budget for service department A is the same amount each month (i.e., no variable costs).

a) What variances from flexible budget allowances, if any, would you expect to find in production department M in connection with the amounts charged to it by each of the service departments and by the plant manager for occupancy costs? What meaning can be attached to each of these variances?

b) What undistributed balances, if any, would you expect to find in the summary account for each of the service departments and for building occupancy? What meaning can be attached to each of these balances?

13. Service department 101 provides services to a number of production departments. The cost budget for the department at a normal volume of 5,000 service hours per month, together with actual departmental charges for the month of March, is as follows (4,000 hours of service were provided to production departments during March):

	Budget at Normal Volume		March Actual
	Amount	Fixed or Variable	
Servicemen labor.........	$15,000	V	$14,000
Supervision.............	2,000	F	2,000
Indirect labor...........	4,000	V	3,000
Supplies................	1,000	V	1,100
Depreciation............	5,500	F	5,600
Rent....................	2,500	F	2,900
Total...............	$30,000		$28,600

Depreciation charged each month is 1 percent of the original cost of equipment installed in the service department. The rental charge is based on the department's pro rata share, based on floor space occupied, of the costs charged to the building service department's accounts during the month.

Production department 76 uses department 101 services, and the foreman in charge of department 76 is expected to control his use of these services. Normal production volume in department 76 is 10,000 machine-hours. Department 76's use of department 101 services is budgeted at one service hour for every 10 machine-hours. A full cost charging rate is used.

Service hours are charged to production departments on the basis of average actual service department cost for the month, multiplied by the number of service hours used during the month. During March department 76 operated a total of 11,000 machine-hours and used 900 hours of department 101 service.

a) Compute department 76's budget allowance for department 101 service:
  (1) At normal volume.
  (2) At 11,000 machine-hours.
b) Compute the service charge to department 76 for March.
c) Analyze department 76's March budget variance in department 101 charges, showing a breakdown between the variance due to factors over which department 76 had some control and the variance due to other causes.

*14. The Tensile Steel Company is overhauling its semivariable overhead budget system in the interest of securing better control over service departments and of charging the cost of these departments to producing departments in the most effective manner possible. Below are budget data for the maintenance and the finance (accounting, payroll, clerical, etc.) departments and operating and cost data for the month of September:

Maintenance Department Budget:
  (1) Normal level of output: 12,000 maintenance labor hours a month.
  (2) Average hourly rate for maintenance workers, $3.50.
  (3) Other maintenance department costs:

Item	Fixed per Month	Variable per Maintenance Labor Hour
Supervision and indirect labor.....	$ 5,000	$0.30
Supplies and tools...............	2,500	0.60
Miscellaneous...................	3,300	0.10
Total.....................	$10,800	$1.00

Finance Department Budget:
  (1) When the factory is operating at a normal level of activity, the factory as a whole employs 1,000 people.
  (2) The budget of the finance department is $18,000 a month plus one dollar for each factory employee.

September Data:

    (1) Maintenance labor hours worked, 13,300.
    (2) Maintenance department costs, $72,900.
    (3) Factory employment, 1,200 employees.
    (4) Finance department costs, $20,000.

a) Specify rules for allocating the costs of the two departments, state their rationale, and illustrate them with the September data.

b) Comment on possible reasons for any variances that arise from your methods of allocating these charges.

*15. The Hutchings Machine Works factory is organized into seven departments: three production departments, and four service and administrative departments. The following data relate to the month of July:

	Direct Overhead	Square Footage	No. of Employees	Equipment Book Value	Executive Time Distribution
Light machinery.......	$30,000	9,000	28	$220,000	30%
Heavy machinery......	54,000	18,000	26	351,000	25
Assembly.............	24,000	21,000	42	120,000	45
Buildings.............	13,000	1,000	6	......	..
Plant accounting......	6,000	1,000	7	8,000	..
Maintenance..........	12,000	1,000	12	15,000	..
Plant management......	10,000	2,000	17	80,000	..

The costs of the four service departments are to be distributed sequentially, in the order given, starting with buildings. The bases for distribution are: buildings—square footage; plant accounting—number of employees; maintenance—equipment book value; and plant management—percentage of executive time spent in each department. As each department's cost is distributed, its accounts are closed and no further charges are made to that department.

Prepare a cost distribution sheet for the month of July.

16. The Cork Corporation operates three plants. The monthly performance reports for the Boston plant for the second quarter of 19x0 showed the following totals:

	April	May	June
Plant credits: Standard cost of products completed..................................	$100,000	$120,000	$140,000
Plant debits:			
Direct plant costs.........................	$ 70,000	$ 83,000	$ 98,000
General overhead—manufacturing division....	20,000	28,800	32,200
Total......................................	$ 90,000	$111,800	$130,200
Plant Balance..............................	$ 10,000	$ 8,200	$ 9,800

The manager of the Boston plant argued that these figures did not present a true picture of his plant's performance because "we are being charged too much general overhead." The monthly overhead charge is designed to distribute to the three plants the total actual general overhead costs of the manufacturing division for the month. The calculation of the monthly charge to the Boston plant was as follows:

	April	May	June
1. Man-hours: all plants.....................	50,000	40,000	42,000
2. Total general overhead: manufacturing....	$100,000	$96,000	$96,600
3. Monthly allocation rate (1)/(2)...........	$2.00/hr.	$2.40/hr.	$2.30/hr.
4. Man-hours: Boston plant................	10,000	12,000	14,000
5. Allocated to Boston plant (3) × (4).......	$ 20,000	$28,800	$32,200

a) Comment on the performance record of the Boston plant during the second quarter of 19x0.

b) How would you change the method of distributing general manufacturing overhead to produce a more meaningful plant performance report?

17. The Tisket Tasket Casket Company (see problem 8–15) derives predetermined service department charging rates at the beginning of each year by applying the cross-allocation method to budgeted costs for the year. The rates for the current year are:

Department A......$2.0788 per service unit.
Department B...... 2.2146 per service unit.
Department C...... 1.6510 per service unit.

a) Compute the total amount charged to production departments during a month in which the following statistics were accumulated:

Service Department	Direct Departmental Charges	Actual Service Consumption (Units)				
		A	B	C	Production	Total
A..........	$11,000	....	1,000	500	6,000	7,500
B..........	19,000	500	....	1,000	9,000	10,500
C..........	22,000	2,500	1,500	....	13,000	17,000

b) What is the net amount over- or underdistributed for each service department during the month? Offer suggestions as to possible explanations of the causes of these variances.

18. The Premier Company (see problem 8–13) derives predetermined service department charging rates at the beginning of each year by distributing budgeted service department costs sequentially. The allocation sequence and the predetermined rates for 19x1 are as follows:

(1) Buildings department............$0.17 per square foot.
(2) Office.......................$140 per employee.
(3) Maintenance department.........$4.80 per maintenance labor hour.
(4) Shipping room................$0.12 per machine.

These rates reflect the following average monthly statistics from the 19x1 budget:

	Floor Space (Square Feet)	Total Employees	Maintenance Labor Hours	Machine-Hours
Department 101............	18,000	50	560	8,000
Department 102............	16,000	40	610	12,000
Department 103............	33,000	100	930	16,000
Department 104............	20,000	60	500	10,000
Office....................	10,000	34	...	.....
Buildings................	1,000	11	...	.....
Maintenance..............	1,000	17	...	.....
Shipping room............	2,000	6	...	.....
Total..................	101,000	318	2,600	46,000

Monthly cost reports are issued to the managers of each of the company's four producing departments and four service departments. Although these reports are to reflect the full cost concept, they are to be used primarily in reviewing the effectiveness of cost control in each department. Production department managers are presumed to share responsibility with the maintenance department manager for the number of maintenance labor hours used.

The following operating and overhead cost data were recorded for the month of November:

	Direct Departmental Overhead	Total Employees	Maintenance Labor Hours	Machine-Hours
Department 101............	$ 12,100	54	600	8,200
Department 102............	21,200	42	650	13,000
Department 103............	18,400	96	900	15,800
Department 104............	15,600	50	550	8,000
Office....................	35,300	33	...	.....
Buildings................	19,200	11	...	.....
Maintenance..............	10,500	18	...	.....
Shipping room............	4,700	6	...	.....
Total..................	$137,000	310	2,700	45,000

Prepare a service department cost distribution sheet for the month of November, using any method of cost distribution that you deem appropriate. Defend your choices.

19. The Barbizon Corporation operates a factory with three producing departments and nine general and service departments. Product costing is on a job order basis. Budgeted monthly factory overhead costs for the coming year are as follows:

	Fixed	Variable	Total
Direct departmental charges:			
Service departments:			
Administration.....................	$11,800	....	$11,800
Office..........................	6,311	$3.00 per employee	6,875
Personnel........................	3,000	....	3,000
Cafeteria........................	1,430	....	1,430
Power...........................	1,130	$0.008 per kwh	2,530
Maintenance.....................	1,770	$4.00 per mainte- nance labor hour	10,570
Building service...................	3,230	....	3,230
Engineering......................	5,078	$1.00 per engineer- ing hour	5,978
Storeroom.......................	1,720	$0.04 per requisition	1,800
Producing departments:			
Machining........................	2,670	$0.13 per machine- hour	3,970
Assembly........................	2,146	$0.15 per direct labor hour	4,522
Shipping........................	945	$0.06 per carton	6,945
Undistributed costs (all fixed):			
Building rent......................			20,000
Equipment depreciation (0.8% of equipment cost)..................			9,600
Property insurance ($0.50 per $1,000 of insured valuation).............			350
Total.............................			$92,600

The amount shown for the cafeteria is the direct deficit—that is, the amount by which cafeteria direct operating costs exceed cafeteria receipts.

Pertinent statistics drawn from the monthly budgets for the coming year are shown in Exhibit I. No floor space statistics are quoted for the power department because it operates its own building. Depreciation on this building is included in the direct costs of the power department.

The producing departments base their product costing rates on the following normal volumes:

Machining.............. 10,000 machine-hours.
Assembly............... 15,000 direct labor hours.
Shipping...............100,000 cartons packed.

The data in Exhibit II relate to the month of August. Floor space figures during August are the same as in Exhibit I and are not repeated. Actual operating volumes for the month of August are:

Machining.............. 9,000 machine-hours.
Assembly.................14,000 direct labor hours.
Shipping.................85,000 cartons packed.

a) Prepare a cost distribution sheet for budgeted costs and derive *full cost* product costing rates for the three producing departments. The com-

Exhibit I

BUDGET DATA FOR NORMAL MONTH

	Floor Space (000 Sq. Ft.)	No. of Employees	Cost of Equipment (000)	Insured Valuation (000)	Kilowatt Hours Used (000)	Maintenance Labor Hours Used	Engineering Hours Used	No. of Requisitions Used
Service departments:								
Administration..........	1	9	....	...	...	....	...	....
Office.................	1	12	$ 15	$ 10	...	50	...	....
Personnel..............	1	4	....	...	...	....	...	....
Cafeteria..............	4	15	20	20	25	150	...	....
Power.................	...	5	200	90	...	200	30	....
Maintenance...........	2	15	5	...	5	....	20	200
Building service..........	1	7	....	...	45	400	...	80
Engineering............	3	7	10	...	4	100	...	70
Storeroom.............	4	3	....	...	...	....	...	....
Producing departments:								
Machining..............	25	30	800	500	85	1,000	650	1,000
Assembly...............	50	83	150	80	11	300	200	600
Shipping...............	8	10	....	...	...	....	...	50
Total....................	100	200	$1,200	$700	175	2,200	900	2,000

pany's data processing facilities are inadequate to make cross-allocations feasible, and costs are to be distributed *sequentially,* as follows:

(1) Distribute building rent on the basis of floor space, equipment depreciation on the basis of equipment cost, and insurance on the basis of insured valuation.

(2) Distribute administration, office, personnel, and cafeteria costs among the other eight departments on the basis of the number of employees in those departments.

(3) Distribute power costs on the basis of the number of kilowatt-hours used.

Exhibit II

ACTUAL DATA FOR AUGUST

	Direct Costs	No. of Employees	Cost of Equipment (000)	Insured Valuation (000)	Kilowatt Hours Used (000)	Maintenance Labor Hours Used	Engineering Hours Used	No. of Requisitions Used
Service departments:	.....	...	....	...	...	....	...	....
Administration........	$12,120	10	....	...	...	....	...	....
Office.................	6,913	12	$ 15	$ 10	...	20	...	....
Personnel............	3,034	4	....	...	...	....	...	....
Cafeteria.............	2,880	14	20	20	24	100	...	....
Power...............	2,658	5	200	90	...	120	5	....
Maintenance.........	10,207	15	5	...	6	....	15	150
Building Service.......	2,867	6	....	...	50	450	...	100
Engineering..........	6,006	7	10	...	3	60	...	50
Storeroom............	1,711	3	....	...	...	....	...	....
Producing departments:	.....	...	....	...	...	....	...	....
Machining............	3,782	28	830	530	82	800	640	920
Assembly.............	4,498	80	170	100	11	350	150	530
Shipping.............	6,145	10	....	...	...	....	10	50
Undistributed costs:	.....	...	....	...	...	....	...	....
Building rent........	20,000	...	....	...	...	....	...	....
Equipment depreciation.............	10,000	...	....	...	...	....	...	....
Property insurance....	375	...	....	...	...	....	...	....
Total.................	$93,196	194	1,250	750	176	1,900	820	1,800

(4) Distribute maintenance department costs on the basis of the number of maintenance labor hours used.

(5) Distribute building service department costs on the basis of floor space.

(6) Distribute engineering department costs on the basis of engineering hours.

(7) Distribute storeroom costs on the basis of the number of requisitions used.

b) Derive product costing rates for the three producing departments on a *variable costing* basis. Use a *sequential procedure,* but remember that the only variable service department costs that should be included in producing department burden rates are those that will vary with product volume. For example, if a service department has many variable cost elements but provides all of its services to production departments in fixed amounts, unrelated to current production volume, then none of its costs should be included in the burden rates of the production departments. You will need to use the following additional information about the variable service department costs:

(1) Variable office costs vary in proportion to the number of employees in all other departments (budgeted at 188 employees for the year).

(2) The number of employees is completely fixed in the power department, engineering department, and storeroom; 80 percent of the number of employees budgeted at normal volume in the maintenance, machining, and shipping departments are variable with volume; 75 of the 83 budgeted assembly department employees are regarded as variable with volume.

(3) Power consumption in the engineering, maintenance, machining, and assembly departments is completely variable.

(4) The budgeted consumption of maintenance labor hours by the machining and assembly departments is 50 percent variable with volume; use of maintenance services by the engineering department is completely fixed.

(5) 20 percent of the number of engineering hours budgeted at normal volume for the machining and assembly departments is variable; use of engineering department services by other departments is entirely fixed.

(6) The number of requisitions used by the machining, assembly, and shipping departments is completely variable.

c) As a result of your work in (b), can you offer any suggestions that would simplify the calculation of variable costing burden rates in this case without reducing their accuracy unduly?

d) Prepare a cost distribution sheet for the month of August, distributing actual full costs in the sequence shown above.

e) Management wishes to prepare departmental cost reports for control purposes. Prepare a cost distribution sheet for August, using whatever allocation method is best suited to management's purposes. State your assumptions as to the controllability of individual cost items.

20. The Gietz-Johnson Company has had difficulties with its overhead allocation practices for some time. The newly appointed controller of the company developed the following plan for allocating the company's general factory and service department costs:

Department	Basis of Allocation
Administration.........Departmental payrolls
Buildings..............Floor space occupied
Power.................Power consumption, using departmental meters
Stores................Dollar value of materials requisitioned
Payroll................Number of employees
Engineering...........Labor costs on basis of daily time distributions; other costs in same proportion

Buildings costs were to be distributed first, to all other departments on the indicated basis. Administration costs were then to be allocated, again to other service departments (except buildings) as well as to production departments. For each of the four remaining service departments, the actual charges accumulated each month were to be distributed directly to the production departments—no inter-service department allocations of the costs of these four departments were to be made.

This plan was presented at a meeting attended by the works manager and the heads of the various production departments. All those attending this meeting seemed to feel that the proposal represented an improvement over existing methods, but several of them raised objections. The manager of the assembly department, for example, argued that although his department accounted for a very large share of total factory payrolls, the administrative attention required by his department was virtually nil. Accordingly, he felt that the proposed allocation of administrative department costs would be grossly unfair.

The manager of the mixing department, on the other hand, found no objection to the proposed allocation of administration costs, but he felt that the charge for stores department costs would be inequitable when applied to his department. Approximately half of the dollar value of materials issued were requisitioned by his department, but most of these were in large bulk quantities, and he felt that a charge based on dollar value of materials would reflect poorly the effect of his operations on stores department costs.

The manager of the light machining department was more critical. He maintained that no matter what method was used, his department would be charged for inefficiences in the service departments. Furthermore, he objected that he had no control over service department costs, and on these grounds he suggested that no allocations be made.

a) Identify the allocation criterion underlying each of the proposed methods of allocation.

b) Prepare a brief report, agreeing or disagreeing with the objections raised by the various production department managers. Are there other weaknesses in the scheme that were not brought out at the meeting?

c) Suggest an allocation scheme that in your opinion best meets the objections raised to the controller's proposal.

Chapter 15

FACTORY OVERHEAD
COST VARIANCES

PREVIOUS CHAPTERS have dealt with two main accounting tasks: (1) the development of product unit cost for planning and inventory valuation purposes; and (2) the accumulation and reporting of cost data for cost control in individual cost centers. Both of these lead to the measurement of factory cost variances, but the amounts are different. The purpose of this chapter is to study the nature of these variances and to discuss some ways of estimating the variance amounts resulting from individual causes.

ANALYSIS OF TOTAL OVERHEAD VARIANCES

In its simplest terms, variance analysis consists of identifying the total overhead variance associated with a given cost center and then breaking this down into two components:

1. A *spending variance,* arising from departures of actual from budgeted costs at actual volume.
2. A *volume variance,* arising from departures of actual from budgeted or normal volume.

Deriving the Total Variance

The total overhead variance, or net variance, arises as a by-product of the use of a predetermined burden rate for product costing. The steps in product costing can be summarized briefly:

1. Establish cost center boundaries so that each cost center's operations are essentially homogeneous.
2. For each cost center of a production department, select a scale on which to measure the volume of activity of that center (e.g., direct labor hours).
3. Estimate the normal (or expected) volume of activity of each cost center for each reporting period, usually a month or similar interval of time (e.g., 4,000 direct labor hours a month).

4. Estimate the direct overhead costs of the cost center at this normal (or expected) volume (e.g., $5,360 at a volume of 4,000 direct labor hours).
5. Include in this cost estimate an estimate of the costs of service departments and general factory overheads that will be allocated to this cost center at this volume (e.g., $6,640 at a volume of 4,000 direct labor hours).
6. Compute a burden rate: estimated cost per unit of volume at normal or expected volume (e.g., ($5,360 + $6,640)/4,000 = $3 per direct labor hour).
7. Apply this rate to individual products passing through the cost center to determine product unit cost (e.g., job No. 4624 requires 10 direct labor hours in the cost center and thus is charged 10 × $3 = $30 for factory overhead).
8. Credit the cost center and charge the work in process account for all the amounts charged to products during the period (e.g., 3,500 hours × $3 = $10,500). This is the *cost absorbed* in the cost center during the period.

The figures in this summary have been derived from the cost center budget data shown in Exhibit 15–1 and should require no further explanation.

Exhibit 15–1

COST CENTER X: OVERHEAD COST BUDGET

	Budget Formula		Budget at Normal Volume (4,000 Direct Labor Hours)
	Fixed per Month	Variable per Direct Labor Hour	
Direct charges:			
Salaries...............	$2,800	...	$ 2,800
Indirect labor:			
Materials handling..............	....	$0.12	480
Idle or lost time.................	....	0.06	240
Overtime premium...............	....	...	.....
Other indirect labor.............	....	0.32	1,280
Supplies........................	....	0.14	560
Total direct..................	$2,800	$0.64	$ 5,360
Allocated:			
Payroll taxes and benefits..........	$ 840	$0.15	$ 1,440
Power........................	....	0.20	800
Maintenance....................	360	0.16	1,000
Floor space....................	800	...	800
Equipment depreciation............	400	...	400
General factory overhead..........	2,200	...	2,200
Total allocated................	$4,600	$0.51	$ 6,640
Total Overhead..................	$7,400	$1.15	$12,000
Burden Rate per Direct Labor Hour....			$ 3.00

The last step listed above almost inevitably leads to over- or under-absorbed overhead in the department. For example, if actual direct overheads in this cost center this month are $5,635 and allocated costs amount to $6,425, the departmental overhead summary, in T-account form, will appear as follows:

Overhead Summary—Cost Center X[1]

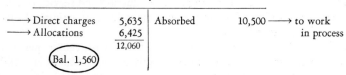

The debit balance of $1,560 in this account indicates that the costs charged to the cost center exceeded the amount absorbed by the month's production. This is the *total overhead variance* and in this case is *unfavorable* in that the cost center has been charged with more costs than its production has absorbed.

This scheme has many variants. At one extreme, represented by many process costing systems, the burden rate is postdetermined rather than predetermined—that is, it represents the actual average cost of the month's production. At the other extreme, the predetermined burden rate is used in preparing product cost estimates, but after-the-fact absorption is omitted except for a year-end adjustment to prepare the books for public financial reporting. In the former case, the total variance is zero by definition, while in the latter it is not computed.

In this chapter, the main discussion will be focused on the intermediate case in which the total overhead variance is calculated periodically, more or less along the lines described above.

Deriving the Spending Variances

The total variance is very different from the variances from flexible budget allowances, developed for use in cost control, and described in

---

[1] The transactions from which these figures are derived can be represented by the following summary entries:

```
Overhead Summary—Cost Center X.............................. 5,635
        Accounts Payable, etc........................................        5,635
    To record direct departmental charges.

Overhead Summary—Cost Center X.............................. 6,425
        Overhead Summary—Service Departments.....................        6,425
    To record costs allocated to cost center.

Overhead in Process..........................................10,500
        Overhead Summary—Cost Center X..........................       10,500
    To record overhead absorbed by production.
```

The allocations might be made on accounting work sheets instead of in the ledger accounts, but the formal entries are presented here for clarity.

Chapter 13. These so-called spending variances arise from a number of causes, including off-normal prices, inadequate or excessive control, and inappropriate cost allocation schemes.

The steps in deriving and reporting spending variances may be summarized briefly:

1. For each cost center, including both production and service centers, select a scale or scales on which to measure the volume of activity of that center (e.g., direct labor hours).

2. Estimate the direct overhead costs of the cost center per period at each of several possible volumes of activity (e.g., $5,040 at 3,500 direct labor hours, $5,360 at 4,000 direct labor hours, etc.). These are the *flexible budget allowances*.

3. Include in the flexible budget allowances an estimate of the costs of service departments and general factory overheads that will be allocated to this cost center at different volumes (e.g., $6,385 at 3,500 direct labor hours, $6,640 at 4,000 direct labor hours, etc.).

4. Accumulate the total direct and allocated charges for each cost element in each cost center for the reporting period (e.g., $12,060, including $5,635 in direct charges and $6,425 in allocated charges).

5. Compute the flexible budget allowances *for the volume of activity actually achieved* (e.g., if actual volume is 3,500 direct labor hours, the budget allowances total $5,040 + $6,385 = $11,425).

6. Compute the difference between actual cost and the volume-adjusted budgeted cost, both in total and for each cost element (e.g., $12,060 − $11,425 = $635, unfavorable). This difference is known as the overhead *budget variance, performance variance,* or *spending variance.*

7. Report the controllable portions of this variance, classified by cost element, to the executive responsible for cost center performance.

The total spending variance, $635, is the sum of the variances in the right-hand column of the report to the cost center manager shown in Exhibit 15–2. Notice that this exhibit is divided into three sections: direct departmental charges, regarded as controllable; partly or indirectly controllable allocated charges; and noncontrollable allocated charges. The sum of the costs in the first two categories is identified as the total responsibility of the cost center foreman; the charges and the $20 variance "below the line" are shown as beyond his control. Thus, although the total performance variance is $635, only $615 of this is identified as wholly or partially controllable.[2]

---

[2] No ledger entries need be made to record the budget allowances, although of course they must be introduced into the data processing system in some way so that reports of the type shown in Exhibit 15–2 can be prepared. A simple plan for entering these amounts into the ledger accounts is presented later in this chapter.

Exhibit 15–2

MONTHLY OVERHEAD COST SUMMARY—COST CENTER X

Month January, 19—	Budget for Actual Volume	Actual Charges	(Over) Under Budget
Salaries......................................	$ 2,800	$ 3,100	$(300)
Indirect labor:			
Materials handling........................	420	410	10
Idle or lost time.........................	210	190	20
Overtime premium........................	....	280	(280)
Other indirect labor......................	1,120	1,125	(5)
Supplies.....................................	490	530	(40)
Total directly controllable................	$ 5,040	$ 5,635	$(595)
Allocated—partly controllable:			
Payroll taxes and benefits..................	$ 1,365	$ 1,525	$(160)
Power.....................................	700	680	20
Maintenance..............................	920	800	120
Total partly controllable................	$ 2,985	$ 3,005	$(20)
Total Responsibility.........................	$ 8,025	$ 8,640	$(615)
Allocated fixed charges:			
Floor space..............................	$ 800	$ 800	
Equipment depreciation....................	400	420	$(20)
General factory overhead..................	2,200	2,200	...
Total fixed charges.....................	$ 3,400	$ 3,420	$(20)
Total Charges..............................	$11,425	$12,060	$(635)

Analysis of the Spending Variance

The spending variance is not precisely analogous to the quantity variances derived in the chapters on standard costing. In fact, under most circumstances it is likely to contain both a price and a quantity element. If the price component is significant, then efforts should be made to remove it, either by pricing overhead inputs routinely at standard prices or by isolating the price variances in variance analysis at the end of the period.

For example, the materials handling labor variance in Exhibit 15–2 was $10, and favorable. Suppose, however, that the standard wage rate for materials handling labor was $2.10 an hour, while the actual rates averaged approximately $1.80. A $420 budget allowance is thus equivalent to a 200-hour allowance at standard rates, whereas the actual charge of $410 represents about 228 hours at the actual wage rate. The spending variance in this item thus could be subdivided as follows:

Actual hours × actual rates........................$410
Actual hours × standard rates (228 × $2.10)......... 479
   MATERIALS HANDLING LABOR RATE VARIANCE....... $ 69
Budgeted hours × standard rates (210 × $2.10)...... 420
   MATERIALS HANDLING LABOR QUANTITY VARIANCE...   (59)
   NET SPENDING VARIANCE, MATERIALS HANDLING
      LABOR...................................... $ 10

Deriving the Volume Variance

The derivation of the spending variances has accounted for $635 of the $1,560 total overhead variance identified at the beginning of this section. The problem is to find out where the remaining $925 came from.

The key to the explanation is to be found in a review of the behavior of overhead costs. For example, the burden rate in the illustration above was based on total overhead charges of $12,000 at a normal monthly production volume of 4,000 direct labor hours. If all these overhead costs were fixed costs, the budget allowance at 3,500 direct labor hours would be $12,000, the same as at 4,000 hours. The $1,500 difference between this total and the amount *absorbed* by the month's production could be due to one factor and one factor only—*volume*. That is, if the burden rate had been based on a volume of 3,500 hours instead of 4,000, the burden rate would have been $12,000/3,500 = $3.43 per direct labor hour and the amount absorbed this month would have been exactly $12,000 (3,500 × $3.43). Thus a variance of this kind results solely from the deviation of actual volume from normal volume and for this reason is called a *volume variance.*

At the other extreme, if all overhead costs had been budgeted as completely variable in proportion to the number of direct labor hours used, the budgeted cost would have been $10,500 (35/40 of $12,000) and there would have been no volume variance. That is, in the case of complete, proportional cost variability, a departure from normal volume affects both the amount budgeted and the amount absorbed, but in the same amount. *Volume variances, in other words, arise only if there are fixed costs or if cost variability is nonlinear.*

The example above presumed a cost behavior between the two extremes of zero and perfect variability. The budget allowances at 3,500 hours totaled neither $12,000 nor $10,000, but $11,425. The difference between this total and the amount absorbed was a volume variance, in this case $925 and *unfavorable* (because volume was less than normal).

The overall variance computation may be summarized in the following manner:

(1) Actual costs charged.............................$12,060		
(2) Budgeted costs for actual volume................ 11,425[2]		
SPENDING VARIANCE (1) − (2).................		$(635)
(3) Costs absorbed by actual volume................ 10,500		
VOLUME VARIANCE (2) − (3).................		(925)
TOTAL VARIANCE (1) − (3).................		$(1,560)

Exhibit 15–3 presents this same information in graphic form. The line labeled "Absorbed" represents the amount absorbed at various volumes. This amount is directly proportional to volume, $3 for each direct labor hour, and thus appears as a straight line on the chart, starting at the double zero at the lower left-hand corner of the chart.

Exhibit 15–3

OVERHEAD COST VARIANCES ILLUSTRATED

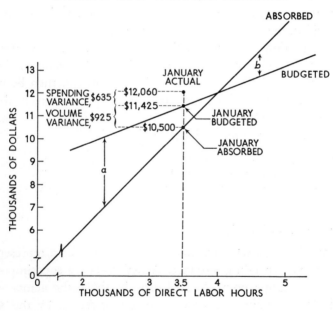

The "Budgeted" line represents the total cost allowed by the flexible budget at various volumes. Because some of the cost center's costs are fixed, this line has a gentler slope than the "Absorbed" line. Cost variability in this case is proportional to volume—$1.15 in budgeted variable costs for each direct labor hour—and thus is shown as a straight line.

The two lines cross at a volume of 4,000 direct labor hours, the normal operating volume of the cost center. Because the burden rate is based on budgeted costs at normal volume, it is not surprising that total absorption should equal the budget at this volume, which is what the intersection of the lines means.

The vertical distance between the budgeted and absorbed lines at any volume represents the volume variance at that volume level and arises solely because actual volume departs from the volume on which the burden rate has been based. Volume variances at volumes in excess of normal volume, such as that marked *"b"* in Exhibit 15–3, represent overabsorption and are classified as favorable. Volume variances at volumes lower than normal, in the zone to the left of the intersection of the lines in the exhibit, represent underutilization of capacity and are referred to as unfavorable. Both the $925 volume variance arising from the illustration and the one marked *"a"* are in this category.

The volume variance can also be derived by analysis of the fixed costs alone if (*a*) there are no steps in fixed cost between actual volume and normal volume, and (*b*) average variable cost is the same for all volumes within this portion of the volume range.

These conditions are met in this illustration. The first step is to determine the fixed cost component of the burden rate, in this case $7,400/4,000 = $1.85 a direct labor hour. This can then be used to compute the amount of fixed cost absorbed by production, in this case 3,500 × $1.85 = $6,475. Comparison of this figure with budgeted fixed cost yields the volume variance for the period:

> Budgeted fixed costs at 3,500 hours $7,400
> Absorbed fixed costs at 3,500 hours 6,475
>   Volume Variance (Unfavorable) . . . . $(925)

Charting the Spending Variance

For completeness' sake, Exhibit 15–3 also includes a representation of the aggregate spending variance. Actual costs are superimposed on this chart as a single point, located directly above the actual volume achieved. The spending variance is then represented by the vertical distance between the actual cost for the period and the point on the budget line corresponding to actual volume, in this case 3,500 direct labor hours.

Reporting the Volume Variance

This discussion has implied that the volume variance is determined in total for each department and is not further subdivided. It would be entirely possible to distribute the volume variance among the various items that make up the department's budget, but there would be little point in making this extra computation. Only the spending variances are affected by the department head's cost control efforts.

In fact, the volume variance is merely a technical by-product of the overhead absorption system. It is computed mainly for negative reasons—to keep it out of the cost center manager's periodic control reports. *It measures neither the effect of volume deviations on costs nor their effect on profits.* At best, it is a measure of the relative utilization of departmental capacity, but physical measures are more readily available, more easily understood, and cheaper to prepare; and computation of the volume variance can ordinarily be discontinued without significant loss of information.

Postdetermined Burden Rates

Burden rates are not always predetermined. Many accounting systems provide for a complete reassignment of the costs of some or all factory cost centers each month. Procedures of this type were described for production centers under process costing in Chapter 5 and for service centers in Chapter 14.

For example, compensation for the $635 unfavorable spending variance in cost center X could be made by increasing the burden rate to provide complete absorption. Cost absorption would thus be based on the average overhead cost for the month: $12,060 divided by 3,500 or approximately $3.45 per direct labor hour. Using this as a burden rate, all costs would be absorbed and the total variance would be zero, defined out of existence.

The main disadvantage of this procedure has been stressed before—that it leads to variations in unit cost that may be very poor guides to managerial action. Variance analysis thus would have to be focused on the unit cost figures, a more difficult process technically and less readily explained to the nonaccountant.

Budgeted versus Normal Volume

A key issue in burden rate determination is whether the volume base should represent an estimate of long-run normal volume or whether it should reflect budgeted current volume. These two concepts are reflected in Exhibit 15–4. This exhibit shows the operating volume statistics for a small paint factory during a six-year period and an estimate for the coming year. Volume in the six years fluctuated between a high of 67,000 gallons a month in 19x2 and a low of 47,000 gallons a month in 19x5. The estimated normal operating volume is 60,000 gallons a month, but the expected volume in 19x7 is 70,000 gallons a month.

Other things being equal, the use of normal volume as the burden rate base will result in larger amounts of under- or overabsorbed burden in individual years than will result from the application of the current volume concept. This has been used to support a current volume base. Advocates of current volume also cite the difficulty of determining a normal volume in the light of uncertainty as to the duration and amplitude of cyclical fluctuations and changes in the total operating capacity of the plant.

Exhibit 15–4

BUDGETED VOLUME AND NORMAL VOLUME

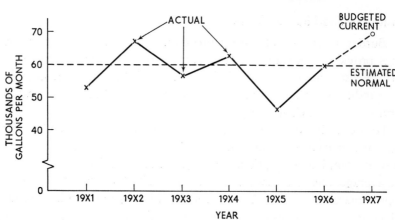

The principal positive argument in favor of normal volume is that it provides product cost data that are more truly representative of the conditions under which the plant will operate during an extended period of time. The advocates of normal volume argue that product cost should include only those costs that are reasonably necessary to manufacture the product. Inefficiencies resulting from underutilization of plant do not fit this concept. Manufacturers cannot expect, in the long run, to earn premium prices to cover inefficiencies of this sort, any more than they can expect to be paid for inefficient factory management. Therefore, balance sheet totals will be overstated if the effect of low volume is allowed to enter the inventory accounts through the medium of high burden rates. Furthermore, it is argued, identical products manufactured in different time periods but under the same conditions as to prices and manufacturing technology should be inventoried at the same cost. Following this line of reasoning, the larger variances that can be expected under the normal volume concept should be allowed to occur because they point up in a highly forceful manner the effects of variations in plant utilization.

The problem of defining normal operating volume still remains, however. Average volume will depend on the period selected for the average and on the overall capacity of the plant. If plant capacity increases, then the normal volume must also be adjusted upward to reflect the greater operating potential. Uncertainty as to future capacity is usually countered by defining normal volume in terms of percentage of capacity. Although capacity itself is difficult to define accurately in absolute terms, some workable definition usually can be derived.

The question of what constitutes a normal percentage of capacity is more troublesome. If the objective is to select a percentage that will reflect average plant utilization during future business cycles, a deviation of the actual average from normal will be regarded as a serious defect in the normal volume base. But this is not necessarily the concept underlying normal volume. Normal may be defined more abstractly as *the percentage of capacity that is regarded by management as essential for efficient, competitive operation.* This is consistent with the criteria used in deciding the size of newly constructed plants, which must include some provision for periods of partial idleness. The definition of the normal plant utilization ratio is inevitably subjective, but any deviation from this utilization level deserves managerial recognition. Only the normal volume concept provides a ready mechanism for identifying deviations of this kind.

Cost Center Summary Accounts

Incorporation of absorbed overhead in the ledger accounts can be done in several ways, of which it is necessary to mention only one. This calls for a separate summary account for each cost center in which to accumulate the amount of overhead absorbed by production. This account is called an *overhead absorbed* or *applied overhead* account.

As work progresses, or at specified intervals, work in process accounts (and job order cost sheets, if any) are debited for overhead absorbed, the amount determined by multiplying the overhead rate by the index of volume. The offsetting credits are made to the overhead absorbed accounts for the individual cost centers. At the end of each reporting period, the difference between the balances in the cost summary and overhead absorbed accounts represents the aggregate overhead variance for the period.

Using the figures from the previous example, the accounts would show:

Overhead Summary—Cost Center X	Overhead Absorbed—Cost Center X

→Direct charges 5,635
→Allocations   6,425
           12,060
	Absorbed 10,500 →
	         to work
	         in
	         process

The total variance is still $1,560, but it is spread over two accounts rather than concentrated in one.

This practice is designed mainly to permit the balances in the overhead summary accounts to show the gross costs of the cost centers. It can also be used to incorporate the basic variance analysis in the accounts. After the flexible budget allowance for the period is credited to the summary account and debited to the absorbed account, the balance in the former is equal to the aggregate spending variance and the balance in the latter shows the volume variance for the period.

VARIANCE ANALYSIS UNDER VARIABLE COSTING

The preceding discussion assumed an absorption costing system of product costing. Under variable costing, the analysis of factory overhead cost variances is much simpler in that volume variances are either eliminated entirely or reduced in magnitude.

Volume Variances under Variable Costing

Volume variances arise only if a predetermined burden rate is used. In variable costing, the burden rate covers only those costs that are expected to vary with volume. If cost center X in the previous example were to be converted to variable costing, the burden rate would be $1.15 a direct labor hour. Budgeted variable costs would also be $1.15 an hour, and no volume variance would arise:

Budgeted variable overhead (3,500 × $1.15)........................$4,025
Absorbed variable overhead (3,500 × $1.15)........................ 4,025
    Volume Variance..$ 0

Because fixed costs are not absorbed in product costs, no volume variance in fixed costs enters the accounts.

A volume variance can arise under variable costing only if the cost function is nonlinear. For example, suppose that the cost structure is as diagrammed in Exhibit 15–5. The cost absorption line is a linear approximation to the anticipated cost behavior, which is nonlinear. The vertical distance between the budgeted and absorbed lines arises because the burden rate is based on a volume different from actual volume. Thus it represents a volume variance.

Exhibit 15–5

VOLUME VARIANCE FROM NONLINEAR COST FUNCTION

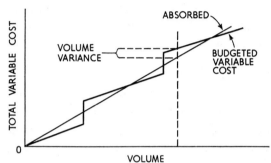

Effect on Spending Variances

It should be emphasized that the introduction of variable costing does not affect the spending variance. The spending variance is the difference between actual costs and the amount budgeted, and neither of these is affected by the choice between absorption costing and variable costing.

Notice that the spending variance need not be separated into fixed and variable categories. The only question is whether the variance is controllable or noncontrollable, and not whether it arises in fixed costs or in variable costs. This is fortunate because in many cases a completely satisfactory distinction between variances in variable costs and variances in fixed costs cannot be made. Many cost items do not fall precisely into either category but must instead be placed in the intermediate class of semivariable costs. That is, it is impossible to decide, at the time of cost recording, whether a particular charge belongs in the fixed category or the variable.

In the illustration, two cost elements (payroll taxes and maintenance) were budgeted as semivariable. While payroll taxes might reasonably be added to the direct labor and indirect labor wage rates, thus splitting the variance into fixed and variable components, no such allocation is possible with maintenance costs. Since it is impossible to do this, it is fortunate that it is not necessary.

OVERHEAD VARIANCES UNDER STANDARD COSTING

The earlier discussion of standard costs largely ignored standard factory overhead costs. Because manufacturing overhead costs do not fluctuate directly and in proportion to changes in operating volume, different techniques (i.e., flexible budgets) have to be developed to provide adequate control information for overhead. When standard costs are used, however, it is customary to develop standard product costs for overhead as well as for direct labor and direct materials.

Burden Rates and Standard Overhead

The concepts underlying standard overhead costs are virtually identical with the concepts underlying the application of overhead to products through the use of burden rates. The volume base for standard overhead is quite clearly a normal volume rather than expected volume for the current year. Standard costs are predicated on normal operating conditions, and changes are seldom made unless factor prices or manufacturing techniques undergo structural changes. In the absence of such structural or permanent changes, a product manufactured in one year should be costed at the same amount as an identical product manufactured in the preceding year. This requires the use of the normal volume concept in setting standard overhead rates.

The main difference between overhead absorption in an actual cost system and overhead absorption in a standard cost system is that under standard costing the overhead assigned to a product depends on some *standard* input quantity required to make the product rather than on the actual input quantity. For example, if the burden rate is $3 per direct labor hour and the product cost standard calls for 1.5 assembly labor hours, the standard assembly overhead cost is $4.50 per unit. This is the amount credited to the departmental accounts no matter whether the actual assembly hours average 1.0 or 2.0 per unit.

Overhead Application

The application of standard overhead costs is best described by an example. Assume that a tabulation of production reports for the month of January indicates that the standard labor hour content of the work performed amounted to 3,400 hours. At a burden rate of $3 an hour, the total overhead absorbed or "earned" during January is $10,200.

The term *earned overhead* implies that the department has "earned" credits for its production during the month. The amount earned is compared with the amount charged to the department to determine the total variance. It is not comparable to corporate earnings because the normal objective in the utilization of standard product cost is to break even or to meet some desired debit or credit balance. Nevertheless, the term is used to describe the standard overhead content of work performed in a manufacturing department.

The total underabsorbed variance in cost center X for the month of January is now $1,860, derived from the account balances:

Overhead Summary—Cost Center X		Overhead Earned—Cost Center X	
Actual	12,060	Earned	10,200

This is $300 greater than the total variance that we measured earlier, because we now are crediting the department on the basis of the *standard* labor hour content of the work performed rather than the *actual* labor hour content.

Two-Variance Analysis of Overhead Variance

Whenever costs are expected to vary in response to changes in *standard* labor hours (or standard machine-hours, standard materials usage, etc.) rather than actual hours, variances from standard overhead cost earned can be analyzed by a two-variance method similar to that developed above.

The flexible budget formula from Exhibit 15–1 yields the following budget allowance for a volume of 3,400 standard or earned labor hours:

$$\text{Budget} = \$7,400 + \$1.15 \times 3,400 = \$11,310 .$$

The variance analysis can then take the familiar form:

(1) Actual costs charged...$12,060	
(2) Budgeted costs for *earned* hours................................ 11,310	
SPENDING VARIANCE (1) − (2)............................	$ (750)
(3) Costs absorbed by earned hours............................ 10,200	
VOLUME VARIANCE (2) − (3)............................	(1,110)
TOTAL VARIANCE (1) − (3)............................	$(1,860)

These variances are all larger than those calculated earlier in this chapter. The amount of overhead absorbed and the size of the flexible budget allowances are now determined by the size of the physical product *output,* as measured by total *earned* hours. Because in this case earned hours fell 100 hours short of actual hours, both the amount absorbed and the amounts budgeted are less than in the earlier illustration. Thus, the variances from actual cost are greater than before.

Three-Variance Analysis of Overhead Variance

The two-variance method is appropriate only if overhead costs vary in response to changes in *output* and are essentially unaffected by changes in the inputs required to achieve a given amount of production. If overhead varies with the quantity of factor *inputs,* however, a three-variance method is called for.

The best of the three-variance methods leaves the volume variance alone but breaks the spending variance down into two parts: an input efficiency variance and a modified spending variance. To avoid confusion, the term *budget variance* will be used here to refer to the latter.

The calculation is simple. Actual labor hours exceeded earned hours by 100 hours. Because overhead costs are expected to vary with *actual* labor hours, this should have increased variable overhead costs by $115 (100 hours at $1.15 an hour, from Exhibit 15–1). In other words, $115 of the $750 spending variances was due to unfavorable direct labor performance. This is the input efficiency variance, in this case known as the *labor efficiency variance* because budgeted costs are a function of labor inputs. Removing this from the spending variance by raising the budget allowance to the 3,500-hour level reduces the budget variance to $635. To summarize:

(1) Actual costs charged...	...$12,060	
(2) Budget at actual hours...	11,425	
BUDGET VARIANCE (1) − (2)...............................		$ 635
(3) Budget at earned hours..	11,310	
LABOR EFFICIENCY VARIANCE (2) − (3)....................		115
(4) Earned at earned hours..	10,200	
VOLUME VARIANCE (3) − (4).............................		1,110
TOTAL VARIANCE (1) − (4).............................		$1,860

This variance analysis is shown graphically in Exhibit 15–6. Once again, the amounts budgeted and absorbed or earned at various volumes are shown as two straight lines, intersecting at normal volume of 4,000 hours. The total variance is the vertical distance between the actual costs for the month and the amount earned, and this is broken down into its three components by measuring the vertical distances between successive pairs of points on the diagram.

Standard costs and flexible budgets are of course intended to state what costs should be under specified conditions. Increasing the cost center's overhead budget allowances by $115 might seem to violate this notion by permitting the manager to escape any responsibility for below-standard labor performance.

This is not true, for two reasons. First, the overhead variance stemming from off-standard labor performance is merely *segregated* from the total variance, not eliminated. The labor efficiency variance is a single figure, clearly identified by cause. The budget variance, on the other hand, is really the sum of a series of variances in individual accounts. Segregation of the labor efficiency variance serves to remove from the accounts the variance stemming from this one cause, thus narrowing the field of search for the causes of the remaining budget variances.

Exhibit 15–6

THREE-VARIANCE ANALYSIS ILLUSTRATED

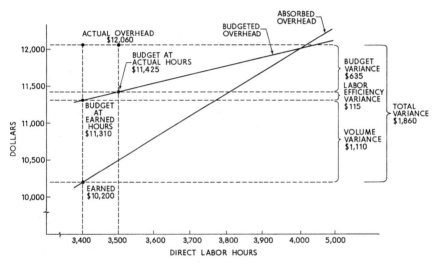

Second, feedback on labor performance is already provided by measurement, reporting, and analysis of labor variances. In fact, control of the labor efficiency variance is not separable from control of the direct labor quantity variance and it might make sense to report the two figures as one. If a machine-hour base were used for the burden rate, on the other hand, the input efficiency variance would be known as a *machine efficiency variance* and would have to be shown separately.

Four-Variance Analysis of Overhead Variances

Earlier in this chapter it was said that the volume variance ordinarily represents the over- or underabsorption of fixed costs. To the extent that it has any meaning at all, the fixed cost component of the burden rate measures the average cost of providing departmental capacity to do business. An unfavorable volume variance, therefore, indicates the amount of capacity costs underutilized. (A favorable volume variance is harder to explain, but it can be said to represent the amount of capacity costs that are doing double duty.)

Assuming that factory capacity is measured in labor hours, it is apparent that the more output achieved in each direct labor hour, the greater the total production capacity of the plant. Thus it can be argued that the effect of direct labor performance on fixed cost *absorption* should be measured to show how much of the factory's capacity has been consumed or released by off-standard labor performance.

To illustrate, the effect of the 100-hour unfavorable direct labor performance in the example is to make this much of the factory's capacity unavailable for other uses. In other terms, one sixth of the volume variance in this case is due to unfavorable labor performance. The fixed cost component of the burden rate is $1.85 an hour ($7,400 in fixed costs divided by normal volume of 4,000 hours), and at this rate a *lost capacity variance* of $185 could be separated from the rest of the volume variance, thus bringing the total to four variances in all.

This fourth variance can be calculated in other ways, but it deserves little attention. It makes sense only if the department is operating at capacity and thus can increase production only if capacity utilization can be improved. In the absence of serious problems of capacity limitation, the two-variance or three-variance method should be completely adequate.

Recording Standard Overhead Costs

No matter what kind of standard costing system is in use, the overhead in process accounts do not serve as a vehicle for deriving departmental cost variances. This is the function of the overhead summary and overhead earned accounts.

For example, the entries to record the month's overhead charges to cost center X can be summarized as follows:

```
Overhead Summary—Cost Center X..............................12,060
     Accounts Payable, etc. ......................................    5,635
     Overhead Summaries—Service Departments....................    6,425
```

Let us assume that cost center X transfers all of its output to the finished goods stockroom and that the products completed by this cost center during the month had a standard overhead cost of $11,000. The transfer can be summarized in the following entry:

```
Finished Goods...............................................11,000
     Overhead in Process—Cost Center X.........................    11,000
```

Let us assume further that the standard overhead cost of the work in process in the cost center at the beginning of the month was $2,600. The department's accounts, after the posting of the previous entries, would appear as follows:

Overhead Summary—Cost Center X			Overhead in Process—Cost Center X			
Charges	12,060		Beg. bal.	2,600	Completions	11,000

No entry, in other words, has been made to reflect overhead cost absorption for the month.

At the end of the month, the inventory count indicates that the work in process in cost center X has a standard overhead cost of $1,800. *The amount of overhead earned during the month is the amount that must be debited to the overhead in process account to achieve this balance:*

Overhead in Process—Cost Center X..............................10,200
  Overhead Earned—Cost Center X............................. 10,200

The accounts now show:

Overhead Summary—Cost Center X			Overhead Earned—Cost Center X		
Charges	12,060			Earned	10,200

Overhead in Process—Cost Center X			
Beg. bal.	2,600	Completions	11,000
Earned	10,200		
	12,800		
End bal. 1,800			

The total overhead variance is now represented by the difference between the balances in the overhead summary and overhead earned accounts and can be analyzed by the methods described earlier. The temptation to debit overhead in process for the number of actual direct labor hours, multiplied by the burden rate ($3,500 \times \$3 = \$10,500$), should be avoided because it only complicates the bookkeeping and introduces a meaningless variance into the account.[3]

SUMMARY

The amounts of overhead assigned to product units through burden rates are usually cumulated in the factory accounts to produce depart-

---

[3] This variance is derived by multiplying the burden rate by the difference between actual hours and earned hours and is equal to the sum of the labor efficiency and lost capacity variances.

mental totals, known as *absorbed overhead* or, in standard costing systems, *earned overhead.* This total almost inevitably differs from the department's actual cost for the month, and this difference is known as the *total overhead variance.*

Part of the total variance is accounted for by differences between actual costs and the amounts shown as the department's flexible budget allowances for the month. These *spending variances* were discussed at some length in Chapter 13. The remainder of the total variance is the *volume* variance, due to deviations of actual from budgeted or normal volume.

A similar system of variance analysis is required by standard product costing, although some refinement of both spending and volume variances is possible. This same kind of treatment can also be afforded the undistributed cost balances of service departments that arise from the use of predetermined charges or predetermined transfer prices, but that analysis has not been repeated here.

DISCUSSION QUESTIONS

1. What factors would you want to consider in deciding whether to use machine-hours, labor hours, labor dollars, or some other volume index as the basis for overhead application?

2. "If large underabsorbed (or overabsorbed) overhead variances occur month after month, the burden rate should be revised to make unit costs more accurate." Comment.

3. In what sense is total standard direct labor cost a measure of production output?

4. To whom would the factory overhead spending variance be reported? How would it ordinarily be subdivided?

5. How is the factory overhead volume variance measured? Does it indicate the effect of volume deviations on total factory overhead costs? Their effect on company profit? What does it represent?

6. What is the meaning of the "labor efficiency variance" that is obtained when a three-variance method of overhead variance analysis is used? What information, if any, does it provide that is not also provided by the direct labor quantity variance?

7. Would subdividing the volume variance by cost element serve any useful purpose?

8. Under what circumstances would factory overhead volume variances arise in a costing system based on the variable costing principle?

9. When the burden rate is based on normal production volume and actual

volume is less than normal volume but greater than the volume for the period, would the factory overhead volume variance be classified as favorable or unfavorable?

10. Under what circumstances will service department cost allocations affect the size of a production department's overhead volume variance?

EXERCISES AND PROBLEMS

*1. The Tiger Corporation employs a flexible budget to provide information for use in the control of manufacturing overhead. For one of its departments the estimated monthly fixed overhead cost is $8,000 and the estimated variable overhead cost per dollar of direct labor cost is $1.20. The average monthly direct labor cost estimated for the year is $10,000.

During the month of August the department's output fell to $9,000 in direct labor cost and the manufacturing overhead was $21,700. Account for the manufacturing overhead, using T-accounts, and develop the relevant variances.

2. Returning from an industry trade show, the production manager of the Tinball Company complained to the plant controller that a friend of his in a competitive company had told him that factory burden rates in the competitor's factory were 50 percent lower than those in use in the Tinball Company. He said: "I know that plant. It is the same age and size as ours and has virtually identical equipment. Wage rates are about the same as ours, and they are running about the same percentage of capacity as we are. How can they be twice as efficient in controlling overhead costs as we are?" How would you answer the production manager? What factors other than efficiency might account for the difference?

3. A company uses a job order costing system with a predetermined burden rate based on normal volume. Overhead costs are budgeted at $10,000 a month plus $1 for each direct labor hour. Normal volume is 10,000 direct labor hours. Actual volume for August was 9,000 direct labor hours, and actual overhead cost totaled $20,700. Job No. 423 was started on August 6 and completed on August 20, with the expenditure of 400 direct labor hours.

a) How much overhead was charged to job No. 423?
b) How much overhead was charged to all jobs during August?
c) What was the total factory overhead variance for August?
d) Break this variance into two parts and explain what each part means.
e) Which of these two parts would probably be further subdivided or shown in greater detail? Indicate the nature of this subdivision.

*4. The burden rate is 200 percent of direct labor cost. A standard costing system is in use. The actual direct labor cost for the month of

---

* Solutions to problems marked with an asterisk (*) can be found in Appendix B.

January was $20,000. Labor in process, at standard, was $8,000 on January 1 and $5,000 on January 31. The standard labor cost of work completed during January was $22,000. Compute the earned overhead for the month.

*5. Overhead costs vary with actual direct labor hours according to the following formula:

$$\text{Overhead} = \$15,000 \text{ per month} + \$1 \text{ per direct labor hour.}$$

Normal volume is 12,000 direct labor hours a month. Actual overhead costs for December were $25,000. Earned or standard direct labor totaled 9,000 hours for the month, and actual direct labor amounted to 8,500 hours.

a) Compute the total overhead variance for the month.

b) Divide the total overhead variance into three parts and explain the meaning of each part.

6. The budget equation for a department is $48,000 a month plus $2 for each actual direct labor hour. During September actual direct labor cost was $39,000 (15,000 hours at $2.60 an hour). Actual overhead was $77,500. The output of the period had a standard cost of:

Labor: 15,500 hours at $2.50 an hour.....................$ 38,750
Overhead: 15,500 hours at $5.00 an hour....................   77,500
         Total..$116,250

Departmental variances are classified as controllable or noncontrollable, favorable or unfavorable. The controllable variances are then totaled, and if the total of the favorable controllable variances exceeds the total of the unfavorable controllable variances, the foreman is paid a bonus amounting to 5 percent of the difference (the "net favorable controllable variance"). If the net controllable variance is zero or unfavorable, the foreman receives no bonus. The foreman has no control over wage rates or volume, but in this problem you may assume that all of the overhead cost items in the department's budget equation are controllable. Materials costs are ignored in this problem.

Prepare a list of the variances you can compute from the above data; indicate for each whether it is controllable or noncontrollable, favorable or unfavorable; and compute the amount of the foreman's bonus, if any.

7. Given the following data, compute factory overhead variances by the three-variance method:

Actual factory overhead..........................$29,000
Standard overhead cost of goods finished............ 27,000
Standard overhead cost of goods in process:
    Beginning of month.......................... 5,000
    End of month..............................   8,000
Burden rate.....................................$3 per direct labor hour
Flexible budget.................................$15,000 + $1.50 per direct
                                                   labor hour
Actual direct labor hours......................... 9,500

8. The Armstrong Process Company manufactures several grades and varieties of product in a single processing operation. It has established standard costs of each of these products from the following information:

Product	Std. Yield per Cwt. Materials	Product Price per Lb.
Prime............................	10%	$0.30
Choice............................	20	0.24
Standard........................	50	0.22
Grounds.........................	10	0.08
Trimmings......................	8	0.05
Waste............................	2	...
Total.......................	100%	...

The standard price of the raw materials is $15 for 100 pounds (cwt.), and the standard processing cost is $2.12 per cwt. The flexible budget for processing costs is based on the formula: $4,800 a week + $1 per cwt.

During the week of November 12, 1,800 hundredweight of materials costing $26,820 were processed at a cost of $6,980. The actual product yield was:

Product	Yield (Cwt.)
Prime..	168
Choice...	370
Standard......................................	910
Grounds.......................................	180
Trimmings....................................	128
Waste..	44
Total......................................	1,800

a) Develop standard product costs for use in costing production.
b) Analyze the week's costs, developing any variances that you deem appropriate.

9. The ABC Company manufactures products in job lots with a standard cost accounting system. The burden rate in the assembly department is $2 per direct labor hour. During the month of March the assembly department was charged with 10,000 direct labor hours at a standard wage rate of $1.75 per hour. It was also charged with manufacturing overhead costs of $22,500. The standard direct labor hour content of products completed or added to work in process in the assembly department during March was 10,500 hours.

The manufacturing overhead budget for the assembly department can be computed from the following formula:

Budget = $9,600 + $1.20 × Standard direct labor hours earned.

a) Compute the normal monthly production volume for the assembly department in terms of standard direct labor hours.

b) Compute the total overhead cost variance for the month of March and analyze it by the two-variance method.

*10. A company has a standard variable costing system with a variable cost burden rate in department X of $1.60 a direct labor hour. Volume in this department seldom exceeds 13,000 direct labor hours or is less than 8,000 direct labor hours. The overhead cost budget for the department is:

Monthly Volume (Standard Direct Labor Hours)	Total Budgeted Overhead Cost
0 to 5,000	$5,000 + $1.60 per direct labor hour
5,001 to 10,000	$6,000 + $1.50 per direct labor hour
10,001 to 15,000	$7,000 + $1.50 per direct labor hour

a) Actual overhead cost totals $20,000, and actual volume is 9,000 standard direct labor hours. Compute and analyze the department's overhead cost variance for the month.

b) If the burden rate is to be used primarily in short-term decision making, should it be $1.60, $1.50, or some other figure?

11. A full costing system is in use, and the overhead budget equation is:

Overhead costs = $100,000 + $3 × Actual direct labor hours.

Other data are:

(1) Normal volume, 50,000 direct labor hours.
(2) Actual overhead cost, $225,000.
(3) Actual direct labor hours used, 40,000.
(4) Standard direct labor hours in actual output, 39,000.

a) Calculate the overhead variances. What managerial use, if any, would be made of each of the variances you have calculated (i.e., who is being evaluated and in what connection)?

b) Calculate the overhead variances that would be appropriate if the overhead budget equation were as follows:

Overhead costs = $100,000 + $3 × Standard direct labor hours.

12. The Siden Company uses a predetermined rate to charge operating departments for the costs incurred in the quality control department. The rate for a current year is 7 cents a standard direct labor dollar on the assumption that inspection and other quality control costs are a function of the complexity of the product, indicated by the standard amount of direct labor required. During March the total standard direct labor recorded in the company's production departments amounted to $270,000. During this month the quality control department reported the following costs and budget allowances:

	Allowance	Actual	(Over) Under
Inspectors......................	$13,600	$12,880	$720
Clerical......................	416	428	(12)
Overtime and shift premium..............	900	952	(52)
Gauges.......................	566	736	(170)
Tools and supplies.................	568	701	(133)
Maintenance.....................	712	742	(30)
Employee benefits.................	2,220	2,019	201
Other.......................	648	484	164
Total......................	$19,630	$18,942	$688

a) Prepare a journal entry to represent the charge to production departments.

b) Compute the total or net variance for the quality control department for March.

c) Prepare a brief summary to explain the sources of this variance.

*13. The Field Company uses standard costs in its manufacturing operations. You are given the following information for the grinding department:

Flexible budget:

Machine-Hours	Manufacturing Overhead Costs
8,000...	$20,000
10,000...	22,000
12,000...	24,000
14,000...	26,000

Standard burden rate = $2 per machine-hour.

Standard manufacturing overhead cost:
Product A..................1 machine-hour per unit = $2 per unit.
Product B..................1.5 machine-hours per unit = $3 per unit.

During April the department produced 4,000 units of product A and 4,000 units of product B. A total of 9,500 machine-hours was recorded during April, and actual manufacturing overhead costs totaled $21,750.

Compute manufacturing overhead variances for the month.

14. The Tinpot Company's factory has a job order costing system. It uses predetermined full cost burden rates and does not use standard product costs. It classifies its manufacturing overhead cost accounts into two categories: class A (wholly fixed), and class B (partly fixed and partly variable). The following data are available:

(1) Normal volume, 20,000 direct labor hours.
(2) Class A costs:
    (a) Budget at normal volume, $20,000.
    (b) Variable costs, none.
    (c) Actual costs for July, $21,100.
    (d) Volume variance for July, $1,400, favorable.

(3) Class B costs:
  (*a*) Budget at normal volume, $30,000.
  (*b*) Variable costs included in (*a*), $1.20 per direct labor hour.
  (*c*) Actual costs for July, $34,000.

a) What was the actual operating volume for July?

b) How much of the costs in each class was assigned to products during the month?

c) Prepare a variance summary for the month, in as much detail as you can derive.

*15. The Destry Corporation uses a full cost, "basic plan" standard costing system to account for its manufacturing costs. The following data relate to the month of June (all figures are in thousands):

Inventories, June 1 (at standard):
  Materials...$30
  Materials in process... 20
  Labor in process.. 10
  Overhead in process...................................... 15
Materials purchases ($25 at standard prices)..................... 23
Direct labor payroll ($34 at standard wage rates)................ 35
Manufacturing overhead....................................... 48
Goods completed (at standard):
  Materials.. 25
  Labor... 32
  Overhead.. 48
Inventories, June 30 (at standard):
  Materials.. 26
  Materials in process.. 19
  Labor in process.. 10
  Overhead in process....................................... 15

The standard burden rate is $1.50 per standard direct labor dollar. The manufacturing overhead cost budget is computed from the formula:

$$\text{Budget} = \$25{,}000 + \$0.50 \text{ per standard direct labor dollar.}$$

a) Enter the above data in appropriate T-accounts.

b) Prepare a variance summary for the month.

16. The T-accounts presented below have been taken from the ledger of a manufacturing company as of the close of the year. December 1 balances and transactions for the month of December have been recorded in these T-accounts, but the accounts have not yet been adjusted to the balances they will carry forward into the next year.

The December 1 balances shown in the inventory accounts represented the standard cost of the raw materials, work in process, and finished goods on hand on that date. Physical inventories were taken as of December 31, and after being priced at standard cost were found to be as follows (no adjustment for these physical inventories has been made in the ledger accounts):

Raw material...$27,690
Labor in process... 29,980
Material in process.. 24,905
Overhead in process....................................... 44,970
Finished goods... 33,540

Taking into account the physical inventories stated above, present your interpretation of each of the balances remaining in the accounts, and if part or all of the balance represents a manufacturing cost variance, indicate whether it is favorable or unfavorable.

Raw Materials			
Bal. Dec. 1	27,265	(3)	12,410
(2)	13,000		

Purchases			
(1)	14,250	(2)	13,000

Direct Labor			
(4)	16,470	(5)	15,250

Labor in Process			
Bal. Dec. 1	30,750	(8)	15,600
(5)	15,250		

Material in Process			
Bal. Dec. 1	25,620	(8)	13,000
(3)	12,410		

Overhead in Process			
Bal. Dec. 1	46,125	(8)	23,400
(7)	22,245		

Manufacturing Overhead Control			
(6)	21,235	(10)	21,490*

Manufacturing Overhead Applied			
(10)	21,490*	(7)	22,245

Finished Goods			
Bal. Dec. 1	37,625	(9)	56,020
(8)	52,000		

* Note: This amount budgeted for the month's production volume.

17. The Blue Ribbon Corporation uses "single plan" standard full costs in accounting for manufacturing costs in one of its plants.

   a) Record the following information in T-accounts for January, 19x1:

   (1) Inventories at standard, January 1, 19x1:
      Materials...$20,000
      Materials in process... 5,000
      Labor in process... 2,000
      Manufacturing overhead in process........................... 3,000
   (2) January materials purchases, $14,500 (total standard cost of items purchased, $14,800).
   (3) Materials requisitioned for production (at standard prices):
      On standard quantity requisitions...........................$12,000
      On supplemental requisitions................................ 1,000
   (4) Freight bill on January materials purchases, $800.
   (5) January direct labor payroll, $9,200 (5,000 actual hours; 5,200 standard hours; the standard labor rate is $1.80 an hour).
   (6) Factory overhead costs incurred or accrued during January, $14,000 (the standard burden rate is $1.50 a direct labor dollar).

(7) Work finished during January:

Standard material cost.......................................$11,000
Standard labor cost.. 9,540
Standard factory overhead cost............................... 14,310
$\qquad$
Total Standard Cost of Work Finished.....................$34,850

b) For the month of January, 19x1, compute, as accurately as you can, two materials variances, two labor variances, and as many overhead variances as you believe relevant. (Overhead budget allowances are computed from the formula:

Budget = $10,000 + $0.90 per standard direct labor hour.)

18. The assembly department of the Hyde Company uses a predetermined burden rate to absorb departmental overhead costs. The burden rate is $3 a direct labor hour. The wage rate for direct labor employees is $2.50 an hour. During the year a total of 20,000 direct labor hours were worked in the assembly department, and $62,000 was charged to the department's overhead account for indirect labor and material, redistributed service department costs, and so forth.

a) By how much was overhead over- or underabsorbed in assembly?

b) By how much would assembly overhead have been over- or underabsorbed if the following events had occurred, while everything else remained the same? (Treat each event as independent; that is, each answer should be based on the effect of each event taken separately.)

(1) An additional 200 hours of direct labor were worked on overtime in the assembly department at time and a half. The Hyde Company adds overtime premiums (that is, the overtime bonus paid in excess of the regular wage rate) to the overhead account of the department in which the overtime is worked.

(2) All direct labor employees received a wage increase of $0.10 an hour beginning in December. A total of 1,100 direct labor hours were worked in December.

(3) The price of food went up during the year, adding $1,000 to the deficit incurred by the employees' cafeteria. All losses from operating the cafeteria are distributed to the producing departments on the basis of their total number of employees. The assembly department has 14 employees out of a total of 100 in all of the plant's producing departments.

19. Inventory balances at the Mooseheart Company factory, all priced at standard cost, were as follows on March 1:

Materials.................................$1,500
Materials in process......................... 600
Labor in process............................ 200
Overhead in process......................... 180

The following transactions occurred during March:

(1) Materials received from vendors: actual price, $1,290; standard price, $1,200.

(2) Materials issued (at standard prices): direct materials, $1,150; indirect materials, $100.

(3) Summary of labor time tickets for the month (at standard wage rates): direct labor, $2,020; indirect labor, $340.

(4) Actual payroll for the month, $2,450 (includes overtime premium, $60, and apprentice pay, $15, to be charged to overhead—these latter two amounts are not included in the figures given in item (3)).

(5) Other overhead charges for the month, $1,300.

(6) Goods completed during March, and standard product costs:

Product	Units Completed	Standard Cost per Unit			
		Materials	Labor	Overhead	Total
X..........	100	$1.00	$2.00	$1.80	$4.80
Y..........	200	1.50	4.00	3.50	9.00
Z..........	300	3.00	2.50	2.00	7.50

(7) The month's flexible budget allowances for factory overhead can be calculated from the following formula:

Overhead costs = $1,000 + 0.4 × Standard direct labor cost.

(8) Standard costs of work in process on March 31:

Materials in process......................$500
Labor in process.......................... 400
Overhead in process...................... 350

a) Enter the opening inventory balances and record the transactions described in items (1) through (6) in appropriately titled T-accounts.

b) Compute aggregate variances for materials, labor, and overhead, and subdivide these in any way you deem appropriate. Indicate for each variance whether it is favorable or unfavorable.

20. The Schuyler Corporation uses a standard costing system in its factory. Statistical studies have shown that variation in overhead costs in department X is more closely correlated with direct labor input than with product output. The departmental burden rate is $2 per direct labor hour, and 15,000 direct labor hours were recorded during November. Additional data are:

	Budget		Actual, November
	Fixed per Month	Variable per Direct Labor Hour	
Supervision..................	$ 5,600	...	$ 5,900
Indirect labor...............	500	$0.60	10,200
Supplies.....................	...	0.25	3,400
Department S service.........	...	0.10	1,750
Building service.............	6,500	...	7,600
Total..................	$12,600	$0.95	$28,850

The standard overhead cost content of work in process was $8,000 on November 1 and $10,000 on November 30. The standard overhead cost content of the work completed and transferred out of the department during the month was $29,500. Production departments are charged for department S service at a rate of $5 per service hour. Production department managers have responsibility for controlling the amount of department S service used. Building service costs are allocated to production departments on the basis of floor space occupied. The actual costs of department S for November averaged $5.20 per service hour.

a) What is the normal volume of activity in department X?

b) What was the total direct labor hours earned by department X during November?

c) What was the effect on total departmental overhead cost of the variation from standard direct labor efficiency during November?

d) What was the overall departmental variance for November?

e) What is the meaning of the variance in "building service" costs for department X?

f) Prepare a brief summary of actual overhead costs and budget allowances for the month reflecting only those variances attributable in whole or in part to *overhead* cost control in department X. (I.e., exclude those variances due to variations from standard direct labor efficiency.)

21. The company has two products, with the following standard costs per unit and the following production for the month of March:

	Product A	Product B
Standard cost per unit:		
Materials.....................................	$ 1	$ 2
Labor...	4	3
Overhead.....................................	8	6
Total.....................................	$13	$11
Units in process (all materials applied, but only one half of labor operations performed and one half of overhead earned):		
Beginning of month.........................	1,000	3,000
End of month..............................	2,000	3,000
Units completed during month.................	4,000	5,000

Factory overhead costs are expected to vary with actual direct labor cost, according to the following formula:

Budgeted overhead per month = $60,000 + 0.50 × (Actual direct labor hours × Standard wage rates)

During the month of March the following costs were recorded:

(1) Materials purchased:
    Standard cost, $20,000.
    Actual cost, $21,200.

(2) Direct materials issued (at standard prices), $17,000.

(3) Direct labor payrolls, actual hours worked:
    At standard wage rates, $31,600.
    At actual wage rates, $34,000.

(4) Miscellaneous overhead costs, $75,000.

a) Prepare a list of variances for the month. Indicate for each whether it was favorable or unfavorable. Show your calculations.

b) Compute the standard cost of work in process at the end of the month.

*22. The Omega Desk Company manufactures one type of desk for office use. At a production of 50,000 direct labor hours, which is considered normal, the overhead costs are expected to be $20,000.

The standard costs for the desk are:

Material:
  30 square feet of lumber at $0.80........................... $24.00
Labor:
  10 hours at $1.75... 17.50
Overhead:
  10 hours at $0.40... 4.00
      Total Standard Cost................................... $45.50

The chief accountant has calculated a semivariable budget for overhead. This budget may be represented by the equation:

$$O.H. = \$8,000 + (\$2.40)\,(A.D.)$$

$O.H.$ = overhead, and $A.D.$ = all desks produced. The latter includes firsts, seconds, and equivalent complete units of work in process.

Some of the desks manufactured cannot be sold as firsts, and they are accounted for as follows. Work in Process is credited with the standard cost of firsts on all desks, but the offsetting debits for seconds are:

Finished Goods—Seconds.................... $35.00 per desk
Loss on Seconds............................ 10.50 per desk

The Loss on Seconds is an overhead account, and the overhead budget includes a standard allowance for this expense.

The transactions for the month of May are:

(1) Material purchased:

  200,000 square feet at $0.77..................... $154,000

(2) Material requisitioned: 180,000 square feet.
(3) Labor:

  53,500 hours at $1.80.......................... $96,300

(4) In addition to the loss on seconds the overhead costs are:

  Depreciation.................................. $ 1,000
  Power and light............................... 2,500
  Taxes.. 750
  Supplies..................................... 8,250
  Insurance.................................... 500
  Salaries..................................... 7,500
      Total................................... $20,500

(5) Production for the month was: 4,800 firsts, 300 seconds, and 600 units in process with all material applied and ⅔ completed with respect to labor and overhead. There was no beginning inventory of work in process.

a) Compute factory cost variances for the month.
b) Which of the above variances would be relevant to the executives responsible for cost control in the factory?

c) Prepare journal entries to represent the company's transactions for the month, including the entries necessary to adjust the work in process accounts to the correct month-end balances. A basic plan system is in use.

23. The Abel Company manufactures three products in two factory departments. Data relating to these products are:

	Product A	Product B	Product C
Standard cost per unit:			
Department I materials....................	$ 1	$ 2	$ 3
Department I labor (at $2 per hour).........	4	6	5
Department I overhead (at $4 per direct			
labor hour)............................	8	12	10
Inventory and production (units):			
Department I work in process, March 1	....	100	200
Completed and transferred to department II,			
March...............................	300	500	400
Department I work in process, March 31....	200	100	....

Work in process at both beginning and end of the month is complete as to materials and half-processed.

Other data for the month were:

Materials issued to department I (at standard prices)..................$ 2,000
Actual direct labor payroll, department I (3,400 direct labor hours)..... 7,100
Actual overhead... 17,000

Overhead costs vary with output rather than with input. At normal operating volume and with actual direct labor hours equal to standard direct labor hours, variable overhead totals $6,000 and fixed overhead amounts to $10,000. It is assumed that variable overhead varies in direct proportion to variations in output.

a) What is the normal operating volume of department I?
b) Prepare a list of variances for department I for the month of March. Be sure to label each variance clearly. Show your calculations.

24. The Poquette Corporation uses standard costing systems in all its plants. Departmental flexible budget allowances are computed monthly, based on standard direct labor hours earned in each department. Each department has three work in process accounts, one each for materials, labor, and overhead. Materials and labor are charged to their respective work in process accounts at standard prices and wage rates. Marketable or reusable scrap is credited to departmental materials in process accounts at standard prices. Factory overhead costs are accumulated in departmental overhead summary accounts, and at the end of the month a charge is made to overhead in process on the basis of standard direct labor hours earned for the month. Completed production is credited to the departmental work in process accounts as finished work is transferred out of the department.

The refining department of the Poquette Corporation's Minneapolis plant processes a certain raw material for use in a number of the company's products. The standard cost of a ton of the refined material is:

Raw materials:

3,400 pounds of concentrate at $0.05....................	$170	
500 pounds of processing chemical at $0.15..............	75	
Less: 1,800 pounds of recoverable residue at $0.02........	(36)	$209
Labor, 3.0 crew hours at $25 per crew hour.................		75
Overhead, 3.0 crew hours at $65 per crew hour.............		195
Total Standard Cost per Ton.........................		$479

The following data summarize the refining department's operations for the month of October:

Materials received in department:

Concentrate.......................................	665 tons
Processing chemical..............................	94 tons
Recoverable residue..............................	370 tons
Actual crew labor at standard wage rates.............$29,200	
Actual crew hours.................................	1,180 crew hours
Actual overhead cost..............................$79,200	
Refined materials completed........................	380 tons

Actual crew hours include 10 crew hours of unproductive time. Standard product cost includes no provision for this kind of unproductive time. The amount of work in process was unchanged during the month.

The number of labor crew hours varies with the number of tons of concentrate used, in the proportions reflected in the standard cost sheet. Overhead varies with the number of actual crew hours, and the flexible budget for the department can be computed from the following formula:

$$\text{Budget} = \$30,000 + \$33.75 \text{ per actual crew hour.}$$

Analyze all variances for the month in as much detail as you can. Use any method of analyzing and classifying the labor and overhead variances that seems appropriate.

25. The Arsene Corporation's factory is engaged in process production. Materials are issued from the storeroom to department 11, from which they are transferred to department 21 after processing. After passing through five more departments, the products are finished in department 47 and transferred to the finished goods stock room.

Costs are recorded in departmental accounts during the month. At the end of each month actual unit cost is computed for each department by process costing methods.

The company has just developed a set of standard costs for this factory but has not yet incorporated them into the accounts.

a) Cost reports are prepared monthly for the department foremen, using the form shown in Exhibit I. Certain information relating to department 47 operations for the month of February has already been entered on this form. Fill in the right-hand column of Exhibit I, using the following additional information (show all your calculations):

(1) Materials losses and shrinkage occur shortly after the start of processing. It is assumed that no further shrinkage will occur in any units in process at the end of any month.

(2) Work in process is complete as to materials, but processing is only half-completed.

Exhibit I

MONTHLY UNIT COST REPORT

DEPARTMENT   47   MONTH February

PHYSICAL:

Pounds in process, start of month........................3,000
Pounds placed in process................................8,240
Pounds in process, end of month.........................2,000
Pounds finished and transferred out.....................9,000
Pounds lost in process.................................. 240

COSTS:	Standard Cost per Pound	Actual Costs	
		Total	Per Pound
Materials:			
Placed in process..............	$1.00	$ 8,640	$
Lost units....................	0.05	...	
Subtotal, materials..........	$1.05	$ 8,640	$
Processing costs:			
Operators....................	$0.70	$ 6,120	$
Helpers.....................	0.15	1,700	
Supervision..................	0.10	935	
Other costs.................	0.30	3,145	
Subtotal, processing costs....	$1.25	$11,900	$
Total Costs....................	$2.30	$20,540	$

b) Prepare an analysis of the reasons for deviations of department 47 costs from standard, with the aid of the following additional information:

(1) All costs are assumed to be proportionately variable with equivalent production except supervision and "other costs." Supervision is budgeted at $1,000 per month; "other costs" are budgeted at $2,000 per month plus $0.10 per equivalent finished pound.

(2) Actual wage rates for operators and helpers during February were equal to standard wage rates.

(3) A minor explosion, resulting from carelessness of a machine operator in the department, caused damages that required immediate emergency repairs. This kept operators and helpers idle for one half day (February had 20 working days). The cost of the idle labor time was not segregated in the accounts. The labor required to repair the machine was performed by the maintenance department, and the cost of this labor has not been charged to department 47. The $200 cost of machine parts used to restore the machine to workable condition, however, was charged to department 47 and was included in "other costs" for February. This kind of damage is extremely rare and product standard costs and flexible budgets include no provision for the costs arising from such damage.

(4) One piece of department 47's equipment, with monthly depreciation of $180, became fully depreciated during the previous month (January). Depreciation charges are a component of "other costs."

(5) Normal production volume for a normal month is 10,000 equivalent finished pounds.

26. The factory of the King Supply Company is organized in four production departments and three service departments. The budget allowances for these departments for the current year, at normal volume, together with other pertinent data, are as follows:

Department	Floor Space	No. of Employees	Dept. 23 Man-Hours Used	Normal Volume per Month	Budgeted Direct Dept. Overhead
Production 11...	20%	80	600	10,000 direct labor hours	$30,000
Production 12...	25	120	900	15,000 direct labor hours	50,000
Production 13...	35	60	1,200	20,000 machine-hours	60,000
Production 14...	9	50	300	5,000 direct labor hours	20,000
Service 21.......	..	6	...	....	10,000
Service 22.......	8	24	...	....	19,000
Service 23.......	3	20	...	3,000 man-hours	15,000

Budgeted service department costs are distributed in sequence as follows:

Department	Basis
Service 21...........................	Floor space
Service 22...........................	Number of employees
Service 23...........................	Service 23 man-hours

a) Prepare a distribution sheet and allocate budgeted service department costs.

b) Compute production department burden rates on the basis of normal monthly volume for each production department, to the nearest tenth of a cent.

27. During April the following data were recorded in the factory of the King Supply Company (see problem 26):

Department	No. of Employees	Dept. 23 Man-Hours Used	Production Volume	Direct Dept. Overhead Cost
11............	75	500	9,000 direct labor hours	$29,000
12............	125	500	16,000 direct labor hours	55,000
13............	58	1,200	21,000 machine-hours	61,000
14............	60	300	6,500 direct labor hours	23,000
21............	6	...	....	8,000
22............	22	...	....	19,000
23............	16	...	2,500 man-hours	13,000

The flexible budgets for the four production departments include the following estimates, in addition to those given in problem 26:

	Dept. 11		Dept. 12		Dept. 13		Dept. 14	
Direct labor hours....	8,000	12,000	12,500	17,500	.....	.....	3,500	6,500
Machine-hours......	.....	.....	.....	.....	17,500	22,500	.....	.....
No. of employees....	68	92	105	135	55	65	38	62
Dept. 23 man-hours..	500	700	800	1,000	1,100	1,300	250	350
Direct overhead......	$27,000	$33,000	$45,000	$55,000	$55,000	$65,000	$17,000	$23,000

Within the volume ranges given in this table, variable overhead costs are expected to vary in proportion to volume.

The costs of service departments 21 and 22 are regarded as wholly fixed. The direct costs of service department 23 are 60 percent variable at normal volume.

Service department costs are distributed monthly on the following bases:

Service 21:   To all departments on basis of budgeted monthly cost/percent of floor space (from problem 26).

Service 22:   To all departments except service 21 on basis of budgeted rate per employee (from problem 26).

Service 23:   To production departments on basis of budgeted rate per man-hour (from problem 26).

a) Prepare an overhead cost distribution sheet for the month of April.

b) Compute the total overhead cost variance for the month for each of the four production departments and the total amount over- or under-distributed for each of the three service departments.

c) Compute flexible budget allowances for each department in as much detail as the data permit, and use these allowances to subdivide the variances derived in (b) into their component parts. Identify each variance as favorable or unfavorable, label it clearly, and comment briefly on each variance that you feel would not be at least partly controllable by the department head.

28. The Carpol Company's factory is organized into four departments: starting, finishing, general factory, and maintenance. The first two of these are production departments, using standard costs. The company manufactures two products, with standard product costs per unit as follows:

	Product A	Product B
Direct materials—starting..........	$ 1	$ 2
Direct labor—starting.............	2	2
Overhead—starting...............	3	3
Direct materials—finishing........	..	1
Direct labor—finishing............	3	6
Overhead—finishing..............	6	12
Total.......................	$15	$26

Materials price and wage rate variances are segregated at the time of acquisition and do not enter the departmental accounts. Products are transferred from the starting department to the finishing department and from the finishing department to finished inventory. The finishing department's materials in process account is charged for the standard cost of all semiprocessed products received from the starting department. No shipments were made from the factory's finished goods stock room during the month. August 1 account balances included materials, $40,000; and finished goods, $10,000. Additional data for the month of August were:

	Starting		Finishing	
	Product A	Product B	Product A	Product B
Units in process, Aug. 1......	0	1,000	200	0
Units completed.............	2,000	8,000	1,800	8,000
Units in process, Aug. 31.....	500	0	400	0

Units in process on any given date in any department are assumed to be 100 percent complete as to materials and 50 percent complete as to labor and overhead *in that department.*

The following transactions were recorded during the month of August:

(1) Purchased materials (standard cost, $54,000)..........................$53,200

(2) Issued materials from storeroom:

	To Starting	*To Finishing*
Direct materials...............................	$17,000	$ 7,800
Indirect materials.............................	2,000	14,500

(3) Accrued payroll liabilities for the entire month for all four departments (including indirect labor)....................................$127,000

(4) Direct labor:

	Starting	*Finishing*
Hours.......................................	10,000	17,000
Standard wage rate per hour........................	$2.00	$3.00

(5) Indirect labor (at standard wage rates):

Starting.........................	$14,000
Finishing.........................	26,000
General factory...................	20,000
Maintenance......................	5,000

(6) Other direct departmental charges:

Starting.........................	$ 5,000
Finishing.........................	60,000
General factory...................	10,000
Maintenance......................	3,000

(7) General factory department costs are charged to the other three departments at the following amounts per month:

Starting.........................	$ 8,000
Finishing.........................	16,000
Maintenance......................	1,000

(8) Maintenance department costs are distributed to the two production departments in proportion to their current consumption of maintenance services. During August maintenance employees worked 800 hours in the starting department and 1,200 hours in the finishing department.

a) Record the opening balances and the month's transactions in appropriate T-accounts. After all the month's transactions have been recorded, the account balances for inventories in process at the end of the month are to be adjusted to a standard cost basis.

b) Given only the above information, prepare a list of variances for the month, with titles that are sufficiently descriptive to identify clearly the nature of each variance.

c) Flexible budget cost allowances for the starting and maintenance departments are computed from the following formulas:

	Starting		Maintenance	
	Fixed per Month	Variable per Direct Labor Hour	Fixed per Month	Variable per Maintenance Labor Hour
Indirect labor..............	$ 6,000	$0.82	$1,240	$3.00
Indirect materials............	...	0.18	...	...
Other direct charges.........	3,000	0.25	1,000	0.20
General factory.............	8,000	...	1,000	...
Maintenance................	1,000	0.25	...	...
Total.................	$18,000	$1.50	$3,240	$3.20

Using this additional information, prepare a detailed breakdown of the overhead variances in each department. Identify, insofar as possible, the causes of each overhead variance that you have developed.

29. The Trim Company uses a basic plan system of standard costing, with all inventories of materials and parts carried at standard prices. The company's factory has two direct production departments, I and II. Direct labor is classified in three basic pay grades, with standard hourly wage rates of $3.00, $2.30, and $1.60, respectively. All payrolls and vendor accounts are paid by the head office; the factory ledger contains a Head Office Control account which is credited for the gross amount of payrolls and vendor invoices, as well as for the cost of any materials or services furnished the factory by the head office.

Overhead costs in both departments are expected to vary with the number of actual direct labor hours. The overhead cost budgets are:

(1) Indirect materials: department I, $0.30 per direct labor hour; department II, $0.35 per direct labor hour.

(2) Indirect labor: department I, $0.10 per direct labor hour; department II, $0.20 per direct labor hour.

(3) Overtime and holiday work premiums: department I, $0.25 for each direct labor hour in excess of 10,000 direct labor hours a month; department II, $0.25 for each direct labor hour in excess of 15,000 direct labor hours a month.

(4) Other overhead: department I, $17,500 per month + $0.60 per direct labor hour; department II, $29,750 per month + $0.40 per direct labor hour.

Normal volume is 12,000 direct labor hours in department I and 20,000 direct labor hours in department II. At these volumes, each department has a burden rate of $2.50 a direct labor hour, and standard product costs have been developed on this basis.

The company's records show the following data for the month of May:

(1) Factory account balances on May 1 (inventories in process are priced at standard):

Materials and Parts..............................	93,000
Materials in Process—Department I................	15,000
Labor in Process—Department I....................	13,000
Overhead in Process—Department I.................	15,000
Materials in Process—Department II...............	18,000
Labor in Process—Department II...................	14,000
Overhead in Process—Department II...............	12,000
Manufacturing Overhead Summary—Department I ..	xxx
Manufacturing Overhead Summary—Department II..	xxx
Manufacturing Overhead Absorbed—Department I ..	xxx
Manufacturing Overhead Absorbed—Department II..	xxx
Materials Price Variance..........................	xxx
Payroll Cost Summary............................	xxx
Variance Summary...............................	xxx
Head Office Control..............................	180,000

(2) Materials and parts received from vendors and issued to production during May:

Item	Received from Vendors			Direct Materials Issued (Units)	
	Units	Std. Price	Amt. Invoiced	Dept. I	Dept. II
Material A..........	1,000	$3.00	$ 3,120	1,400	.....
Material B..........	150,000	0.02	2,880	112,000	.....
Material C..........	10,000	0.40	4,610	8,200	.....
Material D..........	5,000	2.20	10,525	5,200	.....
Material E..........	40,000	0.50	19,680	......	45,000
Material F..........	6,000	1.00	6,350	......	10,000
Part No. 101........	1,500	0.75	1,215	2,100	.....
Part No. 102........	3,500	5.10	18,350	......	2,200
Part No. 103........	4,000	2.30	8,940	2,040	560

(3) Purchases of indirect materials and supplies: actual cost, $15,000; standard cost, $14,370.

(4) Indirect materials issued (at standard prices): to department I, $6,190; to department II, $7,040.

(5) Labor time tickets for the month:

Class	Dept. I Hours		Dept. II Hours	
	Direct	Indirect	Direct	Indirect
Grade 1 ($3.00).........	3,400	100	9,400	250
Grade 2 ($2.30).........	9,300	200	6,000	400
Grade 3 ($1.60).........	5,000	500	5,000	1,000

(6) Actual factory payrolls covering the period from May 1 to May 28 amounted to $101,290, including $2,610 for overtime premium in department I and $2,120 for overtime premium in department II. An additional $4,800 in wages had accrued between May 29 and May 31, including $2,400 premium for holiday work in department II.

(7) Actual manufacturing overhead for the month of May, in addition to items mentioned above, totaled $25,050 for department I and $40,020 for department II.

(8) Physical quantities of products completed:

Catalogue No.	Department I		Department II
	To Dept. II	To Finished Goods	To Finished Goods
216X............	1,000	...	1,100
218X............	....	500	....
222B............	3,000	...	2,800
222F............	1,500	...	1,600
260A............	500	...	400
314T............	....	...	500
406N............	200	...	200

(9) Standard unit costs of these products:

Catalogue No.	Department I Operations				Department II Operations			Total Standard
	Materials	Labor	Overhead	Subtotal	Materials	Labor	Overhead	Cost/Unit
216X..........	$5.50	$2.79	$3.00	$11.29	$7.60	$ 8.30	$10.00	$37.19
218X..........	9.20	8.60	9.25	27.05	...	....	....	27.05
222B..........	3.00	5.85	6.75	15.60	5.00	4.45	4.25	29.30
222F..........	4.55	6.45	7.25	18.25	8.00	14.35	11.25	51.85
260A..........	2.35	4.40	5.50	12.25	6.10	3.80	5.00	27.15
314T..........	...	...	...	....	9.40	16.65	18.75	44.80
406N..........	2.60	7.10	6.75	16.45	...	6.05	7.50	30.00

The standard costs of products completed in department I and transferred to department II are charged to Materials in Process—Department II. Products completed and transferred to finished goods inventory are charged to the Head Office Control account. All variances are closed out at the end of the month, first to the Variance Summary account and then to the Head Office Control account.

(10) Work in process inventories, at standard costs, on May 31:

Materials in process—Department I.................$14,500
Labor in process—Department I.................... 11,200
Overhead in process—Department I................. 10,800
Materials in process—Department II................ 19,400
Labor in process—Department II.................... 15,000
Overhead in process—Department II................ 16,000

a) Prepare the necessary journal entries to record the above transactions, *using only the accounts listed at the beginning of this problem.*

b) Post these entries to T-accounts and compute whatever variances you deem appropriate.

c) Prepare summary variance reports for the two department managers.

Chapter 16

CONTROL OF
NONMANUFACTURING COSTS:
REPETITIVE ACTIVITIES

COST CONTROL PROBLEMS are not restricted to the factory operations of manufacturing firms. Department stores, public accounting firms, and restaurants, to name just a few kinds of nonmanufacturing companies, all need to keep costs under control. The same is true of government agencies and private nonprofit institutions. Even in manufacturing firms, many departments perform nonmanufacturing functions, and their costs, too, need to be controlled. In fact, looking at the economy as a whole, manufacturing activities account for a minor fraction of total economic activity, so that nonmanufacturing costs are actually the more important focus of attention. The purpose of this chapter and the next is to examine the nature of some of the major kinds of nonmanufacturing costs and see what role accounting can play in the control of these costs.

CLASSIFICATION OF NONMANUFACTURING ACTIVITIES

The term nonmanufacturing activities covers a multitude of sins, from research and development through marketing and product distribution to finance, accounting, and administrative activities. The immediate task is to find some basis for classifying these activities that will provide a framework for a discussion of different cost control techniques. The following three-way scheme may provide the answer:

1. Repetitive service activities.
2. Diversified service activities.
3. Independent program activities.

This classification is based on the nature and measurability of the relationships between functional inputs (costs) and outputs (invoices prepared, orders taken, etc.).

Repetitive Service Activities

Repetitive service activities are a close counterpart of direct factory production operations. In this category can be classified all those activities or functions for which relatively homogeneous units of output or *work units* can be clearly identified. Examples include shipping, billing, warehousing, and payroll preparation.

The work load in a repetitive service activity is ordinarily almost entirely a function of factors outside the control of the activity manager—that is, the number of units of service performed depends strictly on the demands imposed by other activities. Because the tasks performed are relatively homogeneous, it is at least theoretically possible to establish standard relationships between output (number of work units) and input (in either physical units or costs).

Selection of work units is not always simple. The output of an activity often can be measured in many different ways, which means that the accountant or other analyst has to decide which unit of measure best suits his particular purpose. For example, in payroll preparation the work unit could be either the number of paychecks, the number of employees, or the number of payrolls drawn up each month. For control reporting, the best unit of measure is the one that correlates most closely with variations in the required inputs, and it is even conceivable that more than one work unit should be measured for some activities because different inputs have different variability patterns.

Diversified Service Activities

Diversified service activities are similar to repetitive service activities in that the services provided are determined largely by the requirements of other activities, but they differ in that the units of output are many, nonstandardized, and constantly changing. Examples include the duties of a good part of the executive force, office management, secretarial work, telephone switchboard operation, and similar tasks. Secretarial output could possibly be measured in terms of the number of telephone calls made, number of letters typed, number of visitors received, and so forth, but there is so little homogeneity within any one of these measures that they offer very little promise for standardization.

It may be apparent that diversified service activities have their counterparts in manufacturing, too. Factory supervision, production scheduling, and factory accounting all fall into this category. This suggests that the control techniques used in manufacturing can also be applied here, a point to which we shall return later.

Independent Program Activities

Independent program activities have few counterparts in manufacturing. Whereas the scope of the activities of the first two categories is determined in large measure by the actual or anticipated service demand, independent program activities in a sense are self-justifying. The reason is that independent program activities are defined as those that are undertaken to obtain results that are deemed desirable in themselves and not because they are required by other activities. For example, whereas invoice typing is made necessary by the shipment of goods, advertising campaigns and direct selling activities can only be justified by the desirability of the results achieved. In other words, output cannot be measured in terms of physical work units but must be measured more qualitatively in terms of the benefits derived from the work done.

Examples of independent program activities are research and development, advertising, and direct selling. Research and advertising typically consist of a number of semi-independent projects or programs moving along on separate time schedules, each with its own particular objective and generally with its own individual budget. Direct selling, on the other hand, might even be recognized as a separate category, on the grounds that it consists largely of repetitive, continuous activities rather than discontinuous projects. All three of these are alike, however, in that they are all characterized by an inverse relationship between cost and results—that is, the level of cost is justified by the qualitative desirability of the results of the expenditure rather than by a technological need to supply certain inputs to meet a service demand.

Broad versus Narrow Classification

Functions or activities can be classified either broadly or narrowly. A broad classification identifies an activity with a certain end-result or service and includes in the definition all of the inputs necessary to accomplish that end-result. A narrower classification scheme insists on homogeneity within the activity.

For example, repetitive service and independent program work, defined broadly, includes some supervision which is in itself a diversified service activity. Furthermore, many independent programs will require repetitive services—e.g., advertising departments ordinarily require a good deal of reproduction work and photo developing and printing. It is better to accept this dual classification, however, than to take the pedantic point of view that the sales manager's job is a diversified service activity and not a part of the independent program of direct selling. A place can be found for both kinds of distinctions.

CONTROL OF REPETITIVE SERVICE COSTS

The activities most closely analogous to direct production operations in the factory are the repetitive service activities. This suggests that similar techniques might be used in cost control: standard unit costs for direct service inputs and flexible budgets for indirect service inputs. Although some difficulties are encountered in applying this approach, it is worthwhile describing the method before finding fault with it.

Defining Activities or Functions

The first step is to identify the activities, tasks, or *functions* performed in each responsibility unit. Whenever possible, the lines of organizational responsibility should coincide with the performance of a given function so as to minimize the difficulty of associating costs with indexes of output. The typical repetitive service department must perform a series of related functions for economy in administration, however, and this requires a careful definition of the various tasks that are assigned to the unit. For example, a study of the operations of a billing and order processing department might reveal the following separate processes:

1. Order recording.
2. Credit reviewing.
3. Invoicing—headings.
4. Invoicing—line items.
5. Order file maintenance.
6. Correspondence.

Examination of a delivery department in one company identified four tasks: truck loading, bulk delivery, route delivery, and bulk unloading.

It may be apparent that this first step can be carried out in varying amounts of detail. For example, the function of invoice typing may be divided into two parts: (*a*) typing the customer's address and other general information; and (*b*) typing the individual invoice lines for the goods shipped. For most purposes, however, the provision of greater detail is subject to the laws of diminishing returns and increasing errors. It is easier to identify the cost of invoice typing than the costs of typing the separate parts of the invoice, and the added refinement may not be worthwhile anyway. The basic criterion should be homogeneity of the task, but it is usually neither possible nor necessary to attempt to apply this criterion rigidly.

Selecting the Work Units

Once the activity or function has been identified, the next step is to select an appropriate work unit. For the order processing department, the work units might be:

Task	*Work Unit*
Order recording	Total orders received
Credit reviewing	Charge orders received
Invoicing—headings	Invoices ⎱ or line items
Invoicing—line items	Line items ⎰
Order file maintenance	Total orders received
Correspondence	Letters written

The nature of the costs may be such that different work units might be appropriate for different expense elements. For example, in the truck delivery department:

Element	*Work Unit*
Loading labor	Total pounds loaded
Gas, oil, and maintenance	Miles
Bulk delivery labor	Miles
Route delivery labor	Deliveries
Bulk unloading labor	Deliveries

In each case it is recognized that the work unit is not entirely homogeneous—for example, bulk delivery labor costs will vary with traffic conditions as well as with miles traveled—but the unit selected is a fairly reliable index of the output requirement and is the best that can be obtained.

Developing Cost Standards: Direct Inputs

The next step is to develop standards for each cost element associated with each of the repetitive service functions. Four different approaches are worth mentioning:

1. Supervisors' approximation.
2. Engineered standards.
3. Recorded experience.
4. Sampling.

Supervisors' Approximation. Asking a supervisor to allocate the various elements of his department's costs among the functions performed is the fastest, cheapest, and probably least accurate method. It may be accurate enough for many purposes, however, and should not be rejected without weighing the costs of other methods and the degree of accuracy necessary.

Engineered Standards.   Engineered standards are at the other extreme and call for very careful and minute investigation of the input requirements for each function. The engineering method most commonly used today is some variant of the Methods Time Measurement (MTM) technique rather than the older stopwatch approach. Under this approach, the operations are first studied to identify the major tasks to be performed. Standard time allowances for each task are then obtained from commercially available tables.[1]

An effort of this sort is usually not justified except as a by-product of a program of work simplification and methods improvement. In other words, the added accuracy of the data derived from engineered standards is ordinarily insufficient by itself to justify the cost and disruption entailed in developing the standards.

Recorded Experience.   It is perhaps natural that some accountants and even some executives feel that the best way to find the cost of various functions is to take a page from the factory's book and set up a system of timecards, supplies requisitions, and perhaps even job orders. Since personnel and materials costs typically account for the lion's share of nonmanufacturing costs, this method could produce the most detailed and most accurate figures on functional costs obtainable from any source.

Leaving the question of accuracy aside for the moment, the analogy with factory operations is perhaps unjustified. Time tickets are used in the factory in job order production typically because the amounts per job order are relatively large and because the conditions of production make it relatively easy to identify certain costs with individual jobs. When these conditions are not met, job time tickets are not prepared. For example, effort is never made to assign the salaries of bookkeepers to individual job orders, nor is there much interest in keeping time tickets for work done on continuous assembly lines, even if the products being assembled are not entirely homogeneous. In other words, job costing is expensive and an alert management will avoid using it if it does not produce data worth their cost or if acceptable data can be obtained by less expensive means.

Furthermore, it is even possible that the accuracy produced by time-

---

[1] For a good illustration of this technique, see Thomas G. Eshelman, "How Hanes Hosiery Uses Clerical Work Measurement," *Management Services,* March–April, 1966, pp. 37–43.

cards and the like is spurious, particularly with respect to salary and wage costs. Unless each task represents a relatively large commitment of resources, the personnel engaged in carrying out the function may find it extremely difficult to identify the time spent. For example, how can a secretary be expected to keep an accurate record of her time spent answering telephones, typing letters, filing, and so forth?

Sampling. The fourth approach relies on performance observations, too, but obtains these observations by sampling rather than by complete enumeration. One form of sampling is to collect funnctional cost data during a test period and then set standards on the basis of the period averages. This approach is applicable only if inputs can be identified with individual activities as they are used.

Another sampling method with more general applicability is called *work sampling.* Space does not permit more than a mention of this technique, but its immediate objective is to provide a reliable estimate of the amount of time spent in various types of productive and nonproductive activities. The method consists largely of recording what people are doing at particular instants of time, selected at random, during some longer time period. For example, the sampling plan may require the recording of the activities being performed by each clerk in the office at 9:12, 10:34, etc. From a set of, say, 30 such samples taken at various times during a week a percentage time distribution can be obtained, and from this the estimated times to perform the various repetitive service activities can be derived.

The work sampling and engineering methods of deriving cost standards are applicable primarily or exclusively to labor costs. Work sampling has both the advantage and the disadvantage of indicating what the costs are rather than what they should be. The disadvantage in this approach is that it gives management little assurance that its costs are reasonable. The advantage is that it provides management with information as to what its money is buying. Furthermore, these studies can indicate trends in functional cost if they are carried out periodically. On the basis of this information, methods improvement and cost reduction programs can be directed at the most crucial activities.

Unit Cost Standards and Flexible Budgets

As in manufacturing, the relevance of unit cost standards to cost control depends on the reliability of the assumption that total cost varies proportionally with variations in the number of work units. If this assumption is seriously in error, then flexible budgets should be used instead.

The short-run cost structures of nonmanufacturing activities in general are characterized by high proportions of fixed costs. Office employees are paid fixed salaries each period, regardless of the work load, subject to occasional overtime payments for extra work. Equipment rentals, depreciation, and space charges are also largely fixed. On this basis it could be argued that unit cost standards should be developed for almost no input elements.

This is too narrow a view. Unit standards should be developed for any input that is reasonably divisible, so that given some time to adjust capacity to the work load, the costs could become variable. This is particularly true of wage and salary costs, which ordinarily represent the lion's share of repetitive service costs. Just as in the factory, the *assumption* of variability serves to identify departures from linearity in the short run. Thus if work loads are running light, average cost will be high and comparisons with unit cost standards will give management the opportunity to review its staffing requirements.

Unit cost standards also serve as a basis for advance planning and decision making when substantial changes in volume are contemplated. It should be repeated, however, that these standard unit costs should be restricted to cost elements that are directly related to the number of work units. Inclusion of an arbitrary allocation of common costs or a unitization of indivisible fixed costs weakens the standard as an indicator of expected or desired cost performance. In other words, aggregate budget allowances rather than standard unit costs should be used for the indirect costs of repetitive service activities.

An illustrative flexible budget for a service department, in this case a warehouse, is shown in Exhibit 16–1. A single work unit has been selected for all of the department's activities, and this is the total number of pallet loads received in and shipped by the warehouse during a period. Budgeted fixed costs per week and average variable costs per load have been derived from a study of the relationships between the various cost elements and the number of loads handled, or "warehouse units."

Recording Actual Costs

The next step is to prepare a chart of accounts for each department or cost center. To permit the isolation of variances for each activity, the chart of accounts would have to provide for separate accumulation of actual cost data for each activity performed within the cost center. The warehouse referred to in Exhibit 16–1 presents no such problems because the department engages in only one activity, but this is not always the case. For example, the same man may perform both the delivery and the unloading functions, and it is extremely difficult to obtain reliable information on how he splits his time between these two activities.

Fortunately, classification of actual cost data by function is not essential. The departmental budget allowance is a composite allowance, reflecting the *total* volume of departmental activity. When more than

Exhibit 16–1

SERVICE DEPARTMENT FLEXIBLE BUDGET

FLEXIBLE BUDGET ALLOWANCES

DEPT. Warehouse   YEAR 1967

Item	Budget Allowances		Normal Budget (10,000 Units per Week)
	Fixed (per Week)	Variable (per Unit)	
Supervision	$122	.....	$ 122
Labor	246	$0.180	2,046
Clerical	55	0.003	85
Overtime	..	0.011	110
Warehouse supplies	..	0.086	860
Office supplies	32	0.002	52
Maintenance	87	0.010	187
Employee benefits	43	0.020	243
Other	52	0.001	62
Total	$637	$0.313	$3,767

one activity is performed, this total represents the actual number of work units performed for each activity. Thus if total costs can be accumulated departmentally, they can be compared with departmental standards. To illustrate, if the cost rates are 25 cents per mile and $1 per delivery and the bulk trucks logged 8,000 miles and made 4,000 deliveries during the month, the budget allowance is:

```
Bulk delivery labor, 8,000 × $0.25................$2,000
Bulk unloading labor, 4,000 × $1.................  4,000
    Total Budget Allowance......................$6,000
```

It should be noted here that some authorities favor routine periodic allocations of historical costs to individual activities. Longman and Schiff, for example, in the leading work in this field, cite six reasons for deriving historical cost data for individual activities:

1. They show, for each activity of the business, total expense and the natural expense components of the total.
2. They show which functions and which items of expense for each function account for the significant changes in total expense from period to period.
3. They contribute materially to the task of tracing factors responsible for changes in expense.
4. They make it possible to pin responsibility for cost performance to specific individuals.
5. They permit development and use of standard costs and comparison of actual costs with standard.
6. They provide the foundation for effective appraisal of marketing policies and for cost analysis by product, customer, and unit of sale.[2]

These are worthwhile objectives, but as always the question is whether the value of the information is worth its costs. This is a question that must always be decided on its merits in each particular circumstance; it may very well be that these objectives can be served adequately by subjecting the major elements of cost to some kind of periodic sampling, ignoring relatively minor items entirely.

Reporting Cost Variances

Control reports for repetitive service activities are much the same as for manufacturing activities. Budget allowances for each reporting period are derived from the predetermined flexible budgets and standard unit costs on the basis of the recorded number of work units. Comparison of actual functional costs with these allowances serves to locate the source of major variances and indicate where further investigation of underlying causes is desirable. When two or more functions are combined in one administrative unit, these comparisons may well be in summary form for the department as a whole, particularly if separate identification of the actual costs of each task or function is impractical. An example of a report of this kind is shown in Exhibit 16–2.

Some companies provide variance information in much greater detail. The system that was cited earlier in this chapter, for example, reports efficiency percentages weekly for each member of the clerical staff engaged in repetitive service operations.[3] All that is necessary to achieve this is to keep records of output (earned standard hours) for each employee. This ordinarily will not be a costly operation, but if these detailed reports are not used regularly it is ordinarily better not to

---

[2] Donald R. Longman and Michael Schiff, *Practical Distribution Cost Analysis* (Homewood, Ill.: Richard D. Irwin, Inc., 1955), p. 125.

[3] Eshelman, *op. cit.*, pp. 41–43.

Exhibit 16–2

SERVICE DEPARTMENT COST REPORT

	DEPARTMENTAL EXPENSE SUMMARY					
DEPT. Warehouse				MONTH AND YEAR March, 1967		
OPERATING VOLUME 36,000 Units				NO. WEEKS 4		

Item	This Month			Year to Date	
	Budget	Actual	(Over) Under	Actual	(Over) Under
Supervision	$ 488	$ 488	. . .	$ 1,680	$(94)
Labor	7,464	7,602	$(138)	26,704	(808)
Clerical	328	310	18	1,115	(22)
Overtime	396	256	140	1,250	136
Warehouse supplies	3,096	2,745	351	9,525	1,311
Office supplies	200	243	(43)	702	(34)
Maintenance	708	815	(107)	2,167	(176)
Employee benefits	892	880	12	3,045	34
Other	244	212	32	840	(38)
Total	$13,816	$13,551	$ 265	$47,428	$ 309

distribute them, so as to avoid deflecting management's attention from the more important aggregate indicators.

From this discussion it should be apparent that the process of budgeting the costs of repetitive service activities is different in no fundamental way from the budgeting of manufacturing costs. In fact many manufacturing departments, such as maintenance and quality control, have the same characteristics as repetitive service departments in the administrative and selling organization. The major difficulties lie in the identification of the appropriate work units and in the relative importance of fixed and variable costs. Because so many of the costs of nonmanufacturing activities are fixed over fairly wide ranges of work volume, the major emphasis must be on cost reduction rather than cost control. That is, long-run cost control is provided primarily by efforts to improve work methods and eliminate unnecessary operations.

Control through Competitive Comparisons

Before leaving the subject of repetitive service activities, some mention should be made of a different kind of control comparison: a comparison of the cost of an activity with performance achieved elsewhere.

One version of this method is the technique of comparing costs of performing similar functions at different locations. This technique has proven more useful in dealing with repetitive service costs of nonmanu-facturing activities than in setting manufacturing cost standards because operations at different locations are often more nearly comparable in the former case. Nevertheless, differences in service volume and in loca-tional factors must be taken into consideration when this technique is applied.

A second possibility is to use market standards, derived from data generated outside the firm. Most companies perform some services that could easily be purchased from outsiders. Typical examples include company print shops, photo services, cafeterias, and power plants, al-though the last of these is more typically regarded as a manufacturing activity. These activities are characterized by readily identifiable service units for which market prices can be estimated with a high degree of reliability. For this reason, the cost of equivalent services performed by outsiders may be useful as an overall bench mark for evaluating the desirability of providing the service internally. For example, the com-pany may own the building in which its offices are located. The rental value of comparable floor space in the same locality is $3.50 per square foot. Multiplying this figure by the number of rentable square feet provides an aggregate standard against which to compare the costs of owning, maintaining, and operating the building, including provisions for interest on invested capital.

Standards of this type do not provide a basis for the control of specific items of cost, but they do indicate overall objectives and meas-ures of effectiveness. Occasionally, they may be useful as summary guidelines for activities that do not fall strictly within the market-substitute category. Almost anything can be hired from the outside, even though the market substitute may not be a realistic alternative for a particular company. For example, service bureaus provide data pro-cessing facilities for companies that either are too small to maintain similar facilities of their own or are unwilling to keep the quantities of equipment necessary to handle peak loads. The prices charged by these service bureaus may in some cases provide a relevant standard for appraising the company's own data processing activities. Firms with substantial data processing requirements, however, can fulfill their nor-mal data processing needs more economically with their own facilities, and service bureau prices are not a reliable cost standard in these cases, although they may provide useful upper limits. Cost standards of this sort typically must be supplemented by others that are more specifically related to the company's own operations.

CONTROL OF DIVERSIFIED SERVICE COSTS

The second category of nonmanufacturing costs is the cost of diversified service activities, also referred to as the cost of administration. Costs of this type may be found in departments classified as repetitive service or independent program departments, as well as in purely administrative departments. They are common inside the factory as well as outside it.

The greatest percentage of diversified service costs is typically represented by salary payrolls, and most such costs are fixed over fairly wide ranges of volume. Variations from fixed budget allowances are unlikely to be significant, except perhaps in such items as travel expense and telephone charges, so that the major instrument of cost control is the preparation of the budget allowances rather than the enforcement of these allowances.

There is little to be gained by any extensive discussion of the procedures for budgeting administrative costs. Most of these costs are of a continuing nature and do not change materially from year to year, except insofar as new procedures are introduced or factor prices change. Department heads prepare estimates of their requirements, generally on the basis of the experience of the most recent period, adjusted for changes in salary rates and the prices of purchased services. Many companies also follow the practice of asking department heads to budget reductions from the costs of the preceding period, so as to offset the increases that result from inflationary forces. Budgetary control reports then serve to indicate any deviations from the planned level of these costs.

The search for means of reducing diversified service costs is not a periodic responsibility, however. Although the annual budget review may provide the stimulus, possibilities for cost reduction should be explored whenever they arise. This is equally true of repetitive service activities, of course, and the dividing line between the two types of activities is often quite narrow. The major problem posed by diversified service costs in this regard is that it is extremely difficult to associate them with specific work units. Cost reduction requires the definition of the function or task performed and an examination to see whether this task can be either eliminated or accomplished at less cost. Because the major element of diversified service costs is the cost of personnel, these efforts are customarily concentrated on job evaluation. Administrative payrolls, if unchecked, have a tendency to grow. Comparisons with previous years are more useful in budgeting this kind of cost than in any other portion of the budget, although even here the consequences of corporate growth tend to reduce the significance of interperiod comparisons.

SUMMARY

Cost control techniques in nonmanufacturing activities are typically much more primitive than those used in the factory. Industrial standards were born in the factory and so was cost accounting, and movement into other areas has been slow.

This may be due to a number of factors, such as the desire of white-collar workers to keep a separate identification from blue-collar workers, the diversity and nonstandardized nature of the output of most nonmanufacturing activities, the commonness of a large proportion of nonmanufacturing cost, and in some cases the reverse causal relationship between output and cost.

This chapter has recognized three separate categories of nonmanufacturing activities—repetitive service, diversified service, and independent program activities—and has discussed the cost control problems of the first two. These two classes of activities are closely analogous to manufacturing activities in that the costs are incurred as a functional response to an externally imposed service demand. Unit cost standards, flexible budgets, and departmental cost reporting techniques can be useful for these activities if the costs are substantial enough to warrant the effort.

The remaining category of activities—independent programs—is a very different matter and requires different approaches. For this reason it will be discussed separately in Chapter 17.

DISCUSSION QUESTIONS

1. Distinguish between repetitive service activities and diversified service activities.

2. What is a "work unit"? For what kinds of nonmanufacturing activities or functions is it both feasible and important to identify work units?

3. Suggest a work unit for each of the following departments and indicate whether you believe that a standard cost for that work unit can be a useful control device:

a) Mail room.
b) Collection department.
c) Credit department.
d) Cashier.
e) Payroll department.

f) Billing department.
g) Purchasing department.
h) Accounts payable department.
i) Legal department.
j) Warehouse.

4. Assuming that an administrative department is multifunctional but that unit standard costs have been developed for each of the functions, is it necessary to record actual departmental costs, function by function, or can costs be recorded by department only, without a functional breakdown? Give your reasons.

5. What is a "market standard"? For what kinds of activities is a market standard likely to be valid? Do market standards need to be supplemented by internal standards? Why or why not?

6. How can employee time distributions obtained by sampling be more accurate than time distributions obtained from complete time records?

7. What purpose, if any, is served by labor time standards in nonmanufacturing activities if all nonmanufacturing employees are on salary?

8. Repetitive service activities have been described as highly similar to factory production activities, yet the application of cost accounting techniques to nonfactory repetitive service activities has lagged far behind their application in the factory. To what do you attribute this lag?

9. To what extent do you feel that flexible budgets are likely to be useful in controlling the costs of office operations?

10. What is the primary means of controlling the costs of diversified service activities?

EXERCISES AND PROBLEMS

1. A warehouse contains 600,000 cubic feet of usable storage space. The normal expectation is that the warehouse will be 80 percent full. Each of the company's products is assigned a specific portion of the warehouse, but this allocation of space can be and often is revised on short notice. The various products differ in weight, in size of container, and in the ratio of pieces handled to pieces in inventory. For a very fast-moving product, for example, the number of pieces handled during a month might be twice the number of pieces in inventory; the ratio for a slow-moving product, on the other hand, might be only 1 to 10. The warehouse costs consist largely of building depreciation, handling equipment depreciation, supervision, insurance, taxes, and handling crew labor.

Outline a procedure whereby the costs of the warehousing operation can be distributed to the various product lines handled. Be prepared to defend your procedure.

*2. The standard cost of the billing operation of the Mannerborn Company is

---

* Solutions to problems marked with an asterisk (*) can be found in Appendix B.

13 cents per invoice line. The billing department's budget is computed from the formula:

$$\text{Budget} = \$1,200 \text{ per month} + \$0.10 \text{ per invoice line.}$$

During April a total of 33,000 invoice lines were prepared at a total cost of $5,000.

a) Analyze the departmental variances for the month.

b) Most of the variable costs in the department represent the salaries of billing clerks. The number of employees is adjusted upward or downward only if a substantial change in the volume of billings is anticipated. Comment on the meaning of the variances derived in (a) above.

*3. The management of the Manley Joyce Company has asked one of the company's accountants to prepare estimates of the cost of processing orders for small quantities of the company's merchandise. The accountant prepared the following estimates of the average cost of order processing per order:

Credit investigation	$0.03
Warehousing	0.16
Shipping	0.25
Billing	0.46
Accounts receivable department	0.15
Cashier	0.18
Total per Order	$1.50

Most of the company's products are priced at a markup of 40 percent over standard manufacturing cost.

a) Using $1.50 as the cost of processing an order, what is the smallest order that the company should accept?

b) To what extent do you believe the above cost estimates provide an adequate basis for deciding on minimum order quanities?

4. The Montgomery Company sells its products in three territories. Management has established the following standard administration expenses to be used in preparing profit and loss statements for each territory:

Credit	$ 5.00 per new account
Collection	10.00 per overdue account
Bookkeeping	0.35 per transaction
Stenographic	0.60 per letter
Other clerical	1.00 per customer account
Executive salaries	0.03 per sales dollar
Other administrative expense	0.02 per sales dollar

The following data were recorded for the month of October:

	Territory A	Territory B	Territory C
New accounts	80	140	100
Overdue accounts	50	60	60
Transactions	10,000	18,000	16,000
Letters	400	500	600
Customer accounts	500	1,000	800
Sales	$200,000	$300,000	$250,000

a) Compute the amount of head office administration cost per dollar of sales in each territory for the month of October.

b) Comment on the usefulness of the comparison of these costs among territories.

5. The Angel Meat Company has studied its selling and administrative expenses to determine the costs attributable to different segments of the company's business. It has found that some of these expenses are fixed, but the bulk of the expenses can be related to one of the following three indicators of sales volume: (1) number of orders, (2) number of items, and (3) number of hundredweight. Classification of expenses on these bases yields the following totals:

| | Fixed per Month | Variable Related to— | | | Total |
		No. of Orders	No. of Items	No. of Cwt.	
Selling expenses............	$20,000	$46,200	$21,600	$ 4,200	$ 92,000
Packing expenses..........	1,000	1,200	1,400	2,400	6,000
Delivery expenses.........	3,000	4,000	5,000	10,000	22,000
Administrative expenses...	15,000	23,400	11,600	6,800	56,800
Total.................	$39,000	$74,800	$39,600	$23,400	$176,800

Analysis of orders received during the analysis period shows the following data:

Size of Order	No. of Orders	No. of Items	Total Cwt.
Less than 50 lbs..........	56,000	81,800	14,000
50–199 lbs..............	58,000	168,200	52,200
200–499 lbs.............	12,000	45,600	37,200
500–999 lbs.............	8,000	48,000	56,000
1,000 lbs. and over........	2,000	16,400	20,600
All Orders...........	136,000	360,000	180,000

Compute the cost per hundredweight for each order size, to the nearest hundredth of a cent. Defend your method of dealing with fixed costs.

6. A company charges the managers of its three product divisions for head office services, using the following charging rates:

Department	Rate
Credit department....................$	0.30 per order
Billing department.....................	0.95 per order
Payroll department....................	2.50 per employee
Accounts receivable department...........	0.40 per order
General accounting department...........	0.30 per entry
Treasurer......................	0.35 per customer remittance
General sales manager..................	2,000.00 per month to each product division
Legal department....................	3,000.00 per month to each product division
Executive management.................	10,000.00 per month to each product division

Statistics for the month of February were as follows:

No. of orders received. 3,900
No. of employees. 860
No. of entries. 9,300
No. of customer remittances. 4,600

Head office expenses and flexible budget allowances for February were:

Department	Actual	Budget
Credit.	$ 1,350	$ 1,400
Billing.	4,150	4,000
Payroll.	2,400	2,200
Accounts receivable.	1,730	1,800
General accounting.	2,910	2,850
Treasurer.	1,680	1,700
General sales manager.	5,630	6,000
Legal.	6,200	9,000
Executive management.	30,400	30,000

Compute and analyze the month's variances for each head office department.

7. A company recently carried out a work sampling study of the operations of its mimeograph room. The observations showed the following percentage distribution of employees' time:

Operating mimeograph machine. 20%
Operating copying machine. 29
Out of room. 10
Telephoning. 5
Writing. 2
Collating. 25
Waiting. 6
Wrapping. 3

During the observation period the wages of mimeograph room employees totaled $2,100. The work load during this same period was:

Mimeo work orders. 5,000
Mimeo stencils processed. 25,000
Mimeo copies made. 500,000
Work orders, copying work. 20,000
Copies made on copying machine. 58,000

Most writing and telephoning is concerned with the status of individual work orders. Although some collating and wrapping is necessary on copying work, almost all of these activities are on mimeograph work.

Compute standard labor costs for mimeographing and copying work, and be prepared to explain and justify each step in your process.

8. The Garver Company has developed standards for its most important clerical operations. The first step was to identify the most important tasks for which standards could be developed, as shown in Exhibit 1.

Assuming that performance was at approximately the same level of efficiency in each of the departments listed, the analysis indicates the relative

Exhibit 1

ANALYSIS OF DEPARTMENTS CONSIDERED FOR MEASUREMENT

Department	Personnel			Total Measurable Hours	Expected Coverage		Equivalent Measurable Employees
	Total	Staff	Measurable		%	Measurable Hours	
Payroll..............	18	2	16	640	74	472.5	11.8
Accounts payable......	12	1	11	440	75	328.5	8.2
Accounts receivable.....	14.4	1	13.4	535	76	409	10.2
Tabulating process......	24	5	19	760	65	497	12.5
Tabulating keypunch....	12	1	11	440	85	374	9.4
Order.................	23	3	20	800	80	641	16.0
Billing...............	27	2	25	1,000	83	830	20.8
Contracts.............	6	1	5	200	76	153	3.8
Mail and file..........	14.5	1	13.5	540	78	420	10.5
Stenographic pool.......	5	1	4	160	80	128	3.2
Total.............	155.9	18	137.9	5,515	77	4,253	106.4

possibilities for savings in each department and the overall possibility for the entire organization. On the further assumption that performance was at 60 percent of normal and that through application of standards it could be raised to 100 percent, the work performed by the indicated 106.4 measurable employees could be handled by approximately 64 employees operating at 100 percent efficiency.

The next step was to set standards. Some of the these standards were set by having employees record time distributions. Others were established by time study, described by one company official as follows:

"In making the time study, the analyst attempts to select clerks or operators who are performing in his opinion at a pace near normal or 100 percent. The operation performed is broken down into measurable units of work called 'elements.' Using a stopwatch, the analyst records in hundredths of a minute the exact time taken to complete each element. He then applies a leveling factor (performance rating), and by the process of averaging or selection, he scales all readings to a normal time. After arriving at a 'norm,' he adds an allowance to compensate for rest periods, fatigue, and delays, to arrive at the final standard time for performing the operation.

"One of the most important considerations in establishing the standard is the application of the leveling factor to the unit times in arriving at normal times. This implies that the standards analyst has a predetermined concept of a normal pace and that all actual times, as indicated by studies, are adjusted to the same concept of normal. Although the ability to level is based on judgment, analysts are carefully trained in leveling, or performance rating, to insure that all standards are based on a consistent and reasonable concept of normal."

Exhibit 2

DAILY TIME AND PRODUCTION REPORT

Time		Elapsed Time		Standard Production		Std. Hrs. per Unit	Std. Hrs. Earned
Start	Stop	Other	On Standard	Code	Quantity		
8:00	9:30		1:50	1	600	0.0022	1.32
9:30	12:00		2:50	3	250	0.0100	2.50
1:00	2:00		1:00	5	100	0.0150	1.50
2:00	5:00	3:00		Machine down			
Total		3:00	5:00			Total	5.32

DATE WORKED: 11/9	EMPLOYEE: John Clark	DATE: 11/10	EFFICIENCY % 106.4

The third step was to record actual times and outputs. Since the inception of the program, employees have been recording the elapsed time on each task on forms such as the one shown in Exhibit 2. The code number indicates the task performed, and the unit output is multiplied by the standard time allowance for this task to obtain the totals shown in the right-hand column of Exhibit 2.

The relationship of earned hours to hours on standard indicates the efficiency for the day, in this case 106.4 percent. By summarizing the results of all of the individuals in an organizational unit, a performance report for the entire unit may be prepared. Exhibit 3 is a fairly typical example of a performance report for a department.

Hours worked by measured employees are broken down into lost time, unmeasured hours, and hours on standard. Lost time hours are those hours lost from a productive standpoint due to machine failure, lack of work, illness and other reasons. Unmeasured hours are hours spent in performing jobs for which standards were not established. Hours on standard are the hours spent in performing operations for which standards are established.

The relationship between hours earned and hours on standard is indicated by the percentage of efficiency. The utilization percentage indicates this same relationship reduced by the effect of the lost-time hours.

a) Comment on the method described above for deriving unit time standards.

b) Comment on the strengths and weaknesses of the reporting system, as summarized above. If you are able to identify any weaknesses, try to suggest ways in which the performance reports could be developed more efficiently or presented more effectively.

(Condensed and adapted from an article by Thomas C. Pitney in the *N.A.(C.)A. Bulletin*)

Exhibit 3

MANAGEMENT ANALYSIS REPORT—ACCOUNTS PAYABLE DEPARTMENT

	Period								
Week ended.........	11/15	11/22	11/29	12/6	12/13	12/20	12/27	1/3	1/10
Number of Employees									
Staff (not measured).	8	9	9	7	7	7	7	7	7
Measured...........	29	26	26	26	25	25	24	24	23
Total..............	37	35	35	33	32	32	31	31	30
Hours Worked (Measured Employees)									
Lost time hours.....	20	10	40	35	30	35	30	40	60
Unmeasured hours...	40	30	20	15	10	15	10	10	10
Hours on standard...	1,100	1,000	980	990	960	950	920	910	850
Standard Hours Produced									
Hours earned........	846	863	871	830	853	847	862	840	848
Measurement Results									
% Efficiency........	77	86	89	84	89	89	94	92	100
% Utilization.......	76	85	85	81	86	86	91	88	93

9. A large distributor of phonograph records and tapes recently established a standard costing system for its warehousing operation. A single large warehouse is used, storing about three million product units and receiving and shipping approximately one million units a month.

Separate standards were developed for the three functions of receiving, packing, and shipping. Materials allowances were developed for each product type by reference to standardization notices for packing methods and adjusted to average quantities where units per carton varied. The labor allowances for the various functions were developed by using a work sampling technique of time study rather than a stopwatch method. An overhead rate was based on the forecast average monthly activity.

The reporting of activity and the number of units processed were obtained, with one exception, from source documents which were already in use. All activity was reported on punched cards. These already identified the product, and it was necessary merely to add a one-digit code to indicate the function. Since several different packing methods were used, an additional three digits were provided for the packing function. To illustrate, the code 6–205–375 on a card for 500 12-inch records would mean that 500 units of product class 205 were packed as specified by packing instruction No. 375.

It was soon discovered that large volume variances were obscuring the

Exhibit 1

STANDARD UNIT COST SHEET

Cost Element	Costs per 100 Units				
	Receiving $	Packing $	Shipping $	Storage $	Total $
Material:					
Cartons and pads.............	.....	0.0004	.....	.....	0.0004
Labor:					
Receiving....................	0.0024	.....	.....	.....	0.0024
Shelving....................	0.0006	.....	0.0006	.....	0.0012
Packing.....................	.....	0.0009	.....	.....	0.0009
Shipping....................	.....	.....	0.0039	.....	0.0039
Overhead:					
Movement expenses...........	0.0090	0.0027	0.0135	.....	0.0252
Storage expenses.............	.....	.....	.....	0.0250	0.0250
Total Standard..............	0.0120	0.0040	0.0180	0.0250	0.0590

Exhibit 2

DAILY LABOR PERFORMANCE REPORT							DATE _____	
Function	Employee Number	Employee Name	Quantity	Units per Hour	Hours		Actual Labor Cost $	Variance $
					Actual	Standard		
1	127	Adams	80,000	10,000	8.0	7.8	17.60	0.44 CR
(Receiving)	143	Poe	98,000	12,250	8.0	8.3	17.60	0 66
	162	Parks	42,000	12,000	3.5	3.5	7.70	...
			220,000		19.5	19.6	42.90	0.22
3	150	Brooks	35,685	4,460	8.0	7.4	18.00	1.35 CR
(Shipping)	180	Sands	14,250	3,562	4.0	3.1	9.00	2.02 CR
			49,935		12.0	10.5	27.00	3.37 CR
4	117	Jones	60,000	7,500	8.0	8.2	15.20	0.38
(Shelving)	162	Parks	30,000	6,667	4.5	4.1	9.90	0.88 CR
			90,000		12.5	12.3	25.10	0.50 CR
6	137	Storm	6,500	929	7.0	7.5	12.60	0.90
(Packing)	138	Groth	6,950	869	8.0	7.9	14.40	0.18 CR
			13,450		15.0	15.4	27.00	0.72
Total			575,290		275.0	289.5	555.50	20.75

*CR indicates unfavorable variance.

data; and therefore the fixed overhead expenses, representing the costs of providing storage space, were segregated and absorbed by a burden rate based on the number of units of product stored. For this purpose, the shelf space occupied by each product was multiplied by a standard cost per square foot of shelf space, based on the past average utilization rate of 80 percent of capacity. A typical standard cost sheet appears in Exhibit 1.

A labor performance report is issued daily in the form illustrated in Exhibit 2. (Because the warehouse is a large one, the actual reports contain many more lines, omitted here to increase the clarity of the presentation.) Both hours and dollars are shown to enable the earning rate to be considered, as the wage rates of the employees vary. The detail by product line or class is not deemed necessary on the daily basis.

Exhibit 3

STANDARD LIQUIDATION
TOTAL WAREHOUSING ACTIVITY—RECAP BY PRODUCT TYPE AND FUNCTION

FOR THE MONTH_____19___

Warehouse Codes	Quantity	Total $	Material Cartons $	Labor				Overhead	
				Receiving $	Shelving $	Packing $	Shipping $	Movement $	Storage $
– 200 ___ (12″ Records)	3,214,218	19,565	425	1,800	900	225	2,500	7,215	6,500
– 300 ___ (7″ Records)	1,872,930	13,312	675	1,200	800	450	1,600	5,387	3,200
– 700 ___ (Tape Reels)	76,375	10,056	530	900	200	300	800	2,926	4,400
– 800 ___ (Tape Cart'gs)	195,250	5,595	870	600	300	825	1,100	3,757	1,900
Totals by Product...........		52,285	2,500	4,500	2,200	1,800	6,000	19,285	16,000
1 ___ ___ (Receiving)	1,220,888	12,349		4,500	800			7,049	
3 ___ ___ (Shipping)	866,421	17,242			1,400		6,000	9,842	
6 ___ ___ (Packing)	198,445	6,694	2,500			1,800		2,394	
8 ___ ___ (Storage)	3,073,019	16,000							16,000
Totals by Function...........		52,285	2,500	4,500	2,200	1,800	6,000	19,285	16,000

A series of cost absorption or "liquidation" sheets is prepared monthly, including the summary shown in Exhibit 3. The column totals are credited monthly to the warehouse accounts and charged, by product, to the cost of sales accounts. Charges for storage are made monthly to individual product classes on the basis of the number of units stored even if no inward or outward movement takes place in that product class. The monthly variances developed are charged to cost of sales after the charges for the standard cost of activity are made. These variances are not distributed among the various product classes.

The overhead statement is issued by object of expense separated into the variable movement expenses and the fixed storage expenses, with actual and

Exhibit 4

WAREHOUSING COST VARIANCE STATEMENT				
FOR THE MONTH _____ 19 __				

Item		Month $	Year to Date $
Material	Standard	2,500	
	Actual	2,450	
	Variance	50	
Labor	Standard	14,500	
	Actual	14,800	
	Variance	300 CR	
Overhead	Standard	19,285	
Movement	Actual	18,900	
	Variance	385	
Overhead	Standard	16,000	
Storage	Actual	15,500	
	Variance	500	
Total	Standard	52,285	
	Actual	51,650	
	Variance	635	

Labor Variance Detail:

	Standard $	Variance $	Standard $	Variance $
Receiving	4,500	100		
Shelving	2,200	50 CR		
Packing	1,800	40		
Shipping	6,000	390 CR		
Total	14,500	300 CR		

budget figures shown for the month and year to date. One additional statement, shown in Exhibit 4, presents the comparison of standard cost liquidation and the actual cost incurred. This report is the summary control report for the operations for the month.

a) What objectives does this system appear to have been designed to serve?

b) What strengths and limitations can you see in this system? If you find any limitations, offer suggestions as to how these might be overcome.

(Condensed and adapted from an article by Frank M. Mastromano in the *N. A. A. Bulletin*)

Chapter 17

CONTROL OF
NONMANUFACTURING COSTS:
INDEPENDENT PROGRAM ACTIVITIES

THE GREATEST CHALLENGE to the industrial accountant is in the design of systems for controlling independent program costs. Independent program activities are characterized by a lack of clearly defined work units and by the absence of a causal relationship that runs from service demand to cost. In other words, the size of the research expenditure is determined not by the need to provide service to other company units but by an administrative decision that the benefits expected from the expenditure are sufficient to satisfy some company decision rule.

Although the lines of demarcation are not clearly delineated, two different kinds of independent program activities can be distinguished:

1. Discrete programs, exemplified by project research and development.
2. Continuous programs, represented by sales promotion activities.

The purpose of this chapter is to discuss some of the problems of achieving cost control over these two types of activities.

Control Criteria

Cost control in independent program activities must be exercised primarily through control over appropriations rather than over expenditures. In this respect, independent program budget schedules come closer to governmental and personal budgets than any other portions of the business budget. Appropriations, once made, serve as planned limits on expenditures, and the conventional budgetary control and reporting techniques are concerned largely with meeting this objective.

Many possible criteria have been suggested to guide management in establishing budgets for independent program activities. Most of them are based on some rule of thumb, such as X percent of sales or $Y per year, but there is only one real test of the advisability of an appropriation—will it produce profits at a rate sufficient to justify the cost?

The main trouble with this test is the difficulty of quantifying it. Much research and a considerable amount of advertising are undertaken as an expression of faith—faith in the ability of money spent on these activities to pay for itself in added future profits—or as an expression of fear—fear that curtailment of expenditure would place the company at a serious competitive disadvantage. Many companies will spend a million dollars on a single advertising campaign without so much as a single question as to the expected results, whereas a $50,000 request for a new automatic production machine must face a rigid battery of profitability tests, approvals, and endorsements.

It is unfortunately true that forecasts of the benefits to be derived from specific programs or projects are subject to considerable error ranges. The same is true of the forecasts of the ultimate costs of some projects, particularly in research. Confronted with this fact, management is often tempted to abandon the profitability approach entirely and select some method that seems to offer security by tying the appropriation to some norm indicative of what others are doing or what has been done in the past. This places an even greater responsibility on the company's analytical staffs to attach profit estimates, even of the roughest sort, to appropriation requests. Errors of estimation are always present in managerial decision making, but it is better to have some indication of expected profitability, no matter how rough, than no guidance at all.

CONTROL OF RESEARCH AND DEVELOPMENT COSTS

Research and development activities can be classified into three main categories: project research, general research, and development. Development work is ordinarily the closest to commercial exploitation, most specific, and subject to the least uncertainty about its results. General research, at the other extreme, often has no specific anticipated commercial applications, is not well specified as to expected inputs and outputs, and is characterized by extreme uncertainty as to its benefits.

Control procedures for general research are ordinarily very simple and reflect a company's faith in its research scientists. Time may even be made available for general research as a kind of fringe benefit, a means of attracting research workers and keeping them content. Activities of this kind will be given little attention in this chapter, which will focus instead on project research and development.

Project Approval

Control procedures for project research and development are essentially of three types: (1) initial approval; (2) progress review; and (3) reapproval.

In a typical case, projects are submitted for approval as part of the annual budget review. Budget results are usually stated in two ways: first by projects, and second by descriptive category of expense, in total for all projects. If the research effort is sufficiently great, separate departmental budgets will also be presented.

Exhibit 17–1 illustrates one kind of project estimate form, in this

Exhibit 17–1

RESEARCH PROJECT ESTIMATE

RESEARCH DIVISION
PROJECT ESTIMATE SHEET

PROJECT NO.   16321   DATE   10/15/66
PROJECT TITLE   Sandfly Attachment   TYPE   New Product
PROJECT SUPERVISOR   G. Hill

Completion Estimate   9 Months   Cost Estimate:

Estimated Annual Profit $30,000

	Labor	$ 8,000
	Materials	7,200
	Equipment	4,800
	Total	$20,000

Task	Phase 1, Specifications		Phase 2, Drawings		Phase 3, Prototype	
	Hours	Cost	Hours	Cost	Hours	Cost
Synthesis and analysis	300	$2,400				
Design specifications	50	400				
Breadboarding	100	700				
Layout	50	350				
Parts list			80	$ 400		
Schematics			150	750		
Test specifications			50	400		
Fabrication					300	$1,200
Assembly					100	300
Wiring					50	300
Test					100	800
Total Labor	500	$3,850	280	$1,550	550	$2,600
Materials and purchased parts	$2,000		$ 500		$4,700	
Equipment	$3,000		...		$1,800	
Completion time	4 months		2 months		3 months	

case covering a small project for the development of a new product. If the research division is departmentalized, this will usually be expanded by a further classification of project costs by department. In this exhibit, project labor costs are subdivided by task, and the tasks are grouped into phases, each phase ending at some readily recognizable point in the development process. The estimated time to complete each phase is shown at the bottom of the sheet, and project totals, including a rough estimate of profit potential, are shown in the summary section at the top of the form. Additional supporting sheets, not shown here, present further detail on the nature of the project and on the derivation of the estimates.

Exhibit 17–2

RESEARCH BUDGET REQUEST FORM

RESEARCH DIVISION
PROJECT BUDGET SUMMARY

YEAR 1967
DATE 12/2/66

| Project No. | Project Supervisor | Costs to Date | Costs This Year | | | | Future Costs | Total Costs | Annual Profit Expected |
			Labor	Materials	Equipment	Total			
16214	P. Jones	$13,500	$21,200	$1,800	$ 600	$23,600	$ 10,000	$ 47,100	$20,000
16285	F. Tons	84,050	15,600	3,400	1,000	20,000	......	104,050	70,000
16312	L. Peters	27,140	5,000	200	....	5,200	......	32,340	10,000
16318	A. Stern	.....	30,000	6,500	2,500	39,000	50,000	80,000	40,000
16320	N. Rossi	.....	10,000	2,000	4,000	16,000	100,000	116,000	60,000
16321	G. Hill	.....	8,000	7,200	4,800	20,000	......	20,000	30,000

Exhibit 17–2 is an example of a form used to summarize the direct costs of all the projects underway or proposed for the coming year. Each project is listed separately. Separate columns are provided for past costs of continuing projects, estimated costs for the current year, estimated costs for future years, if any, expected completion date, and estimated annual profits on completion. This is normally accompanied by a second budget schedule such as that shown in Exhibit 17–3, which summarizes the individual project requests for the current year, together with the overhead costs of the research organization. This is broken down into months for cash budgeting purposes.

Progress Review

One possible approach to the control of research and development costs is to report periodically to each department head the differences between his total budget allowance and actual costs for the period. Unfortunately, these comparisons are of only marginal value. The reason is that most costs are either salaries or closely related to salaries. Total expenditures for these inputs are controlled by decisions to hire personnel, and these, in turn, are the outcome of project approvals. In other words, aggregate expenditure rates are controlled by budget approval, and follow-up budget comparisons of this sort serve only to indicate overall departures from anticipated rates of expenditure.

Exhibit 17–3

CURRENT RESEARCH BUDGET SUMMARY

RESEARCH DIVISION BUDGET SUMMARY	
	YEAR __1967__ DATE __12/2/66__
Description	Annual Total
Project costs: Labor Materials Equipment	$150,000 33,000 39,000
Total Project Costs	$222,000
Executive salaries Clerical Overtime premium Payroll charges Professional services Travel Telephone Insurance Maintenance Shop supplies Office supplies Depreciation Space charges Unclassified	$ 30,000 12,000 8,000 26,000 20,000 5,000 1,500 1,800 4,000 6,000 2,200 5,000 10,000 4,500
Total	$358,000

A second defect in departmental comparisons is that research activity typically focuses on the project rather than on the department. An alternative, therefore, is to compare expenditures with budget allowances periodically on a project basis. For example, a monthly report might take the form illustrated in Exhibit 17–4.

This kind of reporting does serve to identify projects on which rates of expenditure are out of line with preestablished schedules, but it ignores one vital element—progress. Project costs have no meaning

Exhibit 17–4

PROJECT COST COMPARISON REPORT

RESEARCH DIVISION
MONTHLY PROJECT COST REPORT

PROJECT NO. 16321   MONTH April

PROJECT TITLE Sandfly Attachment   SUPERVISOR G. Hill

START DATE 3/6/67

SCHEDULED COMPLETION 11/30/67

	This Month		To Date		
	Actual	Budget	Actual	Budget	Variance
Salaries, professional	$ 800	$ 550	$1,550	$1,000	$ (550)
Salaries, technical	300	220	900	450	(450)
Laboratory services	15	. . .	15	. . .	(15)
Drafting supplies	25	30	95	100	5
Outside services	. . .	. . .	20	. . .	(20)
Purchased parts	350	. . .	350	. . .	(350)
Equipment	1,350	500	3,100	3,000	(100)
Total	$2,840	$1,300	$6,030	$4,550	$(1,480)

except in comparison with the progress achieved toward project objectives. Thus Exhibit 17–4 would seem to indicate that project 16321 is running far in excess of its budget, but it may be that resources were available much sooner than had been anticipated and that more progress had been made than originally scheduled.

Networking

For simple sequential projects like this one, cost and progress reporting is easy to work out. Most such projects can be broken down into stages, with separate cost and time estimates for each. These progress estimates then provide a continuing basis for project review as actual costs charged to the projects are compared with expected costs for the amount of progress reported.

Large projects and even some small ones pose more difficulties. The various parts of the projects are not entirely sequential but require close coordination and careful scheduling. For complex projects, the most useful scheduling tool is the activity *network*.

Networking is a subject in itself, but the basic concept can be spelled out fairly quickly. Exhibit 17–5 is a typical, although very simple, network. The circles represent *events* that occur at specific moments

Exhibit 17-5

PROJECT NETWORK

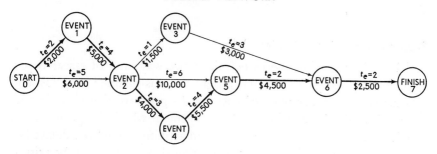

during the course of the project; the connecting lines stand for *activities,* the means of getting from one event to another. The direction of progress toward completion of the project is indicated by arrowheads on the activity lines. The numbers labeled t_e on the activity lines indicate the expected number of weeks required to complete each activity. Thus the network in Exhibit 17-5 indicates that it will take two weeks to get from the start of the project to event No. 1. The expected cost of this activity is $2,000.

Notice that activities are both concurrent and sequential. For example, two separate sets of activities must be completed independently in order to reach event No. 2—these are concurrent sets of activities. The activities linking events 4 and 5 and events 5 and 6, on the other hand, are sequential—the second one cannot be started until the first one is completed.

Networks are used to make the interdependencies visible, to facilitate resource scheduling, and to identify those activities that are likely to be most critical to the timely completion of the project. The activities shown as heavy lines in Exhibit 17-5 constitute the *critical path*—the sequence of activities requiring the longest total elapsed time from start to finish. If the critical path is too long to meet a desired completion date, it may be possible to devote more resources to one or more of the activities on the critical path and thus shorten the total time requirement. Shortening the time required for an activity on one of the *slack paths,* on the other hand, would not advance the completion date at all.

The most widely known networking technique is PERT (Program Evaluation and Review Technique).[1] Most PERT networks or *programs* are very large and require high-capacity electronic computers.

---

[1] For a simple introduction, see Harry F. Evarts, *Introduction to PERT* (Boston: Allyn & Bacon, 1964).

The networking technique can be applied to simpler tasks without the use of computers, however, both inside and outside the research division.

Progress Reporting with Networks

The existence of networks permits a two-way kind of research performance reporting: (1) actual progress versus planned progress, and (2) actual cost versus planned cost *for the progress actually achieved.* Comparisons of the first kind tell management whether a project is on schedule, whether one or more slack path activities have been delayed or have run so far over the time estimates that they are now on the critical path, etc. Comparisons of the second kind indicate whether schedules

Exhibit 17–6

INTEGRATED PROJECT PROGRESS CHART

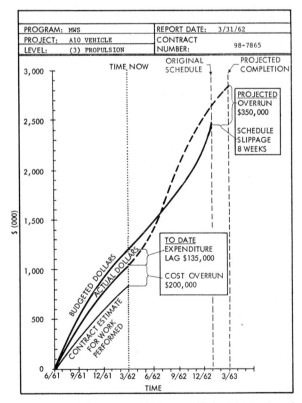

SOURCE: U.S. Department of Defense and National Aeronautics and Space Administration, *DOD and NASA Guide, PERT/COST* (Washington, D.C.: U.S. Government Printing Office, 1962), p. 16 (slightly modified).

have been maintained within the anticipated cost limits. They may also help in project reevaluation.

Exhibit 17–6 is a pictorial version of a progress report of this sort. This focuses attention on three aspects of project performance: (1) total spending to date, against budgeted spending to date (the "expenditure lag"); (2) total spending, against budgeted spending for the work performed ("cost overrun"); and (3) progress to date in comparison with the original plan (indicated by the expected completion delay or "schedule slippage").

Notice that this chart focuses on the future rather than the past. Both costs and completion dates are reestimated and compared with original estimates. These comparisons are then used in deciding whether to continue the projects, modify the objectives, alter the expenditure rates, and so forth.

Charts like the one in Exhibit 17–6 could be constructed for project segments as well as for the project as a whole, as long as the chart of accounts is subdivided to permit recording of actual costs by segments. In the typical case, the clerical cost of recording project costs by individual activities is prohibitive, and so larger groups of activities known as *work packages* are treated as costing units for this purpose.[2]

Project Reapproval

The periodic progress reports not only serve to alert management to departures from plans so that appropriate adjustments can be made but also provide an occasion for reappraisal of project desirability. Projects are typically reviewed annually for this purpose, even if the initial time and expenditure schedules are being met. They may also be reviewed whenever either time or cost overruns become serious enough to call for such a review.

Some projects even include one or more profitability investigation activities in project sequences or networks, and probably more should do so. One reason is that external conditions are constantly changing—a product that would have excited the market when research was started may be completely out of fashion or favor now. Additional expenditures should be made only if they will pay off.

A second reason has a similar impact—as research progresses, the nature and cost of the ultimate product may become much clearer, and

---

[2] See U.S. Department of Defense and National Aeronautics and Space Administration, *DOD and NASA Guide, PERT/COST* (Washington D.C.: U.S. Government Printing Office, 1962), for a description of this and related techniques.

this may not fit the anticipated market conditions as well as the original design/cost expectations.

Finally, progress may be so much slower or so much costlier than originally planned that the revised estimates of future time and costs can no longer be justified by the expected benefits. Once again, the project should be terminated and the resources devoted elsewhere.

Departmental Performance Review

Each project is typically the direct responsibility of a project manager who may or may not have other duties as well. Some companies supplement project cost accumulations with departmental accumulations of direct, as well as indirect, project costs. Each project is identified with a specific department, usually the department to which the project manager is normally assigned. The cost of any work on a particular project that is performed by personnel of other departments in the research division is charged to the project and to the project manager's department as well. The department supplying the service is credited for a corresponding amount. An alternative is to provide for a departmental classification of work performed, by project, so that hours or costs accumulated on all projects in each department can be compared with the hours or costs budgeted for the tasks actually performed on those projects in that department.

The administration of research divisions is an exceedingly complex subject, and one that has only recently been studied by analytical methods. Cost control techniques are only one phase of the greater problem of research administration, albeit an important phase. The discussion in the preceding paragraphs has merely scratched the surface because every company is to a certain extent unique in its research activities. The cardinal point, however, is that no system of control in this field can be successful unless it recognizes that the justification of research is future profit and not merely adherence to arbitrarily established expense budgets.

CONTROL OF MARKETING COSTS

The costs of generating firm orders for delivery of the company's products generally consume a larger portion of the sales dollar than any other nonmanufacturing expense. These are the company's marketing costs or, to use a term often used by accountants, *order-getting costs.*

Order-getting activities are independent program activities, as that term has been used here, and some of them bear striking similarities to research and development activities. Market research is perhaps the most obvious example; media advertising is another. Others differ from research and development in that they are continuous rather than discrete. This second group is exemplified by *direct selling costs* consisting mainly of sales salaries and commissions, travel, entertainment, samples, and dealer aids and other forms of direct assistance to customers. The analysis and control of these costs is extremely complex, and fully meaningful techniques have yet to be developed. Therefore, the following paragraphs should be regarded as introductory and suggestive rather than exhaustive and conclusive.

The Control Problem

The fundamental difficulty in establishing viable control standards for order-getting costs was stated succinctly in a research report of the National Association of Accountants (then National Association of Cost Accountants):

Order-getting costs cannot be budgeted by establishing a simple and direct relationship between sales orders and costs. The principal reason for this is that order-getting activities are a cause rather than a result of sales and the volume of orders obtained depends to some extent upon the amount spent for advertising, sales promotion and selling. This contrasts with the manufacturing cost budget where production costs can be budgeted after the volume of goods to be produced has been determined because the volume of production does not depend upon the amount of money spent for materials, labor, and factory overhead. . . . The lowest unit cost or total cost is not always the preferred objective in controlling order-getting costs because such a cost may fail to yield the most profitable volume which can be attained.[3]

Any effort to establish standard costs per unit of sales is bound to founder on the problem of circular reasoning. The number of calls made or the number or dollar value of orders received may be useful indices of effort or results, but they do not constitute units of output to which a standard cost can be attached. For example, the salesman can reduce cost per call merely by lengthening his stay in a particular city and shortening the duration of each call, but the company's sales may suffer as a result. Sales and the cost of obtaining sales are inescapably interdependent.

While recognizing these difficulties, it is still possible to devise some techniques that will be useful in cost control. Control over direct selling costs is ordinarily exercised in three stages:

---

[3] National Association of Accountants, "Cost Control for Marketing Operations—General Considerations, Research Series No. 25," *N.A.C.A. Bulletin,* Vol. XXXV, No. 8 (April, 1954), pp. 1085–86.

1. Development of budgets.
2. Analysis of results.
3. Analysis of expense rates.

Although the techniques available under each of these stages vary considerably from company to company, it will be profitable to devote some attention to the general characteristics of the control process at each stage.

Budget Preparation

As with research and development, preparation and approval of the marketing budget is the most important determinant of marketing costs. Once the marketing plan is approved, expenditures are likely to follow rather closely.

The marketing plan comprises everything from package size and package design through point-of-sale displays. Many of its elements remain unchanged for fairly substantial time periods—e.g., package design—while others can be changed on a few weeks' or even days' notice—the relative amount of attention to be given by the salesman to his larger customers, for example.

Marketing budgets may be either program-oriented or organizationally centered. If the organization of the sales force coincides with the marketing management structure, the two will be identical. Many companies, however, plan their marketing programs on a product-line or customer-group basis, while their sales forces are geographically structured. This often creates conflicts between marketing management and sales management, as the latter is subject to conflicting demands and pressures from the various product or customer group managers.

Despite all this diversity, one element is universal. Sales and selling expenses are interdependent, and budgets for these items must be developed simultaneously. For example, in a highly participative budget plan, each branch or product manager typically takes as his starting point a sales force of the existing size and develops tentative sales budgets and selling expense budgets for this force. In budgeting such expenses as travel, entertainment, dealer aids, and samples, the manager is aided by historical averages of these expenses in each territory, perhaps supplemented by past averages for different types of customers or different channels of distribution—travel expense per man-day in the field, for example, is often a useful guideline.

The next step is to consider the desirability of increasing or decreasing the number of salesmen or of changing the degree of specialization in the sales force or of altering the amount of attention to be given to different categories of customers or different products. In this task the line manager may need the assistance of staff analysts, both from the accounting staff and from the market analysis group, who try to predict the effects on profits of various proposed changes in the amount or structure of distributional effort. Once this has been done, the revised sales and selling expense budgets are submitted to higher management for review and coordination with production. The final approved budgets then become rough control standards for the ensuing period.

Because changes in market conditions can occur so quickly and because such changes have such a profound influence not only on the desirability of promotional activity but also on factory scheduling and financial management, sales and selling expense budgets are often revised more frequently than other portions of the company's budget—in some cases they are even changed monthly. It is assumed that actual selling expense will approximate the budgeted amounts because these amounts have been determined on the basis of the amount necessary to achieve the budgeted levels of sales and profits. Deviations from budgeted cost are not necessarily favorable or unfavorable—this depends on the results achieved. Therefore, emphasis is placed on the deviation between planned and actual sales margins (sales less cost of goods sold less direct selling expenses) rather than on the absolute level of expense.

It is impossible to do justice to this topic in these few brief paragraphs. Market planning is after all an integral part of the overall planning process. For this reason, further discussion must be deferred to the chapters dealing with financial control systems.

Segment Profit Analysis

The second instrument for use in the control of marketing costs is the analysis of results, in this case sales or, more precisely, the profits contributed by sales. Internal profit reporting and analysis will be discussed in detail in the chapters on financial control systems, but a few comments are in order here.

First, most markets are multidimensional in ways that are significant to marketing management. No unidimensional classification scheme can satisfy all of management's information needs at all times. The most common bases for classification are:

1. By sales territory.
2. By salesman.
3. By product line.
4. By customer group.

5. By size of order.
6. By method of distribution.

Some of these bases are used periodically for routine profit reporting; others are used only infrequently, as the need arises for a special study of some phase of the marketing effort. It is a fairly simple matter to obtain an analysis of sales patterns on any of these bases, either by account coding or, more economically, by sampling the sales documents. This *sales analysis* is a technique widely used by marketing managers to keep themselves informed and assist them in planning future sales activities.[4]

An illustrative district sales report is shown in Exhibit 17–7. Sales, cost of goods sold, and direct field expense (salary, commissions, travel, entertainment, samples, and any other expenses clearly traceable to the individual salesman) are shown for each salesman, while general branch overheads are shown only in total for the branch as a whole.

The difference between sales and the expenses traceable to a particu-

Exhibit 17–7

BRANCH SALES SUMMARY

SALESMAN PERFORMANCE SUMMARY

DISTRICT Boston   MONTH January, 1967

Salesman	Net Sales Billed	Cost of Sales	Salary and Expenses	Profit Contribution		
				Amount	Budget Deviation	% of Sales
Brown	$ 40,000	$ 29,200	$ 2,400	$ 8,400	$ (400)	21.0%
Cannon	31,000	24,300	3,200	3,500	(900)	11.3
Evars	63,000	42,700	4,100	16,200	3,700	25.7
Johnson	30,000	24,200	2,900	2,900	(1,400)	9.7
Kelly	54,000	40,100	4,200	9,700	200	18.0
Lusso	47,000	34,400	3,100	9,500	2,100	20.2
McGregor	76,000	56,000	3,800	16,200	4,000	21.3
Nelson	55,000	41,900	3,300	9,800	500	17.8
Stern	68,000	51,600	3,600	12,800	1,200	18.8
Williams	50,000	36,600	3,000	10,400	(600)	20.8
Total	$514,000	$381,000	$33,600	$99,400	$ 8,400	19.4%
Other branch expenses				12,100	(600)	1.7
District Profit Contribution				$87,300	$ 7,800	17.1%

[4] See National Industrial Conference Board, *Sales Analysis, Studies in Business Policy No. 113* (New York: National Industrial Conference Board, 1965).

lar segment of the business is generally referred to as the *profit contribution* of that segment. The assignment of nontraceable expenses is the subject of distribution cost analysis, to be discussed in Chapter 23. Even a superficial knowledge of the characteristics of nonmanufacturing costs, however, can indicate just how difficult a task this can be. So many of these costs are indivisible capacity costs that any method of cost allocation is bound to be at least partly arbitrary. In most cases, it is better and cheaper to keep the number of allocations to a minimum and make no attempt to measure the unmeasurable—the net profit of any particular segment.

Just to recognize the difficulties inherent in this kind of analysis without trying to resolve them at this point, suppose that a sales force sells several product lines. Salaries, travel, entertainment, and, in fact, most direct selling costs are common costs, not traceable to any one of the product lines in the salesman's book. Salesmen's time reports are not of much assistance in making cost allocations to products, and not only because the salesman finds it difficult to estimate the time spent in promoting any particular product line. The main problem is that direct selling time is a relatively small portion of the salesman's average day. Most of his time he spends waiting in customers' waiting rooms, traveling, listening to the prospect's tale of woe, and performing other necessary but more or less unproductive tasks.

In most cases subtracting one product line from the salesman's order book would not permit him to make a single additional call per day unless the product line is defined so broadly that it makes up a substantial proportion of his stock in trade. Even if product lines are defined this broadly, however, the proportion of time spent promoting any one line does not provide much information that could not be provided by profit contribution figures computed by deducting from product sales all those costs that can be identified readily with that line. Specific product advertising, warehousing costs, and percentage sales commissions are examples of appropriate deductions from product sales. These profit contribution figures then indicate which products are relatively more profitable than others and are therefore deserving of more of the salesman's effort. Conversely, they help identify lines that may need further managerial attention to improve sales appeal or product profitability. Arbitrary allocations of sales salaries and travel expense are unlikely to improve the information content of the product-line profitability statements.

One final problem deserves brief recognition at this point. Promotional effort is often made and its cost dimension recorded in the accounts before the resultant sales revenues are recorded. Sometimes this is due to a time lag between effort and results; sometimes it is due to a time lag between results (sales orders) and accounting recognition of these results (revenues).

Most accounting systems are content to overlook these time lags, trusting in the good judgment of marketing executives and top management to make due mental allowances when reviewing reported results. One alternative that has been suggested is to capitalize marketing costs and take them to expense after an appropriate time lag.[5] Another possibility is to recognize revenues for internal reporting purposes on the basis of orders received, no matter what basis is used for external reporting. This would not solve the problem raised by the first kind of time lag but it would adjust for the second, assuming that the bookkeeping details could be worked out economically.

Expense Rate Analysis

Segment profit analysis is often supplemented by a review of the reasonableness of direct field expenses. Most of the procedures adopted for this purpose focus on the individual salesman or branch territory and rely on the analysis of certain key ratios, such as the following:

Calls per day.
Sales per call.
Travel expense per day.
Selling expense per call.
Miles traveled per day.[6]

The multidimensionality of selling effort and the lack of precise comparability among markets or territories make it difficult to develop a science of ratio analysis. The ratios are valuable insofar as they aid the analyst to identify important patterns, and for this it is the overall picture that is important rather than the absolute size of any one ratio. For example, one salesman may have a high cost per call and few calls per day but a much larger sales volume and a higher profit contribution than his fellows. If the sales territories are comparable, this may indicate the greater effectiveness of a policy of selective selling. Another salesman may have many calls per day and greater-than-average sales per call but a low gross margin, indicating a tendency to sell what is

---

[5] Richard A. Feder, "How to Measure Marketing Performance," *Harvard Business Review*, May–June, 1965, pp. 132–42.

[6] For an exhaustive survey of these ratios, see Spencer A. Tucker, *Successful Managerial Control by Ratio-Analysis* (New York: McGraw-Hill Book Co., Inc., 1961), Chapters vi–ix.

easiest to sell or to cut selling prices and then move on quickly to the next customer.

Many companies include interperiod comparisons in this analysis, but this is of doubtful usefulness. The place for interperiod analysis is in the preparation of the sales plan, and once the latter is formulated it should serve as a better bench mark for comparison. One authority has proposed a form of interperiod incremental analysis relating the *change* in results to the *change* in cost or effort.[7] The concept is useful, but the ability to attribute the change in results to the change in inputs is often limited by the perversity of other profit determinants in refusing to remain constant. We shall look at other methods of analysis more closely in later chapters.

SUMMARY

Independent program activities are those that are undertaken to achieve a discretionary objective—that is, their output is not provided to service either customer orders or current production requirements. They can be undertaken or not, depending on whether the anticipated results satisfy a company decision rule.

Two kinds of independent programs may be distinguished: discrete and continuing. The former is exemplified by research and development activities; the latter by sales promotion and direct selling. For both classes, traditional input/output standards are inapplicable because the input costs are more volume-determining than volume-determined. The most valuable technique for controlling these costs is to test budget proposals by the criterion of expected profits. Once budget allowances for these activities are approved, it is unlikely that actual costs will be materially less than the amounts budgeted. Cost control need be no less effective on this account, but it must be applied at an earlier stage in the budgetary process than is the case for manufacturing operations and repetitive service activities outside the field of manufacturing.

This before-the-fact control can, however, be supplemented by various other techniques. Any program that can be broken down into a number of sequential phases can be monitored by periodic cost and progress reports. For continuous programs, input/output or cost/input ratios may have some usefulness in interunit or intertemporal comparisons. The crucial stage in both cases, however, is the decision to spend, and it is on this stage that control efforts are ordinarily centered.

---

[7] Feder, *op. cit.*

DISCUSSION QUESTIONS

1. What distinguishes independent program activities from repetitive service or diversified service activities?

2. What is the primary technique for controlling research and development costs?

3. "Let's face it. It is ridiculous to talk about control of research costs. We spend what we can afford on research, and if we want to spend more, we hire more people. The only control we can expect is through our employment policy." Discuss this statement.

4. Cost per sales call is an index that is often used to allocate field selling expense to customer groups. Why is this not a useful basis for establishing a standard cost of selling operations for cost control purposes?

5. Inasmuch as the effectiveness of selling activities is measured in part by the volume of sales achieved, why not establish standard selling costs per dollar of sales?

6. What is PERT? What are its objectives? To what extent is it an instrument of cost control? Is it likely to be applicable to field selling activities?

7. Both field selling and product research activities were identified in this chapter as independent program activities. What do they have in common that might justify this treatment? What differences between them would affect the control methods used?

8. How useful are comparisons between budgeted research costs to date and actual costs to date likely to be for cost control purposes? What improvements can you suggest?

9. This chapter has emphasized control rather than profitability analysis, which may require the allocation of activity or functional costs to products, territories, or other revenue segments. To what extent, if any, do such allocations serve a useful cost control objective?

10. Promotional effort is often expended in one period, customer orders are received in another, and sales revenue is recorded in still another. What problems, if any, does this create? How might you try to solve these problems?

EXERCISES AND PROBLEMS

1. The Arlex Development Company is devoted exclusively to missile systems research on cost-plus-fixed-fee contracts for the U.S. Air Force. Inasmuch as the company's profit on any contract is not affected by the costs incurred on that contract, should the company make any effort to develop methods of cost control?

2. Salesmen of the Guston Company submit weekly call summaries to the branch offices, including estimates of the time percentages spent in promoting each of the company's product groups. Assuming that these time

distributions are reasonably accurate, why do they not provide an adequate basis for distributing sales salaries, travel, and entertainment expenses to individual product groups?

3. The travel expense budget for the New Orleans branch of the Winchell Company amounts to $8,500 for the current fiscal year. It is now the last month of the fiscal year, and $8,473 has already been charged to New Orleans branch travel expense. Travel expense vouchers received from the New Orleans branch manager in this morning's mail amount to $286.

   a) As controller of the company, would you refuse to honor the vouchers, notify the president, ask the branch manager for an explanation, charge the amount in excess of budget to another account that has an unexpended balance, or would you take some other action?

   b) If the New Orleans branch manager had consulted you at the beginning of the month, before the travel expenses had been incurred, what action would you have taken?

4. Cost per call is an index that is often used to allocate field selling expense among the company's various product lines or customer groups. Could this provide a useful basis for establishing a standard cost of selling operations for control purposes? If your answer is yes, indicate how it would be used. If your answer is no, indicate why it could not be used for this purpose.

*5. Draw a network to fit the following data and trace the critical path. (Each activity is identified by a two-digit number, the first digit denoting the preceding event and the second digit indicating the event that signals the end of the activity.)

Activity	Estimated Time (Weeks)
01	1
02	3
03	5
14	2
25	4
35	3
46	6
56	2
57	1
69	4
78	2
89	2

6. The Hydro Products Company sells a variety of headache pills, digestion aids, and similar products. The company's sales in February exceeded budgeted sales for the month by approximately 10 percent. This increase was attributed to the success of a new television series that had been launched under company sponsorship on a national television network late in January after the February sales budget had been approved. The summary sales report for February showed the following:

---

* Solutions to problems marked with an asterisk (*) can be found in Appendix B.

Branch	Sales % of Budget	Local Selling Expense % of Sales
Boston......................	108%	3.5%
New York....................	111	3.8
Cleveland...................	110	3.4
Chicago.....................	112	3.4
Atlanta.....................	109	3.6
New Orleans.................	101	3.4
Houston.....................	112	3.4
Denver......................	115	3.5
Los Angeles.................	110	3.5
Seattle.....................	107	3.7

At the monthly sales meeting on March 3, all the branch managers were enthusiastic about the new television series except the managers of the Cleveland and New Orleans branches. The Cleveland manager had to admit that it got results but reported an unusual number of complaints from viewers about the poor taste and stridency of the commercial messages and felt that this should be corrected.

The New Orleans branch manager reported that the series had the highest local Nielson rating of any series, but that he too had noted an unusual volume of viewer complaints and felt that this explained the program's ineffectiveness in his area. His salesmen, he noted, cited the offending commercials as just another example of the company's poor public relations sense and the indifference of headquarters to the problems of the field sales force. Nevertheless, all but three of his salesmen had met their sales quotas which were set approximately equal to the budget estimates, and like all the other branch managers, he was confident that he could exceed budgeted sales levels for the next several months.

The other branch managers also reported a high level of viewer complaints but said that their salesmen felt that these complaints only served to draw further attention to the company's products and thus made their job easier.

The production manager reported that he would have no difficulty in filling orders at the anticipated levels, and the treasurer indicated that adequate funds were available to finance the inventories and receivables required by these added sales.

Statistics on industry sales showed a continuing upward trend, with no significant regional differences. Industry outlays for local sales promotion were approximately unchanged from a year earlier, according to an analysis made by a stock advisory service.

a) At the close of the meeting, the sales manager reported to the president that a problem existed and that he was investigating it. What was the problem and how did the sales manager know that it existed?

b) Suggest several possible causes of the problem and indicate which of these were most likely to be the true causes. Give your reasons.

c) How might the sales manager proceed to investigate these probable causes quickly and cheaply?

7. The Villard Company recently initiated a new product development project estimated to cost \$31,500. The list of activities constituting this project, together with estimates of the number of weeks each activity would take and the cost to carry it out, is shown in the table below. In this table each activity is identified by a two-digit number, the first digit denoting the preceding event and the second digit indicating the event that signals the end of the activity:

Activity	Department	Estimated Time (Weeks)	Estimated Cost
01...........	A	2	\$ 1,100
12...........	A	1	500
23...........	B	3	2,500
24...........	D	7	3,500
25...........	F	2	2,200
34...........	C	3	3,300
35...........	G	1	400
45...........	B	5	4,000
49...........	A	3	1,600
56...........	D	2	900
67...........	C	1	1,200
68...........	E	6	4,200
78...........	G	2	700
79...........	F	4	4,100
89...........	G	3	1,300
Total.........			\$31,500

Eight weeks after this project was initiated, activities 01, 12, 24, and 25 had been completed and activity 23 was approximately half-finished. It was estimated that an additional two weeks and \$1,500 would be necessary to finish activity 23. No other estimates had to be revised. As originally approved, the schedule called for completion of activities 01, 12, 23, and 25 in the first eight weeks, with activity 24 to be five-sevenths finished and activity 34 to be two-thirds finished.

Costs incurred during the first eight weeks were:

Department	Amount
A....	\$1,400
B....	2,400
D....	3,000
F....	2,500
Total....	\$9,300

a) Draw a network to represent this project.
b) List the events through which the critical path passes and indicate the number of weeks which the project was originally expected to take.
c) Prepare a report summarizing costs and performance on this project during the first eight weeks. Has the critical path changed in any way?

8. The following data relate to the activity and performance of salesman Jones last month:

	Last Month				This Territory, Same Month Last Year
	Jones Actual		Jones, Planned	Average, All Salesmen	
	No.	Amount			
Orders received:					
$ 0–$ 250.............	45	$ 3,000	.....	$ 3,100	.....
251– 500.............	20	7,000	.....	8,100	.....
501– 1,000.............	8	6,000	.....	11,200	.....
1,001– 2,000.............	4	5,000	.....	7,800	.....
2,001– 5,000.............	2	8,000	.....	6,300	.....
More than 5,000...........	1	6,000	.....	3,500	.....
Total....................	80	$35,000	$32,000	$40,000	$33,000
Cost of goods sold (at standard)...............		$26,000	$22,500	$28,000	$23,000
Direct expenses...............		2,200	2,250	2,300	2,100
Marketing overhead (5% of sales)....................		1,750	1,600	2,000	1,650
Administrative overhead (8% of sales)....................		2,800	2,560	3,200	2,640
Net Profit....................		$ 2,250	$ 3,090	$ 4,500	$ 3,610
Initial orders received..........	5	$ 1,000	$ 1,500	$ 2,500	$ 1,200
Calls made:					
Group A customers..........	30		40		25
Group B customers..........	20		20		26
Group C customers..........	50		30		45
Total Calls...............	100		90	100	96

Customers are divided for analysis into three categories:
    Group A: regular customers, annual sales volume at least $10,000.
    Group B: prospects, no purchases during previous fiscal year.
    Group C: regular customers, annual sales less than $10,000.
"Initial orders" are the first orders of the year from group B customers. Marketing and administrative overheads are almost entirely fixed costs.

a) Compute the following:
    (1) Sales and expense variances for the month.
    (2) Mr. Jones's contribution to company profits for the month.
    (3) Cost per call: actual and planned for Mr. Jones, all-salesman average, and same territory last year.
    (4) Sales per call: as in (3).
    (5) Profit/sales ratios: as in (3).

b) Using the figures from (*a*), whenever pertinent, and any others that you deem appropriate, analyze Mr. Jones's performance for the month.

9. The Central City branch office of the Superfluous Products Corporation employs a sales force of four salesmen. Each salesman has accounts both in Central City and in a surrounding five-state area. The boundaries of the various sales territories are redrawn periodically to try to equalize territorial sales potentials, but some inequalities are inevitable. Salesmen are paid a straight salary, plus commissions on a few products that require special selling effort.

The branch manager has just received from the accounting department the following data relating to last month's operations:

	Salesman White		Salesman Green		Salesman Black		Salesman Brown	
	Actual	Planned	Actual	Planned	Actual	Planned	Actual	Planned
Orders received:								
Number.........	50	70	100	90	80	80	75	80
Amount (A).....	$8,000	$10,000	$12,000	$11,800	$11,000	$12,000	$11,500	$12,000
Orders canceled:								
Number.........	2	2	3	2	..	2	5	2
Amount (B).....	$ 800	$ 200	$ 200	$ 200	..	$ 200	$ 400	$ 200
Calls made.........	80	90	150	110	90	100	100	100
Cost of goods sold* (C)..........	$5,400	$ 6,660	$ 8,000	$ 8,120	$ 7,700	$ 8,260	$ 7,600	$ 8,260
Direct field expense:								
Salaries..........	$ 600	$ 600	$ 700	$ 700	$ 650	$ 650	$ 620	$ 590
Commissions.....	300	50	60	60	50	60	100	60
Travel and entertainment.......	500	350	320	350	400	350	380	370
Samples........	40	90	150	110	100	100	110	100
Total (D)......	$1,440	$ 1,090	$ 1,230	$ 1,220	$ 1,200	$ 1,160	$ 1,210	$ 1,120
Profit Contribution (A − B − C − D)......	$ 360	$ 2,050	$ 2,570	$ 2,260	$ 2,100	$ 2,380	$ 2,290	$ 2,420

* Based on net orders (orders received minus orders canceled) at standard product cost.

a) Prepare a brief report, commenting on the performance of each salesman last month.

b) Assuming that these data are representative, suggest ways in which changes in salesmen's methods of operation might lead to profit improvement.

c) Identify any additional data you would have liked to have from internal accounting records and indicate whether you think that such data could be obtained at a reasonable cost.

10. The Tancred Corporation has a large research and development division, devoted partly to contract research for government agencies and partly to

company-supported research and development for the company's civilian product lines. Most government contracts are on a cost-plus-fixed-fee basis (CPFF). Company-sponsored work was financed until recently by a blanket appropriation of funds to be spent at the discretion of the vice president–research. The vice president–research made an annual report, summarizing successful projects and commenting on the status and prospects of uncompleted projects.

All professional R & D personnel were required to submit weekly time sheets indicating the number of hours devoted to each project. Similar procedures were used with respect to outside purchases of goods and services and internal materials requisitions. These data sources were used to assign direct costs to individual projects, primarily for cost justification to government auditors and for internal checks on payrolls and materials inventory records. Very little use was made of these data for cost control purposes.

Two years ago the company incurred substantial overruns on two of its major CPFF contracts. Although these overruns were chargeable to the government projects and collectible from the government, the fixed fee or project profit was not increased and the ratio of profit to cost was extremely low. Furthermore, personnel had to be transferred from other projects to meet completion schedules on the overrun projects. After this experience, the company's management appointed a planning and control administrator to devise a system for controlling R & D costs.

Because project labor accounted for the largest share of R & D costs, the administrator concentrated his efforts on this item of cost. The first step was to revise the weekly time sheets to identify not only projects or contracts but individual activities specified in each project or contract. (PERT networks are prepared for all major projects.) This activity breakdown had never been used in cost control.

Each project was subdivided into groups of related activity "packages," and each package was made the direct responsibility of a specific department within the research division, referred to as the "responsible department." In addition, other departments known as "contributing departments" performed services on activities that did not fall directly within their jurisdiction.

For each activity package of each project or contract, the following cost data are reported for each month of the current year and for future years in total:

Original estimates to date.

Actual to date.

Reestimate to data.

Whenever experience indicates that the original estimates are likely to be grossly in error, a reestimate is made for each activity package. This is generally made equal to the actual labor cost up to the reestimation point, plus estimated completion cost. Thus the actual versus reestimate comparison provides information on labor cost performance since the reestimate was made.

The labor cost report forms, known as "control sheets," are issued monthly. They summarize the labor costs of both the responsible department and the contributing departments on each project and activity package and are issued to the managers of the appropriate responsible departments. Departmental summaries of all activity packages within each department's jurisdiction are also prepared. Labor costs of one department on activities that come under the responsibility of another department are credited to the contributing department and debited to the responsible department. Summaries by project and by department are prepared for the vice president–research.

When this report system was devised, it was anticipated that the responsible department heads would identify those activity packages for which labor costs were significantly out of line. They would then meet with heads of the appropriate contributing departments to discuss departures from estimates or budgets. It was hoped that these meetings would be approached in a constructive spirit and that direct intervention by the vice president–research and his staff would be infrequent.

The introduction of this system met with considerable resistance. Department heads resented a system that had been developed by the administrator without their participation. They objected to the amount of time that would be required each month to evaluate progress. The heads of each of the 10 departments designated as responsible departments objected to being charged for work to be performed by contributing departments. Furthermore, the department heads were skeptical that the activity cost estimates could ever be accurate enough to serve any control purpose. Finally, all department heads agreed that mischarges in the weekly time sheets would have to be reduced considerably before the system could work at all.

Despite these objections, the system was put into effect six months ago. Monthly cost review meetings have been stormy, with most of the arguments centering on the accuracy of time sheet allocations. The vice president–research has been called upon repeatedly to adjudicate disputes and to soothe ruffled feelings. The administrator feels that some progress is being made, but he is spending all his time policing the system and has had no time to work on control systems for other elements of research costs.

a) Do you believe that the system now in use in this company can achieve its control objectives once initial antagonisms have been overcome?

b) Can you suggest any improvements in the methods of control reporting and progress evaluation?

c) If you had been appointed planning and control administrator, would you have proceeded any differently in designing the system? Outline any differences you might suggest.

Part IV

Public
Financial
Reporting

Chapter 18

DISPOSAL OF FACTORY COST VARIANCES IN COMPANY FINANCIAL STATEMENTS

THE USE of predetermined costs in inventory accounts leaves a series of balances in variance accounts unallocated to individual products. The purpose of this chapter is to discuss the disposition of these variances in the company's financial statements.

ALTERNATIVE METHODS OF VARIANCE DISPOSAL

Cost variances may be disposed of in three different ways. First, they may be carried on the *balance sheet* as deferred charges or credits to future operations. Second, they may be charged or credited on the *income statement,* either as adjustments to the cost of goods sold or as separate items. Third, they may be *divided* between inventory and cost of goods sold in some way that will make these figures approximate actual historical cost.

Approximating Actual Cost

The choice of disposal method is partly a question of materiality and expediency, but it is or should be mainly dependent on the costing precepts of financial accounting theory. According to one point of view, the use of burden rates or standard costs is an expedient to facilitate data processing or to provide control information. Actual historical costs, according to this point of view, are still essential for inventory costing, regardless of whether these costs are high or low or what the reasons were for the departure of actual historical costs from predetermined averages or standards. The logical conclusion of this argument is to require a division of cost variances between balance sheet and income statement.[1]

Any such division must first relate the variances for the period to the goods produced during the period. Costs attributed in this way to goods that have been sold during the period are then charged or credited on the income statement, while costs attributed to goods on hand as of the end of the period remain on the balance sheet.

To accomplish this adjustment, some companies maintain a dual system of costing individual products—once at standard costs and once at actual costs.[2] This kind of duplication can be avoided, however, by computing an aggregate inventory adjustment on the basis of *average* relationships between variances and total production. Methods of applying such averages are discussed in a later section of this chapter.

Taking All Variances to Income

A second school of thought holds that standard cost is a *better measure* of product cost than actual cost, on the grounds that *all* variances result from departures of actual conditions from normal conditions. (Exceptions are sometimes made for price variances, for reasons to be discussed shortly.) The justification for leaving any cost on the balance sheet as a representation of an asset is a presumption that the present value to the company of future cash flows attributable to this cost is at least equal to the cost. Management's commitment to incur a cost, in other words, presumes that value is not less than cost. If actual costs exceed the amount upon which the commitment was based so that cost exceeds value, then part or all of the excess will have been proven unproductive. An up-to-date standard cost is ordinarily a better measure than actual cost of the commitment implicit in management's decision to manufacture the product.[3]

If this proposition is accepted, then departures from standard cost should not be inventoried on the balance sheet. An up-to-date standard cost represents the costs that are reasonably necessary to turn out

---

[1] For an argument that is generally favorable to costing inventories at average historical cost, see L. J. Benninger, "Accounting Theory and Cost Accounting," *The Accounting Review*, July, 1965, pp. 547–57.

[2] An example of such a "dual plan" of standard costing can be found in Robert I. Dickey (ed.), *Accountants' Cost Handbook* (2d ed.: Ronald Press, 1960), sect. 16, pp. 37–44.

[3] I am indebted to the late Professor Willard J. Graham for this phrasing of the argument. For a more extended discussion of the general principle, see Myron J. Gordon and Gordon Shillinglaw, *Accounting: A Management Approach* (3rd ed.; Homewood, Ill.: Richard D. Irwin, Inc., 1964), chaps. viii and ix.

finished products under current conditions, no more and no less. Goods manufactured in one period should not be inventoried at different costs from those manufactured in other periods as long as the underlying operating conditions remain unchanged. Therefore, all variances (again possibly excepting price variances) should be taken to the income statement for the period in which they arise.

The argument for this approach is perhaps best seen in connection with overhead volume variances. If volume variances are averaged over current production, inventoried unit cost will rise when volume declines and fall when volume expands, as shown in Exhibit 18–1. Because a

Exhibit 18–1

EFFECT OF VOLUME ON AVERAGE FIXED COST

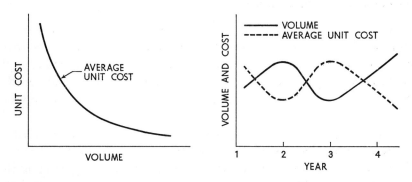

decline in volume usually occurs in response to a generally unfavorable economic outlook for the factory's output, the use of average actual cost will ordinarily lead to high unit cost in poor times when products are difficult to sell and low unit cost in good times. This is a strange result. Asset balances reflect cost, not value, but it is difficult to justify an inventory costing method that yields unit cost figures that move inversely with movements in product value.

The predetermined burden rate was developed at least partly to avoid this paradoxical result. This presumes that the fixed costs from which volume variances stem are costs of providing capacity. The amount absorbed indicates the cost of that portion of capacity used by specific products; the amount unabsorbed is attributable not to the products produced but to those that were not produced. Following this reasoning, none of the cost of idle capacity should be assigned to product inventories.

Clearing favorable volume variances to the income statement is harder to justify. Once again the argument is that each product should be assigned its full share of the costs of providing capacity. Overutilization of capacity is due to currently favorable conditions which change the profitability of the company's products rather than their costs. Just as the costs of idle capacity are assignable to products not produced, so the benefits from supernormal output accrue to the extra products rather than to the normal output.

The main drawback of this latter position is that the volume variance that accompanies supernormal production volume could provide a misleading indicator of income if the production represented a speculative buildup of inventory. This has led some accountants to favor the expensing of unfavorable variances but the spreading of favorable variances over total production for the period.

All Variances to the Balance Sheet

The third possible approach also accepts standard costs as the appropriate measure of *product* cost but maintains that departures from standard are *temporary* and will cancel themselves out if a long enough time period is permitted. Therefore, all variances should remain on the balance sheet until offset in later periods by variances in the opposite direction.

This viewpoint would be valid if variances could all be regarded as the result of random forces. Random fluctuations affect totals during a short period, but the longer the reporting period the greater is the likelihood that residual variances are nonrandom. The presumption that 12 months is a long enough time for random variances other than volume variances to cancel each other, together with uncertainty as to the length and average level of business fluctuations, has generally ruled out any extensive support for this third alternative in annual reporting.

Special Problem: Purchase Price Variances

Unlike other factory cost variances, variances from current materials price standards (and labor rate standards as well) must be small, almost by definition. Barring unusual purchasing department performance, the existence of price variances is a signal that price standards are out of date.

This being the case, standard cost will be a reasonable measure of management's commitment to the purchased goods when price variances are large only in transitory situations or when the buyer makes an irrevocable price commitment far in advance of the delivery date. Therefore, if the amounts are material, some attempt probably should be made to divide the purchase price variance between income statement and balance sheet accounts.

Industry Practice

The accounting profession as a whole has not taken a stand on the desirability or acceptability of various methods of disposing of cost variances. The closest to an official pronouncement on this question was a statement contained in a footnote to an accounting research bulletin issued by the American Institute of Certified Public Accountants: "Standard costs are acceptable if adjusted at reasonable intervals to reflect current conditions so that at the balance-sheet date standard costs reasonably approximate costs computed under one of the recognized bases."[4]

The same bulletin stated further that *"under some circumstances,* items such as idle facility expense, excessive spoilage, double freight, and rehandling costs may be so abnormal as to require treatment as current period charges rather than as a portion of the inventory cost," but it did not say what those circumstances might be or how abnormal the amount would have to be.[5] A more recent statement is more specific but equally permissive: "When standard cost methods of inventory valuation are used, the balances in variance accounts may be used to adjust cost of goods sold if the amounts are immaterial; otherwise they *may* be allocated between inventories and cost of goods sold."[6]

These statements would imply that inventory costs should ordinarily approximate average actual costs and that any significant variances, including volume variances, therefore should be split between income statement and balance sheet accounts. Industry practice, however, does not seem to conform to this pattern. A survey carried out two decades ago, for example, found that an overwhelming majority of the companies surveyed used the normal cost approach to the disposition of variances. Out of 127 companies responding to a questionnaire, 114, or approximately 90 percent, credited overabsorbed overhead variances either to the cost of goods sold or to profit and loss, and 112 charged underabsorbed overhead in the same manner. Furthermore, of 77 companies using standard costs, 58, or 78 percent, carried all materials and labor variances to the income statement and only seven divided all

---

[4] American Institute of Certified Public Accountants, *Accounting Research and Terminology Bulletins, Final Edition* (New York, 1961), fn. to p. 30.

[5] *Ibid.,* p. 29 (italics added).

[6] Paul Grady, *Inventory of Generally Accepted Accounting Principles, Accounting Research Study No. 7* (New York: American Institute of Certified Public Accountants, 1965), p. 102 (italics added).

variances between the income statement and the inventory accounts. The other 12 companies had separate treatment for price and quantity variances or for favorable and unfavorable variances, but all took some variances directly to the income statement.[7] Another survey 12 years later came to substantially the same conclusions,[8] and there is no evidence that current practice is significantly different.

INTERIM FINANCIAL REPORTING[9]

For internal bookkeeping most companies carry variances forward from month to month during the fiscal year and close them out only at year-end. They may or may not be allocated between balance sheet and income statement for interim financial reporting, however, and this raises enough separate conceptual issues to require some attention here.

Sources of Interim Variances

Manufacturing cost variances that arise during the year can be attributed to any of the following influences:

1. *Price influences:* departures of actual factor prices from standard or budgeted prices for the current month.
2. *Quantity influences:* departures of actual consumption of goods and services from standard or budgeted consumption for the output volume achieved during the current month.
3. *Seasonal influences on cost:* differences between the flexible budget allowances for the current month and allowances based on the average month in a normal year.
4. *Seasonal influences on volume:* differences between the normal volume for the current month and one twelfth of normal annual volume.
5. *Cyclical influences on volume:* departures of budgeted production volume for the current month from normal volume for the current month.
6. *Other influences on volume:* departures of production volume from budgeted volume for the current month.

All of this may seem unduly complicated, particularly in that only variances of the second group will ordinarily be reported to individual

---

[7] National Association of (Cost) Accountants, "Costs Included in Inventories, Research Series No. 10," *N.A.(C.)A. Bulletin,* August 15, 1947, pp. 1577–1608.

[8] Osamu Nisizawa, "Inventory Cost Allocation Practices and Concepts," *N.A.(C.)A. Bulletin,* December, 1959, pp. 81–93.

[9] The topic treated in this section is part of a larger group of issues related to interim reporting. See Robert G. Taylor, "A Look at Published Interim Reports," *The Accounting Review,* January, 1965, pp. 89–96; David Green, Jr., "Towards a Theory of Interim Reports," *Journal of Accounting Research,* Spring, 1964, pp. 35–49; and Gordon Shillinglaw, "Concepts Underlying Interim Financial Statements," *The Accounting Review,* April, 1961, pp. 222–231.

cost center managers. All six types will ordinarily be included in some way in divisional and companywide statements, however, and if seasonal or cyclical patterns are strong, failure to separate out the variances stemming from the last four types of influences can lead to incorrect interpretations. Of particular importance are the two seasonal influences which presumably cancel themselves out over the course of the year but may require special treatment for interim reporting.

Seasonal Variations in Costs

Some costs, such as heating and lighting, are subject to seasonal influences. Each month's budget presumably should be adjusted to allow for any such influences, but this will lead to variances between these budget allowances and the allowances that would result from applying to current volume an average of the year's 12 monthly budget relationships.

For example, suppose that a cost center's overhead during four successive fiscal quarters is as follows:

Quarter	(1) Budgeted	(2) Actual	(3) Absorbed	(4) Total Variance (2) − (3)	(5) Spending Variance (2) − (1)	(6) Seasonal Variance (1) − (3)
First	$30,000	$32,000	$27,500	$ 4,500	$2,000	$ 2,500
Second	20,000	21,000	27,500	(6,500)	1,000	(7,500)
Third	20,000	20,000	27,500	(7,500)	....	(7,500)
Fourth	40,000	41,000	27,500	13,500	1,000	12,500
Average	$27,500	$28,500	$27,500	$ 1,000	$1,000	$......

In this illustration volume of production is assumed to be the same each quarter and also equal to budgeted production. Because each quarter's volume is one fourth of normal annual volume, the amount absorbed is the same each quarter and is equal to average budgeted cost. This means that for the year as a whole and for each quarter as well, the volume variance is zero. The quarterly variances are large, however, despite the zero volume variances and the relatively small spending variances. The explanation lies in the seasonal pattern of budgeted costs. The difference between budgeted and absorbed costs for each quarter in this case is not a volume variance but a *seasonal variance*. This does not reflect on the interim efficiency or inefficiency of the enterprise and therefore presumably should be kept out of the quarterly income statement.

Seasonal Variations in Volume

Seasonal fluctuations in volume produce a similar effect. Assume that instead of a steady production volume the company expects to record 30 percent of its annual production in each of the first two quarters and only 20 percent in each of the last two quarters. If this were to happen, then overhead absorption would be as follows:

Quarter	(1) Budgeted	(2) Actual	(3) Absorbed	(4) Total Variance (2) − (3)	(5) Spending Variance (2) − (1)	(6) Seasonal Variance (1) − (3)
First..............	$30,000	$32,000	$33,000	$(1,000)	$2,000	$(3,000)
Second............	20,000	21,000	33,000	(12,000)	1,000	(13,000)
Third.............	20,000	20,000	22,000	(2,000)	....	(2,000)
Fourth............	40,000	41,000	22,000	19,000	1,000	18,000
Average..........	$27,500	$28,500	$27,500	$ 1,000	$1,000	$......

At the end of the year the seasonal variance washes out, but in two of the four quarters it is substantial. This is a normal occurrence, and thus presumably should not be reflected in either the external or the internal interim income statements.

Isolating the Seasonals

Actual volume, of course, does not always follow the predicted seasonal pattern. For example, assume that the burden rate is $2 a direct labor hour, based on an average volume of 13,750 direct labor hours a quarter. Both volume and costs are affected by seasonal influences. Data for the first quarter are:

	Budget	Actual
Production...........	16,500 direct labor hours	15,500 direct labor hours
Costs................	$17,000 + $1.10 × direct labor hours	$32,000

(The cost budget in this table is specific to this quarter, not the average for the year.)

On this basis, the total variance for the quarter is $1,000 and unfavorable:

Actual......................................$32,000
Absorbed....................15,500 × $2 = 31,000
　　　Total Variance............................$ 1,000

The budget for the first quarter is $17,000 + $1.10 \times 15,500 = $34,050. The spending variance is thus $2,050 and favorable, and following the formula developed in Chapter 15, the volume variance is $3,050, unfavorable:

Actual.............................	$32,000	
Budget at actual volume...............	34,050	
SPENDING VARIANCE................		$ 2,050
Absorbed...........................	31,000	
VOLUME VARIANCE................		(3,050)
TOTAL VARIANCE................		$(1,000)

This volume variance is really made up of two elements, however: one reflecting all the seasonal influences and the other the departure of actual volume from the volume budgeted for the quarter. If volume and costs had both been at normal first quarter levels, the variance would have been $2,150:

Absorbed at 16,500 hours = 16,500 \times $2.00 =		$ 33,000
Budgeted at 16,500 hours = $17,000 + 16,500 \times $1.10 =		35,150
Budgeted Volume Variance.....................		$(2,150)

This is the seasonal component of the volume variance. The $900 remainder, representing the difference between the budgeted volume variance and the actual volume variance, is the true volume variance for the quarter. The seasonal variance should always be deferred from quarter to quarter or month to month; the seasonally adjusted volume variance should be taken to the income statement for the current period.[10]

METHODS OF INVENTORY ADJUSTMENT

The division of variances between income statement and balance sheet accounts does not require the recosting of individual jobs or process outputs. An adequate approximation can be obtained by the use of average cost/output ratios.

The Inventory Adjustment Account

Under most procedures, the inventory control accounts continue to represent the standard cost of the items on hand. (In costing systems that do not use product cost standards, the overhead component of

---

[10] This discussion presumes that seasonal adjustments have been made to the budgeted data and that separate flexible budget formulas are therefore available for each interim reporting period or season. The possibility of applying statistical techniques to isolate the seasonal influence, after the fact, is discussed by Werner Frank, "Seasonal Adjustment of Accounting Data," *Management Services*, November–December, 1965, pp. 51–55.

inventory would be shown at the predetermined burden rates.) *The difference between standard cost and the amount to be shown on the company balance sheet is kept in an inventory adjustment account.*

To illustrate, assume that a company prices its inventories by the FIFO method, including an allowance for the appropriate portion of variances of all types. For convenience, this is referred to as the *"actual cost"* of the goods in inventory. Assume further that the overhead cost assigned to the January 1, 1966, inventory quantities was as follows:

	At Standard	At Actual	Difference
Overhead in process..................	$ 500,000	$ 530,000	$30,000
Overhead in finished goods...........	800,000	848,000	48,000
Total........................	$1,300,000	$1,378,000	$78,000

The difference between the actual and standard amounts would then be carried as a debit balance in an inventory adjustment account or accounts:

Inventory Valuation Adjustment

Bal. 1/1	78,000	

A full balance sheet presentation would show:

Overhead in inventories, at standard............................$1,300,000
Plus allowance for actual costs in excess of standard.............. 78,000
    Overhead in Inventories.....................................$1,378,000

Changing Standards

On January 1, 1966, new standards were put into effect and the inventory control accounts were adjusted upward to reflect the new standards. The overhead in inventories at the new standards was:

Overhead in process.........................$ 550,000
Overhead in finished goods.................... 880,000
    Overhead in Inventories...................$1,430,000

This was $130,000 more than the inventory control accounts showed, and the adjustment was accomplished by the following entry:

Overhead in Process....................................50,000
Overhead in Finished Goods............................80,000
    Inventory Valuation Adjustment..................... 130,000

The adjustment account thus showed a $52,000 credit balance:

Inventory Valuation Adjustment

Bal. 1/1	78,000	Adjustment	130,000
		Adj. Bal. 1/1	52,000

This was purely an internal bookkeeping adjustment. The post-adjustment January 1, 1966, balance sheet still showed overhead in inventories at $1,378,000:

Overhead in inventories, at standard...........................$1,430,000
Less allowance to reduce inventories to actual cost............... 52,000
　　Overhead in Inventories.................................$1,378,000

End-of-Year Adjustment: FIFO Method

During 1966, overhead costs were transferred into and out of the inventory accounts at standard, and no entries were made in the valuation adjustment account. This produced the following year-end balances:

Overhead in Process—Standard

Bal. 12/31	450,000

Overhead in Finished Goods—Standard

Bal. 12/31	1,100,000

Inventory Valuation Adjustment

		Bal. 1/1	52,000

Thus, prior to adjustment, the total book value of the overhead in inventories at year-end was $1,498,000 ($450,000 + $1,100,000 − $52,000).

The "actual cost" of the year-end inventories can be approximated in various ways, including the following:

1. Multiply standard overhead cost in inventories by the ratio of actual overhead cost for the entire year to overhead cost earned by production during the year.
2. Multiply standard overhead cost in inventories by the ratio of actual overhead cost for the final months of the year to overhead costs earned by production during those months; the length of the period to be approximately that during which the ending inventory was manufactured (e.g., if standard overhead cost in inventories totaled $1,550,000 and the standard overhead cost earned by production in December, November,

and October totaled $1,450,000, the cost ratios for the fourth quarter could be regarded as a close enough approximation).

3. As in (2), but adjust the overhead costs earned for the seasonal portions of the volume variance, if any.

The first of these is the easiest to apply, while the others are more fully consistent with the FIFO definition. Because the basic method is identical in each case and the differences in many cases will not be material in amount, an example using a simple annual average should serve to illustrate all three.

Assume that factory overhead for 1966 amounted to $5,400,000 while the overhead earned by production totaled $5,000,000. The ratio of actual to earned overhead was thus 108 percent. Applying this ratio to the year-end inventory would yield the following:

	At Standard Cost	Conversion Ratio	At "Actual Cost"
Overhead in process................	$ 450,000	1.08	$ 486,000
Overhead in finished goods..........	1,100,000	1.08	1,188,000
Total........................	$1,550,000		$1,674,000

The "actual cost" total is $176,000 greater than the year-end book value, and the inventory valuation adjustment account should have a debit balance of this amount at year-end. In other words, $176,000 of the $400,000 overhead variance for the year would remain on the year-end balance sheet; the remaining $224,000 would go to the income statement. The entry to close the overhead accounts for the year would be:

```
Inventory Valuation Adjustment...........................  176,000
Cost of Goods Sold.......................................  224,000
Manufacturing Overhead Earned...........................5,000,000
    Manufacturing Overhead Summary......................            5,400,000
```

One further adjustment is necessary. The inventory valuation adjustment account had an opening credit balance of $52,000. In FIFO inventory costing, this attaches to the first goods sold during the year and thus would have to be transferred to the income statement:

```
Inventory Valuation Adjustment...........................   52,000
    Cost of Goods Sold...................................            52,000
```

The inventory adjustment account would then have a debit balance of $176,000. The full balance sheet presentation would be:

Overhead in inventories (at standard)...................................$1,550,000
Plus allowance for actual costs in excess of standard..................... 176,000
    Total..$1,726,000

This adjustment is admittedly an approximation, but it is probably sufficiently accurate for external financial reporting. Greater precision can be obtained by using separate adjustment factors for individual departments, but only at greater clerical cost. It should be remembered that *any* application of overhead to product cost is inexact. The entire burden rate concept is based on the use of average relationships because more direct relationships do not exist. Therefore, if it is company policy to adjust year-end inventories to approximate actual historical cost, the methods just described are entirely valid.

Disposition of Materials Price Variances

No purpose would be served by extending this illustration to direct labor costs, but materials variances are slightly different. The purchase price variance applies to raw materials and parts inventories as well as to the materials content of work in process, finished goods, and the goods that have been sold during the period. This difference requires some discussion.

Once again, full-year averages or partial period averages could be used, but it is simpler to illustrate using the former. The purchase price variance for the year was $600,000, and unfavorable, on a purchase volume of $10,000,000 at standard prices. Ignoring the question of whether a 6 percent variance might be regarded as immaterial, the $600,000 could be spread in proportion to the standard materials cost distribution assumed in the following table:

	At Standard Cost	Conversion Ratio	At Actual Average Prices
Materials and parts inventory......	$ 3,000,000	1.06	$ 3,180,000
Materials in process inventory.....	500,000	1.06	530,000
Materials in finished goods........	1,500,000	1.06	1,590,000
Materials in goods sold (less year-beginning inventory)...........	5,000,000	1.06	5,300,000
Total......................	$10,000,000		$10,600,000

This, of course, presumes that all inventories are carried on a FIFO basis; a LIFO adjustment would start with the materials content of the goods sold and would convert only increments in the inventory figures. With FIFO, however, the inventory adjustment account at year-end should include $300,000 for unfavorable materials price variances. The distribution of the materials quantity variances would of course not extend to the materials and parts inventory and could be based on calculations of the type illustrated for overhead.

End-of-Year Adjustment: LIFO Method

LIFO inventory pricing requires (1) the separate identification of the layer of inventory coming from each year's increment; (2) measurement of the physical inventory increment or decrement for the current year; and (3) estimation of the unit cost applicable to the increments and decrements.

This can be done item by item, but the use of standard cost in the inventory accounts is most readily applicable to composite inventory pools because it provides a ready means of measuring annual physical increments and decrements.[11] For example, the physical inventories in the previous illustration, at 1966 standard costs, increased during the year:

$$
\begin{array}{lr}
\text{End-of-year inventory} & \$1,550,000 \\
\text{Beginning-of-year inventory} & 1,430,000 \\
\hline
\text{Increase in Inventory} & \$\ 120,000 \\
\end{array}
$$

Beginning and ending inventory totals represent two sets of physical quantities multiplied by a single set of standard prices. Because both sets of quantity figures are multiplied by the same prices, the account change represents the combined effect of changes in the inventory mix and changes in the physical quantities of goods on hand. For application of the pooling method, the increment is interpreted to be entirely due to changes in physical quantities, on the grounds that standard costs weight each item in proportion to its importance relative to the others. In other words, it is assumed that two $1 units are fully equivalent to one $2 unit. Without this assumption, the entire pooling concept must be abandoned.

To illustrate the method, suppose that the company adopted LIFO as of January 1, 1966. The book value of the overhead costs in inventory at that time was $1,378,000, which was 96.36 percent of standard cost. At standard prices, the year-end inventory was $120,000 greater than the opening inventory, according to the calculations described in the last paragraph. The problem now is to estimate the "actual" costs of this increment.

---

[11] For an elementary exposition of the pooling method, see Gordon and Shillinglaw, *op. cit.*, pp. 411–15.

The simplest solution would be to price the increment at current standard cost, $120,000:

Base quantity..............................$1,378,000
1966 layer.................................. 120,000
Total Inventory at LIFO..................$1,498,000

This would correspond to the sum of the overhead balances in the inventory accounts and the inventory adjustment account, and no adjusting entry would be needed.

Although many companies take this simple approach, particularly if actual costs are not far from current standards, others include some or all of the current year's variances in the costing of the increment. For this purpose, the simplest approach is to use the ratio of actual to standard costs during the year.

In the example, this ratio was 108 percent for overhead costs, and the 1966 layer would therefore be $1.08 \times \$120,000 = \$129,600$. The LIFO inventory at year-end thus would be $\$1,378,000 + \$129,600 = \$1,507,600$. The total standard cost was $1,550,000, and thus the inventory adjustment account would have to have a credit balance of $42,400 to bring the book value down to $1,507,600. The credit balance carried forward from the beginning of the year was $52,000, however, and this would require a $9,600 debit to this account in the year-end adjusting entries. In other words, the entry to write off the $400,000 unabsorbed overhead for the year would be:

Cost of Goods Sold...390,400
Inventory Valuation Adjustment.............................. 9,600
Manufacturing Overhead Earned............................5,000,000
    Manufacturing Overhead Summary....................... 5,400,000

The calculations for an inventory liquidation are more complicated, but they are facilitated immensely by the availability of standard cost totals. For example, assume that in 1967 the overhead in inventory at standard prices decreased by $150,000. Because both the current standard cost and the LIFO cost of each layer of the inventory are known, measurement of the decrement is simple and straightforward:

	At Standard Cost	Conversion Ratio	At LIFO "Actual Cost"
1966 layer........................	$120,000	108.00%	$129,600
Base quantity......................	30,000	96.36	28,908
Total Decrement.................	$150,000		$158,508

This means that $8,508 would have to be credited to the inventory adjustment account at the end of 1967.

This procedure, of course, is also an approximation. The larger the inventory pool, the less homogeneous it is likely to be and the greater the error of approximation. The use of more than one pool, however, requires some means of dividing the variances among the various pools. Such a division increases the cost of bookkeeping. If the increase in accuracy is slight, this added cost will be hard to justify, particularly in that the adjustment has no managerial significance.

SUMMARY

Most companies write off all variances on the income statement for the year in which they arise. Although convenience is probably often the object, the justification is that variances reflect departures from the conditions upon which purchase or production commitments were based. Only if standards are not current should unfavorable variances be split between balance sheet and income statement, and the same position can be argued for favorable variances.

Many accountants, however, regard standard cost as only a first approximation to actual historical cost and maintain that any factory cost variances of significant amount should be spread appropriately over all production. If this is done, some portion of the current variance will go to the current year's income and some will remain in the asset totals on the year-end balance sheet. Adjustment of inventories from standard cost to average historical cost can be accomplished accurately, insofar as any average can be regarded as accurate, but only at a high clerical cost. Generally satisfactory results can be obtained by pooling inventories and applying average variance ratios to each pool as a whole. Fairly simple methods of applying these averages are available, either for LIFO or for FIFO inventories.

All of these arguments are largely irrelevant in connection with internal management reporting. Management reports should show current variances in their entirety, without regard to the method of disposal for public financial reporting. Only those portions of the current variance that stem from predictable seasonal factors should be excluded from the reports or isolated in the accompanying analysis. Methods of identifying the seasonal components of current variances are discussed in this chapter.

DISCUSSION QUESTIONS

1. From the standpoint of periodic income measurement and inventory cost-ing, what issues are raised by the practice of establishing materials price variances at the time of purchase and carrying these variances directly to the income statement of the period in which the purchases were recorded? How should these issues be resolved?

2. What are the arguments for the use of predetermined burden rates in developing unit cost data for inventory costing?

3. Assuming that all factory overhead variances are taken to the income statement as adjustments to the cost of goods sold, does the selection of the volume base for burden rate determination have any influence on reported income?

4. Assuming that a company wishes to price materials inventories at standard for internal cost bookkeeping but wishes to reflect actual prices in its published financial statements, by what means can both of these objectives be achieved?

5. The use of predetermined charging rates or transfer prices in interdepart-mental cost allocation in the factory often leaves over- or underallocated balances in service department accounts. Discuss alternative methods of disposing of these variances, assuming that the company wishes its publicly reported inventory figures to approximate actual factory costs.

6. The Bently Soft Drink Company's production shows a pronounced seasonal fluctuation. Should overhead variances be shown as adjustments to the cost of goods sold on the company's monthly income statements? If not, what alternative would you suggest?

7. Should factory overhead volume variances be disposed of on the company's published financial statements in a manner different from that used for overhead spending variances? Price variances?

8. Most companies close all variances periodically to the cost of goods sold. A significant minority, however, split the materials price variance, with part going to the cost of goods sold and part remaining in an inventory account. What is the justification for this latter practice?

9. The Carson Corporation uses departmental burden rates, each of them based on direct labor hours as the index of departmental volume. Would the amount of under- or overabsorbed overhead for the plant as a whole be any different if a plantwide burden rate were used? Would the cost of goods sold be different? Explain.

10. Assuming that a company wishes its reported inventory figures to approxi-mate actual costs, would you expect a larger proportion of the year's variances to appear on the income statement if the company's inventories are costed on a FIFO basis than if its inventories are on LIFO? Explain.

11. Overhead costs in a particular factory production department were underab-sorbed by $1,500 during January. This balance is closed out to cost of goods sold at the end of the month.

a) What effect did the use of a predetermined burden rate instead of a postdetermined burden rate have on reported income for January and for February, assuming that inventory cost flows follow the FIFO principle?

b) How would your answer differ if LIFO were in use, assuming that physical inventories remained constant during these two months?

EXERCISES AND PROBLEMS

1. Some authorities on cost accounting advocate a burden rate based on a volume of 100 percent of practical capacity.

a) If this is adopted, would you expect most overhead volume variances to be favorable or unfavorable? Give your reasons in one sentence.

b) A company using this plan has a burden rate of $2 per machine-hour and an unfavorable volume variance of $5,000. Explain briefly, and as precisely as you can, what this unfavorable volume variance means. In what way, if any, might this kind of information be useful to management?

c) What end-of-year adjustments, if any, would be necessary for financial statement preparation if product costs were computed on this basis?

2. Manufacturing overhead costs in a particular department were underabsorbed by $15,000 during 19x1. This balance was charged against revenues on the 19x1 income statement.

a) What effect did the use of a predetermined burden rate instead of actual overhead cost have on reported profit for 19x1 and 19x2, assuming that inventory cost flows follow the FIFO principle?

b) How would your answer differ if LIFO were in use, assuming that physical inventories were the same at the end of 19x1 as at the beginning?

3. The trial balances of the Andrews Company included the following balances at the beginning and end of the year:

	January 1	December 31
Sales revenue....................................		$1,500,000
Labor cost of goods sold........................		200,000
Materials cost of goods sold....................		600,000
Overhead cost of goods sold....................		400,000
Overhead in process............................	$ 50,000	80,000
Overhead in finished goods.....................	100,000	120,000
Manufacturing overhead (debit)................		218,000
Manufacturing overhead absorbed (credit).......		182,000
Operating expenses.............................		250,000
Variances in inventory.........................		....

The company's inventories were costed on a FIFO basis. The burden rate had not been changed for two years, and there was no under- or overabsorbed overhead in the previous year. The burden rate was based on normal volume. Variances in labor and materials costs were negligible.

a) Compute reported income before taxes for the year, on the assumption that the cost of inventories to be reported on the year-end balance sheet is to approximate actual cost rather than normal cost.

b) Perform the operations called for in (*a*), with the same underlying assumptions but based on the LIFO method of inventory costing.

4. The Schouten Products Company uses a single plan standard costing system in its manufacturing operations. For annual financial reporting, however, the company's management wishes to cost inventories at an approximation to actual cost on a first-in, first-out basis. The materials and labor content of all inventories, from raw materials to finished products, is included in a single pool for inventory costing purposes. The inventory accounts are based on standard cost, with a supplemental account to make up the difference between standard and actual costs. On January 1, 1966, these accounts showed the following balances:

```
Materials and labor in inventories (at 1966 standards)............$340,000
Inventory adjustment........................................  10,000
Net Inventories (at FIFO Actual)............................$350,000
```

After adjustments to reflect the annual physical inventory count, the December 31, 1966, trial balance included the following account balances (all debit balances):

```
Materials and labor in inventories............................$396,000
Inventory adjustment........................................  10,000
Materials and labor variances................................  174,000
```

Further investigation revealed that materials and labor variances during the months of September through December, 1966, amounted to $90,200, unfavorable. Total materials purchases and direct labor payrolls for this period, at standard, totaled $410,000.

a) Using only the information above, prepare journal entries to close the summary variance account at the end of 1966 and to adjust the net inventory valuation to an approximation of FIFO actual cost.

b) As of January 1, 1967, the company's standard costs were revised upward, and the new 1967 standards were incorporated into the accounts. The total inventory at 1967 standards was $512,000 on January 1, 1967. Prepare a journal entry to reflect the change in standards.

c) Comment briefly on the desirability of including materials and labor costs in the same costing "pool" for public financial reporting. Comment also on any other strengths or weaknesses of the company's method of approximating FIFO actual cost.

*5. Materials inventories are carried at standard cost, but for public financial reporting the year's variances are spread proportionately between the cost of goods sold and balance sheet accounts. You are given the following data:

(1) Inventories (at standard):

	January 1	December 31
Raw materials..................................	$10,000	$15,000
Materials in process...........................	6,100	5,000
Materials in finished goods....................	8,000	7,000
Materials quantity variance in inventory........	900 (cr.)	?

---

* Solutions to problems marked with an asterisk (*) can be found in Appendix B.

(2) Materials issued, at standard cost, $30,000.

(3) Materials quantity variance (debit), $5,000.

a) Compute the FIFO cost of goods sold for the year.

b) Prepare an end-of-period entry to close out the Materials Quantity Variance account and adjust the Materials Quantity Variance in Inventory account to its appropriate year-end balance.

6. A company maintains three separate accounts for the materials, labor, and overhead content of inventories, plus accompanying accounts for the inventoried portion of cost variances. A standard costing system is in use, and inventories for public financial reporting are costed on a FIFO basis. Data for 19x1 are:

(1) Inventory balances, at standard cost:

	January 1	December 31
Labor in process	$4,000	$ 7,000
Labor in finished goods	8,500	10,500
Labor variances in inventory (debit)	500	?

(2) Direct labor, 8,050 hours (standard wage rate $3 an hour, actual wages, $25,116).

(3) Labor quantity variance for the year at standard wage rates, $3,150 (unfavorable).

a) Compute the standard labor cost of goods sold.

b) Compute the labor cost of goods sold on a FIFO approximate average cost basis. (Suggestion: Deal with quantity variances first.)

c) Prepare a journal entry to close out the year's variances and adjust the inventory accounts to their appropriate year-end balances.

d) Recompute the labor cost of goods sold for the year, assuming a LIFO basis of inventory costing and inventorying only the appropriate portion of the labor rate variance.

7. A company costs its inventories for public financial reporting on a FIFO approximate average cost basis but uses standard cost as the costing basis for internal reporting. For external reporting, the materials content of raw materials, work in process, and finished goods is combined in a single FIFO pool. Data for 19x0 are:

(1) Inventory balances, at standard cost:

	January 1	December 31
Raw materials	$100,000	$130,000
Materials in process	20,000	22,000
Materials in finished goods	60,000	50,000
Materials variances in inventory	5,000 cr.	?

(2) Materials purchased: at actual prices, $297,000; at standard prices, $270,000.

(3) Materials quantity variances, at standard prices, $40,000 (debit).

a) Compute the standard materials cost of goods sold.

b) Assuming FIFO inventory costing, approximately how much of the standard materials cost of goods sold represents the cost of materials issued this year?

c) Assuming FIFO inventory costing and also assuming that the materials cost figures on the year-end balance sheet are to approximate actual average costs for the year, compute the materials cost of goods sold and the materials cost of the year-end inventory.

d) Prepare a journal entry to close out the year's variances and to adjust the Materials Variances in Inventory account to its correct year-end balance.

*8. The Zebra Company used an estimated overhead rate of $2.50 per direct labor hour for 1966. At the end of 1966, after having worked 125,000 labor hours, the company had an underabsorbed overhead of $46,750. It apportioned this in proportion to the labor hours in work in process and finished goods inventories and in cost of goods sold. The labor hours in each of these were:

Work in process	15,000
Finished goods	25,000
Cost of goods sold	85,000
Total	125,000

While auditing the records of the Zebra Company, you find:

(1) A machine costing $10,000 was charged to Manufacturing Overhead; a fixed asset record card for this machine was prepared correctly, however, and depreciation on the machine was correctly charged to manufacturing overhead during the year.

(2) The salary of the president for July ($3,000) was incorrectly charged to Manufacturing Overhead.

(3) Job No. 389 was charged with overhead of $250 which should have been charged to Job No. 298. Both jobs have been completed and sold.

Prepare any necessary adjustments and apportion any under- or overabsorbed overhead resulting from those adjustments.

9. Ivy Caps, Inc., manufactured a line of cloth caps of standard design. Its factory records were based upon standards. The standards in use during 19x2 were as follows (per 100 caps):

Cloth, 35 yards at $1.15	$ 40.25
Lining, 8 yards at $0.80	6.40
Trimmings	3.35
Labor, 60 hours at $1.50	90.00
Overhead, 90% of labor cost	81.00
Total	$221.00

Beginning and closing inventories, production statistics, and costs for 19x2 are tabulated below:

Inventories	December 31, 19x1	December 31, 19x2
Cloth	2,500 yds. at $1.15, $2,875	2,800 yds.
Linings	600 yds. at $0.80, $480	400 yds.
Trimmings	$1,865	$2,100
Caps in process*	4,000 caps, $5,225	8,000 caps
Finished caps	8,600 caps at $2.21, $19,006	7,100 caps

*Complete as to cloth, one-half complete as to linings, trimmings, labor, and overhead.

Production and Costs

Caps started......................................	66,000
Caps completed....................................	62,000
Caps sold...	63,500
Cloth purchases (24,500 yards).....................	$28,910
Lining purchases (5,000 yards).....................	$ 3,950
Trimmings purchases (standard cost, $1,980)........	$ 2,200
Direct labor (40,500 hours)........................	$66,825
Overhead..	$57,600

a) Set up appropriate T-accounts and make entries to record the events of the year.

b) Compute the costs assigned to all December 31, 19x2, inventories: (1) at standard, and (2) including a provision for materials price and labor rate variances.

10. The Grimes Corporation is engaged in the manufacture of metal stampings for the automotive industry. The manufacturing cycle is quite short so that the work in process inventories are small and may be ignored for this problem. A job order cost system is used in the factory. A factorywide burden rate is established quarterly on the basis of the anticipated production volume for the ensuing three months and is used to apply manufacturing costs to the product.

The company ends its fiscal year so as to conform to the model change period in the auto industry, since it normally has no finished goods inventory at this time. The company's cost accountant prepared the following estimates of manufacturing overhead cost:

If Production During Quarter Is—	*Factory Overhead Costs Will Be—*
300,000 units.............................	$420,000
400,000 units.............................	460,000
500,000 units.............................	500,000
600,000 units.............................	540,000
700,000 units.............................	580,000

The estimated production volume for the first quarter was 400,000 units. Actual production during the first quarter totaled 380,000 units, and actual factory overhead costs totaled $456,000. At the end of the quarter 38,000 units were still in finished goods inventory, the remaining 342,000 units having been sold during the quarter.

Estimated production for the second quarter was 600,000 units, and a new burden rate was established on that basis. During the second quarter, the factory produced 620,000 units at a total factory overhead cost of $570,400. Sales during the second quarter totaled 558,000 units, the remaining production being added to inventory.

Finished goods inventory is costed on a FIFO basis during the year.

a) Compute the total overhead variance and the overhead spending variance for each quarter.

b) Indicate for each quarter the amount of manufacturing overhead costs that would be carried to the income statement and the amount that would remain on the end-of-quarter balance sheet:

(1) If cost variances are closed out to the income statement at the end of the quarter.

(2) If the variances are divided between balance sheet and income statement in the same proportion as the absorbed overhead for the quarter is divided between finished goods inventory and the cost of goods sold.

c) Assuming that the burden rate is constant from quarter to quarter, based on a normal quarterly production volume of 500,000 units, indicate for each quarter the amount of manufacturing overhead costs that would be carried to the income statement and the amount that would remain on the end-of-quarter balance sheet, if all cost variances are carried forward on the end-of-quarter balance sheet as deferred charges or deferred credits against the operations of subsequent quarters.

d) Compare the company's financial position and earnings performance as revealed by financial statements prepared by the three methods of variance disposal used in (b) and (c). Indicate which method you prefer and why.

*11. One of the Richardson Company's factory departments consists of a single large machine, accessory equipment, and an operating crew. The costs of shutting the machine down and starting it up again are substantial, so the machine is operated continuusly three shifts a day for seven days a week until inventory levels are deemed excessive or overhaul is urgently needed.

The normal running time is 6,600 hours per year. Because of seasonality of demand, however, running time is not expected to be distributed uniformly over the year, and routine overhauls are scheduled for slack periods when the machine is shut down for other reasons. For 1967, 60 percent of the planned output for the year was budgeted for the first six months.

This company followed the common practice of applying overhead costs to various jobs on this machine by means of a predetermined burden rate per machine-hour. Estimated overhead costs for the year 1967, broken down by fixed and variable components, were as follows:

Fixed charges.....................$ 56,760
Variable charges................. 87,780
Annual Total...............$144,540

Variable charges were assumed to vary in direct proportion to the number of machine-hours.

a) Compute an annual burden rate for 1967.

b) Based on the above information only, what was the balance expected in the over- or underabsorbed overhead account at the end of the first six months?

c) The department recorded 3,800 machine-hours during the first six months of 1967. Given this additional information, what balance would you expect in the over- or underabsorbed overhead account at the end of the half-year?

d) Explain any difference between the amounts given in answer to questions (b) and (c) above.

e) The actual machine overhead costs accumulated during the first half of

1967 totaled $79,915. What was the actual over- or underabsorbed overhead at the end of the half-year?

f) Prepare a table showing the amount of the over- or underabsorbed overhead attributable to each major causative factor.

12. In the Travis Paper Company, as in all paper companies, the principal costs are centered about the paper machines. The company, therefore, attaches great importance to the calculations of machine rates by which manufacturing overhead is allocated to products. Furthermore, the operating executives give considerable attention to the analysis and interpretation of cost figures and in particular to overhead cost variances. In periods of abnormally high or low production, the variances are analyzed to separate controllable from noncontrollable gains or losses.

By running three eight-hour shifts each 24 hours, one of the Travis Paper Company's paper machines has a normal annual volume of 6,000 hours. An hourly machine rate that will adequately distribute budgeted machine overhead to products at this volume is as follows:

$$\text{Fixed charges} \dots \dots \dots \dots \dots \frac{\$61,800}{6,000} = \$10.30$$

$$\text{Variable charges} \dots \dots \dots \dots \frac{\$98,400}{6,000} = 16.40$$

$$\text{Total} \dots \dots \dots \dots \dots \dots \quad \$26.70$$

During the first three months of 19x1, the machine actually ran 1,490 hours; the first quarter ordinarily provides 30 percent of the total year's production. The overhead account for this machine at the end of the quarter showed the following data:

Machine No. 2 Overhead

Fixed charges	14,485	Fixed charges (1,490 × $10.30)	15,347
Variable charges	23,304	Variable charges (1,490 × $16.40)	24,436
	37,789		39,783
		Overabsorbed balance 1,994	

Costs Chargeable to Paper Machine No. 2

Fixed Charges	Normal Annual Charges	Actual 1st Quarter 19x1
Watchman and fire brigade.........	$ 1,800	$ 450
Taxes......................	7,560	1,890
Insurance.....................	4,980	1,245
Depreciation..................	33,000	8,250
Building repairs...............	10,460	1,625
Supervision...................	2,400	600
Accounting and office...........	1,000	250
Laboratory...................	600	175
	$61,800	$14,485

Variable Charges	Normal Annual Charges	Actual 1st Quarter 19x1
Indirect labor......................	$ 5,400	$ 1,318
Supplies...........................	12,260	3,154
Water.............................	1,620	364
Teaming and yard expense...........	6,720	1,520
Stock handling.....................	1,980	430
Repairs to machinery...............	8,160	1,880
Power and light....................	54,220	12,408
Heat..............................	8,040	2,230
	$98,400	$23,304

Determine, insofar as possible, the sources of the $1,994 variance and measure how much of this variance comes from each source. On the basis of your analysis, prepare a brief statement for submission to the general manager.

Part V

Incremental Analysis for Decisions

Chapter 19

FURTHER CONCEPTS IN
DECISION MAKING

MANAGEMENT DECISIONS often rely heavily upon data drawn from the accounting data bank. These data are ordinarily prepared by the methods described in previous chapters. The next five chapters will examine the relevance of accounting data to management decisions and the ways in which these data may have to be modified in particular situations. The purpose of this introductory chapter is twofold: first, to summarize briefly the relationship of accounting data to decisions; and second, to derive a scheme for classifying decision situations based on a previously unrecognized decision dimension—the time dimension.

Alternatives, Increments, and Decision Rules

Because so many chapters have intervened since this topic was introduced, it may be well to review briefly a few points from Chapter 3. First, decisions represent choices among alternative courses of action and must be based on perceived differences among these alternatives. Second, decisions must be made in the face of uncertainty as to the probable outcomes under the various alternatives. Third, every decision reflects the explicit or implicit application of a decision rule or rules to the data representing differences among the alternatives. Fourth, to the extent that the decision rules apply to variables that can be expressed in monetary terms, only differences in the inflows or outflows of cash or its equivalent are relevant; these differences are known as *incremental profits*. It is with this kind of data that accounting is most often concerned, and the analysis that must be undertaken to provide such data is known as *incremental profit analysis*.

Selection of the relevant alternatives can be of crucial importance in this process. In evaluating a particular proposal, the relevant alternative is the best action the company could take if the proposal were to be rejected. This might be to continue operations as at present, to change the existing operations mix, or perhaps even to close down a particular operation entirely.

For example, if a manager requests expansion of the plant to provide capacity for the manufacture of a new product, the relevant alternative may be to operate the existing plant but substitute the new product for an existing product that provides a lower incremental profit contribution. In other words, the investment may have to be justified by the cash flows generated by an existing product rather than by the more lucrative new product.

Most accounting data provided for use in decision making ignore the concept of uncertainty. Product unit cost, for example, is almost always stated as a single figure. Alternative estimates ordinarily can be provided, however, if the uncertainty is great and the decision rule calls for them. These chapters will be concerned primarily with questions of the relevance to decisions of accounting data expressed in monetary terms. Although a simple profit maximization decision rule will be used for illustrative purposes, the principles discussed here are of universal applicability.

Treatment of Allocations

It should be apparent by now that many cost accounting procedures tend to obscure rather than clarify incremental cost patterns. The most important offender is the allocation of common costs to specific costing units. For example, suppose that a company applies factory overhead to products by means of a predetermined burden rate of $2 per direct labor dollar. The industrial engineering department is preparing a proposal to acquire a piece of equipment that is expected to reduce direct labor costs by $4,000 a year. If the burden rate is interpreted literally, this would suggest that the saving in direct labor would be accompanied by a saving of $8,000 a year in factory overhead.

The fact, however, is that the burden rate is based on overall averages under certain specified conditions. It does not pretend to show the change in cost in response to changes in any one of these conditions, be it a change in operating volume or a change in the character of the equipment utilized in production. The change in overhead is highly unlikely to correspond to the ratio indicated by the burden rate. Therefore, effects on indirect costs should be considered explicitly, not by application of an average burden rate which covers a wide variety of costs, each with its own particular response to the contemplated change. Introduction of the new equipment, for example, might increase maintenance and power costs and decrease scrap losses. The *net* saving from this proposal might be greater than the $4,000 saving in direct labor, or it might be less. Only a specific projection of the effects of the proposal on overhead will reveal the direction and extent of the expected changes.

Most accounting systems also provide for the allocation within the company of costs incurred in service or general executive departments, and they may also include cost allocations to reflect transfers of goods and services from one operating division to another. The allocation or transfer pricing methods in use seldom reflect a full causal relationship between the cost and the allocation base, and incremental analysis must recognize this fact.

For example, the Handbuilt Company assigns head office administrative costs to product divisions at a rate of 3 percent of net sales. The company's fertilizer division shows the following income statement:

Sales...	$10,000,000
Cost of sales......................................	7,000,000
Gross margin......................................	$ 3,000,000
Division expenses.................................	2,900,000
Profit contribution...............................	$ 100,000
Head office expense..............................	300,000
Net Loss...	$ (200,000)

In reviewing the profitability of this division, the net loss of $200,000 a year is not precisely relevant. What is wanted is the amount by which company profit would be increased or decreased by the abandonment of this division. If it is estimated that discontinuation of the fertilizer line would reduce head office expense by only $60,000 a year, then this is the amount that should be charged to the division for analysis purposes.

What the $200,000 loss indicates is that this division is not profitable enough to carry its proportionate share of head office expenses, but it does not necessarily mean that the division should be abandoned. If this action were to be taken, then $240,000 in head office expense ($300,-000 now assigned to this division minus the $60,000 potential saving) would have to be reassigned to other divisions. This reallocation might make one or more of these other divisions appear unprofitable, which would produce the same problem all over again.

THE CLASSIFICATION SCHEME

Decision situations can be classified in many ways. Production decisions can be distinguished from marketing decisions, for example, or new product decisions from inventory decisions. Chapter 3 classified decisions on the basis of the relative degree of uncertainty in the cash flow estimates.

All these are useful, but they all overlook the timing of the antici-pated cash flows under the various alternatives. Recognition of this dimension permits classification of decision situations into two catego-ries that have significance for the analyst: *investment problems,* in which the cash flows of more than one time period must be evaluated explicitly; and *tactical problems,* in which only one period's cash flows need be estimated.

Investment Problems

Investment is generally identified with the acquisition of assets. Persons invest in common stocks, in bonds, or in real estate, among other things. A business invests in working capital, plant and equipment, and other assets. The customary definition equates investment by a business with any action that results in an increase in the nonmonetary assets of the business as shown on the balance sheet. An outlay that is written off as an expense is not, by this definition, an investment. This definition unfortunately is neither precise nor very helpful in the analysis of business problems. For this purpose an investment outlay may be defined more satisfactorily as *an expenditure of cash or its equivalent in one time period or periods in order to obtain a net inflow of cash or its equivalent in some other time period or periods.*

For example, suppose that a company has an opportunity to rear-range the layout of one of its factories at an outlay of $50,000. This will permit the company to save $20,000 a year in the manufacture of a product which it expects to produce for the next three years. At the end of that time, a new product model will be introduced which will require a complete retooling and an entirely new plant layout. In other words, the proposed rearrangement expenditures are expected to have a three-year *economic life*—the length of time during which the objects of the expenditure will continue in operation before they will need to be replaced or abandoned as a result of the combined forces of deteriora-tion and obsolescence.

The cash flows in this example can be arranged in a *timetable* like the following:

Years from Now	Cash Inflow (+) or Outflow (−)
0	−$50,000
0 to 1	+ 20,000
1 to 2	+ 20,000
2 to 3	+ 20,000
Total	+$10,000

This is a typical investment problem—a cash outflow is made immediately to get cash inflows in each of the next three periods. The decision cannot be based on the anticipated cash flows for the first period alone.

This definition of an investment problem is broad enough to encompass a substantial variety of situations. Equipment leasing, for example, is essentially a problem of weighing future rental payments against the purchase price of the equipment. In other words, the outflows are in the future while the inflow, in the form of an avoidance of a current outflow to purchase the equipment, is in the present. If this seems difficult, just reverse the pluses and minuses and think of the purchase price of the equipment as a means of avoiding future rental payments. Either way, this is an investment problem.

Plant abandonment is also an investment problem. Continued operation of the plant requires the company to forego the cash that it could release by shutting down, selling plant and equipment, and releasing working capital for other uses. The amount of this released cash appears in the timetable as an inflow $(+)$. Against this must be weighed the cash outflows represented by the cash flow that would be generated by product sales that would be lost by abandonment.

For example, suppose that a company could realize $500,000 if it were to close and sell one of its plants which otherwise could be operated to yield positive cash flows totaling $750,000, spread over the next five years. The comparison could be set up this way:

Years from Now	Abandon	Keep	Difference
0................	+$500,000	0	+$500,000
0 to 1............	0	+$250,000	− 250,000
1 to 2............	0	+ 200,000	− 200,000
2 to 3............	0	+ 150,000	− 150,000
3 to 4............	0	+ 100,000	− 100,000
4 to 5............	0	+ 50,000	− 50,000
Total.........	+$500,000	+$750,000	−$250,000

Thus the total cash flow from continued operations is $250,000 greater than the alternative under consideration, but it comes later. This makes it an investment problem or, more precisely, a disinvestment problem.

Again, this could be regarded as an investment of the current disposal value of the facilities to obtain the cash flows from future product sales. It is merely necessary to reverse the algebraic signs in the table above and the comparison becomes identical to the one considered earlier.

Few investment problems are as simple as the one illustrated above, although it is often permissible to assume that they are. A more typical case is exemplified by the plant acquisition proposal portrayed in Exhibit 19–1. An initial outlay of $1 million for plant, equipment, and

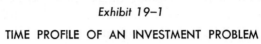

Exhibit 19–1

TIME PROFILE OF AN INVESTMENT PROBLEM

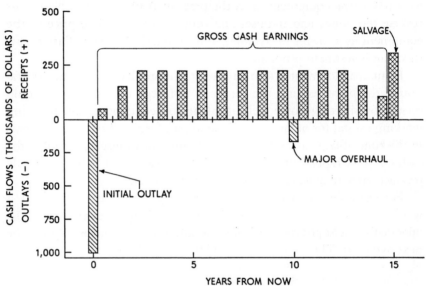

working capital is shown as a shaded block below the zero line at the left of the diagram. The expected annual cash inflows from operating the plant amount to $50,000 in the first year, $150,000 in the second, and $200,000 a year in the 3rd through 13th years. The inflows are expected to decline to $150,000 in the 14th year and to $100,000 in the 15th. All of these inflows or *receipts* are represented by shaded blocks above the zero line.

The economic life of the plant is 15 years, after which it is expected either to be sold or to be rebuilt. The cash value of the plant, equipment, and working capital at that time is expected to be $300,000. This is treated as a cash receipt and is shown as the rightmost shaded block above the line.

Finally, a major overhaul of facilities, costing $150,000, is expected to be necessary at the end of the 10th year. Without this, the company could not obtain the cash inflows of the final five years. This outlay is shown in Exhibit 19–1 as the second shaded block below the zero line.

Another kind of problem that falls into the investment category is the evaluation of proposals for expenditures for research and development. Such expenditures are frequently charged as expense on the income statements for the periods in which they are made and therefore do not meet the accounting definition of investment. The primary justification of corporate research, however, aside from the social objective of supporting the advance of human knowledge, is that it is expected to produce results in the future that will cover the cost of research with something left over for profit. Research outlays thus clearly meet the requirements of our definition of investment. The main difficulty of applying investment analysis techniques to expenditures for research is in deriving the cash flow estimates underlying the analysis of expected profitability. The amount of the outlays required, the amount of potential earnings, and the probability of success are all subject to extremely wide estimating errors. Despite these difficulties, many companies recognize the investment aspects of research and attempt to apply some kind of rough profitability tests to individual project requests, both initially and as the product of the research becomes clearer. These companies feel that it is better to have some form of rough profitability screening than none at all, in the expectation that such screening will cut off unprofitable ventures at an earlier stage and make additional funds available to other activities.

In many problems, the investment aspect is not readily apparent. As an example, a mining company may wish to compare varying rates of ore extraction. Exhibit 19–2 shows the kind of cash flow comparison

Exhibit 19–2

COMPARATIVE CASH FLOWS FROM ORE EXTRACTION

Years from Now	Estimated Cash Flows		Advantage: Slow Mining Minus Fast Mining
	Slow Mining	Fast Mining	
0 to 1	+$ 20,000	+$ 40,000	−$20,000
1 to 2	+ 20,000	+ 40,000	− 20,000
2 to 3	+ 20,000	+ 40,000	− 20,000
3 to 4	+ 20,000	+ 40,000	− 20,000
4 to 5	+ 20,000	0	+ 20,000
5 to 6	+ 20,000	0	+ 20,000
6 to 7	+ 20,000	0	+ 20,000
7 to 8	+ 20,000	0	+ 20,000
8 to 9	+ 20,000	0	+ 20,000
Net Cash Flow	+$180,000	+$160,000	+$20,000

that might be made. In this case, neither alternative taken by itself requires an investment outlay in the usual sense of the term, but in the comparison of the two the selection of the slow rate of extraction will require an "investment" of $20,000 a year for four years before its benefits begin to be felt. Looking at this in a different way, if the fast rate is selected, it will generate an extra $20,000 a year that will be available for investment elsewhere in the company. A choice of the slow rate deliberately foregoes the use of this extra cash in return for later benefits. In investment analysis, the lower receipts of the first four years under the first alternative must be offset against the greater receipts in the last five years.

Tactical Problems

The category of decision situations which we call tactical problems is difficult to define except in negative terms. It includes all problems in which the investment aspect is immaterial—in other words, all problems that need not be treated as investment problems.

Looked at more positively, tactical problems are characterized by a presumption that sound decisions can be based on comparisons of expected cash flows during a single short interval of time, usually a year or less. In other words, it is assumed either that the alternative which promises the most favorable cash flow in the first period will provide the most favorable cash flow in subsequent periods, or that the acquisition of a favorable cash flow in the first period does not commit the company to accept an unfavorable cash flow in subsequent periods.

For example, in deciding whether to increase the emphasis given by the sales force to larger customers, a company might make the following projection for the current year (all figures in thousands):

	Plan A		Plan B		
	Large Customers, 5 Calls per Year	Small Customers, 3 Calls per Year	Large Customers, 6 Calls per Year	Small Customers, 2 Calls per Year	Increment: Plan B − Plan A
Sales..................	$5,000	$3,000	$6,000	$2,500	$500
Variable costs..........	2,000	1,200	2,400	1,000	200
Variable Profit.........	$3,000	$1,800	$3,600	$1,500	$300

Assuming that these estimates are carefully prepared, it appears that total company sales could be increased by $500,000 and total company profit could be increased by $300,000 this year by instructing salesmen to call more frequently on their larger customers, following plan B, and less frequently on smaller customers. Although there may be some cumulative effects of customer contacts, if management feels that these effects are likely to be slight, then the decision can be based solely on the comparison for the current year. Extending the analysis to cover a longer period of time would not change the conclusions of the analysis because one alternative is expected to have greater cash receipts or lower cash outlays than competing alternatives in each and every time period.

This distinction is obviously one of degree. Problems that are generally treated as tactical problems include selection of product mix, sales emphasis, equipment scheduling, and the choice of distribution channels and methods. A decision on one of these problems may be so misguided that tremendous losses may be absorbed in the first few months of operations in comparison with the results that would have been achieved under one of the rejected alternatives. In contrast, an investment may turn out to be so profitable in the first year that all investment outlays can be more than recovered and it does not matter whether estimates of the more distant future are borne out or not. Furthermore, many tactical decisions may have effects that linger beyond a year. An ill-advised product emphasis decision, for example, may set in motion a pattern of sales decline that will be difficult to halt. This does not detract from the validity of the principles of analysis, however. It is a poor estimate rather than a defective analytical method that leads to an incorrect decision.

THE CONCEPT OF PRESENT VALUE

The distinction between investment and tactical problems is not a mere pedantic exercise. It is introduced because investment problems require a more complex kind of analysis than tactical problems. This analysis is based on the notion that time has a cost.

The Importance of Time

Investment problems require computation of the values of the streams of cash flows associated with two or more alternatives. It would be convenient if the anticipated value of each alternative could be measured by the algebraic sum of the cash flows forecasted for that proposal. Unfortunately, this simple expedient would be incorrect. The alternatives differ not only in the *total amount* but also in the *timing* of their cash flows, and sums of money that are either received or paid out at two different points in time cannot be added to or subtracted from each other without adjustment. Other things being equal, *dollars expected to be available only in the distant future are worth less than the same number of dollars now.*

One reason for this is that the dollar received today can be invested to grow to more than a dollar a year from now. The man who gets a dollar now and invests it wisely will have more money a year from now than the man who waits a year for his dollar. A second reason is that the future is uncertain. Other things being equal, the longer the wait, the greater the possibility that conditions will change and the dollar never will be received. This means that an investor who has investment opportunities elsewhere will not provide funds to the corporation unless he can reasonably anticipate receiving some reward for the use of his money.

This fact can perhaps best be illustrated in terms of the familiar compounding of interest in savings accounts. For example, suppose that an investor deposits $100 in a savings bank at the beginning of the year. The bank adds interest to this account every three months, the interest rate being 4 percent a year, or 1 percent each quarter. By the end of the year, the balance in the account will be not $100 but $104.06, computed in the following fashion:

Period	Beginning Balance	Three Months' Interest	Ending Balance
First quarter...................	$100.00	$1.00	$101.00
Second quarter................	101.00	1.01	102.01
Third quarter.................	102.01	1.02	103.03
Fourth quarter...............	103.03	1.03	104.06

The balance in the account has grown by the amount of interest on the sum originally deposited ($100 x 4% = $4), plus interest on the interest credited to the account during the first three quarters, in this case 6 cents. This crediting of interest on previously earned interest is known as *compounding*. In this case, interest has been compounded quarterly, meaning that interest is credited to the saver's account four times a year.

On the basis of this calculation, it may be said that $100 on January 1 is *equivalent* to $104.06 on January 1 of the following year if the interest rate is 4 percent and if interest is compounded quarterly. This equivalence may also be stated in other terms: $100 now is the *present value* of $104.06 a year from now at 4 percent interest, compounded quarterly, and $104.06 a year from now is the *future value* of $100 now. Alternatively, if $104.06 is *discounted* (the reciprocal of compounding) at 4 percent for one year, its *discounted value* or *present value* is $100, again assuming quarterly compounding.

Extending these calculations beyond one year reveals the relationships shown graphically in Exhibit 19–3. The initial $100 will grow to

Exhibit 19–3

FUTURE VALUES EQUIVALENT TO PRESENT VALUE OF $100

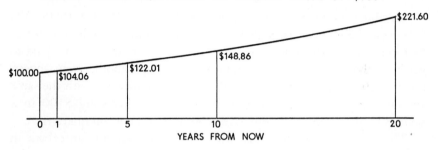

$104.06 at the end of one year, $122.01 at the end of five years, $148.86 at the end of 10, and $221.60 when 20 years have passed, assuming interest compounded quarterly at 4 percent. At higher interest rates the growth would be even greater.

Another aspect of these relationships is that each of the future sums plotted on the chart in Exhibit 19–3 has an identical present value of $100, as summarized in the following table:

Years from Now	Future Amount	Present Value at 4%
0...............	$100.00	$100.00
1...............	104.06	100.00
5...............	122.01	100.00
10...............	148.86	100.00
20...............	221.60	100.00

Knowledge of these relationships permits us to deal with problems in which differences in timing are important because it makes it possible to add or subtract sums that occur at different points in time. For example, suppose that an investor decides that 4 percent is an adequate return on any investments he may make. A promoter approaches him with a proposal to pay him $104.06 one year from now if he will invest $99.50 in the promoter's enterprise now. This proposal can be analyzed in the following fashion:

Date	Cash Inflow (+) or Outflow (−)	Present Value at 4%
Immediately.........................	−$ 99.50	−$ 99.50
One year later......................	+ 104.06	+ 100.00
Difference..........................	+$ 4.56	+$ 0.50

Inasmuch as $100 is the time-adjusted equivalent of $104.06, the $99.50 and $100 can be added together algebraically. The amount to be received is worth more now than the amount that has to be paid to get it, so the proposal is a desirable one. To put it another way, investment of $99.50 in this proposal will provide the investor with the same amount a year from now that he could get by investing $100 in a savings bank account that compounds interest at 4 percent quarterly.

The use of an interest rate as low as 4 percent is highly unrealistic in most business situations because investors demand compensation for assuming business risks. For example, the promoter might promise to pay the investor a percentage of the proceeds of a particular venture. Even though $104.06 may be the investor's best current forecast of the eventual payoff from the investment, the actual payoff may be greater or less than this. To compensate himself for assuming a risk that the amount he will receive at the end of the year will be less than $104.06, he normally demands an expected return on his investment that is greater than he could receive by placing his money in a savings bank account, which is essentially a risk-free investment. In other words, he will ordinarily be unwilling to pay as much as $100 for an uncertain expectation of a $104.06 payoff one year ahead.

Recognizing this, let us now suppose that the investor requires a 10 percent minimum return on investment. By repeating the calculations above, using quarterly compounding at an interest rate of 10 percent per year, we find that $100 now is equivalent to $110.38 one year from now. Conversely, at this higher interest rate, $100 one year from now is equivalent to $90.596 now (0.90596 being the ratio of $100 present value to $110.38 future value). Multiplying this "interest factor" by the expected $104.06 cash receipt at the end of the year, we obtain a present value of $93.35. The comparison now becomes:

Date	Cash Inflow (+) or Outflow (−)	Present Value at 10%
Immediately.......................	−$ 99.50	−$99.50
One year later.....................	+ 104.06	+ 94.27
Difference.........................	+$ 4.56	−$ 5.23

The investor would thus find this proposal unattractive because the present value equivalent of the cash he will receive from his investment is $5.23 less than the $99.50 he would have to pay now to receive the future benefit. Another way of saying this is that if the investor requires a 10 percent return on investment, the future cash receipt of $104.06 is inadequate to repay the original investment plus interest at 10 percent. Generalizing further, it can be stated that the higher the required rate of interest or return on investment, the lower will be the present value of future receipts and the less attractive will be any proposal to invest funds now in anticipation of a future return.

Interest Tables

The mathematical formula on which the previous calculations were based is a simple one:

$$\text{Future value} = \text{Present value} \times (1 + r)^n$$

or

$$F = P(1 + r)^n ,$$

in which r is the rate of interest per period and n is the number of periods that will elapse before the future value can be realized. To find the future value of $100 one year hence, compounded quarterly at an interest rate of 4 percent a year, this formula becomes:

$$F = \$100 \times (1.01)^4 = \$104.06 ,$$

because the period is defined as a quarter of a year and the number of periods is four. This relationship between present and future value is more commonly expressed with present value as the dependent variable:

$$P = \frac{F}{(1 + r)^n} .$$

This equation is, of course, the algebraic equivalent of the preceding one.

Utilization of the present value concept fortunately does not require repeated calculations of the $(1 + r)^n$ component of these formulas. Such calculations have already been performed by mathematicians, and the resulting multipliers are to be found in readily available tables of discounting and compounding ratios, known as interest tables or discount tables.

Two sets of these tables are provided in Appendix A. The set that we shall use in this chapter and the next is based on the principle of *continuous compounding* rather than on periodic compounding, the method used in the preceding illustrations. Without going into the mathematics of continuous compounding (or its converse, continuous discounting), the basic relationship between the two forms of compounding can be seen by expanding our previous example. We saw that if interest is compounded *quarterly* at 10 percent per year, $100 now will grow to $110.38 at the end of one year. If interest is compounded only once a year (*annual* compounding), the future value of $100 one year hence at 10 percent will be only $110. If interest is compounded *monthly,* on the other hand, the future value of $100 now at 10 percent will be slightly greater than $110.38 because interest will be calculated in the second month not only on the original $100 but also on the first month's interest, and so on. The shorter the compounding interval (weekly, daily, hourly), the greater will be the amount of interest accumulated.[1]

Continuous compounding is the limiting case, with the compounding interval at its shortest imaginable length. At a rate of 10 percent, $100 now is equivalent to $110.52 at the end of one year under continuous compounding. At low interest rates and for short periods of time the difference between annual compounding and continuous compounding is very slight, but this difference grows as the interest rate is increased or the time period is lengthened. Continuous compounding is useful in that it permits the development of present value multipliers for sums that are not received or paid out all at once but are spread out in a more or less uniform stream between two points in time. Continuous compounding is also more readily adaptable than discrete compounding to certain kinds of calculations requiring the mathematical operations of integration and differentiation.

Although some authorities on this subject are willing to make a strong stand in favor of one or the other of these forms of compounding, as a practical matter the choice can generally be made on the basis

---

[1] As this book goes to press, some banks are even compounding interest *daily* as a means of raising the effective interest rate without breaching statutory rate ceilings.

of convenience and relevance to a particular problem. In computing bond yields, discrete compounding is generally preferable, whereas in examining equipment investment problems the advantages of continuous compounding are more pronounced. Therefore, although the continuous compounding tables will be used throughout these chapters, a set of tables based on periodic compounding is supplied in Appendix A for the convenience of those who prefer to use them.

Using the Tables

Instructions for the use of these tables are contained in the appendix, but a simple demonstration here may be useful. Assume that a proposal is expected to produce the following cash flows:

	Years from Now	Cash Inflow (+) or Outflow (−)
Initial outlay.................	0	−$40,000
Annual earnings..............	0 to 5	+ 10,000 per year
Salvage......................	5	+ 5,000
Total.....................		+$15,000

One way to compute the present value of the annual cash earnings is to use the multipliers in Table 2 of Appendix A. Because the annual earnings do not come in all at once but are spread throughout the year, their present value is greater than that of end-of-year cash flows. Table 2 is especially constructed to reflect this difference.

Suppose that the company wishes to discover whether this proposal will earn at least 10 percent on the investment. The first figure in the 10 percent column of Table 2 is 0.9516, which means that each dollar of cash received in the first year is worth paying only 95.16 cents for at the beginning of the year. A cash flow of $10,000 is thus worth 0.9516 × $10,000 = $9,516.

Similarly, the second year's cash receipts are worth 0.8611 × $10,-000 = $8,611, and so on for the next three years.

Finally, the salvage value is expected to be received in a single lump sum at the end of five years rather than being spread out over any year. For this kind of cash flow, Table 1 is used. This indicates that at a 10 percent rate of discount each dollar five years from now is equivalent to 60.65 cents now. The present value of $5,000 is thus 0.6065 × $5,000 = $3,032. The value of the proposal as a whole is summarized in Exhibit 19–4.

Exhibit 19-4

USE OF INTEREST TABLES

Years from Zero Date	Cash Inflow (+) or Outflow (−)	Present Value at 10%		
		Table	Multiplier	Amount
0....................	− $40,000	..	1.0000	− $40,000
0 to 1..............	+ 10,000	2	0.9516	+ 9,516
1 to 2..............	+ 10,000	2	0.8611	+ 8,611
2 to 3..............	+ 10,000	2	0.7791	+ 7,791
3 to 4..............	+ 10,000	2	0.7050	+ 7,050
4 to 5..............	+ 10,000	2	0.6379	+ 6,379
5....................	+ 5,000	1	0.6065	+ 3,032
Net Present Value....				+ $ 2,379

This shows that the cash flows anticipated from this proposal are more than adequate to recover the initial outlay of $40,000 plus interest compounded continuously at an annual rate of 10 percent. The present value of the cash flow in excess of interest and amortization requirements is $2,379.

The same answer can be reached in this case by a slightly different route. Because each year's operating cash flow is the same, $10,000, it is not necessary to multiply each one separately. Instead, the multipliers can be added together and then applied in one single multiplication. This is the basis of Table 3 in Appendix A. The multiplier in the five-year row of the 10 percent column in Table 3 is 3.9347. Multiplying this by the annual cash flow of $10,000 yields a present value of $39,347, which is identical to the sum of the first five plus figures in the right-hand column of Exhibit 19-4.

Treatment of Depreciation

Present value is always determined by discounting *cash flows* at a given rate of interest because cash flows represent the resources that are either tied up by a particular decision (cash outlays) or made available for other uses (cash receipts). No deduction is made to allow for annual depreciation charges.

The logic of this practice may perhaps best be seen with the aid of an illustration. A machine costing $10,000 is expected to permit an expansion of output that will increase net cash receipts after taxes by $1,500 a year for 10 years. The initial outlay is entered in the time table in Exhibit 19-5 as a minus item at time zero; the incremental cash receipts

Exhibit 19–5

TABLE OF CASH FLOWS

Years from Zero Date	Cash Inflow (+) or Outflow (−)	Present Value at 8%
0.	− $10,000	− $10,000
0 to 1.	+ 1,500	+ 1,442
1 to 2.	+ 1,500	+ 1,331
2 to 3.	+ 1,500	+ 1,228
3 to 4.	+ 1,500	+ 1,134
4 to 5.	+ 1,500	+ 1,047
5 to 6.	+ 1,500	+ 966
6 to 7.	+ 1,500	+ 892
7 to 8.	+ 1,500	+ 824
8 to 9.	+ 1,500	+ 760
9 to 10.	+ 1,500	+ 702
Net Cash Flow.	+$ 5,000	+$ 526

are shown as plus flows occurring during each of the next 10 years. The total gross cash receipts of the machine during the entire 10-year period is $15,000 *before depreciation*. If it is assumed that the machine will have no salvage value at the end of 10 years, then depreciation charges should total $10,000 during this period, leaving a net lifetime profit of $5,000, and this is the algebraic sum of the figures in the first column. This is more than adequate to meet an 8 percent minimum rate of return on investment, as shown by the present value calculation.

In other words, a method of analysis that deals entirely with incremental cash flows does not ignore incremental depreciation. Incremental depreciation is deducted from expected cash inflows, but not by the methods used in the preparation of company income statements. Instead of deducting annual depreciation charges from annual cash receipts each year during the anticipated life of the facilities, the cash flow method enters the incremental cost of facilities in the timetable as a cash outlay *at the time the outlay is made* and enters estimated end-of-life salvage value in the timetable as a cash receipt *at the salvage date*. The difference between these two figures is depreciation for the entire period.

Incremental Depreciation versus Sunk Cost

This discussion refers, of course, only to *incremental* depreciation —that is, the net cash outlay (initial cash outlay minus salvage or resale value) resulting from holding the asset for a specified period of time. Depreciation charges on facilities already under company ownership are more likely than not to be sunk costs, irrelevant to management decisions.

To illustrate, assume that an automobile company has spent $200 million to design, test, tool, and market a new model. Sales have been disappointing and management is considering discontinuing the model. The first year's operating loss, as shown on the company's internal profit report, was:

Sales..		$400,000,000
Less: Out-of-pocket operating costs....................	$380,000,000	
Amortization of past tooling and development costs.	80,000,000	460,000,000
Net Operating Loss...................................		$(60,000,000)

One mistake would be to conclude that the company must continue the model because it has not yet recovered its initial investment. The $120 million of the original $200 million development cost that has not yet been charged to expense is irrelevant to the decision. The question is not whether all *past* costs have been recovered or charged to expense but rather whether *future* receipts from sale of the product are likely to cover *future* outlays with enough left over to justify continued expenditure of management time and continued investment of liquid resources.

Decision making is not a matter of recovering past costs but of selecting the best of the currently available opportunities. The original decision to develop the new model may have been ill conceived or poorly implemented, but this is not the current issue. The question now is how to allocate the resources that management now has at its command, and the book value of existing facilities is no measure of the resources the company could make available for investment elsewhere if it were to discontinue the model. Book values refer to the past, not to the future, and only future receipts and outlays are subject to management control and thus relevant to decision making.

A second and perhaps more common mistake is to decide that the new model should not be continued unless its future revenues will cover not only future costs but depreciation of past outlays as well. For example, assume that the company is considering the following profit plan for the next year:

Sales..		$450,000,000
Less: Out-of-pocket operating costs....................	$400,000,000	
Amortization of past tooling and development costs.	60,000,000	460,000,000
Estimated Net Operating Loss.......................		$(10,000,000)

A recommendation based on net profit rather than incremental profit would be to discontinue the model rather than incur a $10 million loss, despite the forecast in this instance of a $50 million incremental cash profit.

This illustrates the general rule that annual depreciation charges on existing facilities should normally be treated as sunk costs.

SUMMARY

The main objective of this chapter has been to introduce the concept of present value and to identify the kinds of decision situations in which calculations of present value are appropriate—i.e., the broad category of investment problems, defined as those in which cash outflows must be made in one or more time periods to obtain cash inflows in one or more other periods. The distinction between this kind of decision and so-called tactical decisions provides the framework around which the next four chapters will be organized.

Application of the present value concept to more complex situations, as well as some consideration of such matters as the appropriate discount rate and the derivation of the cash flow estimates, will be the subject of the next chapter.

Most problems have at least some small investment element in them, and almost anything could be classified as an investment problem if small enough time intervals were used. The added accuracy achieved by treating many problems as investment problems, however, is not worth the added computational effort required. For example, if a special promotional expenditure is not expected to produce results until two or three months after it is made, the expenditure could be regarded as an investment outlay and the subsequent sales as future receipts. Because the elapsed time between expenditure and receipt is so short, however, implicit interest on the tie-up of funds is too small to worry about. If the selection among alternatives hinges on differences in capital costs within the first year, then the alternatives must be so close together that the decision should be based on intangible factors that are not reflected in the financial comparisons.

DISCUSSION QUESTIONS

1. Define and state the relationships among the following terms: present value, future value, discounted value, time-adjusted equivalent value.
2. "Cash flows occurring at different points in time cannot be added together without adjustment." Why not?
3. How were investment problems distinguished from tactical problems in this

chapter? Would you agree that the distinction is a useful one for analytical purposes?

4. Would you say that equipment leasing is an example of an investment problem or a tactical problem? Present your reasoning.

5. "Our business is subject to so many uncertainties that we are forced to treat all problems by methods appropriate to tactical problems." What does the author of this statement mean? Do you think that he really applies the decision rule implicit in this statement to all problems that arise?

6. What is the relationship of the "cutoff rate" to investment decisions?

7. The Town of Undershot is not permitted by state law to borrow. All expenditures must be met from current tax revenues. Do you believe that cash flow discounting would be a useful technique for the town's selectmen?

8. Would you classify a plant abandonment decision as an investment problem or as a tactical problem? Why?

9. What is meant by "incremental depreciation"? How would it appear in a cash flow timetable?

10. "Absolute profit figures are never relevant to managerial decision making. Even when we seem to be using absolute profit, what we are really doing is defining incremental profit in such a way that it is equal to absolute profit." Do you agree or disagree? Cite an example in support of your point of view.

11. What is the relationship of opportunity cost to incremental profit?

12. Why do discounting procedures operate on cash flows rather than on net profits after provision for depreciation? Is it true that cash flow discounting ignores depreciation?

13. "Allocations of common costs may be misleading in the short run, but in the long run "cost" must include a portion of all costs, both traceable and common. For investment decisions, therefore, allocations must be made." Do you agree or disagree?

EXERCISES AND PROBLEMS

1. An author received five complementary copies of his book and purchased a sixth copy from his publisher at a price of $6. The author then gave these six copies to various friends and relatives.

   Using an economic concept of cost, and assuming that all six copies were given away simultaneously, how much did it cost the author to give away *each* book? Explain.

*2. Using the continuous compounding tables in Appendix A, compute net present value for each of the following series of cash flows:

---

* Solutions to problems marked with an asterisk (*) can be found in Appendix B.

a) Initial outlay...$100
   Annual cash receipts..$ 15 per year
   Estimated life... 10 years
   Estimated salvage..None
   Discount rate.. 8%

b) Initial outlay...$100
   Annual cash receipts:
      First five years..$ 20 per year
      Second five years.......................................$ 10 per year
   Estimated life... 10 years
   Estimated salvage..None
   Discount rate.. 8%

c) Initial outlay...$110
   Annual cash receipts:
      First five years..$ 10 per year
      Second five years.......................................$ 20 per year
   Estimated life... 10 years
   Estimated salvage..$ 10
   Discount rate.. 8%

d) Initial outlay...$ 80
   Annual cash receipts..$ 15 per year
   Additional outlay, 5 years hence...........................$ 40
   Estimated life... 10 years
   Estimated salvage..None
   Discount rate.. 8%

3. The ABC Company is considering a proposal to purchase materials handling equipment to achieve economies in its warehousing operation. The total cost of the equipment, together with auxiliary investments in pallets and supplies, is $30,000. The equipment is expected to be useful for seven years before replacement becomes economical. Scrap value is expected to be negligible. Annual cash savings are expected to be $5,000 the first year, $6,000 the second year, and $7,000 in each subsequent year as the warehouse reaches full-capacity operation. The ABC Company requires a minimum return on investment of 20 percent a year, before taxes. Assuming that the decision is to be based on before-tax cash flows, should this proposal be accepted?

4. Compute the present value of the following stream of cash flows at an interest rate of 15 percent, using the continuous compounding tables in the Appendix A.

   Outlays:
      Two years before operations commence........................$10,000
      During the year prior to the start of operations........... 50,000
      At the end of 10 years of operations....................... 20,000
   Receipts:
      Each year for the first three years of operations..........   5,000
      Each year for the next 10 years............................   8,000
      Each year for the next five years..........................   5,000
      At the end of 18 years of operations....................... 12,000

5. The Bellingham Company is negotiating to buy the voting stock of the Spinningfleet Company. The balance sheet of the Spiningfleet Company

shows a book value of $14.65 per share of common stock. An appraiser has valued Spinningfleet's assets at an amount equivalent to $18.50 per common share. Spinningfleet's annual earnings amount to $2.55 per share, after taxes, and would be expected to remain at this level if the company were acquired by Bellingham as long as capital expenditures equal to the annual depreciation charge were made each year. The Bellingham Company uses a minimum after-tax rate of return on investment of 15 percent in its capital investment program. What is the stock of Spinningfleet worth to Bellingham?

6. Peter Brown has an opportunity to buy a certain business, paying $50,000 immediately and $20,000 at the end of each of the next five years. It is anticipated that the net cash receipts from the operation of this business will amount to $25,000 a year for the next 15 years and $15,000 a year for the five years after that. Mr. Brown wishes to retire 20 years from now and believes that he can sell the business at that time for $30,000. If he buys the business, he expects to spend $2,000 a year on capital replacements and improvements during the first five years, $3,000 a year during the next five years, $4,000 a year during the third five years, and nothing thereafter.

   The above figures do not provide for any compensation for Mr. Brown's services. If he buys the business, he must leave his present job, in which he is earning $8,000 a year. Furthermore, if he buys the new business, he must liquidate certain investments of comparable risk that now yield a return on investment of 10 percent before taxes.

   Would you advise Mr. Brown to make the purchase? Show your calculations.

7. Frank Destry has been offered the opportunity to submit a bid for the right to provide catering services in a private club. The contract would run for eight years, and Mr. Destry estimates that his net cash receipts from the catering business would amount to approximately $12,000 a year. If he accepts the contract, he will have to make an initial investment of $2,000 in equipment. What is the maximum price that Mr. Destry can afford to bid for the catering privilege, assuming that he requires a 14 percent return on his investment?

8. Building Lessors, Inc., has offered to buy a building that you now own and occupy. The offer price is $1,000,000. The building would be leased back to you at an annual rental of $100,000, to be paid in equal monthly installments for the next 15 years. The lease would provide you with a renewal option for an additional 10 years at an annual rental of $80,000. You estimate that the building will have a market value of $600,000 15 years from now, or $300,000 25 years hence.

   What is the cost of the lease, expressed as a rate of interest, if you expect to occupy the building for the next 15 years? If you expect to occupy it for the next 25 years? (Ignore income taxes.)

9. The Davies Corporation is considering the acquisition of certain attachments to machinery now being used in the manufacture of product A. The

attachments will cost $20,000 and are expected to last five years. The main machinery has a remaining economic life of at least five years. The attachments will permit smaller work crews but will require additional maintenance costs each year. Installation and use of the attachments will have no effect on product quality.

A salesman for the manufacturer of the attachments has prepared the following cost comparison in support of the acquisition proposal:

Item	Present Costs per Year	Costs per Year with Attachments	Saving per Year
Direct materials.................	$ 80,000	$ 80,000	.....
Direct labor....................	40,000	30,000	+$10,000
Maintenance....................	6,000	12,000	− 6,000
Depreciation....................	10,000	14,000	− 4,000
Other factory overhead..........	120,000	90,000	+ 30,000
Total....................	$256,000	$226,000	+$30,000

"Other factory overhead" costs are stated on the basis of the current factory burden rate, minus provision for maintenance and depreciation. This portion of the burden rate amounts to 300 percent of direct labor cost.

The salesman cited the above figures and said, "You can't afford not to buy these attachments. They'll pay for themselves in eight months and give you a tremendous return on your investment." What is your opinion?

10. A single large machine is the only equipment used in one of the departments in the Beaman Company. A fairly large number of products are produced on the machine, and the company is interested in the most economical lot size in which each of the products should be produced. One of the costs that must be considered in arriving at the most economical lot size is the cost of changing the machine over from one product to another—the setup cost. The following information has been obtained for use in computing the setup cost for product A:

(1) Two men from the maintenance department have to spend four hours each to set up the equipment, which is located in department P.

(2) Maintenance department employees have a basic wage rate of $3.50 an hour. It is the company's policy to provide its maintenance force with a 40-hour week, adjusting the size of the maintenance staff only if changes in the size of the work load are substantial and likely to persist.

(3) Department P's machine is operated by a crew of six men whose basic wage rate is $3 an hour. While the machine is being set up, these men perform minor finishing operations and carry out other productive tasks to the extent that such work is available. Experience indicates that they are idle approximately 60 percent of the time required for machine setup.

(4) Department P's costs other than direct materials, the wages of the operating crew, and setup labor are expected to average the following monthly amounts:

Depreciation	$760
Power	280
Space	160
Payroll taxes and insurance	296
Maintenance labor	220
Foremen	600
Operating supplies	300

(5) All payroll taxes and insurance costs on both direct and indirect labor are classified as overhead. They average approximately 8 percent of the gross payroll. Payroll taxes and insurance on setup and maintenance labor are not charged to department P but remain in maintenance department overhead accounts.

(6) Operating supplies and maintenance labor costs charged to department P (as in the table above) are expected to be roughly proportional to the number of productive hours of the operating crew.

(7) Department P's depreciation, power, space, and foremen costs are regarded as fixed costs.

(8) Maintenance department costs other than labor and payroll taxes and insurance are completely fixed.

(9) A typical month has 20 producing days of eight hours each.

Establish the cost of setting up the machines and explain how you derived your figures.

11. The Xema Corporation has been purchasing a certain raw material in small lots at a price of $0.45 a pound. If purchases were made in carload lots, the price would be $0.35 a pound, but Xema's requirements are too small to justify the inventory investment that carload lot purchasing would entail.

The Zobia Corporation has been purchasing a similar raw material, but of lower quality, at a price of $0.37 a pound in half-carload lots. The Zobia Corporation could substitute Xema's raw material for its own if the purchase price were less than $0.37. The purchasing agent of the Zobia Company reasoned that it was ridiculous for both companies to be paying more than $0.35 per pound. He suggested to the Xema purchasing agent that Xema buy in carload lots and sell half of each shipment to Zobia at a price of $0.32. Zobia's trucks would take the material directly from the freight car.

Xema's purchasing agent said that he could justify inventories based on purchases in half-carload lots, but he could never justify to the president of his company the resale of products at less than cost. Is the Zobia proposal sound? Prepare a cost statement that would support your opinion.

12. The Artling Corporation manufactures four products in four identical processing operations. The only differences among the four products are in the raw materials used. The facilities are completely interchangeable, although they differ slightly, with newer machines having higher depreciation and generally lower operating costs than older machines. Processing costs (that is, all costs other than materials costs) are determined by the machines used, not by the product being manufactured.

The company is now considering a proposal to acquire a fifth set of processing facilities to manufacture a new, higher grade of product, using a more expensive raw material that has just come on the market. This proposed set of facilities would be usable on any of the company's products, but it is expected that the proposed new product would be processed on the new facilities.

Data relating to the company's production costs are shown in the table below ("other processing costs" do not include any costs that are common to all of the firm's production activities):

Product	Machine Used	Selling Price per Pound	Materials Cost per Pound	Depreciation Cost per Pound	Other Processing Costs per Pound	Profit Margin per Pound
A........	1	$0.60	$0.15	$0.12	$0.31	$0.02
B........	2	0.66	0.20	0.12	0.30	0.04
C........	3	0.73	0.25	0.13	0.28	0.07
D........	4	0.81	0.30	0.13	0.29	0.09
E*........	5*	0.90	0.35	0.14	0.29	0.12

* Proposed.

Depreciation cost per pound is based on estimated annual production of 200,000 pounds of each product and an estimated life of 10 years. Estimated salvage value of the production equipment is zero; in fact, once the facilities are installed, their only market value is their scrap value.

In support of the proposal to add the fifth product and corresponding facilities, the sales manager of the Artling Company has pointed out that this would increase the company's gross profit margin by $24,000 on an added sales volume of 200,000 pounds annually. Variable selling and administrative costs amount to 5 percent of sales.

Compute the incremental annual cash flow that you would use in deciding whether the proposed investment is adequately profitable. State your reasoning. (Note that you are not asked to indicate whether the proposed investment in new facilities would be adequately profitable to justify the required outlays. This is solely an exercise in estimating the annual earnings data that would enter into the evaluation of this problem. You may ignore income taxes in this problem.)

13. Debonair, Inc., is a manufacturer of lingerie, hosiery, and swimwear. Its growth during the last 10 years has been primarily the result of acquiring previously unprofitable companies and by vigorous efforts at cost reduction and sales expansion, generating satisfactory earnings. The company's common stock is held entirely by members of the Nair family who also serve as executives of the company.

Last month Mr. K. P. Knight, chairman of the board of directors of Knitwear, Inc., a large manufacturer of swimsuits, sweaters, and other women's fashion garments, contacted Mr. J. B. Nair, president of Debonair, Inc., to discuss the feasibility of the acquisition of Debonair by Knitwear. Mr. Nair supplied a set of financial statements for the preceding fiscal year which had been audited by an independent accounting firm. These statements contained little detail but showed that at the end of the year the book value of the common stock in Debonair, Inc., was $47.53 a share. Earnings after taxes were $7.12 a share.

One of Mr. Knight's main objectives in initiating acquisition negotiations was to obtain the services of the Debonair management as a means of improving the profitability of Knitwear's lines. He was also interested in the Debonair product line, which he thought would complement Knitwear's existing lines with little duplication. Accordingly, after examining the audited financial statements and spending several days touring Debonair facilities and talking to Debonair executives, he offered to exchange two shares of Knitwear common stock, which had a current market value of $24 a share, for each share of Debonair stock. He felt certain that his shareholders would ratify an offer on these terms.

Mr. Nair refused to consider this offer, saying that his company's stock was worth at least $70 a share by itself and that the benefits to be realized by consolidating the Debonair line with those of Knitwear made the Debonair stock worth much more than that to Knitwear. Mr. Knight countered by saying that he based his offer price on Debonair's own accounting statements, as audited by independent accountants. Furthermore, he pointed out that any improvement in Knitwear's profitability as the result of the complementarity of the product lines of the two firms would raise the value of the stock to be given to the Nair family. He also pointed out that two of Debonair's plants would be unnecessary to the merged companies and could be disposed of. Accordingly, he argued that his offer was generous in that he was paying for some assets that he did not need.

a) What position would you take in this argument? Do you thing that Mr. Knight's offer was reasonable?

b) Comment on the reliability of historical financial statements for use in investigations of this sort. What additional historical information would you like to have if you were Mr. Knight?

14. The Wingding Company is considering withdrawing one of its products, product X, from the market. The product is manufactured in the company's Altoona plant and requires operations to be performed in three of the departments of that plant. Current production and sales volume is at a rate of 1,000 units of product X a month. The standard cost card for product X shows the following costs per unit:

Materials	$ 1.56
Labor:	
Department 14, 0.8 hours at $2.50	2.00
Department 26, 1.0 hours at $3.10	3.10
Department 29, 0.3 hours at $2.40	0.72
Factory overhead:	
Department 14, $1.80 an hour	1.44
Department 26, $4.20 an hour	4.20
Department 29, $1.30 an hour	0.39
Total Standard Cost	$13.41

The monthly departmental flexible budgets for the three production departments concerned with product X are as follows:

Item	Department 14 Fixed	Department 14 Variable per D.L. Hr.	Department 26 Fixed	Department 26 Variable per D.L. Hr.	Department 29 Fixed	Department 29 Variable per D.L. Hr.
Supervision...........	$1,820	$0.10	$ 4,680	$0.12	$3,890	$0.06
Indirect labor........	....	0.28	.....	1.16	....	0.14
Supplies..............	....	0.12	.....	0.74	....	0.26
Maintenance.........	210	0.05	650	0.10	50	0.01
Depreciation.........	1,000	...	4,200	...	850	...
Other direct charges...	400	0.01	720	0.14	560	0.04
Apportioned charges:						
Bldgs and grounds..	618	...	3,736	...	2,098	...
Power..............	....	0.03	.....	0.03	....	0.03
Factory office.......	....	0.02	.....	0.02	....	0.02
Gen. fact. overhead..	....	0.04	.....	0.04	....	0.04
Total.............	$4,048	$0.65	$13,986	$2.35	$7,448	$0.60
Normal volume per month (direct labor hours)........	3,520		7,560		10,640	

These flexible budget data are based on the presumption that production will be between 75 percent and 125 percent of normal volume. If the department's volume is reduced to less than 75 percent of normal, supervision costs will be decreased by an additional $400 a month in department 114, $920 a month in department 26, and $650 a month in department 29. Other direct charges will be reduced by $200 in each department which goes below the 75 percent level. Department 26 is now operating at normal volume, department 14 is operating at 90 percent of normal, and department 29 is operating at 85 percent of normal. Additional data relating to the costs of the factory service departments are:

Maintenance: All maintenance is charged to production departments at a rate of $4 per maintenance labor hour, and the flexible budgets above are based on this figure. Maintenance department costs are budgeted at a fixed amount per month. This is reduced by $520 if reduced factory volume permits a reduction of 160 hours or more of maintenance labor required, by $1,040 if the maintenance labor requirement is reduced by 320 hours, and so forth, in 160-hour multiples. No maintenance cost reduction will be effected except for full blocks of 160 maintenance labor hours.

Buildings and grounds: Fixed monthly budget.

Power: Studies have shown that power costs vary in the ratio of $0.025 per factory direct labor hour.

Factory office: Fixed monthly budget.

General factory overhead: Fixed monthly budget.

Direct material prices have risen 10 percent since the current standards went into effect, and direct labor rates have increased 8 percent during the same period. Increases in comparable overhead items have been offset by cost reductions so that no variances in factory overheads are budgeted.

Prepare a statement showing the factory costs that would be relevant to a decision between continuing and discontinuing production of product X.

Chapter 20

CAPITAL EXPENDITURE
ANALYSIS

PROBABLY the most important category of investment problems in most firms comprises proposals for the expenditure of funds to build, acquire, replace, or expand long-life productive assets—i.e., *capital* expenditures. The internal investment opportunities available to the firm are reflected in a wide variety of capital expenditure proposals submitted on the initiative of executives at all levels of the organization. In the aggregate, these requests typically exceed the amount of funds available for investment. For this reason, management needs methods and procedures for deciding which proposals should be accepted.

One method of rationing the company's scarce capital funds is to calculate for each proposal the present value of the anticipated cash flows, using the technique described in Chapter 19, and accept only those proposals that seem to promise a positive net present value. Adoption of this method still leaves two sets of problems unresolved:

1. How to define cash flows for this purpose.
2. What rate of discount to apply to these cash flows.

This chapter will examine the first of these in some depth, introduce the basic concepts relevant to the second, and then evaluate briefly several alternative methods of capital rationing. The chapter will close with a brief survey of some of the procedures used to facilitate this rationing process.

ESTIMATES OF PROJECT CASH FLOWS

It is conceptually unnecessary in capital expenditure analysis to distinguish different types of cash flows, because the timetable requires a distinction only between inflows and outflows. For analytical convenience, however, five separate parameters can be recognized, four of them being components of the cash flow stream:

1. The amount and timing of initial investment outlays.
2. The amount and timing of subsequent investment outlays.
3. The amount and timing of operating cash flows.
4. Economic life.
5. End-of-life residual values.

Before examining these, however, we must first examine the relevance of one factor that may influence them all to some extent—the incidence of taxes on business income.

Income Tax Adjustments

For decisions of a tactical nature, income tax considerations are by definition irrelevant because they merely change the amount of the relative advantage of one alternative over another. They do not affect the relative *ranking* of the alternatives. To illustrate, field testing of two possible package designs has indicated that one will yield 10 percent more sales than the other. Investment outlays and operating labor and materials costs for the two alternatives are identical; the only difference is in expected sales volume and therefore in incremental profit. If the before-tax profit differential is expected to be $30,000 a year and the effective tax rate is 40 percent, then the after-tax increment in profit is 60 percent of $30,000, or $18,000.[1] The direction of the superiority is unaffected by the inclusion or omission of the tax effect.

In contrast, the structure of the investment problem is such that income tax effects can be extremely important. In some instances, the tax effects of a decision may be the controlling factor. The main reason for adjusting project profitability estimates for the effect of income taxes is that both the amount and the timing of the tax impact are likely to differ among alternatives. Inasmuch as the characteristic feature of investment problems is that they entail choices among alternatives with differing amounts and timing of cash flows, tax effects are just as important in capital expenditure analysis as any other effects.

For example, suppose that a company is trying to choose between two proposals to invest $100,000. For one of these, the entire $100,000 must be capitalized for tax purposes; for the other, it can be written off immediately as a tax deductible expense. Other things, being equal, the second of these is the better proposal because the tax-deductibility fea-

---

[1] The effective tax rate varies slightly from state to state and is subject to change. For simplicity, a rate of 40 percent will be used throughout this section. Although actual rates are ordinarily in the neighborhood of 50 percent, for illustrative purposes it is clearer to use the 40 percent rate, which produces different figures for income tax and after-tax net income.

ture will reduce the company's current tax bill by $40,000, assuming a 40 percent tax rate, and this amount can be invested productively elsewhere.

It should be noted that an initial tax write-off of this kind merely *postpones* tax payments. There is no tax *saving* unless the effective tax rate in lower in later years. For each proposal the total lifetime tax write-off is $100,000; only its timing differs. The same kind of conclusion could have been reached by using an illustration in which one proposal was subject to straight-line depreciation and the other to some form of declining-charge depreciation for tax purposes. Any device such as immediate deductibility or fast write-off shifts the income deduction to earlier years and thus gives it a higher present value to the taxpayer.

Many countries use tax deductibility as a means of achieving certain social objectives. In the United States, for example, rapid write-off of the cost of depreciable property has been introduced as a means of stimulating investment in such property. A more recent development in this country is the so-called "investment credit," by which a taxpayer is permitted to deduct from his current *tax payments* an amount equal to 7 percent of his total expenditures on certain types of property, up to certain aggregate limits.[2] This kind of thing alters not only the timing of tax payments but their total amount as well.

For example, suppose that a 7 percent investment credit is applicable to the $100,000 expenditure mentioned above. The net initial outlay is thus only $93,000:

Gross outlay	$100,000
Less: Investment credit	7,000
Net Outlay	$ 93,000

Depreciation over the expected useful life of the facilities, however, continues to be based on $100,000. At a 40 percent tax rate, this means that over the life of the facilities, taxes on the company's income will be $40,000 less than they would be if no depreciation deduction were allowed. The total tax deduction is thus $47,000 instead of the $40,000 that would be available in the absence of the investment credit.

Initial Investment Outlays

With this as background, the stage is set for an examination of each of the five parameters listed above. Measurement of the first of these—

---

[2] As this book went to press, the President requested Congress to suspend the investment credit until inflationary pressures eased. The discussion in these paragraphs has been retained, however, in order to show how this kind of device can affect cash flows.

the initial investment outlay—is not always as simple as it might sound. The initial outlay is defined as the net expenditure of cash or its equivalent required by the proposal. This includes all expenditures necessary to carry out the proposal, whether for plant and equipment or for working capital, whether capitalized on the balance sheet or written off immediately as expense for external financial reporting or tax purposes.

For example, a proposal may call for the following expenditures prior to the start of operations:

Equipment	$ 80,000
Installation	10,000
Working capital	5,000
Training and test runs	7,000
Total Expenditures	$102,000

To simplify the calculations, we shall assume that installation, training, and test runs are to be carried out by outside contractors, with payment due for all four of these items when the facilities are placed in full company operation. For convenience, this can be designated as the zero date.

In addition to these cash expenditures, this proposal calls for the use of a machine already under company ownership but now idle. This is one of the resources that would be tied up if this proposal were accepted; the question is how to measure the "outlay" required to obtain these resources for this purpose. This calls for the direct application of the opportunity cost concept first discussed in Chapter 3. Opportunity cost is at least as high as the current market (resale) value of the asset, and in this case this is the measure of opportunity cost. The amount is $12,000. This is regarded as part of the outlay because the company is depriving itself of this amount of cash if it accepts the proposal. A cash receipt foregone is always equivalent to a cash outlay made.

One final element enters into the calculation of the before-tax investment outlay in this example. If the proposal is accepted, a machine now serving a standby purpose can be disposed of. This machine represents resources now unavailable for general use but which will be made available by acceptance of this proposal. Opportunity cost is once again the measure of the resources released, in this case equal to the scrap value of the machine, which is $6,000. The displaced resources, in other words, can finance $6,000 of the gross before-tax outlays required by the proposal.

The net initial investment outlay before taxes can now be computed from the above figures:

Equipment	$ 80,000
Installation	10,000
Working capital	5,000
Training and test runs	7,000
Presently owned surplus equipment to be used (resale value)	12,000
Gross outlay	$114,000
Less: Presently owned operating equipment to be replaced if proposal is accepted (resale value)	6,000
Net Investment Outlay before Income Taxes	$108,000

The tax adjustment will depend on the tax status of the specific facilities. For simplicity, we are assuming a uniform 40 percent tax rate throughout and a 7 percent investment credit on capitalized plant and equipment outlays, including capitalized installation costs. In practice, of course, special capital gains treatment will apply in some cases, and the current tax rate ordinarily will differ substantially from 40 percent, but a straight 40 percent rate will illustrate tax adjustments as well as any other and has the specific advantage of not pretending to more precision than it achieves. A 40 percent rate is better for illustrative purposes than a 50 percent rate because it eliminates the danger of confusing the tax and income after tax figures.

In the illustration, the first two items—equipment and installation costs—are subject to the 7 percent tax reduction, so the cash flows are:

Gross outlay	$90,000
Less: Tax reduction at 7 percent	6,300
After-Tax Outlay	$83,700

The working capital outlays have no special tax treatment, and thus after-tax and before-tax outlays are identical.[3] The training and test-run costs are fully deductible from current revenues, and thus the after-tax cash flow is only 60 percent of the before-tax outlay:

Gross outlay	$7,000
Less: Tax reduction at 40 percent	2,800
After-Tax Outlay	$4,200

The tax effect of retention of the surplus equipment is probably the most difficult to understand. If the company does not accept this proposal, it will be able to dispose of this equipment at a price of $12,000. The book value of this equipment for tax purposes (or, to use technical language, its "adjusted basis") is $20,000. Thus if it is sold, an $8,000 loss will be reported on the income tax return, and this will reduce the company's taxes by $3,200. In other words, the company can realize a

---

[3] This is not always the case. Some countries have special income tax provisions to encourage the investment in inventories, and these would have to be allowed for.

total of $15,200. By accepting the proposal, the company must forego this cash receipt—thus $15,200 must be charged against the proposal as a cash outlay. The calculations can be summarized briefly:

(1) Before-tax cash flow...$12,000
(2) Book value for tax purposes.............................. 20,000
(3) Taxable gain or (loss): (1) − (2)...........................$(8,000)
(4) Tax or (credit): (3) × 40%................................ (3,200)
(5) After-Tax Cash Flow: (1) − (4)...........................$15,200

The tax effect of the disposal of the replaced facilities is similar, but probably easier to understand. Assuming a book value for tax purposes of $1,000, the calculations are:

(1) Before-tax cash flow...$6,000
(2) Book value for tax purposes.............................. 1,000
(3) Taxable gain or (loss): (1) − (2)...........................$5,000
(4) Tax or (credit): (3) × 40%................................ 2,000
(5) After-Tax Cash Flow: (1) − (4)...........................$4,000

These adjustments are all summarized in Exhibit 20–1. In this case the net difference between the before-tax and the after-tax amounts is relatively small, less than 4 percent; in other cases it will be much higher. Some analysts would prefer to recognize a difference in timing between the outlay and the tax adjustment, taking the outlay into the timetable at the zero date and the tax adjustment with the first year's operating cash flows. This is ordinarily an unnecessary complication, first because the time lag before tax payment is relatively short and getting shorter as time goes by, and also because an increase in tax liability ordinarily has approximately the same effect on corporate liquidity as a decrease in cash and thus can be regarded as equivalent to a cash flow.

Exhibit 20–1

CALCULATION OF AFTER-TAX INVESTMENT OUTLAY

Item	Outlay before Tax	Tax Effect	Outlay after Tax
Equipment, installed................	$ 90,000	$(6,300)	$ 83,700
Working capital....................	5,000	0	5,000
Training and test runs..............	7,000	(2,800)	4,200
Surplus equipment used.............	12,000	3,200	15,200
Equipment replaced................	(6,000)	2,000	(4,000)
Total.......................	$108,000	$(3,900)	$104,100

Subsequent Investment Outlays

It is often possible to anticipate, at the time a proposal is made, special outlays in later time periods that are more like investment outlays than operating expenditures. These, too, may be for equipment or working capital, treated as expense or capitalized, and should be adjusted for their tax effects. The only reason for assigning these outlays to a separate category is that they are the easiest cash flows to overlook, and separate recognition at least serves as a partial reminder to look for them. Their conceptual basis is no different from that of the initial outlays, however, and needs no further discussion here.

Economic Life and the Discounting Period

Both this and preceding chapters have referred to economic life rather loosely, with no attempt to define the concept in precise terms. Economic life of any particular asset may be defined as *the time interval that is expected to elapse between the time of acquisition and the time at which the combined forces of obsolescence and deterioration will justify retirement of the asset.* As in human life expectancy calculations, this is a probabilistic notion. Of any group of similar wasting assets, death will come to some soon after birth; others may have lives of 50 years or even longer. Group depreciation for financial reporting is based on this fact, and Internal Revenue audits of depreciation rates frequently require the preparation of actuarial life expectancy tables from historical data. Exhibit 20–2 shows one company's experience with the mortality of a particular type of industrial equipment. In this case the median historical life expectancy was approximately 13 years, meaning that half of the machines lived longer and half were retired before the end of 13 years. The mean life was slightly longer, reflecting the fact that some machines were still in use more than 40 years after installation.

Historical data of this sort may be useful in estimating the economic life of the facilities provided for specific investment proposals, particularly when the proposals are for the replacement of existing equipment. The economic life of an investment project, however, may be very different from the life of any one of the assets required by the project. It may include buildings with a life of 50 years, production equipment with a life of 15 years, test equipment with a three-year life, and working capital the life of which is infinite. The estimated life of such projects is determined not so much by the life of the physical facilities as by the expected duration of the earnings stream generated by the project. This may encompass two or more life cycles of particular kinds of physical assets, or it may be shorter than a single cycle.

Life is usually estimated as the interval before major facilities replacement or renovation will probably be required or before market obsolescence is expected, whichever is shorter. This may be no more than an informed guess, and this solution, therefore, is not entirely satisfactory, but it may be the only solution possible.

To the extent that life is terminated by a progressive evaporation of the source of earnings, it may be possible to estimate life on the basis of

Exhibit 20–2

ILLUSTRATIVE SURVIVAL CURVE FOR INDUSTRIAL EQUIPMENT

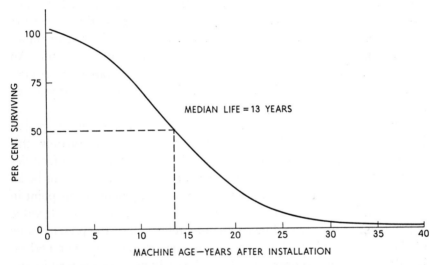

the time pattern of the expected earnings stream. For example, if operating and maintenance costs are expected to rise as facilities age, the stream of anticipated cash flows may decline as time goes by. Life in this case may be estimated by finding the point at which the present value of expected future cash flows is less than the estimated disposal value of the assets. Alternatively, as newer and better equipment becomes available in the future, the spread between the annual costs of operating and maintaining a machine purchased now and the comparable costs of the best machine available for purchase will increase. At some point this cost spread will be great enough to justify replacement, even if operating and maintenance costs of the equipment purchased now have not risen substantially. Equipment replacement formulas embodying this obsolescence effect have been developed by George Terborgh for the guidance of members of the Machinery and Allied Products Institute.[4] These formulas can be extremely useful if a reliable basis exists for predicting the obsolescence pattern.

Assuming for the moment that economic life can be predicted with reasonable accuracy, another problem faces the analyst when the alternatives being compared differ in estimated life. For example, a meat-packer may be faced with the problem of acquiring transportation equipment to move its products from central packing plants to regional distribution points. It can either purchase railroad cars or tractor-trailer combinations. Railroad cars are expected to last 20 years, the tractor-trailers only six. There are two ways of attacking this problem. First, the investment cycle for the shorter life facilities may be repeated as many times as necessary to cover the expected life cycle of the longer-life alternative. Thus the meat-packer would need to use $3\frac{1}{3}$ tractor-trailer cycles to provide comparability with the 20-year railroad car life. An estimate of the salvage value of the fourth tractor-trailer investment would have to be inserted into the timetable at the end of 20 years to make the time periods comparable.

The alternative to this procedure is to define the discounting period in terms of the life of the shorter life alternative. Unfortunately, this requires an estimate of the recoverable value of the longer life facilities at this intermediate point, and intermediate resale values may not be an adequate reflection of the service value of the equipment at this point in time. If used equipment markets were perfect, the estimated resale value at any point in time would be an accurate reflection of the present value of the future services of the equipment, but markets are not perfect. Resale values tend to drop sharply in the early years of ownership and then decline more gradually as the equipment ages. For this reason, the use of intermediate salvage value for long-life equipment is likely to penalize the longer life alternative.

Forecasting of the cost and operating characteristics of future replacements is admittedly difficult. If some basis exists for forecasting a change in equipment prices or technological improvements, these forecasts should be reflected in the replacement cycles for the shorter life alternative. Fortunately, errors in these forecasts are seldom as serious as it might seem. At the discounting rates that are used in capital expendi-

---

[4] For a complete exposition of Terborgh's method, see George Terborgh, *Dynamic Equipment Policy* (New York: McGraw-Hill Book Co., Inc., 1949).

ture analysis, cash flows that take place more than 15 years ahead have relatively little effect on the total present value of the project or on the discounted rate of return. The present value of $100,000 15 years hence, discounted at 10 percent, is only $22,310. This dampens the effect of errors in the salvage value estimates. Nevertheless, every effort should be made to ensure comparability in the life span of mutually exclusive alternatives.

Operating Cash Flows

The income tax adjustment and the explicit recognition of year-to-year variations are the only aspects of the operating cash flows that are unique to investment problems. Net operating cash flows may be either positive or negative, although the ordinary presumption is that they will be positive except perhaps during the first year or two of the project's life.

In many cases, the analyst will have very little basis on which to predict time patterns of the operating cash flows, and will use some formulistic approximation such as uniform annual amounts or linearly declining amounts. The reasonableness of these formulas should always be questioned, and if a better basis can be justified it should be used.

The tax adjustment again requires intimate knowledge of the current state of tax laws and regulations. The earlier illustration, it will be recalled, called for incremental outlays totaling $108,000 before taxes. Of these outlays, $7,000 were deducted immediately from taxable income, and $5,000 represented working capital which is not depreciable. Thus only three determinants of the initial outlay remain to affect taxes on the incremental subsequent operating cash flows:

	Tax Basis	Depreciation Rate for Tax Purposes
Installed equipment cost..........................	$90,000 ⎫	20% of declining
Previously owned equipment incorporated in the project.......................................	20,000 ⎬	balance
Equipment replaced by the project...............	1,000	$500 per year

Notice that in all three items the tax basis differs from the incremental after-tax cash flow entered in the timetable. The surplus equipment, for example, had a before-tax cash flow of $12,000, an after-tax cash flow of $15,200, and a tax basis of $20,000.

Incremental tax depreciation for the first three years of the project's life will be as follows:

	Year 1	Year 2	Year 3
If proposal is accepted:			
Depreciation on new equipment...............	$18,000	$14,400	$11,520
Depreciation on old equipment...............	4,000	3,200	2,560
Total depreciation if proposal is accepted....	$22,000	$17,600	$14,080
If proposal is rejected:			
Depreciation on present standby equipment..	500	500	.....
Incremental Tax Depreciation (Difference).......	$21,500	$17,100	$14,080

The deduction of depreciation on the replaced equipment may be more easily understood if it is recognized as a simple time shift. If the proposal is accepted, the equipment will be replaced and $1,000 will be deducted immediately from taxable income. This was reflected earlier in our calculation of the after-tax investment outlay. If the proposal is rejected, on the other hand, the equipment will be retained and the $1,000 will be deducted from taxable income during the next two years.

Assume now that the incremental before-tax operating cash flows in the first three years are expected to amount to $20,000 a year. This needs to be converted to an after-tax basis by subtracting the incremental tax from the before-tax cash flow. One possible format for doing this is as follows (all figures refer to *incremental* amounts):

Year	(1) Before-Tax Cash Flow	(2) Tax Depreciation	(3) Taxable Income (1) − (2)	(4) Income Tax (3) × 40%	(5) After-Tax Cash Flow (1) − (4)
1.............	$20,000	$21,500	$(1,500)	$ (600)	$20,600
2.............	20,000	17,100	2,900	1,160	18,840
3.............	20,000	14,080	5,920	2,368	17,632

Figures for years beyond the third are omitted here to avoid burying the principles in a mass of numbers. An equivalent alternative is:

Year	(1) Before-Tax Cash Flow	(2) Tax Depreciation	(3) Taxable Income (1) − (2)	(4) Income Tax (3) × 40%	(5) After-Tax Net Income (3) − (4)	(6) After-Tax Cash Flow (2) + (5)
1........	...$20,000	$21,500	$(1,500)	$ (600)	$ (900)	$20,600
2........	20,000	17,100	2,900	1,160	1,740	18,840
3........	20,000	14,080	5,920	2,368	3,552	17,632

This depreciation add-back procedure is familiar to anyone who has prepared a statement of the sources and uses of funds. The analyst should use whichever method he finds more convenient. The results will be identical.

End-of-Life Salvage Value

The final element in the incremental cash flow timetable is end-of-life salvage value. This consists of the after-tax amount realizable from liquidation of the working capital and sale of the facilities. Alternatively, it is equal to the internal value of the assets to the company at the end of the project's life, if this is greater than liquidation value.

Once again, it is a differential amount that is needed. If the proposal calls for replacing certain assets now, these will not be available later. In the example, facilities with a realizable value of $6,000 are to be replaced. If the proposal is rejected, the company is, in effect, investing the after-tax equivalent of this $6,000—this was reflected above in the incremental investment outlay. By rejecting the proposal, however, the company does retain title to whatever residual value is left at the end of the project's life. If this is, say, $1,500, then this is a charge against the proposal. This shows up in a table of alternatives:

	End-of-Project Salvage Value
If proposal is rejected...................	$1,500
If proposal is accepted..................	0
Difference........................	$1,500

To complete this illustration, suppose that the liquidation value of the working capital is equal to its book value for tax purposes ($5,000) and that the equipment required by the proposal has a before-tax residual value of $13,000 and an end-of-life book value for tax purposes of $7,500. The incremental cash flow is:

	(1) Before-Tax Cash Flow	(2) Tax Basis	(3) Taxable Income (1) − (2)	(4) Income Tax (3) × 40%	(5) After-Tax Cash Flow (1) − (4)
If accept proposal:					
Equipment.....................	$13,000	$ 7,500	$5,500	$2,200	$10,800
Working capital...............	5,000	5,000	0	0	5,000
Total residual value...........	$18,000	$12,500	$5,500	$2,200	$15,800
If reject proposal:					
Sale value of standby equipment..	1,500	0	1,500	600	900
Incremental Salvage Value........	$16,500	$12,500	$4,000	$1,600	$14,900

Opportunity Cost

The opportunity cost concept was deliberately injected into the fore-going illustration by incorporating some presently owned facilities into the new proposal. A different way of recognizing opportunity cost is to show each alternative explicitly. For example, a company is considering

Exhibit 20–3

OPPORTUNITY COSTS IN INVESTMENT ANALYSIS

Data Summary

Current after-tax sale value of property..........................	$ 100,000
After-tax cash earnings from parking lot operation...............	8,000 per year
Building construction cost.......................................	1,000,000
After-tax cash earnings from building rentals....................	110,000 per year
After-tax sale value 25 years hence:	
Parking lot...	150,000
Land and building...................................	300,000

Evaluation

Years Hence	Sell Now	Parking Lot	Building Rental
0............................	+$100,000	. . . . . .	− $1,000,000
0 to 1.......................		+$ 8,000	+ 110,000
1 to 2.......................		+ 8,000	+ 110,000
.		.	.
.		.	.
.		.	.
24 to 25.....................		+ 8,000	+ 110,000
25...........................		+ 150,000	+ 300,000
Net Cash Inflow..............	+$100,000	+$350,000	+$2,050,000
Present Value at 10%.........	+$100,000	+$ 85,747	+$ 34,320

a proposal to construct a building on the site of a company-owned parking lot in a growing suburban business area. Three alternatives are recognized: (1) sell the property, (2) continue operating the parking lot, and (3) construct the building. The evaluation of these alternatives is contained in Exhibit 20–3. Assuming that this company requires a minimum rate of return of 10 percent after taxes, the alternative that promises the greatest present value is the alternative of selling the site now. In other words, the investment of $100,000 in land cannot be justified by expected parking lot earnings, nor are the earnings from building rentals sufficient to provide an adequate return on the invest-ment in the building plus the investment in the land.

The other way to handle opportunity cost is to adopt the method used in the previous illustration. Suppose that the immediate proposal is to construct a building. The best alternative, determined by comparing current sale of the land with the profitability of parking lot operation, is to sell the land. Therefore, the project authorization request could condense the comparative cash flow figures into the following form:

Investment outlay:	
Construction costs (after investment credit)..........	$1,000,000
Land value.......................................	100,000
Total..	$1,100,000
Annual cash earnings...............................	$ 110,000
End-of-life recoverable value........................	$ 300,000
Present Value at 10%..............................	−$ 65,680

If the present value of the parking lot alternative were greater than the current sale price, adjusted for taxes, then this greater amount should be deducted as the opportunity cost of the land.

APPLICATION OF THE CONCEPTS

The application of these concepts to capital expenditure decisions encounters problems that are too complex to be treated adequately in a broadly based textbook. This chapter would not be complete, however, without an example to bring together most of the points that have been raised in the preceding pages and to raise one or two additional questions.

Illustrative Proposal: Renovation of Manufacturing Plant

The Bawtry Products Company operates six manufacturing plants, each specializing in a particular type of product. The oldest of these plants, located in Springfield, has long been regarded as inefficient, and its management has just come up with a proposal to spend $580,000 on a major renovation program, after deducting the applicable investment credit. Of this amount, $100,000 can be expensed immediately for tax purposes. The salvage value of equipment and other assets to be discarded is expected to be negligible. All such assets are depreciated on a group basis for tax purposes, which means that in this case scrapping the old facilities will not lead to any recognized gain or loss for tax purposes.

The proposed improvements are expected to reduce factory cash operating costs by approximately $350,000 a year. Tax depreciation charges will be increased by $30,000 a year; annual replacement expenditures (capitalized for tax purposes) will increase by $20,000 a year.

With these expenditures the management feels that the plant could remain in operation for about 15 years before another major renovation would be required. It is estimated that the salvage value of the facilities at the end of 15 years will be $300,000 greater if the expenditures are made than if the plant is to be operated as at present.

Exhibit 20–4

CASH FLOW TIMETABLE FOR PLANT RENOVATICN PROPOSAL

Years from Now	(1) Investment Cash Flows	(2) Operating Cash Flows	(3) Tax Depreciation	(4) Taxable Income (2) − (3)
0.........	−$580,000		$100,000	$ (100,000)
0–15.......	− 20,000 per yr.	+$ 350,000 per yr.	30,000 per yr.	320,000 per yr.
15.........	+ 300,000		330,000	(30,000)
Total......	−$580,000	+$5,250,000	$880,000	$4,670,000

Years from Now	(5) Income Tax Cash Flows (4) × 40%	(6) Cash Flow after Tax (1) + (2) − (5)	(7) Present Value at 10% (6) × App. A
0.................	+$ 40,000	−$ 540,000	−$ 540,000
0–15.............	− 128,000 per yr.	+ 202,000 per yr.	+ 1,569,000
15................	+ 12,000	+ 312,000	+ 70,000
Total.............	−$1,868,000	+$2,802,000	+$1,099,000

The cash flow timetable presented in support of this proposal is shown in Exhibit 20–4. The required return on investment is 10 percent after taxes, and once again a 40 percent tax rate has been used for clarity and simplicity, even though the actual rate ordinarily will be much greater. The only element in Exhibit 20–4 that should need explanation is the $330,000 figure on the last line of column (3). This is the difference between the amounts to be capitalized during the next 15 years ($880,000) and the amounts to be charged as tax-deductible expense prior to the end of the 15-year period ($100,000 immediate write-off plus 15 times $30,000, or a total of $550,000).

Selecting the Right Bench Mark

This proposal would seem to meet the company's minimum return on investment standard, with plenty to spare. The most relevant comparison in this case, however, is not with continued operation of the plant as it stands but with the alternative of discontinuing operations completely. (Other alternatives, such as building an entirely new factory elsewhere, changing the product line, or using different methods of distribution would ordinarily be explored in a decision of this magnitude, but only the abandonment alternative needs to be introduced here for the purpose we have in mind.)

The Springfield plant is now operating at a small annual loss of about $8,000. Depreciation charges amount to about $160,000 a year, so the cash generation is about $152,000 a year. No allocation of head office expenses is included in Springfield's expenses, and this $152,000 represents the amount of before-tax operating cash receipts that would be lost if the plant were to be closed and the product line discontinued. Equipment replacement and plant overhaul expenditures of about $140,000 a year are necessary to keep the plant going. These patterns are expected to continue into the indefinite future unless something is done to change operations radically.

Based on these projections, the after-tax cash flows from annual operations are as follows:

$$\text{Before tax: } \$152,000 - \$140,000 \quad = +\$12,000$$
$$\text{Tax: } (\$152,000 - \$160,000) \times 40\% = + \quad 3,200$$
$$\text{After Tax} \ldots \ldots \ldots \ldots \ldots \ldots \quad +\$15,200$$

(Because this plant reports an operating loss for tax purposes, $8,000 of taxable income elsewhere in the company is thus shielded from taxation and a tax credit of $3,200 results. This is equivalent to a cash inflow.)

The best available evidence is that the plant and equipment can be sold now for about $1,000,000, and the liquidation value of the working capital tied up in the Springfield operation is about $600,000. The book value of these assets for tax purposes is now about $1,300,000. The after-tax cash flow from liquidation thus would be:

$$\text{Before tax: } \$1,000,000 + \$600,000 \quad = +\$1,600,000$$
$$\text{Tax: } (\$1,600,000 - \$1,300,000) \times 40\% = - \quad 120,000$$
$$\text{After Tax} \ldots \ldots \ldots \ldots \ldots \ldots \quad +\$1,480,000$$

The before-tax salvage value at the end of 15 years would be approximately $1,200,000, almost entirely the value of the land and working capital. Book value for tax purposes at that time would be

$300,000 less than it is now, depreciation being $20,000 a year greater than capital additions. The end-of-life salvage value would thus be:

$$
\begin{array}{lr}
\text{Before tax} \ldots \ldots \ldots \ldots \ldots \ldots \ldots \ldots & +\$1,200,000 \\
\text{Tax: } (\$1,200,000 - \$1,000,000) \times 40\% = - & 80,000 \\
\text{After Tax} \ldots \ldots \ldots \ldots \ldots \ldots \ldots & +\$1,120,000
\end{array}
$$

The timetable of the cash flows from the existing operation can be summarized as follows:

Years from Now	Abandon Springfield	Continue Springfield	Difference
0................	+$1,480,000	0	−$1,480,000
0–15.............	0	+$ 15,200 per yr.	+ 15,200 per yr.
15...............	0	+ 1,120,000	+ 1,120,000
Total...........	+$1,480,000	+$1,348,000	−$ 132,000

It is not necessary to do any discounting to find that this plant should be closed unless something can be done to improve its profitability.

What this means is that the appropriate bench mark for the renovation proposal is not the alternative of continued operations as at present. Instead, the relevant alternative is the abandonment alternative. In other words, the renovation profits not only have to justify the renovation expenditure but the disposal value of the facilities as well. The comparison is shown in Exhibit 20–5. The figures in the second column are the sums of the cash flows from continued operation and from the renovation proposal. Because the initial measurements reflected only the increment over continued operations, a pushing back of the bench mark requires a corresponding expansion in the scope of the increment.

The present value column of Exhibit 20–5 shows that the renovation proposal is not the clearly desirable opportunity it originally appeared to be. Instead, it is a borderline proposal, with the present value

Exhibit 20–5

REVISED CASH FLOW TIMETABLE FOR RENOVATION PROPOSAL

Years from Now	Abandon Springfield	Renovate	Difference	Present Value at 10%
0................	+$1,480,000	−$ 540,000	−$2,020,000	−$2,020,000
0–15.............	0	+ 217,200 per yr.	+ 217,200 per yr.	+ 1,687,000
15...............	0	+ 1,432,000	+ 1,432,000	+ 320,000
Total...........	+$1,480,000	+$4,150,000	+$2,670,000	−$ 13,000

of the anticipated cash inflows almost exactly equal to the initial outlay required.

Uncertainty Adjustments

This is the kind of situation that cries out for supplementary data of a different sort, data indicating the degree of uncertainty in the estimates. Two aspects of uncertainty must be considered in the decision-making process:

1. Uncertainty as to future value of an important independent variable (such as aggregate disposable personal income).
2. Uncertainty as to the parameter, or the relationship, between a given value of an independent variable (disposable personal income) and the value of a dependent variable (e.g., product sales).

For example, suppose that aggregate disposable personal income in a given market area is an important factor in determining the level of sales of a new product. Personal income is the net result of many forces operating within this market area, and the exact level of personal income cannot be forecasted with certainty. The best that the forecaster can hope to do is to estimate the probabilities associated with each possible level of personal income. He can make statements as to the *"expected value"* (the average of all possible values, weighted by the percentage probability of each) and the dispersion around this value. From this he can make statements as to probabilities, such as that there is a 95 percent probability that personal income will be between X and Y next year.

As to the second aspect of uncertainty, even if it were possible to predict personal income with complete certainty, the relationship between personal income and sales of the product could be forecast only in terms of probabilities. Again the analyst is faced with the problem of forecasting the frequency distribution of possible outcomes for a given level of personal income.

Dealing with Uncertainty

These uncertainties can be brought into the analysis or considered in a number of ways:

1. By applying management judgment to expected values.
2. By bracketing expected values.
3. By downgrading expected values.
4. By utilizing probability distributions.

Probability distributions may be determined either objectively (by analysis of historical data) or subjectively (by the exercise of management judgment). No matter how they are determined, management's attitudes toward gains and losses may be asymmetrical, as we mentioned in Chapter 3, and probabilities of gains may have to be weighted more or less heavily than probabilities of losses.[5]

Unfortunately, the number of separate estimates required makes unmanageable the application of probabilities to capital expenditure decisions. Instead, many companies try to examine the sensitivity of profits to variations in the size, timing, or duration of the cash flow stream by bracketing the "best" forecast with more pessimistic and more optimistic forecasts.

Exhibit 20–6 shows how this might be applied to the plant renova-

Exhibit 20–6

SENSITIVITY ANALYSIS OF PLANT RENOVATION PROPOSAL

Years Hence	Pessimistic Estimates		Optimistic Estimates	
	Cash Flow after Tax	Present Value at 10%	Cash Flow after Tax	Present Value at 10%
0...............	−$2,200,000	−$2,200,000	−$1,900,000	−$1,900,000
0–15............	+ 190,000 per yr.	+ 1,476,000	+ 250,000 per yr.	+ 1,942,000
15..............	+ 1,400,000	+ 312,000	+ 1,600,000	+ 357,000
Total..........	+$2,050,000	−$ 412,000	+$3,450,000	+$ 399,000

tion proposal. In this case, the optimistic and pessimistic estimates are arrayed fairly symmetrically around the best estimate, and even the pessimistic estimate shows substantial positive cash flows before deduction of interest.

This technique does not yield probability estimates in any sense of the term, but it does give management some idea of how critical the potential estimating errors are. Other estimates could also be inserted if desired—e.g., shorter economic life or declining sales volume—but the introduction of more than two or three alternative estimates is likely to be more confusing than helpful.

CHOOSING THE DISCOUNTING RATE

The preceding discussion deliberately passed over a number of difficult problems that must be solved in the design of a system of capital

---

[5] For a thorough discussion, see Robert Schlaifer, *Probability and Statistics for Business Decisions: An Introduction to Managerial Economics under Uncertainty* (New York: McGraw-Hill Book Co., Inc., 1959).

controls. One of the most crucial of these is the problem of selecting the interest rate at which to discount anticipated incremental cash flows for individual proposals. This topic is perhaps more properly dealt with under the heading of finance or business economics, but a brief introduction is appropriate here.

The Cost of Capital Concept

Capital is not a "one price commodity." The price that must be promised to owners of investment funds to induce them to entrust these funds to a particular undertaking will depend on many factors: the reputation and prospects of the company, the form of the legal relationship between the investor and the company (that is, whether the investor will be a lender or an owner), the duration of the relationship (short-term or long-term lending), and the state of the financial market at the time the company obtains the funds, to mention several of the main factors. For any given company at any given time, however, the price that the company must pay to obtain funds through the issuance of a given type of security is determined by market forces. Generally speaking, this price can be expressed as the percentage expected yield that investors in that type of security demand as a reward for investing their money. From these data on demanded yields, the company can estimate its cost of capital, the cost of attracting funds into the company.

Cost of Debt Capital

The specific cost of debt capital is the rate of interest that equates the present value of the future stream of interest payments (after allowing for income tax effects) and maturity date repayment of face value to the current net proceeds from sale of the debt instruments. For example, assume that bonds with a coupon rate of 5 percent and a 20-year maturity can be sold to net the company $97.53 per $100 of face value. The before-tax cash flows are:

Years after Borrowing	Cash Flow
0	+$ 97.53
1 to 20	− 5.00 a year
20	− 100.00

The interest rate at which the present value of the cash outflows is just equal to the $97.53 net proceeds from the sale of this issue is 5.2 percent, obtained from widely available bond yield tables. After providing for the tax deductibility of interest expense at a tax rate of 40 percent, the after-tax cost of this debt offering is approximately 3.1

percent. All of the components of the yield formula are known, and it is a simple matter to compute the direct cost of debt.

Cost of Equity Capital

Traditional terminology refers to the *cost* of debt and the *return* on equity. In financial accounting, interest is deducted as an expense in computing net profit, but dividends are regarded as distributions of previously retained earnings. These distinctions, however, result from the nature of the legal relationships between the firm and the suppliers of capital, not from any inherent differences in the basic objectives of those who provide capital funds. Stockholders are just as interested in reward as bondholders or other lenders; only the form and legal status of the rewards are different.

The cost of equity capital is far more difficult to estimate because funds obtained from stockholders require no firm contractual commitment as to the level of any future payments by the company. Stockholders do, however, have rights in the residual earnings of the company; and by analogy with the cost of debt capital, the cost of equity capital can be defined as the rate of discount that the marginal stockholder applies to the expected earnings stream to determine the price that he is willing to pay for rights to this earnings stream. Determination of this discount rate requires data on the market price at which a company's common stock is being sold and the future earnings expectations of the stockholders. The latter information being unavailable, the analyst typically falls back on a study of past relationships between market prices and per share earnings, adjusted for any trends that seem to have influenced market price.

As a simple illustration of the concept, if a stock is selling for $50 a share and the company's annual earnings are stable at $5 a share, then this is some evidence that the marginal stockholders in the company are willing to pay $10 for each dollar of earnings. To attract additional funds into the firm, therefore, the company must be able to communicate an expectation that these funds will also earn an after-tax return of at least 10 percent on investment, and perhaps more. This of course is only a crude first approximation to the cost of equity capital. More refined methods are available, but even so, the art of estimating equity costs is in its infancy.[6] Although we shall not discuss this any further, we must recognize the importance of the concept to the capital expenditure decision. The cost of capital estimates that can be made are subject to

---

[6] For further discussion of the concept of the cost of capital, see Ezra Solomon, *The Theory of Financial Management* (New York: Columbia University Press, 1963).

error, but they are sufficiently reliable to be useful in determining the minimum cutoff rate for capital investment decisions.

Combined Cost of Capital

When the cost of each type of debt capital and each type of ownership capital is weighted in proportion to its relative importance in the company's long-range financing plan, the resulting average is the company's combined cost of capital. For example, if the company plans to obtain 30 percent of its long-term funds from creditors and 70 percent from its owners, and if the after-tax capital costs from these two sources are 3 percent and 12 percent, the combined cost of capital is:

Source of Funds	Cost of Funds	Percent of Financing	Combined Cost of Capital
Debt......................	3%	30	0.9%
Equity....................	12	70	8.4
Total..................			9.3%

Just how this figure or its determinants are to be used is the subject of much debate which cannot be reproduced here. The illustrations in this chapter and the problems at the end presume that the cash flows from each proposal will be tested against a profitability criterion reflecting the after-tax combined cost of capital. This means that even if a specific project is to be partly financed from the proceeds of specific borrowing and only partly from general company resources, the combined cost of capital will be used to discount projected cash flows.[7]

The argument for this approach is that although one project may lend itself to specific financing more readily than another, the company's ability to borrow is determined by companywide characteristics. If some projects are financed by specific borrowing, then the company's overall borrowing ability is impaired until additional equity funds are secured. In this light, the apparent cost of the capital borrowed for such projects can be seen to understate the full capital cost of the portion of the project financed by specific borrowing.

This being the case, amounts to be obtained through borrowing should not be deducted from estimated investment outlays, nor should

---

[7] A rate defined in this manner will also be used to appraise proposals for a parent company to invest in a subsidiary. The management of the subsidiary, however, may be justified in using a discount rate different from that of the parent on the grounds that only part of its funds come from the parent company. It will need to develop its own combined rate.

explicit interest on the amounts to be borrowed to finance these outlays be deducted from estimated incremental cash receipts. Thus the outlay appearing in the timetable for a $1 million project to be financed in part by a $700,000 mortgage loan should be $1 million, not $300,000.

Single versus Multiple Cutoff Rates

Another unresolved issue is whether the estimated cost of capital should be applied to all proposals, or whether proposals subject to different degrees of risk should be tested against different minimum return criteria. The argument is made that the individual investor applies different discount rates to the anticipated cash flows attaching to different kinds of potential investments, and that the business firm should do likewise.

This argument is far too complex to be settled here. The approach taken in this chapter uses a single rate across the board. If management wishes to hedge its bets by placing some of its funds in low-risk, low-return investments, it should be aware that these investments do not meet the normal earnings test.

SUBSTITUTE INDEXES OF PROJECT PROFITABILITY

The method of screening capital expenditure proposals by estimating their incremental net present value is not the only method used in practice. Three other methods deserve at least summary treatment:

1. Payback period.
2. Average return on investment.
3. Discounted rate of return.

To keep the presentation as simple as possible, all calculations in this section will be on a before-tax basis. If any of these substitute methods is used, however, it should be applied to after-tax data.

Payback Period

One approach is to compute for each proposal a measure of the length of time that it will take the expected earnings from the proposal to pay back the initial investment outlay. This *payback period* can then be compared with some standard of maximum acceptable payback to determine whether the project is acceptable. Payback period is computed by the following formula:

$$\text{Payback period (years)} = \frac{\text{Investment outlay}}{\text{Average annual cash receipts}}.$$

For example, if the installed cost of a piece of equipment is $50,000 and it will produce cash operating savings of $10,000 a year, it has a payback period of five years:

$$\frac{\text{Investment}}{\text{Annual cash receipts}} = \frac{\$50,000}{\$10,000} = 5 \text{ years}.$$

This figure is simple to compute, but it is inadequate for three reasons. First, it ignores the estimated economic life of the proposed facilities. If the facilities will have to be replaced five years from now, the project will have achieved no net earnings for the company. The company will have invested $50,000 at a zero rate of return.

Second, payback period ignores any time patterns in investment outlays and cash earnings and also ignores any end-of-life recoverable value. For example, if cash receipts are zero in the first year and rise gradually for 10 years so that the 10-year average is $10,000, the proposal will be less valuable than another proposal in which the earnings start out at a high level and gradually dwindle as the facilities get older. Or, if a large portion of the investment outlay is represented by working capital which has high end-of-life recoverability, the project will be more desirable than one in which ultimate salvage value is negligible.

Finally, there is no way of deciding what the maximum payback period should be. The cost of capital is a *net profit* concept, after providing for depreciation on wasting assets, and this can be converted into a maximum payback standard only by making some arbitrary assumptions as to the level of depreciation. The most that payback figures can accomplish is to provide a rough measure of profitability that can be interpreted only in conjunction with separate estimates of economic life.

Average Return on Investment

A second method is to compute for each project the expected average return on investment. This may be defined in many ways, perhaps the most common being expressed by the following formula:

$$\text{Average return} = \frac{\text{Average cash earnings per year} - \text{Depreciation per year}}{\text{Average lifetime investment}}.$$

There are many ways of computing the average lifetime investment. The use of straight-line depreciation for accounting purposes presumes that investment declines in a linear fashion as facilities age, as shown in Exhibit 20–7. The average investment under this assumption is halfway between the amount of the initial outlay and the effective investment at the end of the project's life, measured by the recoverable value of the facilities and working capital at that time. If depreciation is computed by one of the diminishing balance methods, the average investment will be less than this; if annuity method depreciation is used, the average investment will be greater. Average net earnings will be unaffected by the choice of depreciation method; only the earnings distribution over the project's life will be affected.

The assumption most commonly made in computing average return on investment is that average investment can be computed by averaging the beginning and ending investment figures, as in Exhibit 20–7, no

Exhibit 20–7

AVERAGE INVESTMENT: STRAIGHT-LINE DEPRECIATION

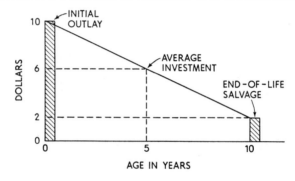

matter what method is actually used to charge depreciation for financial purposes. For example, the project for which payback period was computed earlier required an initial outlay of $50,000 and had no end-of-life salvage value. Average investment is thus $25,000. Assuming that the life of this project is expected to be 10 years, average annual depreciation is $5,000, and the average before-tax return on investment is 20 percent:

$$\frac{\text{Average net earnings}}{\text{Average investment}} = \frac{\$10,000 - \$5,000}{\$25,000} = 20\%.$$

This method does consider the expected life of the facilities, and it does consider the amount of end-of-life salvage. It fails, however, to allow for differences in timing of outlays and earnings. By this method a project in which no earnings appear until the 10th year will show up as equally profitable as a project in which most of the earnings are received in the first few years of the project's life, as long as the average is the same. Only some method of discounting is sufficiently sensitive to these differences in timing to provide a satisfactory measure of project profitability.

Discounted Rate of Return

The most widely used of the various discounting measures of project profitability is the discounted rate of return. This method differs from the present value calculations introduced in the previous chapter in that the discount rate is unknown. The discounted rate of return is defined as

Exhibit 20–8

CALCULATION OF DISCOUNTED RATE OF RETURN

Years Hence	Cash Inflow (+) or Outflow (−)	Present Value	
		At 15%	At 20%
0.........	−$50,000	−$50,000	−$50,000
0 to 1....	+ 10,000	+ 9,286	+ 9,063
1 to 2....	+ 10,000	+ 7,993	+ 7,421
2 to 3....	+ 10,000	+ 6,879	+ 6,075
3 to 4....	+ 10,000	+ 5,921	+ 4,974
4 to 5....	+ 10,000	+ 5,096	+ 4,072
5 to 6....	+ 10,000	+ 4,386	+ 3,334
6 to 7....	+ 10,000	+ 3,775	+ 2,730
7 to 8....	+ 10,000	+ 3,250	+ 2,235
8 to 9....	+ 10,000	+ 2,797	+ 1,830
9 to 10...	+ 10,000	+ 2,407	+ 1,498
Total....	+$50,000	+$ 1,790	−$ 6,768

that rate of discount at which the sum of the positive present values is equal to the sum of the negative present values. In other words, the *net present value* of the cash flows is zero.

Continuing with our simple example of the purchase of equipment for $50,000 to produce annual cash savings of $10,000 a year for 10 years, the discounted rate of return is obtained by discounting all cash flows at at least two rates of interest and interpolating to find the rate at which the algebraic sum of the present values (net present value) is zero. This process is demonstrated in Exhibit 20–8, using tables of interest factors that are contained in Appendix A.

Discounting the cash flows at 15 percent, the present value of the cash inflows exceeds the present value of the immediate outlay by $1,790. This indicates that the project earns more than 15 percent on the investment. Discounting at 20 percent, however, shows a negative present value of $6,768, indicating that the project does not earn 20 percent. The true before-tax rate of return is somewhere in between, approximately one fifth of the distance between 15 percent and 20 percent, or 16 percent.

$$\text{Approximate rate} = 15\% + \frac{\$1,790}{\$1,790 + \$6,768} \times 5\% = 16\% \ .$$

To put this another way, it appears that this project could afford to pay out of its $10,000 annual cash earnings the $50,000 investment outlay plus 16 percent for the cost of capital and still come out even. If the minimum cutoff rate is, say, 15 percent, then this proposal appears to be barely within the range of acceptability.

Discounted Rate of Return versus Present Value

The choice between the discounted rate of return and net present value as the means of summarizing project cash flows hinges on arguments too complex to permit adequate treatment here. A rate of return figure is generally understood more easily than a net present value amount, and it may be preferred on these grounds. Net present value, on the other hand, is simpler to compute and is more consistent with the assumption that management wishes to maximize the value of the enterprise.

In most situations, both methods will point to the same decisions. Differences will occur only if the company cannot accept all of the proposals that meet its minimum standards or, in certain cases, if the company is trying to choose among three or more mutually exclusive alternatives. Demonstration of these points is beyond the scope of this book, but an illustration may demonstrate one error that is sometimes made in the application of the discounted rate of return method.[8] Suppose, for example, that the company's minimum acceptable rate of return is 12 percent before taxes instead of the 15 percent assumed up to now. Also, in addition to the two alternatives on which the previous discussion was based, a third alternative is available: to buy a different kind of equipment at a price of $67,000. The annual cash cost saving with this machine would be $13,000 a year for 10 years instead of $10,000.

The discounted cash flow rate of return on this investment would be approximately 15 percent:

---

[8] Some representative references are James H. Lorie and Leonard J. Savage, "Three Problems in Rationing Capital," *Journal of Business,* October, 1955, pp. 229–39) and Gerald A. Pollack, "The Capital Budgeting Controversy: Present Value vs. Discounted Cash Flow Method," *N.A.A. Bulletin,* November, 1961, pp. 5–19.

	Present Value at 15%	Present Value at 20%
Outlay......................	−$67,000	−$67,000
Inflow ($13,000 a year).......	+ 67,327	+ 56,202
Net Present Value...........	+$ 327	−$10,798

This shows that the cash flows are adequate to cover a cost of capital of 15 percent, with an insignificant amount left over. This is slightly poorer than the 16 percent calculated for the original proposal, and management might therefore conclude that the original proposal to purchase the $50,000 machine is superior. This conclusion would be wrong, however, because what is relevant is not the return on the full $67,000 but rather the return on the *added* $17,000 investment that would be required if this more expensive equipment were to be purchased instead of the equipment represented by the $50,000 outlay. If this added investment produces a rate of return in excess of the company's minimum requirements, then the additional expenditure should be made.

In this case the incremental cash savings available to justify the additional investment outlay are $3,000 a year ($13,000 less the $10,000 obtainable with the lesser expenditure). This works out to a rate of return of approximately 12.7 percent:

	Present Value at 12%	Present Value at 13%
Outlay......................	−$17,000	−$17,000
Inflow ($3,000 a year).......	+ 17,471	+ 16,787
Net Present Value...........	+$ 471	−$ 213

This shows that the incremental cash flows are adequate to cover a cost of capital of 12 percent, with a little left over, but are inadequate to meet a 13 percent rate. The interpolation works out to about 12.7 percent. This rate is in excess of the company's minimum acceptable rate of 12 percent before taxes, and the proposal to buy the more expensive equipment therefore should be accepted.

The net present value method reaches this same conclusion by a simpler route. The cash flow stream for each proposal is discounted at 12 percent, the preferred alternative being the one that offers the greatest present value at this rate. The results of this computation are summarized in Exhibit 20–9 and show that the present value of the excess of earnings over outlays plus interest is $8,709 for proposal B and only $8,238 for proposal A. No differential calculations are necessary, although a difference column is introduced for added emphasis, nor is it necessary to perform trial-and-error calculations to find the discounted rate of return for each proposal and for the increment between them.

Exhibit 20–9

PRESENT VALUE OF MUTUALLY EXCLUSIVE PROPOSALS

	Proposal A	Proposal B	Difference (B − A)
(1) Initial outlay.............	−$50,000	−$67,000	−$17,000
Cash earnings:			
(2) Annual amount.........	+$10,000	+$13,000	+$ 3,000
(3) Present value at 12%			
(2) × Table 3........	+ 58,238	+ 75,709	+ 17,471
(4) Net Present Value			
(1) + (3).............	+$ 8,238	+$ 8,709	+$ 471

In this simple example, either method would lead to the correct solution, but there are circumstances, by no means rare, in which it is not clear in what order to take the various alternatives so as to provide information on incremental rate of return. For example, suppose that there are three alternatives: one requiring no immediate outlay, another calling for an outlay of $60,000 now and $60,000 two years from now, and the third requiring a lump-sum outlay of $100,000 now. The second alternative obviously requires the greatest total investment, but part of this investment can be deferred for two years. The greatest immediate outlay is called for by the third alternative. In this case it is far simpler to apply the present value test to the alternatives than to compute differential rates of return, because the present value method does not require a decision as to the order in which to compare alternatives.

SUMMARY

Capital expenditure proposals need to be tested against company-wide standards of minimum acceptable profitability. These standards are ordinarily related to the cost of capital—the anticipated rate of return that shareholders and other investors demand as the price of providing funds to the company.

The cash flow streams to which profitability tests must be applied should represent the anticipated differential after-tax cash flows associated with the proposal. Four kinds of cash flows can be distinguished: initial investment outlays, subsequent investment outlays, operating receipts and expenditures, and end-of-life salvage value. These differentials should be measured from a bench mark that will be acceptable to the company, and opportunity costs must not be neglected. Finally, in lieu of uncertainty adjustments or statements of probabilities, the analyst may wish to provide management with optimistic and pessimistic estimates of cash flows and present values.

DISCUSSION QUESTIONS

1. Why is authority to approve requests for capital expenditures one of the least extensively delegated powers of top management?
2. Define a capital expenditure. Would you classify research and development costs as capital expenditures? Increased inventory requirements?
3. The controller of the Grover Company has asked a member of his staff to prepare a report on the company's equipment replacement procedure. One of the comments made by the staff member read as follows: "Present procedure overestimates the profitability of replacement proposals because the investment in inventory, receivables, and working cash balances is ignored. We have two dollars invested in these assets for every dollar invested in equipment, and, therefore, the average annual investment as computed (with the previously suggested changes) should be tripled in calculating the rate of return on investment." Discuss this argument.
4. Define the cost of capital. What objections can be raised to measuring the cost of capital by the after-tax yields on the company's debt securities?
5. Public-utility commissions have for many years denied proposed increases in utility service rates if the effect of the increases would be to increase the yield on total investment in utility property after taxes but before payment of interest and dividends to more than 6 percent or 7 percent. What effect is this likely to have on the company's financing policies if the market price of its common stock is approximately constant at 10 times current earnings per share?
6. What information needs to be estimated to compute payback period? Average return on investment? Present value?
7. A stock phrase in economics textbooks some years ago was to the effect that income taxes do not enter into profit-maximization calculations. Under what circumstances is this likely to be true? Why is it false when these conditions are not met?
8. In what way or ways do revisions in income tax regulations permitting a

faster write-off of the cost of depreciable assets provide a stimulant to investment by business firms?

9. "If secondhand equipment markets were perfect, it wouldn't matter what period was selected to represent economic life. The analysis would always reach the same conclusion." Discuss this statement.

10. One objection that has been raised to the use of incremental analysis in appraising proposals to invest additional funds in factories or product facilities that are being operated at a loss is that even if the new investment is profitable on an incremental basis, the facilities as a whole will still be unprofitable. Can this objection be overcome without departing from the incremental principle?

11. A plant has been reporting operating losses consistently, whether it has been operating at practical capacity or at half of capacity. Does this necessarily mean that the plant should be shut down and sold? Explain.

12. "We seldom retire a piece of equipment before it has been depreciated down to its salvage value. If we were to retire property prematurely, we would be losing money, and we're not in business to do that." Comment.

13. "We require a three-year payback or less on all our investments." How do you suppose the management of this company decided to proceed with the construction of a $5 million office building? Is it likely that a payback test was applied?

14. Many expenditures made necessary by the acceptance of plant renovation and modernization proposals will be charged immediately to expense both for tax purposes and for public financial reporting. To what extent, if at all, should they be considered as part of the investment outlays to be justified by anticipated future cash inflows from the proposal?

EXERCISES AND PROBLEMS

*1. For each of the following, compute payback period, average return on investment, discounted rate of return, and present value at 10 percent. All the cash flow figures are stated on an after-tax basis.

a) Initial outlay...$10,000
   Annual cash receipts......................................$ 1,750
   Estimated life..10 years
   Salvage...None

b) Initial outlay...$10,000
   Annual cash receipts:
      First five years.......................................$ 2,000
      Second five years......................................$ 1,500
   Estimated life..10 years
   Salvage...None

c) Initial outlay...$10,000
   Annual cash receipts:
      First five years.......................................$ 1,500
      Second five years......................................$ 2,000
   Estimated life..10 years
   Salvage...None

---

* Solutions to problems marked with an asterisk (*) can be found in Appendix B.

d) Initial outlay...$10,000
Annual cash receipts..$ 1,750
Estimated life...10 years
Salvage..$ 4,000

e) Initial outlay...$10,000
Annual cash receipts..$ 1,750
Estimated life...15 years
Salvage..None

2. You have $100,000 to invest, and two proposals have been submitted for your consideration. Each of the two proposals requires an immediate outlay of $100,000. Proposal A has estimated after-tax receipts of $20,000 a year for the next 10 years. Proposal B will return a lump-sum payment, after taxes, of $1,020,000 15 years from now. Which of these two proposals would you choose? Show your calculations.

3. Company X is considering a proposal to increase the degree of automation in one of its manufacturing departments. The following estimates have been made:

(1) Initial outlay, $100,000, of which $20,000 would be expensed immediately for tax purposes. No "investment credit" would be applicable.

(2) The capitalized portion of the initial outlay would be depreciated for tax purposes at a straight-line rate of 10 percent per year.

(3) The net annual before-tax cash savings would be $22,000, starting immediately after installation.

(4) The facilities would be obsolete at the end of six years of operation, at which time they would be dismantled at a cash cost of $5,000 and sold for scrap. Scrap recovery at that time would be $1,000.

(5) The company's effective income tax rate is expected to be 50 percent.

Compute the following:

a) After-tax initial outlay.

b) Expected after-tax annual cash inflow for the second year.

c) Anticipated effect of this proposal on the company's reported after-tax net income for the third year.

d) After-tax cash flow at the end of six years, when the facilities are dismantled.

*4. Under a new proposal just submitted by the production manager of the Romano Company, the proposed facilities will cost $100,000, half of which will be capitalized for tax purposes. The rest will be expensed immediately. An "investment credit" of 7 percent is applicable to the capitalized portion. Acceptance of the proposal will also require a $10,000 increase in working capital.

Out-of-pocket cash savings are expected to amount to $20,000 per year. Expected life for tax purposes is eight years and the double-rate, declining-balance method is used in computing depreciation. The tax rate is 50 percent.

a) Compute the after-tax initial cash outlay for this proposal.

b) Compute the after-tax cash saving for each of the first two years of the life of the facilities.

*5. A proposal is made to purchase and install a new machine to replace an existing machine. The existing machine has a book value of $20,000, current salvage value of $8,000, and annual depreciation of $3,000. Annual out-of-pocket operating cost is now $10,000.

The replacement machine would cost $50,000 delivered. It would cost $10,000 to train employees to operate the machine, and this amount can be written off immediately for tax purposes. An immediate tax credit of 7 percent of the capitalizable outlay is available as an "investment credit" to reduce current taxes. Annual out-of-pocket operating cost of the new machine would be $3,200.

The first year's tax depreciation on the new machine would be 30 percent of the amount capitalized. The income tax rate is 40 percent.

a) Compute the net incremental after-tax investment outlay required by this proposal.

b) Compute the after-tax net cash operating savings for the first year of operation of the replacement machine.

6. The Laurel Company is investigating the profitability of commercializing a new product which the research division expects to have ready for marketing in about two months. The following estimates have been prepared:

Development costs to date.............................$40,000
Estimated remaining development costs..................... 10,000
Estimated costs of securing patents........................ 1,000
Estimated working capital requirements.................... 50,000

Development and patent costs are charged to expense for tax purposes as they are incurred. The effective income tax rate is 50 percent.

No new equipment will have to be acquired for the manufacture of the new product, but one piece of idle equipment now scheduled for disposal at a salvage price of $5,000 will have to be retained for standby use if the new product is added to the line. This piece of equipment will not be used to manufacture the new product because it cannot meet the close tolerance requirements of the new product, but it will be used to process other company products at times of peak loads. Equipment is depreciated on a group basis, which means that no gain or loss is recognized on retirement of equipment.

Inventories of the new product will also require 10,000 square feet of warehouse space, which is now available in the company's warehouse No. 1. Warehouse No. 1 was built a number of years ago for $500,000, and its present book value is $250,000. It contains 125,000 square feet. The company's warehouse No. 2, built last year at a cost of $1,000,000 contains 200,000 square feet but is fully utilized by other company products. Equivalent warehouse space in the vicinity can now be rented at an annual rental of $1 a square foot. If the new product is not introduced, expansion of the sales of other company products is expected to utilize all presently idle warehouse space within the next two years.

What is the after-tax incremental investment associated with the introduction of the new product? Show and explain your calculations.

7. Compute the after-tax incremental cash flows associated with the following proposal and arrange them in a cash flow timetable.

Proposal: Purchase, install, and operate a new machine, replacing a machine now in use.

Installed price of new machine............................$18,000
Layout rearrangement costs (expensed)..................... 2,000
Salvage value of replaced machine*........................ 1,000

    * Machine to be replaced has a book value of $6,000 and is being depreciated at a straight-line amount of $750 per year.

Annual operating costs (excluding depreciation and allocations of fixed service department and general factory overhead costs):

	Old Machine	New Machine
First 4 years.................	$15,000 per yr.	$11,000 per yr.
Second 4 years...............	17,000 per yr.	12,000 per yr.
Third 4 years................	18,000 per yr.	14,000 per yr.

The market value of either the old or the new machine is likely to be negligible after eight years.

It is expected that the new machine, if purchased, will be used for 12 years. For tax purposes it will be depreciated over this period by the straight-line method. The effective tax rate is 55 percent.

*8. The expected life of a facility proposal is 10 years, the installed cost will be $50,000, and the expected end-of-life salvage value is zero. The equipment will replace facilities now in use that have a book value of $30,000 and a market value of $10,000. The remaining tax life of the old facilities is eight years.

Double-rate, declining-balance depreciation will be used on the new facilities, but the 7 percent "investment credit" is not available for tax purposes. The present facilities are being depreciated by the straight-line method down to an end-of-life salvage value of zero.

Estimated before-tax, before-depreciation cash savings amount to $20,000 per year. The tax rate is 50 percent, and all savings are assumed to take place at the end of each year.

a) Compute the incremental after-tax present value of this proposal at 10 percent, compounded continuously.

b) Compute the incremental after-tax discounted cash flow rate of return on this proposal.

9. A proposal is expected, if accepted, to yield cash savings of $22,000 a year before taxes, spread uniformly during each year. It calls for a before-tax investment outlay of $90,000, to be spent in a single lump sum just before the proposed facilities are placed in operation.

The effective tax rate is 50 percent, both on ordinary income and on capital gains and losses. For this kind of proposal, the company requires a rate of return on investment of at least 10 percent after taxes.

Compute the net after-tax present value of this proposal (treating receipts as positive and outlays as negative cash flows) under each of the following sets of assumptions:

a) The entire investment outlay is capitalized for tax purposes, and—

    (1) Tax depreciation is by the straight-line method, five-year life, $10,000 estimated salvage, and no "investment credit" is available. (In computing the depreciation rate for tax purposes, a zero salvage value is used.)

(2) As in (*a*1), except that tax depreciation is by the double-rate, declining-balance method, five-year life, 7 percent investment credit.

b) As in (*a*2), except that $40,000 of the initial outlay is expensed immediately and is not capitalized for tax purposes.

10. Many companies evaluate at least some of their capital expenditure proposals on a before-tax basis. That is, before-tax cash flows are tested against a standard representing the before-tax cost of capital. The main reason for doing this is to simplify the calculations.

Analyze the following figures relating to a specific proposal, on both a before-tax and an after-tax basis. How, if at all, would your recommendation to management on this proposal be different if you used the before-tax basis instead of the after-tax basis?

(1) The company's cost of capital is 10 percent after taxes; this is assumed to be equivalent to 20 percent before taxes.

(2) Initial investment outlays amount to $80,000, of which $30,000 can be expensed immediately for tax purposes.

(3) The capitalized portion of the initial outlay is subject to special amortization treatment. Fifty percent of the capitalized cost can be written off in equal annual installments during the first five years. The remainder is subject to depreciation at the normal straight-line rate of 6 percent per year, including the first five years.

(4) The investment is expected to produce net cash receipts (before taxes) of $16,500 a year for the first five years, $11,500 a year for the next five years, and $6,500 a year for the third five years.

(5) It is expected that the facilities will be retired at the end of 15 years and that salvage value will be $2,000.

(6) All taxes are to be computed on the basis of a 50 percent tax rate.

11. The Apex Machinery Company's textile division has been operating at a loss for several years, and no prospect for improvement is in sight. The Granby Company has approached the Apex management on several occasions to explore the possibility of acquiring the Apex textile supplies factory and product line as a means of filling out the Granby line, and has now made a firm offer of $1,000,000 for plant, equipment, inventories, trade names, and goodwill. The depreciated cost of these assets on the Apex books is $2,000,000. The Apex Machinery Company plans to transfer responsibility for textile machinery sales to the industrial sales division if the proposed sale of the supplies business goes through.

The estimated annual income statement of the textile division is as follows:

	Machinery	Supplies	Total
Sales.........................	$3,000,000	$7,000,000	$10,000,000
Cost of goods sold.............	2,000,000	5,500,000	7,500,000
Gross margin..................	$1,000,000	$1,500,000	$ 2,500,000
Direct selling expense..........			1,600,000
Division administrative expense			500,000
Head office expense (5% of sales)			500,000
Net Loss......................			$ (100,000)

Management has estimated that consolidation of textile machinery with the industrial line would increase the direct selling expense of the industrial sales division by $400,000 a year and the industrial sales division's administrative expense by $100,000 a year. Head office expenses are unlikely to be changed materially in total by dissolution of the textile division.

The estimated annual manufacturing cost for the textile division's supplies factory is as follows:

Direct materials and purchased parts	$1,500,000
Direct labor	2,000,000
Salaries	600,000
Indirect labor	400,000
Social security and employee benefits	450,000
Factory supplies	100,000
Power, heat, and light	150,000
Property taxes and insurance	100,000
Depreciation	200,000
Total	$5,500,000

If the facilities are sold, it is expected that severance pay and other termination charges will total $150,000. These are treated as current expense for tax purposes. If the facilities are not sold at this time, management estimates that it will still be able to sell them a year from now for approximately the same amount.

Analyze the Granby proposal and make a recommendation to the Apex management. Assume that Apex requires a 10 percent return on its investment after taxes and that the tax rate on earnings is 50 percent.

*12. You are provided the following data to assist you in deciding whether or not to replace an existing piece of equipment. Assume straight-line depreciation for tax purposes.

(1) Old equipment to be retired: book value, zero; no salvage value; $1,000 cost of dismantling and removal (expensed for tax purposes).
(2) Cost of new equipment, installed, $70,000.
(3) Rearrangement costs (expensed for tax purposes), $12,000.
(4) Estimated life five years, no end-of-life salvage value, but $1,000 estimated cost of dismantling and removal.
(5) Estimating operating costs per year:

	Old Equipment	New Equipment
Direct labor	$32,000	$12,000
Supplies	14,000	10,000
Maintenance	8,000	6,000
Supervision	6,000	6,000
Power	4,000	7,000
Other overhead (100% of direct labor)*	32,000	12,000
Depreciation	0	14,000
Total	$96,000	$67,000

* Variable "other overhead" amounts to 60 percent of direct labor dollars at current operating volume; remainder of "other overhead" is fixed.

a) From the foregoing data, estimate the incremental cash flows, after providing for income taxes at a tax rate of 50 percent.

b) If the company requires a minimum return on investment of 8 percent after taxes, is this replacement proposal justifiable?

13. The company is thinking of discontinuing manufacture and sale of product A. Given the following data, indicate whether product A should be withdrawn from the market. Show and label your calculations, and explain your reasoning if necessary.

(1) The projected monthly income statement for product A is as follows:

Sales..		$80,000
Less:		
Cost of goods sold (standard)...............	$64,000	
Selling and administrative expenses..........	25,000	89,000
Net Income (Loss)...........................		$(9,000)

(2) Product A is manufactured in two departments, and its standard unit cost is as follows:

	Dept. X	Dept. Y	Total
Materials..............	$1.00	$0.50	$1.50
Labor..................	1.50	0.75	2.25
Overhead..............	3.00	1.25	4.25
Total.............	$5.50	$2.50	$8.00

(3) The budgeted overhead cost structure in the two departments is as follows ("D.L.$" stands for "direct labor dollars"):

	Dept. X	Dept. Y
Traceable fixed overhead........	$40,000 per mo.	$20,000 per mo.
Traceable variable overhead.....	$0.80 per D.L.$	$0.60 per D.L.$
Allocated costs................	$20,000 per mo. {+$0.20 per D.L.$	$ 6,000 per mo. {+$0.20 per D.L.$
Standard monthly volume.......	60,000 D.L.$	30,000 D.L.$

(Before using these figures, see items [4] and [5] below.)

(4) A study reveals that traceable fixed costs in department Y include a $2,000 step function for each 5,000 direct labor dollars—that is, fixed costs increase by $2,000 a month any time that monthly departmental production volume increases by a full 5,000 direct labor dollars. (If volume increases by 9,000 direct labor dollars a month, the fixed cost increase is still $2,000, but if the increase is 10,000 direct labor dollars, then the fixed cost increase goes up to $4,000 a month.) Traceable fixed costs in department X have no step function.

(5) Of the allocated costs, the only items likely to be eliminated by the discontinuation of product A amount to $500 a month in department X and 6 cents a direct labor dollar in department Y.

(6) Selling and administrative costs charged to product A include (a) $5,000 a month for product advertising, free samples, product display material, etc.; (b) 10 cents per sales dollar for salesmen's commissions and patent royalty payments; (c) 4 cents per sales dollar as an allocation of field selling expenses, market research, etc.; and (d) 11 cents per sales dollar

for the product's share of head office expenses. Total company costs in these latter two categories would be unaffected by the discontinuation of product A.

(7) The sales force estimates that sales of substitute products in the company's line could be increased by $10,000 a month if product A were abandoned. The average ratio of variable profit to selling price for these products is 40 percent, and the increased volume in these lines would not affect fixed costs in any way.

(8) It is estimated that the only investment that would be released by withdrawal of product A from the market would be working capital with a book value of $300,000. This figure includes inventories at their book value of $150,000; before-tax proceeds from liquidation of these inventories would total about $110,000.

(9) The income tax rate is 50 percent and the required minimum rate of return on capital expenditure proposals is 8 percent after taxes.

(10) Remember that all figures except those given in items (8) and (9) are *monthly* figures.

14. The Barnstable Company manufactures and distributes through retail outlets a line of electrical products and appliances. Distribution of the company's products is accomplished through 12 regional branch offices, each of which has responsibility for maintaining adequate inventories, granting customer credit, and for collecting accounts receivable. List prices are established in the head office of the Barnstable Company, but each branch manager has authority to set his own policy on discounts, returns, and allowances to meet competitive conditions in his region.

For a number of years the company has followed the practice of preparing income statements for each branch. The San Francisco branch profit has declined from approximately $50,000 a year five years ago to a loss of $38,000 last year. Last year's income statements for this branch and a somewhat larger branch at Los Angeles were as follows:

	San Francisco	Los Angeles
Gross sales (at list prices)...............	$488,000	$675,000
Discounts, freight, returns, and allowances .	72,000	58,000
Net sales............................	$416,000	$617,000
Manufacturing cost of goods sold (at standard)..............................	293,000	367,000
Gross margin..........................	$123,000	$250,000
Branch expenses:		
Salaries and commissions...............	$ 73,000	$104,000
Travel and entertainment...............	15,000	16,000
Office expense........................	12,000	13,000
Bad debt losses.......................	5,000	3,000
Miscellaneous........................	6,000	5,000
Total branch expenses...............	$111,000	$141,000
Branch margin.........................	$ 12,000	$109,000
Home office charges....................	50,000	74,000
Branch Net Profit (Loss)................	$(38,000)	$ 35,000

Capital invested at the branch consists of $90,000 in receivables (after deducting a provision for uncollectible accounts) and $50,000 in inventories. Because the branch has no depreciable assets, no depreciation charges are included in the branch expenses.

The controller of the Barnstable Company has undertaken an analysis to determine whether it would be profitable to close the San Francisco branch and serve the region from Los Angeles. Analysis of costs and expenses has produced the following estimates:

(1) If the San Francisco branch remains in operation, branch margins at both the San Francisco and Los Angeles branches are likely to remain at last year's levels for the foreseeable future.

(2) If the San Francisco branch were closed, approximately $400,000 in gross sales could be retained by salesmen working out of Los Angeles. Discounts, freight, returns, and allowances on these sales would total $60,000 a year. The product mix in the San Francisco area would be the same at this lower volume as at the current sales volume.

(3) An analysis of the company's factory costs indicate that manufacturing costs are approximately 70 percent variable and 30 percent fixed, at standard volumes.

(4) Salesmen are paid a salary plus commission. Sales commissions are computed at 12 percent of net sales. In addition, each salesman receives a salary of $2,000 a year. If the San Francisco office were closed, two of its salesmen would be added to the Los Angeles sales force. All other sales personnel would be transferred to other positions in the company, as replacements for other employees who are retiring or leaving the company.

(5) Closing of the San Francisco office would eliminate completely all other San Francisco branch expenses, but it is estimated that expenses of the Los Angeles office would be increased by $36,000 per year in addition to the specific items mentioned above.

(6) Home office administrative expense is distributed to the branches at 12 percent of net sales. Past experience has indicated, however, that the variable portion of these expenses is only 4 percent of net sales.

(7) The Los Angeles investment in inventory and receivables would increase by $20,000 and $80,000, respectively, if the San Francisco branch were closed and the San Francisco area were served from Los Angeles.

(8) After taxes at 50 percent, the company's minimum acceptable return on investment is 8 percent.

Solely on the basis of the above information, would you recommend that the San Francisco branch be closed? Should the San Francisco territory be abandoned completely? Show your calculations.

15. Ace Publishing Company is in the business of publishing and printing guidebooks and directories. The company has received a proposal for a five-year contract from an outside printer, under which the volume of work done last year would be printed at a cost of $550,000 per year. From the information that follows, you are to make a recommendation to the board of directors on the question of whether the company should close its print shop and contract with an outside printer for all its printing work, including shipping services.

(1) The company's cost accounts for the preceding fiscal year showed the following balances:

| | Departments | | |
	Publishing	Printing	Shipping
Salaries and wages...............	$275,000	$154,000	$25,000
Materials and supplies.............	50,000	250,000	10,000
Building occupancy...............	75,000	80,000	10,000
Equipment depreciation............	5,000	40,000	5,000
Telephone and telegraph............	12,000	3,700	300
General and administrative.........	40,000	30,000	4,000
Total........................	$457,000	$557,700	$54,300

(2) A review of personnel required reveals the following:
   (a) All printing department personnel could be released except:

   One clerk...................$ 5,000
   Two layout men............. 14,000
   One proofreader.............. 6,000

   (b) All shipping department personnel could be released except one mailing clerk, $4,000.
   (c) One cost clerk whose salary of $6,000 is now included in general and administrative cost could be released.
(3) Termination pay equal to three months' pay would be paid for all released personnel. This pay would be expensed immediately for tax purposes.
(4) The cost of envelopes and stamps for mailing material to an outside printer would be $5,000 per year.
(5) Printing and shipping room machinery having a net book value of $300,000 can be sold for $200,000. This disposal value is unlikely to change materially over the next five years.
(6) If printing is discontinued, the company will retain its present building, but will sublet a portion of the space at an annual rental of $50,000. Taxes, heat, light, and other occupancy costs will remain at current levels.
(7) Long-distance telephone and telegraph charges are identified and distributed to the responsible departments. The remainder of the telephone bill, representing basic service at a cost of $4,000, is now allocated in the ratio of 10 to publishing, 5 to printing, and 1 to shipping. The discontinuance of printing is expected to reduce the basic service cost by $500 per year.
(8) General and administrative expenses include the cost of payroll taxes, retirement insurance premiums, and the like, amounting to approximately 10 percent of salaries and wages. This portion is charged to departments on the basis of total departmental payroll. Payroll taxes, etc., on termination pay (item [3] above) would amount to 8 percent, not 10 percent. All other general and administrative costs would be unaffected by discontinuation of printing.
(9) A $100,000 reduction in required working capital would be made possible by discontinuation of printing.
(10) Volume, prices, and wage rates are expected to remain approximately constant at last year's level for the next five years.
(11) If the company's printing and shipping facilities are retained, annual expenditures for equipment are expected to be $30,000 per year (capitalized for tax purposes), and annual depreciation charges are expected to remain constant at their present levels. (Assume that all property retired is fully depreciated; ignore any scrap values.)

(12) The effective income tax rate is 50 per cent, and the company's minimum rate of return on investment proposals is 10 percent after taxes.

(Adapted from a Uniform CPA Examination)

16. The Sitwell Company manufactures a single product which is sold to manufacturers in New York and Philadelphia. Its only factory has just been destroyed by fire, and it is subcontracting its production until it can acquire new facilities.

Adequate sites are available in both of its market cities and also in Walton, Ky., and Britten, Ga. Walton is the home of Sitwell's major supplier of raw materials, while Britten has offered to supply a new factory building rent-free under a 30-year lease.

The company's former factory was located in New York. A move to another city would not be expected to affect sales at Philadelphia, but it would lead to 10 percent reduction in New York sales volume. Certain relevant data are:

	New York	Philadelphia	Walton	Britten
Annual sales (units)...............	100,000	80,000	...	...
Net selling price..................	$20.00	$18.00	...	...
Freight rate per unit, finished goods:				
To New York....................	...	$0.50	$1.40	$2.00
To Philadelphia.................	$0.50	...	1.50	2.10
Freight rate per unit from Walton,				
raw materials................	0.75	0.70	...	1.20
Wage cost per unit...............	4.50	4.60	4.00	3.00
Other manufacturing costs:				
Materials, per unit.............	5.00	5.00	5.00	5.00
Other variable cost, per unit......	2.00	2.00	1.80	2.40
Fixed costs, per year (except depreciation and interest).......	$ 600,000	$ 600,000	$ 400,000	$ 400,000
Cost of factory site..............	*	800,000	500,000	300,000
Cost of building and equipment......	2,000,000	1,800,000	1,800,000	1,000,000
Working capital required..........	1,000,000	1,000,000	1,000,000	1,400,000
Resale value of land, plant, and equipment, 30 years hence......	2,000,000	1,500,000	1,300,000	300,000
Depreciation, per year†...........	100,000	90,000	90,000	70,000

* New York land now owned has a book value of $500,000 and a market value of $1,000,000.
† Equal to annual replacement outlays.

The useful life of the facilities is expected to be 30 years, no matter where they are located. The company requires a 10 percent minimum after-tax rate of return on investments of this type. Any costs not listed will not be affected by the choice of location. A tax rate of 40 percent is assumed to be applicable to taxable income of all kinds.

a) Given only the data supplied above, where should the new factory be located? Prepare a report to management to support your recommendations.

b) What factors other than those discussed above should be considered in deciding upon a location?

17. The Palfrey Company has just decided to enter full commercial production of a new product to be known as Forbitz, to be manufactured in the Methuen plant. The sales forecast on which this decision was based calls for average sales of 3,000 units of Forbitz a month during the first year, 5,000 units a month during the second year, 10,000 units a month during the third year, and 18,000 units a month in the fourth year and thereafter.

The industrial engineering estimates that were relied upon by management were based on the use of a Macy No. 2 machine. This machine would have a practical capacity of 4,000 units per month (single shift), 7,000 units per month (double shift), and 10,000 units per month for three-shift operation. The machine would cost $50,000, delivered and installed. An additional $2,000 would have to be spent immediately to train operators to use the new machine. The $50,000 would be capitalized for tax purposes, the $2,000 expensed.

The proposal calls for the installation of one Macy No. 2 machine now and a second one three years from now.

In its decision, management gave careful consideration to obsolescence. Past experience seemed to indicate that changes in equipment design would be slow, but that the cumulative effect would force the replacement of *both* machines 10 years from now. In other words, the second machine would last only seven years before replacement would become economical.

The market for used equipment of this type is such that end-of-life resale value is likely to be about 20 percent of original cost for any machine five years old or older.

Monthly operating costs for each machine, other than depreciation, direct department overhead, and floor space charges, would be as follows:

	Units per Month						
	3,000	4,000	5,000	7,000	8,000	9,000	10,000
Materials..............	$3,000	$ 4,000	$ 5,000	$ 7,000	$ 8,000	$ 9,000	$10,500
Labor.................	4,500	6,000	7,650	10,950	12,750	14,550	16,500
Maintenance ($5 per maintenance hour)....	500	500	500	600	700	750	800
General factory administration (10¢ per unit)...............	300	400	500	700	800	900	1,000
Subtotal...........	$8,300	$10,900	$13,650	$19,250	$22,250	$25,200	$28,800

The new machine(s) would constitute a separate cost center, with shift foremen's salaries and other direct departmental charges. With a single machine these direct departmental charges would be $5,000 at 3,000 units a month, $6,000 at 5,000 units a month, and $7,900 at 10,000 units a month. With two machines, operating at a combined rate of 18,000 units a month, the monthly direct departmental charges would be $9,750.

Each machine, together with necessary aisle space, etc., would occupy 500 square feet of factory floor space. The costs of owning and maintaining the factory average $1.50 per square foot per year. The company also rents space in an adjacent warehouse at an annual rental of $1.80 per square foot.

To make room for the new equipment, the plant manager would have to move certain clerical operations out of the main factory building and rent an additional 1,200 square feet of space in a nearby office building at an annual rental of $3 per square foot. No further space adjustments would be necessary when the second machine was installed in three years' time. Costs of moving the office and converting the space would amount to $3,000, an amount that would be charged directly to expense of this year.

The effective income tax rate is 50 percent of taxable income, including any capital gains. Machines are to be depreciated over a 10-year period for tax purposes by the straight-line method, assuming zero salvage value. No "investment credit" is available.

Prepare a table showing the *after-tax incremental cash costs* attributable to owning and operating the machines to make the new product: (*a*) at the date of purchase and installation; (*b*) during each of the 10 years; and (*c*) at the end of the 10-year period. (Note: Although some of the figures are stated as monthly totals, your answer to part (*b*) should be in terms of *annual* cash flows.)

18. The "S" division of a large manufacturing company has the responsibility of supplying other company divisions with a major portion of their requirements for component parts. Some of these parts are manufactured by the "S" division, and some are purchased by the "S" division for transfer to other divisions of the company.

A proposal has been made that the division acquire a large building located in Muncie, Indiana, and equip it for the manufacture of seven large-volume parts now being purchased from outside suppliers. The cost of the building, together with the land on which it is located and a large parking lot, would be $800,000. There is some equipment in the building. and most of this equipment could be used in the proposed operation. Additional costs of equipping the plant and getting it into operation would be as follows:

Machinery	$6,800,000
Tooling	600,000
Rearrangement	500,000
Other preproduction costs	1,200,000
Total	$9,100,000

The $1,700,000 in rearrangement and other preproduction costs could be written off immediately for tax purposes.

The "S" division measures capacity and production output in terms of the aggregate "sales value" of its products. "Sales value" represents the amounts that the "S" division charges other company divisions for products transferred to them. The new Muncie plant would have the capacity to produce goods with a sales value of $17,500,000 each year.

Standard or normal operating volume would have a product sales value of
$13,400,000.

Deliveries of these parts to other company divisions, as contemplated in the company's five-year plan, would be as follows:

Year	Requirements at Sales Value
1	$10,050,000
2	12,060,000
3	14,070,000
4	15,410,000
5	16,750,000

The industrial engineering department of the "S" division has
prepared cost estimates, based on standard volume, for the operation of the
new plant. These estimates are expected to be reasonably close to actual
costs at normal operating volumes. The cost estimates are:

Material	$4,100,000
Direct labor	1,000,000
Indirect labor	1,200,000
Other overhead	1,500,000
Head office charges	1,200,000
Total	$9,000,000

If the "S" division were to continue purchasing these seven parts
from outside vendors, the prices paid to these outside vendors would be
approximately 85 percent of the "sales value" figures quoted above, assuming no change in prices. The company's economic research department has
estimated that the outside purchase prices of these products will increase in
the future by approximately the same total dollar amount each year as the
annual increase in total out-of-pocket operating costs in the new Muncie
plant.

Based on the foregoing information, the industrial engineering
department prepared the following estimate of the profitability of the
posed new plant:

Annual cost savings: $11,390,000 − $9,000,000 = $2,390,000.
Total investment (excluding the portions of rearrangement and other preproduction costs charged off to expense): $8,200,000.
Average investment: ½ total investment = $4,100,000.
Return on investment: $2,390,000 ÷ $4,100,000 = 58.3%.

Upon receipt of the report of the industrial engineering department, the controller of the "S" division decided to obtain some additional
information before presenting the proposal to the "S" division manager:

(1) Depreciation on plant and equipment had been computed on the basis of
the initial investment required and was included in "other overhead"
in the industrial engineering department report.

(2) The expected economic life of plant and equipment is substantially the
same as that embodied in the tax depreciation rates.

(3) Depreciation rates for tax purposes are: buildings, 3 percent; land improvements, 10 percent; machinery, 7 percent; and tooling, 25 percent.
Depreciation is computed on a straight-line group basis with no provision
for end-of-life salvage.

(4) The purchase price of the building would be capitalized as follows: land, $50,000; land improvements, $50,000; building, $600,000; and machinery, $100,000.

(5) Cost variability percentages at standard volume: material, 100 percent; direct labor, 100 percent; indirect labor, 50 percent; other overhead, 20 percent; and head office charges, 0 percent.

(6) The "head office charges" included in the cost estimates cited earlier reflect the industrial engineers' application of the formula now used to allocate divisional head office costs among the various plants and offices of the "S" division. Divisional head office costs are regarded as fixed, but they would increase by approximately $500,000 a year if the Muncie plant were acquired and operated.

(7) Operation of the Muncie plant would require an increase in working capital investment of approximately $1,000,000 immediately, and $50,000 more each year for four years, starting with the beginning of the second year of operations.

(8) Past experience in the division's other plants indicates that, in addition to necessary replacement expenditures (see [9] below), capital expenditures amounting to $100,000 would have to be made during the second year of operations, $150,000 during the third year, and $200,000 during the fourth year and each year thereafter. These expenditures would not increase the plant's capacity but would be necessary to prevent unit costs from rising with increases in wage rates and materials prices. One fifth of these expenditures would be for tooling; the remainder would be for machinery. One-half year's depreciation would be taken for tax purposes on any property acquired during a year.

(9) Tooling replacements would probably amount to about $150,000 a year, starting in the third year of operations. Machinery replacements would begin in the fifth year of operations at $200,000 a year and rise by $100,000 increments annually to $300,000 in the sixth year, $400,000 in the seventh year, and stabilize at $500,000 a year from the eighth year onward. Offsetting retirements of replaced tooling and machinery would prevent depreciation charges from rising as a result of these replacements.

(10) An extensive replacement and modernization program would probably be required during the 14th year of operations, but no cost estimates are now available.

(11) Factory output would probably average about $16,750,000 in terms of sales value of production from the fifth year onward. Standard volume and burden rates would be recalculated at the end of five years.

(12) If the company were to decide to dispose of the Muncie plant and go back to purchasing component parts at some future date, it could probably realize about 80 percent of the book value of the plant and its working capital.

(13) Income taxes are computed at 50 percent, and the division's target return on investment, used in the evaluation of all capital expenditure proposals, is 12 percent after taxes.

a) Comment on the profitability estimate prepared by the industrial engineering department.

b) Prepare your own analysis of the profitability of acquiring and operating the Muncie plant.

CASE 20–1: PORTIA MILLING COMPANY

The Portia Milling Company operated several flour mills in the Midwest. The president of the company had assembled what he felt was an exceptionally competent management team capable of encompassing a much larger operating volume than the company's existing facilities could supply. Accordingly, when he heard that the owner-managers of the Grindell Flour Company were contemplating retirement from the business, he made haste to contact them to open negotiations for the purchase of their business.

The Grindell company had annual sales of approximately $25 million and profits after taxes of about $350,000 a year. Sales and profits had been roughly constant for the last five years, and the Grindell mills had been operating close to their maximum capacity. Grindell's top executives are all members of the same family. Their compensation for the most recent year was:

> J. C. Grindell, president.....................$85,000
> J. P. Grindell, treasurer..................... 75,000
> L. M. Marcus, sales manager............... 50,000
> F. N. Noble, division manager............. 23,000
> R. B. Grindell, division manager........... 23,000

The president and treasurer would retire if the company were to be sold. Mr. Noble, who also serves as the president of a local bank, would undoubtedly leave the company if he were asked to fill a position at the Portia headquarters. Mr. Marcus and R. B. Grindell would be expected to remain with the business if it were acquired by Portia. Mr. Marcus would stay on in the merged company at his current salary and in his current position. R. B. Grindell would be transferred to the Portia head office, also at his current salary.

The Grindell division managers had responsibility for local sales as well as for mill operations. Portia, on the other hand, was organized functionally, with an integrated sales force and mill managers who were responsible for manufacturing only. Portia's mill managers received salaries and bonuses amounting to about $15,000 a year each, and this pattern would be imposed on the two Grindell mills if they were acquired. Two new mill managers would have to be hired to take over the management of the mills from Mr. Noble and R. B. Grindell. No other executives would have to be hired if the Grindell facilities were to be acquired.

Portia's president anticipated that certain other economies could be made if Grindell were acquired. For one thing, consolidation of bookkeeping operations was expected to reduce clerical costs by $40,000 a year.

Secondly, the company would be able to take more complete advantage of the cost advantage of "milling in transit" privileges. Flour can be shipped by rail at the lower rates applicable to grain shipments provided that it has been milled from grain shipped by rail and that the outbound shipment of flour continues to move in the same geographic direction as the grain shipment. Portia's president had made calculations indicating that realigning the areas served by each mill would produce $50,000 a year in freight savings.

Thirdly, acquisition of Grindell's grain elevators, with some idle capacity, would permit Portia to save $20,000 a year in elevator rentals.

Finally, the ability of the company to serve chain bakeries with plants in both territories was expected to increase the sales of the combined companies by $1,000,000 a year and the profits before taxes by $25,000, in addition to the other sources of increased profits discussed above.

Portia's management proposed to make an offer for the inventories, prepaid expenses, facilities, trademarks, and goodwill of the Grindell Flour Company. Grindell's cash, receivables, and certain other assets would not be acquired, nor would Portia assume any obligation for Grindell's liabilities. The price to be paid would be an agreed-upon sum plus the book value of inventories and prepaid expenses at the date of the acquisition. Grindell's inventories and prepaid expenses amounted to $1,200,000 at the seasonal low.

In addition to the purchase price, Portia would have to invest $1,800,000 at the seasonal low to finance the increase in the company's balances of cash and receivables that would accompany this major expansion of its operations.

Funds for all of these items would have to come from the Portia Milling Company's long-term financial resources. The purchase price would be paid with $2,500,000 in 6 percent debentures and the remainder in cash. Capital required for the cash payment would be obtained from the Portia Milling Company's present funds and from the proceeds from the sale of additional shares of stock to the present stockholders. If the acquisition were consumated at a time at which the Grindell inventories and prepaid expenses were greater than their seasonal low, funds to pay for the excess would be obtained by drawing on Portia's line of bank credit. The line of credit was also adequate to finance extra seasonal requirements of cash and receivables.

The Grindell Flour Company's income statement reflected $50,000 in annual interest charges on its funded debt and $100,000 in interest on short-term borrowing to meet peak seasonal needs. Seasonal borrowing requirements were expected to remain approximately the same under Portia management as under Grindell management.

Portia's management estimated that capital expenditures equal to depreciation charges on Grindell facilities and amounting to $100,000 a year would be required to keep the Grindell facilities in economical working condition.

Portia's minimum return on investment was based on an estimate of the company's cost of capital. Its policy was to regard favorably any proposal that was expected to yield a return of 8 percent after taxes on long-term permanent investment. Peak seasonal investment requirements were not treated as investment, but the cost of seasonal borrowing was charged as one of the elements of the cash flows attributed to a proposal.

Although Portia expected the Grindell business to become a permanent integral part of the Portia operations if it were acquired, there was always the possibility that the loss of the close relationship of the business to the Grindell family would lead to some loss in sales. For this reason Portia's president decided to use 10 years as an estimate of economic life, with a resale value of $2,000,000 plus the value of working capital at the end of that time. A tax rate of 50 perecnt was in force at the time of these negotiations and was not expected to change.

Prepare a statement showing the maximum price that Portia could afford to pay for the *physical facilities, trademarks, and goodwill* of the Grindell Flour Company. Also show how much money Portia would have to obtain from its working capital and from sales of its common stock to finance the acquisition.

Chapter 21

INCREMENTAL PROFIT ANALYSIS
FOR TACTICAL PROBLEMS

NOT ALL managerial decisions require the complex analytical techniques that are necessary for the analysis of investment problems. As long as the differential cash flows are expected to have the same algebraic sign in all time periods, the problem can be treated as one of tactics rather than of long-range strategy. Tactical problems often include such questions as whether to sell a product or process it further, whether to make or buy parts and subassemblies, how to ration available capacity among various types of business, or whether to accept an order at a given price. This chapter is designed to demonstrate the ways in which the incremental profit concept can be applied to problems of these types.

BASIC APPROACH TO TACTICAL PROBLEMS

Assuming that the increments can be estimated with certainty, the basic approach to the analysis of tactical problems is as follows:

1. Identify and describe the alternatives.
2. Decide which determinants of cash flow will be affected by the decision.
3. Estimate values for each of these determinants under each alternative.
4. Select the alternative with the most favorable cash flow.
5. List intangible factors that might reinforce or lead away from this choice.

If uncertainty is substantial and either the apparent probabilities of high and low errors are unequal or management's attitude toward gains and losses is asymmetrical, then step (3) should be repeated for other possible states of nature and, if possible, probabilities should be attached to each of these states of nature.

Although these basic ideas about uncertainty were introduced briefly in Chapter 3, uncertainty analysis is too complex for adequate treatment here, and we shall omit any further reference to it. Fortunately, the principles underlying the data requirements for decision making under certainty are also applicable to the uncertainty case. These principles have been developed to a considerable extent in earlier chapters, and the best way to lead into this chapter is to see how they apply to a pair of situations not previously explored.

Incremental Analysis: Depth of Processing

Many companies manufacture products that can either be sold or subected to further processing in company plants. Some of these intermediate products are already in a form suitable for marketing to the ultimate consumer. Meat packing companies, for example, have the option of selling cured hams without further processing and in fact do market large quantities of this product in this form. The meat packer is also free to choose, however, to pack the hams in cans and sell them at a higher price.

A second group of intermediate products requires further processing of some sort before it is suitable for sale to the ultimate consumer. Refined metals, such as aluminum or copper, are good examples of products which the manufacturer must either sell to other processors or process further himself. For this group of products, additional processing is a form of vertical integration, moving the company closer to the consumer. Thus the aluminum manufacturer, seeking direct access to the consumer, may enter the fabrication of such products as cooking utensils or household aluminum foil.

In both instances, the greater depth of processing often requires additional capital investment so that this becomes a problem in investment analysis. No useful purpose would be served by repeating the earlier discussion on investment analysis, however, so we shall examine only the operating cash flows relevant to this kind of problem.

The main question is whether the increment in revenue that results from additional processing is sufficient to cover all the additional costs and still provide an increased contribution to profit. To illustrate, product P is now being sold at a price of $6.90 per unit and at a monthly volume of 20,000 units. Using product P as one of its raw materials, product Q could be sold at a unit price of $9.50. Products P and Q are direct substitutes for each other, and each unit of Q that is sold means one less unit of P that can be sold. The only variable selling costs are salesmen's commissions, computed at 8 percent of net dollar sales. Adequate manufacturing capacity is available to process 10,000 units of product Q per month without additional capital investment.

The plant accountant, working with the plant engineer, has provided the following cost estimates:

	Product P		Product Q	
	Per Unit	10,000 Units	Per Unit	10,000 Units
Materials..........................	$1.40	$14,000	$1.70*	$17,000
Labor and variable overhead:				
Department 14.....................	0.80	8,000	0.80*	8,000
Department 17.....................	1.30	13,000	1.30*	13,000
Department 22.....................	....	.....	1.10	11,000
Total variable cost...............	$3.50	$35,000	$4.90*	$49,000
Added fixed costs—department 22.......				3,500
Total Incremental Cost—Product Q.				$52,500

*Includes the cost of product P.

Fixed costs in all departments except department 22 were excluded from these calculations because they would be unaffected by the diversion of output into further processing. The incremental profit comparisons can now be made:

	Product P	Product Q	Difference
Revenues................................	$69,000	$95,000	$26,000
Less: Sales commissions at 8%..........	5,520	7,600	2,080
Net proceeds from sale..................	$63,480	$87,400	$23,920
Incremental manufacturing costs.........	35,000	52,500	17,500
Incremental Profit......................	$28,480	$34,900	$ 6,420

This indicates that further processing should increase the company's profits by approximately $6,420 a month.

A pure depth of processing problem assumes some limitation on total volume so that sales of the more highly fabricated product can be obtained only at the expense of sales of the intermediate product from which it is made. In the illustration above, this limitation was provided by market substitutability of the product, but it could just as well have been a limitation imposed by the capacity of some key production factor or the capacity of the sales force. Problems are frequently more complicated, however, in that expansion of the *total volume* of the intermediate product is possible. In such cases the *total* incremental profit contribution of the more highly fabricated product is the relevant figure for decision making, less any additional increments in fixed costs that are necessary to handle the increased total volume.

Incremental Analysis: Make or Buy

Another kind of problem that frequently arises is whether it is more profitable to make or to buy component parts that are used in the company's assembled products. At the outset it should be recognized that other factors, such as the need for an assured supply, continuity of delivery, and maintenance of product quality, may lead to manufacture of a part even though cost comparisons favor outside purchase. Requirements may be divided between manufacture and purchase in order to avoid reliance on a single supplier, or to shift the risks of fluctuating needs, or to provide data on the reasonableness of costs or prices. When company policy does not preclude a choice, however, the primary criterion is the effect of the decision on profit.

The make-or-buy decision, like further processing and expansion decisions, often requires the application of the techniques of investment analysis. The investment aspect of these problems, however, is no different from that of other problems, so we shall illustrate make-or-buy analysis by means of an example in which the investment aspects are insignificant.

A steel fabricator maintained, as an adjunct of its maintenance operations, a large machine shop. This shop, employing 95 full-time machinists, helpers, apprentices, and supporting employees, manufactured repair parts on order for use in the plant maintenance program. The typical production run was very small, and despite the fact that most of the repair parts could be machined from scrap and rejected factory products, the maintenance supervisor had long suspected that substantial economies could be achieved by reducing the work force in the shop and purchasing many of the repair parts from outside suppliers.

The task of analyzing the machine shop's operations was assigned to a cost analyst in the methods engineering department. His first step was to study all shop orders for the preceding 12 months to select those parts that appeared in the greatest frequency and in the greatest quanity. Although he did not preclude the possibility that some other items might better be obtained outside, he drew up a list of 66 parts that appeared with sufficient frequency to suggest that purchases to inventory might be an economical alternative to shop manufacture.

Because the machine shop did not maintain a standard cost file, manufacturing cost estimates had to be developed by examination of the shop order tickets. Fortunately, these tickets were available in punched card form, showing both material and labor quantities for each production lot. For each part the analyst obtained average material and labor quantities per unit during the preceding 12 months. Because most of the shop equipment was general-purpose equipment, setup time was relatively small and the labor hour data indicated that lot size had little influence on the labor required per part. Materials quantities were priced at standard prices or at scrap value, depending on the source of the materials; labor hours were priced at rates obtained from the shop's job classification schedule.

Shop overhead was examined with the aid of flexible budget schedules. All general plant fixed overhead allocated to the shop was excluded. Overhead cost was computed by applying the average variable overhead per shop labor hour to average labor hours per unit for each part. Although the shop flexible budget provided for variations in supervisory labor at different volumes of operation, the analyst decided to treat these as fixed until he could rank the parts according to the spread between variable cost and purchase price.

Outside purchase prices for standard catalogue items were obtained from vendor catalogues in the plant purchasing office and adjusted for freight and delivery charges. At least two and usually more vendors were asked to submit bids on the remaining items. In order to insure the representativeness of the bids, separate estimates were obtained by the plant purchasing agent from purchasing officials in other companies in the area. Of the 66 parts studied, it was found that delivered prices were less than variable shop cost for 53 items. The summary comparison for these 53 parts is shown in the following table:

	Group A	Group B	Total
Variable shop cost...........	$53,012	$12,122	$65,134
Purchase cost...............	26,728	6,966	33,694
Direct Saving...........	$26,284	$ 5,156	$31,440
Shop hour reduction.........			12,245 hours

In addition to the direct saving, the 12,245-hour reduction in shop hours would permit a reduction in supervisory labor and other shop fixed costs in the amount of $6,200 a year, making the total saving attributable to outside purchase $37,640 a year.

The magnitude of the spread between purchase cost and variable shop cost was so great that no consideration of inventory carrying costs was necessary, but it also raised the question of whether shop efficiency could not be improved. The maintenance manager had expected to find that many purchase prices were less than full shop cost, including a share of shop and general plant fixed overhead, but he was surprised by the wide spread between prices and variable costs. The cost analyst, anticipating this question, prepared cost estimates for each of the 53 parts in single lots of a size equal to or exceeding annual requirements. Again, however, because setup time was such an insignificant element in cost, lot-size economies were found to be small, averaging about 4 percent, and sufficient savings to justify continued production in the shop could be achieved in only two cases out of the 53. The low outside purchase prices reflected the ability of suppliers to utilize high-speed special-purpose equipment to turn out standard products at high volumes, and the operating volume of the machine shop was insufficient to justify the acquisition of this kind of equipment.

No use was made of full shop cost in this analysis. Of the 13 repetitive repair parts in which the cost comparison favored continued shop production, nine could be purchased at prices lower than full shop cost, but because the shop and all its equipment had to be retained to service the maintenance program, all the fixed costs of shop operation could be ignored. They represented sunk costs that were irrelevant to the make-or-buy decision.

DATA FOR DECISIONS: UNIT PROFIT MARGINS

The accounting data bank is an invaluable source of data for tactical decisions like these. Accounting data may be in either primary or secondary form. Primary data consist of classified totals, unaffected by allocations or averaging of any kind. Secondary data consist of historical or standard unit costs, unit margins, interdepartmental allocations, and even formally recorded forecasts.

One of the most widely used of the secondary data is the product unit profit margin. This can be defined in three ways:

1. *Variable profit:* net selling price less average variable cost per unit (including variable selling and administrative cost).
2. *Attributable profit:* variable profit less an average of the fixed costs that could be eliminated if the product were dropped.
3. *Net profit:* attributable profit less a pro rata share of all other fixed costs.

These measures are typically multiplied by forecasts of physical volume to derive measures of aggregate profit to be derived from alternative courses of action. A variant is to state unit margin as a percentage of the selling price and then multiply this percentage by sales forecasts expressed in monetary terms. These procedures assume linear relationships among cost, volume, and profit, and the question that needs to be examined is when this assumption is likely to be useful and acceptable.

Variable Profit

The first definition of unit profit margin is *variable profit,* also sometimes known as *marginal income* or *P/V income* (P/V being the ratio of variable profit to selling price). It is used primarily as a means of forecasting short-term profit increments. For example, profit/volume ratios are used in Exhibit 21–1 to estimate the profit consequences of

Exhibit 21–1

USE OF PROFIT/VOLUME RATIOS

Product Line	P/V Ratio	Estimated Sales Volume		Estimated Variable Profit	
		Plan X	Plan Y	Plan X	Plan Y
A.....................	30%	$2,500,000	$1,500,000	$ 750,000	$ 450,000
B.....................	50	1,000,000	1,500,000	500,000	750,000
C.....................	40	500,000	800,000	200,000	320,000
Total.................		$4,000,000	$3,800,000	$1,450,000	$1,520,000

two alternative marketing plans. This shows that plan X would produce a lower total variable profit than plan Y, despite its higher sales volume. The reason for this is that plan Y would yield a richer *product mix,* as indicated by the relative sizes of the P/V ratios. For example, $2,-500,000 in sales of product line A yields a variable profit of $750,000 (30 percent of $2,500,000), but this same variable profit can be generated by only $1,500,000 in sales of product line B, with its 50 percent P/V ratio.

It should be emphasized that the P/V ratio is a tool of analysis rather than an absolute indicator of segment profitability. Product line B's high ratio does not necessarily make it the most profitable product, nor does it necessarily call for devoting more promotional effort to this line. Suppose, for example, that product line A is relatively easy to market, and that the shift from plan X to plan Y would increase fixed promotional expenditures by $100,000 a period. The difference in variable profit is only $70,000 a period, and thus plan X would be more profitable by $30,000 a period.

It is even conceivable that the high P/V ratio in product line B is a weakness rather than a strength. If sales volume is sensitive to price, it might be possible to increase company profit by lowering the price in line B, even though this would reduce the P/V ratio. All that a high P/V ratio means is that the segment to which it relates might deserve further emphasis; it does not necessarily indicate that additional resources can be profitably employed in providing that emphasis.

Attributable Profit

Attributable profit figures are designed to be used in the same way as the variable profit figures, but in connection with problems that have a broader scope or a longer time horizon. For example, variable profit may be a satisfactory measure of incremental profit if the problem is to decide which products to have salesmen emphasize in their promotional effort. If the problem is one of deciding whether to discontinue serving a particular category of customers altogether, however, incremental profit must also reflect any fixed costs that can be avoided if these customers are dropped.

In one sense, attributable profit should almost never be calculated. It requires the accountant to estimate the share of divisible fixed factory costs attributable to each product and then requires him to average these costs over the product's normal operating volume. This process assumes that divisible fixed factory costs will vary *proportionately* with volume if enough time is allowed to overcome short-run inertia. This proportionality assumption is probably far from valid for small-volume products and may not be correct even for products that account for a large proportion of factory volume. For these reasons attributable profit figures probably would not be used for any major product abandonment decision—a special item-by-item cost study would be made instead.

Attributable cost and attributable profit data are intended for use in what might be called second-order decisions, in which each product is a relatively minor element. The proposal is not to abandon a product but to enter or withdraw from a particular segment of the market in which several of the company's products are or will be sold. Examining the fixed cost impact of volume changes in each of these products would be prohibitively time-consuming, and the error inherent in the linear basis for attributable cost is small enough to permit it to serve as a basis for this kind of decisions. The development and application of these figures is the subject of Chapter 23.

Net Profit

Net profit is the most nebulous concept of all. It assumes a cost linearity even in the absence of any demonstrable cost/volume relationship at all, linear or nonlinear.

Most companies recognize this, up to a point, in that they make no attempt to assign the fixed portions of nonmanufacturing costs to individual product units. In a majority of manufacturing companies, however, all fixed factory costs are typically unitized, whether attributable or not.

The limitations of net profit figures are essentially the limitations of factory full cost figures that we pointed out in Chapter 8. The allocations necessary to get net profit seldom, if ever, produce figures that correspond to profit variability, either long term or short term. Whenever net profit figures seem to be called for, the analyst would do better instead to work with attributable cost and attributable profit. As we suggested in Chapter 7, this is what the early cost accountants had in mind when they began to develop absorption costing systems and before they were led astray by the notion that every cost had to find a home in some product costing rate.

Use of Unit Full Costs to Estimate Incremental Costs

For any element that is expected to vary with volume in a linear fashion, incremental cost totals can be derived easily by simple multiplication of the unit cost figures. For other cost elements, it is better to work directly with cost aggregates, although estimates of the increments can be derived, if necessary, from unit cost figures.

For example, the incremental cost of an increase in the rate of output can be estimated by multiplying the increment in volume by the variable cost per unit and adding any changes in fixed cost that will accompany the change. To illustrate, suppose that the variable costs of a particular product amount to $1.12 for material, $4.15 for labor, and $1 for variable overhead. To increase the level of output from 10,000 to 12,000 units a month, it is estimated that fixed costs will increase by $1,000 a month. From these data, total differential cost can be computed as follows:

Increase in material cost, 2,000 × $1.12	$ 2,240
Increase in labor cost, 2,000 × $4.15	8,300
Increase in variable overhead, 2,000 × $1	2,000
Increase in fixed overhead	1,000
Total Increase	$13,540
Total increase per unit	$ 6.77

The unit cost approach, on the other hand, starts with *total* cost per unit, including a share of fixed costs, and then adjusts this for over- or underabsorption of fixed overheads at the proposed new volume. Expanding the previous example, total product cost includes manufacturing overhead at $3.18 a unit. Actual factory overhead at a production level of 10,000 units a month is expected to total $34,000, resulting in the $2,200 underabsorption of factory overhead shown in Exhibit 21–2. At a volume of 12,000 units a month, total absorption will be

Exhibit 21–2

DIFFERENTIAL COST DERIVED FROM UNIT COST DATA

	Unit Cost	Total Cost		Differential Cost
		10,000 Units	12,000 Units	
Direct materials..............	$1.12	$11,200	$ 13,440	$ 2,240
Direct labor.................	4.15	41,500	49,800	8,300
Overhead absorbed...........	3.18	31,800	38,160	6,360
Total...................	$8.45	$84,500	$101,400	$16,900
Overhead under-(over) absorbed		2,200	(1,160)	(3,360)
Total Cost..............		$86,700	$100,240	$13,540
Per unit....................		$8.67	$8.35	$6.77

$38,160 ($3.18 × 12,000 units) and actual manufacturing overhead is expected to total $37,000, for an overabsorption of $1,160.

The end result of these calculations is the same as was obtained from the total cost approach, but the second procedure is more cumbersome. Furthermore, there is some danger that the new average cost of $8.35 per unit would be used instead of the $6.77 incremental cost per unit.

BREAK-EVEN AND PROFIT/VOLUME CHARTS

One of the devices that have been developed to present variable profit information to management is the profit graph. Profit graphs, of which there are many variations, are pictorial representations of the relationships between costs, profits, and volume. Taken singly, they assist management in forecasting the probable effect on profit of changes in operating volumes. Comparison of two or more profit graphs helps to dramatize the effects on profits of changes in product prices, product mix, and other variables.

Break-even Charts and Break-even Points

One form of profit graph is the break-even chart, illustrated in Exhibit 21–3. The volume of sales is measured along the horizontal axis, and total costs and total revenues for each sales volume are represented by the vertical distances above the base line. The vertical distance between the total revenue and total cost lines represents the expected profit or loss at that volume (indicated by the shaded areas on the chart).

In this traditional form, the total cost line is depicted as a straight line extending from zero volume to the highest volume shown on the chart. As we have already seen, this is an oversimplification. Variable cost rates are computed for a limited portion of the total output range, covering perhaps that 30 to 40 percent of the total range from zero to

Exhibit 21–3

BREAK-EVEN CHART

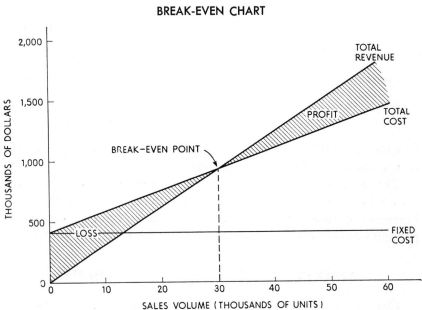

practical capacity within which the company expects to operate. Although the straight-line cost function is reasonably representative within this range, the profit spreads to the left and right of this range have little meaning and are introduced only to facilitate the explanation of the nature of fixed costs. The fixed costs shown on Exhibit 21–3, for example, are the fixed costs associated with sales volume of, say, 20,000 to 40,000 units.

The volume at which the total revenue and total cost lines intersect is known as the *break-even point*. The break-even point may also be calculated algebraicly if the cost and revenue functions are assumed to be linear as they are in Exhibit 21–3, by using the following formula:

$$\text{Break-even volume} = \frac{\text{Fixed costs}}{\dfrac{\text{Revenues} - \text{Variable costs}}{\text{Sales volume}}}$$

For example, assume that fixed costs total $420,000, the price of the product is $30 per unit, and the variable cost is $16 per unit. This means that each unit sold contributes $14 toward absorbing the company's fixed costs. At this rate it will takes sales of 30,000 units to absorb fully the $420,000 in fixed costs associated with operations within the normal volume range. This answer can also be obtained by substituting in the formula:

$$\text{Break-even volume} = \frac{\$420,000}{\dfrac{\$30 - \$16}{1}} = 30,000 \text{ units .}$$

If sales volume is measured in dollars instead of in physical units, the formula becomes:

$$\text{Break-even volume} = \frac{\$420,000}{\dfrac{\$30 - \$16}{\$30}},$$

and the break-even volume in dollars is $900,000. (Note that the denominator of this fraction is the P/V ratio.) The index of volume for most break-even charts is sales dollars rather than physical units because sales generally represent a mixture of many products and a satisfactory physical index cannot be found.

A sales dollar index poses a minor problem in graphic presentation in that the total revenue line is always at a 45-degree angle to the base if horizontal and vertical scales are the same. This means that contemplated changes in product prices will not affect the total revenue line but will affect the relationship between cost and volume, represented by the cost line. An increase in prices requires a downward adjustment of the cost line and vice versa. It is desirable to avoid this by basing the index of volume on a schedule of fixed product prices, that is, in terms of standard sales dollars. Then, if prices are changed, the relationship of cost to the number of units sold represented by the cost line can be left undisturbed. Only the slope of the sales line will be affected.

Significance of the Break-even Point

The point at which the company or a segment of the company breaks even provides neither a standard for performance nor a guide for managerial decisions. Of considerably greater interest are the underlying relationships between volume, costs, and profit on which the break-even chart is based.

Many managers seem to find the break-even point useful, however, as a partial measure of the risks a particular course of action is likely to entail. A decision that will raise the break-even point is often presumed to be riskier than other decisions. This notion is often implemented by the calculation of the *margin of safety* or spread between anticipated volume and the break-even volume.

The break-even concept is often used in another context. Most decisions involve trade-offs or substitutitions of one benefit for another. (Any student who has had to prepare for two examinations on one day should be familiar with this problem.) Lacking really good information as to the probable outcomes under either of two alternatives, the decision maker tries to find the point at which one alternative becomes more favorable than another.

The choice between overtime and second-shift operations, for example, is a break-even decision which can be programmed fairly easily. Second shifts entail additional fixed costs but lower unit variable costs, and the trade-offs between the two are quite clear. Another simple example is the delineation of the normal shipping areas for two plants manufacturing the same product. The "break-even point" in this case is the set of locations between the two plants to which delivered costs from the two points of origin are identical.

Profit/Volume Charts

Another variant of the profit graph is the profit/volume chart, illustrated in Exhibit 21–4. Separate lines for costs and revenues are

Exhibit 21–4

PROFIT/VOLUME CHART

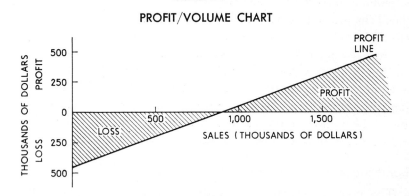

eliminated in this type of presentation by plotting the profit difference only. Volume is again measured along the horizontal axis, and profit or loss is represented by the vertical spread between the profit line and the zero-profit base line. The point at which this line crosses the base line is the break-even point.

This kind of chart is generally simpler than the break-even chart, although what it gains in simplicity it may lose in ease of explanation. It has one advantage over the break-even chart, however, in that either actual or standard sales dollars may be used as the index of volume. Only the net effect of price changes or cost changes is reflected in the profit line.

It should be noted that both kinds of profit graphs assume that sales and production volumes are identical and that beginning and ending inventories are costed at the same prices. In using these charts for forecasting reported net income, changes in these variables will need to be allowed for.

Uses of Profit Graphs

Tactical decisions are customarily based on estimates of the short-run profit effects of alternative courses of action. Variable profit figures or P/V ratios are frequently used as shortcuts in estimation. Profit graphs are useful primarily as a means of visual presentation of information of this type to the executives responsible for decision making. Although the usefulness of profit graphs is severely limited by the assumptions on which they are based, it will be helpful to indicate several ways in which they are used.

Effect of Price Changes. Exhibit 21–5 illustrates the use of a

Exhibit 21–5

EFFECT OF PRICE CHANGE ON PROFIT

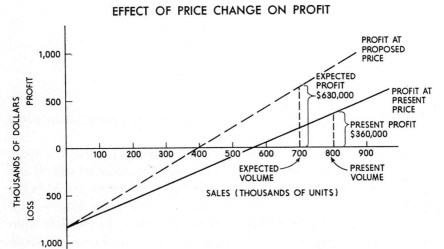

650 Cost Accounting: Analysis and Control

profit/volume chart to present the estimated effect on profit of a change in product selling prices. The broken line in Exhibit 21–5 represents the profit obtainable at various levels of sales at prices that are 10 percent higher than current prices, represented by the solid line. This shows that although increased prices are expected to reduce physical sales volume, dollar profit is expected to increase. The price rise also has the effect of shifting the break-even point to the left. The preparation of this chart requires detailed estimates of the probable effect of the price change on costs and volume, and it may be desirable to supplement the chart by a summary table like the following:

	Present Prices	Proposed Prices
Sales...................	$4,800,000	$4,620,000
Variable cost/sales.............	0.750	0.682
Variable cost..................	$3,600,000	$3,150,000
Fixed cost....................	840,000	840,000
Total Cost...............	$4,440,000	$3,990,000
Net Profit..................	$ 360,000	$ 630,000

Shifts in Product Mix. The profit graph can be used in a similar fashion to illustrate the effects on profit of a change in product mix. For example, the company markets the following three products:

Product	P/V Ratio	Current Sales	Variable Profit
A...................	20%	$ 6,000,000	$1,200,000
B...................	40	3,000,000	1,200,000
C...................	60	1,000,000	600,000
Total...............		$10,000,000	$3,000,000

Deduction of fixed costs of $1,600,000 leaves a net profit before taxes of $1,400,000 per year.

Individual salesmen handle all three lines, but they tend to emphasize product A because its lower price makes it easier to sell. If the product mix could be altered so that the three products were sold in the proportions of 40%–40%–20%, variable profit from $10,000,000 annual sales would be $800,000 from product A, $1,600,000 from product B, and $1,200,000 from product C, for a total of $3,600,000.

Using these calculations, Exhibit 21–6 was drawn for presentation at a sales force meeting. Two separate product mixes were presented, the current 60%–30%–10% mix and a target of 40%–40%–20%. Referring to the chart, the sales manager pointed out that profits would be increased by $600,000 a year if sales volume could be maintained at current dollar levels but with products selling in the target proportions. Even if dollar sales were to fall by as much as $1 million a year, total profit would still rise if the target proportions could be achieved.

Exhibit 21–6

EFFECT OF PRODUCT MIX ON PROFIT

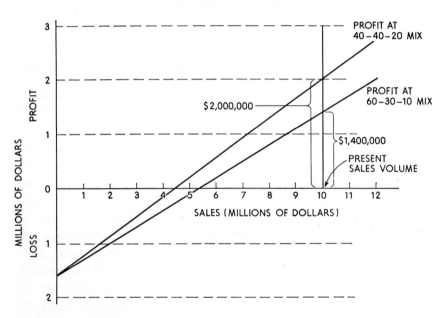

One shortcoming of this kind of presentation is that it does not reflect the costs that might be necessary to accomplish the change. Existing product mix is the result of a combination of circumstances, including prices, competitive conditions, and the market conditions faced by the company's customers. Although it may be possible to disturb this balance simply by instructing the sales force to emphasize certain products at the expense of others, more positive action is frequently necessary. Changes in the fixed costs of distribution or in relative product prices or in the method of compensating salesmen are frequently necessary to secure the desired change in product mix, and such changes tend to reduce somewhat the profit impact of a favorable shift in product mix. If the profit/volume chart is used to illustrate the expected profitability of these actions, the profit lines must be adjusted to reflect the expected effects on fixed costs or on the P/V ratios.

Increased Sales Volume. The most obvious use of the profit graph is to forecast the costs and profits that are likely to result from increases in sales volume. Either of the standard graphs shown in Exhibits 21–3 and 21–4 can be used for this purpose, but the rigid straight-line relationships that have been assumed in the charts that have been presented here are generally much too simplified for practical use. The existence of discontinuities, or steps, in the cost function has already been discussed in an earlier chapter, but there are also many dynamic effects that accompany a shift to a new volume of operations. Some of these are:

1. Increases in fixed selling costs to secure added volume.
2. Decreases in sales price or increased discounts and allowances necessary to achieve higher sales volumes.
3. Increases in variable manufacturing costs due to factors such as bottle-necks, shift differentials, overtime premiums, and the use of untrained personnel.

Furthermore, expansion of sales volume can seldom be achieved without some increase in capital investment requirements. To the extent that the increase can be obtained without acquiring additional plant and equipment, the investment increment may be relatively small in that a large portion of increased needs for inventory and receivables can be offset by the increase in trade payables. Whenever the proposed expansion would necessitate substantial additional capital investment, however, it must be analyzed by the methods appropriate to investment decisions, giving due weight to the cost of money employed. Probably the most satisfactory compromise is to use the profit graph to show the increase in variable profit that would result from a change in volume or price or both, and then compare this on a separate chart with the increases in investment and fixed costs necessary to achieve the added sales.

Problems of Profit/Volume Analysis

The profit graph is only as good as the assumptions that must be made to permit its construction. The conventional straight-line chart is valid only within limited ranges of volume and then only on the assumptions of constant prices, product mix, and cost relationships. Unless it is carefully used, the profit graph is subject to a good deal of misinterpretation. It is useful as a presentation device provided that the underlying analyses have been carefully conducted and the assumptions are clearly stated.

Most of the problems associated with profit/volume analysis may be grouped under four headings:

1. Selecting an index of volume.
2. Estimating the relationship between revenue and volume.
3. Estimating the relationship between cost and volume.
4. Allocating fixed costs to specific segments of the company's operations.

The Index of Volume. The problem of finding a satisfactory index of volume is of course not unique to profit/volume analysis. The volume index is also important in overhead application, flexible budgets, and the establishment of work standards, as we have already pointed out. The volume index for profit/volume analysis is peculiar, however, in that it must necessarily be a composite or aggregate index. This index should be such that a change in the mix of products, channel of distribution, or other variables that does not affect the aggregate index will not affect profit either. An index that meets these specifications is hard to find. By far the greatest number of profit graphs must be drawn on the basis of prior assumptions or forecasts as to such factors as product mix and the relative importance of different channels of distribution. For example, an airline might use passenger-miles as its index of volume, but a weakness of this index is that profit will also depend on the number and length of flights associated with each level of volume.

Revenue Functions. The estimate of revenues associated with each volume is also affected by product mix and channel of distribution mix, in addition to other factors such as the correlation of discounts, returns, and allowances with volume. The typical profit graph is based on the assumption of constant percentage relationships at all levels of activity. This assumption justifies drawing the revenue function as a straight line. The line may be given another shape if investigation uncovers a correlation between volume and other factors affecting net revenue, but such correlations are rare.

Cost Functions. Similar limitations surround the development of single-valued cost functions on the assumption of constant product mix, but here the straight-line presentation is less likely to be satisfactory. The causal relationship runs from volume to cost, and the predictive value of the profit graph is impaired if this response is inaccurately represented. Enough has already been said about the difficulties associated with developing cost functions for the relatively homogeneous activities engaged in by single departments to indicate the even greater difficulties that are encountered for less homogeneous aggregates. The greater the heterogeneity, the more limiting are the assumptions that must be made to permit aggregation.

Fixed Cost Allocations.   The narrowing of the boundaries of the individual segment for which profit graphs are to be constructed increases the proportion of common costs that must be allocated. The greater the allocation to a particular segment, the higher will be the break-even point. This is a problem that need cause no great concern, however, because the precise location of the break-even point has no significance for decision making. Presumably, the purpose of segment break-even points is to increase managerial awareness of the need to cover fixed costs, and almost any method of allocation will serve this purpose. To the extent that profit/volume relationships enter into decision making, the emphasis is on increments, both in the variable profit figures and in fixed costs. No amount of allocation is likely to throw light on this problem.

UTILIZATION OF LIMITED CAPACITY

Scarcity of any kind poses a problem of rationing. In wartime the scarcity of productive resources requires some means of assigning relative priorities so as to insure the flow of resources into their most essential applications. Similarly, when a business finds that its capacity to perform certain functions is fully utilized, it must find some way of rationing the available capacity among alternative uses.

Single Capacity Constraint

If linearity of the cost function can be assumed and capacity can be measured in terms of a single limiting factor, the rationing problem would seem simple. Suppose that two products can be produced in a given set of facilities. One product has a P/V ratio of 40 percent; the other's ratio is 60 percent. The obvious conclusion is to devote all of the capacity to the 60 percent product as long as the shortage continues.

Four objections to this solution can be advanced. First, other short-term alternatives could be considered, such as finding some means of obtaining additional capacity quickly or raising prices on either or both products. Many companies alter the amount of subcontracting of parts and subassemblies as a means of adjusting capacity to product demand, and some even subcontract the entire fabrication process on a portion of their output. Parts or products with the smallest relative margin between purchase price and manufacturing cost are subcontracted first, followed by others with larger and larger cost-price spreads.

Few companies are either willing or able to take the second course and raise product prices to adjust for short-run capacity limitations. Instead, they extend promised delivery times, become more selective in the orders they accept, or adjust their promotional activities to emphasize the most profitable products or channels of distribution. All these are means of administrative rationing, which is always an alternative to rationing through the pricing mechanism.

The second objection is that the P/V ratios may not reflect all the dimensions of profitability. Many customers buy several of the company's products, and any attempt to limit sales to high-margin items may induce these customers to seek alternative sources of supply. In other words, the demand for an individual product may bear either a complementary or substitution relationship to the demand for another product or products.

Closely related to this is the question of intertemporal independence of demand. By withdrawing from the market for one product now, future sales of that product may be lost. This is an investment problem in concept, but in many and probably most cases the costs of reentering a market are so great that explicit investment evaluation is unnecessary.

The final objection is that the linearity assumption does not apply to a shift as large as this. Beyond a relatively narrow limit, increased sales of one product are obtainable only at the cost of additional promotional expenditures. If the productivity of these expenditures could be predicted accurately, the optimum solution could be determined by the kind of analysis portrayed in Exhibit 21–7. The vertical distance between the marginal profit line for product A and the base of the chart represents the added profit that could be derived by devoting a small additional amount of capacity to this product. It is assumed that marginal profit declines as more and more capacity is devoted to this product, reflecting increasing marketing costs for each additional unit sold.

The height of the marginal profit line for product B, on the other hand, indicates the profit that would be lost by diverting capacity away from product B. As long as these two figures are different, the company can gain by substituting one product for another. The optimum solution is thus indicated by the point of intersection of the two curves.

The data available are seldom adequate to any full implementation of this model, which can provide only conceptual guidance. A fairly typical example drawn from practice may illustrate this point. A flour mill has three classes of customers: high-volume chain bakeries, independent commercial bakers, and wholesale distributors of packaged family flour. The mill has been operating with three shifts, seven days a week, for several months, and a number of orders have been lost due to the inability to meet required delivery schedules. Although some salesmen have a higher percentage of family flour and chain bakery business than others, all salesman contact customers in all three categories.

Exhibit 21–7

RATIONING SCARCE CAPACITY

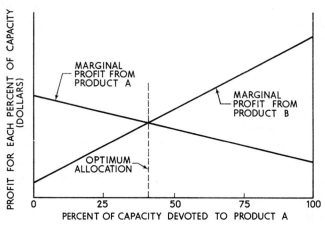

PERCENT OF CAPACITY DEVOTED TO PRODUCT A

Product specifications are different for each group of customers, and for this reason mill hours per hundredweight are also different. Because mill hours are the capacity-limiting factor, this means that relative profitability cannot be indicated adequately by variable profit per hundredweight. The real question is which class of business provides the greatest profit per mill hour. Data relevant to this question are shown in the following table:

	Chain Bakeries	Independent Bakeries	Family Flour
Variable profit per cwt...............	$ 0.0734	$ 0.0896	$ 0.0942
Cwt. per mill hour...................	280	260	245
Variable profit per mill hour.........	$20.552	$23.296	$23.079

This comparison reveals two important facts. First, the chain bakery business is far less profitable than either of the other two categories.

This is no surprise to management because competitive bidding for the trade of the bulk buyers has consistently led to lower prices on this portion of the business. Management is quite satisfied to see that the profit contribution per mill hour on the sales to chain bakeries is as high as it is because the mill could not operate without the substantial volume afforded by this segment of the business. The second fact revealed by the table is that family flour, with a higher variable profit per hundredweight than independent bakery sales, represents a less profitable utilization of capacity. On the basis of this comparison, the company's salesmen might be instructed to continue contacting their more regular customers in each category but to place more promotional effort in the independent bakeries. They might also be authorized to offer firmer delivery promises to the independent bakers than to the wholesale distributors of family flour. The family flour business would not be given up entirely, however, because this would leave idle capacity that could not be filled profitability by expansion of sales in other lines.

Multiple Capacity Constraints

Capacity is seldom unidimensional. Typically, it represents a composite of the separate capacities of various departments or functions of the firm. Whenever a product or other segment of the business utilizes two or more services which have limited service capacity, a more complex form of analysis is required.

To take a simple case, assume that the company has two products, each of which is processed in the same two production departments. The available data are:

Product	Variable Profit per Unit	Machine-Hours Required per Unit		Order Backlog (Units)
		Dept. X	Dept. Y	
A..............	$10	4	2	1,000
B..............	6	1	3	2,500

Capacity is 4,500 hours in department X and 7,500 hours in department Y.

Product A is the more profitable of the two, and one solution would be to produce the 1,000 units of product A, filling in with product B until one department's capacity was reached. Department X's capacity would be critical in this case, and the solution would be:

Product	Output	Capacity Utilized		Variable Profit
		Dept. X	Dept. Y	
A...........................	1,000	4,000	2,000	$10,000
B...........................	500	500	1,500	3,000
Total........................		4,500	3,500	$13,000
Capacity available..............		4,500	7,500	
Idle Capacity..................		0	4,000	

The existence of idle capacity in department Y suggests that it might be profitable to shift some production from A to B, which uses department Y more intensively. If one unit of A were to be dropped, this would permit production of four units of B because it would release four hours of department X capacity. Four units of B contribute $24 of profit instead of $10, for a net gain of $14 for every unit of A that is dropped.

A second possible solution, therefore, would be to produce as much product B as department Y could handle. One unit of product B requires three hours in department Y and thus department Y's capacity would be completely absorbed by 2,500 units of product B and would contribute $15,000 in profit. This is better than the first solution, but this time some of department X's capacity would be idle:

Product	Output	Capacity Utilized		Variable Profit
		Dept. X	Dept. Y	
A...........................	0	0	0	0
B...........................	2,500	2,500	7,500	$15,000
Total........................		2,500	7,500	$15,000
Capacity available..............		4,500	7,500	
Idle Capacity..................		2,000	0	

Once again the opportunity cost analysis is revealing. If a unit of product B were to be withdrawn, this would release capacity in department Y to make 1½ units of product A. The gain would be $15 (1½ × $10); the loss would be $6. Thus a net gain of $9 would result from this shift.

The optimum solution obviously lies somewhere between these extremes. When department X is underutilized, it pays to substitute product A for product B. When department Y is underutilized, it pays to substitute product B for product A. This suggests that the optimum solution will be reached when both departments are fully utilized.

One way to reach this solution is to use the substitution ratio in department Y. By cutting back one unit of product B, capacity is released for $1\frac{1}{2}$ units of product A. This substitution will keep department Y fully occupied and will use five hours of department X's idle capacity:

$$
\begin{aligned}
\text{Added production of A:} \quad & 1\frac{1}{2} \times 4 \quad = 6 \text{ hours} \\
\text{Less: Reduced production of B:} & \ 1 \times 1 = \underline{1 \text{ hour}} \\
\text{Net Increase in Use of Department X} & \ldots.\underline{\underline{5 \text{ hours}}}
\end{aligned}
$$

Because department X had an idle capacity of 2,000 hours, this means that both departments will be fully utilized if 400 units of B are subtracted from the preliminary solution. This will release enough capacity to produce 600 units of A. The profit under this solution is:

$$600 \times \$10 + 2,000 \times \$6 = \$18,600 \,,$$

which is \$3,600 greater than the better of the two previous solutions. This could have been predicted because the benefit from substituting $1\frac{1}{2}$ units of A for 1 unit of B was found to be \$9, and we made 400 of these substitutions.

The feasibility of the solution can be checked by deriving the input requirements:

Product	Units Produced	Hours Required	
		Dept. X	Dept. Y
A.....................	600	2,400	1,200
B.....................	2,100	2,100	6,300
Total.................		4,500	7,500

This same solution can also be derived algebraically in this case. Full utilization of department X can be represented by the following equation:

$$4A + 1B = 4,500 \,.$$

The full utilization equation for department Y is:

$$2A + 3B = 7,500 \,.$$

Two equations in two unknowns can be solved simultaneously to yield the values for A and B that we have already derived.

The knowledgeable reader will have long since recognized this as a special case of a widely used technique known as *linear programming*. This technique can be applied when the number of unknowns exceeds the number of equations. Space does not permit an explanation of this technique here, but it has proved highly effective in the solution of many rationing problems.[1]

SUMMARY

Tactical decisions call for application of the same concepts of incremental analysis as investment decisions without the added complication of present value calculations. The task of the analyst is to identify, insofar as possible, the cash flows likely to be associated with each alternative. Alternative predictions may be made for alternative states of nature if required by management's decision rule.

In deriving these cash flow forecasts, the analyst often finds it useful to use the P/V ratio as a shortcut method of estimating variable costs and revenues. Increments in fixed costs should only be estimated in the form of totals rather than on a per unit basis. P/V ratios may also be used as a means of rationing scarce capacity when profitability functions are expected to be linear.

The analyst often finds it useful to present the results of his analysis in the form of profit/volume charts. Pictures are often easier to understand than tables of numbers. The calculation of break-even points from these charts, however, has usefulness only as a partial indicator of risk and should not be overemphasized.

DISCUSSION QUESTIONS

1. What is the P/V ratio? Would you expect it to be the same at all sales volumes?
2. "A good rule of thumb is to instruct salesmen to concentrate their efforts on products having the highest P/V ratios." Do you agree or disagree? Why?
3. What is the "break-even point"? Describe two methods of determining the break-even sales volume.
4. "The entire concept of the break-even point is fallacious. Businesses are not organized to break even, and the break-even point therefore has no significance in decision making." Discuss.

---

[1] The literature on linear programming and its derivatives is extensive. Two representative references are Harold Bierman, Jr., Charles P. Bonini, Lawrence E. Fouraker, and Robert K. Jaedicke, *Quantitative Analysis for Business Decisions* (rev. ed.; Homewood, Ill.: Richard D. Irwin, Inc., 1965), chaps. xvii–xix; and Alan S. Manne, *Economic Analysis for Business Decisions* (New York: McGraw-Hill Book Co., Inc., 1961).

5. What is meant by a "depth of processing" decision? Under what conditions would you expect to treat this as a tactical problem?

6. "If you take a break-even chart at face value, your only sensible course of action is to operate at full capacity at all times." What is the basis for this statement? What would be the likely result of following this rule?

7. Why are break-even points and P/V ratios for multiproduct firms likely to be less reliable than for single product firms? What peculiar problems must be solved in determining the break-even point for one of the product lines of a multiproduct firm?

8. What are the uses and limitations of cost and profit per unit in incremental analysis?

9. How would you use profit contribution data in analyzing product profitability under conditions of (a) idle capacity? and (b) full capacity?

10. Outline a procedure whereby a sales manager might find a useful application of P/V ratios in preparing his sales plans for the coming budget period.

11. Assuming (a) that the P/V ratios of individual products are constant for all volumes up to practical capacity; (b) that the demand schedules for individual products are independent of each other; (c) that production capacity is limited only by one factor, the number of machine-hours available; and (d) that this capacity is inadequate to permit all orders to be filled, how would you expect productive capacity to be allocated among the company's products?

EXERCISES AND PROBLEMS

1. What effect, if any, would each of the following have on the break-even point and on the P/V ratio?
   a) Increase in total fixed costs.
   b) Increase in physical sales volume.
   c) Decrease in variable cost per unit.
   d) Decrease in selling prices.
   e) Increase in raw materials prices.
   f) Increase in wage rates.

*2. The Cranby Company sells a single product for which the following data are available:

Current selling price..................................	$4.90 per unit
Expected sales volume................................	200,000 units
Budgeted fixed costs..................................	$1.60 per unit
Budgeted variable costs...............................	$2.20 per unit

The company is contemplating an increase in the selling price of its product to $5.40 per unit.
   a) What would be the new break-even point?
   b) How many units would have to be sold at the new price to produce a 10 percent increase in total profit before taxes?

---

* Solutions to problems marked with an asterisk (*) can be found in Appendix B.

*3. The Carillo Company sells two products, A and B, with P/V ratios of 40 percent and 30 percent, respectively, and selling prices of $5 per unit and $2.50 per unit. Fixed costs amount to $100,000 a month. Assuming that each product accounts for one half of the company's dollar sales, how many units of each product must be sold to obtain a profit of $40,000 a month?

4. As a result of an expansion program, Pasabache Industries has excess capacity which is expected to be absorbed by the domestic market in a few years. Twenty-five thousand machine-hours are available for the next year.

It has received inquiries from two firms located abroad. One offers to buy 2,000,000 units of product A at 3.8 cents per unit; the second offers to buy 3,000,000 units of product B at 5 cents per unit. Standard costs for these products are:

	Product A	Product B
Material...............	$0.020	$0.030
Labor...................	.006	.008
Overhead...............	.012	.016
Total..............	$ .038	$ .054

Overhead is applied on a machine-hour basis at the rate of $2 per hour. Seventy-five percent of the overhead is estimated to be fixed. No selling and administrative expense would be allocated to either order; transportation charges are to be paid by the buyer.

One of the two orders will be accepted. Which should it be? Why?

*5. A company is considering the advisability of converting a machine from production of product A to production of product B. The following facts are available:

(1) Product A now sells at a price of $3, and annual sales amount to 100,000 units.
(2) Product B would sell for $5, and annual sales would amount to 120,000 units.
(3) Unit production costs are:

	Product A	Product B
Materials.................	$1.00	$2.00
Labor.....................	0.60	0.50
Factory overhead*.........	0.50	1.00

* Based on a predetermined burden rate of 50 percent of materials cost.

(4) Factory overhead can be expected to vary according to the formula:
Overhead cost = $20,000 + 30% of direct labor cost.
(5) Introduction of product B would require the company to spend an additional $95,000 per year in the sales department for maintenance work in customers' factories and offices.
(6) No other changes in selling and administrative costs would result from the change of products.

(7) The company must choose between the products—that is, the machine would be fully utilized with either product and could not manufacture both.

(8) Sales of the company's other products would be unaffected by this decision.

Assuming that the estimates are reliable, which product should be manufactured and sold? (Show your calculations.)

6. Given the following data prepare a comparative statement of profitability:

Present P/V ratio......................................40%
Present selling price...............................$15.00
Present fixed costs.................................$40,000
Present sales volume.............................10,000 units
Proposed selling price............................$13.50
Estimated sales at proposed price.......................12,000 units
Estimated fixed costs at greater volume.................$42,000

What would be the effect of the proposed price change on the break-even point? Show your calculations.

7. The Plain Talk Company is considering a proposal to purchase from outside vendors certain repair parts that are now being manufactured in the company's own repair shop. None of the present equipment in the shop will be retired if the proposal is accepted because the shop must always be in readiness to perform emergency work and to manufacture other repair parts that are not affected by the current proposal. The size of the parts inventory likewise will not be affected by this decision.

Data for the three repair parts under consideration are as follows:

	Estimated Requirements (Units)	Purchase Price per Unit	Direct Manufacturing Cost per Unit	
			Labor	Materials
Part No. 104.......	120 per month	$4.00	$2.00	$1.80
Part No. 173.......	200 per month	7.00	3.90	2.30
Part No. 221.......	50 per month	8.00	4.80	2.20

Operating costs in the repair shop other than direct labor and materials are budgeted as follows (direct labor cost is regarded as the appropriate index of volume):

	Direct Labor Cost per Month		
	$10,000	$11,500	$13,000
Overhead:			
Supervision....................	$ 1,200	$ 1,200	$ 1,200
Indirect labor.................	2,000	2,300	2,600
Indirect materials.............	500	575	650
Service charges................	3,500	3,575	3,650
Depreciation...................	800	800	800
Other fixed charges	900	900	900
Total overhead................	$ 8,900	$ 9,350	$ 9,800
Overhead/direct labor..........	$ 0.890	$ 0.813	$ 0.754

If the repair shop continues to manufacture these three repair parts, its monthly operating volume for the coming year is expected to average $11,500 in direct labor costs.

Another investigation reveals that if the proposal is accepted, purchasing and handling costs will be increased by $100 a month.

Submit a recommendation on this proposal. Show all calculations.

8. A company has three products which have the following P/V ratios:

Product	P/V Ratio
A	60%
B	40
C	20

Costs of field selling in this company amount to $300,000 per year and are regarded as fixed.

Several months ago the company instructed its salesmen to give more emphasis to products A and B and, in the words of the sales manager, "let product C sell itself." Prior to that time the salesmen had been spending about 20 percent of their time on product A and 40 percent on each of the other two products. Company net income was then at an annual rate of $600,000 per year.

A recent study of a sample of salesmen's call reports has revealed that the salesmen are now spending approximately half of their time on product B and 25 percent on each of the other two products.

Monthly sales, converted to an annual basis, indicate that the shift in sales emphasis seems to have been effective, although total sales volume has declined slightly.

Product	Annual Sales	
	Before Shift	After Shift
A	$1,950,000	$2,000,000
B	2,800,000	2,900,000
C	1,200,000	1,000,000
Total	$5,950,000	$5,900,000

There has been no apparent change in economic conditions or in the actions of competitors. There are no noticeable seasonal influences on the company's sales or expenses, and fixed costs are the same now as they were before the change in sales emphasis policy.

a) What is the forecasted net income on the basis of the new pattern of sales?

b) In what way, if at all, should the new sales emphasis policy be changed? What kind of help could you provide to the sales manager in making this decision, using only the data above? Discuss the problems met in using this kind of data for this purpose. Describe any other kinds of data that you would find useful.

9. The ABC Company is considering the introduction of a new product which is radically different from anything now on the market. Adequate production capacity is available, but introduction of the new product would require the company to invest $120,000 in working capital and to increase its fixed costs of manufacturing, selling, and administering the company by $20,000 a month. The product would be sold at a price of $5 a unit, and variable costs would be $3 a unit.

   a) Assuming that these estimates are correct and that the company requires a 9 percent after-tax minimum return on investment on all proposals of this type, at what volume would the company break even on this product? A 40 percent income tax rate is in effect.

   b) This company tests the desirability of investment proposals by estimating their net present value at a 9 percent rate of discount. Does calculation of the break-even point serve any decision-making purpose under these circumstances? If so, explain how; if not, explain why not.

10. The Galaxy Laundry has a large laundry plant and a number of sales branches throughout a large metropolitan area. It specializes in three types of services: men's shirts (washed and ironed), flatwork (washed and ironed), and family fluff dry (washed, dried, and folded).

    The company is considering a promotional campaign to increase sales by distributing coupons which entitle the customer to have one man's shirt or one pound of flatwork done free, if redeemed within two weeks. Data on costs and prices for the company's three services, together with the expected effect of the offer on physical volume, are shown in the following table:

	Men's Shirts	Flatwork	Family Fluff Dry
Price................................	25¢ each	20¢ per lb.	10¢ per lb.
Standard processing cost................	20¢ each	16¢ per lb.	9¢ per lb.
Variable profit ratio....................	32%	40%	50%
Expected effects of the offer:			
Units processed free..................	10,000	4,000 lbs.	....
Net increase (decrease) in units processed at regular price...........	25,000	12,000 lbs.	(2,000 lbs.)
Net increase (decrease) in customer invoices........................	5,000	1,700	(200)

Although the company will not alter the number of personnel employed in the stores or the main office in response to the expected changes in sales volume, the company's past studies have indicated that store and clerical costs tend to vary in the long run with the number of customer invoices, increasing by $5 for every 100 additional invoices. There are no short-run variable costs of selling and administration.

Past experience has shown that the effects of special offers like this are transitory; no lasting increase in sales volume is expected after the end of the offer period and the number of invoices will return to normal at that time.

The costs of printing and distributing the coupons are expected to amount to $500.

Should the promotional campaign be undertaken? (Show all calculations, clearly labeled.)

11. The Raynor Company manufactures a line of industrial cleaning and disinfecting compounds. One product, known as "Duzit," has a variable cost of 10 cents a pound and is sold at a price of 15 cents a pound. It is manufactured in a department which devotes its entire facilities exclusively to the manufacture of Duzit.

The company uses a variable costing system for product costing, and the wages of the operating crews in the department are classified as fully and proportionately variable with volume. The department's normal fixed costs amount to $2,200 a month, as follows:

Foreman	$ 600
Section supervisors (2)	1,000
Equipment depreciation	400
Floor space	200
Total	$2,200

Normal monthly production is 200,000 pounds.

The department is divided into two parallel sections of equal size, and one of these has been shut down in recent months due to a lack of orders for Duzit. The section supervisor has been laid off along with the operating crews. The other section is now operating at a monthly production rate of only 70,000 pounds, well below its practical capacity of 110,000 pounds per month. It is highly unlikely that sales volume will increase without special efforts such as those discussed below.

a) In each of the following cases, state what costs are relevant to the decision, what course of action you would recommend, whether the company's variable costing system helped you, and whether absorption costing would have given you more useful information. (Note: Treat each of the three cases as independent situations.)

(1) Arco, Inc., offers to buy 30,000 pounds of Duzit per month for six months at a price of 12 cents a pound until Arco completes a plant expansion program that will permit it to satisfy all its requirements for a Duzit-like compound.

(2) The Zipon Company offers to buy 80,000 pounds of Duzit per month for an indefinite period at a price of 11.2 cents per pound. The Zipon Company is not now a buyer of any of the Raynit Company's other products, and the contract would be cancelable by either party on three months' notice. Acceptance of this contract, however, would very likely force Raynor to grant price concessions to its other customers, averaging about 1 cent a pound.

(3) The reason why sales of Duzit have fallen to such a low level is that a competitor has introduced a new product that is a satisfactory substitute for Duzit in most of its applications. This competing product is sold at a price of 10.5 cents a pound. Sales of Duzit at the present price are dwindling rapidly and will be negligible within two months. Two proposals have been made: (a) continue to manufacture Duzit and sell 70,000 pounds a month at a reduced price of 10.5 cents; or (b) discontinue this product and accept an offer of 8.8 cents per pound for the entire current inventory.

b) Inventories of Duzit are costed on a LIFO full cost basis for public financial reporting. Inventories of Duzit amounted to 150,000 pounds on January 1 of the year in which the conditions described above prevailed and 450,000 pounds on December 31 of that year.

(1) What adjustment should be made to the "Fixed Costs in Inventories" account as of December 31?
(2) Do you feel that this end-of-year adjustment is likely to produce a more meaningful figure for reported income than if the adjustment were not made, given the production and market conditions faced by the Raynor Company?

12. The PDQ Company manufactures a line of high-quality office furniture which it sells to dealers in the Middle Atlantic and New England states. Its sales force is divided into two divisions: one covering the five northern New England states and the northern half of Connecticut; and the other covering the District of Columbia, Delaware, Maryland, Pennsylvania, New Jersey, New York, and southern Connecticut. Estimated sales and expenses for the next year are as follows (all aggregate dollar figures in thousands):

	New England Division	Mid-Atlantic Division	Total Company
Sales.............................	$1,200	$900	$2,100
Costs:			
Variable manufacturing:			
Materials........................	$ 300	$225	$ 525
Direct labor.....................	160	120	280
Variable manufacturing overhead....	240	180	420
Variable selling:			
Sales commissions*................	60	45	105
Brochures, etc.....................	120	90	210
Fixed:			
Directly traceable†................	120	120	240
Indirect—allocated................	40	30	70
Total costs.....................	$1,040	$810	$1,850
Profit before taxes.....................	$ 160	$ 90	$ 250
Taxes—50%........................	80	45	125
Net Profit after Taxes.................	$ 80	$ 45	$ 125

* Sales commissions at 5 per cent of sales.
† Directly traceable fixed costs include depreciation as follows:

New England division............................$20
Mid-Atlantic division............................ 30

a) The manager of the Mid-Atlantic division, which is the newer of the two divisions, has proposed that sales promotion in his territory be increased materially by adding a merchandising manager to his staff, two more salesmen, and additional newspaper advertising, the annual fixed cost of these additional efforts amounting to $20,000. He expects that sales would increase 10 percent if this were done, with no change in selling prices. Would you support his proposal? Give reasons for your answer.

b) As an alternative proposal, the manager of the Mid-Atlantic division suggests that prices be reduced by 5 percent (this price reduction would be effective in *both* divisions). If this were done, *physical* sales volume in the Mid-Atlantic territory could be increased by 25 percent without incurring the additional sales promotion costs proposed in (*a*) above. Physical sales volume in the New England division would not be changed as a result of this price reduction. Evaluate the profitability of this proposal.

c) If instead of accepting either of the above proposals the company decided to abandon the Mid-Atlantic territory, what effect would this have on annual cash flows before taxes?

13. The Metal Products Company manufactures three models of a single product. The tentative sales budget for the coming year is as follows:

Model No.	Sales (Units)	List Price	Sales Returns and Allowances
100......................	30,000	$15.00	$1,260
200......................	16,000	18.00	480
300......................	10,000	25.00	410

Sales returns and allowances are assumed to be proportional to sales for each model.

The production and cost budgets for the coming year show the following information:

Model No.	Production (Units)	Variable Costs per Unit	Traceable Fixed Overhead
100.............	30,500	$ 9.871	$38,000
200.............	15,000	10.250	24,000
300.............	10,000	15.436	20,000

Fixed factory overhead that is not traceable to manufacture of any specific model is budgeted at $166,000 for the year. Traceable and nontraceable fixed overhead are lumped together for burden rate purposes and allocated to products at the following rates per unit:

Model 100...$3.40 per unit
Model 200... 5.28 per unit
Model 300... 6.52 per unit

Selling and administrative expenses are regarded as fixed and are budgeted at $100,000 per year.

a) Prepare a statement showing the anticipated profitability of each model at the budgeted sales volumes.

b) Prepare an estimate of the break-even volume for each model. Explain any assumptions that you deem necessary.

c) Prepare an estimate of the break-even volume for the entire company, assuming the product mix contained in the sales budget.

14. The Mossback Company manufactures and sells five products for which the following data are pertinent (all dollar figures are per unit):

	Prod. A	Prod. B	Prod. C	Prod. D	Prod. E
Annual sales (units).............	200,000	1,000,000	500,000	400,000	800,000
Returns and allowances...........	$0.05	$0.03	$0.12	$0.16	$0.10
Variable costs....................	$1.42	$0.84	$2.81	$3.12	$5.22
Fixed costs......................	$0.84	$0.46	$1.95	$2.42	$1.46
Unit price.......................	$2.50	$1.50	$3.95	$5.70	$8.00

The company's productive facilities are general-purpose facilities, and all products require operations to be performed in every department of the factory. Fixed costs, which include selling and administrative expenses as well as factory overhead, are assigned to products on the basis of standard costs per unit. There were no cost variances this year.

a) Prepare a report of profit for the year, by products, and for the company as a whole.

b) What is the break-even volume at the present product mix?

c) Prepare a profit forecast under the assumption that the product mix were to change to the following:

Product	Unit Sales
A...	150,000
B...	800,000
C...	400,000
D...	500,000
E...	1,000,000

d) If fixed selling expenses would have to be increased by $400,000 per year to effect the shift in product mix, would you recommend taking this action?

15. The D. P. Manufacturing Company produces one principal product. The revenue from sales of this product for the current year is expected to amount to $200,000. Cost of goods sold will be as follows:

Direct materials.....................................$40,000
Direct labor...................................... 60,000
Variable overhead................................. 30,000
Fixed overhead.................................... 20,000

In view of continuing upward pressures on costs and expenses and management's conviction that higher selling prices would lead to an unprofitable reduction in sales volume, the management of the company is considering the possibility of redesigning the product to permit lower manufacturing costs per unit. If the product is not redesigned, it is expected that materials prices will be about 5 percent higher next year than this year and that rates for direct labor will average 10 percent higher. Variable overhead varies in proportion to direct labor hours.

number of units sold, with a 15 percent increase in sale price per unit. The

If the product is redesigned according to suggestions offered by the sales manager, it is expected that a 10 percent increase can be obtained in the redesigned product would use a different grade of material, the price of which is expected to be about 5 percent less than the expected price of the materials now used. However, 10 percent more material per unit would be required for the redesigned product. The redesigned product could be manufactured by less highly skilled workmen than are required for the product as it is now designed. The pay rate for the less highly skilled labor next year would be about 10 percent less than this year's pay rate for the more highly skilled workmen, but about 20 percent more labor hours per unit would be required for the redesigned product than for the present product. Variable overhead is expected to increase 10 percent because of price changes and to increase an additional amount in proportion to the change in labor hours. No additional investment would be required to support the change in design.

a) From the foregoing information prepare a statement showing the profitability of the design change.

b) If the product is not redesigned and if the product's average selling price is increased by 8.8 percent, unit sales volume will be reduced by 10 percent next year. Prepare a statement that will indicate whether this alternative should be selected in preference to either redesign of the product or continued sale of the present product at present prices.

(Adapted from a Uniform CPA Examination)

16. The Juniper Dairy Company processes and sells milk to three separate classes of customers: stores, homes, and institutions. There is a separate delivery force for each of these portions of the market. Sales fluctuate from period to period, but the following is a fairly good approximation to expected monthly sales:

Product	Home Delivery		Store Delivery		Institutional Delivery	
	Quantity	Price	Quantity	Price	Quantity	Price
Bottled milk:						
One-half gallons.............	......	...	500,000	$0.35	100,000	$0.35
Quarts.....................	400,000	$0.25	200,000	0.20	50,000	0.20
Bulk milk (gallons)...........	......	...	......	...	250,000	0.65
Ice cream:						
Bayview ½ gallons.........	......	...	100,000	0.50	......	...
Duchess pints..............	20,000	0.40	50,000	0.30	......	...
Duchess gallons.............	......	...	50,000	2.00	20,000	2.00
Heavy cream, quarts...........	......	...	......	...	1,000	1.20
Heavy cream, ½ pints.........	10,000	0.40	20,000	0.32	......	...
Light cream, ½ pints.........	5,000	0.20	10,000	0.16	......	...
Other products, dollars.......	$ 15,000	...	$ 40,000	...	$ 30,000	...

Bottled milk in quarts for home delivery and institutional delivery and heavy cream in quarts are bottled in returnable glass containers. Bulk milk is sold in 10-gallon metal cans, also returnable. All other products are packaged in disposable paperboard containers. Glass container costs are charged to the bottle washing operation; paperboard container costs are charged to the filling operation in the case of milk and cream and are included in processing costs. Processing costs for the coming year are expected to exhibit the following characteristics:

	Milk and Cream				Ice Cream	
	Washing	Pasteur-izing	Filling	Refrig-eration	Bayview	Duchess
Fixed costs per month......	$2,200	$2,850	$2,420	$2,780	$ 950	$1,020
Variable costs.	$0.015/ bottle $0.020/ can	$0.01/gal.	$0.006/ qt. bottle $0.015/ paper qt. $0.021/ ½ gal. $0.005/ ½ pint $0.020/can	$0.007/gal.	$0.317/ ½ gal.	$1.563/ gal. $0.202/ pint

Ice cream costs in the preceding table include the cost of all ingredients, whereas the costs cited for milk and cream do not include the costs of raw milk used. Raw milk prices are determined by the butterfat content of the milk, and on this basis the materials cost of milk is $0.34 per gallon, the materials cost of heavy cream is $1.80 per gallon, and the materials cost of light cream is $1.30 per gallon. "Other products" are purchased by the company at prices that average 75 percent of sale value.

The company has a fleet of 10 trucks engaged in home delivery, six trucks in store delivery, and three trucks in institutional service. Monthly delivery expenses per truck are as follows:

Wages...	$ 600
Gas, oil, maintenance, etc...........................	500
License fees, insurance, taxes........................	100
Depreciation......................................	80
Total......................................	$1,280

The first two of these items are regarded as wholly variable, and the latter two items are regarded as fixed.

a) Prepare an analysis that will indicate the relative profitability of the three parts of the company's business (home, store, and institutional). It may be assumed that all expenses other than those mentioned are fixed. The fixed factory costs listed above include allocations to departments of general factory overhead costs.

b) Prepare an estimate of the incremental cash flow that would be relevant to a decision to abandon or not to abandon the least profitable of the three segments. You may assume that the company's fixed cost other than fixed delivery costs would be reduced by $10,000 a month if any one of the segments was abandoned.

17. The Airtona Chemical Company has for some time derived material X as a by-product of one of its chemical operations. This by-product has been sold at 1 cent a pound to manufacturers of fertilizers, and the proceeds from sale have been credited to the cost of manufacturing the main product. The annual output of material X has been at a rate of approximately 10,000,000 pounds a year, and the company's research engineers have been seeking profitable ways of utilizing this product within the company. Now they think they have found the answer. By combining material X with two other chemicals available from other companies, it can be substituted for material Y, one of the ingredients of another company product, product M. The company's purchases of material Y are now approximately 6,000,000 pounds a year, and this figure has been growing during the last few years.

The process that has been developed for processing material X is amazingly simple, and the additional capital required to introduce the process, excluding inventory requirements, would be negligible. The inventory required would be offset by reductions in material Y inventories that now must be fairly substantial due to erratic delivery patterns from the supplier.

The costs of the additional materials purchases, processing labor, and overhead would be as follows:

(1) One pound of material X, when combined with the processing materials, would be sufficient to produce material that would substitute for two pounds of material Y.

(2) Processing materials, 4 cents per pound of material X processed.

(3) Processing labor, three quarters of an hour per hundred pounds of X, at a wage rate of $2.00 an hour.

(4) Processing would be performed in department 176, which has a burden rate of 60 cents per processing labor hour. Variable overhead costs in this department amount to only 10 percent of total overhead at normal volume.

(5) Fixed costs in department 176 would be increased by approximately $20,-000 a year if the new process were to be introduced.

(6) Material Y is now being purchased at a price of 3.5 cents a pound.

a) Should the company introduce the new process for reclaiming material X if the annual requirements for material Y amount to 6,000,000 pounds? Show your calculations.

b) Would your answer be any different if annual requirements for material Y were 10,000,000 pounds, all other information remaining the same?

c) If the process were to be adopted, do you foresee any change in the method of accounting for material X? Why or why not?

18. The Upson Company manufactures four products in a single factory. Factory volume is considerably lower than normal, and substantial unfavorable overhead variances have resulted. Sales, cost, and expense data relating to the company's four products are as follows:

	Product A	Product B	Product C	Product D	Total
Sales..................	$2,000,000	$2,500,000	$1,000,000	$500,000	$6,000,000
Cost of goods sold:					
Materials.............	$ 300,000	$ 400,000	$ 200,000	$ 40,000	$ 940,000
Labor...............	500,000	600,000	400,000	100,000	1,600,000
Overhead............	600,000	800,000	500,000	100,000	2,000,000
Total cost of goods sold...........	$1,400,000	$1,800,000	$1,100,000	$240,000	$4,540,000
Gross margin...........	$ 600,000	$ 700,000	$ (100,000)	$260,000	$1,460,000
Selling and administrative expenses (15% of sales)............	300,000	375,000	150,000	75,000	900,000
Unadjusted net profit....	$ 300,000	$ 325,000	$ (250,000)	$185,000	$ 560,000
Underabsorbed overhead.					300,000
Net Income before Taxes.............					$ 260,000

Factory overhead is approximately 40 percent variable at normal operating volumes. Variable selling and administrative expenses amount to approximately 5 percent of sales.

The substantial losses reported for product C have led management to consider discontinuing its manufacture, but the company's controller has opposed any such action, saying that company profits would be even lower without product C than with it.

a) Prepare a report that would support the controller's position and provide a better indicator of the relative profitability of each of the company's products.

b) The president of the company agrees with your figures but says that as soon as practical product C should be dropped. "In the long run," he says, "we cannot afford to retain any product that does not cover its costs." At what time would you consider it "practical" to drop product C? What information would you find useful in making such a decision?

c) Is it conceivable that even in the long run it might be profitable to keep product C in the line? Under what conditions?

d) A copy of your report is brought to the attention of the manager of the market research department, who calls you in and tells you that you have overlooked the following relevant facts:

(1) Fifty percent of the sales of product C are for applications in which product D can also be used. If product C were not available, sales of product D could be increased by $400,000 a year without any substantial change in fixed selling expenses.

(2) Twenty percent of the sales of product C are sold in conjunction with product A. These customers would not be able to substitute product D and would seek other sources of supply of product A. It is estimated that sales of

product A would decline by 10 percent if product C were withdrawn from the company's line.

(3) The company's controller has also estimated that a complete abandonment of product C would permit a reduction of fixed factory, selling, and administrative costs in the amount of $100,000 a year. If product C were kept in the line only as a service to product A customers, receiving no direct selling effort or advertising, the reduction in fixed costs would amount to only $40,000 a year.

In view of this additional information, prepare a report indicating whether sales of product C should be continued, or discontinued entirely, or continued only as a service to the small group of product A customers whose busines would be lost if product C were not available.

19. The Able Bakery Company manufactures and distributes packaged cookies throughout New England. The company has two main lines: a lower priced line carrying the Branford label and a higher quality line sold under the Country Oven brand name. The Branford line was introduced a number of years ago to broaden the company's line and provide an entry into the mass market dominated in New England by the nationally advertised brands. The Country Oven brand name has been used since the company's formation 15 years ago, and it is placed on a line of high-quality, high-priced commercial baked goods.

Both lines are sold by the company's single sales force, generally to the same retail outlets. Because of the importance of freshness to sales of the Country Oven products, the company does its own wholesaling; deliveries are made directly to retailers by an outside trucking firm.

Two years ago the company began to accumulate profit and loss information on a product-line basis, and since that time the Branford line has shown persistent operating losses. The preliminary income statements for the last fiscal year were placed in the hands of the executive committee last week and they showed that the Branford line has a gross margin of only 12.6 percent of sales and a substantial net loss, as shown in the table below. The Country Oven line last year had a gross margin of 26.8 percent and a net profit of 8.7 percent of sales, before taxes.

One member of the executive committee said, "These losses have to be stopped. They've been going on for the last two years and probably ever since the first carton of Branford cookies came out of the factory. Let's get out of the Branford line and stick to what we know how to do best."

The other executives agreed that the situation was not good, but they disagreed as to what should be done to improve it. The production manager said, "Without the Branford line my load factor would go down and the cost of the Country Oven line would go up." The sales manager said that what was needed was a new accounting system. All agreed, however, that sales of the Country Oven line were unlikely to be affected, either upward or downward, if the Branford line were discontinued.

a) Assuming that last year's results are likely to be typical of results in the future, what action should be taken? Support your recommendation with figures from the problem.

BRANFORD PRODUCTS DIVISION
Preliminary Income Statement, 19xx

Net sales...	$824,963	100.0%
Cost of goods sold [1]......................................	721,018	87.4
Gross margin..	$103,945	12.6%
Selling and administrative expenses:		
Sales commissions (computed as percent of net sales)............	$ 49,498	
Sales department salaries (allocated between product lines on basis of relative sales) [2]......................................	36,680	
Rent (rental costs of sales offices allocated on basis of relative sales)..	20,196	
Taxes and insurance (levied on finished goods inventories, identified by product line)...	862	
Depreciation (computed at 12% of original cost of sales office equipment, allocated on basis of relative sales).....................	775	
Advertising (brand-name advertising and point-of-sale promotional material)...	29,248	
Travel and entertainment (allocated on basis of departmental sales)...	23,377	
Freight and trucking (payments to truckers based on weight of shipment)..	43,612	
Administrative expenses (allocated on basis of relative sales) [2]....	40,804	
Total expense...	$245,052	29.6
Net Loss...	$141,107	17.0%

Notes:
(1) Eighty percent of the cost of goods sold represents variable manufacturing costs; elimination of the Branford line would reduce fixed manufacturing costs by $68,000.
(2) Elimination of the Branford line would lead to a $30,000 reduction in sales department salaries and a $20,000 reduction in administrative expense.
(3) Average investment in the Branford line, mostly in inventories, amounts to about $50,000.

b) Try to suggest ways in which the company might obtain better information on the effect of discontinuing the Branford line on sales of Country Oven products and on the company's selling expenses.

20. In November, 19x4 the Springfield Manufacturing Company was in the process of preparing its budget for 19x5. As the first step it prepared the following pro forma income statement for 19x4 based on the first 10 months' operations and revised plans for the last two months.

Sales.......................................		$3,000,000
Materials................................	$1,105,000	
Labor.....................................	310,000	
Factory overhead.........................	775,000	
Selling and administrative.................	450,000	2,640,000
Net Income before Income Taxes.............		$ 360,000

These results were better than had been expected and operations were close to capacity, but Springfield's management was not convinced that demand would remain at present levels and hence had not planned any increase in plant capacity. Its equipment was specialized and made to its order; a lead time in excess of one year was necessary on all plant additions.

Springfield produced three products with the following annual sales volumes:

```
100,000 units of product A @ $20.00..................$2,000,000
 40,000 units of product B @  10.00.................   400,000
 20,000 units of product C @  30.00.................   600,000
        Total Sales.....................................$3,000,000
```

Management had ordered a profit analysis for each product and had the following information:

	Product A	Product B	Product C
Material......................	$ 6.00	$ 4.00	$17.25
Labor.........................	2.00	1.00	3.50
Factory overhead...............	5.00	2.50	8.75
Selling and administrative........	3.00	1.50	4.50
Total costs....................	$16.00	$ 9.00	$34.00
Selling price..................	20.00	10.00	30.00
Profit........................	$ 4.00	$ 1.00	$(4.00)

Factory overhead was applied on the basis of direct labor cost at a rate of 250 percent; approximately 20 percent of the overhead was variable and did vary with labor costs. Selling and administrative costs were allocated on the basis of sales at the rate of 15 percent; approximately one half of this was variable and did vary with sales in dollars.

As the next step in the planning process, the sales department was asked to make estimates of what it could sell. These estimates were reviewed and accepted by the firm's consulting economist and by top management. They were as follows:

```
Product A....................130,000 units
Product B....................  50,000
Product C....................  50,000
```

Production of these quantities was immediately recognized as being impossible. Practical capacity in department 1 was 66,000 hours and in department 2, 63,000 hours, and the industrial engineering department concluded that this could not be increased without the purchase of additional equipment. Anticipated sales for 19x5 would require operating department 1 at 136 percent of capacity and department 2 at 121 percent. Standard cost data for the three products, each of which required activity in both departments, were based on the following production rates:

	Product A	Product B	Product C
Department 1.........	2 per hour	4 per hour	4 per hour
Department 2.........	4 per hour	8 per hour	1⅓ per hour

These solutions to the problem of limited capacity were rejected: (1) subcontracting the production out to other firms was considered to be unprofitable because of problems of maintaining quality; (2) operating a second shift was impossible because of shortage of labor; and (3) operating overtime would have created problems because a large number of employees were "moonlighting" and would therefore have refused to work more than the normal 40-hour week. Price increases were also rejected; although they would result in higher profits in 19x5, the long-run competitive position of the firm would be weakened, resulting in lower profits in the future.

The treasurer then suggested that product C had been carried at a loss too long and that it was time to eliminate it from the product line. He argued that if all facilities were used to produce A and B, profits would be increased.

The sales manager objected to this solution because of the need to carry a full line. In addition he maintained that the firm's regular customers had provided and would continue to provide a solid base for the firm's activities and that these customers' needs must be met. He provided a list of these customers and their estimated purchases (in units) which totaled as follows:

$$
\begin{aligned}
&\text{Product A}\dots\dots\dots\dots\dots\dots\dots80{,}000\\
&\text{Product B}\dots\dots\dots\dots\dots\dots\dots32{,}000\\
&\text{Product C}\dots\dots\dots\dots\dots\dots\dots12{,}000
\end{aligned}
$$

It was impossible to verify these contentions but they appeared to be reasonable and, therefore, the president concurred.

The treasurer reluctantly acquiesced, but he maintained that the remaining capacity should be used to produce A and B. Because A produced four times as much profit as B, he suggested that the production of A (that is, the amount in excess of the 80,000 minimum set by the sales manager) be four times that of B (that is, the amount in excess of the 32,000 minimum set by the sales manager).

The production manager made some quick calculations and said that this would result in budgeted production and sales of:

$$
\begin{aligned}
&\text{Product A}\dots\dots\dots\dots\dots106{,}666 \text{ units}\\
&\text{Product B}\dots\dots\dots\dots\dots\ 38{,}667\\
&\text{Product C}\dots\dots\dots\dots\dots\ 12{,}000
\end{aligned}
$$

On this basis the treasurer made the following profit forecast:

$$
\begin{aligned}
&\text{Product A: } 106{,}666 \text{ @ } \$4\dots\dots\dots\dots\dots\$426{,}664\\
&\text{Product B: }\ \ 38{,}667 \text{ @ }\ 1\dots\dots\dots\dots\dots\ \ 38{,}667\\
&\text{Product C: }\ \ 12{,}000 \text{ @ } (4)\dots\dots\dots\dots\dots\ (48{,}000)\\
&\qquad\text{Total}\dots\dots\dots\dots\dots\dots\dots\dots\$417{,}331
\end{aligned}
$$

As this would represent an increase of more than 15 percent over the current year, there was a general feeling of self-satisfaction. Before final approval was given, however, the president said that he would like to have his new assistant check over the figures. Somewhat piqued, the treasurer agreed and at that point the group adjourned.

The next day the above information was submitted to you as your first assignment on your new job as the president's assistant. What product mix should be budgeted for 19x5? Prepare a summary report to support your recommendation.

(Prepared by Professor Carl L. Nelson)

Chapter 22

COSTS FOR
PRODUCT PRICING

A COMPANY's long-term survival depends on its ability to obtain prices for its products that will cover all costs and leave a satisfactory margin of profit, adequate to compensate investors for the use of their funds. Product pricing is not simply a matter of estimating unit cost and adding a markup for profit, however. Costs are important, but they are not all-important. Consumer demand and the competitive environment are frequently far more significant, and in any case they cannot be ignored. Furthermore, as in any question that requires examination of costs, there is no unique measure of cost per unit that is relevant to all kinds of pricing problems.

In this chapter we shall deal with product pricing as a special kind of incremental analysis. Because pricing is such a complex subject, no attempt will be made to examine thoroughly all aspects of pricing or even to cover the entire range of pricing situations. Rather, the emphasis will be on the kinds of information that are relevant to some of the most common pricing problems and particularly on the kinds of cost data that will be useful.

OUTLINES OF THE PRICING PROBLEM

Management's pricing decisions are only one way in which a company can influence the sale of its products. Price is more than a multiplier to be applied to unit sales to determine revenue; it is or can be an active dimension of the company's sales promotion efforts. A situation that seems to indicate a deficiency in the effectiveness of the sales force may actually have arisen because of a poor system of pricing. Conversely, a situation that seems to call for a raising or lowering of price may actually be remedied better by changes in the company's methods of sales promotion. Thus when we speak of a pricing problem we are concentrating on only one of the factors that influence sales. Although it is useful to examine this aspect of the problem separately, we should never lose sight of the fact that pricing and promotional activity are interrelated.

Kinds of Pricing Problems

Pricing decisions must be made in a wide variety of circumstances. One useful classification of pricing problems is in terms of the kind of event that creates the need for a decision, such as the following:

1. A new product has been developed for addition to the line.
2. Historical profit reports indicate that some products, or all products in the aggregate, have been yielding lower profits than management deems necessary for long-run survival.
3. The sales force reports substantial losses in sales volume due to customer resistance to existing prices.
4. An opportunity arises to bid for a special order for a custom product to be manufactured to the buyer's specifications or engineered to meet his specific requirements.
5. An offer is made by a prospective buyer to purchase a product at a specified price.
6. A mass market exists but cannot be penetrated at existing prices.

This list by no means exhausts all the possible circumstances under which pricing decisions must be made. Other problems include the determination of the discount structure for different categories of customers, the relationships between the prices of substitute or complementary products or between the prices of different sizes or qualities of products of a particular type, on-season and off-season differentials, and geographic structures of product prices. Most of the fundamental questions in pricing are met in examining the six kinds of pricing situations listed above, however, and it is on these that we shall concentrate our attention in this chapter.

Economic Theory in Product Pricing

The general approach to product pricing that is implicit in most microeconomic theory (theory of the individual firm and its relation to other firms) is that analysis for pricing is merely a special kind of incremental analysis. The optimum price is the price that will yield the maximum excess of total revenues over total cost.

To illustrate this concept, the economist uses a diagram similar to that shown in Exhibit 22–1. If an unlimited number of units of the product could be sold at the same price, the total revenue line (TR) would be a straight line rising from the zero point in the lower left-hand corner of this diagram. In most market situations, however, it is assumed that additional products can be sold only be reducing prices or increasing promotional effort per unit sold. This means that although total sales revenue will *increase* as more and more units are sold, the *increase* in total revenue will decline gradually as sales expand. For example, if 10 units can be sold at a price of $2, 11 units can be sold at a price of $1.90, and 12 units can be sold at a price of $1.80, we have:

Price	Quantity Sold	Total Revenue	Addition to Total Revenue
$2.00............	10	$20.00	$xxx
1.90............	11	20.90	0.90
1.80............	12	21.60	.70

Lowering the price from $2 to $1.90 increases total revenue by 90 cents; a further price reduction to $1.80 increases total revenue by only 70 cents. In Exhibit 22–1 this falling off in the rate of increase in total revenue is represented by a gradual reduction in the steepness of the total revenue line as further price reductions become less and less effective in stimulating sales. The steepness or rate of climb at any point on this curve is known as its slope at that point.

Exhibit 22–1

TOTAL REVENUE AND TOTAL COST CURVES

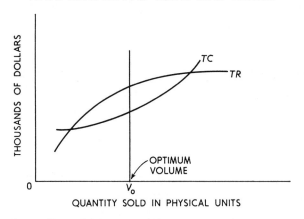

The total cost line (*TC*) in Exhibit 22–1 is the same one discussed in Chapter 3, gradually becoming steeper as volume increases due to the increasing difficulty of expanding output with a given set of productive facilities. As long as total revenue is climbing more rapidly than total cost, total profit will increase with increases in volume. At some point, however, the two rates of climb will become equal, which means that the increase in total cost due to the addition of one more unit of volume is just equal to the increase in total revenue, or a zero increase in total profit. The volume at which this occurs is indicated in Exhibit 22–1 as volume V_0, at which the slopes of the two curves are equal and the curves are parallel. To the right of this point total cost is increasing more rapidly than total revenue, which means that any attempt to increase volume beyond V_0 will reduce total profit. V_0, therefore, is the optimum volume, and the price at which this volume can be obtained is the optimum price.

These relationships can also be expressed in terms of marginal revenue and marginal cost. *Marginal revenue* is defined by economists as the increase in total revenue that results from the sale of one additional unit of product. In the previous example, the marginal revenue from sale of the 11th unit was 90 cents; from sale of the 12th unit it was 70 cents.

Similarly, *marginal cost* is the increment in total cost as the result of increasing volume by one unit. Marginal revenue (MR) and marginal cost (MC) at any volume are determined by measuring the rates of climb or slopes of the total revenue and total cost curves, respectively. (In mathematical terms, marginal revenue is the derivative of total revenue with respect to volume, but definition in terms of rates of climb is sufficiently precise for our purposes.) Because the curves in Exhibit 22–1 are based on the assumption that the slope of the total revenue curve will decrease and that the slope of the total cost curve will increase as volume expands, a line representing marginal revenue will slope downward to the right as volume expands and the marginal cost line will slope upward to the right.

These curves are shown in Exhibit 22–2. Marginal revenue is less

Exhibit 22–2

MARGINAL REVENUE AND MARGINAL COST CURVES

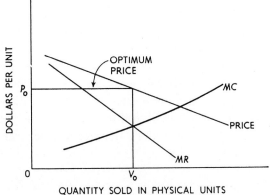

than price because a price reduction lowers the revenue from all units that would be sold at higher prices. For example, if 10 units can be sold at a price of $2 per unit and 11 units can be sold if the price is $1.90, the marginal revenue at a volume of 11 units is $20.90 ($11 \times \$1.90$) minus $20 ($10 \times \$2$), or $0.90. The optimum price is determined by the intersection of the marginal revenue and marginal cost curves. Lowering the price below this level would increase revenues by less than it would increase costs. Raising the price above the optimum would decrease revenues by more than it would decrease costs.

Limitations of the Model

Although this model illustrates the general nature of the incremental profit approach to product pricing, it is very much oversimplified. First, the available data are seldom good enough to give management more than a rough idea of the shape of the revenue curve. Second, revenues depend on many factors other than the company's own price. For example, a company can seldom assume that management's decisions as to price will not induce retaliatory pricing decisions by competing manufacturers. The circumstances under which this assumption is largely valid are those of *monopoly* (no directly competing product in the market) or *monopolistic competition* (many sellers of similar but not necessarily identical products, with no single seller having a large enough share of the market to permit his competitors to identify the effects of his pricing decisions on their sales).

In the intermediate situation, known as *oligopoly* (a market in which a few large sellers occupy a large share of the market), the marginal revenue curve of the individual seller depends on the reactions of his competitors to changes in his selling prices. If the oligopolistic seller finds that his competitors will raise their prices when he raises his and lower their prices when he lowers his, then his revenue curve or "demand curve" takes the same general shape as the demand curve for the market as a whole, except insofar as product differentiation affects the price sensitivity of his sales. If, on the other hand, he finds that his competitors will match his price reductions but will not follow his price increases, than a different situation arises, If one seller tries to raise his prices, his sales will fall off sharply as customers shift their purchases to other firms whose prices have not risen. If he lowers his prices, on the other hand, his competitors will follow suit and the only source of increased revenue will be this seller's share of any general expansion of total industry sales.

This effect is shown in Exhibit 22–3, in which both the price curve or demand curve and the marginal revenue curve are interrupted or "kinked" at the sales volume (V_a) expected at the existing price (P_a). Although marginal revenue at this volume may be greater than marginal cost (as in Exhibit 22–3), any attempt to expand volume by price reductions will produce a substantial drop in marginal revenue. In this illustration the reduced marginal revenue is less than marginal cost, and thus the price reduction would be unprofitable.

Exhibit 22–3

OLIGOPOLISTIC KINKED DEMAND CURVE

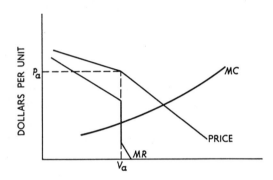

A kink of this sort is likely to appear immediately only if most other firms in the industry are not operating at the limits of practical capacity. If capacity is fully utilized, then competitors might find it profitable to meet any price rises, which would eliminate the kink. If they do not raise their prices but cannot absorb any additional volume immediately, the kink effect will not be felt by the high-price seller until outside capacity has grown sufficiently to permit competitors to take advantage of all the orders that are forthcoming at existing prices. If most sellers suspect the existence of a kink of the kind illustrated here and if they also assume that total industry sales are "inelastic" or relatively insensitive to price reductions, then this is enough to explain why prices in many oligopolistic industries do not decline significantly during periods of idle capacity.

This is not the place to examine oligopolistic price theory in any detail, but the preceding discussion should indicate some of the complexities of pricing in this kind of market. No matter what the market structure, however, the seller must consider the long-run implications of his prices on volume and on the growth of competition. If the seller is able to differentiate his product sufficiently in the minds of his customers, he may be able to price his product consistently higher than those of his competitors, but he must also be alert to the possibility that his competitive advantage will disappear.

Although there are obvious difficulties in deriving the marginal revenue and marginal cost curves required by the economic model, it does provide a useful point of departure for any pricing problem. A good deal of managerial economics consists of providing useful ways of examining problems; it does not insist that a particular method be used to derive the appropriate figures, but it does try to show what character-istics the relevant figures should have.

PRICING STANDARD PRODUCTS

In most companies, the bulk of the company's revenues arises from the sale of standard items in the line—items for which specifications and design are established prior to the solicitation of customer orders. Although the principles of pricing such products are much the same whether the product is a new one just being added to the line or an old one whose market is firmly established, the environmental situation and information base are usually sufficiently different to warrant separate discussion.

Pricing New Products

New products normally present the most difficult pricing problem because the range of uncertainty is so great. The errors in estimates of sales volume at different possible prices may be so large that the result-ing incremental profit comparisons are virtually useless for decision making.

Some companies, however, have used experimental techniques with a great deal of success to produce more reliable estimates of the effect of price on sales. For example, one company recently prepared a new product for national distribution, but before the national market was approached, the product was introduced in three representative regional markets. Every attempt was made to ensure the comparability of the three regions and to standardize the methods of sales promotion. Three prices were selected for testing, one in each market. Analysis of the sales response in the three markets indicated that although profit per unit was highest at the highest of the three prices, product demand was such as to yield a greater total profit at the intermediate of the three prices. The estimated sales and costs are shown in Exhibit 22–4. At a retail price of $2.45, the product was expected to return $54,000 less sales than at a

$1.95 retail price, but the contribution toward fixed costs and profits was expected to be the greatest at the $2.45 price.

There are other ways of deriving sales estimates, of course. One of the most useful approaches is to examine the need that the product will fulfill and to estimate the new product's advantages over other methods of meeting that need at various proposed product prices. For example, if a new machine is developed to mechanize an operation now being performed by manual methods, the price obtainable for the machine is presumably a function of the cost reduction it will make possible. Arraying potential customers in a frequency distribution of present costs will provide some basis for estimating machine sales at various prices.

Exhibit 22–4

ESTIMATED PROFIT/PRICE RELATIONSHIP

	Retail Price, $1.95	Retail Price, $2.45	Retail Price, $2.95
Estimated unit sales...................	800,000	600,000	300,000
Price to dealers......................	$1.17	$1.47	$1.77
Estimated revenues...................	$936,000	$882,000	$531,000
Variable costs:			
Variable manufacturing costs........	$504,000	$378,000	$189,000
Variable selling costs...............	80,160	70,920	40,860
Traceable fixed costs.................	135,000	135,000	120,000
Net Cash Flow.......................	$216,840	$298,080	$181,140

Sales volume in a new product can seldom be created overnight. Sometimes a long period of missionary work is necessary before the product wins acceptance, and substantial losses may have to be absorbed in the meantime. This period of growth may be a significant factor in determining whether the ultimate market is large enough and profitable enough to justify introducing the product at all; early year losses may be regarded as investments to achieve earnings in later years, and the product should be evaluated as an investment problem.

The growth factor may also have an effect on the choice among various alternative current prices. Joel Dean has made a highly useful distinction between two alternative pricing policies which he calls "skimming pricing" and "penetration pricing."[1] Skimming pricing is in effect a policy of high prices during the early period of a new product's

---

[1] Joel Dean, *Managerial Economics* (Englewood Cliffs, N.J.: Prentice-Hall, Inc., 1951), pp. 419–24.

existence, followed by a progressive lowering of prices as the market matures. Penetration pricing, on the other hand, calls for low initial prices to permit rapid acceptance in large segments of the market.

The selection of pricing policy must be based on the characteristics of specific products and markets. High initial prices may be a profitable way to utilize the novelty appeal of a new product when the responsibleness of sales to lower prices is slight, but this possibility carries the danger of inroads by price-cutting competitors as the product catches on and the sensitivity of sales volume to price ("price elasticity of demand") increases. Automobiles, radios, television sets, nylon, and many pharmaceutical products have all gone through a skimming pricing stage before lower prices provided a basis for penetration of mass markets. Skimming pricing also provides a form of insurance against unexpected costs of manufacturing or distribution. It is easier to lower prices than it is to raise them, and manufacturing or engineering difficulties may raise product cost substantially above the estimates during the early shakedown period.

The Role of Unit Cost in Pricing New Products

Thus far no mention has been made of unit cost, yet almost any survey will reveal that prices on new products are often established on a cost-plus basis.

One reason for the appeal of cost-plus formula pricing is that it is fair. The medieval notion of a fair price is still part of our social mythology, and business executives, particularly in large firms, need some means of convincing themselves that their prices are equitable. The cost basis provides this kind of reassurance.

A second reason for the prevalence of cost-plus pricing is that it appears to shield the decision maker from risk. If price is greater than cost, then risk is avoided. Unfortunately, this is a fallacy. Many costs are fixed, and thus unit cost depends on volume. If sales are lower than the level used in computing unit cost for pricing, then actual cost may be greater than the cost-based price. Since in the typical case volume depends to some extent on price, cost-based pricing as a means of risk avoidance is grounded on circular reasoning.

A third reason for the popularity of cost-plus formula pricing is also psychological but has a more rational foundation. The decision maker must make his decisions in the face of a host of uncertainties. He cannot possibly cope with all of these uncertainties, and to keep his sanity he has to find some way of ignoring some of them or of getting others to accept responsibility for dealing with them. He may for this reason accept a pricing formula that seems reasonable on the surface, purely as a means of avoiding the need to deal with this one source of uncertainty.

This form of *uncertainty absorption* would not last long if it seemed to produce consistently unacceptable results. There must be other reasons to explain the durability of a pricing method that appears to ignore demand factors entirely.

Perhaps the best explanation is that a cost estimate may help the decision maker to predict either his competitor's costs or a competitive price. For example, if he has been operating for some time in a market in which markups over cost average 50 percent, as he calculates cost, he may be able to assume that the same relationship will hold on new products.

This kind of thinking is particularly valid in oligopolistic industries. Recognizing that price competition is likely to be self-defeating, the pricer may set a price that he feels will not attract competitors unduly and then focus his competitive efforts on other factors such as delivery, credit terms, and so forth. If every company uses its full cost as a basis for pricing standard products, a substantial measure of price stability can be achieved even under conditions of idle capacity.

A closely related reason for formula pricing is that many firms have so many products that they cannot afford to analyze the price/volume relationships for them all. Once again, by using a pricing rule that seems to work reasonably well, management can devote more time to other dimensions of the marketing mix.

It should be noted that formula pricing does not necessarily mean that market forces are ignored in pricing new products. Anyone who is at all familiar with department store operations, for example, knows that percentage markups over cost vary from department to department and often for different lines of merchandise within a given department. Most differences in markup reflect well-established customs in the trade which guide the pricer toward a competitive price. Furthermore, the customary markups do change from time to time, and most department store buyers who make the pricing decisions are free to alter the markup if they see a reason to do so.

Full Cost versus Variable Cost Pricing Formulas

Most cost-based pricing formulas are so-called *full cost* formulas. The unit cost entered in such a formula is an estimated or standard full manufacturing cost, including provision for fixed costs of both production and factory service departments.

As previous chapters have pointed out, a unit cost defined in this way is subject to two influences that tend to cloud its meaning. First, many interdepartmental factory service department and general factory overhead costs cannot be attributed clearly to particular production departments. They are nevertheless allocated, but on arbitrary bases. Second, unitization of fixed costs requires a selection of normal volume levels in individual departments. This selection is inevitably subjective.

To avoid these two forms of subjectivity, many accountants have turned to variable cost formulas based on the variable costing principle described in Chapter 7. They argue further that restriction of unit cost to the variable costs makes it not only clearer but more relevant to pricing decisions.

Most of the arguments against this solution are misdirected. It is claimed, for example, that prices based on "partial costs" will inevitably be lower than prices based on "full cost." This ignores the fact that full cost ordinarily includes only factory costs and is just as much a partial cost as variable cost. Standard markups over full cost include provision for average selling and administrative expenses; there is no reason why standard markups over variable cost cannot include provision for average fixed costs.

The most telling argument against variable cost pricing formulas for pricing standard new products is that they ignore very real differences in input requirements. It must be remembered that the purpose of the cost element in the pricing formula is to supply guidance as to what a competitive price is likely to be. If a variable cost base accomplishes this, well and good; if not, something else should be tried. Empirical evidence on this point is almost completely lacking, but it might be presumed that long-run normal prices will bear some relation to what we have been calling *attributable cost*. If a company is unlikely to cover the costs attributable to a product, then it ordinarily will not introduce it.

Notice that this is not the same as full product cost. Factory service department costs for which a clear index of attributability is unavailable should not be allocated to production departments. Similarly, the indivisible portion of production department fixed costs should be excluded from product-costing burden rates used for pricing. On the other hand, provision should be made in unit cost for any significant product-related selling and administrative costs for which an attributability index can be found.

If this position is accepted, one final problem still remains—to select an appropriate volume level for unit cost determination. The irrationality of using expected current volume has already been pointed out, but this does not settle the question of how to measure normal volume. As with everything else in this area, the real test is pragmatic—if it works, it's right. A good starting point, however, is what might be called "designed capacity"—for factory costs this is the average operating level assumed by the designers when they were deciding how big a plant to build. It will typically be less than maximum physical capacity and will depend to some extent on industry practice as to number of shifts worked in a normal week.

Use of Unit Cost Targets in Product Design

The preceding discussion has presumed that a price is to be set on a product that has been developed and is ready for commercialization. In many cases, however, selling price is known and the question is what kind of a product can be offered at this price.

For example, the automobile manufacturers often start with a tentative price at which they will want a particular model to sell. Each proposed design is costed, element by element, to test its feasibility at this target price. Features are then added or subtracted, components are redesigned, or new price quotations are sought from parts suppliers until target cost levels are achieved. Clothing manufacturers typically follow a very similar procedure.

The cost estimates used in these calculations are of the same order as those described above, although here the presumption in favor of attributable costing is ordinarily much stronger.

Reviewing Prices of Established Products

Part of the basic rationale for cost-based formula prices disappears once the product is placed on the market. Some of the uncertainty surrounding the initial pricing decision is dissipated by the flow of field sales data. These data seldom provide a very precise indication of price/volume relationships, but they often can point to prices that seem to be out of line, either too high or too low.

Many companies continue to use cost-based formula prices as bench marks against which to compare actual prices. Existing products often differ widely in relative profitability, and routine pricing review can be highly important.

The review of existing prices may take either of two forms: a study of the present and past profit patterns or a projection of the probable effects of price changes. Studies of the first type are frequently made on a routine basis; forward projections are seldom made unless past profits are lower than the desired normal or someone makes a proposal to reduce price as a means of taking advantage of a sales opportunity. One company uses a chart similar to that illustrated in Exhibit 22–5 to identify products with relatively weak earnings positions. It singles out for intensive review any products that fall in the lower left-hand segment of this chart.

This procedure may be objected to on the grounds that products that fall in the upper right-hand segment may present the company with a greater degree of pricing latitude and a greater potential for increased profit. Furthermore, the return-on-investment figure may include so many arbitrary allocations of cost or investment that little significance

Exhibit 22–5

PRODUCT PROFITABILITY CHART

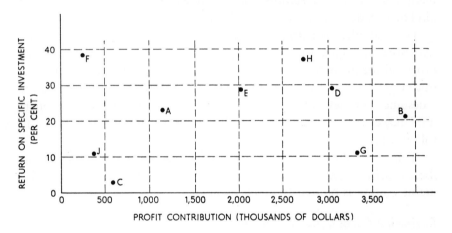

PROFIT CONTRIBUTION (THOUSANDS OF DOLLARS)

can be attached to vertical distances above the base line. Nevertheless, charts of this type or trends of period-to-period movements in product profitability are useful in pointing out possible weaknesses, and this is all that can be asked of any purely historical review. Decisions as to what to do about these weaknesses require estimates of the future and therefore must depart from the record of the past.

Pricing review is seldom entirely separable from the review of the other determinants of product-line profitability, and discussion of this process will be deferred to Chapter 24. Comparison of actual prices with target prices or profitability rankings, however, will not necessarily answer the immediate questions of whether to raise or lower prices or discontinue certain products. Market data are essential to these decisions, and the decision maker will ordinarily need more cost data than single estimates can supply. Ideally, both variable cost and attributable cost should be available, variable cost for short-horizon decisions and attributable cost for long-horizon problems.

Pricing Custom Products

An eastern manufacturer of specialized parts for automotive and industrial equipment manufactured more than 2,000 distinct products during its most recent fiscal year. Approximately half of these products were manufactured to order on the customer's specifications or to meet a specific customer requirement, and this custom business contributed more than half of the company's total sales volume for the year. Except for the standard catalogue items, pricing in this company is largely a matter of bidding or negotiating with individual customers for specific orders or for a planned sequence of deliveries of a custom-designed product. This kind of pricing is typical of a wide variety of products, primarily products to be used by other manufacturers, ranging from ocean-going tankers to salesmen's calling cards.

Pricing this kind of business ordinarily starts with cost estimates prepared expressly for the particular order or contract. A bill of materials and list of operations is prepared by the methods engineering staff or similar group on the basis of the product specifications. A cost estimator then has the task of assigning prices to the estimated physical input requirements. Most custom products represent specialized combinations of fairly standard operations, and standard operating times can be extracted from the current cost files if these are kept reasonably current. Otherwise, detailed estimates of operating times need to be prepared by the engineering or manufacturing staff. Estimated input quantities are then converted into estimated dollar costs with the aid of price lists, wage rate schedules, and, in some cases, inquiries of materials vendors.

At this point we come head on once again with the question of the definition of unit cost. The time horizon for pricing decisions on custom products is ordinarily much shorter than the adjustment period underlying the attributable cost figures, and this argues for the availability of variable cost data. It can be argued, however, that such estimates should be accompanied by estimates of attributable cost. If variable cost data provide a basis for specifying the floor beneath which prices will seldom if ever be reduced, attributable cost data can still perform their major function of providing some indication of what a normal price might be expected to be. A cost estimate summary in this form is shown in Exhibit 22–6. In this example the normal relationship between fixed manufacturing cost and variable cost is $1.20 per machine-hour, fixed selling and administrative cost is applied at a rate of 15 percent of total manufacturing cost, and the profit necessary to produce a target return on investment of 20 percent before taxes is applied at 12 percent of total product cost.

The pricing executive now has the responsibility of deciding whether the market situation will support a price in excess of this "normal" price or whether the normal price must be shaded to permit a successful bid. He will be guided in this by his recent experience in bidding for jobs and by the extent of expected utilization of factory capacity. For exam-

Exhibit 22–6

PRODUCT COST ESTIMATE SHEET

PRODUCT NO. 172–41-B	COST ESTIMATE SUMMARY		PREPARED BY ————	
QUANTITY 1,000			DATE ————	

Materials:		Direct Labor and Machine Time:			
Tooling	$ 507.00	*Dept.*	*Setup*	*Operating*	*Machine-Hours*
Fixtures, etc.	......				
Process	728.00	12	$ 6.25	$ 450.00	200
		14	1.25	175.00	110
Total	$1,235.00	17	2.50	130.00	150
		22	3.00	650.00	300
		24	1.25	85.00	20
		Total	$14.25	$1,490.00	780

Direct manufacturing cost	$2,739.25
Variable manufacturing overhead	548.00
Variable administrative costs	54.80
Total specific cost	$3,342.05
Fixed manufacturing overhead at $1.20 per machine-hour	936.00
Fixed selling and administrative at 15% of manufacturing cost	641.71
Normal profit at 12% of cost	590.37
Target Price	$5,510.13

ple, if the company is operating at high levels of capacity utilization, the pricer will not do much price shading below the normal level except possibly on orders that appear likely to lead to repeat business when greater available capacity exists. If recent bids at normal levels have found ready acceptance, he will feel justified in increasing the provision for profit on bids for new work. If substantial idle capacity exists, however, and full cost bidding has been failing to secure orders, the pricing executive faced with the choice of losing the order or quoting a price that is lower than the normal level is likely to accept the latter course and bid at some point intermediate between the estimated specific cost of the order and the normal price.

This description should provide ample support for the statement that pricing is an art rather than a science. The pricing executive must be alert to general market conditions and to differences among customers in their willingness to pay higher prices. Even when substantial idle capacity exists, it is not uncommon to find many orders priced at or above normal levels because all sections of the company's markets are not subject to the same competitive conditions.

Price Discrimination

Business executives face many other kinds of pricing situations, but we have space to consider only one more question—price discrimination. Price discrimination consists of charging different prices to different customers, and the term is intended to have no ethical overtones. Some discrimination can be defended on social grounds; some cannot.

For example, a uniform price charged both to customers across the continent and to those next door is nondiscriminatory according to the definition in the preceding paragraph, but it can be regarded as socially undesirable because it deprives the next-door customer of his locational advantage. For this reason, discrimination is often defined as differences in the net proceeds from sales to different customers, after deducting freight and delivery costs.

The private benefit from price discrimination is probably obvious. Suppose that a customer will buy one television set if the price is $200 but will buy two sets only if he can get the second set for $110. The cost attributable to the manufacture and sale of a television set is $80. In this situation, the company can make $30 more if it can sell the two sets at the buyer's maximum price than if it has to adhere to a one-price policy:

Selling Price		Total Revenue	Total Cost	Profit
First Set	Second Set			
$200	. . .	$200	$ 80	$120
200	$110	310	160	150
110	110	220	160	60

Successful price discrimination always requires an ability to segment the market and to prevent shifts of customers from one segment to another. Petroleum marketers generally find it difficult to confine gasoline price wars to narrow areas because price concessions made at one station lead to demands from other station operators in adjacent areas for equivalent reductions. The safest way to prevent erosion of the price structure through individual price concessions is through product differentiation. Price concessions on standard products are difficult secrets to keep, but when product differences are present, it is much more difficult for individual customers to find out whether price concessions are being granted. The product differentiation must appear to be important, of course, so that other buyers do not regard the cheaper product as a satisfactory substitute for the standard item.

Price discrimination can be either systematic, in the form of standard discounts or price concessions to certain classes of customers, or sporadic, as the seller responds with special price concessions to meet specific competitive conditions. Both forms of discrimination are restricted in the United States by the provisions of the Robinson-Patman Act. This act provides that price discrimination between customers is unlawful if it is likely to lessen competition substantially unless the price differential can be justified by a cost differential or unless the lower price is made in good faith to meet a price quoted by a competitor. The vague wording of the statute leaves ample room for interpretation, and a substantial body of litigation has arisen on the three questions of lessening competition, cost justification, and price cutting in good faith. Nevertheless, the basic intent of the provision is fairly clear—that some justification must be present for price discrimination among customers, whenever the effect may be to lessen competition.

We shall examine briefly in the next chapter some of the principles to be followed in analyzing cost differentials to justify price differentials for Robinson-Patman Act purposes. It should be noted, however, that few companies have been able to justify their price differentials by evidence on cost differentials. The best defense is to differentiate the product sufficiently so that the product sold at a lower price is not a perfect substitute for the standard product. There is nothing in the law to require that markups be uniform for all products. One authority on antitrust law has stated: "If in fact there is an actual and substantial difference in grade and quality of two commodities, they may be sold at different prices, and the difference in price apparently need not be measured by the difference in cost, consumer acceptance, value or any other standard." [2]

Companies whose share of specific product markets is relatively small are less vulnerable to Robinson-Patman charges than companies with large market shares because it is more difficult to substantiate a charge of probable lessening of competition on the basis of a small

---

[2] Mathias F. Correa, "Discrimination in Prices," in *How to Comply with the Antitrust Laws,* edited by Jerrold G. Van Cise and Charles Wesley Dunn (New York: Commerce Clearing House, 1954), pp. 152–73, at p. 159.

market share. In any case, however, the seller must consider the related possibilities of weakening the general price structure or spoiling the market for future sales. Of these, the first is the more dangerous. If excess capacity exists in the future, the company will probably be willing to grant the same kind of price concessions it finds profitable now. If, on the other hand, the excess capacity disappears in the future, the company will not be willing to grant price concessions in order to obtain added sales, and therefore the possibility of spoiling future markets may not be a serious objection.

SUMMARY

Application of the profit maximization decision rule to pricing decisions requires data on price/volume and cost/volume relationships. In the absence of the former, most companies fall back on pricing formulas, most of them based on estimates of product unit cost.

These pricing formulas seem illogical, and often are, but their main purpose is to assist management in determining what a "normal" price might be. For pricing new products to be added as standard items in the regular product line, management may wish to follow a "skimming pricing" policy by setting a price in excess of the normal price, or a "penetration pricing" policy by setting price at or near the normal level.

Cost estimates for this purpose are perhaps most logically based on the attributable cost concept, although the real question is which formula provides the best indication of the normal price. If attributable cost or its conceptually weaker cousin, full cost, is used, it should be supplemented by data on variable cost for use in decisions with shorter time horizons. The pricer must then use his own judgment as to what markup to seek. Judgment is the essential ingredient in product pricing; cost data are merely aids to the exercise of this judgment.

DISCUSSION QUESTIONS

1. Prepare an argument that will justify the use of standard full cost plus a standard markup as the basis for pricing a new product.
2. Describe the procedure for determining the optimum price, assuming that all relevant information is known with certainty.
3. "I lose money on every item I sell, but my success is due to the fact that I am able to sell so much." Explain the paradox contained in this statement.
4. Under what circumstances will it be profitable to sell all products at a loss or some products at a loss?
5. It has been suggested that full cost pricing provides the company with a rational basis for allocating plant capacity when that capacity is inadequate

to handle the entire flow of orders. Describe how this might be done. Can you suggest another method of accomplishing the same objective?

6. Many companies quote prices on a full cost basis. Discuss the implications of using burden rates based on normal output and on expected output for this purpose.

7. A company's pricing committee establishes a tentative price to be charged for a new product and then asks the controller to prepare an estimate of the P/V ratio for that product. If the P/V ratio is less than a certain level, the price is increased. Discuss this procedure.

8. "If I accept an order at a price that is less than full cost, the difference will have to be added to the costs of other orders and that will decrease their profitability unless I raise their prices. As far as I'm concerned, every order has to bear its fair share of overhead." How would you reply to this statement?

9. Discuss the implications of interdepartmental cost allocations as they might influence product pricing.

10. The term "discrimination" carries a connotation of unfairness in everyday usage. "Price discrimination" as used by economists, merely means charging different prices in different sectors of the company's markets. The Robinson-Patman Act does not outlaw all price discrimination but only certain kinds. Under what circumstances is a policy of price discrimination likely to be most effective in increasing the firm's profits? Why are export markets often regarded as a safer place to practice price discrimination than domestic markets?

11. Discuss the respective roles of "science" and "art" in pricing custom products.

12. "There is no such thing as full cost pricing because full cost cannot be determined without first estimating volume and volume cannot be estimated before specifying a price." Discuss this statement.

13. Under what circumstances might a break-even chart help a manager arrive at a selling price for one of his products?

14. How would you go about estimating the "value" of your product to your customers?

15. "Variable cost provides a pricing floor, but it has no other role in product pricing." Comment.

16. Are attributable cost figures more reliable for product pricing than full cost?

17. "If we used variable costing figures in pricing all of our products, we'd be bankrupt within a year." What assumptions did the speaker make? Do you agree? Comment.

EXERCISES AND PROBLEMS

1. The manager of the industrial sales division of the Ortega Company has been called upon to explain why his division's sales have not been increasing as rapidly as sales of competing companies. He offered in explanation the fact that competitors were quoting lower prices and argued that he couldn't meet those prices unless the company reduced the amount of head

office expense allocated to his division. He said, "This is a low-margin business, but you allocate head office expense on the basis of sales. If you allocated on the basis of gross margin, that would cut my expenses by more than 50 percent and I could compete with anybody."

Comment on this argument. Do you think the allocation basis should be changed?

2. The Fantasi Corporation is engaged in setting the price to be established on a new product. It is estimated that sales of 10,000 units would give the company approximately the same share of this particular market as it has been able to maintain in the markets for the company's other products. The sales manager believes that he can obtain this share if the price is not more than 10 percent higher than $13.50, the price at which the most closely competitive product is now being sold. No estimates of sales volume at other prices are available.

The company's policy is to establish prices on new products at factory cost plus 40 percent to cover selling and administrative expenses and provide a profit. Factory cost is defined as direct labor and materials plus overhead. The burden rate for the department in which the new product will be processed is $3.46 per direct labor hour. Direct costs will be $2.50 for materials and 1.5 hours of direct labor at $1.80 an hour.

a) What price should the company establish?

b) Would your answer be affected if competing products were priced at $12.50? If so, quote a new price under these circumstances.

c) Would your answer differ if the competitive price were $10? Explain.

3. The Weiss Company manufactures a highly machined precision part that is used in the manufacture of certain kinds of industrial equipment. The selling price is $350. Standard cost is as follows:

Material, 30 pounds at $2	$ 60
Direct labor, 30 hours at $2.50	75
Variable overhead	30
Fixed overhead	40
Total Standard Cost per Unit	$205

The company was recently offered an order by a Canadian concern for 200 units at a price of $250 each. Freight charges and Canadian import duty, to be paid by the seller, would have totaled $15,000. There was no danger that units shipped to Canada would be reshipped to Weiss's domestic customers because of high U.S. tariffs on imports of this product.

The Canadian company had never done business with the Weiss Company, and the sales manager pressed strongly for the sale on the ground that this was an opportunity to expand into a new market. The controller was out of town when this offer came in and was not consulted. The president turned down the sales manager's recommendation and instructed him to reject the offer.

Due to a number of factors, unabsorbed overhead variances amounting to $5 a unit have been budgeted for the coming year. Labor and materials quantity variances have been negligible, but the standards do not reflect recent increases in materials purchases prices and wage rates. Materials prices have increased 3 percent above standard, and wage rates have increased 5 percent. Wage and price changes affecting overhead costs account for $1 of the budgeted underabsorption of overhead.

a) Do you agree with the president's decision? Support your position with arguments based on data provided above.

b) Are there any considerations that might justify a course of action other than that which you have supported?

4. The Rabid Company makes animal traps, and last year it sold 80,000 traps at a price of $4 each. Selling and administrative expenses amounted to $28,000, and manufacturing costs averaged $3 a unit. This year's tentative budget indicates that if price is unchanged and the sales organization is not expanded, 70,000 units will be sold. Selling and administrative expenses will increase by 2 percent, and average manufacturing costs per unit will increase by 15 percent.

The sales manager has proposed that the price be reduced to $3.50 and that he be permitted to hire an additional salesman at a cost of $5,500 a year. This he feels would put the company in a more competitive position and would yield sales of 100,000 units a year. The company's accountant estimates that expansion of volume to 100,000 units would reduce average manufacturing cost per unit to 82 percent of the level now budgeted for this year.

What is the incremental profit or loss on the sales manager's proposal?

5. The sales manager of the Franglais Company has been asked to submit a price quotation for 100,000 units of a product used by one of the Franglais customers.

The out-of-pocket cost of filling the order, if it can be obtained, is $90,000. Three possible prices are being considered, $1, $1.25, and $1.50. The sales manager is not certain how busy competitors' factories are, but in the light of their bids on recent jobs he thinks that the chance of their operating at a rate as high as 80 percent of capacity or higher is only 20 percent. Similarly, he believes that the probability that competitors are operating at 60 percent of capacity or less is 30 percent.

He estimates that if competitors' operating rates are 80 percent or higher, he can secure the order at any bid up to and including $1.50. If competitors are operating between 61 percent and 79 percent of capacity, a price of $1.25 or less will secure the bid, but if competitors' operating rate is 60 percent or less it will take a bid of $1 to land the order.

Prepare a payoff table to reflect these data. Assuming that the decision rule is to maximize the expected value of the monetary return, which bid should be submitted?

*6. The Magellan Company has been selling its product at a price of $0.80 and has decided to investigate the profitability of increasing the price to compensate the company for recent increases in operating cost. The controller of the company has analyzed the company's costs, and although he recognizes that his analysis is imperfect, he has derived the following cost estimates:

---

* Solutions to problems marked with an asterisk (*) can be found in Appendix B.

Monthly Output (Units)	Operating Costs	
	Fixed Cost	Marginal Cost per Unit
50,000 and less...............	$10,000	$0.60
50,001–60,000................	10,000	0.61
60,001–70,000................	10,000	0.62
70,001–80,000................	11,000	0.64
80,001–90,000................	11,000	0.67
90,001–100,000...............	11,000	0.71
100,001–110,000..............	12,000	0.75
110,001–120,000..............	12,000	0.79
120,001–130,000..............	13,000	0.85

The market research department has recently studied prices and performance of competitive products and has derived an estimate of the effect of price on sales volume. The manager of market research has presented the following figures to the controller hesitantly, saying that he doesn't know how reliable they are but that they are the best he can do. He adds that in good years sales would exceed these figures, but on the average he thinks his estimate would be borne out.

Price per Unit	Monthly Unit Sales
$0.75............................	100,000
0.80............................	90,000
0.85............................	80,000
0.90............................	70,000
0.95............................	60,000
1.00............................	50,000

Prepare a statement that will indicate the most profitable price at which the product might be sold.

7. The Aybec Foundry Company is feeling the effects of a general over-capacity of the foundry industry in the Boston area. Its monthly production cost budget for the next six months is based on an output of only 500 tons of castings a month, which is less than half of practical capacity. The prices of castings vary with the composition of the metal and the shape of the mold, but they average $140 a ton. The condensed monthly production cost budget at the 500-ton level is as follows:

	Core Making	Melting and Pouring	Molding	Cleaning and Grinding
Labor........................	$ 6,000	$ 8,000	$3,000	$2,000
Variable overhead.............	3,000	1,000	1,000	1,000
Fixed overhead...............	5,000	9,000	2,000	1,000
Total Labor and Overhead..	$14,000	$18,000	$6,000	$4,000
Labor and overhead per direct labor hour.................	$7.00	$4.50	$4.00	$3.20

Operation at this level has brought the company very close to the break-even point. The lack of work also means that some of the most highly skilled workers will probably have to be laid off, and the production manager is worried that he might find it difficult to get them back when volume picks up later on. Accordingly, when he learned that a customer was soliciting bids for a large casting order, he called in the plant accountant and instructed him to prepare a bid "at cost." He reasoned that if he could keep his work force together, that would be enough profit for the contract.

The order is for 90,000 castings, each weighing about 40 pounds, to be delivered on a regular schedule during the next six months. Materials required would cost $1 per casting after deducting scrap credits. The labor requirements would be:

Department	Direct Labor Hours per Casting
Core making	0.09
Melting and pouring	.15
Molding	.06
Cleaning and grinding	.06

Variable overhead would bear a normal relationship to labor cost in the melting and pouring department and in the molding department. In core making and cleaning and grinding, however, the extra labor requirements would not be accompanied by proportionate increases in variable overhead. Variable overhead would increase by $1.20 for every additional labor hour in core making and by 30 cents for every additional labor hour in cleaning and grinding. Standard wage rates are in effect in each department, and no labor variances are anticipated.

To handle an order as large as this, certain increases in fixed factory overhead would be necessary, amounting to $1,000 a month for all departments combined. No increases in selling and administrative expense are anticipated, but the company uses a standard selling and administrative expense rate of $12 per ton of castings in its pricing work. Production for this order would be spread evenly over the six-month period.

a) Prepare a revised monthly factory cost budget, reflecting the addition of this order.

b) What is the lowest price that the plant manager could quote without selling at a loss? Show your calculations.

*8. The Hammer Company manufactures a product that it distributes through its own sales branches in the midwestern United States. The company's president, Mr. Martin, was recently approached by a West Coast distributor who was interested in obtaining a franchise for distribution of the product in seven western states not now served by the company. The distributor proposed that he purchase the product from Hammer at a price of $32.50 F.O.B. the Hammer factory, and offer it for sale to retailers at a price of $42.50. He would pay freight charges to the West Coast, averaging $3.50 per unit. No sales commissions would have to be paid on these sales. Mr. Martin promised that he would consider the offer.

The product is now sold to retailers in Hammer's present market area at a price of $44 delivered. Sales commissions are computed at 5 per cent of sales. Freight averages $1.50 per unit. Other selling and administrative costs are regarded as fixed, and amount to $4.50 per unit. Manufacturing cost amounts to $29.50 per unit, as follows:

Materials	$18.70
Labor	3.00
Variable overhead	3.30
Fixed overhead	4.50
Total	$29.50

Manufacturing capacity is adequate to handle the increased volume, which Mr. Martin estimates would amount to 1,000 units a month, but fixed factory overhead would probably increase by $1,500 a month.

a) Would you advise Mr. Martin to accept the arrangement suggested by the West Coast distributor?

b) What factors other than those mentioned above should be considered in making this decision?

9. The Texto Company manufactures a variety of machined metal products. About half of the company's annual volume is provided by standard items, manufactured to inventory and listed in the company's sales catalogue. The remainder is provided by custom products, produced to meet customers' orders and customers' specifications. Often the customer does not know exactly what kind of product will best meet his needs, and the Texto Company's sales engineers will be called in to help design a product.

Pricing of special orders is the responsibility of the sales manager, subject to certain guides and policy limitations. If factory capacity is inadequate to process all orders, the manufacturing vice president first requests a deferred delivery date for some orders. If this is unacceptable to the customers, the matter is referred to the president to decide which orders to accept. Although some flexibility exists in scheduling the production of the company's standard items, at periods of peak loads these typically must be given priority.

During a recent period of relatively slack demand, the sales manager was able to obtain two larger orders for custom products. The Mafia Company had placed an order for 25,000 fittings of a special design on which the sales manager had quoted a price of $10.56 each. All design work had been performed by the customer, who also presented detailed drawings and would provide some technical assistance in manufacturing. The second order for 10,000 fittings had been received from the Welks Company at a quoted price of $25.80 each. Most of the design modifications necessary to meet the company's specifications had been worked out by Texto sales engineers and the Texto Company's drafting room. The cost to Texto of this design work had amounted to $4,810.

Neither order could be placed in the backlog, and the manufacturing vice president reported that he could meet the required delivery schedule for either order but not for both. To do even this, he would have to reschedule some production, but he had received authorization from another customer to spread promised deliveries over a longer period and he felt that this would give him room to schedule one of the new orders. Although manufacture of the valves for the Welks Company would require more than twice as much labor as the Mafia job, most of this excess would be in departments which could expand their rates of output fairly readily. Labor requirements for the two orders were virtually identical in each of the critical limited-capacity departments.

The two orders were referred to the president who asked the controller to provide him with information on which to base a decision as to which order to accept. The data provided by the controller, working with the plant engineer, are as follows:

	Mafia Fittings	Welks Valves
Unit price.....................	$10.560	$25.800
Factory cost:		
Materials....................	$ 1.283	$ 3.513
Labor........................	2.428	6.078
Overhead.....................	3.316	8.144
Total factory cost...........	$ 7.027	$17.735
General overhead..............	1.307	3.299
Sales engineering............	.....	0.481
Total Unit Cost..........	$ 8.334	$21.515

In response to a question from the president, the controller estimated that the amount of variable factory overhead included in these figures was $1.926 per unit for the Mafia fittings and $3.744 per unit for the Welks valves. He also said that he had derived the general overhead figures by taking the average selling and administrative expenses per dollar of factory cost in that year's budget, excluding sales engineering expenses which he charged only to the Welks order. General overhead costs were almost entirely fixed.

a) Prepare a statement that will show which of these two orders would have been more profitable.

b) Comment briefly on any other considerations that might have influenced the president in making his decision.

10. The Garibaldi Products Company is currently operating its plant at approximately single-shift capacity. The plant produces a wide range of products, and the income statement for a typical month is as follows:

Sales...		$850,000
Cost of sales:		
Direct materials..................................	$450,000	
Direct labor......................................	110,000	
Indirect labor....................................	50,000	
Overtime premium.................................	2,200	
Payroll taxes and charges...........................	16,200	
Factory supplies...................................	24,000	
Property taxes and insurance.........................	12,000	
Depreciation......................................	18,000	
Maintenance......................................	4,000	
Other..	7,600	
Total cost of sales...............................		694,000
Gross margin......................................		$156,000
Selling and administrative expense:		
Salaries..	$ 30,000	
Supplies..	5,000	
Depreciation......................................	3,000	
Other..	7,000	
Total selling and administrative expense..............		45,000
Net Profit from Operations............................		$111,000

The company's general pricing policy is to estimate direct labor and direct materials costs per unit, add any costs that are specifically identifiable with the specific product being priced, and then add an amount equal to 250 percent of the estimated direct labor cost. The total of these items is the unit price. If volume is normal, at these prices the company can maintain its earnings per share and dividend rates at levels that are deemed satisfactory.

Despite the fact that the plant is running at capacity, the sales manager has not relaxed his efforts to find new customers. One potential customer who for several years has expressed interest in the company's products but has always refused to place an order because of a price differential over a competitor's substitute product has finally agreed to give Garibaldi Products a try. He made this offer: "You quote a price of $47 per hundred, and I can get the product I am now using at $40 per hundred. I'll split the difference with you on an order for 50,000 units a month for three months. If your product does what you say it will do, I'll stay with you, but only as long as your price is no more than $3.50 a hundred more than I would have to pay somebody else."

The standard cost card for this product calls for the following:

	Cost per Hundred
Materials................................	$21.80
Labor—stamping..........................	1.75
Labor—trimming..........................	2.20
Labor—finishing..........................	3.25
Overhead—stamping.......................	2.80
Overhead—trimming.......................	1.98
Overhead—finishing.......................	3.90
Total Standard Cost....................	$37.68

Departmental burden rates are based on standard direct labor cost and include a provision for overtime premium at 2 percent of standard direct labor dollars. The production planning department estimates that if this order is accepted, one half of the stamping department operations, 10 percent of trimming operations, and 80 percent of finishing operations will have to be performed on overtime. Overtime is paid for at a rate of time and a half.

The flexible budgets for the three departments indicate variable overhead costs (including overtime premiums at normal budgeted amounts) as follows:

Department	Per Direct Labor Dollar
Stamping	$0.40
Trimming	.50
Finishing	.60

If this order is accepted, however, it is estimated that variable factory overhead will increase by 10 percent more than the flexible budget indicates, over and above any direct labor overtime premiums in excess of normal. Selling and administrative expenses will not be materially affected by acceptance of the order.

a) Prepare a statement that will indicate whether it would be profitable to accept this order, considering only the operations of the next three months.

b) What price would you have to quote if you used the company's pricing rule?

c) Assume that your answer to (*a*) indicated that the order should be accepted and that this customer will continue buying the company's product after the end of the three-month period, but only at discount prices. Discuss the longer term implications of accepting this customer's business.

d) Assume that your answer to (*a*) indicated that the order should not be accepted. Assume also that the company sells other products that have a ratio of variable cost to selling price of 80 percent. In what way, if any, would your analysis be changed?

11. The Oppenheim Company is just completing the construction of a new facility to manufacture a new product. This product is intended for sale to manufacturers of a wide variety of civilian and military products in which it would be used as a component part, ordinarily hidden from the view of the ultimate consumer.

Competing products sell at prices ranging from $3.80 to $4.80, but differences in product specifications and design make direct comparisons difficult. Furthermore, the company believes that there is some price shading for large volume customers, but has thus far been unable to determine its extent.

Sales in this market are quite difficult to forecast, at least in part because individual orders tend to be fairly large and the loss of one order can make the difference between a good forecast and a highly inaccurate one.

In making the decision to enter this market, the Oppenheim management believed that it would be able to sell 150,000 units a month within three years after commencing operations if its prices were competitive. Market conditions have changed materially since the initial decision was made, and even with heavy promotional outlays at the outset, the company is not confident that it can meet the original sales target.

The company's reputation for product quality and delivery performance is such, however, that the sales manager has suggested setting a premium price of $5 a unit. He is quite confident that he can sell 80,000 units a month in the first year at that price. In fact, he thinks it unlikely that he could sell more than 80,000 units a month in the first year, no matter how low a price were set. Buyers in this market try out new components in their less popular lines, often waiting two or three years before incorporating components of improved design into their major products, and this latter portion of the market tends to be highly price sensitive.

It is estimated that materials will cost 80 cents per unit at monthly volumes of 100,000 units or less and 70 cents per unit if monthly volume is in excess of that figure. Labor costs will amount to $1.40 per unit. Factory overhead is to be budgeted at $90,000 per month plus 42 cents per unit. By-products from the process are expected to yield 24 cents per unit of the main product manufactured. The plant's output can be increased to 250,000 units a month, but for all output in excess of 200,000 units a month labor cost will increase to $1.70 per unit and variable overhead will rise to 65 cents per unit.

An intensive sales promotion campaign is now being prepared to launch the new product. Advertising and special promotion activities costing $750,000 will be spread over the first year of the new product, in addition to salesmen's commissions of 5 percent of sales. Thereafter it is expected that selling costs attributable to the new product will be $20,000 a month plus commissions. No change in administrative or other nonmanufacturing expenses is expected to accompany the introduction of the new product.

The company's selling and administrative expenses (including advertising and salesmen's commissions), together with its reported net income before taxes, have in the past averaged about 40 percent of manufacturing cost. This comes very close to a pricing formula that the company has used on many occasions: budgeted manufacturing cost at normal volume plus 45 percent.

a) Compute unit cost on whatever basis you feel would be most helpful to management in setting an initial price on this product. Prepare a summary report to present this figure and any others that you would want management to see, including any charts or diagrams that you would find useful in getting your analysis across.

b) Approximately what price would you like to see the management of the Oppenheim Company set on this product? What reasons underlie your recommendation?

12. The president of the Gregson Products Company makes all the product pricing decisions. He is now trying to decide on a price to be placed on a

new type of floor wax, called "Flow-On," that has just been perfected by the company's research department. Although there are a number of competing brands of liquid floor wax now on the market, the company has not previously marketed any kind of floor wax. The company's products are distributed in a seven-state regional market, rather than nationally.

Labor, materials, and manufacturing overhead costs at different volumes are expected to average as follows:

	Cost per Gallon				
	10,000 Gal./Wk.	15,000 Gal./Wk.	20,000 Gal./Wk.	25,000 Gal./Wk.	30,000 Gal./Wk.
Materials..........	$1.00	$1.00	$0.95	$0.95	$0.95
Labor.............	0.50	0.45	0.40	0.40	0.43
Factory overhead...	1.55	1.05	0.80	0.69	0.68
Total Cost per Gallon.......	$3.05	$2.50	$2.15	$2.04	$2.06

These costs are also typical of those facing the company's major competitors.

The manufacturing process is such that it requires 24-hour, three-shift operation of the production facilities. Changes in the rate of output are achieved by increasing or decreasing the number of processing units in service. In designing the facilities, the company's engineers were asked to design for efficiency at "normal" operating level of 25,000 gallons per week, or 80 percent of maximum physical capacity. The company's efficient competitors are able to achieve about an 80 percent utilization, on the average.

The company's salesmen are paid on a flat salary basis. Introduction of this new product, however, would require the permanent addition of two new salesmen at an average salary of $180 per week each. All other selling and administrative costs would be unchanged by the introduction of this new product. On a companywide basis, the selling and administrative cost averages about 30 percent of manufacturing cost. If the company's profitability targets were met, company net income would be approximately 20 percent of manufacturing cost, but in the past few years the reported net income has averaged about 15 percent of factory cost.

The company's research people are convinced that "Flow-On" is superior to any existing liquid floor waxes. The leading competing product sells at a retail price of $5 per gallon. At the prevailing trade discount of 40 percent off list, the manufacturer's realization at this price is $3 per gallon. The other five brands in the company's market area are less popular and sell at retail prices ranging from $3.95 to $5.35. No quality product is marketed at a price of less than $4.75, and sales of the $5.35 product have been rather small, although it is marketed by a well-established manufacturer of branded household products.

The sales manager is planning an extensive promotional campaign to launch the new product. He is convinced that he can sell 25,000 gallons of "Flow-On" per week once the product is established, as long as the price is no higher than that of the leading competitor. This would represent a market share of about 15 percent, but the impact on competitors would be lessened considerably by expansion of total sales of floor waxes in this area as a result of the extra promotion of the new brand.

The president is less optimistic than the sales manager. He, too, hopes for a sales volume of 25,000 gallons per week but does not expect to reach this level of operations until normal growth of the market expands industry sales sufficiently several years hence. He thinks that 20,000 gallons a week is more likely as long as prices are competitive, and sales might even be as low as 15,000 gallons per week.

a) As controller of the Gregson Products Company, you have been asked to supply the president with a figure representing the cost per gallon of "Flow-On." Prepare a short report, providing the figure(s) that you think is (are) most likely to be relevant in this situation and explaining to the president what your figures mean and why you selected them.

b) There is no time for experiments that would test the price elasticity of demand. *No one in the company can give you any information other than that supplied above.* What price would you establish and why?

13. The Lundstrom Company's factory consists of three production departments and two service departments with the following normal monthly overhead costs:

	Production Departments			Service Departments	
	A	B	C	M	N
Direct overhead:					
Variable...........	$ 5,200	$16,000	$10,500	$ 7,500	.....
Fixed—divisible....	6,000	4,500	2,000	.....	.....
Fixed—indivisible..	800	1,500	3,000	2,000	$10,000
Allocated (full cost basis):					
General factory.....	2,000	2,000	2,000	.....	.....
Department M.....	1,000	4,000	5,000	.....	.....
Department N......	5,000	2,000	2,500	500	.....
Total...........	$20,000	$30,000	$25,000	$10,000	$10,000
Normal volume......	20,000 dir. lab. hrs.	10,000 dir. lab. hrs.	12,500 ma- chine- hours	2,000 serv- ice hours	100,000 sq. ft.

Consumption of service department M's services is regarded as a divisible fixed cost in department A and as proportionately variable with volume in departments B and C. General factory overheads are entirely fixed and largely indivisible.

Product X has just been developed by the Lundstrom Company and is now ready for commercialization. It will be listed in the company's next product catalogue, and orders will be taken for immediate or deferred delivery at list price.

Product X will compete with more than 100 products offered by 36 competing companies in the Lundstrom market area. Its biggest competition will come from the Deane Company's product P, which now sells 5,000 units a month, about 35 percent of the potential market for product X, at a unit price of $45. Lundstrom's market share in other product lines in its own region ranges from 5 percent to 35 percent, with most products between 10 and 15 percent. Prices in this market have been relatively stable for several years.

Product X has a number of significant advantages over product P and other competing products already on the market, and competitors will not be able to match these distinctive features for at least a year. The Lundstrom sales department is enthusiastic about the new product and feels that at a competitive price product X could achieve a good share of the market, perhaps as much as 15 percent, during the first year. Whether it could keep or increase its market share in subsequent years would depend in part on customers' experience with the product and in part on competitors' responses to product X.

The company's development engineers estimate that after an initial six-month learning period, production inputs for a unit of product X will be: direct materials, $5; direct labor, $15; department A, three direct labor hours; department B, 1½ direct labor hours; and department C, two machine-hours. Errors in the engineers' estimates at this stage of product development have generally been within 10 percent of actual costs in the past, and underestimates have been just as frequent as overestimates.

Markups over factory cost on the company's other regular products average about 40 percent of full factory cost and generally range between 25 percent and 45 percent.

Most selling and administrative expenses will be the same no matter what price is set on product X. Selling costs attributable to this product are expected to amount to about $5,000 a month, not counting any special price "deals" that might be made to stimulate sales during the introductory period.

a) Prepare a unit cost estimate or estimates that you feel would help management arrive at a price for product X. Discuss your reasoning.

b) Recommend a selling price for product X. Support your recommendation, using figures from the problem to whatever extent you deem appropriate.

c) How, if at all, would your answer to (a) differ if the decision were whether to accept a single order for 100 units of product X to be shipped to a customer outside Lundstrom's ordinary sales area at a time when factory capacity in each department is only 75 percent utilized?

d) Assuming that product X is now in the line, selling 500 units a month, and that factory production capacity is not fully utilized, what unit cost figure would you use in a rough test of the desirability of discontinuing production and sale of product X? Explain.

CASE 22–1: CLOVIS, S.A.*

Clovis, S.A. manufactures a line of roller skates which it sells in France and other European countries. The company has just received a proposal from Empire Importing Company of New York to introduce Clovis skates into the U.S. market, but at lower net prices than the company now receives on its European sales.

Clovis has no foreign subsidiaries, all foreign sales being made through independent wholesale distributors in the various countries. The company sells three models of detachable skates (detachable skates are attached to the wearer's regular street shoes by means of straps or clamps) and four models of shoe skates (skates fastened at the factory to special skating shoes). The company's requirements of all of these models are manufactured in the company's plant at Lyon, France.

Annual sales volume is now approximately 3 million pairs of detachable skates and 500,000 pairs of shoe skates. Shoe skate sales have remained approximately constant for the past several years, but unit sales of detached skates have declined by approximately 25 percent from the level of a few years ago, despite successive price reductions in most European markets, as competitors have increased their shares of the market at Clovis's expense. The overall European market is about the same size as it was a few years ago.

Empire Importing is convinced that it can market the Clovis detached skates in the United States as high-quality items. Typical cost and price data for one of these, Model TM-5, are shown in Exhibit 1. The other two detachable models have similar cost/price relationships in the three countries listed in the table. Markups over manufacturing cost in other European countries are less than in Switzerland but greater than in Italy. Cost/price relationships for the shoe skates are somewhat different, but Empire Importing does not believe that they could be marketed effectively in the United States, at least at this time, and thus data on these models need not be considered in evaluating this proposal.

The proposal is to offer the products for sale through department stores and discount houses in the eastern part of the United States. Empire Importing would sell Model TM-5 to retailers at a price of $3.50 per pair (approximately 17.15 francs), plus freight from New York. Empire would pay Clovis 9.20 francs per pair, plus all shipping charges and U.S. import duties, estimated at 4.50 francs per pair for the TM-5. It would be responsible for all advertising and sales promotion in the United States, would bear all U.S. credit risks, and would have exclusive rights to market Clovis skates East of the Mississippi River for a period of five years.

Mr. J. R. Martell, Clovis's sales manager, is strongly attracted by this proposal. Empire executives are convinced that they can sell 100,000 pairs of

---

skates this year and that within three years they will be able to increase their U.S. volume to 300,000 pairs per year. Manufacturing burden is now under-absorbed, and capacity exists in the Lyon factory to manufacture more than the 300,000 pairs per year required to supply Empire Importing. The burden rates from which the unit cost figures in Exhibit 1 were derived were based on an annual volume of about 3,600,000 pairs of detachable skates and 500,000 pairs of shoe skates. Most fixed overheads are not traceable to any one product, but represent capacity costs for the combined production of detached and shoe skates and skate parts.

Exhibit 1

SELECTED PRICE AND COST DATA

(All Figures in French Francs per Pair)

	France	Switzerland	Italy
Price data—Model TM-5:			
Retail price......................	24.00	30.08	24.30
Wholesale price..................	18.00	22.00	18.10
Factory price....................	13.80	15.12	10.35
Cost data—Model TM-5:			
Manufacturing cost:			
Variable cost..................	6.70	6.70	6.70
Fixed cost.....................	2.10	2.10	2.10
Selling and administrative expense			
—fixed.......................	1.50	1.50	1.50
*Average shipping costs..........	1.50	1.80	2.10
*Import tariff..................	...	1.51	1.65
Approximate retail price range:			
Competing products..............	20.50–34.00	22.13–42.56	9.41–23.52
All Clovis models................	20.50–30.50	26.67–36.89	18.82–24.30†

* Paid by wholesale distributor; factory prices do not cover shipping costs or import duties.
† Model TM-6, Clovis's most expensive model, is not marketed in Italy.

The present level of fixed costs could probably be maintained if sales were to increase by 100,000 pairs a year, but additional supervisory and clerical person-nel would be required to handle a larger increase. Clovis's accounting depart-ment has assembled estimates that the accompanying increases in total fixed costs would average approximately 180,000 francs per year from the second year onward. Variable manufacturing cost per pair would be approximately as shown in Exhibit 1.

Mr. Pepincourt, Clovis's president, is not entirely convinced of the wisdom of entering the U.S. market on this basis. The company's policy has been to market no product at less than full cost, although in some countries such as Italy the profit margin above full cost has been very thin. Furthermore, expansion into the U.S. market would mean that Clovis would have to spend approximately 150,000 francs three or four years from now to replace certain items of factory equipment now in use. If the company does not accept the Empire Importing proposal or find other ways to increase volume, production lines can be reorganized at negligible cost, thereby making it possible to dispose of this equipment now. Thus the Empire proposal would commit Clovis to an investment which Mr. Pepincourt is reluctant to make. On the other hand, the working capital necessary to support the company's entry into the United States would be negligible.

The equipment referred to in the previous paragraph has no salvage value at the present time, but depreciation on it is included in factory fixed costs at 15,000 francs per year. Other fixed costs associated with this equipment amount to approximately 60,000 francs a year.

Shipping charges and European tariffs are high enough so that reexportation of Clovis skates from New York to Europe would not be feasible, but Mr. Pepincourt is worried nevertheless that if he agrees to this proposal his sales manager will begin to propose major price concessions in other markets as well.

Should Clovis skates be introduced in the United States at the price proposed by Empire Importing Company? Be sure to consider the arguments advanced both by Mr. Martell and by Mr. Pepincourt.

Chapter 23

DISTRIBUTION COST ANALYSIS

MOST marketing policy or strategy decisions—which products to emphasize, what distribution channels to use, what kinds of customers to approach, what discount structure to adopt, etc.—require careful analysis of the company's nonmanufacturing costs.

Some of these decisions call for estimates of the costs associated with individual segments of the company's revenues. For example, the company's management may wish to have information on the profitability of individual sales territories or of small orders or of sales made through its own retail stores. Other marketing problems call for estimates of the costs and revenues associated with new ways of doing business. For example, a company which now sells only through wholesalers is thinking of setting up its own wholesaling operation to deal directly with retailers and needs estimates of the effect of this action on its total costs and total revenues.

For both kinds of problems, estimates of manufacturing costs are ordinarily derived from the product unit costs derived by the methods described earlier in this book. Cost totals are obtained by multiplying either full cost, average variable cost, or attributable cost per unit of product by the number of product units associated with each revenue segment or method of doing business. The problem to which we turn in this chapter is to develop comparable methods for nonmanufacturing costs. This is generally referred to, somewhat inaccurately, as *distribution cost analysis.*[1]

The General Approach

The "product" of a nonmanufacturing activity is the unit of service performed. Some of these services are performed specifically for one

---

[1] For an extended discussion of these methods, see Donald R. Longman and Michael Schiff, *Practical Distribution Cost Analysis* (Homewood, Ill.: Richard D. Irwin, Inc., 1955), chaps. viii–xiv.

revenue segment or another, and their costs can thus be traced directly to those segments. The costs of a fleet of delivery trucks, for example, can often be traced entirely to retail sales or wholesale sales, or to one region or another.

Even here, however, the simple traceability criterion is not entirely adequate. A cost that is traceable to the New England region may not also be traceable to any one group of customers or product line within the region. If the problem is to examine the profitability of a particular customer group, some other means must be found to estimate the costs of serving that group.

To satisfy this need, the distribution cost analyst starts by developing unit costs for the "products" of departments outside the manufacturing

Exhibit 23–1

ASSIGNMENT OF NONMANUFACTURING COSTS TO REVENUE SEGMENTS

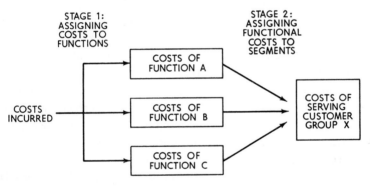

area—i.e., unit costs for individual activities or *functions.* Examples of these "functions" are invoice writing, credit review, payroll preparation, and customer delivery.

Once functional unit cost has been estimated, cost can be estimated for any revenue segment as long as the number of units of functional service required by those revenues can be estimated. This process is diagrammed in Exhibit 23–1.

The process described here is not entirely unfamiliar to anyone who has mastered the principles of accounting for manufacturing costs. Before factory service department costs can be assigned to individual products they normally must be analyzed to determine how much service is provided to each of the factory production departments through which the products flow. Substitute "production department" for "function" and "product" for "customer group" in Exhibit 23–1 and the similarity becomes apparent.

Developing Functional Unit Cost

Cost estimation is thus a two-stage process, the first stage being the development of functional unit costs and the second being the assignment of functional costs to individual revenue segments. Although functional cost analysis was covered in Chapter 16, two points deserve special comment here before we go on to the segment cost analysis that is the main content of the chapter.

First, functional services are often measured indirectly, in units of some *governing factor* or factors appropriate to the particular functional cost element. The governing factor should be one that correlates closely with the cost of carrying out the functional activity. For example, the governing factor for an employee recreation function might well be the number of company employees.

Selection of such units is ordinarily not very difficult, the only practical problem arising because so many different factors are selected for the various functions that obtaining statistics would become a massive job. The typical solution is to try to reduce the number of measuring rods so that one index will serve a number of functions. Thus although number of orders received may be a less perfect measure of the work load in the credit review function than the number of credit inquiries made, it may be accurate enough to eliminate the need for separate collection of the second set of statistics.

The second problem encountered in unitizing functional costs is that very few nonmanufacturing costs are proportionately variable in the short run. The materials cost component is ordinarily small, and the adjustment period for labor costs is typically much longer than in the case of factory costs. This means that unit costs in most cases must be based either on the attributable cost concept or on full cost. Our preference for the former has been expressed repeatedly in earlier chapters, but is it particularly pronounced here. So many manufacturing costs are joint costs—costs incurred to service two or more functions or two or more segments simultaneously—that full cost cannot be regarded as even an approximation to long-run incremental unit cost.

The rule throughout this chapter, therefore, will be to include in functional unit cost only those cost elements that seem sufficiently divisible to justify the assumption of proportionate change in response to substantial changes in the total volume of functional activity.

ASSIGNING FUNCTIONAL COSTS TO SPECIFIC PRODUCT LINES

The first illustration of segment cost analysis to be introduced here is the assignment of costs to individual product lines. For product-line costing, the general approach described in the preceding paragraphs can be translated as follows:

1. Identify all costs traceable to specific products, distinguishing between those that are:
   a) Variable with volume in the short run.
   b) Fixed in the short run but variable with volume in the long run.
   c) Indivisible and thus relatively fixed in the long run but avoidable if the product line is discontinued or withdrawn.

2. For all other cost elements, estimate the number of units of service provided by each service function in support of each product line—"units of service" will ordinarily be measured by the number of units of the governing factor for each service function.

3. Multiply the number of governing factor units in each function by:
   a) Attributable unit cost if the problem is long term.
   b) Variable unit cost if the problem is short term.

The total cost assigned to a product line in the first and third of these steps provides the raw materials for the profitability analysis. As previous chapters have pointed out, incremental cost can be defined only when the alternative solutions to a particular problem have been specified. For the traceable costs, for example, only the first subcategory of traceable costs should be included in product cost if the problem is short term, while all three subcategories should be included if the continuation of the entire product line is in question.

It might be noted at this point that a possible fourth subcategory of traceable costs would be those that are both indivisible and unavoidable in the event of discontinuation of the product line. These mostly represent depreciation charges on major facilities and are reflected in incremental cash flows only if abandonment and continuation would require different levels of investment outlays in the future. If such investment differentials are present, then a discounted cash flow analysis should be undertaken.

An Illustration

A simplified example should serve to illustrate the method. Suppose that a company has three product lines which it wishes to rank on a profitability basis. The purpose of this analysis is to identify those products that deserve the most short-run promotional effort, as well as those that appear to have weaknesses that if not corrected will endanger their long-run survival. For these purposes, both variable profit and attributable profit are to be computed.

The first preliminary to product-line analysis is the classification of functional costs as either product-related or customer-related. Authorities on distribution cost analysis are generally agreed that virtually all distribution costs are determined, directly or indirectly, either by characteristics of the product or by characteristics of the customer, and only product-related costs are relevant to the study of product-line profitability.

This does not mean that all costs can be assigned unequivocably either to specific customer groups or to specific product lines. The many nonmanufacturing costs that are joint costs with respect either to products or to customers cannot be assigned to any one group in a meaningful way. They are related only to products in general or customers in general, and the temptation to unitize them should be resisted.

To continue the example, suppose that a study of nonmanufacturing activities in this company has provided the following estimates of product-related costs:

	Variable Costs	Attributable Fixed Costs
Sales commissions..........	$0.01 × gross sales	....
Product handling..........	$0.02 × pounds of product	$0.0075 × pounds of product
Storage value.............	....	$0.0230 per year × average inventory value
Storage space.............	....	$1.40 per year × square feet required
Inspection................	$3.60 × inspection hours	....

In addition, two groups of cost elements—product management expenses and the costs of samples and product sales brochures—are completely traceable to individual product lines and thus require no allocations. All customer-related costs, as well as nonattributable fixed costs, have been excluded completely from the analysis. These are expected to average approximately 30 percent of aggregate budgeted sales volume for the coming year.

The following forecasts have been made for the company's three product lines for the coming year:

	Product Line A	Product Line B	Product Line C
Gross sales...................	$1,000,000	$800,000	$750,000
Variable factory cost..........	$ 500,000	$450,000	$350,000
Attributable fixed factory cost...	$ 50,000	$ 30,000	......
Average inventory valuation	$ 300,000	$182,000	$160,000
Product weight...............	2,000,000 lbs.	400,000 lbs.	300,000 lbs.
Warehouse space required......	50,000 sq. ft.	6,500 sq. ft.	5,000 sq. ft.
Inspection hours.............	20,000 hrs.	2,000 hrs.	2,500 hrs.

Application of the unit cost factors to these estimates yields the product-line profit forecasts shown in Exhibit 23–2. Notice how the ranking of product line A has been changed by the introduction of nonmanfacturing costs into the analysis. Just looking at manufacturing costs would give the impression that product line A would have a variable profit ratio of 50 percent of sales and an attributable profit ratio of 45 percent. Comparable ratios for product line B would be 43.8

Exhibit 23–2

PRODUCT-LINE PROFIT FORECASTS

	Product Line A		Product Line B		Product Line C	
	Amount	%	Amount	%	Amount	%
Gross sales.....................	$1,000,000	100.0	$800,000	100.0	$750,000	100.0
Variable product costs:						
Factory......................	$ 500,000	50.0	$450,000	56.2	$350,000	46.7
Sales commissions..............	10,000	1.0	8,000	1.0	7,500	1.0
Product handling..............	40,000	4.0	8,000	1.0	6,000	0.8
Inspection...................	72,000	7.2	7,200	0.9	9,000	1.2
Total variable product cost	$ 622,000	62.2	$473,200	59.1	$372,500	49.7
Variable profit..................	$ 378,000	37.8	$326,800	40.9	$377,500	50.3
Attributable fixed costs:						
Factory......................	$ 50,000		$ 30,000		......	
Product management...........	23,000		21,000		$ 22,000	
Samples and brochures.........	8,000		7,000		10,500	
Product handling..............	15,000		3,000		2,250	
Storage value.................	6,900		4,186		3,680	
Storage space.................	70,000		9,100		7,000	
Total attributable fixed cost....	$ 172,900	17.3	$ 74,286	9.3	$ 45,430	6.0
Product margin..................	$ 205,100	20.5	$252,514	31.6	$332,070	44.3

percent and 40 percent. Product line A is a heavy consumer of nonmanufacturing services, however, and recognition of these shows that product line A's variable profit ratio is slightly lower than that of product line B, and its attributable profit or product margin is substantially lower.

Treatment of Independent Program Costs

A careful review of this example will show that the allocated costs represented repetitive service activities only. The only costs shown for other types of functions were product management and samples and brochures, both of which required no allocation because they could be traced to individual product lines.

The most controversial of the omissions in this example are the costs of independent program activities such as product research, advertising, and direct selling. Two issues are encountered here: (1) the degree of relationship between current cost and current revenue; and (2) the attributability of individual cost elements to specific product lines.

Matchability. Selling costs and product research costs are typically recorded prior to the period in which revenues are recognized. These time lags should be recognized in product profitability analysis. Product research, for example, should be assigned to the product lines to which it can be traced as a determinant of attributable profit. In concept, it should be identified with future product-line revenues rather than estimated current revenues because it is the former that will indicate whether further investment in the product line is profitable. Charging it against current revenues, however, only indicates whether current profit margins are adequate to justify the current level of product research. Even at the product-line level, research outlays often exhibit a considerable degree of stability, and the practice of charging current outlays against current revenues at least has the advantage of indicating how much of a profit growth will be required to justify current outlay rates.

Attributability. The second issue is how much of the costs of independent programs can be attributed to individual product lines. In most cases, the only costs that can be so attributed are those that can be *traced* to specific product lines. Some allocations are occasionally justified, such as each product line's proportionate share of a newspaper advertisement which it cosponsors with another product line. The problem here as elsewhere, however, lies in determining what constitutes a proportionate share. For example, suppose that a salesman promotes three separate product lines when he visits customers' offices. The annual sales plan may provide that he spend 50 percent of his time on product line A, 30 percent on line B, and 20 percent on line C. It would be unwise to argue, however, that his salary should be allocated in these proportions in preparing estimates of product profitability. In the first place, all of the costs of travel and waiting time are joint costs of the various product lines; thus any allocation should be limited to that portion of salesmen's time which is actually devoted to selling specific products. In the second place, allocation of these costs is unnecessary. One of the major reasons for computing product profitability is to provide guidance to marketing management in how to allocate its promotional efforts. Allocation of the cost of these efforts is unnecessary because by the time it is feasible the key decisions have already been made.

Treatment of Interest Costs

Interest costs could enter into distribution cost analysis from four sources: interest on investment in plant and equipment, interest on investments in warehouse and office space, interest on receivables, and interest on inventories. Two issues arise here: (1) should interest costs be allocated at all; and (2) if so, how should interest be calculated?

No hard-and-fast rule can be advanced in response to the first of these. Interest can seldom be included with the proportionally variable costs because investment requirements are seldom proportional to sales volume. For the purpose for which the attributable profit figures in the example were developed, introduction of interest charges as fixed costs would have caused no harm. If the profit figures were to be used in a cash flow timetable for a capital expenditure justification, however, the interest component would have to be added back to the indicated profit to get the cash flow. (Cash flow discounting, it will be recalled from Chapter 19, is applied to cash flows before interest charges.) To avoid confusion, interest charges are typically excluded from general-purpose allocations.

If interest is allocated, it should be charged on the basis of the investment attributable to each product line, at an interest rate that reflects the firm's overall cost of capital. In other words, it should not reflect a full allocation of joint investments and it should not be based on the specific interest to be accrued on external debt during the coming period. This ordinarily means using a before-tax interest rate of 20 percent or even more.

Treatment of Space Costs

In the example, a charge of $1.40 a year was made for each square foot of warehouse space required for any given product line. It should be emphasized that this did not represent the average internal cost of the company's warehouses. The concept of opportunity cost is highly relevant here, and this may be as low as zero or as high as the market value of comparable quantities of warehouse space.

Historical versus Forecasted Allocations

Only forecast data were used in the example above, but it is probably safe to say that most distribution cost analysis is applied to historical data for one or more time periods.

In one sense, all distribution cost analysis is based on historical data. Estimated time distributions, whether based on complete time records or sample data, are merely projections of the past. The principal purpose of segment analysis is to assist management in decision making, and thus the justification for using the historical data for any given time period must be that they produce useful forecasts of the future. When distribution cost analysis confines itself to the physical and dollar statistics for a given time period, however, the tie to the past is tightened and rigidified. A better approach is to use average cost for a particular time period only when it is easy to compute and likely to be representative of the future. Time distributions in any one period are particularly suspect as a basis for forecasting and typically should be used only in post-mortem reviews of past operations.

Consistency with Incremental Approach

If carried out as described here, product cost analysis is in no sense inconsistent with the incremental approach to decision making advocated in preceding chapters. The methods outlined in this chapter are designed to get better data on cost increments. The introduction of attributable cost figures is intended to serve the purposes for which many accountants have computed full cost in the past, without falling prey to the defects of full cost.[2]

No one should pretend that this approach contains the magic formula that will automatically produce the right cost for every situation.

---

[2] For a discussion of the pros and cons of full costs in product cost analysis, see Martin Mellman, "Marketing Cost Analysis—Its Relationship to Factory Costing Methods," *N.A.A. Bulletin*, January, 1962, pp. 25–33; and Robert K. Jaedicke, "Marketing Cost Analysis—A Reply," *N.A.A. Bulletin*, July, 1962, pp. 57–61.

Attributable cost, in particular, is only an approximation to the truth, and if abandonment of a product line were ever to be considered, the assumptions underlying the cost estimates must be queried.

Maintaining Analytical Perspective

The usefulness of this kind of analysis should not be overstated. Just how much effort a company should make to incorporate nonmanufacturing elements in product unit cost depends on the impact that allocations of these elements is likely to have on management decisions. Our own inclination is to focus on the main elements of product-related costs and ignore the rest. If these product-related elements are relatively small, they may even be ignored altogether.

Obtaining the Data

Different methods of deriving functional cost figures were discussed in Chapter 16. Statistical data can also be collected internally to direct the allocation of functional costs among the various product lines or other segments of the company's sales.

These methods of data gathering, however, leave a serious gap in the data base for managerial decision making because they pertain directly only to one of the alternatives being considered—continuation of the status quo. To put this a different way, the average cost of distributing a unit of product is relevant to a decision only if costs and revenues are likely to be affected in the same proportions by the choice between alternatives.

Although the focus of this chapter is on the behavior of distribution costs, the other side of the picture should not be overlooked. Data on revenue responses to a particular decision are often obtained by experimentation. For example, most large food manufacturing companies test-market new products in a limited number of cities before placing them in general distribution, to gauge consumer response and the profitability of different marketing techniques. One test market may be saturated with local advertising, while sales promotion in another area may use point-of-sale displays only. Differences between sales in the two areas may help to indicate the profitability of specific local advertising campaigns.

This kind of experimentation cannot be discussed adequately here, but it ought to be noted that the crucial determinant of incremental profit is more likely to be the impact of the decision on sales volume and mix than its impact on the cost of servicing this incremental volume and mix. Any serious student of accounting should attempt to familiarize himself with these methods.[3]

COST ANALYSIS BY SIZE OF ORDER

A product-line classification was chosen as the first illustration of distribution cost analysis because product-line analysis was already familiar from earlier chapters. In a sense, it was a poor starting point, however, because most problems calling for distribution cost analysis relate to some dimension of the customer mix.

One important form of customer-related analysis is the estimation of the costs of handling orders of different sizes. This "unit of sale" analysis can be used by management in such matters as setting minimum order sizes, establishing a quantity discount structure, or altering methods of promoting and distributing products to small-order customers.

Basic Method

Estimates of the costs of handling orders of different sizes can be obtained from the functional cost totals, derived by the methods described earlier. Every functional cost element which has a governing factor that depends on the number, size, or other dimension of customer orders is germane to the analysis. Other items should be rigorously excluded. The cost of writing a customer invoice, for example, is clearly an order-related cost; the salary of the marketing vice president just as clearly is not.

A thorough example would have so many cost elements that a whole chapter would be required to discuss it.[4] To illustrate the method, however, let us assume that functional cost analyses have revealed the following unit cost totals:

Governing Factor	Unit Cost
Number of orders	$1.00 per order
Value of orders	0.001 per dollar
Number of product units ordered	0.03 per unit
Number of order lines	0.01 per line

This table, of course, represents the summation of all of the functional cost elements governed by each of the factors listed; a full example would have to list each function separately.

---

[3] An interesting discussion of the objectives of these studies and the results of a number of them is in Charles H. Sevin, *Marketing Productivity Analysis* (New York: McGraw-Hill Book Co., Inc., 1965), especially chaps. iv–viii.

[4] For example, see Longman and Schiff, *op. cit.,* chap. xi.

The next step is to find out how many units of each of these governing factors are associated with orders of various sizes. For example, a sample of orders might yield the following statistics:

Size Class	Number of Governing Factor Units			
	Orders	Order Value	Product Units	Order Lines
$ 1–$ 99........	50,000	$ 1,000,000	200,000	100,000
100– 199........	20,000	2,600,000	500,000	60,000
200– 499........	20,000	5,600,000	1,100,000	80,000
500 and up......	10,000	6,000,000	1,200,000	50,000
Total............	100,000	$15,200,000	3,000,000	290,000

Because the question in this case is how much it costs to obtain and service an order, these statistics next should be restated as averages, as follows:

Size Class	Average Number of Governing Factor Units per Order			
	Orders	Order Value	Product Units	Order Lines
$ 1–$ 99........	1	$ 20	4	2.0
100– 199........	1	130	25	3.0
200– 499........	1	280	55	4.0
500 and up......	1	600	120	5.0
Average..........	1	$152	30	2.9

The final step is to multiply these statistics by the unit cost figures cited earlier. The end result is the unit cost of an order, as summarized below:

Size Class	Costs Attributed to—				Total Cost per Order
	Each Order	Value of the Order	Number of Units in the Order	Number of Order Lines	
$ 1–$ 99....	$1.00	$0.02	$0.12	$0.02	$1.16
100– 199....	1.00	0.13	0.75	0.03	1.91
200– 499....	1.00	0.28	1.65	0.04	2.97
500 and up..	1.00	0.60	3.60	0.05	5.25
Average.....	$1.00	$0.152	$0.90	$0.029	$2.08

Orders that contribute less product profit contribution (variable profit or attributable profit) than the amounts shown in the right-hand column are not covering their costs.

In practice, this analysis could be further simplified by consolidating two or more governing factors that are highly correlated. In this example, for instance, the number of units in each order correlated very closely with the value of the order. This can be checked by computing average value per unit, which in this case is virtually constant. Another simplification would be to omit insignificant variables, in this case the number of order lines.

A variant on this approach is to derive by statistical correlation or regression analysis, mathematical relationships between size of order as the independent variable and the various governing factors as dependent variables. This would avoid the obvious error of saying that a $99 order costs $1.16 while a $100 order costs $1.91. Unfortunately, the correlation is unlikely to be good enough to use, and in most cases the method described here is the only possibility.

The Quantity Discount Problem

The preceding analysis could serve as a basis for the establishment of a quantity discount schedule. From an economic point of view, the quantity discount structure is a means of discriminating among different segments of the market to obtain a greater total revenue from a given physical sales volume than could be derived from a one-price policy. This form of price discrimination has long been accepted practice in the regulated electric power industry. Outside the public utility field, however, public policy has been to discourage systematic discrimination of this sort, principally through the provisions of the Robinson-Patman Act mentioned in Chapter 22. One way to justify quantity discounts in Robinson-Patman proceedings is to show that they do not exceed demonstrable cost differentials.

Few attempts at cost justification of quantity discounts have been successful, but this does not mean that they could not be successful if the discount structure itself were established on a cost basis.[5] Most cost studies designed to defend a company's discount structure have been conducted after the Federal Trade Commission filed its complaint, and thus it is not surprising that discounts and cost differentials have failed to coincide.

---

[5] For an exhaustive study of this question, see Herbert F. Taggart, *Cost Justification, Michigan Business Studies, Vol. XIV, No. 3* (Ann Arbor, Mich.: Bureau of Business Research, University of Michigan, 1959).

To illustrate briefly how cost data might be used in justifying quantity discounts, suppose that the company in the previous illustration has offered quantity discounts as follows:

Size of Order	Discount
$ 1–$ 99	None
100– 199	3%
200– 499	5
200– 499	5
500 and up	7

If this structure is to be justified, the cost differential *per dollar of order value* must be at least as great as the percentages indicated. In other words, if it costs 10 percent less per order dollar to process a $600 order than to process a $20 order, then any discount of 10 percent or less is justifiable on a cost basis. The computed cost differentials in this example are:

Size Class	(1) Average Order Value	(2) Average Cost per Order	(3) Average Cost per Order Dollar (2) ÷ (1)	(4) Cost Differential from Base Class $0.0580–(3)
$ 1–$ 99	$ 20	$1.16	$0.0580	......
100– 199	130	1.91	.0147	$0.0433
200– 499	280	2.97	.0106	.0474
500 and up	600	5.25	.0088	.0492

This table shows that the 3 percent discount offered to customers purchasing in $100–$199 quantities is more than justified by the cost savings attributable to these larger orders (4.33 percent). The discounts offered to customers buying in larger quantities cannot be justified in this way, however. The 5 percent discount offered to the third class of invoices is 0.26 cents greater than the cost differential, and the gap is even wider in the case of the top discount category.

A moment's reflection will indicate that these cost differentials per order dollar are not created by those functional cost elements that vary directly with order dollars. These average 60 cents for a $600 order and 2 cents for a $20 order, or 1 cent per order dollar in both cases. In more general terms, the costs that are relevant to the quantity discount structure are those that are order-related but do not vary proportionately with the size of the order. When order size is measured in dollars, the relevant costs are those that do not vary in proportion to the *dollar value of the individual order* but do vary with the *number of orders or order elements.*

Attributable Cost versus Full Cost

Most authorities on cost justification for Robinson-Patman Act cases prefer to use full cost figures for that purpose. One reason may be that they believe that full cost figures are conceptually preferable. Another is that the Federal Trade Commission accountants are accustomed to working on a full cost basis, and this will make it easier to come to an agreement on technical matters. Another may be that differentials in full cost are likely to be larger than differentials in attributable cost, and thus a larger proportion of the discount structure can be justified.

The foregoing illustration, in contrast, employed the attributable cost concept throughout. Variable cost was rejected on the grounds that most decisions to be based on unit costs for different order sizes have a longer time horizon and a broader scope than would be appropriate to variable cost figures. Full cost, on the other hand, was rejected for reasons that have been cited repeatedly in this and previous chapters—it has no clear analytical meaning.

Exclusion of Manufacturing Cost Differentials

No mention has been made thus far of possible differentials in manufacturing costs for orders of different sizes. The reason is that in most cases manufacturing cost per unit is a function of the *total* volume of production rather than of the volume generated by any one order.

For example, suppose that the company has two orders for the same product, one for 100 units and the other for 1,000 units. Manufacturing costs attributable to production of these units are:

Volume (Units)	Total Cost	Unit Cost
100....................	$10,000	$100
1,000....................	80,000	80
1,100....................	86,900	79

In this case the incremental cost of the 100-unit order could be either $100 or $69 a unit, depending on whether the larger order was also in the shop at the same time. (The $69 figure is the average cost of increasing production from 1,000 units to 1,100 units.) Similarly, the incremental cost of the 1,000-unit order could be either $80 or $76.90. In other words, cost differentials between orders of different sizes do not include differentials in manufacturing costs unless circumstances require that each order be produced separately or else different versions of the product are sold to the customers in the various order-size brackets.

This indeterminacy of cost does not necessarily mean that production cost differentials should not be reflected in price differentials if the Robinson-Patman Act is not applicable. If the 100-unit customer's business can be taken for granted and if the large order cannot be obtained without giving the customer a $20 discount, the cost figures will support this discount. The basic decision factors, however, are marketing factors, namely, the sensitivity of unit sales to price in individual segments of the market.

OTHER APPLICATIONS

The variety of problems that call for distribution cost analysis is very large. In each case the appropriate method of analysis will be very similar to the methods outlined in this chapter, and no purpose would be served by expanding the list of illustrations. It is merely necessary to describe a pair of highly disparate applications to show the universality of the method.

Bank Service Charges

Commercial banks render a variety of services for their demand depositors. Many of these services, such as lines of credit and safe deposit boxes, are provided under separate agreements with the depositor; others are provided automatically as long as the depositor has a balance in his account.

Although most banks have some degree of monopoly power and some banks have a good deal of insulation from direct competition, banking in general is a highly competitive business and fees that are out of line with competitive practice can lead to a substantial loss of business. A bank in a competitive environment is seldom free to raise its service charges far above a compensatory level.

Data on the cost of servicing customers' accounts provide the bank's management with guidance in its pricing policies. If costs exceed service prices by a significant margin, the time may be ripe for an upward adjustment of the price structure. Alternatively, management may wish to question its service policies and operating methods to see if costs can be reduced.

Once again the appropriate approach is to develop estimated or standard costs of performing various functions, and then use these rates to determine the costs of various services. For example, a committee of the New York Clearing House Association several years ago published a pamphlet in which three classes of account-related costs were recognized:[6]

Fixed maintenance costs.
Variable maintenance costs.
Activity costs.

Fixed maintenance costs are the costs of "maintaining depositors' account records, regardless of size of account balances or degree of account activity," and they include the costs of such activities as opening and closing accounts and maintaining signature card files. The pamphlet also sees fit to include in this category the costs of rendering services that benefit all depositors as a group, a category that would not fit in under the attributable cost doctrine.

The *variable maintenance costs* are those, like deposit insurance, which tend to vary with the size of depositors' account balances. Once again it is unfortunate that the category was expanded to include activities *presumed* to be of benefit to depositors in proportion to the size of account balances, and most of the illustrations in the pamphlet fell into this latter group. Acceptance of attributable cost as a guiding concept makes this second group superfluous, as all costs that vary with the size of the depositor's account can be treated as *activity costs,* the costs of performing varying amounts of specific banking services for the depositor.

The Clearing House pamphlet identified 30 separate activities likely to be undertaken in servicing regular demand deposit accounts. Repetition of this list here is unnecessary, but the main items were:

Paying checks drawn on the depositor's account.
Cashing checks drawn on other banks.
Processing checks submitted for deposit.
Accepting currency for deposit.
Supplying wrapped currency.
Issuing account transcripts.

By identifying the amount of each of these kinds of activities required by a given class of customers, the bank's management can identify cost-price relationships that are out of line and take whatever action it deems appropriate under current circumstances.

Vending Machine Profitability

As one final example of distribution cost analysis, a company engaged in the sale, supply, and servicing of vending machines recently

[6] The New York Clearing House Association, Committee on Accounting Procedures, *Bank Cost Accounting Principles and Procedures* (New York: The New York Clearing House Association, 1961). The references in this chapter are mainly to chap. vii, pp. 40–50.

undertook a study to determine the costs associated with four of its most important types of equipment. The machines were further grouped by type of location—e.g., offices, light industrial factories, heavy industrial factories, supervised public locations, and unsupervised public locations. The company's study recognized eight major classes of activities:

Selling.
Delivery and installation.
Financing.
Field maintenance.
Shop maintenance.
Repainting and reconditioning.
Bookkeeping.
Repossession.

Using some sample data and some data drawn from the routine historical accounting records, the company developed unit costs for activities in each of these classes, as well as records of functional consumption for each of the 20 machine type/location combinations (Type A—Offices, Type B—Offices, Type A—Light Industrial Factories, etc.).

This analysis provided the company's management with information on which to base its machine rental charges. (The company's objective was to break even on the machine, relying for its profits on products sold in the machine.) Such a study might also reveal that certain types of equipment are more suitable than others in given kinds of locations or that some kinds of locations are so hard on the machines that the profitable course of action is to withdraw from those locations altogether.

SUMMARY

Many problems in marketing management call for estimates of the profitability of specific segments of the company's revenues. Most of these problems call for the analysis of distribution costs.

The first step in distribution cost analysis is the estimation of the costs attributable to the performance of individual nonmanufacturing functions. Next, selection of the governing factor or factors for each of these functions permits the derivation of functional unit cost or costs. Finally, the analyst must estimate the number of each of the governing factors associated with the particular segments of the business being studied, and multiply these numbers times the functional unit cost estimates.

Some of these analyses focus on individual products, but most of them deal with some dimension of the customer mix—size of order, channel of distribution, location, industry, etc. It is in analyses of this sort that the concept of attributable cost is most needed. Variable cost is too narrow to fit the scope of the decisions to be made, while joint costs are ordinarily so numerous that full cost has no analytical meaning whatsoever.

In reaction to years of neglect in this area, enthusiasts for distribution cost analysis may overstate their case. This kind of analysis is expensive, and it is easy to undertake it too often or carry it to too fine a degree of detail. Means are justified only by the ends to be served, and the analysis should be carried only as far as the application seems to require.

DISCUSSION QUESTIONS

1. List the steps the analyst must take in functional cost analysis.

2. What special difficulties hinder the measurement of functional unit cost that were not encountered in the measurement of product unit cost in the factory?

3. Which functional costs, if any, should be unitized for use in distribution cost analysis?

4. What is a "governing factor"? How does it relate to the "work unit" defined in Chapter 16?

5. What is the relevance of the divisibility of fixed costs to segment cost analysis?

6. Should salesmen's salaries be allocated among product lines or among customer groups on the basis of salesmen's time records? Give your reasons.

7. Should distribution costs be assigned to revenue segments on the basis of predetermined rates or on the basis of the actual costs of the current period?

8. What kinds of costs are most likely to create a need for different pricing or marketing policies for small orders?

9. To what extent would distribution cost analysis provide data that are relevant to so-called product combination decisions—e.g., which products to emphasize in the marketing program?

10. A department store's management wishes to decide which products to display and sell at certain high-traffic locations in the store. Is distribution cost analysis likely to be of much help for this purpose?

11. American railroads have witnessed a sharp and continuing drop in rail passenger business since the end of World War II. Increases in passenger fares, curtailment of services, and tax abatements have been inadequate, it is

claimed, to permit the railroads to break even, much less to earn an adequate return on capital invested in passenger facilities. What problems would you encounter in trying to estimate the company's earnings from passenger business and how would you try to overcome these problems?

EXERCISES AND PROBLEMS

1. The controller and sales manager of the Krucut Manufacturing Company are seeking a means of revising the present method of assigning selling and administrative expenses to the company's products. The present method is to divide total expense by total sales, using the resulting ratio to assign these expenses to individual products. The sales manager has suggested that these allocations be discontinued entirely because they present a false picture of product profitability. The controller has replied that the president wouldn't stand for that inasmuch as he has insisted repeatedly that every product must bear its fair share of selling and administrative expense. According to the sales manager, "We have to do something. The plant is only working four days a week as it is, and the way the reports are now prepared the Old Man is likely to tell us to stop selling the entire line of foundry supplies because it is showing a big net loss. If we drop that line, we'll really be in the soup and the whole company is likely to go in the red. The Old Man should be grateful that we can cover the full cost of manufacturing the foundry supplies line even at the high factory burden rates you are using."

   Suggest a method of allocation that might satisfy the sales manager and also meet the president's requirement that every product bear its fair share of selling and administrative expenses.

2. The payroll section of the accounting department of the Hookrug Company consists of a supervisor, an assistant supervisor, and approximately 15 payroll clerks. Payroll preparation is not highly mechanized, and most of the work is done by the clerks working with standard deduction tables and the employees' master personnel cards.

   The amount of time spent by a clerk in preparing a payroll line—that is, computation of gross pay, deductions, and net pay for a single employee— depends on a number of factors, but the number of payroll lines is a good index of the volume of activity in this operation.

   An average clerk can process a maximum of 3,600 payroll lines a month, but this rate cannot be kept up for more than two or three months. The company's rule of thumb has been to hire payroll clerks on the basis of expected average work loads over the next six months. In a normal month each payroll clerk would be expected to process between 3,300 and 3,400 payroll lines.

   The monthly operating costs of the payroll section vary to a certain extent from month to month, although all clerical employees are salaried. Costs and volume in a normal or average month and in the month of March were as follows:

	Normal Month	March
Volume (payroll lines)...........	50,000	55,000
Costs:		
Supervisor.....................	$ 715	$ 715
Assistant supervisor..............	500	500
Clerks.........................	6,000	6,650
Supplies.......................	2,000	1,650
Equipment rental...............	1,500	1,500
Floor space....................	450	550
Total Costs...................	$11,165	$11,565

The only costs that vary directly with volume in the short run are supplies costs. A full-time supervisor would be required for this section even if its volume were to fall to 40 percent of normal. The assistant supervisor shares responsibility for maintaining orderly work flows and in addition spends approximately half of her time working directly on payrolls to help handle peak loads and deal with particularly difficulty cases. If the departmental work load were to fall to 30,000 payroll lines a month the assistant supervisor would no longer be needed but if volume were to expand beyond 70,000 payroll lines an additional assistant would be needed.

Equipment rental costs shown in the table above represent approximately one third of the rentals paid by the company for a number of general-purpose bookkeeping machines, used by the billing, accounts receivable, and accounts payable sections as well as by the payroll section. As the company's business has grown, the number of bookkeeping machines installed has increased, more or less in proportion to the growth in volume. Machine rentals are shown in the monthly budgets as a fixed cost, however.

Floor space charges represent the average cost of building depreciation, taxes, insurance, heat, light, janitorial service, etc., allocated among departments on the basis of floor space occupied. The present office space available to the accounting department is regarded as adequate for the foreseeable future, even if office work loads increase substantially.

The Northeast Sales Region of this company normally employs 1,000 people, 400 of whom are paid monthly, the remaining 600 being paid weekly. (A normal month includes 4⅓ weekly paydays.) During March the Northeast Sales Region had 380 employees on the monthly payroll and 660 on the weekly payroll. Five weekly payrolls were prepared during the month.

In preparing a statement of the profitability of the Northeast Sales Region during the month of March, how much of the cost of the payroll section should the accountant deduct from regional revenues? Indicate clearly the basis on which you calculated the charge and state your reasons for selecting that basis.

*3. The delivery department of the Egbert Company operates under a departmental budget which recognizes three separate functions: (1) loading and unloading, (2) truck operation, and (3) truck repairs. Costs directly

---

traceable to each of these functions are charged to functional accounts. All other fixed charges, mainly supervision of the department's operation and rent on the garage and truck repair shop, are charged to general department accounts and not to specific functions.

The departmental budget for the current year is based on the following data:

	Loading and Unloading	Truck Operation	Truck Repairs	Undistributed Fixed Charges
Normal monthly volume	380 man-hrs.	11,000 miles	11,000 miles	...
Variable cost per unit:				
Labor..................	$2.40	$0.31	$0.05	...
Supplies and parts........	...	.15	.02	...
Outside repairs...........	...	...	.04	...
Employee benefits........	.24	.031	.005	...
Total Variable.........	$2.64	$ .491	$ .115	...
Fixed costs per month:				
Labor..................	...	...	...	$ 900
Rent....................	...	...	...	400
Depreciation.............	$ 20	$ 500	$ 100	...
Insurance................	5	125	45	20
Taxes...................	1	20	80	...
Employee benefits........	...	...	...	90
Total Fixed............	$ 26	$ 645	$ 225	$1,410

The loading platform occupies 10 percent of the rented space, the repair shop occupies 15 percent, and the remaining 75 percent is used as a garage. Normal driving speed is 15 miles per road hour, not including unloading time.

During the month of May the department's trucks logged 12,000 miles in 820 hours of road time exclusive of unloading time. Loading and unloading operations consumed 400 man-hours. The department's accounts showed the following costs for the month:

	Loading and Unloading	Truck Operation	Truck Repairs	Undistributed Fixed Charges
Labor.....................	$ 940	$3,690	$ 450	$ 920
Overtime premium.........	...	...	10	240
Supplies and parts..........	...	1,710	160	...
Outside repairs............	...	...	310	...
Employee benefits..........	94	369	46	116
Rent......................	...	...	...	400
Depreciation..............	20	522	100	...
Insurance.................	5	130	45	24
Taxes.....................	1	20	80	...
Total.................	$1,060	$6,441	$1,201	$1,700

Bulk deliveries during the month accounted for 9000 miles, 500 hours of road time, and 200 hours of loading and unloading time. Express deliveries accounted for the remaining mileage and time. Prepare an analysis showing the cost to be distributed to these two segments of the company's business. Be prepared to defend your treatment of fixed costs.

4. As part of the preparation for its defense in a Robinson-Patman case, C. E. Niehoff & Company conducted a series of time and motion studies of order-processing operations. Seventeen orders of varying sizes were selected for study, and the processing times were obtained for each of these by a time-study engineer. The engineer then added 25 percent to these observed times to allow for personal needs and fatigue. The total processing times, priced at standard wage rates for individual operations are listed in the table below:

Order No.	No. of Items	No. of Packages	Net Billing	Processing Cost	Cost per Dollar (in Cents)
44524...............	1	2	$ 12.00	$ 1.1909	9.92
44525...............	6	23	37.66	1.3141	3.49
44576...............	20	29	45.14	1.9457	4.31
44575...............	8	49	56.51	2.0506	3.66
45968...............	33	69	125.20	2.6529	2.11
44572...............	25	116	134.47	3.2335	2.33
46162...............	37	171	206.79	3.6094	1.74
44577...............	36	86	208.64	3.3236	1.59
44573...............	63	163	223.76	4.7155	2.11
45969...............	49	110	259.80	3.8108	1.47
45945...............	56	163	305.01	5.4135	1.77
46161...............	49	236	341.79	4.4516	1.30
44991...............	68	391	496.98	7.1486	1.44
45078...............	81	334	523.22	8.6659	1.66
45301...............	101	623	785.80	10.7736	1.36
45079...............	94	598	811.57	11.4696	1.41
44993...............	89	469	846.66	10.3696	1.23

Source: Herbert F. Taggart, *Cost Justification* (Ann Arbor: University of Michigan, Graduate School of Business Administration, Bureau of Business Research, 1959), p. 408.

a) On a sheet of graph paper, plot processing costs per dollar of net billing against size of order (measured by net billings) and draw a line of relationship freehand, as accurately as you can.

b) Assuming that these are the best data available, indicate how you would use these figures in:
   (1) Setting a minimum order size.
   (2) Estimating the profitability of different customer groups.

c) Comment on the methods used to obtain the data and their adequacy for the purposes outlined in (b).

5. The Henlo Company has separate sales divisions for each of its product lines. The company's factories are not specialized by product lines but serve all divisions to varying degrees.

One division, the Hardy Products Division, sells its products in part through wholesalers and in part through retail dealers. Wholesalers pay a lower price than retailers to compensate them for warehousing, advertising, and other sales-related functions that would otherwise have to be performed by the Hardy Products Division. The following data can be regarded as typical of a full year's activity under the present rate structure:

	Wholesale Business	Retail Business
Revenue from sales......................	$500,000	$700,000
Cost of goods sold......................	$420,000	$420,000
Number of salesmen's calls...............	500	4,500
Number of invoice lines.................	45,000	255,000

Additional data:

(1) The division's six salesmen are all on salary. When adjusted for changes in salary rates and outside price levels, the cost of sales solicitation per salesman (salaries, travel, and samples) has remained roughly constant from year to year. The number of salesmen has been increased from three to six in the past few years as Henlo's business volume has expanded. The solicitation costs of obtaining the sales listed in the preceding table total $84,000 a year.

(2) A call on a wholesaler takes approximately one and one-half times as long as a call on a retailer. Wholesalers are also farther apart than retailers, and in an experiment conducted two years ago, the company found that a salesman assigned full time to wholesale accounts made calls at an average annual rate of 450 calls a year, whereas a salesman working full time on retail accounts made calls at the rate of 900 calls a year.

(3) The Hardy Products distribution network consists of 25 wholesalers, serving 500 retailers, and 400 additional retailers served directly by Hardy Products.

(4) Costs of inventory record keeping, order receiving and filling, invoicing, accounts receivable bookkeeping, and collecting total $138,000 a year. These are regarded as fixed but have increased from year to year in parallel with the increase in the number of invoice lines.

(5) Advertising expenditures amount to $62,000 a year. Advertising is directed exclusively to retailers and could be discontinued entirely if all sales were made through wholesalers. Advertising's purpose in this case is to keep the company's name familiar to retailers. Increased advertising would be unlikely to increase sales, but decreased advertising would very likely lead to a reduction in sales volume.

(6) Inventory storage costs which are incurred exclusively to service retailers amount to $24,000 a year. Storage costs consist entirely of warehouse rent, based on the amount of space used. These costs tend to increase from year to year, roughly in proportion to increases in the standard cost of goods sold.

(7) The cost of goods sold is approximately 30 percent fixed and 70 percent variable. The fixed costs are largely indivisible.

Assuming that the data above are typical of the costs and effectiveness of wholesale and retail distribution if the Hardy Products Division is to distribute its products exclusively through one channel of distribution or the other, which one should it choose? If wholesale distribution is selected, the additional wholesalers would be approximately as effective in promoting Hardy products as the present wholesalers. Show your computations and state any assumptions you have made.

6. A company has two products, X and Y, for which the following data are available:

	Product X	Product Y
Selling price per unit.......................	$5.00	$2.00
Standard manufacturing cost per unit:		
Materials................................	$0.50	$0.45
Labor....................................	1.00	0.50
Overhead.................................	1.50	0.75
Total....................................	$3.00	$1.70
Units produced and sold per month............	50,000	200,000
Sales discounts and allowances per month......	$12,500	$ 4,000
Advertising and other direct selling costs per month................................	20,000	20,000
Salesmen's commission per unit...............	$0.25	$0.05

Additional information:

(1) Both products use the same manufacturing facilities, and all present facilities would still be required if only one of these two products were manufactured.

(2) At normal volume, variable overhead costs constitute 80 percent of manufacturing overhead.

(3) Manufacturing variances are apportioned between the two products on the basis of relative total standard direct labor cost per month. The manufacturing variances reflected in the net income (loss) figures above are:

Overhead volume, $3,000 per month—unfavorable.

Quantity and spending, $45,000 per month—unfavorable.

These variances are not traceable to individual products and are not regarded as variable with output.

(4) Costs of sales promotion, general company administration, etc., not otherwise specified above are regarded as fixed and are not traceable to either product. They amount to $52,000 a month and are allocated between the two products on the basis of relative gross sales dollars. Elimination of *either* product would permit a reduction in these costs of $10,000 per month.

(5) No change in annual sales volume is expected in the near future.

(6) The income tax rate is 50 percent on all taxable income, gains, and losses.

(7) In evaluating capital expenditure proposals, the company applies a return on investment standard of 10 percent, after taxes.

a) Prepare an income statement for each product that will fully distribute all company expenses, with subtotals for variable profit and attributable profit. Compute net income (loss) per unit, before taxes.

b) If the company were to discontinue the manufacture of product X, it could reduce working capital by $10 million. Discontinuation of product Y would release $2 million in working capital for other uses. None of the company's other assets would be released by the abandonment of either product. On the basis of this information and the data given above, would you recommend discontinuation of product X? Product Y? State your reasoning. (Do not attempt to evaluate the desirability of discontinuing both products and going out of business entirely—not enough data are provided.)

7. A company manufactures and sells three products. Its market is divided into three sales regions for which the following monthly data are typical:

	Region A	Region B	Region C
Orders:			
Number of orders..................	800	900	1,500
Number of units:			
Product X........................	2,000	1,000	10,000
Product Y........................	8,000	14,000	7,000
Product Z........................	5,000	5,000	10,000
Shipments:			
Weight (pounds)...................	27,000	31,000	57,000
Number of customers..............	2,000	2,200	3,000
Number of new customers..........	50	55	100
Number of employees..............	15	16	20
Sales discounts granted...........	$ 1,000	$ 2,000	$ 4,000
Field selling expense..............	8,000	9,000	10,000
Branch office expense.............	4,000	4,500	5,000
Freight and delivery...............	2,000	2,500	1,500

Factory cost, selling price, and sales commissions on each of the company's three products are:

	Selling Price	Standard Factory Cost	Salesmen's Commissions
Product X.............	$ 5	$4	$0.25
Product Y.............	10	6	.50
Product Z.............	2	1	.10

Variable factory costs represent 75 percent of total factory cost at normal volume. Sixty percent of the fixed factory costs are reasonably divisible.

Unit costs have been developed for a number of the activities performed by the head office, as follows:

Payroll................................	$ 6.00 per employee per month
Order processing.......................	1.20 per order
Packing and shipping...................	0.03 per pound
Credit review..........................	12.00 per new customer
Cashier................................	0.25 per customer
General accounting.....................	0.35 per customer

These unit costs represent cost elements that are almost entirely fixed in the short run but are divisible and thus variable in response to large changes in volume. They do not include highly indivisible costs such as space rental.

Other head office expenses not previously mentioned are highly fixed and have the following normal monthly amounts:

Executive salaries............................	$20,000
Secretarial salaries...........................	5,000
General office expenses.......................	30,000
Advertising..................................	8,000
Computer system:	
Central processor..........................	3,000
Peripheral equipment......................	2,000

Records of computer utilization show that three of the services listed above are heavy users of the computer system, with the following utilization percentages:

	Central Processor	Peripheral Equipment
Payroll preparation.............	5%	10%
Order processing...............	1	15
General accounting.............	2	8

The employees in the three sales regions constitute 10 percent of total company employment; the computer time in the table above refers to all company payrolls combined. Computer system costs are fixed and not significantly divisible.

Prepare a statement that in your opinion will best indicate the relative profitability of the three sales territories. Comment on any analytical problems you encountered and justify your solutions to these problems.

8. The Western Appliances Limited income statement for the year ended December 31, 19x1, appears below:

Sales (1,900,000 units).............................			$3,800,000
Cost of sales.....................................			2,280,000
Gross profit......................................			$1,520,000
Packing and shipping:			
Shipping containers............................	$ 91,750		
Packing and shipping labor expenses...............	221,250		
Freight-out....................................	375,750	$688,750	
Selling expenses (excluding advertising):			
Sales manager's salary...........................	$ 15,200		
Salesmen's salaries.............................	32,000		
Salesmen's commissions..........................	24,000		
Agency commissions.............................	30,000		
Bad debts.....................................	11,500	112,700	
Advertising:			
Local newspapers...............................	$ 43,500		
National magazines.............................	57,000	100,500	
Administrative expenses (fixed).....................		64,750	966,700
Net Operating Profit..............................			$ 553,300

The company manufactures a single product in a variety of colors. The selling price is $2 a unit.

The product is distributed in four market areas—A, B, C, and D.

District A is the district in which the manufacturing plant and offices are located. No salesmen are employed. Orders are received through the mail and by telephone, and customers send their trucks to the plant to pick up their orders when ready.

District B is located 100 miles from the plant. The company employs four salesmen in this area, each on a commission basis. The company also places a one-quarter-page advertisement once each week in the local newspaper.

District C is located 200 miles from the plant. The company employs eight salesmen in the area, each on a salary basis. The company takes one quarter of a page three times a week in the local paper in district C; the cost per insertion is twice as much as that in district B.

District D is an agency. It is 400 miles distant from the plant. The company shares with the agency the cost of a quarter-page weekly advertisement in the local paper on a 1:3 ratio, the space cost being the same as in district B.

The product is packaged in containers of three different sizes: namely, 16's (small), 32's (medium), and 48's (large), and shipments are made in case lots only. It is assumed that each order calls for one case.

Sales commissions are paid on a flat percentage of sales basis.

The following unit costs per case have been determined:

	Small	Medium	Large
Container.	$1.00	$1.50	$2.00
Packing and shipping labor expenses.	3.00	3.50	4.00
Freight-out (cost per 100 miles).	2.00	3.50	5.00

A statistical analysis of the marketing operation during 19x1 shows the following:

	Total	District A	District B	District C	District D
Number of orders:					
Small cases.	22,500	2,500		20,000	
Medium cases.	30,500	5,000	7,500	15,000	3,000
Large cases.	11,750		7,500		4,250
Provision for bad debts—					
% of sales.		¼ of 1%	⅛ of 1%	⅜ of 1%	½ of 1%

a) Prepare a set of statements showing the profitability of each sales district. Describe and defend the basis on which costs were assigned to each district.

b) Prepare a set of statements showing the profitability of each case size. Describe and defend the basis on which costs were assigned to each size group.

c) It has been proposed that an additional $50,000 a year be spent on local advertising in district C. By how much must the sales volume of the district increase to warrant such an expenditure?

   (Adapted from an examination prepared by the Society of Industrial
                               and Cost Accountants of Canada.)

9. The Mitchell Products Company manufactures two products, Hank and Yank. These are distributed through a single sales force, organized into two territories with branch offices in Cleveland and Chicago. Hank is sold in 50-gallon drums to all customers in both territories. Yank is sold in 24-can cartons to "commercial" customers in the Cleveland territory and to "trade" customers in both territories. Finished products are shipped directly from the company's Cleveland factory to warehouses located adjacent to each branch. The Cleveland branch office and the company's head office are both located at the Cleveland factory. All billing, accounting and general administration are performed in the head office.

Products are billed to the branch offices at standard manufacturing cost. Salesmen are paid a salary plus commission. Unit prices, costs, and sales commission rates are:

	Hank	Yank
Price........................	$80 per drum	$10 per carton
Standard cost..................	$48 per drum	$ 8 per carton
Salesmen's commission...........	6% of sales	3% of sales

Freight charges from Cleveland to Chicago are $1 per drum for Hank and $0.10 per carton for Yank.

Unit sales and other statistics for the month of June were as follows:

	Cleveland		Chicago		Total
	Trade	Commercial	Trade	Commercial	
Sales in units:					
Hank (No. of drums)...	5,000	1,250	4,375	1,000	11,625
Yank (No. of cartons)..	7,000	1,000	8,000	....	16,000
Free samples distributed:					
Hank................	10	1	15	2	28
Yank................	20	....	15	....	35
Orders received..........	500	700	400	500	2,100
Invoice lines............	900	800	700	600	3,000
Customer accounts.......	1,000	1,500	800	900	4,200
Credit and collections.....	20%	30%	15%	35%	100%
Number of employees.....		80		70	
Warehouse inventories:					
Hank (drums).........		8,000		7,500	
Yank (cartons)........		12,000		10,000	

Direct branch expenses for the month of June, in addition to those to be derived from the above data, were as follows:

	Cleveland	Chicago
Branch salaries.....................	$20,000	$18,000
Travel..............................	15,000	10,000
Entertainment:		
Trade............................	2,000	2,100
Commercial.......................	300	200
Warehousing........................	4,000	4,600
Other branch expenses................	10,000	11,000

Branch warehousing costs are budgeted as follows:

	Cleveland	Chicago
Fixed costs...........................	$2,400	$2,800
Variable costs:		
Per drum shipped....................	$ 0.20	$ 0.25
Per carton shipped..................	0.04	0.05

Four cartons of Yank occupy the same amount of warehouse space as one drum of Hank.

No breakdowns of other items of branch expense are available, but branch salesmen have submitted the following data for the month:

	Cleveland	Chicago
Number of calls:		
Trade.....................................	700	800
Commercial............................	500	400
Percentage of time:		
Hank....................................	90%	85%
Yank....................................	10%	15%

Head office expenses for the month, together with budget information for the various head office departments, are shown in the following table:

	Budget		Actual for June
	Fixed per Month	Variable per Month	
Executive salaries....................	$30,000	....	$30,000
Billing..............................	800	$0.40 per inv. line	2,100
Accounts receivable..................	1,200	0.10 per cust. acct.	1,500
Cashier (½ charged to factory)........	6,000	....	5,800
Payroll (¾ charged to factory)*.......	4,000	5.00 per employee	7,200
Advertising†.......................	10,000	....	10,500
Credit and collection.................	2,000	3.00 per order	8,000
Other.............................	13,000	....	13,900

* There were 450 factory employees during June.
† Ninety percent of advertising is for Hank, and 80 percent is directed to trade customers.

a) Prepare analyses of the profit contribution made by each territory, by each product, and by each class of customer during the month.

b) Prepare an income statement for the company for the month.

Part VI

Profit Planning and Control Systems

Chapter 24

PROFIT PLANNING
AND INTERNAL REPORTING

MANAGEMENT exerts control over a company's operations at three stages: before the fact, through its planning decisions; during operations, through direction, supervision, and coordination; and after the fact, through its responses to various kinds of feedback data. This last stage blends imperceptibly into the first, and the cycle begins anew.

These processes were first discussed in Chapters 1 and 2 before the concepts and methods of cost accounting were introduced. The application of planning and feedback reporting to operating costs was developed in some detail in Part III, and now it is time to return once more to these questions, focusing on the planning, measurement, and reporting of *profit performance*.

PROFIT PLANNING

Control of business operations starts with the formulation of company goals and subgoals. Goals may be established at any level and for any dimension of performance that management deems important. For example, a lower level executive may have such diverse goals as the reduction of the accident rate in his department, meeting materials yield standards, and getting four of his employees through a skill-improvement program. The industrial relations manager may aim for reduced employee turnover, improvement of the employee grievance procedure, and the negotiation of a new union contract within a specified cost limit and without a strike. The company's president, in turn, may strive for an overall rate of return objective, the completion of plans for a 10 percent expansion of capacity, and so on.

Although we are concerned here only with the establishment of profit goals, this is not to imply that other dimensions of performance are not important. Monetary and nonmonetary objectives are not even independent of each other, as any manager must recognize who wishes to establish and meet standards of what he conceives to be his responsibilities to society. If good architectural design is going to add 5 or 10 percent to the cost of a new factory, for example, the manager has a difficult problem in balancing conflicting objectives.

By concentrating on cost and profit performance, the accountant is often accused of measuring things that are easiest to measure and ignoring the rest. Valid though this criticism may be, profitability is still the central objective and the *sine qua non* of company survival, growth, and community service. The means used to plan for profits are well worth study.

Purposes of Profit Goals

All company goals probably have the same basic purposes:

1. To motivate executives toward achievement of the goals.
2. To guide executives by spelling out what has to be done to achieve the goals.
3. To provide a bench mark against which to compare actual achievements.

Profit goals are typically embodied in periodic *profit plans* or *profit budgets*. These plans consist not only of the profit figure itself but also include the means that are contemplated to achieve that profit. A large pharmaceutical firm, for example, includes in its profit plan such details as how many visits each of its sales representatives will make to each category of customers, which products will be emphasized, in which sizes and forms, how many free samples will be distributed, and so on.

Establishment of the profit plan, in other words, simultaneously establishes the methods to be used to achieve it, at least in broad outline. Profit targets that represent the long-run desires of top management but which are not expected to be met during the coming period are not profit plans, as that term is usually used.

Setting Profit Objectives

Although the managerial guidance and measurement bench-mark purposes of profit plans may be apparent, the motivational objective may not. Most profit plans today are established jointly by profit-responsible executives, their subordinates, and their immediate superiors. The purpose of this multilevel participation is partly to secure a more carefully thought-out profit plan and partly to increase the motivational impact of the resulting plan. Participation, the argument runs, will lead the subordinate executive to accept the plan more readily and to commit himself more unreservedly to its achievement.

Some reference to the literature bearing on the connection between participation and performance was made in Chapter 12, and that discussion will not be repeated here. Although the behavioral scientists are not entirely agreed on the implications of the various empirical studies that have been made, one interpretation is that if participation in profit planning is to affect performance, it must succeed in increasing the executive's sense of identification with a larger group which accepts profit generation as a desirable goal.[1] Executives of many companies believe that it does just that.

One point that is often misunderstood in this connection is the role of higher management. Some people have interpreted participation to mean a complete abdication of responsibility by managers at higher levels in the organization. This is certainly not the intent. For one thing, one manager's plan is an integral part of his superior's plan, so that the latter cannot abdicate responsibility even if he wants to. Secondly, participation is likely to further company goals only if some leadership force steers it in that direction. In a typical planning procedure, the manager and his subordinates discuss the plans as they are being developed, and the subordinate is expected to convince his boss that the plan he finally submits is not only feasible but also is as profitable a plan as can be designed, consistent with the manager's nonprofit objectives.

In the final analysis, each manager has to use participation in the way it seems to work best. Individuals' personalities differ, as do their natural styles of leadership. Whereas one executive may offer frequent suggestions to his subordinates, another may operate strictly as a reviewing agent, trying to find weaknesses in the plans submitted to him, or constantly demanding more detail or more evidence until he is satisfied with what his subordinate has done.

Program versus Organic Budgeting

Profit plans can be developed on either a program basis or an organizational basis. In organization-based or *organic* budgeting, primary responsibility for planning is vested in line executives who supervise the personnel who will implement the plan. In program budgeting, on the other hand, the focus is on individual product lines or customer groups, with a separate plan being prepared for each as a responsibility of a program executive. The budget component for a given organization

---

[1] Selwyn Becker and David Green, Jr., "Budgeting and Employee Behavior," *The Journal of Business,* October, 1962, pp. 392–402; and George J. Benston, "The Role of the Firm's Accounting System for Motivation," *The Accounting Review,* April, 1963, pp. 347–54.

unit is determined jointly by the various programs that affect that unit.

The choice between these two approaches depends largely on the locus of responsibility for profit planning. Program budgeting is typically encountered when the organization structure has been modified to provide for one or more program executives. We have already encountered one such executive, the research project manager. More significant for profit planning, however, is the so-called *product manager.*

The position of product manager has existed in some industries such as meat-packing for a long time, but only in recent years has it come into widespread use. It has arisen in companies in which a completely product-oriented organization structure would be inefficient, so that individual product programs have to share in the resources of factories or other organization units. In many such companies, management has come to believe that the line organization structure is not conducive to aggressive and coherent product program development, and has superimposed a set of product managers on the conventional line organization.

The product manager is typically responsible for both product and profit planning. He has at least advisory responsibility for selecting channels and methods of distribution and for selecting advertising and promotional material for his product line. He often acts as liaison man between the production and sales departments, but he seldom has any direct authority over either. A meat-packer, for example, has a beef department, a pork department, a lamb department, and others, each with its own manager, even though most of the production and selling activity is conducted in multiprogram operating units.[2]

Because the product manager has no troops of his own, program budgeting can be a very delicate affair.[3] The line managers, particularly in marketing, have to reconcile the often conflicting demands of the various product managers. Because the line managers will have ultimate responsibility for the implementation of the various programs, and often for their results as well, they must work simultaneously with the various product managers to make sure that their commitments are

---

[2] A concise tabulation of a typical product manager's responsibilities is to be found in Michael Schiff and Martin Mellman, *Financial Management of the Marketing Function* (New York: Financial Executives Research Foundation, 1962), pp. 28–31.

[3] The structure of government agencies often makes program budgeting particularly difficult, but this is one of the most interesting developments in governmental budgeting to come along in recent years. See David Novick, *Program Budgeting in the Department of Defense* (Santa Monica, Calif.: The RAND Corp., 1964).

mutually consistent. With more people to satisfy at one time, the difficulty of planning becomes multiplied.

The Role of the Budget Director

As the foregoing would imply, profit planning is a responsibility of line management. The task of pulling together all the elements of a profit plan, however, ordinarily falls to the lot of the budget director or controller. The amount of detail and the number of interrelationships among components of the plan in a large corporation can be enormous, and the budget director has no easy task. Some of the work of reconciling conflicting demands and eliminating internal inconsistencies (e.g., planned sales in excess of production capacity) can be shifted to the product managers, if the company has them, but the budget director still has a difficult job.

The budget director or controller is also responsible for designing and securing support for the procedural aspects of profit planning, mainly the questions of what is to be budgeted, when, and by whom. This is ordinarily done by the budget staff, working closely with operating executives from beginning to end. The final installation is likely to be summarized in a budget manual or manuals, spelling out deadlines for various budget components, assigning responsibilities for budget preparation, prescribing forms, and describing the overall budget pattern. For example, Exhibit 24–1 shows the budget flow chart from the budget manual of a large decentralized company, indicating relationships between local management and the corporate staff. This is followed by a detailed time schedule of due dates for various parts of the plan.

Even if profit plan components have been reviewed carefully and critically all the way up the line within a given segment of the organization, the corporate controller or budget director often has the authority to subject the proposals to his own tests of feasibility and profitability. He is always free to seek clarification or question whether other alternatives have been investigated, and in some cases he even has the power to ask individual managers to revise their programs.[4] It must be emphasized that in taking any actions of this sort *the controller is acting as the agent of line management* and is applying tests that they would apply. The difference is probably not too great because top management often

---

[4] For further discussion of these points, see Neil W. Chamberlain, *The Firm: Micro-Economic Planning and Action* (New York: McGraw-Hill Book Co., Inc., 1962), chap. xi.

Exhibit 24–1

PLANNING SEQUENCE AND COORDINATION CHART

H E A D Q U A R T E R S   L O C A L

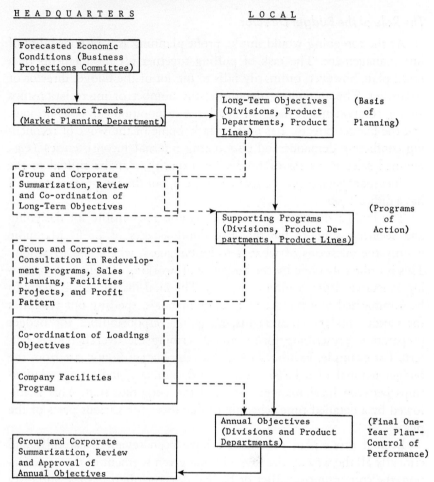

relies heavily on the controller for profitability criteria in any case. When the controller does not exercise this kind of rejection authority, a top management budget committee is often formed for the same purpose, but once again the analytical work itself is still within the province of the controller or budget director.

Plans as Guides to Management Action

The usefulness of goals and plans in guiding day-to-day managerial decisions should not be overemphasied. Conditions change in unexpected ways, and management's actions must tie in to the latest perception of reality. It would make no sense, for example, for a company to negotiate a loan in September merely because the annual plan formalized 10 months earlier had forecast a cash shortage at that time.

The process of developing comprehensive plans is too cumbersome to be repeated weekly or even monthly, the management has to use a more piecemeal approach to short-period planning. Just as company goals are reflected in periodic financial and operating plans, so these plans must be converted into schedules to make them operational. Schedules serve as instructions to operating personnel and are revised quarterly, monthly, weekly, or even in some instances daily.

The original plans, in other words, serve primarily as a fixed point of reference in a changing world. Departures from these plans are inevitable, and the real question is what forces have caused these departures. Without the fixed reference point, the quantification of change would be much more difficult.

REPORTING PROFIT RESULTS

Establishment of profit goals for various segments of a company's business also presumes the existence of a system for reporting internal profit results to the affected executives. These reports serve primarily to identify variances from planned results. Analysis of these variances can often help management find ways to change its operations so as to increase profits during the ensuing periods.

Profit Concepts for Internal Profit Reporting

Because management's decisions and actions typically center on individual *segments* of the enterprise—products, territories, customer groups, programs, etc.—these segments are also the focus of the periodic profit reports.

The profit contributed by any one segment can be measured on at least four different bases:

1. *Variable profit:* revenues less the variable costs attributable to these revenues.
2. *Contribution margin:* variable profit less traceable fixed costs.
3. *Attributable profit:* profit contribution less the nontraceable fixed costs that could be eliminated if the segment were to be abandoned.
4. *Net profit:* attributable profit less a pro rata share of all other nontraceable fixed costs.

Contribution margin and attributable profit are both intended to represent the direct profit that would be lost if the particular revenue segment were abandoned, but only the former can be measured routinely

Exhibit 24–2

PRODUCT PROFIT CONTRIBUTION STATEMENT

	All Products	Regular Products		Custom Products	
		Amount	% of Net Sales	Amount	% of Net Sales
Net sales........................	$2,000,000	$1,640,000	100.0	$360,000	100.0
Variable costs (standard):					
Factory........................	$1,097,600	$ 836,600		$261,000	
Order filling....................	65,100	52,600		12,500	
Total variable costs.............	$1,162,700	$ 889,200	54.2	$273,500	76.0
Variable profit....................	$ 837,300	$ 750,800	45.8	$ 86,500	24.0
Product-traceable fixed costs.........	$ 195,400	$ 148,500		$ 46,900	
Labor and materials variances.......	7,900	10,600		(2,700)	
Contribution margin...............	$ 634,000	$ 591,700	36.1	$ 42,300	11.8
Common fixed costs:					
Factory........................	$ 137,200				
Selling and administrative.........	283,500				
Net Income before Tax.............	$ 213,300				

without significant ambiguity. Furthermore, the focus of these reports is less on the absolute level of cost or profit and more on variances between planned and actual. For this kind of analysis, allocations of common fixed costs to individual product lines or other revenue segments serve no useful purpose. Therefore, historical segment profit reports can safely stop at contribution margin or *profit contribution,* as it is often called.

Exhibit 24–2, for example, makes no attempt to allocate nontraceable costs to individual product lines. The columns representing segment profit are carried down only to the contribution margin level, the amount available to cover the nontraceable fixed overheads and provide a margin for profit for the company as a whole. Company net income is the sum of these segment profit contributions, less the total of the fixed costs not traceable to individual segments.

Comparison Reports

The profit report shown in Exhibit 24–2 is of limited usefulness because it provides no comparison bench mark, but the profit contribu-

Exhibit 24–3

DISTRICT PROFIT PERFORMANCE REPORT

DISTRICT SALES AND EXPENSE SUMMARY

DISTRICT Boston   MONTH January, 1967

	Budget	Actual	Deviation	Actual % of Sales
Net sales billed	$500,000	$514,000	$14,000	100.0
Cost of sales	375,000	381,000	(6,000)	74.1
Gross margin	$125,000	$133,000	$ 8,000	25.9
District office costs:				
Branch salaries	$ 2,500	$ 2,500	. . .	0.5
Sales salaries	25,000	25,500	$ (500)	5.0
Travel	8,000	6,800	1,200	1.3
Entertainment	1,000	1,300	(300)	0.2
Local advertising	500	500	. . .	0.1
Storage and delivery	7,000	7,300	(300)	1.4
Branch office expense	900	1,100	(200)	0.2
Other	600	700	(100)	0.1
Total district cost	$ 45,500	$ 45,700	$ (200)	8.8
District Profit Contribution	$ 79,500	$ 87,300	$ 7,800	17.1

tion concept can be applied in comparative statements as well. Exhibit 24–3, for instance, shows a report that might be issued to the district sales manager as an overall summary of his district's profit contribution. The business segment in this case is the company's sales in this company's Boston district rather than companywide sales of a specific product line as in Exhibit 24–2. The format is the same, however, in that no allocations of head office fixed costs are charged against the individual district's revenues.

A glance at this report will tell the district manager that his actual sales volume was $514,000, that this gave him a gross margin $8,000 larger than his profit plan called for, and that his district profit contribution for the month was $7,800 greater than his profit objective.

While this kind of report is useful as an overall summary, it does not provide the district manager with any explanation of the *sources* of the main deviations. Another report that he might receive is shown in Exhibit 24–4, to permit him to monitor the performance of his individual salesmen. Although many companies limit such summaries to sales volume alone, the interjection of product costs and traceable fixed expenses can add a significant dimension to the sales figures. Salesman Kelly, for example, sold $4,000 more than Williams during the month but showed a $700 smaller profit contribution. Williams, on the other hand, failed to meet his profit objective for the period, as did three of the other salesmen.

Some companies prefer to show figures for the comparable period of the previous year in addition to the deviations from the profit plan. No serious objection can be raised to this practice as long as it does not lead

Exhibit 24–4

DISTRICT SALESMAN REPORT

				Profit Contribution		
Salesman	Net Sales Billed	Cost of Sales	Salary and Expenses	Amount	Budget Deviation	% of Sales
Brown	$ 40,000	$ 29,200	$ 2,400	$ 8,400	$ (400)	21.0%
Cannon	31,000	24,300	3,200	3,500	(900)	11.3
Evars	63,000	42,700	4,100	16,200	3,700	25.7
Johnson	30,000	24,200	2,900	2,900	(1,400)	9.7
Kelly	54,000	40,100	4,200	9,700	200	18.0
Lusso	47,000	34,400	3,100	9,500	2,100	20.2
McGregor	76,000	56,000	3,800	16,200	4,000	21.3
Nelson	55,000	41,900	3,300	9,800	500	17.8
Stern	68,000	51,600	3,600	12,800	1,200	18.8
Williams	50,000	36,600	3,000	10,400	(600)	20.8
Total	$514,000	$381,000	$33,600	$99,400	$8,400	19.4%
Other branch expenses				12,100	(600)	1.7
District Profit Contribution				$87,300	$7,800	17.1%

SALESMAN PERFORMANCE SUMMARY

DISTRICT Boston   MONTH January, 1967

to *de facto* displacement of the current year's profit plan as the relevant bench mark. Graphic presentations of year-to-date performance against planned performance are also useful supplements to the tabulated figures in most cases.

The district manager might receive another report summarizing the same data but arranged as in Exhibit 24–5, if he is expected to influence product mix actively. Notice that in this exhibit a much smaller percentage of expenses is assigned to individual segments of the district's business. Salesmen's salaries and expenses are traceable to individual salesmen but not to individual product lines. Local advertising, on the other hand, in this instance is completely product-traceable and thus moves "above the line."

Exhibit 24–5

DISTRICT PRODUCT SALES REPORT

PRODUCT CONTRIBUTION REPORT							
DISTRICT Boston					MONTH January, 1967		

Product Line	Net Sales Billed		Cost of Sales	Other Product Expenses	Profit Contribution	
	Actual	Variance			Actual	Variance
White Shield	$204,000	$26,000	$136,000	$500	$ 67,500	$14,000
Red Label	133,000	(50,000)	103,000	. . .	30,000	(11,000)
Commercial	177,000	38,000	142,000	. . .	35,000	5,000
Total	$514,000	$14,000	$381,000	$500	$132,500	$ 8,000
Other branch expenses					45,200	(200)
District Profit Contri-bution					$ 87,300	$ 7,800

It is unnecessary, of course, to carry all reports down to the same final profit or variance figure. The tie-in has been made here, however, to emphasize that a single set of figures has been combined in several ways to illustrate different facets of the problem.

Reports for Higher Management

Profit reports for higher levels of marketing management are similar in structure to those just illustrated, but the level of aggregation is higher. For line management, the basic segmentation is typically along organizational lines, as in Exhibit 24–6. A product manager would receive a similar type of report, limited to his own product line.

Sales management may also get routine or special profit reports on such bases as customer group or channel of distribution. Such reports are often restricted to gross sales or variable product profit unless the importance of other expenses is great enough to justify some form of distribution cost analysis, as described in the previous chapter.

It will be noticed that none of these performance reports has shown any factory cost variances. Manufacturing performance measures become an integral part of routine profit reports only at the level at which manufacturing and marketing responsibility are joined. In a straight line organization, this may be at the divisional or top-management level. When product managers are used, they may see the results of manufacturing as well as marketing operations. The product manager's report, however, should show manufacturing cost variances only if they

Exhibit 24–6

MARKETING DIVISION PERFORMANCE REPORT

DISTRICT SALES PERFORMANCE SUMMARY
(000 Omitted)

MONTH January, 1967

District	Net Sales Billed	Cost of Sales	District Selling Expense	District Profit Contribu- tion	Budget Deviation	Contri- bution % of Sales
Boston	$ 514	$ 381	$ 48	$ 85	$ 8	16.5%
New York	946	603	84	259	25	27.4
Baltimore	472	365	51	56	(33)	11.9
Atlanta	348	260	42	46	5	13.2
Pittsburgh	588	434	63	91	3	15.5
Cleveland	627	472	58	97	(2)	15.5
Total	$3,495	$2,515	$346	$634	$ 6	18.1%
Head office expense:						
Management				$ 40	$ 1	
Market research				26	(1)	
Advertising				103	10	
Other				23	(3)	
Total head office expense				$192	$ 7	5.5
Net Marketing Margin				$442	$13	12.6%

depend at least partly on characteristics of the product line or methods of distribution. Excessive unfavorable factory cost variances, for example, may signify an ultraliberal product modification policy which may be worthy of the product manager's attention. Alternatively, if it shows that the factory cannot meet cost standards in a particular line, consideration may be given to changing product specifications, raising prices, or something else.

Top-Management Reports

At least one and sometimes two or even more additional management levels are superimposed on the sales management level to which this series of reports was carried. The sales manager, for example, may report to a product division manager who has line responsibility for both sales and production of a particular set of product lines. The division manager, in turn, is answerable to company top management, which requires still another report structure.

Top management's or division management's main focus is on the performance of major organization units within its jurisdiction. Reports organized on this basis can be backed up by supplementary schedules which classify profit in other ways, but these alternative classification schemes should not be allowed to displace the organizational report entirely. To do justice to the subject of divisional and top-management profit measurement, however, more space must be provided than can be spared in this chapter. We shall return to this topic in depth in Chapter 25.

PROFIT VARIANCE ANALYSIS

Most internal profit statements include some form of analysis or commentary on the deviations between actual and budgeted performance. The commentary may call attention to unusual events that had significant favorable or unfavorable effects on reported income during the period, and it may indicate whether these effects are expected to continue and what actions management is taking to cope with or capitalize on the situation.

These qualitative commentaries are often supported and supplemented by quantitative breakdowns of the aggregate profit variance in each segment of the business. The form that this profit variance will take will depend on the nature of the company and of its product line, as well as the preferences of its management. The scheme described in the following pages is thus only a rough model, to be adapted as circumstances seem to warrant.

Levels of Causality

An ideal variance analysis would identify the ultimate or primary cause of each element of the overall profit variance. Thus, so much would be attributed to orders lost due to price competition, so much to higher materials prices resulting from an increase in rail freight tariffs, and so on.

Unfortunately, although this can often be done for a portion of the total variance, it cannot be done for all or even for the lion's share of the total in most cases. The variance analysis, therefore, usually has to focus on intermediate causes or symptoms rather than on the primary causes. Examples of categories into which profit variances ordinarily can be split are:

1. Deviations from budgeted selling prices (sales price variances).
2. Deviations from budgeted physical sales volume (sales volume variances).
3. Deviations from budgeted product sales mix (sales mix variances).
4. Deviations from budgeted input prices (input price variances).

5. Deviations from standard costs and flexible budget allowances (input quantity and spending variances).

6. Deviations due to product costing procedures, accounting adjustments, etc.

These variances are not necessarily independent of each other—selling price and sales quantity variances are particularly interdependent—but they are, as one authority put it, convenient ways of "bringing to the attention of the reader the results of the market situation."[5]

Variance Analysis: An Example

A fully realistic variance analysis would require a far more complex example than we have space for. Let us assume, therefore, a company with only two product lines, a single sales force, and a one-department factory. All cost relationships are wholly linear. The company follows the variable costing principle in product costing but uses a supplemental burden rate to absorb fixed costs for public financial reporting. The following *standard* relationships have been established:

	Product Line A (% of List Price)	Product Line B (% of List Price)
Sales discounts and allowances...........	1.5	1.0
Variable factory costs...................	55.0	35.0
Fixed factory costs.....................	15.0	6.0
Variable selling and administrative costs	5.0	5.0

The profit plan for the month of July contained the following figures:

Sales (at standard list price):
Product line A.......................................$108,000
Product line B.. 60,000
Production (at standard list price)[6]:
Product line A.. 100,000
Product line B.. 60,000
Fixed selling and administrative costs.................... 35,000
Factory cost variances (overabsorbed).................... 600

The budgeted factory cost variance in this case was a *production volume* variance, computed as follows:

Fixed factory overhead absorbed by production:
Product line A: 15% × $100,000........................$15,000
Product line B: 6% × $60,000.......................... 3,600
Total absorbed....................................$18,600
Budgeted fixed factory overhead.......................... 18,000
Budgeted Overabsorption (Volume Variance)..............$ 600

---

[5] Harold C. Edey, *Business Budgets and Accounts* (2d ed.; London: Hutchinson University Library, 1960), p. 49.

[6] The factory production budget ordinarily would not be measured in dollars of gross sales value, but this measurement has the advantage here of reducing the complexity of the illustration without discarding anything of substance.

In other words, the factory production schedule during July called for a volume in excess of normal. No other cost variances were budgeted for the period.

The company's income statement for the month of July is shown in Exhibit 24–7. The format adopted for this exhibit differs substantially

Exhibit 24–7

COMPARATIVE INCOME STATEMENT
FOR THE MONTH OF JULY

	(A1) Actual	(A2) Budget	(A3) Variance
Gross sales (at standard list prices).................	$175,000	$168,000	$ 7,000
Less:			
Sales discounts and allowances....................	$ 3,100	$ 2,220	$ (880)
Standard variable factory cost of goods sold.......	85,250	80,400	(4,850)
Variable selling and administrative expense.........	8,600	8,400	(200)
Total variable expense.........................	$ 96,950	$ 91,020	$(5,930)
Variable profit......................................	$ 78,050	$ 76,980	$ 1,070
Other charges and credits:			
Standard fixed factory cost of goods sold............	(21,300)	(19,800)	(1,500)
Factory volume variance.........................	2,160	600	1,560
Other factory cost variances, net...................	(1,960)	...	(1,960)
Fixed selling and administrative expense............	(35,650)	(35,000)	(650)
Net Income before Taxes...........................	$ 21,300	$ 22,780	$(1,480)

The ( ) in the right-hand column denotes an unfavorable variance.

from that suggested earlier in this chapter and is designed solely to facilitate the presentation that follows. The exhibit reveals a $1,480 net unfavorable profit deviation from the profit plan for the month of July, and it is this figure which needs further investigation and explanation.

Sales Volume Variance

The $7,000 variance in gross sales indicates that aggregate sales volume was $7,000 greater than the original budget. The question is what effect this had on reported income.

If the increase in sales volume had been divided between products A and B in their budgeted proportions, then sales discounts and allowances, cost of goods sold, and variable selling and administrative expenses should have increased in the same proportions. These ratios, computed from the July budget, were as follows:

	Budgeted	
	Amount	% of Sales
Standard sales discounts and allowances.................	$ 2,220	1.32
Standard variable cost of goods sold.....................	80,400	47.86
Standard variable selling and administrative expense.......	8,400	5.00

Multiplying these percentages times the *actual* gross sales for the month indicates the variable profit that would have been expected if the $7,000 sales increase had been divided between the two product lines in their budgeted proportions:

```
Gross sales.......................................$175,000
Standard sales discounts and allowances..................$  2,310
Standard variable factory cost of goods sold..............  83,755
Standard variable selling and administrative expense........   8,750
Variable Profit......................................$ 80,185
```

The sales volume variance is the difference between this figure and the variable profit originally budgeted for the month:

	Variable Profit Budget at—		Sales Volume Variance
	Actual Volume	Budgeted Volume (from A2)	
Gross sales....................	$175,000	$168,000	$ 7,000
Standard sales discounts and allowances.........	$ 2,310	$ 2,220	(90)
Standard variable factory cost of goods sold......	83,755	80,400	(3,355)
Standard variable selling and administrative expense.......	8,750	8,400	(350)
Variable Profit.............................	$ 80,185	$ 76,980	$ 3,205

In other words, a volume increase of $7,000 would normally be accompanied by a $90 increase in sales discounts and allowances, a $3,355 increase in the variable factory cost of goods sold, and a $350 increase in variable selling and administrative expense. Thus if all of these relationships had been maintained during this period, the $7,000 increase in volume would have increased variable profit by $3,205. This is the sales volume variance for the month.

Sales Volume Variance under Absorption Costing

The preceding calculation is strictly applicable only in a variable costing system. In absorption costing an additional element is present:

the effect of sales volume variations on the amount of fixed factory costs charged against the revenues of the period.

In this case, for example, the planned cost of goods sold included $19,800 in fixed factory costs, or 11.786 percent of planned sales. Applying this ratio to actual gross sales yields a standard fixed cost of goods sold of $20,625. The revised computation of the sales volume variance now appears as follows:

	Profit Budget at—		
	Actual Volume (B1)	Budgeted Volume (from A2) (B2)	Sales Volume Variance (B3)
Gross sales...........................	$175,000	$168,000	$ 7,000
Standard sales discounts and allowances.........	$ 2,310	$ 2,220	(90)
Standard cost of goods sold:			
Variable.....................	83,755	80,400	(3,355)
Fixed.......................	20,625	19,800	(825)
Standard variable selling and administrative expense.....................	8,750	8,400	(350)
Fixed selling and administrative expense.........	35,000	35,000	....
Net Income before Taxes.....................	$ 24,560	$ 22,180	$ 2,380

This measure of the sales volume variance shows the impact of volume on reported income under absorption costing, not on cash flow. The $825 increase in the fixed component of the cost of goods sold does not mean that sales volume has increased cash outlays by this amount. Segregation of this component of the volume variance does not serve any useful purpose, however, and it will not be segregated in this illustration.

Sales Mix Variance

It will be noticed that the only parameter that was allowed to vary in the preceding calculation was sales volume. A second influence that might be examined is the effect of variations in *sales mix* or *product mix*—i.e., the relative proportions in which sales of the two product lines were recorded.

Analysis of July sales indicates the following breakdown by product line (at standard list prices):

Product line A..........................$120,000
Product line B........................ 55,000
Total............................$175,000

At standard costs, these sales would yield the following profit:

	Product Line A		Product Line B		Total Product Profit Budget (C5)
	% of Gross Sales (C1)	Product Profit Budget (C2)	% of Gross Sales (C3)	Product Profit Budget (C4)	
Gross sales....................		$120,000		$55,000	$175,000
Standard sales discounts and allowances...................	1.5	$ 1,800	1.0	$ 550	$ 2,350
Standard cost of goods sold:					
Variable.....................	55.0	66,000	35.0	19,250	85,250
Fixed.......................	15.0	18,000	6.0	3,300	21,300
Standard variable selling and administrative expense........	5.0	6,000	5.0	2,750	8,750
Profit Margin.................		$ 28,200		$29,150	$ 57,350

In other words, at the *actual* sales mix, the standard profit margin (before deducting fixed selling and administrative expense) was $57,-350. The difference between this figure and the standard profit margin calculated above for a *budgeted* sales mix is the *sales mix variance:*

	Product Profit Budget at Actual Volume and		Sales Mix Variance (D3)
	Actual Sales Mix (from C5) (D1)	Budgeted Sales Mix (from B1) (D2)	
Gross sales...............................	$175,000	$175,000	....
Standard sales discounts and allowances........	$ 2,350	$ 2,310	$ (40)
Standard cost of goods sold:			
Variable...............................	85,250	83,755	(1,495)
Fixed.................................	21,300	20,625	(675)
Standard variable selling and administrative expense...................................	8,750	8,750	....
Profit Margin............................	$ 57,350	$ 59,560	$(2,210)

The shift in mix toward a larger proportion of the lower margin product line A thus had the effect of depressing net income by $2,210.

Sales Price Variance

All of the previous calculations were based on list prices and standard sales discounts. Not all sales were made at standard net prices, however, and the variance reflecting this fact is the sales price variance, the difference between budgeted prices and the actual prices received for the actual volume and mix. Because price variations in this case are reflected in the sales discounts and allowances account, this variance can be derived by comparing the actual discounts and allowances from column A1 ($3,100) with discounts and allowances budgeted for the increased volume and changed sales mix (from column D1, $2,350). In this case, the sales price variance was $750 and unfavorable.[7]

Operating Cost Variances

The remaining departures from the original profit plan can be analyzed by the methods described in considerable detail in earlier chapters. Only a quick summary of these variances is needed here to round out the illustration.

As Exhibit 24–7 shows, the factory volume variance during July was $2,160, and favorable. This was $1,560 greater than the $600 volume variance originally budgeted, indicating that production volume was in excess of the amount originally planned. This $1,560 was credited to the income statement, and thus reported net income was $1,560 higher than the plan called for.

The other factory cost variances in Exhibit 24–7 totaled $1,960, unfavorable. The original budget included no provision for these, and thus the entire amount represented a departure from the profit plan. In practice, this would be subdivided by factory departments, but in this illustration the factory is assumed to have only one department, thus eliminating that complication. The variance would also be divided into materials, labor, and various overhead components, and each of these could be further subdivided into input price and cost control performance variances, but provision of all these details would only complicate this illustration needlessly.

A similar set of calculations could be performed for selling and administrative expenses. The budgeted selling and administrative expenses were:

> Variable...................... $ 8,400
> Fixed......................... 35,000

In deriving the sales volume and mix variances, the budget allowance for the variable component was adjusted to the actual sales volume and

---

[7] Volume, mix, and price variances can be computed in different sequences to produce different results, but an explanation of these calculations would be tedious beyond reasonable limits. We prefer to use standard prices in all calculations of volume and mix variances to give them month-to-month comparability, but otherwise the sequence in which the variances are computed is arbitrary.

sales mix, or $8,750. In other words, variable selling and administrative expense should have increased by $350 to match the $7,000 increase in aggregate sales volume, and this higher figure thus provides the flexible budget allowance for the evaluation of cost performance. Actual costs for the month, taken from Exhibit 24–7, thus yield the following variances:

	Actual	Volume-Adjusted Budget	Cost Variance
Variable selling and administrative expense..............................	$ 8,600	$ 8,750	$ 150
Fixed selling and administrative expense....	35,650	35,000	(650)
Total............................	$44,250	$43,750	$(500)

Variance Summary

The variances developed in this section are summarized in work sheet form in Exhibit 24–8. This report would ordinarily be too detailed for presentation to management, but it has the virtue here of showing the internal consistency of the analysis. The rows and columns do add up to the right totals. In practice, a list of the main variances, perhaps with accompanying comments, is ordinarily preferable, even if it does not permit the executive to see how the numbers were derived.

SUMMARY

Profit planning is basically a device to force management to lift its sights from immediate pressing problems and study the implications of forecasted future states of nature for the management of the business. It is believed that doing this will give management time to weigh alternative courses of action, free from the pressure of immediate events, and to work out means of reaching agreed-upon goals.

The profit plan that is adopted serves as a target throughout the planning period, although as conditions change it may become less and less relevant as a set of operating instructions. It does serve another useful purpose, however, as a bench mark against which to measure actual profit performance as the period goes by.

The profit contribution approach has been developed to serve this latter purpose. Its main strength is that it reports to any given manager

Exhibit 24-8

PROFIT VARIANCE SUMMARY

	Total Variance from Profit Plan (Col. A3)	Sales Volume Variance (Col. B3)	Sales Mix Variance (Col. D3)	Sales Price Variance (Col. E3)	Factory Volume Variance	Factory Cost: Price and Performance Variance	S & A Cost: Price and Performance Variance
Gross sales..........................	$ 7,000	$ 7,000	.....	$(750)	.....	.....	.....
Sales discounts and allowances.........	(880)	(90)	$ (40)	.....	.....	.....	.....
Standard variable cost of sales.........	(4,850)	(3,355)	(1,495)	.....	.....	.....	.....
Variable selling and administrative expense...	(200)	(350)	.....	.....	.....	.....	$ 150
Factory cost variances................	(400)	.....	.....	.....	$1,560	$(1,960)	.....
Standard fixed cost of sales...........	(1,500)	(825)	(675)	.....	.....	.....	.....
Fixed selling and administrative expense......	(650)	.....	.....	.....	.....	.....	(650)
Total........................	$(1,480)	$ 2,380	$(2,210)	$(750)	$1,560	$(1,960)	$(500)

The ( ) denotes an unfavorable variance
Numbers in the column headings refer to the columns of previous tables.

only those figures that are clearly traceable to the segment of operations in which he is interested, without arbitrary allocations of common costs. Many costs that are common to reporting units at one level, of course, will be traceable to individual reporting units at the next level, so that no operating costs are ordinarily left out of the profit reports issued to top management.

The profit report in itself, even if it contains a finely detailed breakdown of deviations from the profit plan, element by element, will be of limited usefulness unless some explanation of these deviations is forthcoming. The last section of this chapter has outlined in a rather mechanistic way one method of analysis that will quantify the effects of intermediate causes, such as sales volume reductions, price increases, etc. This kind of analysis can be very useful, but no one format can be advertised as universally applicable. The analyst needs to tailor his methods to the situation, the requirements of his management, and the resources available to him.

DISCUSSION QUESTIONS

1. What are the objectives of product-line profit planning? Is participation by middle management in this process consistent with these objectives?

2. What is the role of the product manager in an otherwise functionally organized company? What problems of profit responsibility are faced in this type of organization?

3. What are the advantages of contribution margin over net profit as a measure of product profitability in routine profit performance reports? What are its disadvantages?

4. What role can the budget director play in profit planning?

5. The management of your company wishes to analyze deviations from budgeted profit to determine how much of the variance is due to price concessions, changes in aggregate volume and changes in product mix, and how much is due to other factors. How can P/V ratios be useful in this connection?

6. Is variable costing in the factory likely to make the profit analyst's job easier or more difficult? Justify your answer.

7. State the argument for measuring sales volume and mix variances on the basis of standard selling prices rather than actual selling prices. Can a counter-argument be made for the use of actual selling prices?

8. Is the analysis of profit variances likely to interest anyone except the accountants who carry it out? If so, how can it be used?

9. In what sense do typical breakdowns of the overall profit variance merely identify the symptoms rather than the underlying causes of the variances? Is this a damaging indictment? Does it impair the usefulness of profit variance analysis?

10. The cost of goods sold in a multiproduct company is reported at standard unit costs on the monthly profit performance report. Revenues are listed at actual selling prices, and it is not feasible to reprice all items sold at budgeted or list prices for comparison purposes. Outline a procedure for isolating the profit impact of variances in sales volume, sales mix, and selling prices, insofar as this can be done from the available data.

EXERCISES AND PROBLEMS

*1. From the information below, compute the amount of the profit variance due to variations in (*a*) selling prices, (*b*) sales volume, and (*c*) other factors, in as much detail as you deem appropriate.

	Budget	Actual
Sales.................................	$60,000	$60,500
Cost of goods sold:		
Direct material......................	$10,000	$11,200
Direct labor.........................	13,000	14,700
Factory overhead.....................	13,000	14,100
Total cost of goods sold.............	$36,000	$40,000
Gross margin.........................	$24,000	$20,500
Selling and administrative expenses......	18,000	18,500
Net Profit...........................	$ 6,000	$ 2,000
Units sold...........................	10,000	11,000

Additional information:

(1) Materials prices and wage rates were at budgeted levels.
(2) Production volume and sales volume were identical.
(3) Factory overhead is budgeted at $7,800 plus 40 percent of direct labor cost.
(4) Selling and administrative expenses are assumed to be wholly fixed.

2. The Antic Products Company recently reorganized the operations of one of its largest processing departments. A considerable amount of semiautomatic equipment was installed, permitting an increase in the overall volume of production and a substantial reduction in direct labor costs per unit of product processed in this department. After the new equipment had been in use for about six months the plant controller submitted a memorandum to the effect that although the savings in direct labor seemed to be at the anticipated levels, the ratio of departmental overhead to direct labor had increased tremendously and that this was eroding the labor savings.

Upon investigation, you have been able to determine the following facts:

* Solutions to problems marked with an asterisk (*) can be found in Appendix B.

	Prior to Reorganization	Subsequent to Reorganization
Sales value of production per month......	$900,000	$1,125,000
Production costs per month:		
Direct materials.....................	$225,000	$ 306,000
Direct labor........................	450,000	328,000
Depreciation.......................	20,000	40,000
Other factory overhead..............	92,000	114,000
Total Production Costs.............	$787,000	$ 788,000

Selling prices, product mix, materials prices, and wage rates had not changed appreciably in the last year, and production and sales volume were substantially equal in each period.

The flexible budget for "other factory overhead" in use prior to the reorganization was $69,500 plus 10 percent of direct materials used. No new flexible budgets have been established, but it is estimated that the fixed portion of other factory overhead has been increased by $5,000 a month as a result of the installation of the new equipment.

Prepare a report, using figures and comments, to account for the changes in factory cost. Was the plant controller's objection well founded?

3. Woodbridge, Inc., after several years of profit, showed a loss of $2,000,000 in 19x3, accompanied by a severe cash shortage. Woodbridge seethed with activity as a result: new financial controls were installed, and a new sales manager was hired. By the end of 19x4, the new organization was fully operating and Mr. James Woodbridge, the company's president, was optimistic about the future despite the 19x4 loss of $1,300,000 on sales of $5,000,000.

Looking ahead, Mr. Woodbridge was convinced that the firm could attain a volume of $10,000,000 in a few years, with the following profit results:

Sales............................		$10,000,000
Variable production costs..........$5,000,000		
Fixed production costs............. 2,000,000		
Variable selling costs.............. 1,000,000		
Fixed selling costs................ 1,000,000	9,000,000	
Net Income before Taxes...........	$ 1,000,000	

Variable costs were expected to vary in proportion to changes in physical volume. Standard product costs in the factory were established on the basis of the physical volume required for an annual sales volume of $10,000,000. All production cost variances were to be taken directly to the income statement for the period in which they arose.

The initial profit budget for 19x5 called for sales of $6,500,000 (at standard prices) and a net loss (before taxes) of $400,000. Actual volume for 19x5 was $7,000,000, also at standard prices. At this volume a loss of $200,000 was budgeted, but the company's cash position had improved so much by the end of 19x5 that Mr. Woodbridge thought the company might even have broken even. Therefore, he was aghast when he received the following income statement:

Sales (at actual prices)...............		$6,860,000
Standard cost of goods sold..........$4,900,000		
Selling expenses..................... 1,720,000		
Factory overhead volume variance.... 900,000		
Other factory cost variances.......... 30,000	7,550,000	
Net Loss..........................		$ 690,000

"What happened?" he gasped. Tell him, in as much detail as possible.

4. A company's gross margin dropped precipitously from the first quarter to the second quarter of the year:

	First Quarter	Second Quarter
Sales....................................	$84,960	$86,014
Cost of goods sold:		
Direct materials........................	$15,399	$15,565
Direct labor..........................	21,771	24,328
Factory overhead......................	45,135	46,581
Total cost of goods sold...............	$82,305	$86,474
Gross Margin (Loss)...................	$ 2,645	$ (460)

Sales volume was approximately equal to production volume in both periods. Earned standard hours totaled 106,200 in the first quarter and 115,300 in the second quarter.

a) Reconstruct the statement on the basis of costs per earned standard hour.

b) Show the factors which accounted for the fall in gross margin and suggest the possible causes. Quantify your answer as much as possible. (Adapted from an Institute of Cost and Works Accountants examination)

5. A large oil refiner sets annual price and volume objectives for each product and then computes volume, price, and mix variances from actual sales data. Sales revenue data for one such product are as follows:

	(1) Sales Volume (in Units)	(2) Sales Volume (in Dollars)	(3) Average Price (2) ÷ (1)
Trade class 1:			
Actual................	2,414	$21,449	$ 8.88
Plan.................	2,000	17,244	8.62
Variance............	414	4,205	0.26
Trade class 2:			
Actual................	1,500	11,568	7.71
Plan.................	1,500	12,259	8.17
Variance............	....	(691)	(0.46)
Trade class 6:			
Actual................	500	3,625	7.25
Plan.................	600	5,123	8.54
Variance............	(100)	(1,498)	(1.29)
Total, all trade classes:			
Actual................	4,414	36,642	...
Plan.................	4,100	34,626	8.45
Variance............	314	2,016	...

a) From these data, compute volume, price, and trade mix variances in sales revenue. Explain your method of analysis.

b) Comment on the managerial usefulness of these variances. Would you recommend any changes in the basis on which volume, mix, and price variances are computed?

(Adapted from a National Industrial Conference Board exhibit)

*6. The Dorsey Corporation has prepared the following performance summary for its industrial division for the month of December:

Net sales...		$2,000,000
Cost of goods sold:		
Labor...	$ 400,000	
Materials.....................................	100,000	
Overhead (actual)..............................	1,000,000	
	$1,500,000	
Overhead overabsorbed..........................	100,000	
Product costs................................	$1,600,000	
Decrease in inventory..........................	160,000	
Cost of goods sold...........................		1,760,000
Gross margin......................................		$ 240,000
Less: Selling expenses.............................	$ 300,000	
Administrative expenses......................	50,000	350,000
Profit (loss) on sales.............................		$ (110,000)
Add: Factory overhead overabsorbed.................		100,000
Net Income (Loss) before Taxes....................		$ (10,000)

(1) Manufacturing overhead costs are all traceable to the division.

(2) At normal operating volumes, variable manufacturing overhead costs are approximately 30 percent of total manufacturing overhead costs in the industrial division. Variable overhead cost per labor dollar is not affected by fluctuations in production volume.

(3) The volume variance in manufacturing overhead costs in the industrial division was favorable, amounting to $20,000.

(4) Variable selling expenses amount to 4 percent of industrial sales. All administrative expenses are fixed.

(5) $50,000 of fixed selling expense and $5,000 of administrative expense are traceable to the industrial division; all other fixed selling and administrative expenses come from allocations.

(6) An absorption costing system is in use in the factory. The ratio of the variable cost content of work in process and finished goods inventories to the total costs of these inventories is the same as the ratio of variable manufacturing cost to total "product costs" for the division for the period. Price level changes may be assumed to be negligible.

a) Compute the following:

(1) Factory overhead performance variance.

(2) Budgeted fixed manufacturing cost.

(3) Variable profit ratio.

b) Prepare a profit contribution statement in good form, summarizing the results of the month's operations.

7. The XYZ Company sells its products through two channels of distribution: through dealers and direct to the ultimate consumer. In addition, it bills its customers for the work performed for those customers by its customer engineering department. The company operates a single factory with three production departments and four small service departments.

The sales manager has been receiving monthly sales reports for each of these three business segments, but no attempt has been made to compute or report profit figures for individual segments.

From the following data, prepare a summary profit report, showing the profits of each division individually and of the company as a whole. Use whatever format you feel is appropriate and be prepared to defend your choice.

(1) Sales revenues:
   Dealer sales, $28,000.
   Direct sales, $36,000.
   Customer engineering, $15,000.
(2) Standard cost of goods sold:
   Dealer sales: variable costs, $11,000; fixed costs, $4,000.
   Direct sales: variable costs, $13,000; fixed costs, $5,000.
(3) Total factory costs:
   Direct materials: earned, $10,000; actual, $10,500.
   Direct labor: earned, $12,000; actual, $13,200.
   Factory overhead: earned, $17,000; actual, $20,400.
(4) Factory overhead volume variances included in (3) above: $3,000 (unfavorable).
(5) Cost variances in opening inventory, none.
(6) Commissions on direct sales, $2,700.
(7) Dealer discounts, $10,500.
(8) Other direct field expenses (fixed):
   Dealer sales department, $1,000.
   Direct sales department, $4,500.
   Customer engineering department, $15,800.
(9) Product advertising (budgeted at 3 percent of direct and dealer sales), $2,500.
(10) Time spent by customer engineers on work not billable to customers:
   For dealer sales customers, $600.
   For direct sales customers, $150.
(11) General sales division overheads, $1,500.
(12) Administrative expenses, $4,900.

8. The Bristow Products Company costs its products by the absorption costing principle, including in burden rates a provision for fixed factory overhead. Sales during 19x2 were substantially greater than in 19x1, but the 19x2 income statement prepared by the company's accountants revealed a substantial reduction in reported income. The company's selling prices had not changed, nor had there been any significant change in the sales mix. Furthermore, factory burden rates were the same for the two years.

The company's president was disappointed by the year's profit results and asked the controller to investigate the situation and "find out what went wrong." The comparative statements follow:

	19x1	19x2
Sales....................................	$4,000,000	$4,750,000
Cost of goods sold:		
Inventory, January 1......................	$1,225,000	$2,592,000
Manufacturing costs:		
Direct materials.........................	1,480,000	1,381,000
Direct labor............................	1,788,000	1,676,000
Absorbed overhead—variable.............	494,000	462,000
Absorbed overhead—fixed.................	1,026,000	959,000
Total...............................	$6,013,000	$7,070,000
Inventory, December 31....................	2,592,000	2,992,000
Total cost of goods sold...............	$3,421,000	$4,078,000
Gross margin.............................	$ 579,000	$ 672,000
Selling and administrative expense:		
Variable...............................	$ 240,000	$ 288,000
Fixed...................................	205,000	208,000
Total...............................	$ 445,000	$ 496,000
Net profit before adjustment...............	$ 134,000	$ 176,000
Unabsorbed manufacturing overhead...........	54,000	126,000
Net Profit...............................	$ 80,000	$ 50,000

The fixed manufacturing overhead included in inventories was:

January 1, 19x1.........................$245,000
January 1, 19x2......................... 545,000
December 31, 19x2...................... 628,000

a) Prepare comparative income statements for the two years, following the variable costing principle.

b) Prepare a short table, indicating the effects on reported income of volume and other factors that would explain the $30,000 reduction in net profit in 19x2.

9. Monthly budget and product standard cost data for the Foster Company are as follows:

(1) Profit budget:

	Product A	Product B	Total
Gross sales (list price)..................	$60,000	$200,000	$260,000
Discounts.............................	1,200	8,800	10,000
Net sales.............................	$58,800	$191,200	$250,000
Cost of goods sold (standard costs).......	48,000	140,000	188,000
Gross margin..........................	$10,800	$ 51,200	$ 62,000
Selling and administrative expenses.......			30,000
Manufacturing cost variances............			......
Net Income before Taxes...............			$ 32,000

(2) Standard product cost:

	Product A	Product B
Direct materials........................	$1.00	$1.00
Direct labor........................	1.00	2.00
Overhead...........................	2.00	4.00
Total........................	$4.00	$7.00

(3) Factory overhead budget: $78,000 + 0.5 × Standard direct labor cost.

(4) Budgeted production volume:

Product A.....................12,000 units
Product B.....................20,000 units

(5) Selling and administrative expense budget:

$22,400 + 0.01 × Gross sales + 0.02 × Net sales.

The actual results for the month of November were as follows:

(6) Profit realized:

	Product A	Product B	Total
Gross sales (list prices)................	$55,000	$210,000	$265,000
Discounts.............................	500	20,000	20,500
Net sales............................	$54,500	$190,000	$244,500
Cost of goods sold (standard costs).......	44,000	147,000	191,000
Gross margin.........................	$10,500	$ 43,000	$ 53,500
Selling and administrative expense........			35,000
Manufacturing cost variances...........			2,500
Net Income before Taxes...............			$ 16,000

(7) Actual production volume:

Product A.....................11,000 units
Product B.....................20,000 units

(8) Actual factory overhead: $104,000.

Prepare an analysis of the month's operations, indicating insofar as possible the sources of the $16,000 departure from budgeted profit. List prices in effect for products A and B during November were those used in preparing the profit budget.

10. The Randall division of the Walters Company reported divisional net income as follows for the first six months of the current fiscal year:

	Budget	Actual	Deviation
Gross sales—list prices.................	$8,000,000	$7,400,000	$(600,000)
Sales discounts.........................	(400,000)	(600,000)	(200,000)
Sales allowances.......................	(200,000)	(150,000)	50,000
Net sales..............................	$7,400,000	$6,650,000	$(750,000)
Cost of goods sold:			
Standard product cost.................	$4,800,000	$4,530,000	$ 270,000
Purchase price variances...............	250,000	235,000	15,000
Underabsorbed overhead...............	200,000	180,000	20,000
Factory labor and materials variances..	....	(20,000)	20,000
Net cost of goods sold..............	$5,250,000	$4,925,000	$ 325,000
Gross margin..........................	$2,150,000	$1,725,000	$(425,000)
Division expenses:			
Controllable..........................	$ 800,000	$ 790,000	$ 10,000
Noncontrollable......................	300,000	305,000	(5,000)
Total division expenses..............	$1,100,000	$1,095,000	$ 5,000
Contribution margin....................	$1,050,000	$ 630,000	$(420,000)
Head office charges....................	320,000	350,000	(30,000)
Net Profit............................	$ 730,000	$ 280,000	$(450,000)

The manager of the Randall division is concerned with the failure to achieve budgeted profits and has asked you to analyze the situation and report back to him. You have found the following additional information:

(1) List prices were not changed during the period.
(2) Budgeted sales for the company's three product lines were:

Product Line	% of Total Gross Sales	Ratio of Standard Product Cost to List Price	Ratio of Standard Variable Factory Cost to Standard Factory Cost
A...........	50%	70%	80%
B...........	30	60	85
C...........	20	35	70

(3) Budgeted sales discounts and allowances were assumed to be proportional to gross sales.
(4) Factory fixed costs were budgeted at $1,195,000 for the six-month period.
(5) The standard cost of budgeted and actual production was as follows:

Product Line	Budgeted	Actual
A.................	$2,800,000	$2,750,000
B.................	1,500,000	1,500,000
C.................	700,000	600,000

(6) The entire budgeted underabsorbed overhead was attributed to factory volume variances.

(7) Actual sales for the six-month period were:

Product Line	Gross Sales	Discounts	Allowances	Net Sales
A................	$3,900,000	$190,000	$80,000	$3,630,000
B................	2,300,000	140,000	50,000	2,110,000
C................	1,200,000	270,000	20,000	910,000

(8) Physical quantities of materials purchased were in accordance with the amounts originally budgeted.

(9) The variable portion of controllable division expenses are estimated to amount to 3 percent of gross sales.

(10) Sales of product line A are expected to vary in proportion to the Federal Reserve index of production, which was 5 percent less than the forecast for the six-month period.

(11) A competitor recently introduced a new product, directly competitive with the main item in product line C and priced 25 percent lower than the Randall division's list price for the comparable product. The division's sales manager estimates that his market share for product line C has dropped from a budgeted 60 percent to 40 percent, despite efforts to meet competition by increased price discounts.

Prepare an analysis of the deviation of actual from budgeted net profit, indicating insofar as possible the sources of this deviation. Make any interpretive comments that seem appropriate.

CASE 24–1: TREFLAZ, S.A.*

Treflaz, S.A. was a large distributor of a wide range of consumer and industrial products in Switzerland. Products were sold to wholesalers, retailers, and directly to large institutional consumers (such as hospitals and laboratories). The organization was divided into 11 product sales departments, each responsible for the sale of a particular group of products, and 12 service and administrative departments.

Sales department X reported the following sales, cost of goods sold, and operating expenses for the month of September, 1959:

(000 Sfr.)

Net sales............................340.4
Cost of goods sold....................191.0
Operating expenses.................... 95.4

Each sales department prepared a budget at the beginning of each year. Because of seasonal factors, department X's September budget differed slightly from one twelfth of the annual budget for the fiscal year 1959–60. The figures were:

(000 Sfr.)

Budgeted net sales, entire year.........3,900.0
Budgeted net sales, September......... 318.0

Cost of goods sold was budgeted on an annual basis by multiplying budgeted annual physical unit sales of each product by standard cost or purchase price per

---

* Copyright 1965 by l'Institut pour l'Etude des Méthodes de Direction de l'Entreprise (IMEDE), Lausanne, Switzerland. Reproduced by permission.

unit. This was then expressed as a percentage of budgeted net sales for the department. The resulting ratio was multiplied by budgeted monthly sales to compute budgeted cost of goods sold for each month. For department X in 1959–60 the figures were:

> Budgeted cost of goods sold, entire year, percent
> of budgeted net sales.......................... 54.4%
> Budgeted cost of goods sold, September (54.4% ×
> budgeted net sales)..........................173,000 Sfr.

Operating expenses were divided into four categories:

Direct:	traceable to specific sales departments.
Allocated:	allocated to sales departments by formula.
Freight:	traceable to specific sales departments.
Reserves and interest:	provisions for costs that will not be known with certainty until some future period, plus imputed interest on working capital.

Flexible budgets were prepared for expenses in each of these four categories, on the bases described in Exhibit 1. These budgets for 1959–60 can be summarized in the formula:

Budgeted operating expense = 30,200 Sfr./month + 19.4% × net sales,

and the budget allowances for 1959–60 were:

> *(000 Sfr.)*
> Entire year (budgeted net sales of 3,900,000 Sfr.)..1,118,600
> September (budgeted net sales of 318,000 Sfr.).... 91,900

Actual operating expenses charged against department X's revenues for September totaled 95,400 Sfr., as detailed in the right-hand column of Exhibit 1.

Budgeted net sales were stated on the basis of standard list prices† in force at the beginning of the fiscal year. Actual net sales were recorded on the basis of the amounts actually billed customers, but a supplementary record was kept of the standard list prices of all goods sold. For September, actual net sales at standard list prices amounted to 355,500 Sfr.

a) Prepare a summary report analyzing department X's profit variance for the month of September, in as clear and as concise a form as possible. This report should show, among other things, the total variance from budgeted profit, the effect of deviations from budgeted physical sales volume, the effect of deviations from budgeted or standard list prices, and the amounts due to ineffective cost control and other causes, to the extent that these effects can be identified. (Note: You need not accept the company's classifications into direct, allocated, etc., if you feel that some other classification would be more meaningful.)

b) Do you agree with the company's methods of charging expenses to department X? Give your reasons.

c) Which variances should be reported to the department managers?

---

† The company actually kept a record of actual sales at gross or dealer prices and *computed* standard net prices by multiplying these by a predetermined average discount percentage. The result is approximately the same as that described here.

Exhibit 1

DEPARTMENT X

Budgeted Operating Expenses for Fiscal Year 1959–60 and Actual Expenses for September, 1959

	Budgeted		Basis for Charging Department	Actual Expenses Sept. (000 Sfr.)
	Fixed Amount per Year (000 Sfr.)	Variable % of Sales		
Direct cost of department X:				
Salaries and premiums.........	84.0	...	Traceable	6.9
Commission of representatives..	....	3.0	"	10.2
Fringe benefits...............	16.8	...	"	0.3
Office supplies................	12.0	...	"	1.9
Depreciation on equipment and furniture..................	9.2	...	"	0.8
Price lists, brochures..........	3.6	...	"	1.3
Travel and entertaining........	24.0	...	"	1.9
Postage, telephone, and telegraph.....................	24.0	...	"	2.3
Demonstrations and samples....	2.4	...	"	...
Quality control and research....	54.0	...	"	4.5
General selling expense........	18.0	...	"	2.6
Subtotal................	248.0	3.0	....	32.7
Cost allocated to department X:				
Buildings (depreciation, maintenance, etc.)..............	67.2	...	Fixed sum	5.6
Management.................	....	2.0	Fixed %	6.8
Data processing.............	....	2.8	"	9.5
Inventory handling...........	....	4.4	"	15.0
Subtotal................	67.2	9.2	....	36.9
Freight........................	....	1.8	Traceable	3.3
Reserves, interest:				
Provision for advertising.......	....	4.2	Fixed %	14.4
Provision for bad debts.........	....	0.5	"	1.7
Provision for unsalable inventories.....................	....	0.2	"	0.7
Provision for free replacement of goods sold..............	....	0.5	"	1.7
Interest on inventories.........	27.3	...	*	2.9
Interest on accounts receivable..	19.5	...	*	1.1
Subtotal................	46.8	5.4		22.5
Total....................	362.0	19.4		95.4

*Charge based on fixed percent of departmental inventories and receivables; all other "fixed %" charges are based on actual net sales.

Chapter 25

DIVISIONAL PROFIT
REPORTING

As THE size of the business firm and the complexity of its operations have grown, the desirability of having routine profit reports on a divisional basis has become increasingly apparent. In this chapter and the next we shall examine the nature of divisional profit reporting, some of the problems to be encountered in preparing these reports, and a number of concepts that have been developed to deal with these problems.[1]

ORGANIZATIONAL SETTING

Divisionalization results from the need for imposing at least one level of organizational superstructure between top management and operating and technical departments in order to facilitate coordination and direction of the company's activities. Day-to-day operating problems are too diverse for direct top-management control except in companies that are quite small, so departments are grouped into divisions each of which then becomes a major segment of the company.

Bases for Divisionalization

Divisionalization may take one or a combination of several forms, the choice depending partly on the history of the company's growth and partly on considerations of the company's policies and objectives. The divisional structure may be based on the functions performed, with separate divisions for sales, manufacturing, engineering, and finance, or it may be based largely on market distinctions, with separate divisions for the company's various sales territories or product lines or customer

---

[1] For a much more extended discussion of this topic, see David Solomons, *Divisional Performance: Measurement and Control* (New York: Financial Executives Institute Research Foundation, 1965).

groups. Exhibit 25–1 shows a simplified functional organization structure. Five executives report directly to the president and constitute the executive committee: the treasurer, the controller, and three vice presidents responsible for manufacturing, sales, and engineering, respectively. The president also has an administrative assistant who takes on some of the detail of the president's office and performs special studies for use in policy formation. A personnel relations manager also reports to the president.

A market-oriented division structure may be organized around individual product lines, or geographic regions, or categories of customers.

Exhibit 25–1

FUNCTIONAL ORGANIZATION STRUCTURE

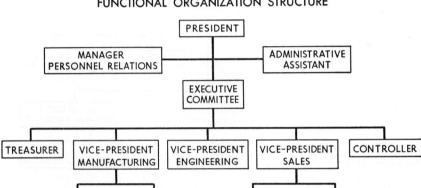

Product divisions are most common when manufacturing facilities tend to be specialized by product line or when product distribution calls for separate sales forces for individual product lines. For example, one manufacturer of home heating equipment and household appliances has separate divisions for each of these lines. Geographic divisions are generally indicated if marketing problems differ more among regions than among products and if the technical problems of engineering and manufacturing the company's products are sufficiently homogeneous to justify reduced specialization of the output of individual factories. Customer divisions arise primarily because of differences in problems of product distribution to different customer groups.

Exhibit 25–2 illustrates a division structure based on separate product lines. Seven executives report directly to the president: treasurer, controller, vice president–research, director–management services, and three operating vice presidents. Company operations are centered around three separate product lines, each under a vice president who has overall responsibility for sales and production in his division.

Two of these divisions, the defense products division and the industrial products division, are organized internally along functional lines. The structure of these functional organizations differs between the two divisions because of differences between them in the nature of their products and of the markets that they serve, but the nature of the responsibility of each of the functional heads is similar to that of their corporate counterparts in the functional organization structure illus-

Exhibit 25–2

PRODUCT-LINE ORGANIZATION STRUCTURE

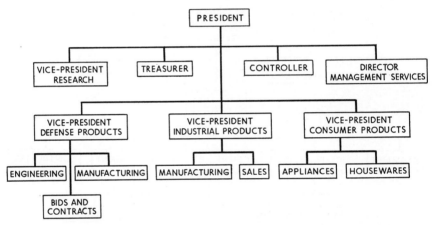

trated in Exhibit 25–1. The consumer products division, on the other hand, is subdivided further around two distinct groups of consumer products that are marketed through separate sales forces and manufactured in separate production facilities.

Divisional Decentralization

A company is *divisionalized* whenever certain related activities are grouped together for administrative direction and control by high-level executives. Whenever this is accompanied by the delegation to division managers of the responsibility for a segment of the company's profits, then the company is said to be *decentralized*. The hallmark of the decentralized company is its subdivision into a number of smaller, relatively self-contained entities that are equipped to operate in substantially the same manner as independent firms dependent on their own profit performance for economic survival. The creation of these semiautonomous units, often referred to as *profit centers,* has three major objectives:

1. To provide a basis for delegating portions of top management's decision-making responsibility to executives who have closer operating familiarity with individual products or markets.
2. To bring subordinate executives into more direct contact with the ultimate profit objectives of the firm.
3. To provide an integrated training ground for the top managers of the future.

Perhaps the most important of these is to overcome the sheer weight of the decision-making responsibility in a large corporation. With operations spread over a vast geographical area and encompassing hundreds of products and thousands of customers, central management cannot hope to be completely and continuously in direct personal contact with every segment of the company's business. To provide flexibility and adaptability to changing conditions, it has become increasingly necessary to delegate substantial powers to executives who can maintain a closer, more detailed familiarity with individual products or markets. In other words, decentralization aims to recreate in the large organization the conditions that give life and flexibility to the small company without sacrificing the advantages of size—diversification of risk, centralized financing, and specialization in the planning and advisory functions of management.

A second objective of decentralization is to bring subordinate executives into more direct contact with the ultimate profit objectives of the firm. A strictly manufacturing executive sees all problems as production problems with a cost overlay. A marketing executive focuses his attention on sales volume and distribution cost. In a centralized organization these viewpoints come together only at the top of the pyramid. Decentralization is one way of attempting to bring them together at lower levels.

Closely related to this is a third objective of decentralization, namely, to provide a more comprehensive training ground for the top managers of the future. The ranks of the top executives are continually being thinned by death and retirement, and there is a need for replacements who have been schooled in various aspects of business management and are thereby better prepared to face the major problems that can be resolved only at the top-management level. This kind of experience is best obtained at lower levels where the inevitable mistakes are likely to be smaller.

Requirements for Profit Decentralization

Divisionalization, whether the company is centralized or decentralized, requires careful examination and definition of four major elements:

1. The boundaries within which each division is free to operate without interference from other divisions and the relations that are to exist between divisions.
2. The scope of each division manager's decision-making authority and responsibility and his relationship to top management.
3. The criteria by which each division manager should be guided in making decisions on matters that fall within his jurisdiction.
4. The measures that will be used to evaluate the performance of each division manager in carrying out his responsibilities.

In a decentralized company, the third and fourth of these are defined in terms of divisional profit, and the major problem is to work out the details of the definitions. Before discussing this problem, however, it is necessary to examine briefly the first two elements, both concerned with intraorganization relationships.

Divisional Boundaries. The ideal basis for profit decentralization exists whenever a division can be virtually self-contained, with its own manufacturing and distributive facilities and relatively few transfers of product internally among divisions. In other words, decentralization is at its best whenever a division's operations come closest in scope and depth to those of separate independent companies. In these circumstances, the profit reported by each division is largely independent of operating performance in other divisions of the company, thus facilitating the interpretation of reported profits.

Unfortunately, these ideal conditions are often unattainable. Organization structure cannot be determined solely by the need for profit separability. Other factors, such as economies of common use of sales forces or facilities, may override the desirability of separating profit centers from each other. In these circumstances, the problem is to seek means of measurement and evaluation that will achieve a satisfactory compromise between conflicting objectives. Management has the task of deciding whether departures from the ideal are sufficiently serious to make profit decentralization unworkable. A single manufacturing plant may serve several product or regional sales divisions, for example, and although the sales divisions may be organized on some sort of profit-centered basis, it may be very difficult to devise a workable basis for profit measurement of the manufacturing operation.

Exhibit 25–3

COMPANY X, MANUFACTURING DIVISION

Income Statement for the Quarter Ending March 31, 19xx
(In Thousands of Dollars)

	Budget	Actual
Volume:		
Trade.....................................	$ 630	$ 665
Industrial...............................	1,921	2,142
Total volume.........................	$2,551	$2,807
Cost of production:		
Trade.....................................	$ 386	$ 390
Industrial...............................	1,457	1,853
Total cost of production...............	$1,843	$2,243
Gross earnings:		
Main factory...........................	$ 420	$ 285
Albany..................................	182	169
Rochester..............................	106	110
Total gross earnings...................	$ 708	$ 564
Division expenses:		
Salaries................................	$ 90	$ 95
Pensions................................	56	55
Other..................................	54	51
Total expenses........................	$ 200	$ 201
Net Profit before Taxes....................	$ 508	$ 363

Delegation of Authority. Effective decentralization requires that division executives be granted the authority to control at least some of the major determinants of profit performance. Decentralization in some companies goes no deeper than the allocation of total company profit among divisions, with real authority being retained in the hands of central management. In these cases the responsibility of division managers for the profits shown on their monthly reports is little more than a responsibility for costs or dollar sales or whatever else is subject to each manager's authority. The monthly profit reports are issued almost entirely to dramatize and perhaps glamorize operations.

One company, for example, recently adopted a profit reporting system in which a profit was reported for its manufacturing division. The first quarterly statement for the division is shown in Exhibit 25–3. In this company the manufacturing division manager and his subordinate plant managers had no control over the volume of production or over the prices at which products were transferred to other company divisions. Their only control was over costs and expenses. The reported profit, therefore, was not indicative of managerial performance in the division, although it may have served other purposes.

There is no hard-and-fast rule as to just what kinds of authority must be delegated to justify the use of the term "decentralized." One company may delegate authority to drop or add products; another may delegate pricing authority. Both may legitimately be called decentralized if the intent is clear. Decentralization is partly an attitude, an attempt to restore to operating executives in a large company the close connection between operations and profit that is never far from the center of attention in a small company.

No matter how it is defined, decentralization never represents a complete delegation of authority. Even in the most decentralized companies, top management retains some vestige of authority, particularly over financing and capital expenditures. In any case, divisional autonomy is limited by the need to conform to overall company policies and by the need for coordination. In some companies, the amount of authority delegated will be slight, but as long as division executives are given some latitude to apply a profit criterion to decisions, there is some element of decentralization.

Service Centers in Decentralized Companies

Both at the corporate level and within each profit center there are units that are not organized on a profit responsibility basis. These are called *service centers* or *budget centers* to distinguish them from profit centers. For example, referring back to Exhibit 25–2, the organization chart provides for a research division and a treasurer's department. In each of these the executive in charge is responsible for costs but not for profits. Although Exhibit 25–2 is too abbreviated to show them, each product division also has staff departments, such as divisional accounting or marketing research, which act in an advisory capacity to the division managers. The managers of these departments are also responsible for costs, but they generally have no direct profit responsibilities.

Advisory services need not always be organized in service centers, although that is the typical pattern. The corporate organization chart illustrated in Exhibit 25–2 shows a staff department which departs from this pattern. The manager of the management services division reports directly to the president. This division is organized as a profit center. It consists of a number of staff groups whose services are provided on a competitive basis. For example, one of the departments in this division is a photo and reproduction shop which performs a wide variety of blueprinting, photostating, and printing of reports, forms, and so forth on demand for other parts of the company organization. In this operation it competes with outside organizations to which its customers within the company have free access. It is expected to justify its existence by providing services of a quality and at prices which compare favorably with those offered by outside competition. The manager of each of these service departments and the director of the division are held responsible for the profits of their operations in much the same manner as the vice president in charge of a product division is held responsible for his division's profits.

OBJECTIVES OF DIVISIONAL PROFIT REPORTING

The measurement and reporting of profits on a divisional basis has three objectives:

1. To help division managers and their superiors appraise the financially measurable aspects of *managerial* performance in the division.
2. To provide top management with a measure of the profitability of the *resources* invested in the division.
3. To guide division managers toward decisions that will increase company profit.

Appraisal of Executive Performance

Managerial performance has many dimensions of which current profit performance is only one. The divisional profit report, therefore, provides only a partial basis for executive appraisal. Profit measurement is essential, however, whenever substantial decision-making authority is delegated to division heads. This conclusion is based on three points. First, the company as a whole is assumed to have an income objective. Second, the division is a segment of the company which also has an income objective. Third, the managers of any business unit are always accountable to the suppliers of capital, in this case to company top management. In view of the postulated income objective, this accountability must be regarded as primarily accountability as to the amount of *income* produced.

Evaluation of Resource Profitability

The evaluation of managerial performance should be clearly distinguished from the evaluation of the profitability of the *resources* committed to division management's care. The president may be completely satisfied with the performance of his division managers even though resource profitability in some divisions is extremely low.

Top management's interest in resource profitability stems from its responsibility to the company's shareholders to allocate resources profitably. If divisional income is inadequate to meet management's objectives, then ways should be sought to improve profitability. If efforts in this direction are unavailing, then presumably the resources should be diverted to other uses.

Guidance to Divisional Executives

Divisional profit reports guide divisional executives by providing feedback on what has happened, and the previous chapter was mostly an examination of how they might satisfy this objective. These reports also provide guidance in a second and less direct way by showing division managers how their past decisions have affected their divisions' reported profits. Knowing that divisional profits will be reported, the manager will presumably try to forecast the impact of his decisions on the reported profit of his own division and choose those solutions that will increase this figure.

PROFIT REPORTING FOR ACTIVITY EVALUATION

Both top management and division management have use for measures of activity profitability. Division management is concerned mainly with the details of performance, along the lines discussed in the preceding chapter. Top management's interest in divisional activity evaluation centers on:

1. Reviewing the aggregate profitability of the resources invested in each division.
2. Identifying profitability trends for individual divisions.
3. Ranking divisions in order of relative profitability.

For these purposes, reported profit is typically translated into ratios of one kind or another. The most widely used ratios are margin on sales and return on investment:

$$\text{Margin on sales} = \frac{\text{Profit}}{\text{Sales}}.$$

$$\text{Return on investment} = \frac{\text{Profit}}{\text{Investment}}.$$

While margin on sales ratios are often highly revealing in trend analysis, they do not indicate *resource* profitability because they ignore the amount of resources committed to the division. For example, two divisions of a company might show the following profit record:

	Division A	Division B
Sales...................................	$10,000,000	$5,000,000
Profit...................................	2,000,000	500,000
Investment............................	10,000,000	2,000,000
Percentage margin on sales.............	20%	10%
Percentage return on investment.........	20%	25%

Division B ranks lower than division A on the basis of sales, profit, and margin on sales, but it yields a return on investment considerably greater than that of division A.

The primary question in activity evaluation is whether profits are adequate to support the investment in the activity; if not, the activity should be abandoned and the funds directed elsewhere. This kind of comparison calls for the same minimum return-on-investment standard used by management in capital expenditure decisions.

Measures of historical return on investment do not represent incremental cash flows and thus cannot be used directly in decision making. Any comparison of such measures with a companywide minimum return-on-investment standard is useful primarily as an attention-directing device. For this purpose, measures of divisional return on investment need to reflect all of the elements implicit in the standard—in other words, *net profit* divided by *net investment*.

Measurement of Divisional Profit

Both numerator and denominator of the return-on-investment ratio present problems of measurement. Ideally, reported profit for activity evaluation should measure the profit that would have been lost if the division had not existed. Unfortunately, any such measure would require more drastic changes in accounting measures than most companies would find feasible.

For example, it would be necessary to credit *two* divisions for *all* the revenues from a given sale if the sale would have been lost if *either* division had not been in existence. Alternatively, if abandonment of division X would merely divert the customer to division Y, then the revenues from that customer would not be credited to division X at all under this scheme. Effects of these kinds are so difficult to program into the routine income measurement procedures that no such attempt is made.

Return-on-investment computations typically require some form of net profit calculation. Starting with the revenues recorded in division accounts, the following expense deductions are ordinarily made:

1. Cost of goods sold.
2. Division-traceable nonmanufacturing expense.
3. Other nonmanufacturing expense.

The main difficulty, of course, lies in measuring the fixed component of the third of these categories. The allocations of fixed costs should be based as closely as possible on the concept of attributable cost, and should reflect the proportion of service department capacity that could be eliminated if the particular division were to be spun off. This concept is difficult to apply, but if allocations are to be made this is the only basis that makes any sense.

This still leaves a gap in the allocation structure, leaving unallocated those fixed costs that bear no apparent relationship to division activity. Probably the best allocation scheme for these items is allocation in proportion to divisional investment. Such allocations have no economic significance, but they have the negative advantage of leaving unchanged the relative return-on-investment rankings of the various divisions.

Measurement of Divisional Investment

Three questions of major importance in the measurement of divisional return on investment need examination here:

1. The definition of invested capital.
2. The effects of price level fluctuations.
3. The assignment of assets to divisions.

Definition of Invested Capital. Divisional investment may be defined in many ways, the most important being (1) the division's share of corporate stockholders' equity, (2) total assets, (3) net investment, and (4) traceable assets. Stockholders' equity is the book value of the owners' investment in the assets of the firm. Total assets represents all assets of the division, including a share of corporate cash and other assets that are administered centrally. Net investment is the division's share of total assets less noninterest-bearing current liabilities—in other words, the division's share of the total investment of stockholders and lender creditors. Traceable assets includes all assets that can be identified specifically with the division, regardless of their physical location.

Stockholders' equity is clearly inapplicable as a measure of divisional investment. The funds provided to a division cannot be identified specifically as debt funds or equity funds. The financing mix is a characteristic of the corporation and is the same for all divisions. Division management is entrusted with a portion of the company's total capital which consists of both debt and equity, and any distinction at the division level is unavoidably arbitrary.

Certain subsidiaries, it is true, engage in their own financing, and for these an argument can be made for using the parent company's equity as the investment base, on the grounds that this equity was provided from parent company funds, both debt and equity.

Net investment and *total assets* are substantially identical in concept, although not in absolute amount. Both require allocations of centrally administered assets. Of the two, net investment is more closely comparable to the cost-of-capital figures underlying minimum investment standards because it includes only those funds that are provided to the firm specifically for an interest-like return—i.e., owners' equity, long-term debt, and short-term interest-bearing debt.

Defining divisional investment as *traceable assets* avoids the allocation of centrally administered assets to individual divisions, but it makes comparisons among company divisions vulnerable to intracompany variations in asset administration. For example, one division may handle all its own inventories and receivables, whereas another may utilize central billing and warehousing and thereby bury some of its investment in the common pool. For this reason, most companies prefer to use some variant of total assets or total investment.

Assignment of Assets to Divisions. Many of the assets that relate to the activities of a specific division can be traced to that division from the organizational account classification. In addition to these, every company has some assets that are administered centrally, either because they are necessary to perform central office or service functions or because central administration represents a more efficient use of resources.

At this juncture we should distinguish between assets that are truly common to more than one division and those that presumably could be traced to specific divisions by a finer subdivision of the account codes. Cash, for example, can never be traced satisfactorily to the operations of individual divisions, whereas it is often possible to identify receivables by division even though billing and accounts receivable operations are performed centrally.

Centrally administered assets of this latter type may be subcoded in the accounts to permit divisional identification. If this step is regarded as excessively costly, at least two solutions are available. First, the percentage distribution might be approximated by sampling techniques—for example, a sample of open customer accounts might be taken to approximate the true distribution of all receivables among divisions. Second, studies might be undertaken to determine the statistical relationship between asset balances and divisional activity. For example, receivables might be found to bear a fixed relationship to sales volume, the exact ratio differing for each division because of differences in terms, collection policies, or industry customs. This second method is likely to be inferior to sampling because statistical relationships frequently get out of date.

Assets that are truly common to more than one division present a more difficult problem. The relevant investment base for activity evaluation is the amount that is uniquely devoted to the support of the division's operations. For common assets, the allocation criterion that satisfies this definition is the criterion of avoidable investment—that is, what portion of the common investment would be unnecessary if this division were not present?

Implementation of this concept is extremely difficult, but an effort should be made. Without allocations, the investment base becomes traceable assets, expanded by the use of account coding, sampling, and statistical analysis to reduce the amount of unallocated common assets to the bare minimum and eliminate interdivisional differences in the use of the services of central asset administration. Many common assets, however, are not unrelated to division activity. Company cash requirements, for example, bear some relationship to the size and structure of division operations. Allocations of such items should be based on statistical analysis whenever possible. Even though the results of such analyses cannot be precise, they are far more relevant to activity evaluation than arbitrary averages can ever hope to be.

Of course, if statistical analysis fails to reveal any usable relationships, then arbitrary allocations are probably necessary. These allocations add nothing to the ability of the return on investment ratio to reflect the profitability of the division's assets, but they are one way to make internal return on investment roughly comparable to company-wide ratios. Any allocation of this kind, however, should have no effect on divisional ranking. The best way to accomplish this is to distribute the remaining common investment as a uniform percentage of the assets that can reasonably be attributed to the division. This reduces all ratios proportionately and leaves the relative ranking undisturbed.

Effects of Price Level Fluctuations. After a period of inflation, long-life property is a mixture of assets acquired at many different price levels. Divisions with an older asset mix will have a lower historical cost investment base and lower depreciation charges than younger divisions and therefore will tend to report a higher return on investment. This may serve to cover up a deteriorating profit situation until price levels stabilize and investment replacement at higher prices begins to make itself felt in lower return on investment figures.

This problem differs in no fundamental way from the price level problem in external financial reporting and seems no nearer to solution. If there is any difference at all, it is that few division managers have major responsibility for so-called holding gains and losses on their asset portfolios, but this is relevant to the use of divisional profit figures in managerial evaluation rather than in activity evaluation, which is the concern of this section.

Costing inventories at current standard cost and long-lived assets at some approximation to current replacement cost by the use of explicit index numbers or otherwise might be a good solution to the problem of interdivisional comparability, but the expense of making the replacement cost calculations is unlikely to be justifiable except as part of a companywide adjustment for public reporting purposes. (Some of the large Dutch companies do in fact make such adjustments both for internal and for external reporting.) The only alternative seems to be the exercise of judgment in evaluating the reported figures, and this may be the only practical possibility for most companies.

Alternative Sources of Profit Standards

In addition to the uniform, across-the-board return-on-investment standard implied in the previous discussion, most companies develop specific standards tailored to the circumstances in which each division operates. One such standard is provided by examining the return on investment reported in the published financial statements of competing firms. Unfortunately, these are companywide data and may represent product mixes far different from that of the related company division, and this impairs their usefulness. Despite these imperfections as well as those of internal return-on-investment calculations, however, information on competitive performance may be extremely important in pointing out the need for and the possibility of profit improvement.

Differential return-on-investment standards may also be applied to different divisions to reflect top management's attitudes toward risk or the desirable pattern of future expansion. Some companies, for example, place a high premium on growth through the development of new products by applying lower standards to divisions that are in the initial stages of growth than are applied to older, more mature divisions. Other companies take just the reverse position and demand higher yields in the newer and therefore presumably riskier fields than in established lines. Standards of this type are difficult to derive by objective means, and instead are established by managerial judgment. They may still be useful, nevertheless, as visible expressions of managerial policy.

Gross Assets versus Depreciated Cost

One final question needs to be considered, whether physical property is to be stated at original cost (gross assets) or at book value (net after depreciation). Gross valuation has long since gone out of use for company financial reporting, and for good reasons, but many companies have adopted it in recent years for internal return on investment reporting.

Two main arguments are advanced in favor of the gross assets approach. First, intercompany differences in depreciation policy may impair the validity of intercompany return-on-investment comparisons if depreciation allowances are deducted from the investment base. Second, intracompany and year-to-year differences in the age of depreciating facilities may vitiate internal comparisons that are based on net book value. For example, a division with an older property mix will have a lower net asset base than a relatively new division with new plant and equipment. If earning power does not decline with age, then the net book value approach will tend to lower the newer division's position in the interdivisional ranking. Moreover, as the division grows older, its net book value will decline in relation to original cost and it will show an upward trend in return on investment.

The other side of the argument is at least equally persuasive. If earning power is not steady but declines as facilities age, then net book value will provide a better base for internal return-on-investment comparisons. Furthermore, if depreciation charges reflect, as they should, the patterns of service potential expiration, then book value will be a better measure of the assets committed to the division's activities than original cost. Finally, one end purpose of these calculations is to provide a profitability measure comparable to external, companywide measures, and these generally reflect a net asset definition.

Whether earning power increases or declines is a question of fact, often undeterminable. Use of the gross assets approach, however, seems to deny the validity of the depreciation concept, and of the fact that depreciation occurs there seems little doubt. If divisions differ in depreciation policy, the appropriate response would seem to be to adjust the policy, not abandon the concept.

PROFIT REPORTING FOR MANAGERIAL EVALUATION

It needs to be emphasized and reemphasized that *these divisional return-on-investment measures are not directly relevant either to man-*

agerial resource allocation decisions or to the appraisal of current managerial performance. The former require incremental profit data, while the latter call for modifications in the measurement scheme which we shall examine in the next section. Routine historical measures of net profit ratios to net investment serve only to direct attention to divisions in which favorable or unfavorable profit levels or trends require special study.

Divisional profit reports are also prepared for use by division management to monitor divisional operations and by top management in appraising the performance of division management. The requirements of these reports thus need to be considered separately.

Requirements of Managerial Evaluation Standards

Standards to be used in evaluating the profit performance of division managers need to meet two major requirements: (1) current attainability by competent division managers, and (2) consistency with the degree of divisional profit controllability. It is not necessary that they be uniform for all divisions within the company, except insofar as uniformity means a uniform observation of the two basic requirements for all divisions. Neither is it necessary that they be based on past performance within the company or contemporary performance in other companies. Their essential characteristic is that they provide a basis for evaluating how well management has utilized the resources at its command in the environment in which it has operated.

Attainability. The first requirement of a sound profit standard—attainability by competent division management—is somewhat difficult to define in unambiguous terms. Each division is to a certain extent unique with respect to the conditions that affect its performance. Profit differences can be created by variations in the age or condition of production facilities, by differences in local wage structures, transportation costs, and raw material prices, by differences in the types of products handled or customers served, or by differences in the degree of competition faced in the marketplace. To judge the manager of a pharmaceuticals division by the same profit standard that is applied to the performance of the manager of a fertilizer division runs completely counter to the concept of standards as measures of reasonably attainable performance. Furthermore, the standard that is applicable in one year may be entirely inappropriate in another if market or operating conditions have changed significantly. Nothing can undermine a profit measurement system more quickly than a standard that is not in tune with current operating realities. It may serve adequately as a target or long-range objective, but it is not a standard of satisfactory managerial performance.

Controllability. The second criterion, the need for consistency with the extent of divisional profit controllability, applies with equal force to the standard and to the measure of divisional profit. Both the measure of profit and the standard with which it is to be compared should be defined so as to exclude any variances that are not to some significant extent within the control of the division managers.

This criterion must be interpreted with a dash of common sense. No variable is ever completely and absolutely controllable; controllability always means the ability to influence an item of cost or revenue within limits, and these limits may be either very broad or extremely narrow. No measure of profit, no matter how carefully defined, can hope to be a precise reflection of a manager's effectiveness in profit control. The danger lies in trying to avoid the problem by adopting a profit definition that eliminates so many of the possible sources of variances that the manager is relieved of most of his profit control responsibilities.

For example, changes in local property taxes are clearly outside the scope of divisional controllability, as is the amount of most central administrative expense allocated to the divisions. Variations in divisional sales, however, are an important aspect of managerial performance even though they may result in large part from changes in general business conditions. To define controllability so narrowly as to exclude this latter kind of variation would be to reduce profit comparisons to mere statements of cost variances. Changes in the business environment can and should be considered in *evaluating* profit deviations, but not in *computing* those deviations. The difference is significant. There is little that the division manager can do to influence local property assessments, but he is expected to react to market changes so as to take advantage of favorable opportunities or reduce the impact of unfavorable developments.

Additional Measurement Constraints

Managerial performance reports, as indicated above, need to exclude noncontrollable items. In addition, they must meet two other constraints:

1. Divisional profit should not be increased by any action that reduces total company profit or decreased by any action that increases total company profit.
2. Each division's profit should be as independent as possible of performance efficiency elsewhere in the company.

The first of these must be specified because of the guidance or motivational impact of divisional profit reports. Actions that would increase divisional profits while decreasing company profits are the result of what is known as *suboptimization.* Suboptimization of one kind or another is difficult to avoid and often remains undetected, but every effort should be made to insure that the structure of historical profit reports does not encourage it. It takes a strong manager to make decisions that will reduce his reported profit, even if he is convinced that they will benefit the company as a whole. This issue will receive a good deal of attention in Chapter 26.

The independence requirement has an evaluation implication which may be apparent. If one service or profit center's unit costs exceed or are less than the budgeted amounts, this has no bearing on the managerial performance of the managers of the profit centers using these goods or services. Such deviations must be excluded from the evaluation reports in one way or another.

Profit Budgets versus Return-on-Investment Standards

Most companies that have moved far enough in the direction of decentralization to prepare divisional profit reports express divisional profits as percentages of divisional investment. These return-on-investment ratios are then compared with similar ratios for prior periods or other divisions or with some desired companywide return-on-investment ratio.

A division of one company, for example, presented the following report, covering the first nine months of its 1967 fiscal year (all figures are in thousands of dollars) :

	Current Month	Year to Date	12 Months	
			1966	1965
Net sales............................	$ 876	$ 8,432	$ 8,712	$ 9,014
Cost of sales........................	502	4,993	4,775	4,654
Gross margin........................	$ 374	$ 3,439	$ 3,937	$ 4,360
Division expenses....................	212	1,946	1,817	1,763
Net Profit before Taxes...............	$ 162	$ 1,493	$ 2,120	$ 2,597
Current assets, net...................	$ 4,012	$ 3,936	$ 3,410	$ 3,690
Fixed assets, gross...................	9,322	9,229	8,970	8,430
Total Investment.....................	$13,334	$13,165	$12,380	$12,120
Return on Investment (Annual)........	14.6%	15.1%	17.1%	21.4%

Trend analysis of these data and comparison with the company's 25 percent before-tax return on investment objective indicate a serious and deteriorating profit situation in this division. Although this is useful information, the return-on-investment standard is of little relevance to the objective of managerial performance evaluation because so many factors other than ineffective managerial performance might account for the low level of profits.

The most serious defect of uniform companywide return-on-investment standards for this purpose is that they violate the criterion of *attainability*. The manager of a division operating in a depressed market, for example, is likely to regard uniform companywide return-on-investment standards as unattainable and therefore unfair. The manager of a division in an expanding market, on the other hand, can often meet one of these uniform standards with relative ease. For this reason, a division manager who reports an 8 percent return on investment may actually be doing a better managerial job than another manager who reports 30 percent. In the previous example, the division may actually be increasing its share of its markets in the face of widespread industry overcapacity, and under these circumstances a 15 percent return on investment may be exceptionally good.

Uniform return-on-investment standards are also inappropriate for managerial evaluation because they do not reflect adequately the degree of divisional profit *controllability*. The true return on the investment required by any division is indeterminate because many assets and operating costs that are necessary to support the operations of a division are administered centrally rather than by the division managers. Allocation of these items to individual divisions is inescapably arbitrary; they are neither controllable by the division managers nor objectively traceable to the operations of particular divisions. As a result, the return-on investment ratios are not truly comparable to targets drawn from reported performance of other companies or from estimates of the company's own cost of capital. Failure of one division to achieve the target return on investment may merely mean that that division has been assigned too large a share of these common costs or common investments.

All of this leads to the conclusion that *budgeted profit* provides a better profit standard for managerial performance evaluation than any uniform ratio applied across the board. This is implicitly recognized by many companies that express their standards in terms of ratios but vary the ratio from division to division. A carefully conceived profit budget is by definition attainable with good management under expected operating conditions. The budget may be as high or as low as these conditions seem to warrant.

One large decentralized company sums up its profit and return-on-investment budgets in the form shown in Exhibit 25–4. This form has the advantage of combining a flexible current objective, based on plans originating within the division itself, with a record of the immediate past and an indication of how the division plans to meet the future.

Profit and return-on-investment budgets of this type need to be supported by detailed schedules of the underlying components. These detailed profit budgets, moreover, provide a basis not only for determin-

Exhibit 25–4

BUDGETED PROFIT OBJECTIVES

Objectives	1967 Annual Objectives	Long-Term Objectives			Performance	
		1968	1969	1970	1966	1965
Gross sales billed						
Total gross assets—average						
Asset turnover						
Income before taxes						
Percentage return on total gross assets						

ing net variations from budgeted performance but also for analyzing the elements that together account for the net variation. Step-by-step breakdown of the return-on-investment ratio into component ratios, such as margin on sales and asset turnover, is useful, but it is not nearly as informative as item-by-item analysis of cost and sales deviations from budget.

The use of desired performance ratios as profit standards stems from a confusion of long-run desirability with short-run attainability, or a confusion of managerial evaluation with activity evaluation. These are not identical. Merely because management desires a certain return on investment does not make this a valid standard for use in evaluating current managerial performance, although it may have some relevance in examining the profitability of the activities that make up the division. The continuing emphasis on these ratios leads to time-consuming and fruitless efforts to allocate centrally administered investments, despite the fact that the periodic performance report is not intended to be and in fact cannot be a faithful indicator of the profitability of investment in the division.

Investment Carrying Charges

Advocates of the return-on-investment approach to divisional profit reporting and evaluation rely heavily on the argument that the use of divisional profit budgets, established without reference to the amount of invested capital, reduces the accountability of the division manager for the prudent use of capital funds. Clearly, some mechanism must be provided to regulate internal capital investment. Capital is invested to produce profits. If profit expectations are inadequate, the investment should not be made. Investment control, however, is not achieved primarily through routine historical comparisons:

1. Most of the division's plant and equipment investment remains substantially unchanged for long periods and is thus not currently controllable.
2. Control over current capital expenditures is achieved by project review and justification procedures that emphasize future expectations rather than past performance; the major portion of these decisions is made at the top-management level rather than by the division managers.

Control over the division manager's exercise of his limited authority in these projects is best accomplished by incorporating provisions for planned cost reductions and profit improvement in the operating profit budget. This should be accompanied by procedures that will require division managers to justify new capital expenditures on the basis of anticipated profitability and to limit severely expenditures on projects that cannot meet such tests.

There is, however, one portion of divisional investment which is subject to a substantial degree of current control at the division manager level, and this is the investment in working capital, particularly investments in inventories and receivables. The division manager may be able to control receivables by selecting his customers and by regulating his efforts to collect overdue accounts. He can influence inventory levels by changing reorder levels and by adjusting production schedules. Variations in controllable investment, however, do not customarily enter the profit budgets because the normal accounting procedure is to make no charge for implicit interest on capital investment.

One solution to this problem that has been adopted by a number of companies is to include a provision for interest on controllable investment in the divisional profit budgets and to charge interest to divisions on the basis of actual controllable investment balances. This procedure serves to emphasize to the division managers the importance of invest-ment control over these elements. It also ties in very nicely with the inventory control formulas used by many companies to achieve a bal-ance between the costs of carrying inventories and the economies of long production runs and stable production levels.

Manipulation of Divisional Profit

One of the most serious objections that has been leveled at the entire concept of the profit evaluation of managerial performance is that the divisional profit figures are capable of substantial short-period juggling of time-shiftable costs. Supplies and indirect manufacturing materials, for example, may be charged to expense either at the time of purchase or at the time that they are issued from inventory. To the extent that unrecorded inventories of these items fluctuate, currently recognized expense will be an inadequate reflection of current operating costs. This particular problem is unlikely to be serious for periods as long as one year, but for monthly or even quarterly reporting they will influence the absolute level of profits and return on investment. Maintenance costs fall into the same category, although the time required to average these out is likely to be considerably longer insofar as maintenance expendi-tures may be deferred or advanced at management's discretion.

It must be admitted that this problem has not been completely solved. Some central administration of such items as maintenance is probably required, but the degree of central interference in divisional affairs is an extremely ticklish problem. Perhaps the best weapon that top management has is its authority to review and modify divisional budgets, but this is not a complete solution to the problem. This only serves to emphasize the fact that the evaluation of managerial perform-ance has many dimensions and that no single figure, profit or otherwise, is enough in itself.

RECONCILING MANAGERIAL AND ACTIVITY EVALUATION MEASURES

Many of the components of the return-on-investment figures used in routine activity evaluation are irrelevant to managerial evaluation, as we have already noted, because they are not currently controllable by division management. The accounting system must provide some means of reconciling these differences and eliminating noncontrollable vari-ances from the periodic profit reports used for managerial evaluation.

Defining Income as Controllable Profit

One possibility is to include only controllable items in the divisional profit report. In other words, the accountant should now recognize the concept of *controllable profit* in addition to the three concepts of variable profit, contribution margin, and net profit discussed in the preceding chapter. The relationships among these four concepts are illustrated in Exhibit 25–5.

From this exhibit, it can be seen that controllable profit is what is left after deducting from sales revenue all variable costs plus those fixed costs which can be controlled by division management. Some of these fixed costs may be specific costs of individual products, but most of them

Exhibit 25–5

FOUR PROFIT CONCEPTS ILLUSTRATED

Sales...	.$760,000
Less:	
Variable cost of goods sold.......................................	.$270,000
Variable divisional selling and administrative expense............	30,000
Variable profit...	.$460,000
Less: Controllable divisional overhead...........................	200,000
Controllable profit...	.$260,000
Less: Fixed, noncontrollable divisional overhead..................	150,000
Contribution margin..	.$110,000
Less: Allocation of extradivisional fixed expenses—noncontrollable...	50,000
Net Profit before Taxes...	.$ 60,000

are normally joint costs of all or several of the products of the division. They include such items as engineering, production planning, supervision, and sales management salaries.

Although these controllable fixed costs are not entirely relevant to many current tactical decisions, collectively they make up an area in which the division manager can exercise control. In addition, the division manager may find ways to increase profit by either increasing or decreasing the level of fixed costs that are subject to his control. For example, an increase in the size of the sales force may be justified by the added profit that results from increased sales. Addition of a parts inspector may be justified by the reduced variable product cost due to a lower rejection rate for finished products. These decisions are different from the daily operating decisions regarding price, product mix, and equipment utilization, but they are an important aspect of the job of division management. Controllable fixed costs should not, in any circumstances, be eliminated from the divisional profit reports.

Contribution margin, on the other hand, is too inclusive a concept for use in the evaluation of current managerial performance in that it includes some divisional costs that are not currently controllable. For example, certain fixed costs are imposed on the division by top management or by decisions of prior years, such as the division manager's salary, depreciation, property taxes, and insurance, and these are not currently controllable at the division level. Although some of these noncontrollable fixed costs (depreciation and property taxes, for instance) reflect the past investment decisions of management and thus throw light on its overall record, this aspect of performance is more effectively appraised through special reviews of capital outlays than it is through the current data on profit performance.

Suppressing Noncontrollable Variances

The only difficulty with this first solution is that top management ordinarily wants one report to reflect the profit performance both of the division and of its management. If variances in the controllable fixed costs arise, therefore, they will appear on these dual-purpose reports. Even if the reports are designed so that noncontrollable items are listed "below the line," variances in these items are likely to attract management's attention.

One alternative is to adjust the profit budget after the fact to eliminate any deviations in noncontrollable items. For example, if allocations of central office costs exceed the initial budget allowance, the allowance may be increased to offset the difference.

The other and generally preferable method is to design the allocation procedures by which nontraceable costs get into the division profit reports so as to eliminate any deviations before they are reported. The principles on which such allocations should be based were described in Chapter 14 and can be applied here with only minor changes in wording:

1. *Predetermined transfer prices* for services with measurable consumption units.
2. *Predetermined activity charges* for the variable component of the costs of service centers and central office centers which lack readily traceable outputs.
3. *Predetermined fixed charges* equal to the amounts budgeted for the fixed component of the costs of service centers and central office centers which lack readily traceable outputs.

The desirability of adjusting the cost recording procedures rather than the profit standards is most apparent in the case of service center costs that are indirectly controllable by the profit center managers. The use of predetermined rates per unit of service eliminates the price effect from these charges and restricts deviations to those stemming from the quantity or mix of services consumed. If these services are priced at average historical cost, the task of separating the price from the quantity effect may be extremely difficult, particularly if the service in question is not one that can be measured in a single homogeneous physical unit such as pounds or man-hours.

SUMMARY

Many companies have found it desirable to decentralize decision-making responsibility in a number of semiautonomous divisions. The managers of these divisions need profit reports to judge the effects of past actions and to provide data for future planning. Top management needs divisional profit reports for use in evaluating the performance of division management, to guide and motivate division management toward profit goals, and to monitor the profitability of resources invested in the various divisions.

Routine measures of resource profitability are almost never directly usable in top-management investment/disinvestment decisions but can only point to the need for special attention. For this purpose, comparisons with uniform, companywide return-on-investment standards is appropriate.

The operating cost and investment allocations necessary to derive return-on-investment figures have little bearing on managerial evaluation. Instead, a measure of controllable profit is required. Furthermore, divisional circumstances vary so widely that managerial performance has to be judged against tailor-made division profit plans rather than against the uniform return-on-investment standard.

As long as a clear distinction is made between these two major purposes of profit reporting and the requirements of each are kept in mind, there is no reason why a rational divisional profit measurement system cannot be worked out within the context of the company's profit planning program.

DISCUSSION QUESTIONS

1. Can a company be divisionalized without being decentralized? Distinguish between the two terms.
2. What reasons can you suggest for the adoption of a decentralized organization structure?

3. Distinguish between profit centers and budget or service centers. Under what circumstances can a service department be treated as a profit center?

4. Inasmuch as division profit reports are historical, whereas managerial decisions must look to the future, in what sense can these reports serve division management as guides to decision making?

5. What attributes should be possessed by a sound system of internal profit reporting?

6. If measures of divisional investment are desired, how would you define divisional investment? Indicate the reasons for your rejection of alternative definitions.

7. How do price level fluctuations affect interdivisional return on investment comparisons?

8. Outline in detail a procedure for evaluating divisional profit performance, assuming that divisional profit standards are provided by detailed budgets rather than by a uniform return on investment ratio.

9. What criteria should be satisfied by a divisional profit standard for managerial evaluation? Indicate why each is important.

10. It has been suggested that a well-designed system for charging interest on investment to individual profit centers cannot only substitute for return on investment ratios but can also provide more meaningful profit reports. Discuss this proposal and indicate how it would have to be applied if it is to be successful.

11. Distinguish between managerial profit evaluation and activity profit evaluation. Discuss the relevance of monthly profit reports to each of these kinds of evaluation.

12. What problems must be solved if management decides that divisional profit must be defined as net profit? Outline an approach for the solution of these problems.

13. The Culver Company has established 20 percent as a desired minimum return on divisional investment, before income taxes. The company's plastics division is currently reporting a return on investment of 12 percent before taxes, reflecting a slight improvement over the performance of previous years. Indicate what use you would make of these figures and how you would proceed to analyze them.

14. The legal department of the Exhow Company is now treated as a budget center. The company's controller has suggested that this department be designated a profit center, with individual division managers being free to retain outside legal counsel or to dispense with legal services entirely. The controller says: "In the final analysis, it is management that decides whether to initiate lawsuits, whether to defend lawsuits or settle out of court, and whether to develop new products that are competitive with products covered by patents controlled by other companies. The function of the legal department is clearly subsidiary to these responsibilities of management. Therefore, why not leave the amount of legal services to be used up to the judgment of division management?" Prepare an answer for this proposal.

15. It has been suggested that the introduction of large-scale electronic comput-

ers which are capable of simultaneous analysis of many aspects of managerial problems will eventually reverse the trend to decentralization and will tend to reconcentrate decision-making responsibility in top management. Discuss the implications of this point of view.

EXERCISES AND PROBLEMS

1. The asset and liability records of the Deutsch Instruments Company show the following account balances (in thousands of dollars):

	Un-distributed	Division A	Division B	Division C
Cash........................	$360	$ 10	$ 20	$ 15
Receivables..................	400	...	....	....
Inventories..................	...	300	450	400
Plant and equipment..........	100	500	1,500	1,000
Allowance for depreciation.....	(40)	(200)	(700)	(300)
Total Assets..............	$820	$ 610	$1,270	$1,115
Accounts payable..............	$ 30	$ 80	$ 140	$ 100
Accrued liabilities.............	30	20	30	25
Bonds payable................	200	...	....	....
Total Liabilities...........	$260	$ 100	$ 170	$ 125

No further divisional identification of undistributed asset balances is possible, but the president of the company has insisted that divisional net profits be expressed as a percentage of divisional investment, including a share of undistributed investment. Further information on company activities for the most recent year follows (in thousands of dollars):

	Division A	Division B	Division C
Net sales........................	$1,500	$2,400	$2,100
Division payroll.................	400	600	500
Materials received..............	500	800	800
Head office expense distributed....	80	120	100
Division net profit..............	150	300	380

Compute net investment for each division and justify the methods that you have used in your computations.

2. The Ray Manufacturing Company is decentralized in several divisions, including the textile products division. The following statistical information relates to the company as a whole and the textile products division for the month of June. All budget data have been taken from the planning budget for the month.

	Entire Company		Textile Products	
	Budget	Actual	Budget	Actual
Number of employees............	5,000	4,600	800	780
Total payrolls..................	$ 3,500,000	$3,175,000	$ 480,000	$ 485,000
Factory payrolls................	$ 2,400,000	$2,200,000	$ 375,000	$ 365,000
Net sales......................	$10,000,000	$9,000,000	$1,500,000	$1,600,000

Actual head office selling and administrative expenses are fully distributed among the divisions each month. All head office expenses are assumed
to be fixed with respect to volume. Budgeted and actual head office
expenses, together with the relevant allocation bases, were as follows
during the month of June:

	Basis	Budget	Actual
Accounting department...............	Employees	$120,000	$115,000
Manufacturing department............	Factory payrolls	60,000	62,000
Marketing department................	Net sales	50,000	51,000
Advertising.........................	Net sales	200,000	280,000
Executive offices....................	Total payrolls	70,000	68,000

a) Prepare a head office expense budget for the textile products division,
based on budget data only, and compute the amount of head office
expenses to be charged to the division for the month.

b) Compute the variances in the charges for these five items that will appear in the textile products division profit report for the month. What
effect do they have on divisional return on investment? What relevance
do they have either to activity evaluation or to managerial performance evaluation?

3. The Top Equipment Company is organized into several autonomous divisions. The valve divisions sells all of its output to outside customers and
buys all of its materials and parts from outside suppliers. The asset and
liability sections of the division's last two balance sheets and its income
statement for the most recent year are given below. This income statement is considered indicative of the division's profit potential for the
future:

Balance Sheet Data

	January 1, 19xx		December 31, 19xx	
Cash..............................		$ 380,000		$ 400,000
Accounts receivable................		450,000		520,000
Inventory.........................		780,000		850,000
Land, buildings, and equipment......	$2,280,000		$2,300,000	
Less: Allowance for depreciation....	1,110,000	1,170,000	1,200,000	1,100,000
Total Assets..................		$2,780,000		$2,870,000
Wages, accounts, and taxes payable...		$ 300,000		$ 350,000
Mortgage loan payable.............		550,000		500,000
Total Divisional Liabilities......		$ 850,000		$ 850,000

Income Statement 19xx

Sales..		$4,250,000
Less: Cost of goods sold............................	$3,410,000	
Selling and administrative expense.................	470,000	3,880,000
Division profit contribution...........................		$ 370,000
Less: Allocated headquarters expense....................		120,000
Division Net Income before Taxes......................		$ 250,000

Notes:

(1) The cost of goods sold figure includes $110,000 in annual depreciation charges.

(2) Wages, accounts, and taxes payable are all traceable to the vale division.

(3) The mortgage loan payable calls for interest at a rate of 5% and is a long-term obligation of the Top Equipment Company, secured by a mortgage on the land, buildings, and equipment of the valve division. This loan would be paid off if the division were to be liquidated. Interest on this loan is not charged to the valve division.

(4) Liquidation expenses, including such items as terminal pay of employees and losses from liquidation of inventory and receivables, would total $320,000.

(5) The disposal value of the land, buildings, and equipment is approximately $820,000.

(6) Replacement cost of the fixed assets is considerably in excess of their book value. The replacement of the existing facilities with equivalent brand-new facilities would cost approvimately $3,700,000.

(7) Annual outlays on plan and equipment necessary to maintain the division's competitive position would amount to $160,000 if the division were to continue in operation.

(8) Headquarters expenses are allocated among the company's divisions as a uniform percentage of divisional sales.

Compute divisional rate of return (*a*) on a going concern basis, and (*b*) on a liquidation basis. Comment on the differences between the two figures and indicate how you think they would be used.

4. Burpee Baby Products is a wholly owned subsidiary of a large pharmaceutical company. Three quarters of the firm's annual sales are made at a uniform rate over the six-month period May to October, the remainder being distributed equally and uniformly over the period November to April. Over the past decade, sales volume has increased in direct proportion to the number of births in the United States.

The company's fiscal year ends on March 31. This year's profit plan shows the following breakdown of total costs:

Manufacturing cost of goods sold:			
Materials (including packaging)................	$240,000		
Direct labor....................................	240,000		
Indirect labor and supervision..................	240,000		
Depreciation of plant...........................	240,000		
Other manufacturing overhead...................	240,000	$1,200,000	50%
Selling and distribution expenses.................		960,000	40
General and administrative expenses..............		240,000	10
Total Costs...............................		$2,400,000	100%

Inquiry reveals that indirect labor and supervision are 50 percent variable with output, depreciation is computed on a production basis, and other manufacturing overhead is essentially fixed. All of these costs are charged to manufactured products by means of annual burden rates based on machine-hours. The operation is highly mechanized. The plant is only a few years old and has a maximum capacity approximately double its present output.

The company's products are not subject to deterioration in storage, and it has been the practice to manufacture at a uniform rate throughout the year, thus building up finished goods inventories steadily from November through April and liquidating these over the subsequent six months.

In comparing the operating performances of this and other subsidiaries and separate divisions, the parent company uses as its principal performance index annual "return on invested capital" figures computed by the formula:

$$\frac{\text{Net income}}{(\text{Beginning total assets} + \text{Ending total assets}) \div 2} = \% \text{ return.}$$

Thus measured, the performance of Burpee Baby Products has for several years been the poorest of any unit in the group. This fact has been a source of particular concern because the Burpee plant is newer and presumably more efficient than that of any other unit.

Early this year, Burpee hired a new controller who was asked to give particular attention to means for improving the return on investment. After considerable study of the problem, he has proposed that the annual production plan be modified to eliminate insofar as possible any manufacturing for inventory. He has stated that under the present system and with an annual manufacturing cost of goods sold of $1,200,000, the capital unnecessarily tied up in finished goods inventories can be computed as follows:

Month	Production Cost	Cost of Sales	Cost of Excess Inventory
November.............	$ 100,000	$ 50,000	$ 50,000
December.............	100,000	50,000	100,000
January...............	100,000	50,000	150,000
February.............	100,000	50,000	200,000
March................	100,000	50,000	250,000
April.................	100,000	50,000	300,000
May..................	100,000	150,000	250,000
June..................	100,000	150,000	200,000
July..................	100,000	150,000	150,000
August...............	100,000	150,000	100,000
September............	100,000	150,000	50,000
October..............	100,000	150,000	–0–
Total.............	$1,200,000	$1,200,000	$1,800,000

Average excess inventory for year: $1,800,000 ÷ 12 = $150,000

The production manager has objected to this proposal on the grounds that uneven production would adversely affect labor costs. Hiring new personnel each year only for the busy season would increase training costs and, even so, give a less efficient labor force. Moreover, since the plant now operates a full day shift and a partial night shift, the change would necessitate either a third shift or overtime during the peak months with consequent additional pay premiums and additional supervisors. He suggests also that the controller's figure of $150,000 must be overstated because 30 cents out of every dollar of manufacturing cost is fixed and will therefore be incurred regardless of when the goods are produced.

The president of Burpee Baby Products has retained you as a consultant. He would like from you a clear statement of the problem, or problems, and suggestions as to how it, or they, might be solved.

5. The sales manager of the Valli Products Company is preparing a tentative sales budget for the coming year. The bulk of the company's organization is concentrated in two divisions, a sales division and a manufacturing division. The manufacturing division consists of a small head office staff and two factories, one for each of the company's two product lines, known as the Valor line and the Valmaid line. The sales division consists of the sales manager and his central staff, two product managers and their staffs, and a field sales organization.

The field sales force is organized by branch territories, with each salesman responsible for covering all present and potential customers in his portion of the territory assigned to his branch. The salesmen report a branch manager. Branch managers report directly to the sales manager, but they also receive sales promotion advice and assistance from two product managers, each of whom is responsible for one of the product lines.

Sales, standard cost of sales, and branch expenses are reported monthly for each branch. Sales, cost of sales, and salesmen's commissions are also classified by product line; most other branch expenses are not allocated between product lines. Each product manager has a small staff responsible for providing technical assistance to purchasers of products in his product line. He also controls expenditures against annual budgets for advertising and product development and improvement.

This divided responsibility for sales promotion at times places a strain on the sales organization as each product manager attempts to induce the field sales force to devote more time to his product line. Each salesman receives an annual bonus computed on the basis of his branch's reported profit, and the product managers vie with each other in pointing out the profitability of their respective lines.

The tentative budget for the sales division for the coming year, as prepared by the sales division controller from budget estimates submitted by responsible executives within the division, is as follows (all figures are in thousands of dollars):

	Valor	Valmaid	Undistributed	Total
Sales	$35,000	$20,000	....	$55,000
Cost of sales	21,000	14,000	....	35,000
Gross margin	$14,000	$ 6,000	....	$20,000
Commissions	1,400	800	....	2,200
Other branch expenses	100	50	$ 2,800	2,950
Product manager expenses	300	200	....	500
Other divisional expenses	.....	.....	2,680	2,680
Divisional Profit	$12,200	$ 4,950	$(5,480)	$11,670
Percentage of sales	34.8%	24.7%	....	21.2%

The Valmaid product manager was immediately concerned over the effect of these figures on branch managers' and salesmen's willingness to push Valmaid sales. He asked the division controller to find out what had happened to his profit margin, which had never been less than 30 percent and had often been higher in the past. The controller discovered that the cost of sales for each line had been prepared by the manufacturing vice president on the basis of sales forecasts compiled from the branch managers' tentative budgets. These forecasts had indicated that whereas the Valor line plant would be operating at virtually full capacity for the next year, the Valmaid plant would be seriously underutilized. The tentative factory cost budgets from the coming year showed the following (all figures in thousands of dollars):

	Valor	Valmaid
Standard costs:		
Direct labor..	$ 5,000	$ 4,000
Direct materials..................................	8,000	3,000
Factory overhead...............................	9,000	6,000
Total standard cost............................	$22,000	$13,000
Volume variance.................................	(1,000)	1,000
Net Cost of Goods Manufactured....................	$21,000	$14,000

Factory overhead costs are approximately 70 percent fixed at standard volume in the Valmaid plant and 50 percent fixed at standard volume in the Valor plant. Sales commissions are proportionate to dollar sales. All other division expenses are substantially fixed.

a) Given the existing profit measurement system, prepare a statement that will indicate to salesmen the relative profitability of the two lines insofar as this relates to the bonus calculation.

b) Compute the effect on total company profit of increases in sales volume in each of the two lines.

c) A salesman believes that by giving more attention to the Valmaid line he can increase its sales by 20 percent, but that if he does so, he will lose $1.10 in Valor sales for every dollar of additional Valmaid sales. Assuming that the annual bonus is 10 percent of net branch profit before taxes, how would you advise the salesman to act? Is this action in the best interests of the company?

d) Discuss the company's treatment of manufacturing volume variances. Should these be charged to the sales division? To the product managers? To the sales branches?

e) From what you know of this company's operations, are there any changes in organization structure that might be considered? Discuss these changes. Are there any other changes in the profit reporting structure that you might suggest?

6. Two years ago the executive committee of the Armchair Club decided to establish four profit centers within the club: (1) dining room (2) bar (3) cigar counter, and (4) hotel service. Wages, salaries, materials, and

other items are charged directly to the appropriate profit center whenever possible, as are revenues from members and guests. Administrative salaries, rent expense, and other items of a general nature are not distributed to the profit centers, nor are members' dues and initiation fees. The only charges between profit centers are for free meals for employees. Each of the other profit centers is billed by the dining room at menu prices. No attempt is made to segregate the cost of these meals from the cost of other meals served in the dining room.

The club's annual financial statements for the last two years are shown in the following table:

	Dining Room	Bar	Cigar Counter	Hotel Services	Administration
19x2					
Revenues......................	$294,318	$94,290	$ 8,673	$16,472	$ 72,254
Expenses:					
Materials...................	$130,332	$42,684	$ 8,298	.....	.....
Salaries and wages...........	121,787	16,645	1,721	$ 394	$ 38,337
Employees' meals............	20,638	1,334	277	.....	2,777
Payroll charges..............	8,762	1,166	128	26	2,729
Supplies.....................	5,009	510	639	86	1,690
Laundry and cleaning........	13,771	727	.....	357	364
Rent........................	.....	.....	.....	.....	42,000
Other.......................	5,726	2,760	.....	.....	6,184
Total expenses............	$306,025	$65,826	$11,063	$ 863	$ 94,081
Departmental Profit...........	$(11,707)	$28,464	$(2,390)	$15,609	$(21,827)
19x1					
Revenues......................	$268,731	$89,171	$ 8,522	$11,033	$ 71,684
Expenses:					
Materials...................	$122,020	$40,358	$ 8,245	.....	.....
Salaries and wages...........	113,386	15,785	1,587	$ 382	$ 36,304
Employee's meals............	17,282	1,189	250	.....	2,835
Payroll charges..............	7,084	954	100	22	2,197
Supplies.....................	4,711	532	592	74	1,418
Laundry and cleaning........	13,044	690	.....	390	69
Rent........................	.....	.....	.....	.....	40,000
Other.......................	4,337	1,860	145	.....	6,675
Total expenses............	$281,864	$61,368	$10,919	$ 868	$ 89,498
Departmental Profit...........	$(13,133)	$27,803	$(2,397)	$10,165	$(17,814)

Hotel services revenues are derived partly from overnight room rentals ($1,780 in 19x1 and $1,459 in 19x2) and from rentals of the club's meeting rooms to outside organizations ($8,923 in 19x1 and $14,712 in 19x2). The club's cashier also serves as manager of the cigar counter and one quarter of his salary is allocated to cigar counter expenses. Administrative expenses include the costs of janitorial services for the entire club amounting to $6,426 in 19x1 and $7,034 in 19x2. Retail prices of items sold by the cigar counter are approximately 120 percent of the wholesale purchase prices of these items.

 a) Prepare a brief report for the club's board of directors, commenting on operations for 19x2, analyzing any items that you think would be of interest to the board.

 b) A recent membership vote on the question of raising dining room prices revealed strong sentiment against any further increases. The board of directors has asked you to examine the possibility of eliminating the dining room deficit by discontinuing dining room service. Does the reported loss for the dining room provide an adequate basis for computing the effect of such an action? If not, indicate what other estimates would have to be made.

7. Delphi Instrument Company acquired the assets of Apollo Electronics Inc. late in 1965. The operations of Apollo continued under the name of the Apollo division and John Avakian, the former president of Apollo Electronics, was made a vice president of Delphi, in charge of the Apollo division. Unlike the other principal officers of Delphi, however, Mr. Avakian was not elected to the board of directors, nor did he have a rug on the floor of his office as did the officers who had been with Delphi prior to the merger.

Shortly after the merger Mr. Avakian approached the president of Delphi, a personal friend of long standing, and said: "If I can make a $250,000 profit in the Apollo line this coming year, how about putting a rug in my office?" Both men realized that the general economic outlook for the next few months was relatively unpromising, but the Apollo Division was scheduled to introduce a new line of products in the next few months to be known as the Apollo Sunlite line, and the greater profit margins on this new line gave Mr. Avakian a fairly good chance of meeting his profit goal.

The Sunlite line was introduced early in 1966, phased with orders so that all of the old instruments would be sold before deliveries on the new line were made. Unfortunately, production cutbacks in customers' factories were more severe than had been ancitipated, and Mr. Avakian was disappointed to see $440,000 of inventory write-offs in the old Apollo line. Furthermore, orders for the Sunlite line were not coming in as rapidly as had been expected. The most painful development as far as Mr. Avakian was concerned, however, was that factory burden rates had just been increased drastically as the Delphi controller took action to "correct a chronic unabsorbed overhead problem." Mr. Avakian was convinced that the unabsorbed overhead could be traced directly to the Delphi line, which consisted primarily of low-volume, high-margin items that suffered even more from order cancellations than the Apollo lines. The controller was unmovable, however, and the revised burden rates remained in effect.

By November of 1966, electronic instrument sales had picked up substantially, except in the Delphi line. In looking over the October income statement, Mr. Avakian noted that the doubling of burden rates had not solved the controller's "unabsorbed overhead problem." Still with the hope of paving his office with broadloom, Mr. Avakian dictated the following memorandum to Delphi's president.

"The latest profit forecast indicates that the Apollo division will report a profit of $160,000 or possibly more when the books are closed at the end of this year, on sales of approximately $1.5 million. This figure reflects the 1966 burden rates which are one and one-half times the rates in force at Apollo prior to the merger. Although the Apollo lines are no longer manufactured exclusively in the old Apollo plant, which is now only one plant in the manufacturing division, the changes in manufacturing methods in the last year have been negligible and just enough to offset a 3 percent rise in wage rates. I still think that I am entitled to my rug, and the following calculations back me up.

	1963	1964	1965	1966 (Est.)
Direct labor/materials (K).............	0.26	0.26	0.27	0.27
Sales prices/materials (R).............	2.35	2.38	2.57	2.81
Overhead/direct labor (Z).............	1.23	1.34	1.57	2.35
Gross margin—% (M)................	33%	32%	34%	32%

"Materials prices have remained approximately constant for the past four years and in some cases have actually decreased slightly due to the economies of bulk purchasing. Labor costs have risen only slightly despite annual wage rate increases, as a direct result of improvements in methods and more effective cost control. The increasing ratio of sales prices to materials costs in the last two years is almost solely attributable to price increases. Offsetting this is the increase in the overhead/direct labor ratio that followed the merger. If the 1965 overhead rate of $1.57 per direct labor dollar were applied to 1966 sales, the Apollo gross margin would be approximately 40 percent rather than 32 percent, and on sales of $1.5 million this would add $120,000 to the Apollo division's profits. You can prove this to yourself by using the following formula:

$$\text{GROSS MARGIN} = \text{SALES} - \text{LABOR} - \text{MATERIALS} - \text{OVERHEAD}$$

Substituting the ratios referred to above, this formula becomes:

$$\text{Gross margin} = \text{Sales} - \frac{K \cdot \text{Sales}}{R} - \frac{\text{Sales}}{R} - \frac{ZK \cdot \text{Sales}}{R}.$$

Dividing all of these items by sales, we get:

$$\text{Margin/sales } (M) = 1 - \frac{K + ZK + 1}{R} = 1 - \frac{K(Z+1)+1}{R}.$$

If we use 1966 values for all of these items except the overhead ratio and the 1965 value for that, we get a margin of 39.7 percent:

$$M = 1 - \frac{0.27\,(1.57+1)+1}{2.81} = 0.397, \text{ or } 39.7\%."$$

How would you reply to Mr. Avakian's memorandum? Do you think he has earned his rug? What flaws, if any, do you detect in his reasoning?

8. The following financial report was prepared for the Hepplewhite division of the Duncan Company for the first two months of the 19x1–x2 fiscal year which began on March 1, 19x1 (all figures are in thousands of dollars):

	Comparative Results of Business			
		Two months to April 30		
	Actual, April, 19x1	Forecast 19x1	Actual	
			19x1	19x0
Sales:				
Product A	$190	$ 500	$ 453	$484
Product B	223	700	522	377
Product C	65	100	132	91
Product D	12	50	28	39
Total sales	$490	$1,350	$1,135	$991
Cost of sales:				
Product A	$112	$ 300	$ 266	$312
Product B	107	336	251	183
Product C	38	58	76	44
Product D	6	25	14	22
Total cost of sales	$263	$ 719	$ 607	$561
Gross profit on sales	$227	$ 631	$ 528	$430
Expenses:				
Home office commissions	$ 28	$ 66	$ 66	$ 66
Selling	58	128	121	79
Administrative	27	52	61	63
Development	27	77	63	106
Total expenses	$140	$ 323	$ 311	$314
Net profit before taxes	$ 87	$ 308	$ 217	$116
Taxes at 50%	44	154	109	58
Net Profit	$ 43	$ 154	$ 108	$ 58

| | Comparative Financial Condition | | |
	2/28/x1	4/30/x1	Change
Assets:			
Cash	$ 16	$ 20	$ 4
Receivables	277	101	(176)
Inventories	2,451	2,324	(127)
Fixed assets—net	1,295	1,291	(4)
Deferred charges—net	19	(67)	(86)
Total assets	$4,058	$3,669	$(389)
Accounts payable	189	94	(95)
Net Investment	$3,869	$3,575	$(294)
Return on investment	10.8%	17.5%	+6.7%

Additional Information:

(1) Home office commissions reflect predetermined payments for central administrative services rendered.

(2) Development expenses consist of current research division charges to projects which have been requested and approved by the Hepplewhite division.

(3) Cash balances represent imprest funds only. All payrolls and most payments to vendors are made by the home office.

(4) Accounts receivable and accounts payable consist of billings and invoices in transit between Hepplewhite and the home office.

(5) All materials, work in process, and finished product inventories of the Hepplewhite division, together with plant and equipment listed in the corporate property records as belonging to Hepplewhite, are shown on the Hepplewhite statements. There is no allocation of centrally administered assets.

(6) The company uses 10 percent after taxes as its cost of capital in capital expenditure decisions.

(7) Factory flexible budget allowances for March and April amounted to $282,000, overhead absorbed totaled $308,000, and actual overhead totaled $273,000; over-absorbed overhead as of April 30 accounts for part of the credit balance in deferred charges.

(8) The standard before-tax P/V ratio is 50 percent for product A, 60 percent for product B, 55 percent for product C, and 50 percent for product D. All expenses other than the cost of goods sold are assumed to be fixed with respect to volume.

a) Comment on the reporting system used for the Hepplewhite division. How well does it provide a measure of managerial performance? Of investment performance?

b) Prepare a revised report for the two-month period, incorporating any improvements that you deem desirable and feasible, given only the information above.

9. The Burton Beneficial Company is a manufacturing firm with three divisions and a home office in New York. The company is decentralized, with each division manager responsible for the profits of his division. The company's consolidating income statement for an entire year is shown in Exhibit 1. (In this exhibit, both "managed" and "committed" costs are regarded as wholly fixed; there are no variable overhead costs.)

The company's inventories are carried on the books at their variable cost, calculated on a last-in, first-out basis. If current costs had been used during the period instead of LIFO cost, the cost of goods sold for the various divisions would have been as follows:

Division A—$25,000   (no change)
Division B—   9,000
Division C— 15,000

Depreciation is, of course, recorded on a historical cost basis. If depreciation had been charged on the basis of replacement costs during the period, the depreciation for the various divisions would have been as follows:

Division A—$10,000
Division B—   4,000
Division C—   5,000

Exhibit 1

THE BURTON BENEFICIAL COMPANY

Consolidating Income Statement

	Consolidated	Consolidating Adjustments	Home Office	Division A	Division B	Division C
Sales—outside	$100,000			$60,000	$25,000	$15,000
Interdivisional sales		$(20,000)		.....	5,000	5,000
Total sales	$100,000	$(20,000)		$60,000	$30,000	$30,000
Manufacturing costs:						
Product costs—outside sales:						
Direct labor	$ 7,000			$ 2,000	$ 3,000	$ 2,000
Raw materials	7,000			3,000	2,000	2,000
Raw materials—intercompany purchases	.....	$(20,000)		20,000		
Product costs—intercompany sales:						
Direct labor	6,000				1,000	5,000
Raw materials	5,000				2,000	3,000
Total cost of goods sold	$ 25,000	$(20,000)		$25,000	$ 8,000	$12,000
Committed costs:						
Depreciation	12,000			9,000	2,000	1,000
Rents and royalties	1,000			500	300	200
Insurance	1,000			300	400	300
Other fixed overhead	5,000			3,200	800	1,000
Managed costs—manufacturing:						
Operating costs	9,000			5,000	3,000	1,000
Policy costs	6,000			3,000	2,000	1,000
Total manufacturing costs	$ 59,000	$(20,000)		$46,000	$16,500	$16,500
General and administrative costs:						
Managed costs:						
Research and development	$ 5,000		$ 3,000			$ 2,000
Other	8,000		7,000			1,000
Committed costs:						
Administrative salaries	6,000		$ 6,000			
Rent	1,000		1,000			
Depreciation	1,000		1,000			
Home office allocation	.....		(18,000)	$ 9,000	4,500	4,500
Total general and administrative costs	$ 21,000		$	$ 9,000	$ 4,500	$ 7,500
Selling costs:						
Managed costs:						
Advertising	$ 4,000		.....	$ 2,000	$ 1,500	$ 500
Sales department costs	3,000		1,000	1,000	800	200
Committed costs:						
Fixed sales overhead	3,000		1,000	1,500	500	.....
Total selling cost	$ 10,000		$ 2,000	$ 4,500	$ 2,800	$ 700
Income before income tax	$ 10,000		$ (2,000)	$ 500	$ 6,200	$ 5,300
Provision for income tax	5,000		5,000			
Net Income	$ 5,000		$ (7,000)	$ 500	$ 6,200	$ 5,300

The home office carries an investment account for each division, reflecting the net investment in that division on a historical cost basis. The investment accounts did not vary substantially during the year in question and at year-end had the following balances:

	Original Cost	Replacement Cost
Division A............	$100,000	$120,000
Division B.............	60,000	80,000
Division C.............	40,000	100,000

The figures in the second column reflect an estimate of the current replacement cost of the net assets of each division.

The division managers constantly argue over who is doing the better job. The manager of division A, for example, says that the net income figure for his division is a poor indication of his performance. In the first place, he points out that his division purchases goods from the other two divisions on which they make a profit. In addition, he notes that his division's cash flow is the highest, and this is highly significant. He is also suspicious of the accounting practices of the other divisions, claiming that their accounting departments make more profits than their operations. Finally, he complains about the method of allocating home office general and administrative expense. The other division managers also have a variety of complaints.

a) Analyze the performance of the three divisions, and prepare a brief report in which the divisions are ranked according to their profitability to the company.

b) Comment on any aspect or aspects of the company's reporting system that you found particularly desirable or undesirable. What do you think is the difference between "managed" and "committed" costs?

(From a problem prepared by Professor John C. Burton)

Chapter 26

INTRACOMPANY TRANSFER PRICING

ONE OF the most difficult problems in decentralization and internal profit measurement is to devise a sound, workable scheme for pricing the goods and services that are transferred from one company unit to another. From a profit measurement viewpoint, the ideal profit center is one that buys all its raw materials and parts from outside companies and sells its entire output on the market, with no intracompany purchases or sales. Under these circumstances there is no transfer pricing problem and internal profit measurement is relatively simple. Unfortunately, convenience in profit measurement cannot be the dominant criterion in establishing profit centers and interdivisional transfers do take place. The prices at which these transfers are recorded can have a substantial impact on the profit reported for each division, particularly if the physical volume of internal transfers is large.

ISSUES IN TRANSFER PRICING

The prices used to record transfers of goods between divisions serve two main purposes:

1. Before the fact, to guide division managers toward decisions that will lead to an economic allocation of resources.
2. After the fact, as one determinant of the profit attributed to each profit center.

Resource Allocation

A free economy relies to a large extent on the market as a means of securing an economic allocation of resources. Competition among independent economic entities, each of which has a profit objective, and each of which faces alternative customers or sources of supply, is relied upon to promote the social welfare by directing production to those firms that are most efficient in the use of resources. If one firm is able to use resources more effectively than another, it will be able to pay a higher price for these resources and thus draw them away from less productive uses. This is known as the "market test" of efficiency in resource allocation.

This competitive process is typically tempered by various forms and degrees of governmental intervention, including subsidies to such industries as shipping and agriculture, regulation of such industries as transportation, power, and communications, and even direct government ownership of productive facilities. In some cases minimum resource prices are set by government action, and there are likely to be regulations governing the ways in which resources are used—for example, maximum workweek laws, minimum sanitation requirements, and the like. Nevertheless, the basic resource allocation mechanism of a private enterprise economy is competition in resource and product markets. Economic value is measured by market prices, and resources go to those who can use them most effectively in meeting consumer demands.

The integration of two successive production processes removes this market test of economic efficiency. The transfer price, derived internally, replace the independent market transaction as a means of directing the allocation of economic resources. The social implications of this integration process are the concern of national economic policies, particularly in the field of antitrust law and enforcement, and are beyond the scope of this text. The managerial implications, however, are our concern, and we must examine transfer price policies in this light.

When one division manufactures an "intermediate product"—that is, a product that is or can be transferred to another division within the company for further processing—there must be some mechanism for deciding whether further processing is desirable and, if so, how much of the intermediate product to divert to this use. In a centralized company, the central decision-making authority can examine the incremental cost of further processing and compare it with the probable increment in sales value of the final product over that of the intermediate product. In a decentralized company, however, the manager of the final product division treats the price at which the intermediate product is transferred to him as an incremental cost.

The transfer price establishes the cost of the buying division's raw materials. When combined with the estimated costs of processing the materials and marketing the output, this cost can be compared with estimated end-product market values to determine the estimated profitability of various possible courses of action. The transfer price also guides the management of the supplying division by establishing the sales value of one of its outputs to one of its customers. This value can be compared with the net value of other uses of the supplying division's capacity to determine their relative profitability.

Another type of resource allocation decision is the make-or-buy decision. The company has the option of manufacturing a certain part, subassembly, or intermediate product or of buying it from an outside supplier. Given the available facilities, the question is one of comparing outside purchase prices with incremental internal manufacturing costs. When the company is decentralized, however, the intermediate product may be made by one division and the final product by another. The manager of the final product division, given authority to decide such matters, will compare outside purchase prices with internal transfer prices and base his decision largely on this comparison.

Suboptimization and the Opportunity Cost Criterion

The transfer price will serve its decision-making objectives satisfactorily only if it will lead division management to make the same decisions that headquarters management would make if it had the time to study the problem and if it had full access to all the data available to the managers of both divisions. If the transfer price leads to departures from this ideal, it is said to cause *suboptimization.*

As an example of suboptimization, suppose that a supplying division can sell a product (product X) to an outside customer for $1,000, less incremental selling costs of $180. Alternatively, the supplying division can transfer product X internally to another of the company's divisions which will use it as a raw material in the manufacture of product X'. The buying division can sell product X' to an outside customer for $1,800, against which it must charge the cost of "materials" (product X) and also $850 in further processing and marketing costs. For some reason, a transfer price of $1,100 has been established for product X.

If he based his decision on the transfer price, the manager of the buying division would choose not to buy product X and process it into product X', basing his decision on the following calculation:

Potential revenues		$1,800
Incremental costs:		
Materials (product X)	$1,100	
Processing and selling	850	1,950
Estimated Processing Loss		$ 150

Given all of the above information, however, a manager responsible for both divisions would decide that the interdivisional transfer would be in the company's best interests:

Estimated revenues, processed product X′.....................	$1,800
Less: Estimated revenues, unprocessed product X.............	1,000
Incremental processing revenue.........................	$ 800
Estimated processing and selling costs, processed product X′..$850	
Less: Estimated selling costs, unprocessed product X.......... 180	
Incremental processing and selling costs..................	670
Estimated Incremental Processing Profit.....................	$ 130

The reader by now will recognize this as simply another application of the concept of *opportunity cost*. If the supplying division had priced its output to the buying division at $820 (product X's outside sale value less incremental selling costs), the manager of the buying division would have arrived at the profit-maximizing solution:

Estimated revenues..		$1,800
Estimated costs:		
Materials (product X)..................................$820		
Processing and selling................................. 850		1,670
Estimated Incremental Processing Profit.....................		$ 130

This solution presumes that the supplying division could not sell *both* to the outside customer *and* to the internal buying division. Suppose, however, that the supplying division had adequate capacity to serve both, and that if it did sell to *both* customers, its incremental processing cost would be $500 for *each*. The supplying division could not find a customer for the second unit of product X at a net price in excess of $500. Finally, let us assume that the buying division could obtain only $1,500 from its outside customer for product X′. Under these circumstances, the buying division would not buy product X at a price of $820:

Estimated revenues..		$1,500
Estimated costs:		
Materials (at net market price)..........................$820		
Processing and selling................................. 850		1,670
Estimated Incremental Processing Loss.....................		$ 170

Taking all the available data into consideration would lead to just the opposite result—the material should be subjected to further processing:

Estimated revenues..		$1,500
Estimated costs:		
Materials (at incremental cost)..........................$500		
Processing and selling................................. 850		1,350
Estimated Incremental Processing Profit.....................		$ 150

The difficulty in this case is that $820 is not a good measure of the opportunity cost of a unit of product X. The manufacture of a unit of X for transfer to the buying division would require an expenditure of

$500; it would not force the supplying division to sacrifice a sale to an outside customer at any higher price. Thus $500, not $820, is the appropriate measure of opportunity cost in this situation.

In other words, an economical resource allocation solution could be reached in either of these situations by division managers acting independently, but only if the transfer price was equal to opportunity cost. This is the general rule: *an appropriate transfer price for managerial guidance in decision making is one that approximates opportunity cost.*

Performance Measurement

Transfer prices have a second impact, this time on the image of the division and of its management that will be transmitted to top management. When transfers of goods are made, a portion of the revenue of one profit center becomes a portion of the cost of another. This means that the price at which transfers are made can influence the earnings reported by each profit center. For example, a division's income statement might show the following items:

Sales—trade....................................		$1,000,000
Sales—intracompany.............................		600,000
Total sales.................................		$1,600,000
Cost of goods sold:		
Materials—vendors.........................	$300,000	
Materials—intracompany......................	400,000	
Labor.......................................	150,000	
Overhead....................................	250,000	
Total cost of goods sold.....................		1,100,000
Gross Margin................................		$ 500,000

Both revenues and cost of goods sold are heavily influenced by the prices at which internal transfers are made. If the division manager's performance is to be measured in part by reported profit, then he has a direct interest in the transfer prices that are to be established. Nothing can undermine a profit measurement system more quickly than forced transfers at prices that are regarded as unfair by the participating profit center managers.

Fairness, of course, is a relative matter. The manager of a buying division wants to purchase at the lowest prices, and the manager of a selling division wants to sell at the highest prices. What seems fair to one may seem highly unfair to the other. What is important, however, is that the system should provide measures of divisional profit that are objectively determined and as free from administrative bias as possible. No profit measure is entirely alibi-proof, but the objective should be to remove insofar as possible the transfer price as an alibi for poor profit performance.

BASES FOR TRANSFER PRICING

Many different bases for transfer pricing have been tried or proposed, and none can be said to be the "right" one under all circumstances. The principal alternatives are:

1. Full cost (or full cost plus).
2. Marginal or variable cost.
3. Market price.
4. Market-based negotiated price.
5. Market price minus commission.
6. Variable cost plus subsidy.

Other schemes have been presented, mainly based on the principle of securing some division of joint divisional profit by means of mathematical formulas, but examination of the six in the above list will cover most of the main issues.

Full Cost

Full cost is probably the oldest method of transfer pricing. In costing transfers between units within a profit center or between units in a centralized company, the principle of full cost has become firmly established, and it might seem only logical to extend this principle to profit center transfers. At the outset, let us dispose of one set of objections to full cost by defining it as *standard* full cost rather than historical average cost. This eliminates one source of delay in processing transfers and eliminates the perverse effect that fluctuations in productive efficiency in one unit can have on the reported profit of another. Furthermore, it permits a division manager to know in advance what price he will receive or what price he will pay for transferred goods, thus eliminating one source of uncertainty and permitting a division manager to predict more accurately the effects of his decisions on his reported profit.

The major defect of full cost as a basis for transfer pricing is that it fails to provide a sound guide to decision making. The manager of a division which receives intermediate products from another division treats the transfer price as a variable cost of his own operation. As we have pointed out earlier, he will not buy unless the price that he can receive from the sale of the final product is enough to cover the transfer price plus any additional processing and marketing costs that he may incur. The overall effect of the transaction might be to increase total company profit, but the full cost transfer price will obscure this fact.

To cite another example, suppose that a division manager is faced with the problem of choosing between an outside vendor and an internal supplying division for all or part of his requirements of a certain intermediate product. He has authority to choose his sources of supply, and his financial performance is to be judged on the basis of divisional reported profit. The intermediate product is transferred at a full cost transfer price of $12, but it can be obtained from an outside vendor at a price of $10 per unit, delivered. Given these conditions, the division manager has an incentive to purchase the product outside, other things such as reliability and quality being equal:

Internal price	$12.00
Outside price	10.00
Apparent saving	$ 2.00

But now suppose that the internal supplying division is operating at 60 percent of capacity and that the incremental costs in this division amount to $9 per unit. If the product is purchased outside, the supplying division will lose a $3 contribution toward its fixed costs and the loss in total company profit will thus be $1 per unit. In this case full cost transfers are in sharp conflict with the principle of decentralized decision making which requires that the buying division manager be granted control over his sources of supply. If there is complete rigidity in the transfer price, the only way that top management can prevent an action that would reduce company profit is to abrogate the buying division manager's authority and order him to purchase internally. If this is done, however, it is difficult to hold the buying division manager responsible for his division's reported profit.

Full cost may have a further distorting effect on executive decisions. As long as a division manager is operating below practical capacity—that is, on the relatively flat portion of his average variable cost curve—he will be willing to produce to satisfy both internal and external demands for his goods. But if he is pressing the limits of his capacity, he will be likely to favor the outlet for his goods that offers him the highest current revenue. Under these circumstances, market prices for the intermediate product are most likely to be higher than full cost, and unless a higher authority intervenes, sales to the outside market are likely to take precedence over internal transfers. The usual result is that the full cost transfer price system breaks down at this point as top management steps in to insure the flow of goods to other divisions.

The fact is that full cost transfer prices are incompatible with the resource allocation objectives of a decentralized company. They do not provide a sound basis on which top management can delegate decision-making authority to division managers—authority over sources of supply and outlets for each division's products. For this reason full cost transfer prices are generally restricted to situations in which this authority is not granted, in fact, to companies or divisions that are not really decentralized. In such cases full cost, or full cost plus a specified markup, is used to divide the total revenue from the sale of the company's products among divisions in such a way as to provide each division with an illusion of profit. Under these circumstances, the profit reported by a manufacturing division, for example, reflects only the effect of volume and the effectiveness of cost control. A useful purpose may be served by expressing these factors in an overall profit figure, but this is by no means a comprehensive concept of profit. In this way, full cost transfer prices may serve the profit awareness objective of internal profit measurement, but they fail to meet the other objectives discussed in the preceding chapter.

Marginal or Variable Cost

Transfer prices based on marginal cost or average variable cost are designed specifically to answer the objections raised to full cost transfer prices. Again, for the reasons cited earlier, we shall define these costs as standard costs rather than historical costs. Marginal and variable cost, of course, are not the same thing, but difficulties of measurement and the likelihood of a close parallelism over wide segments of the operating range have led most accountants to assume them equal. Because this situation is a special case of the more general marginal cost case, our immediate purpose can be served by examining marginal cost as a basis for transfer pricing.

A marginal cost transfer pricing system works in the following manner.[1] Each division manager is provided with a schedule representing the marginal cost of each of his supplying divisions at various volumes of operations. This provides him with a basis for calculating the prices he must pay for additional quantities of the intermediate products. To these he adds his own marginal cost figures to determine a composite marginal cost schedule for the final products. He then adjusts his volume to the level at which the additional or marginal revenue from the sale of an additional unit of the final product is just adequate to cover total marginal cost. To use a more common frame of reference,

---

[1] For a full exposition of the marginal cost method, see Jack Hirshleifer, "On the Economics of Transfer Pricing," *Journal of Business,* Vol. XXIX, No. 3 (July, 1956), pp. 172–84.

the division manager will accept additional orders for the final product as long as the price received exceeds combined marginal cost, assuming that additional orders do not require price reductions on the business already obtainable at higher prices. When there is a market for the intermediate product, the respective amounts to be sold in the final and intermediate markets can be determined by finding that point at which the marginal cost of manufacturing the intermediate product is just equal to the marginal revenue from sale of the intermediate product and is also equal to the net marginal revenue (marginal revenue less marginal processing cost) from sales of the final product.

To use a simple example, assume that division A buys product X from division B for use in the manufacture of product Y. One unit of X is used in the manufacture of each unit of Y. The managers of the two divisions have the following marginal cost schedules for their respective divisions:

Units per Month	Marginal Cost per Unit	
	Division B	Division A
13,000 and less..............	$1.50	$1.00
14,000......................	1.55	1.00
15,000......................	1.60	1.05
16,000......................	1.65	1.10
17,000......................	1.70	1.15
18,000......................	1.75	1.20
19,000......................	1.80	1.25
20,000......................	1.85	1.30

The resource allocation decision in this company is to be made by the manager of division B, and he receives the following schedules of marginal revenues:

Units per Month	Marginal Revenue per Unit		Net Marginal Revenue per Unit Product Y*
	Product X	Product Y	
6,000 and less........	$2.00	$4.00	$3.00
7,000................	1.90	4.00	3.00
8,000................	1.80	4.00	3.00
9,000................	1.70	4.00	3.00
10,000................	1.60	3.75	2.75
11,000................	1.50	3.50	2.50
12,000................	1.40	3.20	2.20
13,000................	1.30	2.85	1.85
14,000................	1.20	2.55	1.55
15,000................	1.10	2.00	0.95

* Marginal revenue less marginal cost in division A.

Taken independently, the manager of division B could justify production and sale of 11,000 units of X in outside markets because up to that volume marginal revenue exceeds marginal cost. Similarly, it would seem profitable to manufacture 14,000 units of X for conversion into product Y because up to that volume the net marginal revenue from sales of product Y exceeds the marginal cost of the intermediate product, product X. If both of these were to be done, however, total production of X would be 25,000 units a month and the marginal cost of X would exceed the marginal revenue obtainable from either market. Therefore, a system of priorities must be established to decide how many units of X should be devoted to each use.

In this example, product Y has the first priority on output of X as long as net marginal revenue (marginal revenue from sales of product Y less marginal costs in division A) is greater than $2. In other words, as long as a unit of X can produce a net addition to company profit greater than $2 by incorporating it in product Y, then no sales of X should be made in the intermediate product market. A total of 12,000 units of Y can be sold before the net marginal revenue from sales of Y falls below $2. At an output of 12,000 units of X, marginal cost of X is $1.50 and production is profitable.

At this point the marginal revenue from sale of X ($2 per unit) becomes greater than the net marginal revenue from the diversion of X into the manufacture of Y ($1.85), and production of additional units of X must be justified in terms of the profitability of such sales. By increasing production to 13,000 units of X, the manager of division B can meet the requirements for product Y and also sell 1,000 units of X at a marginal revenue of $2 and a marginal cost of $1.50. In fact, he can increase production to 19,000 units, supplying 12,000 units of X to division A and selling 7,000 units of X on the market, before the marginal revenue from sales of X falls below the $1.85 net marginal revenue to be derived from the sale of additional product Y. Sale of the 7,000th unit of X produces a marginal revenue of $1.90 and a marginal cost of $1.80, so this is profitable.

Increasing production of Y to 13,000 units adds net marginal revenue of $1.85 and also brings production of X up to the 20,000 unit level, at which marginal cost equals $1.85. It is unprofitable to expand production of either product beyond this point because additional revenue will be less than additional cost. Therefore, the optimum output of X is 20,000 units a month and the optimum output of Y is 13,000 units a month.

The difficulties of developing marginal cost and marginal revenue schedules that change with volume in this way are substantial. Few companies have cost structures that are delineated clearly enough to justify anything but a constant marginal cost assumption, and marginal revenue is even more of a mystery. Within some volume limits, however, marginal cost may indeed be constant, and within these limits marginal cost may be a reasonable measure of opportunity cost.

A second defect is even more fundamental in that in some situations a marginal cost transfer pricing system cannot be administered without abrogating the decision-making autonomy of the various profit centers. For example, if marginal cost increases with volume, it will depend on the *total* demands of the buying division and the supplying division's external customers. Thus *neither* division can make its output decisions independently. A division is thus essentially a cost center rather than a profit center to the extent that it obtains or supplies products internally.

Some sophisticated systems today attempt to circumvent this to some extent by using linear programming to derive for each internal customer a schedule of transfer prices for various transfer volumes, based on the assumption that aggregate volumes for other purposes remain at specified levels. The buying division manager then makes his own purchase commitments on the basis of these schedules. This can lead to suboptimization, but companies that have adopted this technique feel that aggregate volume changes will not be abrupt enough to destroy the general validity of the figures, as long as the figures are recomputed fairly frequently.

Capacity operations place additional strains on a marginal cost transfer pricing system. When the supplying division is operating at capacity, the net revenue available from outside customers often appears to be greater than marginal cost. In theory, this could not happen because the firm would increase its rate of output until marginal cost equaled marginal revenue. In fact, the firm's knowledge of its marginal costs is almost never good enough to extend the cost schedule to this point or else the firm is unwilling or unable to engage in subcontracting or other high-cost devices to expand its short-run capacity to deliver products.[2] As a result, when the supplying division is operating at capacity, top management may have to permit the division manager to depart from the previously calculated marginal cost or else may have to direct him to divert his production to internal customers at a sacrifice in his reported

---

[2] Economic capacity can be defined as the volume at which marginal cost becomes high enough to exceed average cost. Joel Dean, *Managerial Economics* (Englewood Cliffs, N.J.: Prentice-Hall, Inc., 1951), p. 305. Common definitions of practical capacity assume implicitly that expansion of operations to this point is not feasible.

profit. Under the former solution, the marginal cost basis for transfer pricing is acknowledged to be inadequate; under the latter, divisional authority is abrogated.

The third defect of a straight marginal cost transfer pricing system is that it ignores the performance measurement aspects of internal profit reporting. As long as marginal cost is lower than average full cost, under marginal cost transfer pricing all divisions will show a loss except those divisions that make sales to the outside market. If these divisions also supply intermediate products to other units within the corporation, then their profit reports will reflect a mixture of "profits" on outside sales and "losses" on internal sales.

Reported losses need have no ill effects at all on the use of divisional profit statements in the evaluation of managerial performance, provided that evaluation is based on achievement of predetermined goals which have been established in a critical, creative manner. Unfortunately, no matter how intellectually it is committed to this point of view, management often finds it emotionally difficult to accept a low profit figure as evidence of good or satisfactory performance. Furthermore, executive promotion often seems to come faster, the monetary rewards are greater, and people are easier to recruit in divisions with good profit records, and a transfer pricing system that a division manager feels is unfairly depriving him of these advantages is likely to breed resentment.

The activity evaluation aspect may be even more important, particularly during periods of idle capacity. Here all the profits on internally transferred goods will be lodged in the internal buying divisions, and the supplying divisions may find it correspondingly more difficult to justify capital expenditure proposals.

If marginal cost or something like it is to be used as a basis for transfer pricing, some means must be found for overcoming these defects. Before examining the possibilities of doing this, however, we should round out the picture by examining the various systems based on market price.

Market Price

If the profit centers were, in fact, independent businesses, any transfer of intermediate products would require a market transaction for which a market price could be recorded. The independent firm is judged on its ability to buy and sell at market and make a profit. If a purchase price is too high, the independent firm will not buy, and if its selling prices are too high, it will not sell. Profit centers are not independent businesses, and some transactions do not go through the market, but in certain circumstances it may be possible to maintain the self-regulating conditions of the market by pricing these internal transfers at market prices. If a division cannot afford to pay market prices, it should not be permitted to buy internally at less than market, and if it can sell outside at market, it should not be required to sell internally for less. In other words, a division should not be subsidized by other divisions merely because it cannot produce a profit if transfers are made at market prices.

This argument is a strong one, but certain conditions are necessary to make it fully valid. The implicit assumption in the use of market prices is that these prices truly represent the opportunity cost of the intermediate product. In the strictest sense, market price is truly representative of opportunity cost only if intermediate markets are perfectly competitive—that is, if the company's activity in the market, either in buying or in selling, has no influence on the market price. If the company's sales of the intermediate product act to depress market prices, then the marginal revenue from those sales will be less than market price; if the company's purchases force market prices upward, marginal cost will be greater than market price.

Perfectly competitive conditions exist only in the rarest of circumstances, so in a strict sense, market price is almost never a fully adequate basis for transfer pricing. Management must always deal with an imperfect world, however, and the main question is not whether a transfer pricing system is perfect but rather whether it is sufficiently reliable to be workable. In general, a market price transfer system may be regarded as workable whenever the intermediate product is one which is traded actively and in substantial quantities at prices that approximate those available in published quotations.

The number of instances in which published market prices can be used as transfer prices without adjustment is very small. Markets for many intermediate products are established only through promotional effort and negotiation with prospective purchasers. For others, published prices are available, but they represent such a small quantity of transactions that they cannot be regarded as reasonable approximations to opportunity cost. Finally, product differentiation may make it difficult to find market quotations that are strictly relevant to any one company's transfer price problem. In these circumstances, some solution other than quoted market price must be sought.

Market-Based Negotiated Prices

Most transactions between independent firms are not made at publicly quoted prices but at prices in which there is an element of negotiation. At a minimum this consists of obtaining bids from two or more potential suppliers and placing orders with the firm that seems to offer the most favorable package. This suggests that an analogous procedure might be adopted for internal transfer pricing, leaving the respective division managers free to negotiate with each other to determine the appropriate price. Only if the division managers are unable to come to an agreement on price will top management be called upon to intervene in what is called "umpiring."

Four conditions are necessary to make a negotiated transfer price system workable:

1. There must be some form of outside market for the intermediate product.
2. Any available market information should be communicated to both parties to the negotiation.
3. Both parties must have freedom to deal outside.
4. Top management must indicate its support of the principle of negotiation.

All four of these conditions must be present if the transfer pricing system is to satisfy the resource allocation objective perfectly, but some relaxation is possible without destroying the system's ability to meet the performance evaluation objective.

In a sense, these conditions are also part of the definition of a profit center. Delegation of profit responsibility is possible only insofar as it is accompanied by the delegation of authority to make decisions that determine profitability, including the selection of sources of supply and the pricing of the division's products, within the framework of general company policies. This authority may be restricted in various ways, but it cannot be completely withheld if the various divisions are to operate as profit centers. When both input and output prices are determined at higher levels, as they are for many sales divisions or subdivisions, the resulting profit figures may still be useful as a means of summarizing the promotional and cost control activities of the unit managers, but they provide little useful guidance to managerial decision making.

The existence of an outside market for the intermediate product is important in negotiation because it provides both parties with an alternative. Dissemination of information relating to this outside market should reduce the bargaining range and permit negotiation to take place in an atmosphere conducive to producing transfer prices that are fair approximations to opportunity cost. In the absence of an outside market, the bargaining range is likely to be considerably wider because the buying and selling divisions are in the position known to economists as bilateral monopoly—that is, the market for the intermediate product consists of two firms, one buying and one selling, and neither has an outside alternative. The buyer may buy or not buy or, at the extreme, he may equip his division to manufacture the intermediate product. The seller may sell or not sell or, at the extreme, he may equip his division to manufacture the final product. Under these conditions the market price is likely to be indeterminate within a fairly wide range, and relative profit of the two divisions will depend on the bargaining ability of the respective division managers.

The fact that many intermediate products are to a certain extent unique raises questions as to what constitutes an outside market. For products that are not standard items in the product line of potential outside suppliers, the only way that real market price information can be obtained is through the solicitation of bids. If these bids never result in sales, outside suppliers may be reluctant to bid or may submit nominal bids merely as a formality. One way to avoid this difficulty is to make a sufficient quantity of outside purchases to offer the bidder a real possibility of acceptance. Another way, less satisfactory but occasionally the only real alternative, is to estimate market prices by analysis of cost-price relationships in related products. The automobile companies have applied this technique with some success to many of the parts and subassemblies that are purchased internally only.

It should be reemphasized that the mere existence of an outside market for the intermediate product is insufficient to secure the success of a negotiated transfer price system. Even if the market is there, the lack of real freedom to buy or sell outside tends to weaken the effectiveness of negotiation as a means of promoting sound resource allocation. In the circumstances that make published market prices unacceptable and that therefore require negotiation, opportunity cost cannot be determined with sufficient reliability unless there is some way to test the market. Freedom to enter the market provides the necessary mechanism. If a buying division can purchase outside for a certain price, freedom to go outside will permit him to negotiate a price internally that will reflect this opportunity. He may even be willing to pay a price in excess of market in order to obtain the advantages of an assured supply, better quality control, and reduced purchasing costs, but this merely expands the effective bargaining range.

Freedom to buy outside is particularly important when substantial capacity for the manufacture of the intermediate product exists internally, capacity that would be made idle if the products were to be acquired outside. Paradoxical as this may seem, it is under conditions such as these that it is most important to have internal transfer prices that best reflect the company's opportunity costs. Without buying freedom, transfer prices are less likely to feel the pressure of competitive forces and will remain higher than they should be to guide the manager of the buying division in his pricing and output decisions. With his costs kept at artificially high levels, he will be unable to accept orders that would prove profitable to the company as a whole.

It should be remembered that freedom to deal outside does not necessarily mean that a substantial volume of purchases will actually be made from outside suppliers when idle internal capacity exists. Freedom must be accompanied by an obligation to negotiate internally. The buying division will normally prefer to buy from another unit of his company if he can obtain intermediate products at competitive prices. On the other side, the supplying division that is faced with idle capacity should be willing to reduce transfer prices to retain the business as long as some margin remains over the incremental costs of serving the internal customer. Admittedly, the manager of the supplying division is in a poorer bargaining position at this point. Although he has the option of seeking additional business outside to utilize his capacity, if idle capacity is widespread in the markets for the intermediate products this may not be a very effective weapon in negotiation. What the division manager should consider is whether he would make a larger profit or a smaller loss by accepting an internal order at a reduced price instead of rejecting it. Given this, there is no reason why freedom to deal outside will result in underutilization of capacity unless it is more profitable to the company to do so.

The fourth requirement for a successful negotiated transfer price system—strong top-management support—is essential to reduce the amount of umpiring that top management is called upon to do. A system of negotiation can be undermined quickly if top management is ready to step in and arbitrate disputes whenever they arise. Appealing to the umpire is a form of dodging responsibility. Unless top management makes it clear that appeals for arbitration will reflect unfavorably on the executive ability of the negotiators, umpiring is likely to become frequent and the resulting transfer prices will serve as unreliable guides to resource allocation decisions.

Market Price Minus

Effective negotiation is not always possible because one or more of the requisite conditions cannot be met. The absence of outside markets is the most serious drawback to negotiation because, as we have seen, buyer and seller have no alternative sources of supply or markets. One transfer pricing basis that has been used frequently when the buying division is largely a marketing organization and the selling division manufactures products for sale through the buying division is the market price minus a sales commission.

The absence of a market for the intermediate products means that these divisions are not profit centers but rather pseudo-profit centers in which decision-making authority is restricted within fairly narrow limits. Nevertheless, as we have pointed out, the advantages of creating an awareness of profit and of providing a summary measure of financial performance in profit terms may justify separate profit reporting of these two units. If the company were to market its products through independent distribution companies, the price paid for marketing services would be represented by the spread between the final market price of the product and the net proceeds to the manufacturer. This suggests that something similar might be adopted when the marketing organization is not independent but is an internal operating unit. After deducting from revenues the marketing division's commission on sales, the residual is credited to the manufacturing division.

Under this sytem the basic resource allocation decisions are made by top management, not by the managers of the affected divisions. List prices and standard markups are established by top management. The sales division manager may or may not be given authority to grant price concessions, but if he is given this authority, any price concessions that he may make are not reflected in the transfer price. The reason for this is that sales management is evaluated on its ability to perform the marketing function. Changing the transfer price eliminates the fixed point of reference dividing the manufacturing from the selling function. Just as manufacturing cost standards are not changed monthly to conform to the latest cost experience, transfer prices should not be changed to reflect factors that are subject to the control of only one of the parties to the transaction. Allowing actual prices to influence the transfer price has the effect of guaranteeing a profit to the sales division, with the manufacturing division absorbing most of the losses from depressed market conditions.

This discussion should point up the basic weakness of the market minus scheme of transfer pricing. It fails to provide a reliable guide to decision making and through its effects on reported divisional profit may actually distort operating decisions. Because there is no independent market for the manufactured product except through the sales organization, decisions as to what products to manufacture and what products to emphasize must be made on the basis of an examination of manufacturing and selling operations combined. Top management may raise or lower the transfer prices of individual products that it wishes the sales divisions to discourage or promote, but once the transfer prices are set, sales management will direct its activities with a view toward improving its reported profit. The manufacturing division becomes merely a service unit, supplying products to the sales division on order. The sales minus device is useful primarily when decision-making authority is essentially centralized. It subjects the sales organization to rough tests of profitability, but for the manufacturing division it provides a profit measure that is of limited significance.

Variable Cost Plus Subsidy

In our earlier discussion, the use of marginal cost as a basis for transfer pricing was criticized: first because it is inconsistent with the concept of decentralization, second because it results in concentrating all profit in the final product or sales divisions, leaving all preceding divisions with reported losses, and third because the data required to establish marginal cost curves are generally not available. Market or market-based negotiated prices are the only prices that are fully consistent with the concept of decentralization and profit center autonomy. Unfortunately, the availability and accessibility of intermediate markets which make systems of this sort workable are frequently absent. Nevertheless, management may still wish to report profit on a divisional basis in order to get divisional executives thinking in terms of profit rather than cost or sales volume.

Under these circumstances, in which internal buying and selling divisions are inextricably interdependent, some companies have turned to a modification of the marginal cost approach. This approach substitutes standard variable cost per unit for marginal cost and adds a monthly lump-sum subsidy to cover the fixed costs of the internal supplier of the intermediate product. This subsidy normally also includes a provision for profit so that as long as the supplying division adheres to budgeted performance it will report a profit.

A system of this kind can be made quite workable as long as it is clearly understood that the supplying divisions are essentially budget centers rather than profit centers. The main difficulty arises when the supplying division markets a portion of its output directly to outside markets. The lump-sum subsidy under these circumstances amounts to a reservation of a portion of the supplying division's capacity by the final product division, and the question of how much to reserve is extremely difficult. For example, suppose that a division has been selling half of its output internally and half to outside customers, and that the subsidy has been established on the basis that this allocation will continue. During the year the final product division finds that its sales are running ahead of budget, and the manager requests additional quantities of the intermediate product. If the supplying division has idle capacity, this additional demand can or should be met at standard variable cost and no distortion of the supplying division's profit should result. But if the supplying division is operating at or near capacity, the additional volume for the final product division can be obtained only by diverting capacity from outside sales of other products of the supplying division or by incurring costs in excess of standard variable cost, perhaps by increased subcontracting or by increased use of overtime or by use of less productive stand-by equipment. In this hybrid situation, who makes the decisions and how are these decisions reflected in the transfer prices?

There are no clear-cut answers to these quesions. Because much of the output of the supplying division is sold to outside customers, it may be regarded as a modified profit center, with a considerable degree of authority to make decisions as to production and sales. Perhaps the best solution is to provide for direct negotiation between the supplying division and the final product division. Because he wishes to make as favorable a profit showing as possible, the supplying division manager will be unwilling to accept any price that will not cover his opportunity costs of increasing his deliveries to the final product division. If the increased output can be obtained only by curtailing production of other products now being sold outside the company, he will demand the same dollar markup over variable cost from his internal customer that he would lose by restricting sales to his outside customers. If he can expand his total output, he must demand a price that is at least adequate to cover the incremental cost of production by the more costly methods. The final product division manager will be willing to pay these higher prices for additional quantities of product only if their sales value is adequate to cover the transfer price plus any additional costs that he may incur in further processing and distribution.

Thus when a division is operating at capacity, supplying both inside and outside markets, there is a market price mechanism for resource allocation even when there is no independent market for a specific intermediate product. But when the supplying division is operating at less than full capacity, market forces are inoperative in determining the transfer price, and the standard variable cost plus subsidy may be the only practicable approach.

RECORDING INTERNAL TRANSFERS

No matter how transfer prices are derived, the accounting system must provide a means of adjusting internal company data to the cost basis used for public financial reporting. If the transfer price is less than inventoriable cost, as in variable cost transfer pricing, then a portion of fixed cost ordinarily must be applied to goods remaining in inventory at the end of the accounting period. If transfers are at market or negotiated prices, any excess of transfer price over inventoriable cost must be subtracted from inventory and profit accounts in consolidation.

Even if transfers are made at standard full cost, interdivisional sales must be eliminated from the income statement in consolidation. The most typical procedure is to record intracompany sales and outside customer sales in separate accounts. A similar distinction is made between internal and external purchases. This not only assists in consolidation but also provides information to management on the relative importance of intracompany transactions.

Under this approach, the entries to record a shipment from one division to another could take the following form:

On the supplying division's books:

Accounts Receivable—Buying Division	1,500	
Intracompany Sales		1,500
Cost of Goods Sold—Intracompany	1,000	
Inventory		1,000

On the buying division's books:

Inventory—from Supplying Division	1,500	
Accounts Payable—Supplying Division		1,500

Suppose now that four fifths of these goods are sold by the buying division to an outside customer for $1,800. The entries on the buying division's books would be:

Accounts Receivable—Outside Customers	1,800	
Sales Revenue		1,800
Cost of Goods Sold—Outside Customers	1,200	
Inventory—from Supplying Division		1,200

If the intracompany sales are handled in this manner, an end-of-period adjusting entry would have to be made, such as:

Intracompany Sales..1,500	
Cost of Goods Sold—Intracompany.............................	1,000
Cost of Goods Sold—Outside Customers.........................	400
Inventory Adjustment Allowance...............................	100

The Inventory Adjustment Allowance account is of course a contra account to the inventory accounts for external financial reporting. The effect of this entry would thus be to eliminate the intracompany transactions from both the companywide balance sheet and the income statement, but divisional income would still be computed from the divisional books, unadjusted.

SUMMARY

Although it is possible to meet some of the objectives of profit decentralization within the framework of a functional organization structure, most decentralized companies are organized around products or regions or customer groupings. In many companies, the move to decentralization has been promoted by managerial dissatisfaction with the ability of the functional organization to permit substantial delegation of top-management's decision-making authority and to provide an adequate training ground for future top management.

From a profit measurement point of view, it is the lack of satisfactory intermediate markets, more than any other single factor, that makes it extremely difficult to decentralize effectively on a functional basis. Many transfer pricing problems would disappear if the division structure could be reorganized around product lines. Transfers within each division could then be made at full standard cost or incremental cost—the functional subexecutives in each division would not be expected to make final decisions on make or buy or sell or process further. This would be the province of the division manager and his staff who could look at the problem without worrying about the realism of the transfer prices within the division. It is easy enough to forget that profit decentralization is not a substitute for the other control techniques of budgeting and standard costing but an extension of them. Within each decentralized division or profit center, just as in the completely centralized firm, functional performance continues to be measured in these more traditional terms.

Some imperfection in the transfer pricing mechanism is unavoidable, but a workable system of profit decentralization can be designed if four points are recognized. First, it should be recognized that divisional profit measurement is intended to serve several purposes: to guide and motivate division management in decision making, to provide a partial basis for evaluation and control of managerial performance, and to supply a rough measure of divisional profitability for top management's use in resource allocation and long-range planning. Second, the divisional boundaries should be established in such a way as to reduce the number of interdivisional transfers and to permit effective market checks on the realism of transfer prices. Third, the measure of divisional profit should be based on the principle of controllability, either eliminating noncontrollable charges entirely or making them in such a way as to lead to no variances from profit standards. And finally, the profit standard for managerial evaluation should be based on budgeted data, specifically attuned to the current operating potentialities of each division, independent of long-run normal desired yields on invested capital.

DISCUSSION QUESTIONS

1. Why is it important that a "good" transfer price system be introduced? In other words, in what kinds of problems does the method of establishing transfer prices affect the interpretation of accounting data?

2. Discuss the problems of preparing annual financial reports to stockholders when internal transfers are priced at other than inventoried cost. How would you proceed to solve these problems?

3. How does the transfer price problem with respect to transfers between two profit centers differ from the transfer price problem with respect to transfers between two departments within a single profit center (e.g., charge of power department costs to production departments within the same plant)?

4. The hot roll division of the Algy Steel Company transfers a portion of its output to the fabricating division where it is processed further into finished products for sale to industrial customers. The material transferred is credited to the hot roll division and charged to the fabricating division at standard cost plus 10 percent. What problems do you foresee arising out of this practice?

5. What conditions must be met to make workable a system of negotiated intracompany transfer prices?

6. Does full standard cost provide an adequate basis for pricing interdivisional transfers if the supplying division is operating at capacity?

7. It has frequently been argued that permitting a division to go outside to buy products or parts for which ample manufacturing capacity exists in other divisions of the company will reduce company profits if it results in substantial idle capacity in the supplying divisions. Appraise this argument.

8. What problems do you foresee in attempting to apply the marginal cost method of transfer pricing?

9. What are the advantages and disadvantages of basing transfer prices on published market prices? Under what circumstances are market price transfers likely to be reasonably satisfactory?

10. One writer on transfer pricing has proposed that interdivisional transfers be priced at current market prices for any products for which market price quotations are readily available. These market prices would be determined by the corporate controller and his staff. Each month the latest list of transfer prices would be distributed to the division managers, and these prices would then be used to price all transfers of the affected products during the coming month. Comment briefly on this proposal, indicating your opinion as to how well it is likely to meet the criteria for a sound transfer pricing scheme.

11. In what way might advance recognition of transfer pricing problems influence management's decisions as to the divisional structure of the decentralized organization? Explain.

12. What is meant by the term, "pseudo profit center?" What are the reasons for establishing such units?

13. The general manager of the international division of the Zaybo Company complains that he cannot sell many of the company's products in foreign markets if he has to pay the domestic division the same prices it charges to domestic distributors. He recommends that the transfers be made at standard variable cost, with an additional subsidy payment based on budgeted factory fixed costs at normal operating volumes. Discuss this proposal.

EXERCISES AND PROBLEMS

1. The Apex Machinery Company manufactures and distributes a line of textile machinery and supplies and a line of machinery for nontextile industrial trades. The company's operations are organized as shown in the following chart:

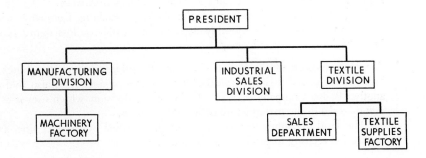

All machinery, including both textile and industrial trades machinery, is manufactured in the machinery factory of the manufacturing division. The textile division manufactures its own supplies in its supplies factory but purchases all its requirements of machinery from the manufacturing division. The machinery is highly technical and cannot be obtained from independent manufacturers.

The management of the Apex Machinery Company wishes to prepare profit reports for each of the company's three divisions, and you have been asked to recommend a transfer pricing system. The manufacturing vice president has suggested that machinery be transferred at standard manufacturing cost plus 10 percent. The industrial sales division has suggested list price less 25 percent, an arrangement that is common among manufacturers' agents in this market. You need not recommend either of these proposals if you feel that some other arrangement would be superior.

2. The Chicago Packing Company operated a small packing plant. The departmental organization included, among others, the following departments: cattle killing, dressed beef, hide, offal, beef casing, and glue. Cattle were slaughtered in the first department. The various parts of the animal were then passed on to other departments for further processing. The carcass was sent to the dressed beef department, the hide to the hide department, and so on.

For control purposes, each department was treated as a separate business. Departmental costs were accumulated in a departmental ledger. Each department "sold" its product to the next in line. Thus the cattle killing department was credited for the market price of carcasses turned over to the dressed beef department, the latter department being charged for a like amount. The dressed beef department, at the completion of its processing, "sold" the beef to the distributor and was credited for the selling price.

Any department in the chain was authorized to buy part of its raw material outside or to sell part or all of its finished product outside, although in many departments the number of outside transactions each year was negligible. Intermediate product markets were uneven—for example, very little trading in undressed carcasses occurred, whereas there were highly active markets for such items as hides and offal.

By the method of accounting followed, it was possible to compute departmental profits and losses. It was felt that such profits and losses were the best possible basis for measuring departmental performance.

Discuss the control policy of the Chicago Packing Company with respect to the use of the monthly departmental profit or loss figure as an index of departmental efficiency.

3. The Hull division of the Ballou Company manufactures and distributes a broad range of industrial chemicals. One of these, product X, is also sold to another Ballou Company division, the Hingham division, which uses it as a raw material in the manufacture of several products.

The Hull division's income statement is classified by product line, and the section relating to product X is as follows:

Sales—outside (100,000 lbs. @ $2)		$200,000
Sales—Hingham (50,000 lbs. @ $1.80)		90,000
Total sales		$290,000
Product-traceable costs:		
Variable manufacturing costs ($0.90/lb.)	$135,000	
Sales commissions—outside sales	10,000	
Depreciation	20,000	
Other traceable fixed costs	40,000	205,000
Product profit contribution		$ 85,000
Share of divisional fixed costs		60,000
Net Profit before Taxes		$ 25,000

Common fixed costs, including such items as executive salaries and sales branch operating expenses, are allocated among the division's product lines at a flat 40 cents a pound.

An outside supplier has offered to supply the Hingham division with a product similar to and a perfectly satisfactory substitute for product X, at a firm contract price of $1.60 a pound, delivered at the Hingham factory. The Hingham division manager has proposed that the interdivisional transfer price of product X be reduced to $1.60 to meet the competing offer. Otherwise, he threatens to purchase the substitute product from the outside vendor.

The manager of the Hull division has refused to meet this price on the grounds that this is less than his cost. You are a staff assistant to the manager of the Hingham division, and he has asked you to draft a short memorandum to the Hull division manager in support of the proposed $1.60 price.

4. The Jackman Corporation manufactures and sells a line of fastening devices for commercial and industrial use. It has one factory, located in Des Moines, Iowa, and six regional sales offices scattered throughout the United States. The factory's entire output is marketed through the sales division, which also markets a line of eyelets, tacks, staples, and other supplies purchased from other manufacturers.

In addition to the manufacturing and sales vice presidents, three other men report directly to the president—the controller, the purchasing agent-traffic manager, and the director of research. Aggregate sales volume is currently running at a rate of $5 million a year, of which about $1 million is in purchased products, the remainder coming from the Jackman factory.

Although the top management of this company works closely as a group, the president is convinced that profit decentralization would have advantages in giving everyone a clearer view of the profit criterion for business decisions. Specifically, he wants to make the manufacturing and sales divisions into profit centers, with each regional sales office also regarded as a profit center. The other three divisions would be treated as service centers.

a) Design a transfer pricing system that will meet the president's objectives with the least danger of suboptimization and explain how it would work and why it is better and more feasible than other plans.

b) Comment on the desirability of adopting a profit center structure in this company.

5. The Alma Products Company is decentralized into a number of operating divisions. In the words of the company's controller, under this arrangement "practically absolute authority is granted to the division to carry on its everyday operations." The controller described the company's interdivisional transfer pricing system in the memorandum quoted in the following paragraphs.

"Our plan is to use market price as the intercompany pricing base where the material is a prime one that can be purchased from an independent source in the same form and quality as obtained from the affiliated unit. The controller's organization doesn't set the price in this case. Representatives of the buying and selling units sit down and develop prices with just as evident interest on either side as would be shown if they were dealing with someone outside of the family.

"On all other items we have used cost as the basis of transfer value between divisions. This transfer value is established for a quarterly period and is the sum of current manufacturing cost and a percentage thereof to cover other allocable items not ordinarily included in the manufacturing cost of the product. This latter arrangement has the effect of putting all of the gross profit into the company that does the selling and which must stand the selling and merchandising expense. Just so there won't be any question about it, the buying divisions' representatives look just as caustically at the costs involved as they would if they were doing the job of manufacturing from the very beginning. It is in this type of transaction that the controller's responsibility enters, as in our organization he has the job of creating the cost base upon which the price is established."

a) Discuss the soundness of this system in view of the company's announced practice of delegating to divisional executives "practically absolute authority" for decision making.

b) What purpose is served by having buying division representatives look "caustically" at transfer prices that are established by the controller's organization? What problems do you foresee under this arrangement and how do you think they can be solved?

(Based on an article by L. R. Feakes in *The Controller*)

6. Professor E. G. Heide recently received the following letter from a former student:

"Dear Professor Heide:

"I found your paper on Divisional Profit Standards very much to the point. We are working on our divisional reporting structure now, and much that you say seems to fit our situation.

"In my limited experience so far, the most difficult aspect of this problem has always been the matter of transfer pricing. I wonder if you could comment on the merit of the following approach which I believe takes into account the effect of below-capacity operation of the supplying division in a market where price and to a large extent market share are constant. This, you will admit, is the case in many industries today, especially where oligopolies exist.

"Consider division A, whose operations can be described as shown on the diagram labeled Exhibit 1.

"Division B wishes to purchase a quantity M of material produced by A, whose cost curves are shown, and whose output, not counting the contemplated interdivisional transfer, is limited to Q, its 'share of market.' A forced purchase of the material at market price by division B would be, in effect, a 'windfall profit' for division A; while purchase at marginal cost would cause division A to lose money. I would suggest that the additional income to A that could result from B's purchase of the material at market cost be divided evenly between A and B, resulting in a transfer price above A's average cost—i.e., a profit to A—and below the market cost, i.e., a saving for B.

Exihibit 1

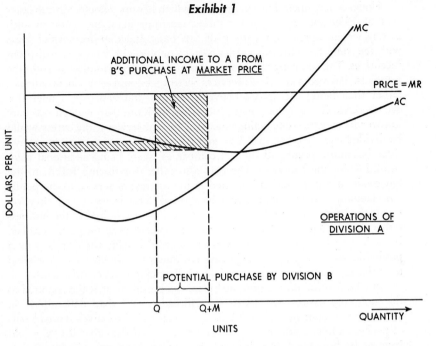

ADDITIONAL INCOME TO A FROM
B'S PURCHASE AT <u>MARKET</u> <u>PRICE</u>

PRICE = MR

MC

AC

DOLLARS PER UNIT

OPERATIONS OF
DIVISION A

POTENTIAL PURCHASE BY DIVISION B

Q   Q+M

QUANTITY

UNITS

"If the purchase price were set at average cost, A's manager would have no incentive to make the transfer of material, while if the price were set at market cost, B might prefer to go 'outside' for marginal reasons like 'service,' and if so, would adversely affect corporate earnings. The 50–50 split could become a matter of company policy, and thus avoid negotiations each time a transfer cost has to be established.

"I look forward to hearing from you."

Draft a reply for Professor Heide's signature.

7. R.E.A. Express (new trade name adopted in 1960 for Railway Express Agency, Inc.) was formed in 1929 as a joint facility of the nation's leading express-carrying railroads which bought the express properties of American Railway Express Company. The predecessor business was formed in 1918 as a unification of seven then-existent separate express companies, including American, Adams, Southern, and Wells Fargo, some of them dating back to the founding of the express industry in 1839.

The original agreement between the present company and the express-carrying railroads provided that it would have neither a profit nor a loss. After all its expenses—except those for rail transportation—had been paid from gross receipts, the balance was turned over to the railroads as payments for the transportation of express. The direct expenses of the express company generally consist of about 80 percent for labor, and the company in recent years has been caught between spiraling wage rates and the growth of competing means of small shipment transportation.

Under a new operating arrangement which became effective in the latter part of 1959 and providing for three transition steps, the company ultimately was to operate on a profit or loss basis under uniform agreements with the some 156 railroads parties thereto, acting with its own set of profit incentives. The company was to buy transportation services directly from the railroads. Payments for these services were to be agreed upon in advance rather than being the spread between receipts and expenses. Under this arrangement, if the agency were able to obtain more than enough revenues to cover its expenses (including payments for rail service), the excess would be divided equally between R.E.A. and the railroads, the express company's share becoming profit and the rail companies' share being additional compensation for their services. The plan also called for freeing R.E.A. to use any mode of transportation it elected in the interest of service to the public and economy of operation. It was to be allowed to retain for capital improvements the proceeds from the sale of assets no longer required in the business rather than including these amounts in the remittances to the carriers as had been the previous practice. And as a first step in placing the company on a profitable basis, R.E.A. proposed to ask the Interstate Commerce Commission to authorize immediate rate increases for less-than-carload shipments.

In commenting on the proposed plan, the president of R.E.A. pointed to the mounting express deficits of the railroads, more than $40 million in 1958—the amount by which R.E.A. payments failed to cover railroad out-of-pocket express costs, and which for a time raised fears that R.E.A. would have to be liquidated. He observed that under the proposed plan, R.E.A. would be able for the first time to earn a profit (or sustain a loss) and its management and staff would know it. With no income of its own, its management had lacked the discipline and incentive of a profit and loss statement.

In an interview prior to the I.C.C. hearing, R.E.A.'s president stated: "Long before 1954 I had come to the conclusion that the company had to be on an independent footing, rather than operate as the alter ego of 173 railroads. I never felt that management of R.E.A. had enough responsibility given to it. We tried to put the business on a sound economic basis in 1954 and to give management full responsibility, but the crisis was not severe enough to get the railroads to agree."

Give your opinion on the problem faced by R.E.A. Express and on the merits of the plan offered to meet it. Comment specifically on the transfer pricing aspects of the proposal.

*8. The Sandringham Products Company is decentralized into two principal operating divisions. Each division has its own manufacturing facilities and its own sales force. Each division records sales to the other division separately from sales to outside firms and has separate cost of goods sold accounts for internal and external sales. Separate inventory control accounts are not maintained for internally and externally manufactured products and parts, but physical inventory records permit segregation of inventories into these two categories.

---

* Solutions to problems marked with an asterisk (*) can be found in Appendix B.

Purchases by one division from the other are recorded in the supplying division by debiting its Head Office Control account and crediting Sales—Inside. The buying division credits its Head Office Control account and debits Inventories—Materials. Cost of sales is recorded by the supplying division at standard product cost. All payrolls are processed centrally, and the divisions are charged at standard wage rates.

On December 31, 19x0, the divisional accounts included the following items:

Accounts	Division A	Division B
Sales—Outside........................	$(12,462,000)	$(8,924,000)
Sales—Inside.........................	(539,000)	(1,616,000)
Cost of Sales—Outside................	7,087,000	5,978,000
Cost of Sales—Inside.................	364,000	1,342,000
Inventories—Materials................	512,000	586,000
Inventories—Work in Process..........	604,000	523,000
Inventories—Finished Goods...........	925,000	982,000
Materials Price Variances............	67,000	21,000
Materials Quantity Variance..........	23,000	(13,000)
Labor Performance Variance...........	(8,000)	12,000
Factory Overhead Control.............	2,105,000	2,016,000
Factory Overhead Absorbed............	(2,426,000)	(1,897,000)

A tabulator run of the inventory cards indicates that the costs of materials and finished goods on hand include costs of materials and products transferred between divisions. Work in process counts also reveal that a portion of the costs of these inventories relates to internally transferred products. Analysis of these data reveals the following information:

	Division A	Division B
Internally supplied materials in inventories:		
At transfer prices......................	$234,000	$102,000
At standard cost........................	161,000	88,000

Selling and administrative expenses amounted to $3,848,000 for division A and $3,110,000 for division B. Head office expenses, amounting to $1,424,000 in 19x0, are not allocated to divisions.

An inventory valuation adjustment is made on the head office books quarterly to eliminate intracompany profits from company financial statements. The charge is to an Inventory Valuation Adjustment account, with an offsetting credit to a Provision for Intracompany Profit in Inventories account. This entry is reversed after quarterly statements have been prepared. The Inventory Valuation Adjustment account and all variance accounts are closed annually to profit and loss. On January 1, 19x0, prior to the reversing entry, there was a credit balance of $122,000 in the Provision for Intracompany Profit in Inventories account.

a) Prepare the January 1, 19x0, reversing entries and December 31, 19x0, entries to eliminate intercompany transactions from the financial statements of the Sandringham Company for the year 19x0.

b) Prepare reports showing profit or loss attributed to each division and an income statement for the company as a whole for the year 19x0.

c) Assuming that each division had budgeted sales of $12,000,000 for the year, budgeted cost of sales of $7,000,000, and selling and administrative expenses of $3,400,000, prepare a brief analysis of departures from budget for each division. You may assume that production and sales volumes were identical and that no manufacturing variances were budgeted.

9. The Foley Corporation has two sales divisions—domestic and foreign—both supplied by plants of the company's manufacturing division. The company's plants manufacture two products—Dennite and Portex—which are transferred to the domestic division at standard manufacturing cost plus 10 percent and to the foreign division at standard manufacturing cost. The domestic division also distributes a product known as Biltex, manufactured by the Curite Company. The divisional profit reports for the month of August show the following (all figures in thousands):

	Domestic Division		Foreign Division		Manufacturing Division	
	Actual	Budget	Actual	Budget	Actual	Budget
Sales:						
Dennite........	$15,442	$17,000	$2,176	$2,000	$13,130	$12,960
Portex.........	8,963	9,000	1,518	1,400	7,824	7,870
Biltex..........	3,369	3,000	...	...	...	...
Total sales...	$27,774	$29,000	$3,694	$3,400	$20,954	$20,830
Standard cost of sales:						
Dennite........	$10,802	$11,560	$1,416	$1,400	$12,072	$11,910
Portex.........	6,743	6,750	1,225	1,120	7,226	7,256
Biltex..........	2,695	2,400	...	...	...	...
Total cost of sales....	$20,240	$20,710	$2,641	$2,520	$19,298	$19,166
Division gross margin......	$ 7,534	$ 8,290	$1,053	$ 880	$ 1,656	$ 1,664
Manufacturing variances.....	...	...	...	...	1,022	410
Selling and administrative expense......	3,584	3,800	916	900	...	...
Division Net Profit (Loss)..	$ 3,950	$ 4,490	$ 137	$ (20)	$ 634	$ 1,254

Manufacturing division billings to the domestic division amounted to $11,638,000 for Dennite and $6,578,000 for shipments of Portex. The remainder of the manufacturing division sales were to the foreign division. Billing prices used in computing budgets were the same as those used in pricing interdivisional transfers. Biltex is purchased under an agreement whereby purchase and resale prices are fixed at a given level for an entire year.

It has been estimated that variable costs amount to approximately 72 percent of the standard manufacturing cost of Dennite and 78 percent of the standard manufacturing cost of Portex, and the consolidated flexible budget for the manufacturing division, adjusted to August production volumes, reflects these percentages. (The "budget" figures shown for the manufacturing division in the table above refer to planning budgets rather than flexible budgets.) The budgeted variances included $242,000 for materials price variances (unfavorable) and the remainder for volume variances. The actual price variances totaled $305,000 during the month.

The variable portion of division selling and administrative expense is assumed to average 5 percent of sales in each of the two sales divisions. Included in the selling and administrative expense charges are allocations of head office fixed costs. These charges were budgeted at 4.0 percent of sales and charged at 4.1 percent of sales during the month of August.

a) Compute the net profit before taxes of the Foley Corporation for the month of August. All variances are to be charged or credited to profit and loss.

b) Analyze, insofar as possible, the profits reported by each division and prepare a summary indicating the reasons for profit deviations from budget.

c) It has been suggested that the foreign division is not earning an adequate return on investment. Prepare a statement, using only the figures given above, that would be useful in considering this question.

10. Division A manufactures and sells product X both to outside customers and to division B. Both division A and division B are regarded as profit centers, and each manager is expected to try to maximize divisional profit.

Division A has no marketing organization of its own, but instead sells its products to outside customers through a network of manufacturer's agents. The manufacturer's agents maintain no inventories, but are responsible for investigating customers' credit ratings, billing, and collections.

Product X is priced to customers at 95 cents a pound. The agents' commission on sales of this product is 25 cents a pound, leaving 70 cents a pound for division A. Experiments conducted several months ago indicated that reducing customer prices by 10 cents a pound (to 85 cents) and agents' prices by 15 cents a pound (to 55 cents) had no noticeable effect on the number of pounds sold to outside customers. The agents have also said that sales to their customers would fall considerably if the price were to be raised, but no attempt has been made to verify this.

Division A's sales to division B are billed at 70 cents a pound. The transfer price is set by the manager of division A and is not subject to negotiation. All sales are in batches of 1,000 units each.

Division B uses one pound of X in the manufacture of each unit of its product, product Y. The demand function for product Y is as follows:

Price	Units Sold per Week
$2.00	1,000
1.60	2,000
1.40	3,000
1.25	4,000
1.10	5,000
0.95	6,000
0.80	7,000

Division A is now selling 10,000 pounds of X each week to its outside customers. The following cost estimates have been prepared for the two division managers. Each division manager has access to his own cost data only—he does not see the cost estimates for the other division.

	Division A		Division B
Pounds Produced per Week	Total Production Cost	Units Produced per Week	Total Production Cost*
10,000	$6,000	0	$1,000
11,000	6,400	1,000	1,500
12,000	6,800	2,000	1,850
13,000	7,200	3,000	2,200
14,000	7,600	4,000	2,550
15,000	8,000	5,000	2,900
16,000	8,400	6,000	3,250
17,000	9,000	7,000	3,700

* Exclusive of the cost of product X.

a) How many pounds of product X would division B be likely to buy each week at a price of 70 cents a pound?

b) Assuming that the division managers were instructed to negotiate the transfer price, what transfer price do you think might result? How many pounds of product X would division B buy at this price? Would it make any difference if each negotiator had access to the information available to the other? (The price to outside customers would not be affected by these negotiations.)

c) How many units of product Y would be manufactured if a single division manager were responsible for the activities of both of these divisions? Compare this figure with the one derived in (b) and comment on the similarity or difference.

11. The industrial products division of the Samavel Company has been required, since its inception, to purchase from other company divisions any component part or product that it requires and that is manufactured by those divisions for sale to outside customers. For special parts, not manufactured by other divisions for sale to outside customers, the industrial products division has been required to use internal sources if other divisions have

adequate capacity and facilities. As a result, approximately 85 percent of the materials cost in industrial products plants has represented parts and processed materials transferred from other divisions. Such transfers have been made at standard product cost.

Early last year the president of the Samavel Company issued the following directive:

MEMORANDUM TO: Division Managers

SUBJECT: Interdivisional Transfers

1. To place all divisions on a more competitive footing, each division manager is hereby authorized to negotiate with outside vendors for the purchase of all processed materials, component parts, and products now purchased from other divisions of the company, except (a) products sold directly under the company's brand names without further processing, and (b) components and processed materials on Schedule T-146, for which specifications and drawings are classified company confidential.
2. Before any order is placed with an outside vendor for an item currently being supplied from another division, that division must be given a chance to meet the outside price and promised delivery schedule. No such procedure need be followed on orders in amounts of less than $500.
3. Before any order is placed with an outside vendor for a new item, all divisions should be notified and given a chance to bid on the item. This procedure need not be followed for orders amounting to less than $500.
4. Transfers between divisions will continue to be made at standard cost for all items that have not been covered by the negotiations referred to in paragraphs 2 and 3 above. These standard costs are to be approved in all cases by the corporate methods department. Negotiated prices that are less than standard cost will be reported to the accounting department-department on Form PR-12-60, and do not require review by the corporate staff.
5. The cooperation of all personnel is requested to make this system effective. Each division will keep a record of outside purchases and the savings accomplished thereby.

Shortly after this memorandum was circulated, the president called a meeting of division managers to explain the new procedure and to answer questions that had arisen. The manager of the small machinery division was skeptical. He said, "Does this mean that if I have idle capacity I can be forced to transfer at less than standard cost? It seems to me that that is just the time when I need transfers at standard cost more than ever to help me absorb my overhead." Most of the other division managers were more sympathetic to the new system, although they were not certain exactly how it would work.

Upon his return from this meeting, the manager of the industrial products division instructed the divisional controller to obtain outside quotations on a metal housing used in one of the division's products. This housing was then being cast in the small machinery division's foundry at a standard cost of $22.17 per casting. The castings were then machined to required tolerances in the industrial products division, and the standard cost of this operation was $6.18. Inquiries at local foundries produced a bid from the Gray Foundry Company of $23.75 per casting, plus $175 for the cost of an aluminum pattern. These castings would be produced by a more modern process and would not require any machining in the industrial products division. Annual requirements were expected to average 500 castings.

The manager of industrial products then prepared the following cost estimate and submitted it to the small machinery manager, noting that unless the indicated price could be met, the order would be placed with Gray Foundry:

```
Cost of outside purchase:
  Pattern..............................$    175.00
  Castings—500 at $23.75.................  11,875.00
      Total purchase cost....................$12,050.00
  Less: Cost of machining—500 at $6.18.......   3,090.00
  Maximum transfer price..................$ 8,960.00 = $17.92 per casting
```

The manager of the small machinery division exploded when he received this estimate. "This is just what I was afraid of. You don't even know whether these people can live up to their promises and you want me to accept an order at less than cost. How do you expect me to cover my overhead? They are only quoting you this price to get your business, and once you are on the hook, they will raise their prices. As long as I have idle capacity, it is foolish to go outside—the whole company will suffer if you do very much of this. Against my better judgment, however, I'll quote you a price of $19.62. This doesn't cover depreciation on foundry equipment, and it's as low as I can go."

The industrial products manager rejected this offer and placed an initial order for 200 castings with the Gray Foundry Company, whereupon the small machinery manager appealed to the president, claiming that the new system was unworkable and unreasonable.

The president had hoped to avoid participation in disputes of this kind, but since this was the first case he felt that it warranted his attention. A staff assistant was assigned to study the problem and he made the following breakdown of standard costs:

	Variable Cost	Fixed Costs	Total Standard Cost
Casting..........	$17.95	$4.22	$22.17
Machining.......	4.15	2.03	6.18

He also found that materials price variances in the foundry were likely to be unfavorable, amounting to $0.12 per casting.

a) Prepare an analysis that will indicate whether future castings should be acquired from the Gray Foundry Company or from the small machinery division.

b) Discuss the transfer pricing policy outlined in the president's memorandum, commenting on any features that you feel should be changed.

c) Would you expect the new policy to require any substantial amount of top-management mediation to settle disputes of the kind arising in this problem? Explain.

12. The Falmouth division of the Briarcliff Company manufactures all its own products, together with a line of metal stampings sold through the company's Rahway division. The stampings are "sold" by Falmouth to Rahway at 88 percent of list price. The income statements for the Falmouth division

and for the Rahway division for the month of October are shown in the following tables:

FALMOUTH DIVISION

	Stampings	Other	Total
Deliveries....................	$205,398	$186,442	$391,840
Cost of deliveries			
At standard................	$160,922	$ 97,116	$258,038
Cost variances*.............	(13,772)	(8,311)	(22,083)
Net cost of deliveries...........	$147,150	$ 88,805	$235,955
Gross profit..................	$ 58,248	$ 97,637	$155,885
Administrative expense.........	16,200	9,777	25,977
Net Profit....................	$ 42,048	$ 87,860	$129,908

* Prorated to product lines on the basis of standard cost.

RAHWAY DIVISION

	Stampings	Other	Total
Sales revenue.................	$230,658	$584,321	$814,979
Cost of sales.................	205,398	409,025	614,423
Gross margin..................	$ 25,260	$175,296	$200,556
Controllable expenses*.........	25,962	65,776	91,738
Controllable profit (loss).......	$ (702)	$109,520	$108,818
Noncontrollable expenses*......	2,513	6,367	8,880
Net Profit (Loss)..............	$ (3,215)	$103,153	$ 99,938

* Prorated to product lines on the basis of sales revenue.

Although these statements summarize stampings operations for one month only, the figures shown are fairly typical. A major portion of the profit on sales of stampings is reported on the statements of the Falmouth division; the Rahway division seldom reports a profit on the stampings portion of its business.

A consultant brought in to study the problem raised by this situation recommended that the stampings be transferred to the Rahway division at full standard cost, with an additional transfer of a share of the manufacturing volume variance. The reasoning was that, inasmuch as the Rahway division is responsible for sales volume, any variances due to volume should be assigned to that division. The volume variance in October amounted to $9,191, and was favorable. In addition, the consultant proposed that the Rahway division be assigned a charge to cover a portion of the budgeted administrative expenses of the Falmouth division. Separable selling expenses of the Falmouth division are negligible, inasmuch as the remainder of the division's output is sold to an independent sales subsidiary of the Briarcliff Company. The monthly administrative expense budget for the Falmouth division was $25,200, of which $15,900 was allocated to the stamping line.

Using this approach, the consultant recommended a revision of the monthly profit reports and illustrated his proposal with the October figures:

FALMOUTH DIVISION

	Stampings	Other	Total
Deliveries:			
At standard cost............	$160,922	$ 97,116	$258,038
Volume variance adjustments*	(5,732)	(3,459)	(9,191)
Administrative expense			
charged†.................	15,900	9,300	25,200
Net billings...................	$171,090	$102,957	$274,047
Cost of deliveries:			
Manufacturing.............	$147,150	$ 88,805	$235,955
Administrative.............	16,200	9,777	25,977
Total cost of deliveries.....	$163,350	$ 98,582	$261,932
Division Profit Contribution....	$ 7,740	$ 4,375	$ 12,115

    * Prorated to product lines on the basis of standard cost.
    † Predetermined charge, based on average monthly budget.

RAHWAY DIVISION

	Stampings	Other	Total
Sales revenue.................	$230,658	$584,321	$814,979
Cost of sales..................	171,090	409,025	580,115
Gross margin..................	$ 59,568	$175,296	$234,864
Controllable expenses*........	25,962	65,776	91,738
Controllable Profit............	$ 33,606	$109,520	$143,126

    * Prorated to product lines on the basis of sales revenue.

In justification of this approach, the consultant's report contained the following statement: "The profit contribution figure for the Falmouth division thus represents the performance of the Falmouth division in its area of responsibility—manufacturing. The earnings of the Rahway division, in turn, are independent of manufacturing efficiencies and reflect only the success of the Rahway division in carrying out its function. Whenever Rahway makes (or loses) a dollar for the company, its reported earnings will go up (or down) by a dollar. The proposed method is equivalent to a method whereby transfers would be made at amounts equal to variable standard cost, plus a fixed charge for the budgeted fixed costs, in other words, variable costing, without requiring the incorporation of variable costing into the inventory cost records. The important feature of the plan is that it emphasizes the important 'contribution to overhead and profit' for each product line and for each division. This method also entails the transfer of the bulk of stampings profits from the Falmouth division, where they are now shown, to the Rahway division. This should not be a cause of concern, however, if it is remembered that Falmouth is *not expected* to show any positive profit contribution under this system."

When the consultant's report was received, the manager of the Falmouth division objected immediately. He said, "This completely destroys the profit center concept, insofar as my division is concerned. As far as I can see, all you have achieved is a transfer of profits from one division to two others and I come out on the short end of the transfer. If we really believe in decentralization, I have to share in the profits of products that are manufactured in my plant."

The manager of the Rahway division recognized the consultant's proposal as a great improvement over the existing system, but he was worried about the "volume variance adjustment" item. He said, "That's fine now, because Falmouth is operating at more than normal capacity, but what happens if sales of stampings hold up but the market for all the other Falmouth products, over which I have no control, goes into a slump? It seems to me that there is something wrong here, but I'm not enough of an accountant to put my finger on it."

The president of the Briarcliff Company has asked you to prepare a report, analyzing the consultant's proposal and considering the objections raised by the two division managers and making whatever recommendations for modification of the proposal you deem appropriate.

CASE 26–1: HOPPIT CHEMICAL COMPANY

The Moorhouse division of the Hoppit Chemical Company has 14 chemical plants located in various parts of the United States. Its profit contribution after deducting all divisional overheads runs about $50 million a year, and in exceptionally good years this may even reach $75 million.

The company's Allworth division is much smaller, with only two plants and an annual profit contribution of about $2.5 million. Four years ago, the Allworth division constructed a new plant on a site adjacent to one of the main plants of the Moorhouse division. At the time construction of the new plant was begun, the Moorhouse plant was producing and was expected to continue producing 10 million pounds of a product known as amalite. Amalite was obtained by converting the waste residue thrown off in the production of the Moorhouse plant's main products. Prior to the construction of the new Allworth plant, amalite had been manufactured intermittently whenever its market price was high enough to justify the conversion expenditures. The market for amalite had been weak for some time, however, and the Hoppit market research department forecasted that this condition would continue to prevail for many years to come as amalite was gradually displaced by petroleum derivatives in one of its main uses. Under these circumstances, it seemed a good move to build the new plant to convert amalite into another chemical product with a considerably higher market value.

A transfer price system was devised and accepted by the managers of both divisions when the new plant went into production. This system provided that prior to the start of each quarter the Moorhouse division would quote a set of prices for different quantities of amalite to be delivered during that quarter. These prices were to be based primarily on the estimated incremental costs of processing different quantities of Moorhouse waste into amalite. For example, during the first two years the plant was in operation, a typical transfer price schedule was as follows:

Quarterly Transfers (Pounds)	Total Transfer Price
1,000,000 or less.......$400,000	
1,000,000–2,500,000....$400,000 + $0.30 per pound in excess of 1,000,000 pounds	
More than 2,500,000...$850,000 + $0.40 per pound in excess of 2,500,000 pounds	

The transfer pricing system also provided that if the anticipated market price of amalite for the quarter were to exceed the incremental costs of converting waste into amalite, then the market price would be used as the transfer price for the ensuing quarter.

The Allworth plant was not completely dependent on Moorhouse amalite for raw materials. It could also use another commercially available product known as flemite. The market price of flemite was considerably higher than the transfer prices prevailing during the first two years of the new plant's operations, however, and flemite was not used.

Each year each division manager in the Hoppit Chemical Company is required to prepare a profit plan. In drawing up their plans, the Allworth and Moorhouse managers get together and agree on a forecast of the transfer prices expected to prevail during the coming year—this price schedule is then built into the divisional profit plans for the year.

Shortly after the beginning of the current year, the market price of amalite took a sudden jump to 50 cents a pound. This price was then established by Moorhouse as the transfer price for the second quarter. Because flemite was available at a price of 45 cents, however, Moorhouse sold most of its amalite on the market and bought flemite to meet its supply commitment to the Allworth plant. Both division managers agreed that this was in the best interest of the Hoppit Chemical Company.

At the same time, however, Mr. C. P. Jones, the Allworth division manager, refused to approve the transfer charge at 45 cents on the grounds that this would create a substantial profit variance amounting to approximately $250,000 a quarter, through no fault of anyone in the Allworth division. As Mr. Jones pointed out, when the plant was constructed he could have signed a long-term contract with outside suppliers of amalite at a price of 40 cents a pound, but he was not allowed by Hoppit's top management to do so. Mr. Jones felt that Moorhouse was under an obligation to continue to supply amalite or a substitute at a price within the range that was forecasted when the plant was built.

Mr. John England, Moorhouse's chief cost analyst and the man responsible for the transfer price calculations, did not agree. "Even if they had signed a contract like that," he said, "we would still have to make our decisions on the basis of current market conditions. If Allworth can't make an incremental profit on the basis of current market prices, then the plant should be shut down until materials prices go back down or selling prices of the Allworth products go up. If we let them have this stuff at 40 cents, the company could be losing as much as 5 cents on every pound they use."

a) Do you feel that Mr. Jones is justified in asking for a long-term price commitment from Moorhouse, or is Mr. England right in saying that the transfer price should always reflect current market conditions?

b) Should the transfer pricing system be changed, and if so in what way? Can you identify any other defects in the system? Explain your reasoning.

Appendixes

Appendixes

Appendix A

COMPOUND INTEREST TABLES

THE tables in this appendix contain the multipliers or conversion factors necessary to convert cash flows of one or more periods into their equivalent values at some other point in time. The basic explanation of the reasons for conversion is given in Chapter 19. Only the mechanical details of how the numbers in the tables should be used are explained here.

CONTINUOUS COMPOUNDING TABLES[1]

The first five tables are based on continuous compounding and are the tables used in the illustrations in the text. In continuous compounding, interest is added to principal continuously rather than once each year or once each quarter. The mathematical formulas on which these tables are based are given as footnotes to the various tables.

Arranging the Basic Data

The figures shown in these tables are the amounts of "factors" by which to *multiply* time-identified cash flow totals to derive their present values. To facilitate the application of these tables, dollar figures relating to investment proposals should be arranged in the form of a timetable. Net cash outlays should be identified by a minus sign; net cash receipts should be identified by a plus sign.

Lump-sum receipts or outlays should be identified as occurring a specified number of years subsequent to a "reference date" (zero date in the timetable). Receipts or outlays that are spread out more or less uniformly during a period of time should be identified as occurring between the two appropriate points in time (e.g., from four to five years after the reference date). If the reference point selected occurs after the first substantial outlays are to be made, then the outlays should be

---

[1] Based on interest tables prepared for the Atlantic Refining Company by J. C. Gregory. Used by permission of the company.

identified as occurring a specified number of years prior to the reference date or spread out during a specified year prior to the reference date.

The net algebraic sum of all the cash flows indicates the net lifetime profit of the proposal at zero interest. Discounting or compounding these cash flows at some rate of interest serves to charge interest against the proposal.

Selection of Zero Point

The reference date is usually selected as the date on which a proposed investment first goes into operation or as the date on which the first substantial outlays will be made. If a number of related or competing proposals are being studied, a single reference date or zero point should be selected for them all.

Description of Tables

Each of the first five tables in this Appendix provides interest factors that will discount future cash flows to a common reference point or zero date. These five tables are:

Table 1: Present value of $1, received or paid in a lump sum.
Table 2: Present value of $1, received or paid in a uniform stream during individual years.
Table 3: Present value of annuity of $1, received or paid in a uniform stream during individual years.
Table 4: Future value of $1, received or paid in a lump sum prior to reference date.
Table 5: Future value of $1, received or paid in a uniform stream during individual years prior to reference date.

Table 1 is to be used for discounting receipts or outlays that occur in a lump sum a given number of years subsequent to the reference date. In other words, this is the table to be used to discount, say, the anticipated outlay of $10,000 five years hence for the purchase of replacement pallets for use in connection with forklift trucks the purchase of which is now under consideration.

Table 2 is to be used for discounting receipts or outlays that are spread out at a more or less uniform rate during a given year. For example, this is the table to be used to discount each year's savings in labor costs that are expected to result from the use of forklift trucks. These savings do not occur all at once in a lump sum but are realized more or less continuously throughout the year.

Table 3 (pp. 868–69) is to be used for discounting receipts or outlays that occur at a relatively constant rate, both annually and within each year, from the zero point to the end of the indicated time interval. For example, if the forklift truck proposal is expected to yield net cash savings in labor costs of $2,000 a year for seven years, Table 3 should be used. The cash flow to be multiplied by the discount factor contained in this table is the annual receipt or outlay rather than total receipts or outlays during the entire annuity period.

Table 4 (p. 867) is to be used for compounding receipts or outlays that occur in a lump sum a given number of years prior to the reference date. For example, this is the table to be used to compound the cost of land to be purchased a year or more prior to its use if the reference date for this particular proposal has been established as the date of first operation of the proposed facilities.

Table 5 (p. 867) is to be used for compounding receipts or outlays that are spread out at a more or less uniform rate during a given year prior to the reference date. For example, this is the table to be used to compound the costs of construction during the construction period if the reference date for the proposal has been established as the date of first operation of the proposed facilities.

Calculation of Present Value

To compute present value at the reference date at a given rate of interest, simply multiply each item in the timetable by the applicable factor and find the discounted algebraic sum. The discounted value of each cash flow retains the sign of the corresponding undiscounted value.

The present value of a simple timetable of cash flows discounted at a 10 percent rate is determined in the following manner:

Time Period	Cash Flow	Table Number	Discount Factor at 10%	Present Value at 10%
0.....................	−$1,000	..	1.0000	−$1,000
0–1....................	+ 500	2	0.9516	+ 476
1–2....................	+ 500	2	0.8611	+ 430
2.....................	+ 150	1	0.8187	+ 123
Total.............	+$ 150			+$ 29

This problem may also be solved by using Table 3 instead of Table 2:

Time Period	Cash Flow	Table Number	Discount Factor at 10%	Present Value at 10%
0.....................	−$1,000	..	1.0000	−$1,000
0–2....................	+500/yr.	3	1.8127	+ 906
2.....................	+ 150	1	0.8187	+ 123
Total.............	+$ 150			+$ 29

Thus the present value of this stream of cash flows at 10 percent is $29. Alternatively, it might be stated that the present value of the cash receipts exceeds the present value of the cash outlays by $29. This is the present value of the cash "surplus" that would remain if interest of 10 percent had to be paid on the capital invested in this project.

Calculation of Discounted Cash Flow Rate of Return

Discounted cash flow rate of return, sometimes known as the "profitability index" of a proposal, is defined as the rate of interest at which the present value of the cash outlays associated with a proposal is just equal to the present value of its anticipated cash receipts. This is the maximum rate of interest that the company could afford to pay from the earnings of a particular proposal and still break even. This rate of interest can be located by the process of trial and error:

1. Find one rate of interest at which the net algebraic present value is positive.
2. Find another higher rate of interest at which net present value is negative.
3. Interpolate between the two.

A useful rule of thumb in selecting the rate of interest for the first trial is to use the rate indicated by dividing average net receipts per year during the first half of the expected life of the project by the initial investment outlay required. Thus if a project is expected to last 10 years, initial investment is $10,000 and expected earnings during the first five years amount to $2,000 per year, the first trial might be run at a 20 percent interest rate.

If the net present value at the initial trial rate is positive, then the second trial rate should be higher than the first, and vice versa. Once two present values have been found, one negative and one positive, the true discounted cash flow rate of return can be approximated by interpolation. For example, assume that the cash flows expected from a proposal have been discounted at interest rates of 20 percent and 15 percent, and that the net present values at these rates are −$1,354 and +$358, respectively. From this we know that the true rate is somewhere between 15 percent and 20 percent. The algebraic difference between −$1,354 and +$358 is $1,712, and thus the true rate is approximately 358/1,712 of the distance between 15 percent and 20 percent, a distance of five percentage points. In equation form:

$$\text{Rate of return} = 15\% + (358/1{,}712 \times 5\%) = 17.1\% .$$

Interest Factors Not Included in Tables

The tables present interest multipliers for most of the interest rates and time intervals that will be required, but in some instances it may be necessary to find multipliers not presented in these tables. It is possible to do this by simple multiplication and substitution, without need to resort to mathematical derivation formulas. A few examples will indicate how readily these extensions can be made (in most cases, alternative methods of calculation are shown—the numbers in parentheses in each case indicate the table from which the interest multiplier is drawn):

Lump Sum: 26 years after zero point at 10%:

(1) 25 years at 10% $\times$ (1) 1 year at 10% =
$$0.0821 \times 0.9048 = 0.0743$$

(1) 13 years at 10% $\times$ (1) 13 years at 10% =
$$0.2725 \times 0.2725 = 0.0743$$

(1) 10 years at 26% $= 0.0743$

(1) 20 years at 13% $= 0.0743$

Spread Out: 25 years to 26 years after zero point at 10%:

(2) 14 years to 15 years at 10% $\times$ (1) 11 years at 10% =
$$0.2347 \times 0.3329 = 0.0781$$

(2) 9 years to 10 years at 10% $\times$ (1) 16 years at 10% =
$$0.3869 \times 0.2019 = 0.0781$$

Spread Out Annuity: 26 years at 10%:

(3) 25 years at 10% $+$ (2) 24 years to 25 years at 10% $\times$
(1) 1 year at 10% =
$$9.1790 + (0.0863 \times 0.9048) = 9.2571$$

Lump Sum: 6 years before zero point at 10%:

(4) 2 years at 30% $= 1.8221$

(4) 3 years at 20% $= 1.8221$

(4) 1 year at 10% $\times$ (4) 5 years at 10% $= 1.1052 \times 1.6487 = 1.8221$

Reciprocal of (1) 6 years at 10% $= 1/0.5488$ $\qquad = 1.8221$

Spread Out: 6 years to 5 years before zero point at 10%:

(5) 1 year to zero date at 10% $\times$ (4) 5 years at 10% =
$$1.0517 \times 1.6487 = 1.7339$$

(5) 2 years to 1 year at 10% $\times$ (4) 4 years at 10% =
$$1.1623 \times 1.4918 = 1.7339$$

DISCRETE COMPOUNDING TABLES

The final two tables are based on discrete compounding in which interest is added to principal at the end of each time period. As with the continuous compounding tables, the cash flows should first be arranged in the form of a timetable.

To use these tables, the cash flows must be assumed to occur on specific dates—e.g., at one year after the zero date—rather than being spread out continuously between successive dates. The two tables are:

Table 6: Present value of $1, received or paid in a lump sum, discounted once each period.

Table 7: Present value of an annuity of $1, received or paid as a series of lump sums at the end of individual periods, discounted once each period.

COMPOUND INTEREST FORMULAS

The formula for the present value (P) of a future sum at the end of t years (F_t), discounted once a year at an annual rate of interest r, is as follows:

$$P = F_t \times \frac{1}{(1 + r)^t} .$$

If interest is compounded more often than once each year, the interest rate per compounding interval is reduced proportionately. For example, if interest is compounded semiannually, the formula becomes:

$$P = F_t \times \frac{1}{\left(1 + \frac{r}{2}\right)^{2t}} .$$

This can be restated in general terms by letting m represent the number of compounding intervals per year:

$$P = F_t \times \frac{1}{\left(1 + \frac{r}{m}\right)^{mt}} .$$

If m/r is represented by the letter k, this becomes:

$$P = F_t \times \frac{1}{\left(\left(1 + \frac{1}{k}\right)^k\right)^{rt}} .$$

As the length of the compounding interval ($1/k$) becomes shorter, then k becomes larger. As k approaches infinity, the quantity $(1 + \frac{1}{k})^k$ approaches the limit e, which is the base of the so-called natural logarithms. In other words, with an infinitely short compounding interval, the present value formula becomes:

$$P = F_t \times \frac{1}{e^{rt}} .$$

Formulas underlying Tables 2, 3, 4, and 5 can be derived by analogous procedures.

TABLE 1

Present Value of $1, Received or Paid in a Lump Sum at Date *t*, Discounted Continuously for *t* Periods

t	5%	6%	7%	8%	9%	10%	11%	12%	13%	14%	15%	20%	25%	30%	40%
1	0.9512	0.9418	0.9324	0.9231	0.9139	0.9048	0.8958	0.8869	0.8781	0.8694	0.8607	0.8187	0.7788	0.7408	0.6703
2	0.9048	0.8869	0.8694	0.8521	0.8353	0.8187	0.8025	0.7866	0.7711	0.7558	0.7408	0.6703	0.6065	0.5488	0.4493
3	0.8607	0.8353	0.8106	0.7866	0.7634	0.7408	0.7189	0.6977	0.6771	0.6570	0.6376	0.5488	0.4724	0.4066	0.3012
4	0.8187	0.7866	0.7558	0.7261	0.6977	0.6703	0.6440	0.6188	0.5945	0.5712	0.5488	0.4493	0.3679	0.3012	0.2019
5	0.7788	0.7408	0.7047	0.6703	0.6376	0.6065	0.5770	0.5488	0.5220	0.4966	0.4724	0.3679	0.2865	0.2231	0.1353
6	0.7408	0.6977	0.6570	0.6188	0.5827	0.5488	0.5169	0.4868	0.4584	0.4317	0.4066	0.3012	0.2231	0.1653	0.0907
7	0.7047	0.6570	0.6126	0.5712	0.5326	0.4966	0.4630	0.4317	0.4025	0.3753	0.3499	0.2466	0.1738	0.1225	0.0608
8	0.6703	0.6188	0.5712	0.5273	0.4868	0.4493	0.4148	0.3829	0.3535	0.3263	0.3012	0.2019	0.1353	0.0907	0.0408
9	0.6376	0.5827	0.5326	0.4868	0.4449	0.4065	0.3716	0.3396	0.3104	0.2837	0.2592	0.1653	0.1054	0.0672	0.0273
10	0.6065	0.5488	0.4966	0.4493	0.4066	0.3679	0.3329	0.3012	0.2725	0.2466	0.2231	0.1353	0.0821	0.0498	0.0183
11	0.5770	0.5169	0.4630	0.4148	0.3716	0.3329	0.2982	0.2671	0.2393	0.2144	0.1921	0.1108	0.0639	0.0369	0.0123
12	0.5488	0.4868	0.4317	0.3829	0.3396	0.3012	0.2671	0.2369	0.2101	0.1864	0.1653	0.0907	0.0498	0.0273	0.0082
13	0.5220	0.4584	0.4025	0.3535	0.3104	0.2725	0.2393	0.2101	0.1845	0.1620	0.1423	0.0743	0.0388	0.0202	0.0055
14	0.4966	0.4317	0.3753	0.3263	0.2837	0.2466	0.2144	0.1864	0.1620	0.1409	0.1225	0.0608	0.0302	0.0150	0.0037
15	0.4724	0.4066	0.3499	0.3012	0.2592	0.2231	0.1921	0.1653	0.1423	0.1225	0.1054	0.0498	0.0235	0.0111	0.0025
16	0.4493	0.3829	0.3263	0.2780	0.2369	0.2019	0.1720	0.1466	0.1249	0.1065	0.0907	0.0408	0.0183	0.0082	0.0017
17	0.4274	0.3606	0.3042	0.2567	0.2165	0.1827	0.1541	0.1300	0.1097	0.0925	0.0781	0.0334	0.0143	0.0061	0.0011
18	0.4065	0.3396	0.2837	0.2369	0.1979	0.1653	0.1381	0.1153	0.0963	0.0805	0.0672	0.0273	0.0111	0.0045	0.0007
19	0.3867	0.3198	0.2645	0.2187	0.1809	0.1496	0.1237	0.1023	0.0846	0.0700	0.0578	0.0224	0.0087	0.0033	0.0005
20	0.3679	0.3012	0.2466	0.2019	0.1653	0.1353	0.1108	0.0907	0.0743	0.0608	0.0498	0.0183	0.0067	0.0025	0.0003
21	0.3499	0.2837	0.2299	0.1864	0.1511	0.1225	0.0993	0.0805	0.0652	0.0529	0.0429	0.0150	0.0052	0.0018	0.0002
22	0.3329	0.2671	0.2144	0.1720	0.1381	0.1108	0.0889	0.0714	0.0573	0.0460	0.0369	0.0123	0.0041	0.0014	0.0002
23	0.3166	0.2516	0.1999	0.1588	0.1262	0.1003	0.0797	0.0633	0.0503	0.0399	0.0317	0.0101	0.0032	0.0010	0.0001
24	0.3012	0.2369	0.1864	0.1466	0.1153	0.0907	0.0714	0.0561	0.0442	0.0347	0.0273	0.0082	0.0025	0.0007	0.0001
25	0.2865	0.2231	0.1738	0.1353	0.1054	0.0821	0.0639	0.0498	0.0388	0.0302	0.0235	0.0067	0.0019	0.0006	.....
30	0.2231	0.1653	0.1225	0.0907	0.0672	0.0498	0.0369	0.0273	0.0202	0.0150	0.0111	0.0025	0.0006	0.0001	.....
35	0.1738	0.1225	0.0863	0.0608	0.0429	0.0302	0.0213	0.0150	0.0106	0.0074	0.0052	0.0009	0.0002	.....	.....
40	0.1353	0.0907	0.0608	0.0408	0.0273	0.0183	0.0123	0.0082	0.0055	0.0037	0.0025	0.0003	.....	.....	.....
45	0.1054	0.0672	0.0429	0.0273	0.0174	0.0111	0.0071	0.0045	0.0029	0.0018	0.0012	0.0001	.....	.....	.....
50	0.0821	0.0498	0.0302	0.0183	0.0111	0.0067	0.0041	0.0025	0.0015	0.0009	0.0006	0.0000	.....	.....	.....

P = present value
F_t = future sum at date t
e = 2.71828 (approximate)
r = annual rate of interest as a decimal
t = number of years from zero date

$$\left(P = F_t \times \frac{1}{e^{rt}} \right)$$

TABLE 2

Present Value of $1, Received or Paid in a Uniform Stream during Individual Years, Discounted Continuously to Zero Date

$(t-1)$ to t	5%	6%	7%	8%	9%	10%	11%	12%	13%	14%	15%	20%	25%	30%	40%
0 to 1	0.9754	0.9706	0.9658	0.9610	0.9563	0.9516	0.9470	0.9423	0.9377	0.9332	0.9286	0.9063	0.8848	0.8640	0.8242
1 to 2	0.9278	0.9141	0.9005	0.8872	0.8740	0.8611	0.8483	0.8358	0.8234	0.8112	0.7993	0.7421	0.6891	0.6400	0.5525
2 to 3	0.8826	0.8608	0.8396	0.8189	0.7988	0.7791	0.7600	0.7413	0.7230	0.7053	0.6879	0.6075	0.5367	0.4741	0.3703
3 to 4	0.8395	0.8107	0.7829	0.7560	0.7300	0.7050	0.6808	0.6574	0.6349	0.6131	0.5921	0.4974	0.4179	0.3513	0.2482
4 to 5	0.7986	0.7635	0.7299	0.6979	0.6672	0.6379	0.6099	0.5831	0.5575	0.5330	0.5096	0.4072	0.3255	0.2602	0.1664
5 to 6	0.7596	0.7190	0.6806	0.6442	0.6098	0.5772	0.5463	0.5172	0.4895	0.4634	0.4386	0.3334	0.2535	0.1928	0.1115
6 to 7	0.7226	0.6772	0.6346	0.5947	0.5573	0.5223	0.4894	0.4588	0.4299	0.4029	0.3775	0.2730	0.1974	0.1428	0.0748
7 to 8	0.6874	0.6377	0.5917	0.5490	0.5093	0.4726	0.4385	0.4069	0.3775	0.3502	0.3250	0.2235	0.1538	0.1058	0.0501
8 to 9	0.6538	0.6006	0.5517	0.5068	0.4655	0.4276	0.3928	0.3609	0.3314	0.3045	0.2797	0.1830	0.1197	0.0784	0.0336
9 to 10	0.6219	0.5656	0.5144	0.4678	0.4254	0.3869	0.3519	0.3201	0.2910	0.2647	0.2407	0.1498	0.0933	0.0581	0.0225
10 to 11	0.5916	0.5327	0.4796	0.4318	0.3888	0.3501	0.3152	0.2839	0.2556	0.2301	0.2072	0.1227	0.0726	0.0430	0.0151
11 to 12	0.5628	0.5016	0.4472	0.3986	0.3553	0.3168	0.2824	0.2518	0.2244	0.2000	0.1783	0.1004	0.0566	0.0319	0.0101
12 to 13	0.5353	0.4724	0.4169	0.3680	0.3248	0.2866	0.2530	0.2233	0.1970	0.1739	0.1535	0.0822	0.0441	0.0236	0.0068
13 to 14	0.5092	0.4449	0.3888	0.3397	0.2968	0.2593	0.2266	0.1981	0.1730	0.1512	0.1321	0.0673	0.0343	0.0175	0.0045
14 to 15	0.4844	0.4190	0.3625	0.3136	0.2713	0.2347	0.2030	0.1757	0.1519	0.1314	0.1137	0.0551	0.0267	0.0130	0.0030
15 to 16	0.4608	0.3946	0.3379	0.2895	0.2479	0.2123	0.1819	0.1558	0.1334	0.1143	0.0979	0.0451	0.0208	0.0096	0.0021
16 to 17	0.4383	0.3717	0.3151	0.2672	0.2265	0.1921	0.1630	0.1382	0.1172	0.0994	0.0842	0.0370	0.0162	0.0071	0.0014
17 to 18	0.4169	0.3500	0.2938	0.2467	0.2070	0.1738	0.1460	0.1225	0.1029	0.0864	0.0725	0.0303	0.0126	0.0053	0.0009
18 to 19	0.3966	0.3296	0.2739	0.2277	0.1892	0.1573	0.1308	0.1087	0.0903	0.0751	0.0624	0.0248	0.0098	0.0039	0.0006
19 to 20	0.3773	0.3104	0.2554	0.2102	0.1729	0.1423	0.1172	0.0964	0.0793	0.0653	0.0537	0.0203	0.0076	0.0029	0.0004
20 to 21	0.3588	0.2923	0.2381	0.1940	0.1581	0.1288	0.1049	0.0855	0.0697	0.0568	0.0462	0.0166	0.0060	0.0021	0.0003
21 to 22	0.3414	0.2753	0.2220	0.1791	0.1445	0.1165	0.0940	0.0758	0.0612	0.0494	0.0398	0.0136	0.0046	0.0016	0.0002
22 to 23	0.3247	0.2593	0.2070	0.1654	0.1320	0.1054	0.0842	0.0673	0.0537	0.0429	0.0343	0.0111	0.0036	0.0012	0.0001
23 to 24	0.3089	0.2442	0.1930	0.1526	0.1207	0.0954	0.0755	0.0597	0.0472	0.0373	0.0295	0.0091	0.0028	0.0009	0.0001
24 to 25	0.2938	0.2300	0.1800	0.1409	0.1103	0.0863	0.0676	0.0529	0.0414	0.0324	0.0254	0.0075	0.0022	0.0006	0.0001

$$\left(P = F_i \times \frac{e^r - 1}{r e^{rt}} \right)$$

TABLE 4

Future Value of $1, Received or Paid in a Lump Sum *t* Years Prior to Zero Date, Compounded Continuously for −*t* Years

t	5%	6%	7%	8%	9%	10%	11%	12%
−1..................	1.0513	1.0618	1.0725	1.0833	1.0942	1.1052	1.1163	1.1275
−2..................	1.1052	1.1275	1.1503	1.1735	1.1972	1.2214	1.2461	1.2712
−3..................	1.1618	1.1972	1.2337	1.2712	1.3100	1.3499	1.3910	1.4333
−4..................	1.2214	1.2712	1.3231	1.3771	1.4333	1.4918	1.5527	1.6161
−5..................	1.2840	1.3499	1.4191	1.4918	1.5683	1.6487	1.7333	1.8221

t	13%	14%	15%	20%	25%	30%	40%
−1............	1.1388	1.1503	1.1618	1.2214	1.2840	1.3499	1.4918
−2............	1.2969	1.3231	1.3499	1.4918	1.6487	1.8221	2.2255
−3............	1.4770	1.5220	1.5683	1.8221	2.1170	2.4596	3.3201
−4............	1.6820	1.7507	1.8221	2.2255	2.7183	3.3201	4.9530
−5............	1.9155	2.0138	2.1170	2.7183	3.4903	4.4817	7.3891

$$F = P_t \times e^{rt}$$

TABLE 5

Future Value of $1, Received or Paid in a Uniform Stream during Individual Years Prior to Zero Date, Compounded Continuously to Zero Date

t to (*t* + 1)	5%	6%	7%	8%	9%	10%	11%	12%
−1 to 0............	1.0254	1.0306	1.0358	1.0411	1.0464	1.0517	1.0571	1.0625
−2 to −1............	1.0780	1.0943	1.1109	1.1278	1.1450	1.1623	1.1800	1.1980
−3 to −2............	1.1333	1.1620	1.1915	1.2217	1.2528	1.2845	1.3173	1.3507
−4 to −3............	1.1913	1.2338	1.2779	1.3234	1.3708	1.4197	1.4704	1.5229
−5 to −4............	1.2524	1.3101	1.3705	1.4337	1.4998	1.5689	1.6414	1.7171

t to (*t* + 1)	13%	14%	15%	20%	25%	30%	40%
−1 to 0.......	1.0679	1.0734	1.0789	1.1070	1.1361	1.1662	1.2296
−2 to −1......	1.2161	1.2347	1.2535	1.3521	1.4588	1.5743	1.8343
−3 to −2......	1.3850	1.4202	1.4564	1.6514	1.8731	2.1249	2.7365
−4 to −3......	1.5773	1.6337	1.6920	2.0171	2.4051	2.8684	4.0824
−5 to −4......	1.7962	1.8792	1.9659	2.4636	3.0883	3.8719	6.0902

$$F = A_t \times \left[\frac{(e^r - 1)e^{rt}}{re^r} \right]$$

TABLE 3

Present Value of Annuity of $1 a Year for *t* Years, Received or Paid in a

t	5%	6%	7%	8%	9%	10%	11%
1	0.9754	0.9706	0.9658	0.9610	0.9563	0.9516	0.9470
2	1.9032	1.8847	1.8663	1.8482	1.8303	1.8127	1.7953
3	2.7858	2.7455	2.7059	2.6671	2.6291	2.5918	2.5553
4	3.6253	3.5562	3.4888	3.4231	3.3591	3.2968	3.2361
5	4.4239	4.3197	4.2187	4.1210	4.0263	3.9347	3.8460
6	5.1835	5.0387	4.8993	4.7652	4.6361	4.5119	4.3923
7	5.9061	5.7159	5.5339	5.3599	5.1934	5.0342	4.8817
8	6.5935	6.3536	6.1256	5.9089	5.7027	5.5068	5.3202
9	7.2473	6.9542	6.6773	6.4157	6.1682	5.9344	5.7130
10	7.8692	7.5198	7.1917	6.8835	6.5936	6.3213	6.0649
11	8.4608	8.0525	7.6713	7.3153	6.9824	6.6714	6.3801
12	9.0236	8.5541	8.1185	7.7139	7.3377	6.9882	6.6625
13	9.5589	9.0265	8.5354	8.0819	7.6625	7.2748	6.9155
14	10.0681	9.4714	8.9242	8.4216	7.9593	7.5341	7.1421
15	10.5525	9.8904	9.2867	8.7352	8.2306	7.7688	7.3451
16	11.0133	10.2850	9.6246	9.0247	8.4785	7.9811	7.5270
17	11.4516	10.6567	9.9397	9.2919	8.7050	8.1732	7.6900
18	11.8685	11.0067	10.2335	9.5386	8.9120	8.3470	7.8360
19	12.2651	11.3363	10.5074	9.7663	9.1012	8.5043	7.9668
20	12.6424	11.6467	10.7628	9.9765	9.2741	8.6466	8.0840
21	13.0012	11.9390	11.0009	10.1705	9.4322	8.7754	8.1889
22	13.3426	12.2143	11.2229	10.3496	9.5767	8.8919	8.2829
23	13.6673	12.4736	11.4299	10.5150	9.7087	8.9973	8.3671
24	13.9762	12.7178	11.6229	10.6676	9.8294	9.0927	8.4426
25	14.2700	12.9478	11.8029	10.8085	9.9397	9.1790	8.5102

$$\left(P = A_t \times \frac{e^{rt} - 1}{re^{rt}} \right)$$

A_t = annual amount of annuity for *t* years

Uniform Stream during Individual Years, Discounted Continuously for *t* Years

12%	13%	14%	15%	20%	25%	30%	40%
0.9423	0.9377	0.9332	0.9286	0.9063	0.8848	0.8640	0.8242
1.7781	1.7611	1.7444	1.7279	1.6484	1.5739	1.5040	1.3767
2.5194	2.4841	2.4497	2.4158	2.2559	2.1106	1.9781	1.7470
3.1768	3.1190	3.0628	3.0079	2.7533	2.5285	2.3294	1.9952
3.7599	3.6765	3.5958	3.5175	3.1605	2.8540	2.5896	2.1616
4.2771	4.1660	4.0592	3.9561	3.4939	3.1075	2.7824	2.2731
4.7359	4.5959	4.4621	4.3336	3.7669	3.3049	2.9252	2.3479
5.1428	4.9734	4.8123	4.6586	3.9904	3.4587	3.0310	2.3980
5.5037	5.3048	5.1168	4.9383	4.1734	3.5784	3.1094	2.4316
5.8238	5.5958	5.3815	5.1790	4.3232	3.6717	3.1675	2.4541
6.1077	5.8514	5.6116	5.3862	4.4459	3.7443	3.2105	2.4692
6.3595	6.0758	5.8116	5.5645	4.5463	3.8009	3.2424	2.4793
6.5828	6.2728	5.9855	5.7180	4.6285	3.8450	3.2660	2.4861
6.7809	6.4458	6.1367	5.8501	4.6958	3.8793	3.2835	2.4906
6.9566	6.5977	6.2682	5.9638	4.7509	3.9060	3.2965	2.4936
7.1124	6.7311	6.3825	6.0617	4.7960	3.9268	3.3061	2.4957
7.2506	6.8483	6.4819	6.1459	4.8330	3.9430	3.3132	2.4971
7.3731	6.9512	6.5683	6.2184	4.8633	3.9556	3.3185	2.4980
7.4818	7.0415	6.6434	6.2808	4.8881	3.9654	3.3224	2.4986
7.5782	7.1208	6.7087	6.3345	4.9084	3.9730	3.3253	2.4990
7.6637	7.1905	6.7655	6.3807	4.9250	3.9790	3.3274	2.4993
7.7395	7.2517	6.8149	6.4205	4.9386	3.9836	3.3290	2.4995
7.8068	7.3054	6.8578	6.4548	4.9497	3.9872	3.3302	2.4996
7.8665	7.3526	6.8951	6.4843	4.9588	3.9900	3.3311	2.4997
7.9194	7.3940	6.9275	6.5097	4.9663	3.9922	3.3317	2.4998

TABLE 6

Present Value of $1, Received or Paid in a Lump Sum, Discounted Once Each Period for t Periods

(Important: These are not the discount factors used in the text illustrations)

t	5%	6%	7%	8%	9%	10%	11%	12%	13%	14%	15%	20%	25%	30%	40%
1	0.952	0.943	0.935	0.926	0.917	0.909	0.901	0.893	0.885	0.877	0.870	0.833	0.800	0.769	0.714
2	0.907	0.890	0.873	0.857	0.842	0.826	0.812	0.797	0.783	0.769	0.756	0.694	0.640	0.592	0.510
3	0.864	0.840	0.816	0.794	0.772	0.751	0.731	0.712	0.693	0.675	0.658	0.579	0.512	0.455	0.364
4	0.823	0.792	0.763	0.735	0.708	0.683	0.659	0.636	0.613	0.592	0.572	0.482	0.410	0.350	0.260
5	0.784	0.747	0.713	0.681	0.650	0.621	0.593	0.567	0.543	0.519	0.497	0.402	0.328	0.269	0.186
6	0.746	0.705	0.666	0.630	0.596	0.564	0.535	0.507	0.480	0.456	0.432	0.335	0.262	0.207	0.133
7	0.711	0.665	0.623	0.583	0.547	0.513	0.482	0.452	0.425	0.400	0.376	0.279	0.210	0.159	0.095
8	0.677	0.627	0.582	0.540	0.502	0.467	0.434	0.404	0.376	0.351	0.327	0.233	0.168	0.123	0.068
9	0.645	0.592	0.543	0.500	0.460	0.424	0.391	0.361	0.333	0.308	0.284	0.194	0.134	0.094	0.048
10	0.614	0.558	0.508	0.463	0.422	0.386	0.352	0.322	0.295	0.270	0.247	0.162	0.107	0.073	0.035
11	0.585	0.527	0.475	0.429	0.388	0.350	0.317	0.287	0.261	0.237	0.215	0.135	0.086	0.056	0.025
12	0.557	0.497	0.444	0.397	0.356	0.319	0.286	0.257	0.231	0.208	0.187	0.112	0.069	0.043	0.018
13	0.530	0.469	0.415	0.368	0.326	0.290	0.258	0.229	0.204	0.182	0.163	0.093	0.055	0.033	0.013
14	0.505	0.442	0.388	0.340	0.299	0.263	0.232	0.205	0.181	0.160	0.141	0.078	0.044	0.025	0.009
15	0.481	0.417	0.362	0.315	0.275	0.239	0.209	0.183	0.160	0.140	0.123	0.065	0.035	0.020	0.006
16	0.458	0.394	0.339	0.292	0.252	0.218	0.188	0.163	0.142	0.123	0.107	0.054	0.028	0.015	0.005
17	0.436	0.371	0.317	0.270	0.231	0.198	0.170	0.146	0.125	0.108	0.093	0.045	0.023	0.012	0.003
18	0.416	0.350	0.296	0.250	0.212	0.180	0.153	0.130	0.111	0.095	0.081	0.038	0.018	0.009	0.002
19	0.396	0.331	0.277	0.232	0.194	0.164	0.138	0.116	0.098	0.083	0.070	0.031	0.014	0.007	0.002
20	0.377	0.312	0.258	0.215	0.178	0.149	0.124	0.104	0.087	0.073	0.061	0.026	0.012	0.005	0.001
21	0.359	0.294	0.242	0.199	0.164	0.135	0.112	0.093	0.077	0.064	0.053	0.022	0.009	0.004	0.001
22	0.342	0.278	0.226	0.184	0.150	0.123	0.101	0.083	0.068	0.056	0.046	0.018	0.007	0.003	0.001
23	0.326	0.262	0.211	0.170	0.138	0.112	0.091	0.074	0.060	0.049	0.040	0.015	0.006	0.002	....
24	0.310	0.247	0.197	0.158	0.126	0.102	0.082	0.066	0.053	0.043	0.035	0.013	0.005	0.002	....
25	0.295	0.233	0.184	0.146	0.116	0.092	0.074	0.059	0.047	0.038	0.030	0.010	0.004	0.001	....
30	0.231	0.174	0.131	0.099	0.075	0.057	0.044	0.033	0.026	0.020	0.015	0.004	0.001	....	....
35	0.181	0.130	0.094	0.068	0.049	0.036	0.026	0.019	0.014	0.010	0.008	0.002	....	....	....
40	0.142	0.097	0.067	0.046	0.032	0.022	0.015	0.011	0.008	0.005	0.004	0.001	....	....	....
45	0.111	0.073	0.048	0.031	0.021	0.014	0.009	0.006	0.004	0.003	0.002	....	....	....	....
50	0.087	0.054	0.034	0.021	0.013	0.009	0.005	0.003	0.002	0.001	0.001	....	....	....	....

$$P = F_t(1 + r)^{-t}$$

TABLE 7

Present Value of an Annuity of $1 a Period for *t* Periods, Received or Paid
as a Series of Lump Sums at the End of Individual Periods, Discounted
Once Each Period for *t* Periods

(Important: These are not the discount factors used in the text illustrations)

	5%	6%	7%	8%	9%	10%	11%	12%	13%	14%	15%	20%	25%	30%	40%
1	0.952	0.943	0.935	0.926	0.917	0.909	0.901	0.893	0.885	0.877	0.870	0.833	0.800	0.769	0.714
2	1.859	1.833	1.808	1.783	1.759	1.736	1.713	1.690	1.668	1.647	1.626	1.528	1.440	1.361	1.224
3	2.723	2.673	2.624	2.577	2.531	2.487	2.444	2.402	2.361	2.322	2.283	2.106	1.952	1.816	1.589
4	3.546	3.465	3.387	3.312	3.240	3.170	3.102	3.037	2.974	2.914	2.855	2.589	2.362	2.166	1.849
5	4.329	4.212	4.100	3.993	3.890	3.791	3.696	3.605	3.517	3.433	3.352	2.991	2.689	2.436	2.035
6	5.076	4.917	4.767	4.623	4.486	4.355	4.231	4.111	3.998	3.889	3.784	3.326	2.951	2.643	2.168
7	5.786	5.582	5.389	5.206	5.033	4.868	4.712	4.564	4.423	4.288	4.160	3.605	3.161	2.802	2.263
8	6.463	6.210	5.971	5.747	5.535	5.335	5.146	4.968	4.799	4.639	4.487	3.837	3.329	2.925	2.331
9	7.108	6.802	6.515	6.247	5.995	5.759	5.537	5.328	5.132	4.946	4.772	4.031	3.463	3.019	2.379
10	7.722	7.360	7.024	6.710	6.418	6.145	5.889	5.650	5.426	5.216	5.019	4.192	3.571	3.092	2.414
11	8.306	7.887	7.499	7.139	6.805	6.495	6.207	5.938	5.687	5.453	5.234	4.327	3.656	3.147	2.438
12	8.863	8.384	7.943	7.536	7.161	6.814	6.492	6.194	5.918	5.660	5.421	4.439	3.725	3.190	2.456
13	9.394	8.853	8.358	7.904	7.487	7.103	6.750	6.424	6.122	5.842	5.583	4.533	3.780	3.223	2.468
14	9.899	9.295	8.745	8.244	7.786	7.367	6.982	6.628	6.302	6.002	5.724	4.611	3.824	3.249	2.477
15	10.380	9.712	9.108	8.559	8.061	7.606	7.191	6.811	6.462	6.142	5.847	4.675	3.859	3.268	2.484
16	10.838	10.106	9.447	8.851	8.313	7.824	7.379	6.974	6.604	6.265	5.954	4.730	3.887	3.283	2.489
17	11.274	10.477	9.763	9.122	8.544	8.022	7.549	7.120	6.729	6.373	6.047	4.775	3.910	3.295	2.492
18	11.690	10.828	10.059	9.372	8.756	8.201	7.702	7.250	6.840	6.467	6.128	4.812	3.928	3.304	2.494
19	12.085	11.158	10.336	9.604	8.950	8.365	7.839	7.366	6.938	6.550	6.198	4.844	3.942	3.311	2.496
20	12.462	11.470	10.594	9.818	9.129	8.514	7.963	7.469	7.025	6.623	6.259	4.870	3.954	3.316	2.497
21	12.821	11.764	10.836	10.017	9.292	8.649	8.075	7.562	7.102	6.687	6.312	4.891	3.963	3.320	2.498
22	13.163	12.042	11.061	10.201	9.442	8.772	8.176	7.645	7.170	6.743	6.359	4.909	3.970	3.323	2.498
23	13.489	12.303	11.272	10.371	9.580	8.883	8.266	7.718	7.230	6.792	6.399	4.925	3.976	3.325	2.499
24	13.799	12.550	11.469	10.529	9.707	8.985	8.348	7.784	7.283	6.835	6.434	4.937	3.981	3.327	2.499
25	14.094	12.783	11.654	10.675	9.823	9.077	8.422	7.843	7.330	6.873	6.464	4.948	3.985	3.329	2.499
30	15.372	13.765	12.409	11.258	10.274	9.427	8.694	8.055	7.496	7.003	6.566	4.979	3.995	3.332	2.500
35	16.374	14.498	12.948	11.655	10.567	9.644	8.855	8.176	7.586	7.070	6.617	4.992	3.998	3.333	2.500
40	17.159	15.046	13.332	11.925	10.757	9.779	8.951	8.244	7.634	7.105	6.642	4.997	3.999	3.333	2.500
45	17.774	15.456	13.606	12.108	10.881	9.863	9.008	8.283	7.661	7.123	6.654	4.999	4.000	3.333	2.500
50	18.256	15.762	13.801	12.233	10.962	9.915	9.042	8.305	7.675	7.133	6.661	4.999	4.000	3.333	2.500

$$P = A \left[\frac{1 - (1 + r)^{-t}}{r} \right]$$

Appendix B

SOLUTIONS TO SELECTED PROBLEMS

Chapter 3

3–3.

Output Rate	Average Total Cost	Average Fixed Cost	Average Variable Cost	Marginal Cost
1...................	$11.00	$10.00	$1.00	$1.00
2...................	6.00	5.00	1.00	1.00
3...................	4.33	3.33	1.00	1.00
4...................	3.50	2.50	1.00	1.00
5...................	3.00	2.00	1.00	1.00
6...................	2.67	1.67	1.00	1.00
7...................	2.43	1.43	1.00	1.00
8...................	2.25	1.25	1.00	1.00
9...................	2.22	1.11	1.11	2.00
10...................	2.30	1.00	1.30	3.00

3–7. *a*) Amounts in thousands:

	$p = 0.1$ State 1	$p = 0.2$ State 2	$p = 0.4$ State 3	$p = 0.2$ State 4	$p = 0.05$ State 5	$p = 0.05$ State 6
If spend.....	-10	-5	0	$+5$	$+10$	$+15$
If don't spend.....	0	0	0	0	0	0

b) Expected value:

Spend		Don't Spend
0.1 × −10,000 = −1,000		0
0.2 × − 5,000 = −1,000		0
0.4 × 0 = 0		0
0.2 × + 5,000 = +1,000		0
0.05 × +10,000 = + 500		0
0.05 × +15,000 = + 750		0
Total...... + 250		0

3–8.

		Revenue	Cost		Profit
At 75,000 units level	at $2.50	$187,500	at $2.00	$150,000	$37,500
At 50,000 units level	at $3.00	150,000	at $2.25	112,500	37,500
Incremental revenue		$ 37,500			
Incremental cost				$ 37,500	
Incremental profit					$ 0

3–13. *a*) Costs for six-day operation:

	Total/Wk.	Average/Cwt.
Fixed: $\quad\quad\quad\quad$ 6 × 2,100 =	$ 12,600	$0.35
Wheat: $2.17 × 2.35 × 6,000 × 6 =	183,582	5.10
Variable: $0.17 × 6,000 × 6 $\quad$ =	6,120	0.17
Total	$202,302	$5.62

Profit margin: $5.70 − $5.62 = $0.08/Cwt.

b) Costs for seven-day operation:

	Total/Wk.	Average/Cwt.
Fixed	$ 12,810	$0.305
Wheat	214,200	5.100
Variable	8,100	0.193
Total	$235,110	$5.598

Increment in revenue: 6,000 × $5.70 $\quad$ =	$34,200
Increment in costs: $235,110 − $202,302 =	32,808
Increment in Profit	$ 1,392/week

Chapter 4

4–3. *a*)

Materials (21,000 × $0.66)	$13,860
Materials returned (800 × $0.66)	(528)
Labor (2,000 × $2.15)	4,300
Overhead	8,000
Total	$25,632

$$\text{Unit cost} = \frac{\$25,632}{9,800} = \$2.62 \, .$$

b)

Work in Process	26,160	
$\quad$ Materials Inventory		13,860
$\quad$ Wages Payable		4,300
$\quad$ Factory Overhead		8,000
Materials Inventory	528	
$\quad$ Work in Process		528
Finished Goods	25,632	
$\quad$ Work in Process		25,632

4–5. *a*)

Materials	$ 800
Labor	200
Overhead ($9 × 60)	540
Total	$1,540

b)

Actual	$100,000
Absorbed (10,000 × $9)	90,000
Underabsorbed	$ 10,000

4–11. *a*)

Raw Material and Stores				Work in Process			
Bal.	12,650	(2)	7,250	Bal.	8,320	(6)	12,650
(1)	4,500	Bal.	9,900	(2)	6,320		
				(3)	3,300		
Bal.	9,900			(5)	4,950	Bal.	10,240
				Bal.	10,240		

Finished Goods			
Bal.	11,100	(8)	14,500
(6)	12,650	Bal.	9,250
Bal.	9,250		

Accounts Payable, Etc.		
	(1)	4,500
	(4)	2,700
	(7)	1,835

Accrued Payroll		
	(3)	7,780

Cost of Goods Sold		
(8)	14,500	
(11)	560	

Factory Overhead Summary			
(2)	930	(10)	5,510
(3)	1,880		
(4)	2,700		

Factory Overhead Absorbed			
(10)	5,510	(5)	4,950
		(11)	560

Selling and Admin. Expense		
(3)	2,600	
(7)	1,835	

Accounts Receivable		
(9)	19,350	

Sales Revenue		
	(9)	19,350

b)

ACE APPLIANCE COMPANY
Statement of Income for the Month Ending October 31

Sales......................................	$19,350
Cost of goods sold (Schedule A)...........	15,060
Gross margin.............................	$ 4,290
Selling and administrative expenses........	4,435
Net Income (Loss).......................	$ (145)

Schedule A: Cost of Goods Sold

Direct materials...........................		$ 6,320
Direct labor..............................		3,300
Factory overhead:		
Indirect material.......................$	930	
Indirect labor..........................	1,880	
Miscellaneous..........................	2,700	
Total factory overhead................$	5,510	
Less: Underabsorbed overhead........	560	4,950
Total factory costs charged to production...		$14,570
Less: Increase in work in process:		
Work in process, October 31.............$10,240		
Work in process, October 1..............	8,320	(1,920)
Cost of goods finished....................		$12,650
Add: Decrease in finished goods:		
Finished goods, October 1...............$11,100		
Finished goods, October 31..............	9,250	1,850
Cost of goods sold.......................		$14,500
Add: Underabsorbed overhead............		560
Cost of Goods Sold (Adjusted)...........		$15,060

Chapter 5

5–4. *a)*

	Materials	Labor
Units completed	9,000	9,000
Incomplete units, 5/31	800	480
Less: Incomplete units, 5/1	(1,000)	(400)
Output Divisor	8,800	9,080

b)

	Materials	Labor
Units completed	9,000	9,000
Incomplete units, 5/31	800	480
Output Divisor	9,800	9,480

5–7. *a)* Average operating cost/pound $= \dfrac{\$2,755}{14,500} = \$0.19/\text{pound}$.

Equivalent pounds $= 13,500 + 2/3 \times (1,500) = 14,500$.

Materials costs/pound $= \dfrac{\$9,600 + \$3,300}{15,000} = \$0.86/\text{pound}$.

Total cost/pound $= \$1.05$.

b)

Inventories—Material A			
Bal	24,000	(2)	9,600
(1)	12,500	Bal	26,900
Bal	26,900		

Inventories—Material B			
Bal	9,000	(2)	3,300
		Bal	5,700
Bal.	5,700		

Work in Process			
(2)	12,900	(5)	14,175
(4)	2,755	Bal.	1,480
Bal.	1,480		

Finished Goods			
(5)	14,175	(6)	14,175

Head Office Control			
(6)	14,175	Bal.	33,000
		(1)	12,500
Bal.	34,080	(3)	2,755
		Bal.	34,080

Factory Overhead			
(3)	2,755	(4)	2,755

5–9.

	Mixing		Refining	
	Total	Per Unit	Total	Per Unit
Costs:				
Materials:				
Received	$ 49,500	$0.495	$138,000	$1.500
Lost unit adjustment	xxx	0.005	xxx	0.033
Adjusted materials cost	$ 49,500	$0.500	$138,000	$1.533
Processing costs:				
Labor	$ 57,300	$0.600	$ 42,500	$0.500
Other	38,200	0.400	38,250	0.450
Total	$ 95,500	$1.000	$ 80,750	$0.950
Total Costs	$145,000	$1.500	$218,750	$2.483
Cost distribution:				
Transferred	$138,000		$198,670*	
In process, 1/31	7,000		20,080	
Total Costs Distributed	$145,000		$218,750	

* Adjusted to absorb rounding error.

5–14.

Mixing:

Transferred out	10,000 units at $2.00	$ 20,000
	78,000 units at $2.05	159,900
		$179,900
In process, 11/30	12,000 units at $2.05	$ 24,600

Refining:

Transferred out	8,000 units at $3.00	$ 24,000
	78,000 units at $3.04	237,120
		$261,120
In process, 11/30	10,000 units at $3.04	$ 30,400

Finishing:

Transferred out	12,000 units at $3.50	$ 42,000
	77,000 units at $3.56	274,120
		$316,120
In process, 11/30	9,000 units at $3.56	$ 32,040

Chapter 6

6–3. One alternative would be to credit department X with $20, but the answer in this particular case should be not to distribute the scrap credit at all on the grounds that the amount is immaterial.

6–5. *a*) Burden rate $= \dfrac{\$144,000}{\$2,400,000} = \$0.06/\text{purchase price}$.

b)

Materials Inventory	238,500.00	
Accounts Payable		225,000.00
Purchasing Costs Applied		3,937.50
Freight-In Costs Applied		7,500.00
Receiving Costs Applied		2,062.50

c) Variances:

Purchasing	$3,937.50 − $3,600.00 =	$ 337.50 overapplied
Freight-in	7,500.00 − 4,500.00 =	3,000.00 overapplied
Receiving	2,062.50 − 1,900.00 =	162.50 overapplied
Total		$3,500.00 overapplied

To the extent that the costs of each of these operations are fixed, the the heavier-than-average volume of purchases would lead to over-application of these costs. One twelfth of annual volume would be $200,000, while actual purchases totaled $225,000. On freight-in, a more likely explanation is that more goods were bought on a de-livered-price basis or were bought from nearby suppliers.

6–7. *a*)

ITEM: Material #1467A								UNIT: Each	
	In			Out			Balance		
Date	Quantity	Price	Amount	Quantity	Price	Amount	Quantity	Price	Amount
April 1							200	$0.500	$100.00
2	500	$0.550	$275.00				700	.536	375.00
4				50	$0.536	$ 26.80	650	.536	348.20
8				200	.536	107.20	450	.536	241.00
12	500	.510	255.20				950	.522	496.20
16				400	.522	208.80	550	.522	287.40
18				50	.522	26.10	500	.522	261.30
25				250	.522	130.50	250	.522	130.80
28	1,000	.501	500.60				1,250	.505	631.40

b)

	In			Out			Balance		
Date	Quantity	Price	Amount	Quantity	Price	Amount	Quantity	Price	Amount
April 1							200	$0.500	$100.00
2	500	$0.550	$275.00				500	.550	275.00
4				50	$0.500	$ 25.00	150	$ .500	$ 75.00
							500	.550	275.00
8				150	.500	75.00	450	$ .550	$247.50
				50	.550	27.50			
12	500	.510	255.20				500	.510	255.20
16				400	.550	220.00	50	$ .550	$ 27.50
							500	.510	255.20
18				50	.550	27.50	500	$ .510	$255.20
25				250	.510	127.50	250	$ .510	$127.70
28	1,000	.501	$500.60				1,000	.501	500.60

ITEM: Material #1467A   UNIT: Each

6–9. *a)* Most systems leave all labor-related costs in overhead, but a conceptually superior solution would be to include in the labor charging rates a provision for those labor-related costs that vary approximately in proportion to wages or labor hours. If you have not done this, give it a try before reading the rest of this solution.

Using an inclusive labor charging rate the wage surcharges would be:

	Hourly Employees	Salaried Employees
Payroll taxes......................	6.0%	5.0%
Hospital insurance.................	2.0	2.0
Holidays and vacations............	7.5	7.5
Total........................	15.5%	14.5%

Overtime premiums are excluded because they are not subject to the same rules of behavior as the other items.

On this basis, jobs should be charged $20,000 × 115.5% = $23,-100, indirect labor for hourly employees would be $4,620, indirect labor for salaried employees would be $5,725, and overtime premiums would be $3,500. (Payroll taxes have to be paid on overtime premiums, too, if these are within the taxable limits, but this problem was written to assign all payroll taxes to the straight-time accounts.)

b)

Work in Process....................................	23,100	
Indirect Labor—Hourly Employees.....................	4,620	
Indirect Labor—Salaried Employees....................	5,725	
Payroll Summary................................		29,000
Provision for Payroll Taxes........................		1,690
Provision for Holiday and Vacation Pay		2,175
Provision for Hospital Insurance Premiums...........		580
To record cost distribution for the month.		

Payroll Summary....................................	29,000	
Overtime Premium...................................	3,500	
Income Tax Withheld.............................		4,800
F.I.C.A. Tax Payable.............................		1,465

Hospital Insurance Premiums Payable...............	600
Accrued Wages Payable..........................	25,635
To record the month's payroll.	

Provision for Payroll Taxes...........................	2,440	
Provision for Hospital Insurance Premiums..............	600	
F.I.C.A. Tax Payable............................		1,465
Unemployment Tax Payable.......................		975
Hospital Insurance Premiums Payable...............		600
To record the accrual of surcharges on current payrolls.		

c)
Provision for Holiday and Vacation Pay.................	200.00	
Income Tax Withheld.............................		13.80
F.I.C.A. Tax Payable.............................		8.40
Hospital Insurance Premiums Payable...............		3.10
Accrued Wages Payable..........................		174.70
To record the payroll.		

Provision for Payroll Taxes...........................	8.40	
Provision for Hospital Insurance Premiums..............	3.10	
F.I.C.A. Tax Payable.............................		8.40
Hospital Insurance Premiums Payable...............		3.10
To record the accrual of surcharges on payroll.		

(These sums have previously been charged to operating cost accounts on an estimated cost basis. At the end of the year the "provision" accounts will have negligible balances if the rates were correct.)

Chapter 7

7–4. *a*) Absorption costing:

	19x5	19x6
Cost of goods sold:		
Direct labor............................	$ 50,000	$ 51,000
Direct materials........................	100,000	102,000
Fixed factory overhead..................	60,000	61,200
Variable factory overhead...............	40,000	40,800
Cost of goods sold—normal............	$250,000	$255,000
Less: Overabsorbed overhead..............		12,000
Cost of Goods Sold, Net..................	$250,000	$243,000

b) Variable costing:

	19x5	19x6
Cost of goods sold:		
Direct labor............................	$ 50,000	$ 51,000
Direct materials........................	100,000	102,000
Variable factory overhead...............	40,000	40,800
Variable cost of goods sold............	$190,000	$193,800
Fixed factory overhead..................	60,000	60,000
Total Charge to Income..................	$250,000	$253,800

7–5.

	Price	Direct Costs	Variable Overhead	Fixed Overhead
A.............	$20	$9	$1.00	$3.00
B.............	19	8	1.50	4.50
C.............	18	7	2.00	6.00
D.............	17	6	2.50	7.50

Profit margins:

	Full Costing		Variable Costing	
	Per Unit	Per-cent	Per Unit	Percent
A.............	$7	35	$10.00	50
B.............	5	26	9.50	50
C.............	3	17	9.00	50
D.............	1	6	8.50	50

7–8. *a)*

Sales..		$172,000
Variable cost of goods sold:		
Inventories, January 1...............................	$ 20,000	
Cost of goods finished..............................	86,000	
	$106,000	
Less: Inventories, December 31.....................	25,000	
Variable cost of goods sold........................		81,000
Variable manufacturing margin.......................		$ 91,000
Variable selling expenses............................		35,000
Variable profit......................................		$ 56,000
Fixed expenses:		
Manufacturing.....................................	$ 30,000	
Selling and administrative.........................	29,000	59,000
Net Loss..		$ (3,000)

b)
$$\frac{\text{Fixed overhead}}{\text{Variable mfg. cost}} = \frac{\$30,000}{\$86,000} = 34.884\%.$$

Fixed cost in inventories, December 31 = $25,000 × 34.884% = $8,721.

The Fixed Overhead in Inventories account must be debited by $3,721, i.e., this amount must be transferred from expense to inventory, with a resultant increase of $3,721 in reported income before taxes.

7–10. *a)*

	1st Quarter	2nd Quarter
Sales...	$300,000	$450,000
Cost of goods sold...................................	220,000	330,000
Gross margin..	$ 80,000	$120,000
Less:		
Selling and administrative expenses...................	$ 25,000	$ 27,000
Underabsorbed overhead............................	....	36,000
Total deductions..........................	$ 25,000	$ 63,000
Profit..	$ 55,000	$ 57,000
Ending Inventory.....................................	$110,000	$ 44,000

b)

	1st Quarter	2nd Quarter
Sales	$300,000	$450,000
Cost of goods sold	100,000	150,000
Gross margin	$200,000	$300,000
Less:		
Selling and administrative expenses	$ 25,000	$ 27,000
Fixed overhead	180,000	180,000
Total deductions	$205,000	$207,000
Profit (Loss)	$ (5,000)	$ 93,000
Ending Inventory	$ 50,000	$ 20,000

c)

	Full Cost	Direct Cost
Sales	$450,000	$450,000
Cost of goods sold	330,000	150,000
Gross margin	$120,000	$300,000
Less:		
Selling and administrative expenses	$ 27,000	$ 27,000
Fixed costs	...	180,000
Total deductions	$ 27,000	$207,000
Profit	$ 93,000	$ 93,000
Ending Inventory	$110,000	$ 50,000

Chapter 8

8–1. Dept. X charging rate $= \dfrac{\$2,000}{20,000} + \$0.20 = \$0.30/\text{service unit}$.

Component of departmental burden rates:

Dept. 1: $1,000 \times \$0.30/10,000 = \$0.03/\text{direct labor hour}$.
Dept. 2: $5,000 \times \$0.30/\ 8,000 = \$0.1875/\text{direct labor hour}$.
Dept. 3: $8,000 \times \$0.30/20,000 = \$0.12/\text{machine-hour}$.
Dept. 4: $6,000 \times \$0.30/15,000 = \$0.12/\text{direct labor hour}$.

8–7.

	Melting and Pouring	Molding	Core Making	Cleaning and Grinding
Indirect labor	$1,000	$300	$100	$300
Supplies used	50	50	200	100
Taxes:				
Machinery and equipment	4	1	3	4
Building	3	12	3	6
Compensation insurance	20	15	6	24
Power	10	x	10	30
Heat and light	10	40	10	20
Depreciation:				
Building	8	32	8	16
Machinery	20	5	15	20
	$1,125	$455	$355	$520

8–11.

Building cost: $\$60,000 \times \dfrac{120 \text{ sq. ft.}}{75,000 \text{ sq. ft}}$ ....$ 96

Depreciation on machine cost: $\$4,000 \times 10\%$ 400

Power charges: $20 \times 2,500$ hrs. $\times \$0.015$ 750

Taxes.. 10

Insurance.. 12

Stores and supplies...................................... 38

Repairs.. 35

Tools and jigs.. 169

Planning cost.. 69

Foremen.. 131

Indirect labor.. 70

Total ....$\$1,780$

Normal machine-hours.............................. 2,500

Normal machine-hour rate (per machine-hour)........$\$0.712$

Note: The number of hours worked during the previous year is irrelevant, since all significant factors have been considered in arriving at the normal work load—2,500 hours.

8–15. *a*) Dept. A: $\dfrac{\$12,000}{6,000 \text{ units}} = \$2.00/\text{unit}$.

Dept. B: $\dfrac{\$18,000}{8,000 \text{ units}} = \$2.25/\text{unit}$.

Dept. C: $\dfrac{\$20,000}{12,000 \text{ units}} = \$1.67/\text{unit}$.

b)

	Dept. A	Dept. B	Dept. C	Production
Direct charges...............	$12,000	$18,000	$20,000	xxx
Allocations:				
Service dept. A............	(12,000)	1,800	1,200	$ 9,000
Service dept. B............		(19,800)	2,949	16,851
Service dept. C............			(24,149)	24,149

Charging rates:

Department A: $12,000/8,000 = $1.50/service unit.

Department B: $19,800/9,400 = $2.1064/service unit.

Department C: $24,149/12,000 = $2.0124/service unit.

c)   Dept. A = $2.0788/unit.

Dept. B = $2.2146/unit.

Dept. C = $1.6510/unit.

Computations:

$$\text{Rate}_A = \frac{\$12,000 + 600 \times \text{Rate}_B + 2,000 \times \text{Rate}_C}{8,000} \tag{1}$$

$$\text{Rate}_B = \frac{\$18,000 + 1,200 \times \text{Rate}_A + 1,000 \times \text{Rate}_C}{10,000} \tag{2}$$

$$\text{Rate}_C = \frac{\$20,000 + 800 \times \text{Rate}_A + 1,400 \times \text{Rate}_B}{15,000} \tag{3}$$

$$8,000 \text{ Rate}_A = 12,000 + 600 \times \text{Rate}_B + 2,000 \times \text{Rate}_C \quad (1)$$
$$\text{Rate}_A = 1.5 + 0.075 \text{ Rate}_B + 0.25 \text{ Rate}_C \quad (1a)$$

Substituting this in equations (2) and (3):

$$10,000 \text{ Rate}_B = 18,000 + (1,800 + 90 \text{ Rate}_B + 300 \text{ Rate}_C)$$
$$+1,000 \text{ Rate}_C$$
$$9,910 \text{ Rate}_B = 19,800 + 1,300 \text{ Rate}_C \quad (2a)$$
$$15,000 \text{ Rate}_C = 20,000 + (1,200 + 60 \text{ Rate}_B + 200 \text{ Rate}_C)$$
$$+ 1,400 \text{ Rate}_B$$
$$14,800 \text{ Rate}_C = 21,200 + 1,460 \text{ Rate}_B \quad (3a)$$

Solving (2a) for Rate_B:

$$\text{Rate}_B = \frac{19,800}{9,910} + \frac{1,300}{9,910} \text{ Rate}_C$$

Substituting in (3a):

$$14,800 \text{ Rate}_C = \$21,200 + \frac{1,460 \times 19,800}{9,910}$$
$$+ \frac{1,460 \times 1,300}{9,910} \text{ Rate}_C$$
$$\text{Rate}_C = \$1.6510/\text{unit}$$

Substituting this in (2a):

$$9,910 \text{ Rate}_B = 19,800 + (1,300 \times \$1.6510)$$
$$\text{Rate}_B = \$2.2146/\text{unit}$$

Substituting in (1a):

$$\text{Rate}_A = \$1.5 + 0.075 \times \$2.2146 + 0.25 \times \$1.6510$$
$$\text{Rate}_A = \$2.0788/\text{unit}$$

Chapter 9

9–4.   Aviation gasoline: $\left(\dfrac{\$\ 50,000}{\$460,000} \times \$440,000\right) \div 8,000$ bbl.
$$= \$5.978 .$$

Motor gasoline: $\left(\dfrac{\$210,000}{\$460,000} \times \$440,000\right) \div 42,000$ bbl.
$$= \$4.783 .$$

Kerosene: $\left(\dfrac{\$\ 44,000}{\$460,000} \times \$440,000\right) \div 10,000$ bbl.
$$= \$4.209 .$$

Distillate fuels: $\left(\dfrac{\$\ 80,000}{\$460,000} \times \$440,000\right) \div 20,000$ bbl.
$$= \$3.826 .$$

Lubricants: $\left(\dfrac{\$\ 50,000}{\$460,000} \times \$440,000\right) \div 5,000$ bbl.
$$= \$9.565 .$$

Residual fuels: $\left(\dfrac{\$\ 26,000}{\$460,000} \times \$440,000\right) \div 10,000$ bbl.
$$= \$2.487 .$$

9–6.   Total cost:

Material A	$12.00
Material B	7.50
Labor	6.00
Overhead	10.50
Total	$36.00

Product	Price	Value	% of Value	Allocation	Cost/Unit
I..................	$0.60	$18.00	37.5	$13.50	$0.45/lb.
II..................	.40	24.00	50.0	18.00	.30/lb.
III................	.30	6.00	12.5	4.50	.225/gal.
Total.............		$48.00	100.0	$36.00	

9–8.

Category	Value	%	Cost
Sheets, unused..................	$ 10,000	6.250	$ 8,250
Blocks........................	40,000	25.000	33,000
Singles, rare....................	84,000	52.500	69,300
Singles, unused, common........	20,000	12.500	16,500
Singles, used—catalogue........	5,000	3.125	4,125
Singles, used—bulk.............	1,000	0.625	825
Total....................	$160,000	100.000	$132,000

9–10. *a)*

Product	Value	%	Costs
Whole milk..................	$54,431.80	64.63	$51,774.45
Cream for sale...............	18,358.69	21.80	17,463.76
Cream for butter.............	5,394.67	6.41	5,134.99
Skim milk..................	6,027.68	7.16	5,735.80
Total..................	$84,212.84	100.00	$80,109.00

b) Losses:

	100 lbs. @ $ 1.01 =	$101	
	3 lbs. @ 78.00 =	234	
	Total	$335	

This represents the *value* of the product lost, not the effect of losses on average unit cost. This is the method actually used in the creamery from which the data for this problem were drawn.

9–13.

	Materials	*Processing*
Equivalent production:		
Finished output:		
Product A...............................	$ 8,000	$ 8,000
Product B...............................	12,000	12,000
Ending work in process:		
Product A: 2,000 × ½ × $0.80.............	800	400
Product B: 2,000 × ¼ × $2.40.............	1,200	600
Total................................	$22,000	$21,000
Joint cost..................................	$ 7,920	$ 9,240
Cost: Percent of market value.................	36%	44% = 80% total
Unit cost:		
Product A: 80% × $0.80 = $0.64		
Product B: 80% × 2.40 = 1.92		

Chapter 10

10–6.
Actual labor cost.................1,900 × $1.85 = $3,515
Actual hours × standard wage rate 1,900 × $1.80 =   3,420
   Wage rate variance....................................$ 95 unfavorable
Standard hours × standard wage
      rate.......................2,000 × $1.80 =   3,600
   Labor performance variance........................... 180 favorable
Total Variance...$ 85 favorable

10–8.
    Labor usage variance:
      1,500 units of A @ 2 hours = 3,000 hours @ $3...$ 9,000
      4,000 units of B @ 3 hours = 12,000 hours @ $3.. 36,000
      Standard usage of labor........................$45,000
      Actual usage of labor 14,500 hours @ $3.......... 43,500
      Favorable usage variance....................... $ 1,500
    Labor rate variance:
      Standard cost of labor worked: 14,500 hours @ $3.$43,500
      Actual payroll................................ 44,000
      Unfavorable rate variance.....................   (500)
    Net Labor Variance............................. $ 1,000

10–9.
    Units finished: 3,000 × $3   = $9,000
    Ending inventory: 800 × ¼ × $3   =   600
                            $9,600
    Less: Beginning inventory: 500 × ½ × $3   750
    Standard direct labor cost of month's output......$8,850

10–12. *a)*
                                       Unfavorable Favorable
    Material price variance.....................$6
    Labor rate variance........................ 2
    Material usage variance.................... 5
    Labor usage variance...................... $3

b)

Miscellaneous Credits		Raw Material			Material in Process		
(1)	106	(1)	100	(2)	105	(2)	105
(3b)	70					(4)	85
						(6a)	5
						Bal.	15
		Bal.	15				

Payroll Costs		Labor in Process				Finished Goods	
(3b)	70	(3a)	68	(3a)	68	(4)	63	(4)	148

Payroll Costs			Labor in Process				Finished Goods	
(3b)	70	(3a)	68	(3a)	68	(4)	63	(4) 148
		(3c)	2	(6b)	3	Bal.	8	
				Bal.	8			

Variances

(1) MPV 6	(6b) LQV 3
(3c) LRV 2	
(6a) MQV5	

10–15. *a)*

Raw Material and Supplies

Bal. 9/1	58,500	(5)	46,650
(2)	44,620	Bal. 10/1	56,470
Bal. 10/1	56,470		

Material in Process

Bal. 9/1	6,700	(3)	40,350
(5)	46,650	(6)	700
		Bal. 10/1	12,300
Bal. 10/1	12,300		

Labor in Process

Bal. 9/1	2,400	(3)	22,300
(4)	23,600		
(6)	1,000	Bal. 10/1	4,700
Bal. 10/1	4,700		

Accrued Wages

(8)	23,600	(4)	23,600

Control

Bal. 9/1	99,700
(2)	42,380
(8)	24,400

Finished Goods

Bal. 9/1	32,100	(7)	63,500
(3)	62,650	Bal. 10/1	31,250
Bal. 10/1	31,250		

Cost of Goods Sold

(7)	63,500

Material Price Variance

(2)	2,240

Labor Quantity Variance

(6)	1,000

Materials Quantity Variance

(6)	700

Wage Rate Variance

(8)	800

b)

Materials price variance	$2,240	Favorable
Wage rate variance	(800)	Unfavorable
Materials quantity variance	(700)	Unfavorable
Labor quantity variance	1,000	Favorable
Net Variance	$1,740	Favorable

Chapter 11

11–3. *a*) $2 \times 30 + \$3 \times 45 + \$5 \times 25 = \$320$.

b)

Product	Costs Earned		Mix Variance
	Actual Mix	Standard Mix	
A..........................	$ 3,200	$ 2,970	$ 230
B..........................	7,200	6,682	518
C..........................	4,750	6,188	(1,438)
Total......................	$15,150	$15,840	$ (690)
Actual cost................	17,300	17,300	
Yield Variance.............		$(1,460)	
Total Variance.............	$(2,150)		

The yield variance can be further broken down into two parts:

Actual cost of processing 5,000 pounds.............	$17,300
Standard cost of processing 5,000 pounds...........	16,000
Processing cost variance........................	$(1,300)
Standard cost of lost units: 50 × $3.20...........	(160)
Total Yield Variance........................	$(1,460)

11–5.

Actual labor cost..............................	$30,000
Actual labor hours at standard rates..............	29,000
Labor rate variance.........................	$(1,000)
Actual labor hours at standard rates, standard mix	
(9,000 hours × $3.50)........................	31,500
Labor mix variance..........................	2,500
Standard labor cost............................	32,000
Labor quantity variance.....................	500
Total Labor Variance......................	$ 2,000

11–8. *a*)

Variances (all unfavorable):	
Materials prices....................	$ 8,000
Materials quantity.................	4,000
Labor rates........................	2,000
Labor quantity.....................	5,600
Total........................	$19,600

b)

(1) Materials....................................	123,000	
Purchase Price Variance......................	8,000	
Accounts Payable......................		131,000
(2) Materials in Process..........................	140,000	
Materials............................		140,000
(3) Materials Quantity Variance...................	12,000	
Materials............................		12,000

(4) Materials...................................... 8,000
    Materials Quantity Variance................ 8,000

(5) Labor in Process.............................. 80,000
    Labor Quantity Variance...................... 5,600
    Payroll Cost Summary...................... 85,600

(6) Accrued Wages Payable........................ 8,200
    Payroll Cost Summary..................... 8,200
    (Reversing entry.)

(7) Payroll Cost Summary......................... 79,500
    Cash................................... 79,500

(8) Payroll Cost Summary......................... 16,300
    Accrued Wages Payable.................... 16,300

(9) Finished Goods...............................198,900
    Materials in Process...................... 122,400
    Labor in Process......................... 76,500

Materials				Materials in Process			
(1)	123,000	(2)	140,000	(2)	140,000	(9)	122,400
(4)	8,000	(3)	12,000				

Labor in Process				Purchase Price Variance			
(5)	80,000	(9)	76,500	(1)	8,000		

Materials Quantity Variance				Labor Quantity Variance			
(3)	12,000	(4)	8,000	(5)	5,600		

Payroll Cost Summary				Accrued Wages Payable			
(7)	79,500	(5)	85,600	(6)	8,200	Bal.	8,200
(8)	16,300	(6)	8,200			(8)	16,300

Finished Goods	
(9)	198,900

Note: The labor rate variance in this problem is represented by the balance in the Payroll Cost Summary account.

11–11. a)

	Std. Cost per Cwt. Material B	Cost/ Value	Cost Allocated		Standard Cost	
			To Y	To Z	Y/Lb.	Z/Gal.
Material.....	$12.00	50.00%	$10.00	$2.00	$0.200	$0.1000
Labor.......	1.50	6.25	1.25	0.25	0.025	0.0125
Total...	$13.50	56.25%	$11.25	$2.25	$0.225	$0.1125

b) Inventories:

	May 1	May 31
Materials............................	$ 600.00	$ 1,200
Labor..............................	37.50	75
Total costs in process...............	$ 637.50	$ 1,275
Material B...........................	8,400.00	10,800
Product Y...........................	3,825.00	2,700
Product Z...........................	1,800.00	1,575
Total Inventories..................	$14,662.50	$16,350

Variances:

Materials:

Materials costs earned*......................$47,800.00		
Materials issued @ standard price............. 45,600.00		
Materials yield variance.................		$ 2,200.00
Materials price variance 400,000 lbs. @ $0.01..		(4,000.00)

Labor:

Labor costs earned ....$ 5,937.50		
Standard labor hours required by actual		
materials inputs†......................... 5,662.50		
Effect of materials variance..............		275.00
Actual labor hours at standard rates.......... 5,400.00		
Labor performance variance..............		262.50
Actual labor costs......................... 5,800.00		
Labor rate and crew variance.............		(400.00)
Total Variance.............................		$(1,662.50)

* Costs Earned:

	Quantity	Materials	Labor
Product Y.....................	205,000 lbs.	$41,000.00	$5,125.00
Product Z.....................	62,000 gal.	6,200.00	775.00
In process...................	5,000 lbs.	600.00	37.50
Total..................		$47,800.00	$5,937.50

† To calculate the labor required to process the month's input, we first have to calculate the amount of processing done:

To finish processing opening inventory..........................	2,500 lbs.
To start and finish processing units received during month........	370,000
To start processing remainder of units received during month......	5,000
Total Processing Load...................................	377,500 lbs.

At a rate of one crew hour for every 600 pounds of material B, the crew-hour requirement for the actual materials throughput is 629⅙ crew-hours, or $5,662.50.

Chapter 12

12–5. The 6.3-pound product is half of 90 percent of the weight of the materials. The original weight, therefore, must be 14 pounds. The cost calculation is:

Materials input: 14 pounds × $1.00....................	$14.00
Less scrap: 1.4 pounds × $0.10........................	0.14
Net materials cost/unit............................	$13.86
Cost per Pound of Product.........................	$ 2.20

12–6. Initial mix: cost 80¢/gal.
After boiling: cost 80¢/3/4 gal. = $1.067/gal.
                sugar   0.040/gal.
                    Total $1.107/gal.

After filling: $1.107/.98 gal. = $1.129/gal. = $0.141/pint.

Chapter 13

13–4. *a*) The first step in this problem is to adjust January–June power costs
for the rate increase:

> January: $1,000 × 1.1.................$1,100
> February: 1,100 × 1.1................ 1,210
> March: 1,300 × 1.1................ 1,430
> April: 1,200 × 1.1................ 1,320
> May: 1,200 × 1.1................ 1,320
> June: 1,100 × 1.1................ 1,210

If you used the least-squares method, you found that the sum of the
adjusted cost observations was $14,880, the sum of the volume ob-
servations was 48,000 machine-hours, the sum of the products was
$60,204,000, and the sum of the squares of the volume observations
was 195,420,000. This yields the following formula:

Power costs = $440 + $0.20 × machine-hours.

The allowances obtained with this formula are:

Machine-Hours	Power Cost
2,500	$ 940
3,500	1,140
4,000	1,240
4,500	1,340
5,500	1,540

b) The allowances for the extreme volume limits are shown in the table
in (*a*) above. The main question here is whether allowances for the
2,500 and 5,500 machine-hour levels can be derived by extrapolation
from data that do not extend to or near these extremes. Another
question on all the figures is whether enough observations are available for reliable estimates. This can be checked by statistical tests,
but sometimes it is necessary to proceed with whatever data are
available, even if statistical requirements are not met.

13–7. *a*) Only the first three overhead cost items listed are likely to be of any
significance in evaluating the cost control performance of the department supervisor, and of these nonproductive time and other indirect labor have the greatest impact. Depreciation and building
service charges are uncontrollable and have no bearing on managerial
evaluation in this department.

b) Labor costs did not go down with decreasing volume. There are
many possible reasons for this. This may merely be a time lag—
management may have decided not to cut the labor force to meet
the volume reduction in the hope that volume would recover quickly.

This should be examined more critically if volume continues at these newer and lower levels. We cannot ignore any one month's reports, but we need to examine them in the context of a longer period of time. Even two months is likely to be too short a period for random forces to have averaged themselves out.

The other item in which the variance has increased is depreciation, and this should be labeled as noncontrollable.

Chapter 14

14–9. *a*) Charging rates:

$$\text{Plant operation} = \frac{\$22,110}{67,000 \text{ sq. ft.}} = 33\cancel{c}/\text{sq. ft.}$$

$$\text{Factory office} = \frac{\$19,490 + 3,000 \times \$0.33}{64 \text{ employees}} = \$320/\text{employee} \, .$$

$$\text{Storeroom} = \frac{\$24,460 + 10,000 \times \$0.33 + 2 \times \$320}{100 \text{ percent}}$$

$$= \$284/\text{percent} \, .$$

Cost distribution sheet:

	Plant Opera-tion	Factory Office	Store-room	Milling	Machining	Painting	Assembly
Direct...........	$22,110	$19,490	$24,460	$40,000	$35,000	$42,000	$30,000
Allocations:							
Plant operator.	(22,110)	990	3,300	5,940	3,960	4,950	2,970
Factory office..		(20,480)	640	8,960	4,480	3,520	2,880
Storeroom.....			(28,400)	7,384	2,840	6,816	11,360
Total..........				$62,284	$46,280	$57,286	$47,210

b)

Milling Department Overhead......................	40,000	
Machining Department Overhead...................	35,000	
Painting Department Overhead....................	42,000	
Assembly Department Overhead...................	30,000	
Factory Office Costs.............................	19,490	
Plant Operation Department Costs................	22,110	
Storeroom Costs................................	24,460	
Sundry Accounts...........................		213,060
To record actual overhead costs.		

Milling Department Overhead......................	22,284	
Machining Department Overhead...................	11,280	
Painting Department Overhead....................	15,286	
Assembly Department Overhead...................	17,210	
Factory Office Costs...........................		19,490
Plant Operation Costs........................		22,110
Storeroom Costs.............................		24,460
To record cost redistribution.		

14–14. *a*) Charge variable maintenance costs on the basis of $4.50 per maintenance labor hour. Charge the fixed component on the basis of normal monthly hours per production department. (Criteria of facilities provided and usage.)

Charge fixed finance department costs on the basis of each department's share of normal employment, the variable component at $1 per actual equivalent full-time employee. (Criteria of facilities provided and variability.) Actually, because costs are so nearly totally fixed, the entire charge might be predetermined on the grounds of lower clerical cost.)

Maintenance:

	Charged to Production	Actual	Variance
Fixed........................	$10,800	.....	....
Variable.....................	59,850	.....	....
Total.....................	$70,650	$72,900	$2,250

Finance:

Fixed........................	$18,000	.....	....
Variable.....................	1,200	.....	....
Total.....................	$19,200	$20,000	$ 800

14–14. *b*) The maintenance department variance reflects either poor cost control, rising wage rates, and so forth, or transitional effects of changing from one level of service volume to another. There is no volume variance as such, but it should be remembered that volume variances of a sort may arise when volume is changing rapidly and management either has not had time to adjust or has decided for other reasons not to adjust.

The finance department's variance may be interpreted in a similar fashion, except that it is not service provided but the number of employees that gives rise to transitional variances.

14–15.

	Buildings	Plant Accounting	Maintenance	Plant Management	Light Machinery	Heavy Machinery	Assembly
Direct costs..	$ 13,000	$ 6,000	$ 12,000	$ 10,000	$30,000	$54,000	$24,000
Buildings....	(13,000)	250	250	500	2,250	4,500	5,250
Plant accounting...		(6,250)	600	850	1,400	1,300	2,100
Maintenance.			(12,850)	1,333	3,667	5,850	2,000
Plant management...				(12,683)	3,805	3,174	5,704
Total....					$41,122	$68,824	$39,054

Chapter 15

15–1. $\text{Burden rate} = \dfrac{\$8,000 + 1.20 \times \$10,000}{\$10,000} = \$2/\text{DL}\$$.

Manufacturing Overhead				Manufacturing Overhead Absorbed			
(a)	21,700	(c)	18,000	(c)	18,800	(b)	18,000
		Budget				Volume	
		variance	2,900			variance	800

Actual..21,700
Budget..18,800
 Budget variance...............................   2,900 Dr.
Absorbed..18,000
 Volume variance...............................   800 Dr.

15–4. Earned direct labor dollars: $\$22,000 - (\$8,000 - \$5,000) = \$19,000$. Earned overhead: 200 percent of $\$19,000 = \$38,000$.

15–5. *a*) Actual......................................$25,000
 Earned (9,000 × $2.25)........................ 20,250
  Total Variance........................... $4,750

$\text{Burden rate} = \dfrac{\$15,000 + \$12,000}{12,000} = \$2.25/\text{direct labor hour.}$

b) Actual.......................................$25,000
 Budget at actual hours......................... 23,500
  Budget variance........................... $1,500 unfavorable
 Budget at earned hours......................... 24,000
  Labor efficiency variance....................   500 favorable
 Earned....................................... 20,250
  Volume variance...........................   3,750 unfavorable
   Total Overhead Variance.................. $4,750 unfavorable

15–10. *a*) Actual......................................$20,000
 Budget....................................... 19,500
  Spending variance........................ $500 unfavorable
 Earned....................................... 14,400
  Volume variance + budgeted unvarying
   costs....................................$ 5,100
  Less: Budgeted unvarying costs.............. 5,000
    Volume variance......................   100 unfavorable
  Total Variance.............................. $600 unfavorable

The volume variance is due to the step function. The burden rate includes 10 cents to cover the cost of the step. At 9,000 standard direct labor hours, the total absorption for the step is 0.10 × 9,000 = $900, or $100 less than the step.

b) The marginal rate is either $1.50, $1.70, or even higher, depending on the size of the volume increment. The $1.60 figure is a compromise that will not even satisfy the financial accounting objective of avoiding systematic underabsorption of variable and step-function costs. (Only at volumes of 5,000 direct labor hours or less or at 10,-000 or 15,000 direct labor hours will unfavorable volume variances be avoided.)

15–13. Because overhead costs vary with *actual* machine-hours, a three-variance system should be used:

Actual..	$21,750	
Budget at actual hours..........................	21,500	
Budget variance..............................		$ 250 unfavorable
Budget at standard hours........................	22,000	
Labor efficiency variance......................		500 favorable
Earned..	20,000	
Volume variance.............................		2,000 unfavorable
Total Variance.............................		$1,750 unfavorable

15–15. *a)*

Materials Inventory				Mat'ls Price Variance		Accounts Payable, Etc.	
Bal.	30	(6)	29	(1)	2	(1)	23
(1)	25					(4)	48
		Bal.	26				
Bal.	26						

Materials in Process				Labor in Process				Overhead in Process			
Bal.	20	(5)	25	Bal.	10	(5)	32	Bal.	15	(5)	48
(6)	29	(7)	5	(3)	34	(8)	2	(9)	48		
		Bal.	19			Bal.	10			Bal.	15
Bal.	19			Bal.	10			Bal.	15		

Payroll Cost Summary				Manufacturing Overhead Control				Manufacturing Overhead Absorbed			
(2)	35	(3)	34	(4)	48	(9)	41	(9)	41	(9)	48
						(10)	7	(11)	7		

Wages Payable			Finished Goods			Materials Quantity Variance		
		(2) 35	(5)	105		(7)	5	

Labor Quantity Variance			Overhead Volume Variance			Overhead Budget Variance		
(8)	2			(11)	7	(10)	7	

b) Unfavorable variances:

Materials quantity variance....................................	$5	
Labor quantity variance......................................	2	
Labor rate variance..	1	
Overhead spending variance..................................	7	$15
Favorable variances:		
Materials price variance.....................................	$2	
Overhead volume variance....................................	7	9
Net Variance,,,		$ 6

15–22. *a*) Materials price variance: 200,000 ×

$$($0.77 - $0.80)\dots\dots\dots\dots\dots\dots\dots\dots\dots\dots$$ $6,000 favorable

Materials quantity variance:

Inputs: 180,000 × $0.80.......................$144,000

* Earned: (4,800 + 300 + 600) × $24........... 136,800

Materials quantity variance..................   7,200 unfavorable

Labor rate variance: 53,500 × ($1.80 − $1.75).....   2,675 unfavorable

Labor quantity variance:

Inputs: 53,500 × $1.75.......................$ 93,625

* Earned: (4,800 + 300 + 400) × $17.50.......... 96,250

Labor quantity variance....................   2,625 favorable

Overhead:

Actual: $20,500 + (300 × $10.50)..............$ 23,650

Budgeted: $8,000 + $2.40 × 5,500.............. 21,200

Overhead spending variance..................   2,450 unfavorable

* Earned: 5,500 × $4.......................... 22,000

Overhead volume variance...................   800 favorable

Total Variance........................ $2,900 unfavorable

> * The work in process accounts are credited for the full standard costs of all desks, including the seconds. Losses on seconds are included in the overhead variance.

b) Presumably the two quantity variances and the overhead spending variance, suitably subdivided.

c) (1) Raw Materials Inventory..............................160,000

Accounts Payable..............................   154,000

Materials Price Variance.........................   6,000

(2) Work in Process—Materials.............................144,000

Raw Materials Inventory..........................   144,000

(3) Work in Process—Labor............................. 93,625

Labor Rate Variance.............................. 2,675

Wages Payable....................................   96,300

(4) Manufacturing Overhead............................. 20,500

Vouchers Payable.............................   20,500

(5) Finished Goods—Firsts.............................218,400

Finished Goods—Seconds........................... 10,500

Loss on Seconds.................................. 3,150

Work in Process—Materials.......................   122,400

Work in Process—Labor..........................   89,250

Work in Process—Overhead.......................   20,400

(5*a*) Manufacturing Overhead............................. 3,150

Loss on Seconds.................................   3,150

(6) Materials Quantity Variance.......................... 7,200

Work in Process—Materials.......................   7,200

(7) Work in Process—Labor............................. 2,625

Labor Quantity Variance.........................   2,625

(8) Work in Process—Overhead............................. 22,000

Manufacturing Overhead.........................   22,000

(9) Overhead Spending Variance.......................... 2,450

Overhead Volume Variance.......................   800

Manufacturing Overhead.........................   1,650

Chapter 16

16–2.   Costs earned, 33,000 at 13¢ = $4,290

Costs budgeted.............. 4,500

Volume variance........... $210

Actual costs................. 5,000

Spending variance.........   500

Total Variance.............. $710

Normal volume is 40,000 invoice lines, and at this level the budget is $5,200. A substantial portion of the budget variance may be due to temporary reductions in volume. What it does show, however, is that costs are excessive for the volume of business being done and if the low volume is expected to continue, some reduction in the clerical staff should be considered.

16–3.   Price = 1.4 × standard manufacturing cost .
Gross margin = 0.4 × standard factory cost = $\frac{0.4}{1.4}$ × Price .

Break-even order size = $\frac{\$1.50}{0.4/1.4}$ = $5.25 .

Many fixed costs are included in the averages quoted, including standard manufacturing costs. The true break-even order size is probably less than $5.25. Furthermore, many costs are related to factors other than the number of orders and some larger orders might even prove unprofitable.

Chapter 17

17–5.

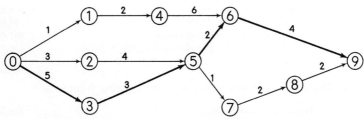

CRITICAL PATH: 0-3-5-6-9 = 14 WEEKS.

Chapter 18

18–5. *a*) Materials costs earned = $30,000 − $5,000 = $25,000.

Assuming that materials quantity variances are proportional to costs earned, the variance ratio is $5,000/$25,000 = 20 percent. Applying this ratio to ending work in process and finished goods inventories:

To work in process: $5,000 × 20%	$ 1,000
To finished goods: 7,000 × 20%	1,400
	$ 2,400
Remainder, to cost of goods sold	$ 2,600
Cost of goods sold:	
Costs earned	$25,000
Decrease in work in process	1,100
Decrease in finished goods	1,000
Cost of goods sold at standard	$27,100
Materials quantity variance:	
From prior year	(900)
From this year	2,600
Adjusted Cost of Goods Sold	$28,800

b)   Materials Quantity Variances in Inventories..........3,300
       Cost of Goods Sold................................1,700
              Materials Quantity Variances...................   5,000

18–8. $10,000 of the underabsorbed overhead came from the misclassification
of the machinery cost and $3,000 from the misclassification of the presi-
dent's salary. The entry to correct these two errors is:

Plant and Equipment.................................10,000
Administrative Salaries............................. 3,000
       Work in Process.....................   1,560
       Finished Goods.....................   2,600
       Cost of Goods Sold.............................   8,840

No entry is required to correct the third error, although for data bank
purposes the job order cost sheets should be corrected.

18–11. *a)* Variable costs: $87,780/6,600.......................................$13.30
       Fixed costs: $56,760/6,600.................................... 8.60
              Burden Rate per Machine-Hour..................................$21.90

b) Budgeted costs based on 60 percent of 6,600 hours, or 3,960 hours
for 6 months:

Fixed costs (half of total)....................................$28,380
Variable costs ($13.30 × 3,960)............................. 52,668
       Budgeted costs at expected volume.........................$81,048
       Absorbed costs at expected volume (3,960 × $21.90).......... 86,724
Seasonal Variance.......................................$ 5,676

c) Budgeted costs based on 3,800 hours during 6 months:

Fixed costs (half of total)....................................$28,380
Variable costs ($13.30 × 3,800)............................. 50,540
       Budgeted costs at actual volume...........................$78,920
       Absorbed costs at actual volume (3,800 × $21.90)........... 83,220
Actual Volume Variance.................................$ 4,300

d) The variance was $1,376 less favorable than expected, due to a lower
than normal first-half volume.

e) Actual costs. $79,915
     Absorbed costs... 83,220
              Total Overhead Variance (Overabsorbed).........................$ 3,305

f) Actual costs...$79,915
     Budgeted costs at actual volume (*c*)............................... 78,920
              Spending variance..$ (995)
     Seasonal variance (*b*)... 5,676
     Unanticipated volume variance..................................... (1,376)
              Net Overabsorbed.......................................$ 3,305

Chapter 19

19–2. These solutions are based on the continuous compounding tables in
Appendix A.

a)

	P.V. at 8%
Outlay....................	−100.00
Earnings.................	+103.25
Net P.V.................	+ 3.25

b)

	P.V. at 8%
Outlay....................	−100.00
Earnings:	
10 yrs. at $10..........	+ 68.83
5 yrs. at $10..........	+ 41.21
Net P.V.................	+ 10.04

c)

	P.V. at 8%
Outlay....................	−110.00
Earnings:	
10 yrs. at $10..........	+ 68.83
5 yrs. at $10..........	+ 27.62
Salvage..................	+ 4.49
Net P.V.................	− 9.06

d)

	P.V. at 8%
Outlay now..............	− 80.00
Earnings................	+103.25
Prop-up.................	− 26.81
Net P.V.................	− 3.56

Chapter 20

20–1.

Payback	*Average Return*	*Discounted Return*	*Present Value*
a) 5.7 yrs.	15.0%	12.5%	+$1,062
b) 5.0 yrs. or 5.7 yrs.	15.0	13.6	+ 1,449
c) 6.25 yrs. or 5.7 yrs.	15.0	11.5	+ 675
d) 5.7 yrs.	16.4	14.9	+ 2,534
e) 5.7 yrs.	21.7	16.0	+ 3,595

20–4. *a)*

Cost of machine...	$100,000
Less: Tax reduction on portion expensed ($50,000)...................	(25,000)
7% tax credit on portion capitalized........................	(3,500)
Plus: Working capital required.....................................	10,000
Net Initial Outlay..	$ 81,500

b)

	Year 1	*Year 2*
(1) Before-tax reduction in operating costs.................	$20,000	$20,000
(2) Cost subject to depreciation for tax purposes.............	50,000	37,500
(3) Tax-allowed depreciation (25% of (2)).................	12,500	9,375
(4) Taxable saving ((1) − (3)).........................	7,500	10,625
(5) Tax (50% of (4)).................................	3,750	5,313
(6) After-tax cash receipts ((1) − (5)).....................	$16,250	$14,687

20–5. *a)*

	Gross	*Tax*	*Net*
Purchase price...............................	$50,000	.....	$ 50,000
Training.....................................	10,000	$(4,000)	6,000
Investment credit............................	.....	(3,500)	(3,500)
Salvage (old machine).......................	(8,000)	(4,800)	(12,800)
Incremental Outlay......................	$52,000	$(12,300)	$ 39,700

b)

Gross cash savings before tax............................	$ 6,800
Tax depreciation:	
New: 30% of $50,000.............................$15,000	
Old... 3,000	
Increased depreciation.............................	(12,000)
Taxable saving...	$ (5,200)
Tax reduction at 40%...	(2,080)
After-Tax Incremental Cash Savings...................	$ 8,880

20–8. *a*) Initial outlay:

Cost of machine..		$50,000
Less: Sale value of old machine.........................	$10,000	
Tax reduction on retirement loss on old machine....	10,000	20,000
Net Initial Outlay.....................................		$30,000
Present value at 10% of after-tax future cash savings (see table below).......................................		67,010
Net Present Value......................................		+$37,010

Calculation of discounted cash flows:

(1) Years Hence	(2) Net Book Value of New Machine	(3) Tax Depreciation	(4) Depreciation on old Machine	(5) Increase in Depreciation	(6) Taxable Income	(7) Income Tax	(8) After-Tax Cash Flow	(9) Present Value at 10%
1.........	$50,000	$10,000	$ 3,750	$ 6,250	$ 13,750	$ 6,875	$ 13,125	$11,876
2.........	40,000	8,000	3,750	4,250	15,750	7,875	12,125	9,927
3.........	32,000	6,400	3,750	2,650	17,350	8,675	11,325	8,390
4.........	25,600	5,120	3,750	1,370	18,630	9,315	10,685	7,162
5.........	20,480	4,096	3,750	346	19,654	9,827	10,173	6,170
6.........	16,384	3,277	3,750	− 473	20,473	10,237	9,763	5,358
7.........	13,107	2,621	3,750	− 1,129	21,129	10,564	9,436	4,686
8.........	10,486	2,097	3,750	− 1,653	21,653	10,826	9,174	4,122
9.........	8,389	1,678	—	1,678	18,322	9,161	10,839	4,406
10.........	6,711	1,342	—	1,342	} 13,289	6,645	13,355	4,913
10.........	5,369	5,369	—	5,369				
Total......		$50,000	$30,000	$20,000	$180,000	$90,000	$110,000	$67,010

(3) 20% of (2).
(4) 12.5% of $30,000 (remaining book value).
(5) Col. 4—Col. 3.
(6) $20,000 cash flow less increase in depreciation (col. 5).
(7) 50% of col. 6.
(8) $20,000 less col. 7.
(9) Col. 8 × Table 1, Appendix A.

b) Rate of return: slightly greater than 30%.

20–12. *a*) Investment required:

Equipment...		$70,000
Rearrangement..	$12,000	
Dismantling..	1,000	13,000
Less: Tax credit......................................		(6,500)
Net Outlay Required..............................		$76,500

Operating savings per year:

Direct labor...	$20,000
Supplies...	4,000
Maintenance...	2,000
Power...	(3,000)
Other overhead......................................	12,000
Total...	$35,000
Tax depreciation.....................................	14,000
Taxable savings......................................	$21,000
Tax at 50%..	10,500
After-Tax Cash Savings.............................	$24,500

End-of-life, after-tax dismantling costs amount to $500, but since this would be the case under either alternative, this amount can be ignored.

b)

Time	Cash Flow	P.V. at 8%
0	−$76,500	−$ 76,500
0–5	+ 24,500/yr.	+ 100,965
Total P.V.		+$ 24,465

Replacement is justifiable.

Note: This assumes that the old equipment could be used for another five years at the operating costs shown, or rather that the differential operating costs would remain at the predicted level.

Chapter 21

21–2. *a*) Break-even volume $= \dfrac{\text{Total fixed costs}}{\text{Price} - \text{Variable cost}} = \dfrac{\$320,000}{\$3.20}$

$= 100,000$ units.

b) Desired profit $= \$220,000 + \$22,000 = \$242,000$.
New P/V margin $= \$3.20/\text{unit}$.

Target sales volume $= \dfrac{\$242,000 + \$320,000}{\$3.20} = 175,625$ units.

21–3. Average P/V ratio $= 35\%$.
Fixed costs $+$ profit $= \$140,000$.

Desired sales $= \dfrac{\$140,000}{0.35} = \$400,000$.

	A	B	Total
Sales	$200,000	$200,000	$400,000
Variable costs	120,000	140,000	260,000
Variable profit	$ 80,000	$ 60,000	$140,000
Fixed costs			100,000
Net Profit			$ 40,000

Unit sales:
A..........40,000 units
B..........80,000 units

21–5.

	Product A	Product B
Price	$3.00	$5.00
Variable cost:		
Materials	$1.00	$2.00
Labor	0.60	0.50
Overhead	0.18	0.15
Total	$1.78	$2.65
Variable Profit/Unit	$1.22	$2.35
Total variable profit	$122,000	$282,000
Change in fixed costs	......	95,000
Incremental Profit	$122,000	$187,000

Conclusion: Change over to Product B.

Chapter 22

22–6.

Price	Sales (Units)	Sales Revenues	Fixed Costs	Variable Costs	Total Costs	Profit Margin
$0.75	100,000	$75,000	$11,000	$62,500	$73,500	$ 1,500
0.80	90,000	72,000	11,000	55,400	66,400	5,600
0.85	80,000	68,000	11,000	48,700	59,700	8,300
0.90	70,000	63,000	10,000	42,300	52,300	10,700
0.95	60,000	57,000	10,000	36,100	46,100	10,900
1.00	50,000	50,000	10,000	30,000	40,000	10,000

The most profitable price is $0.95/unit.

22–8. *a*)

	West Coast	Midwest
Sales.............................	$32.50	$44.00
Variable costs:		
Materials........................	$18.70	$18.70
Labor...........................	3.00	3.00
Variable burden..................	3.30	3.30
Freight..........................	....	1.50
Commissions....................	....	2.20
Total Variable Cost............	$25.00	$28.70
Variable Profit.....................	$ 7.50	$15.30

The indications are that the company could increase its profit by $7,500 — $1,500 a month, or $6,000. All present fixed costs can be charged against existing sales in making this decision.

b) One factor that definitely should be considered is whether the West Coast distributors would reship the products to distributors in the Midwest. The delivered cost in the Midwest would be $36. This is substantially less than the price now quoted to Midwest dealers, but whether it is low enough to tempt the West Coast distributors to set up a clandestine distribution outlet in the company's present market areas is not clear. It is fairly certain that reshipment by West Coast *dealers* is unlikely, nor is it likely that ultimate industrial purchasers who have consuming plants in both areas would find it profitable to buy in the West and reship to the Midwest. There may be some questions on these points in the edges of the company's sales territory, but the issue is probably not serious. The West Coast distributor would be unlikely to risk the loss of a franchise on which he has made a good deal of promotional effort, unless, of course, he is finding his West Coast operations unprofitable.

Another problem is how to react to complaints by Midwest retailers when they hear of the lower West Coast retail price. There is probably no Robinson-Patman problem because this is in the nature of a trade discount and the areas are noncompeting, but dealers might exert pressure to get a reduction in the $44 price.

Another more fundamental question, of course, is whether the company could go into the West Coast and perform the distribution function more economically—or whether the product would sell as well at $44 as at $42.50 on the West Coast.

Chapter 23

23–3.

	Bulk	Express
Variable cost (at actual):		
Loading-unloading	$ 517	$ 517
Truck operation*:		
Labor	2,250	1,440
Supplies and parts	1,284	428
Employee benefits	225	144
Truck repairs	732	244
Total Variable	$5,008	$2,773

* Labor and employee benefits costs for truck operation distributed on basis of road time; supplies and parts costs distributed on basis of mileage.

The variable costs may also be computed on the basis of predetermined rates. In the case of truck repair costs, this may be a more accurate reflection of the costs than those actually recorded this month.

It makes little sense to allocate the undistributed fixed costs to the various functions and even less to divide these between bulk and express shipments. The fixed costs of *truck operation* probably should be allocated on the basis of total hours, including loading and unloading time as well as road time. The reason for this is that the company could probably use fewer trucks if one class of business or the other were to be discontinued, and that capacity is probably more a function of time than of miles. On this basis, the express deliveries should be assigned 520/1,220 of the fixed costs of truck operation, or $286, with the remaining $386 being assigned to bulk deliveries. The fixed costs of loading and unloading and of truck repairs are unlikely to be affected substantially by large changes in the volume of business in either type of delivery.

Chapter 24

24–1. Budgeted profit margin/unit:

Sales	$6.00
Direct materials	$1.00
Direct labor	1.30
Variable overhead	.52
Fixed overhead	.78
Profit margin	$2.40

Variance analysis:

Increased sales volume: 1,000 × $2.40 * = $ 2,400   favorable
Factory overhead volume variance * . . . . . .   (780) favorable
Reduced price: 11,000 × $.50 =   (5,500) unfavorable
Materials usage variance. . . . .   (200) unfavorable
Labor performance variance. . . . .   (400) unfavorable
Overhead budget variance. . . . .   (420) unfavorable
Overhead labor efficiency variance. . . . .   (160) unfavorable
Selling and administrative variance. . . . .   (500) unfavorable
     Total Variance. $(4,000) unfavorable

         * Can be combined in a single figure in this case.

24–6. *a*) (1) Actual. $1,000
     Total variance. . . . .   100 favorable
     Absorbed. $1,100
     Volume variance. . . . .   20 favorable
     Budget. $1,080
     Spending variance. . . . .   80 favorable

(2) Budgeted fixed cost: $1,080 − 30% of $1,100 = $750

(3) Variable cost:
     Labor. $400
     Materials. 100
     Overhead (30%). 330
         Total. . . . .$830 = 830/1,600 of product cost

     83/160 × $1,760 = $913
     Selling expense (4%).   80
         Total variable. $993
     Variable profit = $2,000 − $993 = $1,007 = 50.35%.

***b*)** Sales. $2,000
     Variable costs:
         Manufacturing. $913
         Selling. 80   993
     Variable profit. $1,007
     Traceable fixed costs:
         Manufacturing. $750
         Selling and administrative. 55   805
     Performance variance (favorable). . . . .   (80)
     Profit Contribution. . . . . $ 282

Chapter 26

26–8. *a*) Reversing entry, January 1:

(1) Provision for Intracompany Profit in Inventories. 122,000
       Inventory Valuation Adjustment.   122,000

Eliminating entries, December 31:

(2) Division A Sales—Inside. 539,000
       Division A Cost of Sales—Inside.   364,000
       Division B Cost of Sales—Outside.   175,000

(3) Division B Sales—Inside. 1,616,000
       Division B Cost of Sales—Inside.   1,342,000
       Division A Cost of Sales—Outside.   274,000

(4) Inventory Valuation Adjustment. 73,000
       Provision for Intracompany Profit in Inventories. .   73,000

(5) Inventory Valuation Adjustment..................... 14,000
      Provision for Intracompany Profit in Inventories. .   14,000

b) Thousands omitted:

	Division A	Division B	Company
Sales—outside.......................	$12,462	$ 8,924	$21,386
Sales—inside.........................	539	1,616	. . .
Total sales.....................	$13,001	$10,540	$21,386
Cost of sales—outside...............	$ 7,087	$ 5,978	$12,616
Cost of sales—inside.................	364	1,342	. . .
Inventory valuation adjustment......	. . .	. . .	(35)
Total cost of sales...............	$ 7,451	$ 7,320	$12,581
Gross margin—outside...............	$ 5,375	$ 2,946	$ 8,805
Gross margin—inside................	175	274	. . .
Total gross margin..............	$ 5,550	$ 3,220	$ 8,805
Manufacturing cost variances.........	239	(139)	100
Adjusted gross margin...............	$ 5,789	$ 3,081	$ 8,905
Division selling and administrative expenses........................	3,848	3,110	6,958
Contribution margin..................	$ 1,941	$ (29)	$ 1,947
Head Office expenses.................			1,424
Net Profit before Taxes..............			$ 523

c) Thousands omitted:

	Division A			Division B		
	Budget	Actual	Variance	Budget	Actual	Variance
Sales.........................	$12,000	$13,001	$1,001	$12,000	$10,540	$(1,460)
Cost of sales—standard........	7,000	7,451	(451)	7,000	7,320	(320)
Standard gross margin........	$ 5,000	$ 5,550	$ 550	$ 5,000	$ 3,220	$(1,780)
Manufacturing variances:						
Materials prices..............	.....	$ (67)	$ (67)	.....	$ (21)	$ (21)
Materials usage..............	.....	(23)	(23)	.....	13	13
Labor performance..........	.....	8	8	.....	(12)	(12)
Overhead....................	.....	321	321	.....	(119)	(119)
Total manufacturing variances..	.....	$ 239	$ 239	.....	$ (139)	$ (139)
Adjusted gross margin.........	$ 5,000	$ 5,789	$ 789	$ 5,000	$ 3,081	$(1,919)
Division expenses.............	3,400	3,848	(448)	3,400	3,110	290
Contribution Margin...........	$ 1,600	$ 1,941	$ 341	$ 1,600	$ (29)	$(1,629)

	Division A	*Division B*
Percent gross margins:		
Inside sales......................	32.5%	17.0%
Outside sales.....................	43.1	33.0

Index

INDEX

.

This book has been set in 12 and 10 point Garamond #3, leaded 1 point. Chapter titles are in 18 point Spartan Medium caps. Chapter numbers and part titles and numbers are in 24, 30, and 42 point Weiss Series I. The size of the type page is 27 by 46½ picas.